THE INTERNATIONAL CRIMINAL COURT AND AFRICA

Africa Legal Aid Series, Volume 4

THE INTERNATIONAL CRIMINAL COURT AND AFRICA

One Decade On

Edited by
EVELYN A. ANKUMAH

intersentia
Cambridge – Antwerp – Portland

Intersentia Ltd
Sheraton House | Castle Park
Cambridge | CB3 0AX | United Kingdom
Tel.: +44 1223 370 170 | Fax: +44 1223 370 169
Email: mail@intersentia.co.uk
www.intersentia.com | www.intersentia.co.uk

Distribution for the UK and Ireland:
NBN International
Airport Business Centre, 10 Thornbury Road
Plymouth, PL6 7 PP
United Kingdom
Tel.: +44 1752 202 301 | Fax: +44 1752 202 331
Email: orders@nbninternational.com

Distribution for Europe and all other countries:
Intersentia Publishing nv
Groenstraat 31
2640 Mortsel
Belgium
Tel.: +32 3 680 15 50 | Fax: +32 3 658 71 21
Email: mail@intersentia.be

Distribution for the USA and Canada:
International Specialized Book Services
920 NE 58th Ave. Suite 300
Portland, OR 97213
USA
Tel.: +1 800 944 6190 (toll free) | Fax: +1 503 280 8832
Email: info@isbs.com

The International Criminal Court and Africa. One Decade On

ISBN 978-1-78068-417-8
D/2016/7849/102
NUR 828

British Library Cataloguing in Publication Data. A catalogue record for this book is available from the British Library.

FOREWORD

To understand *The International Criminal Court and Africa: One Decade On* it is important to comprehend the past as a yardstick for the present and future. In the evolution of international criminal law one decade is hardly a blink in the eye of time. Seen in its proper historical perspective there has been more progress made during the last several decades toward deterring massive inhumanities than in all past centuries of recorded history. The Nuremberg war crimes trials after the second world war took a major step forward in 1946 when war-making, that had previously been hailed a national right, was condemned as a supreme international crime for which the responsible leaders should be held to account in a court of law. That conclusion, affirmed by the UN General Assembly, was reaffirmed when the Statute for a new International Criminal Court (ICC) was overwhelmingly acclaimed in Rome in 1998 and again a dozen years later, by silent consensus at an amendment conference in Kampala, Uganda in 2010.

However, many powerful states were not really willing to surrender what they insisted was their sovereign right to decide for themselves when they would use armed might to protect their perceived national interests. They found fault with every proposed definition that would allow the ICC to exercise its jurisdiction over aggressors. It was finally agreed in Kampala that further consideration of an amendment enabling the ICC to try aggressors should be postponed until some unspecified date no sooner than 2017. No completion date was mentioned. As long as combatants in armed conflicts insist that they alone can judge the morality and legality of their deeds there is no way to end conflicts through the rule of law. Respected independent judicial institutions with clear laws and enforcement powers are essential for a more tranquil world.

The amendments agreed to 'by consensus' at Kampala should be ratified. Failing to do so would completely undercut the work done at Kampala. Major substantive differences were submerged since additional ratifications would be mandatory before any amendments would become binding. To be sure, even after other contrived hurdles are surmounted, the existing loopholes, including the right of defendants to 'opt in or opt out', diminishes prospects for holding wrongdoers to legal account. How much longer can massive armed cruelties be tolerated and remain unpunished? If the rule of law is to be upheld, it is a prudent safeguard to seek another route to by-pass definitional difficulties that reluctant governments have been unable or unwilling to resolve for almost 70 years. Enough is enough!

Africa Legal Aid (AFLA) and collaborators are to be congratulated for analysing many issues that remain contentious. Nuremberg recognised that crimes are committed by individuals and correctly held that law must apply equally to everyone. The scholarly authors probe the perplexities of eliminating existing immunities that protect guilty political leaders from prosecution. The dilemma of Justice versus Reconciliation remains unresolved. New African states denounce perceived discriminations and form unions to protect regional African interests. Respected ICC prosecutor, Fatou Bensouda writes in support of justice and gender rights for all. Juta Bertram-Nothnagel presents a sweeping analytical overview of some key unresolved issues. Some of the articles re-examine the tragedy of Rwanda where – to its everlasting shame – the world community failed to prevent genocide. Cultural and economic disparities compound difficulties. Writers urge compensation to human rights victims yet no one knows who will pay the bill. It would have a deterrent effect if those who caused the harm could be forced to pay for the injuries.

There can be no instant evolution or painless revolution and perfection is not to be expected. Newly formed human rights courts, whether international, national or hybrid should be seen as prototypes that will have to be improved over time. What is vital now is that respected institutions be given authority and support to enable them to bring to justice those responsible for the most egregious crimes against the human person. Criminal law cannot stop all crimes but it certainly has a significant deterrent effect. The UN Charter allows armed force in self-defence or pursuant to a Security Council mandate, but if not one of those pre-conditions exists, the use of armed force is illegal and should be condemned. The nature and destructive power of the weapon is irrelevant; it emphasises the urgency for more effective controls. Illegal use of force in violation of the UN Charter should no longer be tolerated anywhere.

There is really no compelling need to wait for the aggression definition to become actionable. The prohibited conduct can also be condemned now as 'other inhumane acts' that are already punishable under the ICC Statute as Crimes against Humanity. Many supportive nations have already included ICC mandates into their national criminal codes. In fact that is a common-sense requirement of the complementarity principle discussed herein. Stopping crimes against humanity begins at home.

Yet another supplementary approach is recommended in the timely article by Manuel Ventura and Amelia Bleeker who describe the new African Union protocol. Universal Jurisdiction provides a traditional basis for trials in any court that apprehends perpetrators of prohibited deeds that are so atrocious that no derogation from the humanitarian rules can be tolerated. Piracy is an early example. For jeopardising commerce all who sailed on the pirate ship risked hanging from the yardarm. The prevailing list of other crimes now generally recognised as subject to universal jurisdiction includes genocide, apartheid, torture, enslavement and a host of other atrocious offences. Surely, illegal use of armed force against innocent civilians is worthy of at least equal protection. Those whose primary concern is for universal peace should lend support to every reasonable interpretation designed to protect universal human rights universally.

The common sense of humankind should serve as a guide for the protection of humanity. An ideology cannot be killed by a gun. Before peace can be secure it is necessary to change the mind and hearts of those who are ready to kill and die to protect their own particular religious, nationalistic, economic or other cherished cause. Things that were considered impossible have become realties in the new cyberspace era. It remains to be seen whether science and technology will be used to improve or to destroy human lives. The task cannot be easily or quickly achieved – but it can be done. The abolition of slavery, emancipation of women, the end of colonialism and apartheid, are a few illustrations of the awakening of the human conscience.

When I was 27 years old, as a Nuremberg prosecutor, I obtained convictions of 22 high-ranking Nazi officers responsible for the calculated slaughter of more than a million innocent men, women and children. The victims were murdered because they did not share the race, religion or ideology of their executioners. I was deeply convinced such actions had to be eliminated by enforceable rules of law. I still feel the same way now in my 97th year. My guiding spirit remains my persistent determination to never stop trying to make this a more humane and peaceful world for everyone. Can the readers of this book do anything less?

Benjamin B. Ferencz
Last Surviving Prosecutor of the Nuremberg Trials

EDITOR'S NOTE

This fourth volume in the Africa Legal Aid (AFLA) book series is dedicated to the International Criminal Court (ICC) and its significance for Africa. Almost two decades ago, African states played an important role in the establishment of the ICC. More than a decade after the Court became operational, one can only conclude that African nationals play a key role in its work – Africans sit on the ICC bench, the current Prosecutor is an African – as is the President of the Assembly of States Parties. No continent has more states parties to the Rome Statute than Africa. Most importantly, and controversially, almost all cases brought before or taken up by the Court concern the perpetration of international crimes on African soil.

The ICC's focus on Africa has been much debated. Former United Nations Secretary-General, Kofi Annan, once observed that: 'it is the culture of impunity and individuals who are put on trial at the ICC, not Africa as a continent'. Critics however do not always share this view, and often speak in terms of the ICC targeting Africa. After cases were initiated against incumbent African Heads of State, the critique on the ICC intensified. The willingness of many African states to cooperate with the ICC decreased, while debates on the role of the ICC in Africa were increasingly politicised. Calls were made for Africans to take criminal law matters in their own hands and to work towards establishing an African criminal law system.

The authors who contribute to this volume all recognise the current problems the ICC faces, and its troubled relationship with Africa. Yet, they all seem to be of the view that one decade of activity is simply too short to pass a final judgment on the Court and the contribution it has made and can make to the progressive development of international criminal justice. The authors do not side with the populist pessimist movement that just condemns and opposes the ICC and its role in Africa. Rather, they take a realistic, cautious and optimistic approach. They use their unique specific knowledge, expertise and experiences as the basis for reflections on the current problems and their possible solutions.

This volume contains contributions which analyse in depth the ICC's activities and developments in the last decade. It addresses a range of specific topics concerning the functioning of the Court such as complementarity, impunity, the role of both prosecution and defence, the role of victims, gender crimes, and the nexus between the ICC Statute and human rights. It also explores issues of specific relevance to Africa – particularly the crime of aggression, the role of the African Union, and the role of alternative justice mechanisms, and considers what lessons can be learnt from other criminal courts, notably the International Criminal Tribunal for Rwanda. The book contains a comprehensive bibliography and is as such an authoritative source of reference on international criminal justice.

On behalf of AFLA, I thank each and every author for having contributed so readily and so richly in substance. The customary disclaimer applies: the views expressed in the various contributions are personal to the authors. They do not necessarily reflect AFLA's views or policy on international criminal justice, nor do they necessarily reflect the views of individual AFLA board members, and partner organisations.

This publication could not have been issued without the commitment and tireless efforts of individuals working behind the scenes. I owe a debt of gratitude to Rachael Nelson-Daley for her invaluable and meticulous work. Many thanks to Tamara Emer, Fiona Lau, and Lucile Paupard for their part in bringing this publication to fruition. Last but not least, my heartfelt thanks to A.P. van der Mei for all that he has done to support this publication.

Evelyn A. Ankumah
The Hague
March 2016

ABOUT THE EDITOR

Evelyn Ankumah is the Founder and Executive Director of Africa Legal Aid (AFLA). She is the author of *The African Commission on Human and Peoples Rights: Practice and Procedures*, which is the first monograph on the African human rights system. Originally published by Kluwer Law International in 1996, the book was later published in French and Arabic. She is also the editor of the *AFLA Quarterly*, with more than 40 issues to date and AFLA's Book Series with four volumes to date. Ms Ankumah has authored a forthcoming memoire, *Hague Girls*.

PREFACE

This volume is dedicated to a topic that has dominated a large part of my professional life and that is close to my heart: justice, notably criminal justice, in Africa and for all Africans. Of course, criminal justice and international criminal justice are not exclusively African goals and values. They are universal in scope and nature. Yet, there is no denying that Africa so far has played a central role in the development of international criminal law. One of the ad hoc tribunals was set in place in response to the Rwandan atrocities, the work of the International Criminal Court (ICC) so far has been devoted to African situations and there is no other continent with more hybrid and special criminal law bodies than the African continent – The Special Court for Sierra Leone, the International Crimes Division of Uganda's High Court and the Extraordinary African Chambers in Senegal.

Practice so far demonstrates that it is far from easy to actually hold alleged perpetrators of international crimes accountable. Gathering adequate evidence for crimes under investigation is often a formidable task. The various international tribunals seem increasingly mired in politics, especially where it concerns cases against Heads of State or other high-ranking government officials. If one adds that some of the most powerful and populous nations still refuse to participate in the battle against impunity, then one might be tempted to agree with pessimists who believe there is no real future for international criminal justice.

I am not such a pessimist. I do believe that there is a future for international criminal law. Criminal justice has only been on the international political agenda for two decades or so; the ICC has only been operational for a little over a decade. Creating an effective international criminal law system requires time. In fact, if one looks at the overall achievements of the last two decades or so, and places these in a broader historical perspective, one may conclude that quite impressive progress has been made. In the early 1990s the creation of an international criminal court seemed like a dream that was unlikely to become reality in the short term, if ever. There is a growing list of persons convicted before international tribunals and hybrid courts. The culture of silence in which sexual and gender based crimes are often shrouded is being challenged by activists, prosecutors and others.

NGOs have played a significant role in the quest to promote accountability and end impunity for gross human rights abuses, and the notion that persons who commit international crimes should not enjoy impunity is now firmly embedded in the minds of people. More than ever before, international criminal justice is now on the global agenda.

The contributions in this book all start from this presumption that international criminal justice indeed has a future and that there is a need to improve the current international justice system. The editor deserves to be complimented for having composed a well-balanced and comprehensive list of topics that, taken together, present an excellent overview of the current debates on the ICC and, more broadly, international criminal law as it relates to Africa and its people. Academics, practitioners, policymakers and all those interested in criminal justice in Africa will benefit from the rich and well-written contributions.

Navanethem Pillay
Immediate Past United Nations High Commissioner for Human Rights

CONTENTS

LIST OF ABBREVIATIONS

ABA ROLI	American Bar Association's Rule of Law Initiative
AC	Appeals Chamber
ACJ & HR	African Court of Justice and Human Rights
ACT	Accountability, Coherence and Transparency Group
Adelaide L. Rev.	Adelaide Law Review
AfCHPR	African Court on Human and Peoples' Rights
AFLA	Africa Legal Aid
Afr. Hum. Rts. L.J.	African Human Rights Law Journal
Am. J. Int'l L. / AJIL	American Journal of International Law
AMIB	African Union Mission in Burundi
AMIS	African Union Mission in the Sudan
AMISEC	Mission for Support to the Elections in the Comoros
AMISOM	African Union Mission in Somalia
ANC	African National Congress
Ann. Surv. of Int'l and Comp. L.	Annual Survey of International & Comparative Law
APC	All Progressive Congress
APSA	African Union's Peace and Security Architecture
ASF	African Standby Force
ASIL	American Society of International Law
ASP	Assembly of States Parties
AU	African Union
AUPD	African Union High Level Panel on Darfur
BBC	British Broadcasting Corporation
BCLR	Butterworths Constitutional Law Reports
BCS	Bosnian Croatian Serbian
BMJ	British Medical Journal
British YB of Int'l Law	British Yearbook of International Law
Brook. J. Int'l L.	Brooklyn Journal of International Law
Buff. Hum. Rts. L. Rev.	Buffalo Human Rights Law Review
CADSP	Common African Defence and Security Policy
CALS	Centre for Applied Legal Studies

CAR	Central African Republic
CAT	Committee Against Torture
CEWS	Continental Early Warning System
CFPU	Child and Family Protection Unit
Chi. J. Int'l L.	Chicago Journal of International Law
CID	Directorate of Criminal Investigations
CIPEV	Commission of Inquiry on Post-Election Violence
Colum. Hum. Rts. L. Rev.	Columbia Human Rights Law Review
COMESA	Common Market for Eastern and Southern Africa
Convention I	(Geneva) Convention (I) for the Amelioration of the Condition of the Wounded and Sick in Armed Forces in the Field
Convention II	(Geneva) Convention (II) for the Amelioration of the Condition of Wounded, Sick and Shipwrecked Members of Armed Forces at Sea
Convention III	(Geneva) Convention (III) Relative to the Treatment of Prisoners of War
Convention IV	(Geneva) Convention (IV) on the Protection of Civilian Persons in Time of War
COVAW	Coalition on Violence against Women
COW	Coalition of the Willing
CRC	Convention on the Rights of the Child
CSIR	International Convention Center
CUP	Cambridge University Press
DG	Directorate General
DCAF	Geneva Centre for the Democratic Control of Armed Forces
DPP	Director of Public Prosecutions
DRC	Democratic Republic of Congo
Duke J. Comp. & Int'l L.	Duke Journal of Comparative & International Law
Duke L.J.	Duke Law Journal
DV	Domestic Violence
EAC	East African Community
EACJ	East African Court of Justice
ECCAS	Economic Community of Central African States
ECCC	Extraordinary Chambers in the Courts of Cambodia
ECHR	European Convention on Human Rights
ECOWAS	Economic Community of West African States

ECtHR	European Court of Human Rights
EU	European Union
FES	Friedrich Ebert Stiftung
FGM/C	Female Genital Mutilation/Cutting
FICHL	Forum for International Criminal and Humanitarian Law
FIDA	Women Lawyers Association
FIDH	International Federation for Human Rights
FNI	*Front des Nationalistes et Intégrationnistes*
Fordham Int'l L.J.	Fordham International Law Journal
FPLC	*Forces Patriotiques pour la Liberation du Congo*
FRPI	*Forces de Résistance Patriotique d'Ituri*
FSU	Family Support Unit
GCU	Gender and Children Unit
HRC	Human Rights Council
HRCe	Human Rights Centre at the University of California, Berkeley
HRVIC	Human Rights Violations Investigation Commission
Hum. Rts. L. Rev.	Human Rights Law Review
Hum. Rts. Q.	Human Rights Quarterly
IACHR	Inter-American Convention on Human Rights
ICC	International Criminal Court
ICCPR	International Covenant on Civil and Political Rights
ICD	International Crimes Division of the High Court of Uganda
ICGLR	International Conference on the Great Lakes
ICJ	International Court of Justice
ICJS	International Criminal Justice System
ICL	International Criminal Law
ICLQ	International and Comparative Law Quarterly
ICLR	International Criminal Law Review
ICTR	International Criminal Tribunal for Rwanda
ICTY	International Criminal Tribunal for the Former Yugoslavia
IDPs	Internally Displaced Persons
IGAD	Inter-Governmental Authority on Development
IHL	International Humanitarian Law
IHRL	International Human Rights Law
IJTJ	International Journal of Transitional Justice

ILC	International Law Commission
IMT	International Military Tribunal at Nuremberg
Int'l Hum. Rts. L. Rev.	International Human Rights Law Review
Int'l LJ	International Law Journal
IRRI	International Refugee Rights Initiative
IS	Islamic State
ISA	International Student Association
ISS	Institute for Social Studies
Iswap	Islamic State's West Africa Province
J Int Criminal Justice / JICJ	Journal of International Criminal Justice
U.S.F. J.L. & Soc. Challenges	University of San Francisco Journal of Law & Social
JEM	Justice and Equality Movement
JLOS	Justice, Law and Order Sector
JSI	Judicial Studies Institute
KNDR	Kenya National Dialogue and Reconciliation
KPTJ	Kenyans for Peace with Truth and Justice
LJIL	Leiden Journal of International Law
LRA	Lord's Resistance Army
LSS	Language Services Section
LSU	Language Services Unit
MAES	African Union Electoral and Security Assistance Mission to the Comoros
MASSOB	Movement for the Actualization of the Sovereign State of Biafra
Max Planck Y.B. U.N. L.	Max Planck Yearbook of United Nations Law
MDC	Movement for Democratic Change
MEND	Movement for the Emancipation of the Niger Delta
Mich. St. U.-DCL	Michigan State University-Detroit College of Law
J. Int'l L.	Journal of International Law
MICT	Mechanism for International Criminal Tribunals
MIOC	Military Observer Mission in the Comoros
MISCA, later MINUSCA	*Mission internationale de soutien en Centrafrique*
MLC	*Mouvement de libération du Congo*
MONUC	United Nations Organization Mission in the Democratic Republic of the Congo
MOSOP	Movement for the Survival of the Ogoni People

MP	Member of Parliament
MRND	*Mouvement républicain national pour la démocratie et le development*
NATO	North Atlantic Treaty Organisation
NCCR	National Centre of Competence in Research
NCICC	Nigerian Coalition of the International Criminal Court
NDPVF	Niger Delta People's Volunteer Force
NGC	National General Council
NGHC	North Gauteng High Court
NGO	Non-governmental Organisation
NPA	National Prosecuting Authority
NURC	National Unity and Reconciliation Commission
OAU	Organisation of African Unity
ODM	Orange Democratic Party
OHCHR	Office of the High Commissioner for Human Rights
OMCT	World Organisation Against Torture
ONMOG	Neutral Military Observer Group to Rwanda
OPC	Oodua People's Congress
OPCD	Office of Public Counsel for the Defence
OSCE	Organisation for Security and Co-operation in Europe
OSU	Operations Support Unit
OTJR	Oxford Transitional Justice Research
OTP	Office of the Prosecutor
Ottawa L. Rev.	Ottawa Law Review
PAP	Pan-African Parliament
PCLU	Priority Crimes Litigation Unit
PEV	Post Election Violence
PJ	Principal Judge
PNU	Party of National Unity
PRDP	Peace Recovery and Development Plan
PRI	Penal Reform International
PSC	Peace and Security Council
PSU	Protection Strategies Unit
R2P	Responsibility to Protect
REC	Regional Economic Communities
RPE	Rules of Procedure and Evidence
RPF	Rwanda Patriotic Front

SACC	Constitutional Court of South Africa
SADC	Southern African Development Community
SALC	Southern Africa Litigation Centre
SAPS	South African Police Service
SBS	Special Broadcasting Service
SCA	Supreme Court of Appeal of South Africa
SCSL	Special Court for Sierra Leone
SGBV CU	Sexual and Gender-based Violence Crimes Unit
SLA	Sudanese Liberation Army
SOA	Sexual Offences Act
SRSG	United Nations Secretary General's Special Representative
SRSG-SVC	United Nations Office of the Special Representative of the Secretary-General on Sexual Violence in Conflict
SS	*Schutzstaffel*
SSC	Supreme Court of Canada
STIC	Court Interpretation and Translation Section
Suffolk Transnat'l L. Rev.	*Suffolk Transnational Law Review*
Theoretical Inq. L.	Theoretical Inquiries in Law
TIA	Trial on Indictment Act
TNA	The National Alliance Party
TRIAL	Track Impunity Always
UCLA J. Int'l L. & Foreign Aff.	University of California Los Angeles Journal of International Law and Foreign Affairs
UK	United Kingdom
UN	United Nations
UNAMID	United Nations African Union Mission in Darfur
UNAMIR	United National Assistance Mission in Rwanda
UNCAC	United Nations Convention against Corruption
UNFPA	United Nations Populations Fund
UNGA	United Nations General Assembly
UNICEF	United Nations International Children's Fund
UNOMUR	United Nations Observer Mission Uganda-Rwanda
UNPREDEP	United Nations Preventive Deployment Force
UNSC	United Nations Security Council
UNSCR	United Nations Security Council Referrals
UNTAET	United Nations Transitional Administration in East Timor

UNTOC	United Nations Convention against Transnational Organized Crime
UPC	*Union des Patriotes Congolais*
UPDF	Uganda People's Defence Fund
UPF	Uganda Police Force
URP	United Republican Party
USSR	Union of Soviet Socialist Republics
Va. J. Int'l L.	Virginia Journal of International Law
VPRS	Victims Participation and Reparations Section
VUB	Vrije Universiteit Brussel
VWU	Registry's Victims and Witnesses Unit
WACPS	Women and Children's Protection Service
WCD	War Crimes Division
WWII	World War II
Yale J. Int'l L.	Yale Journal of International Law
ZANU-PF	Zimbabwe African National Union – Patriotic Front
ZEF	Zimbabwe Exiles Forum
ZSC	Zimbabwe Supreme Court

LIST OF AUTHORS

Roland K.G. Amoussouga is Head of Integrated Office of the United Nations Multidimensional Stabilization Mission in the Central Africa Republic (MINUSCA), and former Chief of External Relations and Strategic Planning at the International Criminal Tribunal for Rwanda (ICTR).

Kjell F. Anderson is a researcher at the Netherlands Institute for War, Holocaust, and Genocide Studies (NIOD).

Cécile Aptel is Senior Legal and Policy Advisor at the Executive Office of the UN High Commissioner for Human Rights, and Associate Professor of International Law at The Fletcher School of Law and Diplomacy, Tufts University.

Fatou Bensouda is the Prosecutor of the International Criminal Court (ICC).

Jutta F. Bertram-Nothnagel is Director of Relations with Intergovernmental Organizations at the International Association of Lawyers (UIA).

Amelia J. Bleeker is a Barrister and Solicitor of the High Court of New Zealand, and LLM candidate at Leiden University.

Kamari M. Clarke is Professor of Anthropology at the University of Toronto.

Benjamin Cohen is an Associate with Shearman & Sterling LLP, and Former Student Researcher at the Crimes against Humanity Initiative

Max Du Plessis is Associate Professor at the University of Kwazulu-Natal School of Law.

Julie Freccero is the Associate Director of the Sexual Violence Program at the Human Rights Center of the University of California Berkeley School of Law.

Idayat Hassan is Executive Director of the Centre for Democracy and Development.

Alexander Heinze is Assistant Professor at the University of Göttingen School of Law, and Senior Research Assistant at the Department of Foreign and International Criminal Law.

Elizabeth Ibanda-Nahamya is Judge of the International Crimes Division of the High Court of Uganda.

Brigid Inder is Executive Director of Women's Initiatives for Gender Justice.

George Kegoro is Executive Director of the Kenya Human Rights Commission.

Xavier-Jean Keïta is Principal Counsel at the Office of the Public Counsel for Defence (OPCD) of the International Criminal Court (ICC).

Akbar Khan is Secretary-General of the Commonwealth Parliamentary Association.

André Klip is Professor of Criminal Law at the University of Maastricht.

Sanji Monageng is President of the Appeals Division of the International Criminal Court (ICC).

Renifa Madenga is a PhD Candidate at the Southern and Eastern African Centre for Women's Law (SEARCWL), and a former Legal Officer at the International Criminal Tribunal for Rwanda (ICTR).

Anne-Sophie Massa is a Legal Advisor at the Dutch Ministry of Security and Justice.

Angela Mudukuti is an International Criminal Justice Lawyer at the Southern African Litigation Centre (SALC).

Godfrey M. Musila is Head of International Criminal Law Research at the International Nuremberg Principles Academy.

Leo C. Nwoye is Assistant Appeals Counsel at the Office of the Prosecutor (OTP) of the Mechanism for International Criminal Tribunals (MICT).

Benson C. Olugbuo is Programme Manager at the Centre for Democracy and Development, and a Research Associate at the Public Law Department of the University of Cape Town.

Chris M. Peter is Professor of Law at the School of Law of the University of Dar es Salaam, and a member of the United Nations International Law Commission (ILC).

Leila N. Sadat is the Henry H. Oberschelp Professor of Law at Washington University School of Law, Director of the Whitney R. Harris World Law Institute, and Special Adviser on Crimes against Humanity to the ICC Prosecutor.

Kim T. Seelinger is the Director of the Sexual Violence Program at the Human Rights Centre of the University of California Berkeley School of Law.

Lorraine Smith van-Lin is an International Criminal Law Expert, and former International Bar Association (IBA) Programme Director on the ICC.

Mia Swart is Professor of International Law at the University of Johannesburg.

Manuel J. Ventura is an Associate Legal Officer at the Appeals Chamber of the Special Tribunal for Lebanon, the Director of the Peace and Justice Initiative in The Hague, and Adjunct Fellow at the University of Western Sydney.

FIGHTING IMPUNITY

African States and the International Criminal Court

Chris Maina PETER*

The African leaders behind the move to extract the continent from the jurisdiction of the International Criminal Court are effectively seeking a licence to kill, maim and oppress their people without consequences.
– Desmond Tutu

It is the culture of impunity and individuals who are put on trial at the ICC, but not Africa as a continent.
– Kofi Annan

1. INTRODUCTION

In October 2013, the African Union (AU) called a special session to address the African position with relation to the International Criminal Court and particularly, the ongoing case against the President of the Republic of Kenya and his Deputy. At this meeting, it was *inter alia*, alleged that the ICC has been targeting African countries and exercising double standards by avoiding others who should be prosecuted as well. It was eventually resolved that no sitting African Head of State or Government should be arraigned in any court. The relevant authorities should wait until the ruler has completed his or her tenure. This is an interesting proposition because Africa does not only have feudal monarchs with life tenures, but also 'democratically' elected Presidents and 'civilianised' military rulers who have amended

* The author is most grateful to Ms Irina Gerassimova, the Chief, Specialized Reference Unit, Library of the United Nations Office in Geneva, Switzerland where this work was done for immense assistance; Dr Juliana Masabo, Lecturer in Law, School of Law, University of Dar es Salaam for commenting on the article in draft form; and Ms Evelyn A. Ankumah for updating the work.

the Constitutions of their countries to allow them to rule forever. In such a situation, how long will ICC and victims of serious violations of human rights wait – forever?[1]

The aim of this work is to interrogate the love and hate relationship between the AU and The Hague based ICC and in particular the activities of this Court in the continent. Special focus however will be the Republic of Kenya where the current Head of State faced charges[2] and his Deputy is facing charges before the Court in The Hague in connection with the post-election violence in that country of 2007–2008. However, this will be examined in the context of how the international community has addressed serious violations of human rights over the years without the existence of a permanent institution.

2. THE INTERNATIONAL COMMUNITY AND SERIOUS HUMAN RIGHTS VIOLATIONS

2.1. AD HOC MECHANISMS AND SERIOUS HUMAN RIGHTS VIOLATIONS

One area in which international law has been weak is in the address of criminal law at international stage and particularly where the scale of the violation is high. Thus, for many years, no global mechanism could be established to address these situations.

The solution to this obvious lacuna has been establishment of ad hoc institutions to deal with serious human rights violations whenever they have occurred, spontaneously on a situation-by-situation basis. This system did not help in development of a system and rules to guide it in such situations.

A number of institutions were established in this way to address serious violations of human rights.[3] These include the Leipzig War Crimes Trial of 1921, which tried several German military commanders of the First World War;[4] the International Military Tribunal that conducted the Nuremberg Trials of prominent members of the political, military, and economic leadership of the

---

1 One African diplomat noted that the suggestion that leaders should be prosecuted when they leave office is full of mischief. What if they do not get out of power? See Mutambo, 'What AU Positions on Kenya Mean', *Sunday Nation* (Nairobi), 20 October 2013, p. 40.

2 In December 2014, the Prosecutor of the ICC filed a notice to withdraw charges against Mr Kenyatta 'given the state of the evidence' without prejudice to the possibility of bringing a new case should additional evidence become available, Statement of the Prosecutor of the International Criminal Court on the Withdrawal of Charges against Mr Uhuru Kenyatta, ICC Press Release, 5 December 2014, available at: www.icc-cpi.int.

3 On profiles of some of these institutions see Williams 2012; and Kuosmanen 2007.

4 See Mullins 1921; and Yarnall 2011.

defeated Nazi Germany in 1945–46;[5] the International Military Tribunal for the Far East 1946, the Tokyo War Crimes Tribunal, convened in 1946 to conduct the Tokyo Trials of the leaders of the Empire of Japan for conspiracy to start and wage war and other war crimes;[6] the International Criminal Tribunal for the Former Yugoslavia (ICTY), established in 1993 to prosecute serious crimes committed during the wars in the Balkans and try their perpetrators;[7] and the International Criminal Tribunal for Rwanda (ICTR), established in November 1994 by the United Nations Security Council through Resolution 955 in order to try individuals responsible for the Rwandan Genocide and other serious violations of international law in Rwanda between 1 January and 31 December 1994.[8]

Other institutions of lesser prominence are the Special Panels of the Dili District Court (also called the East Timor Tribunal), a hybrid international and East Timorese tribunal created in 2000 by the United Nations Transitional Administration in East Timor (UNTAET) to try cases of 'serious criminal offences', including murder, rape, and torture, which took place in East Timor in 1999;[9] the Extraordinary Chambers in the Courts of Cambodia, also known as the 'Khmer Rouge Tribunal', a national court established pursuant to an agreement between the Royal Government of Cambodia and the United Nations to try senior members of the Khmer Rouge for serious violations of Cambodian penal law, international humanitarian law and custom, and violation of international conventions recognised by Cambodia, committed during the period between 17 April 1975 and 6 January 1979;[10] and the Special Court for Sierra Leone, an independent judicial body set up to 'try those who bear greatest responsibility' for the war crimes and crimes against humanity committed in Sierra Leone after 30 November 1996 during the Sierra Leone Civil War.[11]

---

5 Woetzel 1962; Taylor 1993; and Ginaburgs and Kudriavstev (eds.) 1990.

6 Minear 1971; Rolling and Cassese 1993.

7 This Tribunal was established vide United Nations Security Council Resolution 827 of 25 May 1993. On this Tribunal see *inter alia*, Cassese 1996; Morris and Scharf 1995; Lescure and Trintignac 1996; and Kerr 2004. On one of its well-known detainees see Dawson 2010, p. 385.

8 Peter 1997, pp. 675–683; Van Den Herik 2005; and Wilson 2011, p. 351.

9 On this tribunal see *inter alia*, Katzenstein 2003, p. 245; Beauvais 2001 p. 1101; and De Bertodano 2003, p. 226.

10 See Van Heughten and Verhoeven 2011; Chon and Thet 2010; Meng-Try and Sim 2001.

11 See Jalloh 2007; and Wharton 2011, p. 217. The most celebrated case decided by this Court is that of the former President of Liberia Charles Ghankay Taylor (*The Prosecutor against Charles Ghankay Taylor*, SCSL-2003-01-I). See Nouwen 2005, p. 654; Deen-Racsmany 2005, p. 299; and Tejan-Cole 2009, p. 205. Taylor has been found guilty of all the 11 counts of war crimes and crimes against humanity and has been sentenced to 50 years in prison. See Sesay and Mahony 2012, pp. 22–23; and Davies 'Unfinished Business', Vol. 46 No. 518 *New African*, June 2012, p. 8. Also interesting is the new book Waugh 2012.

2.2. UNIVERSAL JURISDICTION AS A STOP-GAP MEASURE TO ADDRESS IMPUNITY

The emergence and application of the principle of universal jurisdiction in the 1990s which did away with the whole question of *locus standi* and place of crime for purposes of assuming jurisdiction in cases involving serious crimes was a rude shock to African rulers.[12] Victims of human rights violation in the continent approached courts in Europe and their cases were entertained under this principle and warrants issued against some of the prominent and long reigning rulers in the continent. This part examines the principle itself and its application in Africa and the reaction of the rulers to the principle.

2.2.1. The Principle in Principle

The principle of universal jurisdiction provides that there are certain types of offences which are so serious that those alleged to have committed them should be prosecuted wherever they are on the globe.[13] This is irrespective of where the offences were committed or the nationality of the suspects or the victims.[14] These offences include genocide, torture, war crimes, and crimes against humanity. A considerable portion of the international community takes this principle quite seriously.[15]

Therefore, suspects have had warrants of arrest issued against them in some jurisdictions for offences alleged to have been committed elsewhere. Where suspects have arrived in states where such warrants have been issued they have been arrested and prosecuted with ease, with courts assuming jurisdiction without questions asked or resort to undue technicalities.[16] The most famous suspect to have been arrested through invocation of the principle of universal jurisdiction was the former President of Chile, Lieutenant General Augusto José

12 See African Union, *Report of the Commission on the Use of the Principle of Universal Jurisdiction by Some Non-African States as Recommended by the Conference of Ministers of Justice/Attorneys General*, presented at the Assembly of the African Union Eleventh Ordinary Session held at Sharm el-Sheikh, Egypt, on 30 June–1 July 2008 (AU Doc. Assembly/AU/ 14 (XI)).

13 Many seminal works have been written on this principle. See for instance Macedo 2004; and Abbi-Saab 2003, p. 596.

14 Summers 2003, p. 63.

15 There are a few dissenting voices against this principle. See Kissinger 2001, p. 86. This work is also reproduced in Driscoll 2004, p. 93.

16 See Princeton Project on Universal Jurisdiction, *The Princeton Principles on Universal Jurisdiction*, Princeton, 2001; Chatham House, *Universal Jurisdiction for International Crimes*, 2008; Africa Legal Aid 2002. The text of the Cairo-Arusha Principles is available at: www.africalegalaid.com/resources. Adopted under the auspices of Africa Legal Aid (AFLA), the Principles have been coined the 'voice of Africa on universal jurisdiction': Africa Legal Aid 2001; African Union and European Union, *AU-EU Technical Ad hoc Expert Group on the Principle of Universal Jurisdiction Report*, 2009.

Ramón Pinochet Ugarte.[17] Warrants of arrest were issued in Spain for torture and other serious offences committed in Chile during his tenure of office. On arrival in the United Kingdom for medical treatment, Pinochet was arrested on the basis of the Spanish warrants of arrest.[18]

The British courts assumed jurisdiction and his case went before several courts[19] before reaching the House of Lords which underlined the importance of the principle of universal jurisdiction and refusing to recognise the doctrine of sovereign immunity[20] on account of the seriousness of the offences he was alleged to have committed. Pinochet was saved by the British government on the basis of bad health and allowed to return to Chile.[21]

2.2.2. Universal Jurisdiction and Africa

In the recent past, some courts in Europe have been issuing warrants of arrest against some African Heads of State and senior government officials. This follows complaints by victims of torture, genocide, war crimes and crimes against humanity committed in the continent. Any attempt to plead diplomatic or sovereign immunity has not received a sympathetic attention. This is basically due to the seriousness of the offences involved.

These arrest warrants have mainly been issued in France and Belgium. Among those touched by the application of this principle are the former President of Gabon, the late Omar Bongo, and the President of Congo, Denis Sassou Nguesso. Furthermore, Germany arrested Ms Rose Kabuye, the former Chief of Protocol of President Paul Kagame of Rwanda, on arrival at Frankfurt Airport on the basis of a warrant issued in France under this principle. Indeed, President Kagame was very upset by this event. It did not only impact the official visit to Germany but also worsened the already strained relationship between Kigali and Paris.[22] The issue of warrants of arrest against African leaders incensed the AU. The AU Assembly at its Eleventh Ordinary Session held on 30 June and 1 July 2008 in Sharm el-Sheikh, Egypt received a study of the Commission on the use of

---

17 General Pinochet and his case have been extensively analysed. As a sample see Roht-Arriaza 2005; Wilson 1999, p. 930; Kaleck 2008–2009, p. 927; and Perez 1999–2000, p. 175.

18 See *Regina v. Bow Street Magistrate, ex parte Pinochet Ugarte* [1999] 2 All ER 97. See Hawthorn 1999, pp. 253–258; and Munoz 2008.

19 See *inter alia, Regina v. Bow Street Metropolitan Stipendiary Magistrate & Others, ex parte Pinochet Ugarte* (1) [1998] 4 All ER 897; and *Regina v. Bow Street Metropolitan Stipendiary Magistrate & Others, ex parte Pinochet Ugarte* (3) [1999] 2 WLR 827. See also Roht-Arrianza 2009, p. 77.

20 On sovereign immunity and how it functions see *inter alia*, Fox 2008; and Fox 2003, p. 297.

21 The whole process under which General Pinochet went under the principle of universal jurisdiction is captured and analysed in Burbach 2003.

22 See McGreal, 'Top Rwandan Aide Chooses French Terror Trial', *The Guardian* (UK), 10 November 2008; *The Sunday Times* (Kigali), 'Lifting of Judicial Restriction on Kabuye, We Remain Vindicated', 27 September 2009; and Y'Gihanga, 'Reflections: France, Truth Passes Through Fire Without Getting Scathed', *The Sunday Times* (Kigali), 4 October 2009.

the Principle of Universal Jurisdiction by Some Non-African States as previously recommended by the Conference of Ministers of Justice/Attorneys General.[23] As a result, the Assembly commissioned a team of independent experts to study the application of this Principle in relation to Africa. This team was made of three experts from the AU and three from the EU.[24] This team whose report was presented to the African Union went through the Principle and made a variety of recommendations on how its application could be improved and balanced in order to avoid possible bias and double standards.[25]

What is important from the preceding development is the reality that African leaders were compelled to act to address matters which were beyond their control. This aspect was key precisely because the principle of universal jurisdiction challenged the invocation of sovereign immunity as a shield in cases of serious violations of human rights. With time, as the importance of human rights gains ground, the principle of universal jurisdiction is gaining ground at an even faster rate. As a clear and accepted exception to the doctrine of sovereign immunity it makes dictators sleepless. They have to choose their destinations quite carefully across the globe, particularly when they are sure that warrants of arrest have been issued somewhere and are just awaiting execution.

3. THE INTERNATIONAL CRIMINAL COURT – AIM AND PURPOSE

3.1. INTRODUCING THE COURT – FUNCTIONS AND JURISDICTION

The ICC effectively came to existence in 2002 following the coming into force of the Rome Statute of 1998 which establishes it.[26] The ICC is the first permanent criminal justice institution.[27] For a long time, there was reluctance on the part of

23 See Assembly/AU/14 (XI) of July 2008.

24 The team of independent experts was made of the following: from the European Union side were Professor Antonio Cassese (Italy); Professor Pierre Klein (Belgium); and Dr Roger O'Keefe (Australia). From the African Union side were Dr Mohammed Bedjaoui (Algeria); Dr Chaloka Beyani (Zambia); and Professor Chris Maina Peter (Tanzania). The Secretariat was made of Mr Ben Kioko, Legal Counsel, AU Commission; Mr Fafré Camara, Legal Officer, AU Commission; Dr Sonja Boelaert, Legal Adviser, European Commission; and Mr Rafael de Bustamante Tello, UN and ICC Desk, General Secretariat of the Council of the EU.

25 See African Union and European Union, *AU-EU Technical Ad hoc Expert Group on the Principle of Universal Jurisdiction Report*, 2009.

26 Doria 2009; and Triffterer 1999.

27 See the Rome Statute for an International Criminal Court 1998 as corrected by *procès-verbaux* of 10 November 1998; 12 July 1999; 30 November 2000; 17 January 2001; and 16 January 2002. On the genesis of the Court see Simbeye 2004, Chapter One; and Van der Mei 2003, p. 6.

the international community to have such an institution. Whenever confronted with serious violations of human rights,[28] the tendency by the international community has been to establish ad hoc mechanisms to address individual situation.[29]

As the first permanent institution of its kind in the history of international criminal justice, the main focus of the ICC is on the most serious crimes of concern to the international community as a whole.[30] According to Article 5 of the Rome Statute, the ICC is supposed to exercise jurisdiction with respect to the following crimes: the crime of genocide; crimes against humanity;[31] war crimes; and the crime of aggression.[32]

In order for the ICC to exercise its jurisdiction, these crimes should have been committed either in the territory of a member state, by nationals of a member state or when the United Nations Security Council (UNSC) acting under Chapter VII of the United Nations Charter refers a specific situation to the ICC.[33] The jurisdiction of the Court is addressed in Articles 12, 13 and 14 of the Rome Statute which address the precondition to exercise of jurisdiction, exercise of jurisdiction, and referral of a situation by a state party respectively. Under the Statute, it is therefore possible for the Court to exercise jurisdiction over nationals of other states who are not party to the Statute, but have committed a crime on the territory of a state that has ratified that Statute.

3.2. COMPLEMENTARITY TO NATIONAL CRIMINAL JURISDICTIONS AS THE BACK ROCK OF THE ICC

According to the Rome Statute, all the offences which are handled by the ICC, namely, the crime of genocide, crimes against humanity, war crimes, and the crime of aggression (as enumerated in Article 5 to the Rome Statute) are

28 On these crimes see Smeulers and Grunfeld 2011; and Van der Wolf 2011.

29 Among the ad hoc institutions established to address international crimes prior to the establishment of the International Criminal Court in 1998 include: Leipzig War Crimes Tribunal of 1921; The Nuremberg International Military Tribunal, 1945; the Tokyo International Military Tribunal for the Far East 1946; International Criminal Tribunal for Former Yugoslavia, 1993; and International Criminal Tribunal for Rwanda, 1995. Other ad hoc Tribunals with specific national outlook are the Special Panels of the Dili District Court (also called the East Timor Tribunal) was the hybrid international, 2000; the Extraordinary Chambers in the Courts of Cambodia, commonly known as the 'Khmer Rouge Tribunal'; and the Special Court for Sierra Leone. See Goy 2012, p. 1.

30 See United Nations 2004, p. 24; Schabas 2004, p. 69. See further, Ankumah and Kwakwa 2005.

31 There are initiatives to have this crime elaborated vide a separate convention. See Stranton 2011, p. 345.

32 The crime of aggression was elaborated in the Rome Statute Review Meeting in Kampala, Uganda in 2010. See Trahan 2011, p. 48.

33 Weldehaimanot 2011, pp. 208–235.

supposed to be dealt with in the states where they occur.[34] It is only when the state where these crimes occur fail, ignore or are unwilling to deal with them that the ICC comes in.[35] This is the meaning of the complementary nature of the Court. It is captured beautifully in the Preamble and Articles 1 and 17 of the Rome Statute.

It is important to emphasise this point in order to underline the fact that the question of ICC targeting any state does not arise. The Court comes into picture only when the national criminal jurisdiction fails to address the crimes enumerated in the Rome Statute.

It has been explained time and again that due to the principle of complementarity,[36] the measurement of the performance of the ICC should not be the number of cases in its docket and the number of the cases it has completed. The lesser the cases the ICC handles is an indication that the principle of complementarity is working – if national criminal jurisdictions take charge of cases relating to serious violations of human rights.[37] Therefore, the duty of the Court is to guide national criminal machinery on how to handle cases involving serious human rights violations within their jurisdiction and empower them through training and advice where necessary. This is what has been described as positive approach to complementarity.[38] At the same time, the Court will not close its eyes where there are obvious attempts to scuttle justice at national level.

3.3. THE ICC AND IMMUNITY TO RULERS – PROSECUTION OF THE HEAD OF STATE

The ICC is another headache for the African rulers. This is because this Court compliments what has been developed under the principle of universal jurisdiction.[39]

The Kenya's Foreign Affairs Minister Ms Amina Mohamed, while briefing the media in Addis Ababa asked a rhetorical question – where have you seen a Head of State being prosecuted while in office?[40] The question is not entirely irrelevant.

34 See Stahn and El Zeidy 2011.

35 A good example of this situation is the Republic of Kenya which failed to establish a mechanism to deal with the 2007 post-election violence, notwithstanding several reminders. The ICC was forced to take over the prosecution of the suspected masterminds of this violence. See Brown and Sriram 2012, p. 244. Also see Yang 2005, p. 121.

36 This principle did not begin with the ICC. It has a long history as traced in El Zeidy 2011, p. 71; and Jurdi 2011.

37 On how this principle works and its implications in practice see El Zeidy 2002, p. 869; Newton 2001, p. 20; Solera 2002, p. 145; Tallgren 1998, p. 107; Kleffner 2008; El Zeidy 2008, p. 403; and Schabas 2008, p. 5.

38 See Moreno-Ocampo 2011.

39 See Arbour 2003, p. 585.

40 Quoted in 'President Kenyatta cannot be prosecuted while in office, AU says', *The Standard* (Nairobi), 14 October 2014. See also Peter, 'The AU, African States and the International Criminal Court', *Guardian on Sunday* (Tanzania), 20 October 2013.

It is based on customary international law mindset. The question of providing immunity to the Head of State and some of his/her close associates and frequent emissaries like the Foreign Minister has bedevilled the international community for years and continue to be debated even today.[41]

In the recent past, the position of customary international law was discussed by the Appeals Chamber of the International Criminal Tribunal for the former Yugoslavia in the *Prosecutor v. Tihomir Blaskic* case.[42] The issue here was whether state officials could be subpoenaed to appear before the Tribunal or whether they enjoyed immunity. The Tribunal ruled that state officials acting in their official capacity enjoy a 'functional immunity', which is a well-established rule in customary International law.' Prof. Hernández notes that this is an exception to the general rule as international criminal courts have tried persons who, for the purposes of this report, could be categorised as 'officials.' She goes on to warn that even when that exception is invoked, it has to be done restrictively as it is justified on the basis of the characteristics of such persons and the offices they occupy.

There is no doubt that Minister Mohamed was trying to play down the presence and effects of Article 27 of the Rome Statute which specifically provides that the official capacity of a person is irrelevant. This is not a new provision.[43] Its aim was and still is to check impunity by those holding high offices in the land.[44] This provision surprises many because they have always taken it for granted that the Heads of State or Government enjoy various forms of immunity as long as they are in office.[45] It is therefore difficult to appreciate the fact that

41 Currently, the United Nations International Law Commission is considering this very subject. The topic is *Immunity of State Officials from Foreign Criminal Jurisdiction* and is being handled by Prof. Concepción Escobar Hernández as Special Rapporteur. On her latest product see United Nations General Assembly, International Law Commission, *Third Report on the Immunity of State Officials from Foreign Criminal Jurisdiction* 2 June 2014 (Doc. A/CN.4/673). Incidentally, the issue of immunity of the Head of State is equally controversial at domestic level and a rich jurisprudence has been developed in the process. See Ratemo 'Immunity of President', Vol. 50 No. 6 *The Nairobi Law Monthly*, June 2014, p. 50; and Njiru, Boniface, 'Fumbling over the Head of State Immunity', No. 1 *The Platform* (Nairobi), December 2014, p. 32.

42 ICTY, *Prosecutor v. Blaskic*, Appeals Chamber, IT-95-14-AR 108, 29 October 1997.

43 It has been in the Rome Statute since 1998 when the Statute was adopted and indeed, when the Republic of Kenya became a party to the Statute. Kenya signed the Rome Statute on 11 August 1999; ratified it on 15 March 2005 and the Statute became binding on the country on 1 June 2005. The same argument applies to the 34 African states that are party to the Rome Statute of 1998, which establishes the International Criminal Court. Surely they must have read the Statute before signing it and eventually ratifying it. If they were serious and listened to their legal advisers carefully, they should have noted all important provisions of the Statute, including Article 27 which does away with immunity to politicians of all levels.

44 See Akande 2004, p. 407.

45 On immunities enjoyed by senior state officials and their limitations see *inter alia*, Fox 2012, p. 127; Bianchi 1994, p. 195; Bojic 2005; Cassese 2002, p. 853; Koivu 2001, p. 305; Penrose 2000, p. 193; and Mallory 1986, p. 169.

people holding these offices could actually be prosecuted while still in the Office. Article 27 of the Rome Statute creates a new revolution in governance and accountability on the part of state officials.

4. AFRICA AND THE ICC

4.1. AFRICA AND SERIOUS VIOLATIONS OF HUMAN RIGHTS

At independence in the 1960s, the majority of the new African rulers believed that the journey was over. They were stepping into the shoes of the colonial rulers, and therefore they had no intention of behaving otherwise. They were to behave like their predecessors. However, unlike the colonial regime which was at least accountable to the metropole, the new rulers were accountable to nobody but themselves – not even to their own people. That was the beginning of tyranny in the continent.

Therefore, while the 1960s were years of hope, the 1970s turned into a nightmare for the majority of Africans. It was during this period that dictators like Idi Amin of Uganda, Emperor Bokassa of the so-called Central African Empire, and Macias Nguema of Equatorial Guinea ruled with an iron hand. The rest of Africa looked on helpless but somehow giving these dictators tacit support. The best that could be done was the adoption of the African Charter on Human and Peoples' Rights in 1981[46] to address human rights violations in the continent. The institution adopted for the implementation of the Charter – the African Commission on Human and Peoples' Rights – was to a very large extent toothless. The Court that followed to fortify the Commission in 1998[47] was not useful either as it began with its hands tied at the back, by keeping the people, through civil society, technically out of its reach.

It seemed that only efforts from beyond the continent could make a difference for the people of Africa. The application of the principle of universal jurisdiction, the UN backed tribunals and the establishment of the first global court to address serious violations of human rights have all proved able to bite. They seem to worry both rulers 'in power' and their protagonists in 'the bush' as well. Several of them are being sought for torture, war crimes, crimes against humanity and related offences.

---

46 Also sometimes called the 'Banjul Charter', the African Charter was adopted in Nairobi, Kenya on 27 June 1981 and entered into force on 21 October 1986 [CAB/LEG/67/3/Rev 5]. See Ankumah 1996; Kufour 2010; and Ssenyonjo 2012.

47 The Protocol on the Establishment of an African Court on Human and Peoples' Rights was adopted in Ouagadougou, Burkina Faso, on 9 June 1998 and entered into force on 25 January 2004. The first judges of the Court were sworn in in July 2006.

This section is an attempt to map this sad journey of the continent from innocence of independence through consolidation of impunity to the attempts to rein in the dictators and tyrants in State House or the similar characters in the bush. Concentration will be on the ongoing cat and mouse game between the continent's rulers and the International Criminal Court.

4.2. THE RISE AND CONSOLIDATION OF IMPUNITY IN AFRICA

Following the declaration by the then British Prime Minister Harold Macmillan of the wind of change blowing in the African continent and the rest of the British Empire, Africans were excited and expectant of a bright future. However, they were disappointed. Apart from the foreign sponsored coups d'état through mercenaries and killing of African leaders, those who remained in power and the others who followed proved to be worse.

What indirectly and not intentionally encouraged African leaders into dictatorship and impunity was the Charter of the former Organisation of African Unity (OAU) of 1963.[48] This Charter, in good faith and with the intention of protecting the continent, included a provision which was to be abused openly in the latter years. That is Article 3(2) which provided for the 'non-interference in the internal affairs of States.' Having just emerged from colonial rule, the continent was protective of its newly won independence, hence the introduction of this provision in the OAU Charter.[49] The issue was not the validity of the new states' concerns about their security, but rather the interpretation of that clause by the new rulers. The question of security was equally important because governments had been overthrown or killed[50] within months of coming into office while some of the departed powers had sponsored mercenaries[51] to create problems for their former colonies.

The 'non-interference in the internal affairs' clause, which was intended to be a shield in the hands of the African rulers, was almost immediately turned into a sword against the people of the continent. Almost all African states introduced

48 See Biswaro 2012; Abegunrin 2009; Naldi 1989; Desta 2007; Dagash 2006.

49 The Charter of the Organisation of the African Unity is reproduced in Hamalengwa 1988, at p. 28.

50 One sad case is that of the Democratic Republic of Congo whose Prime Minister Patrice Lumumba was killed a short time after independence; the country has never really recovered from the events leading to his death. It is only now – more than 40 years later – that Belgium is admitting a conspiracy to kill Lumumba in a belated apology. See De Witte 2001. Also relevant is Hoare 1968 which provides mercenary Mike Hoare's story of his activities in the Congo in the 1960s.

51 Paid mercenaries have been a menace in the continent. On the work of mercenaries in Africa see *inter alia* Peter 1984, p. 373. Unfortunately, mercenaries have been reinvented and given a new name – 'civilian contractors' in war zones. See Cahill 2007; and Ontiti 2005, p. 152.

detention laws which would allow them to detain real and perceived opponents indefinitely.[52] These laws were almost the same though carrying different labels. They gave those holding the reins of power wide and unlimited discretion. One could be detained for 'utterances which are dangerous to the good government and its institutions'[53] or 'conducting oneself so as to be dangerous to peace and good order'[54] or 'acting in a manner prejudicial to the defence or the security of the State'.[55] With such wide-worded formulations used, the sky was the limit and the African rulers could do as they wished to their people.

The coming of the military onto the political scene in the continent pushed the abuse of the internal affairs clause to new absurd heights.[56] In the 1970s, while Idi Amin was killing innocent human beings in Uganda – and it was common knowledge – the Organisation of African Unity, playing the ostrich's game of hiding its head in the sand, crowned Amin by electing him the Chairman of the Organisation in 1975.

Military dictatorships were complemented by one-party political systems in the 'democratic' regimes all over the continent. Rulers were standing for election competing with shadows in the so-called 'Yes' and 'No' elections. Thus, the continent has from South to North and East to West large numbers of people who should never have been allowed anywhere near the seat of power.

As one-party political systems or military dictatorships are no longer in fashion, the continent has witnessed warlords and guerrilla leaders exchanging military fatigues for designer suits and 'civilianising' themselves and seeking for peoples' mandate in elections[57] whose results are in most cases suspect. Some of the dictators have been removed[58] while others have been rigging elections

---

52 On preventive detention in Africa see *inter alia*, Harding and Hatchard 1993; Martin 1974; Kalunga 1978–1981, p. 281; Quigley 1978–1981, p. 11; Peter 1997, p. 113 and p. 8; Lugakingira and Peter 2008, p. 292.

53 This is what is provided in the Kenyan Public Security Act, 1966.

54 For other discretionary language used in legislation of this nature in Malawi, Ghana, Uganda, Zambia, Nigeria, and The Gambia, and in Sierra Leone before the war, see Howard 1986, pp. 152–159.

55 This formulation is used in the Preventive Detention Act 1962 of Tanzania which is still in force. See Martin 1974, p. 85.

56 A case in point is the chaos brought about by military takeovers in Nigeria. See Maier 2000.

57 Former President Jerry John Rawlings of Ghana, Former President Hosni Mubarak of Egypt, Former President Olusegun Obasanjo of Nigeria, President Yoweri Museveni of Uganda, President Joseph Kabila of the DRC and President Paul Kagame of Rwanda can be counted among former military officers who have 'civilianised' themselves. On the behaviour of the African leadership in the last forty or so years see Othman 2000.

58 Among those removed include Hissène Habré of Chad now in Senegal; and Mengistu Haile Mariam of Ethiopia now in Zimbabwe. The latest dictator to be shown the door by people's power is Blaise Compaoré who ruled Burkina Faso by iron fist from 1987 until 31 October 2014 when the Burkinabé people said enough is enough and he had to flee the country. For years, the government in Senegal with silent approval by the AU had failed to prosecute Hissène Habré, former President of Chad, a long-term fugitive from international justice residing in Dakar as a free man. This forced Belgium to approach the International Court of Justice for guidance. In a decision rendered in July 2012, the Court directed Senegal either to

for decades and have been lording it over their people for over twenty years and still going strong.[59] It is against some of these that warrants of arrest have been issued by both national[60] and global courts.[61]

4.3. EMBRACING HUMAN RIGHTS IN ORDER TO FEEL GOOD

The adoption of the African Charter on Human and Peoples' Rights in 1981 and the Protocol on the African Court on Human and Peoples' Rights in 1998 was not an indication of change of heart on the part of the African rulers, but of their desire to appease the foreign donors and feel good while dictating and squeezing the people as usual.

The adoption of the African Charter on Human and Peoples' Rights was merely an exercise in public relations. The majority of African rulers were pointing fingers at those who were extreme – Idi Amin, Macias Nguema, Jean Bedel Bokassa and the like – in order to shift focus away from what they were doing at home against their own citizens.[62] While these extreme rulers could not be excused in any way, they were convenient scapegoats. Otherwise, brutalisation of the African people in the hands of their 'leaders' continued unchecked.

Most initiatives touching on human rights are at best lip service without any serious intention of ensuring that these rights are respected, protected and promoted in the continent. This is clearly indicated by the kind of limitations imposed on institutions established in the continent. For instance, when the

---

prosecute or extradite Habré to Belgium (*Questions Relating to the Obligation to Prosecute or Extradite (Belgium v. Senegal) Merits, 20 July 2012*). This decision prompted Senegal to act. After a long delay, eventually on 2 July 2013, Hissène Habré was charged with crimes against humanity, torture and war crimes and placed in pre-trial detention by the Extraordinary African Chambers established within the courts of Senegal to prosecute international crimes committed in Chad between 7 June 1982 and 1 December 1990. The other fugitive being sought in his own country, having been convicted *in absentia*, is the former Ethiopian strongman Mengistu Haile Mariam who has been living in Zimbabwe for years under the protection of President Robert Gabriel Mugabe. Interestingly the current Chadian President Idriss Deby characterised the arrest of Habré as a step towards 'an Africa free of all evil, an Africa stripped of all dictatorships.' On these two issues see Kegoro, 'African Human Rights Court Needs More than Just a Secretariat to Deliver', Vol. 2 No. 11 *The Nairobi Law Monthly*, 2011, p. 102; Deguefe 2006, Chapter 10; Mayfield 1995, p. 553; and Tiba 2007, p. 513.

59 Among the rulers still clinging to power after many years in office are Teodoro Obiang of Equatorial Guinea, since 1979; José Eduardo Dos Santos of Angola, since 1979; Robert Mugabe of Zimbabwe, since 1980; Paul Biya of Cameroon, since 1982; Yoweri Museveni of Uganda, since 1986; King Mswati III of Swaziland, since 1986; Idris Deby of Chad, since 1990; and Denis Sassou Nguesso of Congo, since 1997 (having previously ruled 1979–91).

60 Courts in France and Belgium have issued warrants against Denis Sassou Nguesso, and the late Omar Bongo (President of Gabon) under universal jurisdiction.

61 See for instance the case of the *Prosecutor v. Omar Hassan Ahmed Al-Bashir*, ICC-02/05-01/09, 12 December 2011 by the International Criminal Court against the President of Sudan.

62 See *inter alia*, Viljoen and Odinkalu 2006.

African Charter was adopted the possibility of establishing a court of law to strengthen the protection of rights was ruled out. The implementation of the Charter was to be done through a Commission which at the end of the day was to eventually report to the Summit of the Heads of State and Government of the then Organisation of African Unity (OAU) and now of the African Union (AU). So, it was essentially the African rulers who would have the last word on fellow rulers without an independent arbiter intervening in a decisive manner.

Even when a Court was eventually established, it was not without restrictions.[63] This court was to complement the Commission[64] but individuals and the civil societies organisations were blocked from accessing the Court in contradiction to the easy access to the Commission. According to Articles 5 and 34 of the Protocol establishing this Court, an individual or a civil society organisation can access the Court only if the respondent state has made a special declaration allowing that. At present, out of the 54 members of the African Union, only seven have made this form of declaration. These are Burkina Faso, Côte d'Ivoire, Ghana, Malawi, Mali, Rwanda and the United Republic of Tanzania. This is a clear indication of not being committed to human rights in the continent and their protection and promotion. African states and their rulers want to discuss and generally talk about human rights in the continent but not to walk their talk.

Another problem is at the level of enforcement of the decisions of the Court. Again, in this aspect the Protocol is extremely weak. While the Protocol gives the Court the power to award remedies for human rights violations including the payment of fair compensation or reparation,[65] the problem is the execution of the Court's decisions. This is supposed to be done by the Council of Ministers on behalf of the Assembly.[66] This is a desperate situation which should be interpreted more generously to allow the victim of a human or peoples' right violation to enforce the compensation part of the judgment of the Court in the national courts.[67]

This is not a surprising situation. It arises out of the age-old tendency of the African leadership to see itself as being above the law, as lawmaker and judge, giving orders but not receiving them. For them, it is inconceivable to take your

63 The issue of an African Court on Human and Peoples' Rights was raised during the 30th Summit of the Heads of State and Government of the Organisation of African Unity (OAU) in Tunis in 1994. The general feeling was that things were not moving smoothly in the continent as far as human rights were concerned. The Protocol prepared for the establishment of the Court was adopted by the 34th Ordinary Session of the Assembly of the Heads of State and Government of the OAU held in Ouagadougou, Burkina Faso in June 1998. See Kioko 1998, p. 70; Bekker 2007, p. 151; Pityana 2003, p. 110; and Ouguergouz 2003, p. 79.

64 See Malila 2011, p. 551.

65 See Article 26(1). It has been noted that this position is broader than all the current mandates to afford remedies to victims of human rights abuse. See Shelton 1999, p. 177.

66 Article 27 of the Protocol.

67 See Shelton 1999, p. 295.

elder and leader to court. The Head of State is seen as 'the wise man', 'a father figure': why drag him to court? It is this attitude towards the courts of law that hindered earlier development of a proper continental dispute settlement mechanism.

4.4. EARLY LOVE AND FALL OUT – AFRICA AND THE ICC

The ICC has a very close relationship with the African continent. In fact, African states were solidly behind the initiatives of establishing the court. They came out in large numbers to support the Rome Statute negotiations and they constitute the highest ratification block of the Statute. Sixty percent of African states have signed and ratified the Rome Statute.[68] Incidentally, currently all cases before the court are also from the continent.[69] Half of the situations before the Court have been referred by African states themselves[70] while others have been referred to the Court by the UNSC. There have also been some initiatives from the ICC itself.[71]

The establishment of the International Criminal Court through the Rome Statute of 1998 was celebrated in the continent as it was seen as a solution in the never-ending civil wars. However, when the Court began inquiring into the conduct of some of the rulers, it became a thorn in the flesh.

Currently, the International Criminal Court has opened investigations into eight situations in Africa. These are the Democratic Republic of the Congo; Uganda; the Central African Republic; Darfur, Sudan; the Republic of Kenya; the Libyan Arab Jamahiriya; the Republic of Côte d'Ivoire; and Mali. Of these eight, four were referred to the Court by the concerned states parties to the

68 This point is made articulately by Cote d'Ivoire President Alassane Ouattara when he says: "Africa is not reluctant when it comes to the ICC. This idea is false. Out of 54 member states, 34 have signed up to the Treaty of Rome; in other words, the majority. I think I can justifiably state that most African countries are not in favour of impunity." See De Lavarene, 'President Alassane Ouattara: We are Regaining our Former Glory', Vol. 47 No. 533 *New African*, November 2013, p. 28.

69 States in Africa which are in one way or the other touched by the ICC include the Democratic Republic of the Congo; Uganda; the Central African Republic; Sudan; Kenya; Libya; Côte d'Ivoire; and Nigeria. Some situations have been referred to the Court by the states themselves while others have been referred by the United Nations Security Council and others by the Court itself. All of them are at different stages of handling. See http://en.wikipedia.org/wiki/International_Criminal_Court visited on 14 August 2012.

70 One of the cases which have been brought to the Court by an African state is that of the Lord's Resistance Army in Uganda. Following a reference by the Government of Uganda a Warrant for the Arrest of Joseph Kony was issued on 8 July 2005 and amended on 27 September 2005 by Pre Trial Chamber II – ICC-02/04-01/05-53. See El Zeidy 2005, p. 83; Akhavan 2005, p. 403; Traylor 2009–2010, p. 23; Arsanjani and Reisman 2005, p. 385; Happold 2007, p. 159.

71 The ICC has received complaints relating to alleged crimes from over 100 countries across the globe. By Power of Attorney from the Union of the Comoros, a law firm referred the situation on the Comorian-flagged *MV Mavi Marmara* vessel to the Court, prompting the Prosecutor to initiate a preliminary examination.

Rome Statute and members of the African Union namely Uganda, Democratic Republic of the Congo, Central African Republic and Mali. Two were referred by the United Nations Security Council, i.e. Darfur and Libya. It is only two of these cases which were begun *proprio motu* by the Prosecutor. These are Kenya and Côte d'Ivoire. The fact that a half of African cases pending at the ICC were referred to the Court by African states on their volition proves that there is lack of sincerity in blaming ICC. It would make sense to concentrate on the innocence or guilt of those taken to The Hague as it makes little sense to accuse the Police of arresting one set of 'thieves' but not the others. That does not make the arrested 'thieves' innocent just because the other 'thieves' have not been arrested.

4.4.1. The Al-Bashir Warrants

The problem between the ICC and the African continent was triggered by the situation in Darfur region in the Sudan.

In 2004, the UN Secretary General established the International Commission of Inquiry on Darfur as directed by the UN Security Council via Resolution 1564 (2004) of 18 September 2004.[72] The resolution, adopted under Chapter VII of the UN Charter gave the Commission the following four tasks:

(1) to investigate reports of violations of international humanitarian law and human rights law in Darfur by all parties;
(2) to determine whether or not acts of genocide have occurred;
(3) to identify the perpetrators of violations of international humanitarian law and human rights law in Darfur; and
(4) to suggest means of ensuring that those responsible for such violations are held accountable.

The Commission's focus was on incidents that occurred between February 2003 and mid-January 2005.

The findings of the Commission established that the Government of the Sudan and the Janjaweed are responsible for serious violations of international human rights and humanitarian law amounting to crimes under international law. The Commission established without doubt that Government forces and militias conducted indiscriminate attacks, including killing of civilians, torture, enforced disappearances, destruction of villages, rape and other forms of sexual violence, pillaging and forced displacement, throughout Darfur. As these acts

72 The members of this Commission were: Mr Antonio Cassese, from Italy (Chair); Mr Mohammed Fayek, from Egypt; Ms Hina Jilani, from Pakistan; Mr Dumisa Ntsebeza, from South Africa; and Ms Theresa Striggner-Scott, from Ghana.

were widespread and done in a systematic way they amounted to crimes against humanity.[73]

In its report to the Security Council, the Commission recommended that the situation of Darfur was grave and thus should be referred to the International Criminal Court in accordance with Article 13(b) of the Rome Statute. The Security Council referred the matter to the ICC through Resolution 1593 of 31 March 2005[74] and following investigations by the Office of the ICC Prosecutor, an application for a warrant of arrest was made on 14 July 2008 by the then Chief Prosecutor of the ICC, Luis Moreno Ocampo, against the President of the Sudan Omar Hassan Ahmad Al-Bashir for bearing individual criminal responsibility for genocide, crimes against humanity and war crimes committed since 2003 in Darfur. President Al-Bashir was accused of *inter alia*, masterminding and implementing a plan to destroy three main ethnic groups namely, the Fur, Masalit and Zaghawa through a campaign of murder, rape and deportation which amounted to genocide. The ICC issued the 1st Warrant of Arrest against President Al-Bashir on 4 March 2009.[75] Again, on 12 July 2010, the ICC's Pre-Trial Chamber I issued a second warrant of arrest against President Al-Bashir, considering that there were reasonable grounds to believe him to be responsible for three counts of genocide committed against the Fur, Masalit and Zaghawa ethnic groups.[76]

It is this second warrant that woke up the African rulers as it became clear to them that sitting African Heads of State and Government could face prosecution – something unimaginable for ages. This new situation sent jitters across the continent and particularly among African rulers.[77] As a result, they all rallied behind the beleaguered President, promising assistance as one of their own. It was quite clear to them that allowing the President to go on trial

---

73 The main victims of these massive violations of rights were from the Fur, Zaghawa, Massalit, Jebel, Aranga ethnic groups which could be closely identified with black Africans but not Arabs. Al-Bashir called them 'Zurgas' or Africans in an attempt to disguise the crimes he was committing against the people of the Sudan. See Mamdani 2009, p. 85.

74 See Happold 2008, p. 226; Odinkalu 2009; and Mamdani 2009.

75 In the warrant, the Court listed five counts of crimes against humanity (murder, extermination, forcible transfer, torture and rape) and two counts of war crimes (intentionally directing attacks against a civilian population as such or against individual civilians not taking part in hostilities, and pillaging). See *The Prosecutor v. Omar Hassan Ahmad Al-Bashir*, Decision on the Prosecution's Application for a Warrant of Arrest against Omar Hassan Ahmad Al-Bashir, Public Redacted Version, ICC-02/05–01/09, 4 March 2009. See Dworkin and Iliopous, 'The ICC, Bashir, and the Immunity of Heads of State' 2011, www.crimesofwar.org/commentary/the-icc-bashir-and-the-immunity-of-heads-of-state/ (accessed on 1–07–2012); and McCausland and Rojo 2010, pp. 464–470.

76 See *The Prosecutor v. Omar Hassan Ahmad Al-Bashir*, Second Decision on the Prosecution's Application for a Warrant of Arrest, ICC-02/05–01/09, 12 July 2010. See also Tehindrazanarivelo 2012 p. 397; Jones 2009–2010, p. 13; Williams and Sherif 2009, p. 71; and Saxum 2009–2010, p. 1.

77 See Baker 2004, p. 1487.

would open an unstoppable flood and the Court would come for the next ruler ... *ad infinitum*.[78]

Some states in the continent and particularly those which are parties to the Rome Statute found themselves in the dilemma. On the one hand, the ICC was asking them to cooperate and arrest the fugitive if he visited their countries. On the other, they felt a duty of maintaining solidarity with others in the African Union and its pledge to protect Al-Bashir.[79] Be as it may, with this case there is no doubt that the die was cast – the collision between the Court and the African Union was a clear eventuality.

The African Union has been solidly behind the President of the Sudan in his struggles against the ICC and the international community.[80] As an organisation, it requested the ICC to postpone the issue of President Al-Bashir at least for one year.[81] They invoked Article 16 on deferral of investigation or prosecution. This provision reads as follows:

> No investigation or prosecution may be commenced or proceeded with under this Statute for a period of 12 months after the Security Council, in a resolution adopted under Chapter VII of the Charter of the United Nations, has requested the Court to that effect; that request may be renewed by the Council under the same conditions.

Through this provision, they wanted the Court to defer enforcement of the arrest warrant issued against President Al-Bashir for at least one year, a request that was flatly rejected by the Court which insisted that President Al-Bashir should surrender himself.

The next attempt was the UN Security Council, which remained silent on this matter preferring to be non-committal. As a result, in July 2009 the African Union Summit decided to be defiant by urging its members not to cooperate with the Court. As for the African states which are parties to the Rome Statute the Summit:

> DECIDE[D] that in view of the fact that the request by the African Union has never been acted upon, the AU Member States *shall not cooperate* pursuant to the provisions of Article 98 of the Rome Statute of the ICC relating to immunities, for the arrest and surrender of President Omar El Bashir of The Sudan.[82]

---

78 See the analysis of the thinking of African rulers in Odero 2011, p. 145. Also relevant is Anangwe, 'Kenyatta's Case at the ICC Re-ignites Neo-colonial Debate', Vol. 4 No. 10 *The Nairobi Law Monthly*, November 2013, p. 28; and Jabre and Moni, 'Is Africa on Trial? ... the Role of ICC Examined', Vol. 46 No. 519 *New African*, July 2012, p. 42. For four highly critical but not necessarily accurate essays against the ICC see Hoile, 'Is the ICC fit for Purpose?; Vol. 46 No. 515 *New African*, March 2012, p. 8.

79 Eberechi 2009, p. 53; and Tladi 2009, p. 57.

80 See Ssenyonjo 2013, pp. 389–394.

81 See Jalloh 2011, p. 5; and Eberechi 2011, p. 51. See also Nmehielle 2011, p. 209.

82 African Union, Assembly/AU/Dec.245(XIII) Rev.1, para. 10.

Ever since the issue of these two warrants Al-Bashir has become a fugitive with very limited freedom notwithstanding his presidency. Wherever he goes the law is behind him. He is very careful in choosing his destinations.[83] He visited Malawi under the late President Bingu wa Mutharika, who was then the Chair of the AU, and that was a major embarrassment to the country; the ICC wrote Malawi seeking explanation why it failed to arrest the Sudan's President during his visit. Also, Al-Bashir visited Kenya in 2010 to attend the inauguration of the new Constitution. He managed to leave the country before being served with an arrest order issued by a Kenyan High Court Judge.[84] The presence of Al-Bashir spoilt a festive occasion to celebrate a new beginning and President Mwai Kibaki was thoroughly embarrassed as members of the civil society had rushed to the courts of law to seek the arrest of the Sudanese President but got the court order after he had already left the country.[85]

There have been official protests against countries which have hosted him instead of arresting and surrendering him to the Court. Among these are Djibouti, Chad, Kenya and Malawi.[86] They have however been praised and commended by the African Union for not cooperating with the ICC.[87] In June 2015 Al-Bashir travelled to Johannesburg to attend the African Union Summit. Upon his arrival, the Southern African Litigation Centre (SALC), a small civil society organisation filed an urgent application to have Bashir arrested and transferred to the ICC. The South African government ignored an order of the Guateng High Court in Pretoria that Al-Bashir remain in South Africa pending the Court's final determination. Bashir escaped with the assistance of the South

---

83 On the plight to dictators see Weller 1999, p. 599.

84 See the case of *Kenya Section of the International Commission of Jurists v. Attorney General of Kenya and Another*, High Court of Kenya at Nairobi, Miscellaneous Criminal Application No. 685 of 2010. On this interesting case which is now on appeal before the Court of Appeal of Kenya see Odete 2013, p. 47; and Gathii, 'Why Bashir Appeal Faces Uphill Task', Vol. 3 No. 1 *The Nairobi Law Monthly*, January 2012, p. 46.

85 On 28 November 2011, Justice Nicholas Ombija, a Puisne Judge of the High Court of Kenya, delivered his ruling on an application for issuance of a provisional warrant of arrest against President Omar Al-Bashir. The application had been filed by the Kenyan Section of the International Commission of Jurists, (ICJ Kenya) which had joined both the Attorney General and the Minister for Internal Security as the Respondents. This warrant is still valid which means that General Al-Bashir can be arrested at any time he sets foot in the country. See *The Kenyan Section of the International Commission of Jurists v. The Attorney General, Minister of State for Provincial Administration and Internal Security*, Miscellaneous Criminal Application No. 685 of 2010, [2011] eKLR, kenyalaw.org/Downloads_FreeCases/84203.pdf. See also *The Guardian* (UK), 'Kenya defends failure to arrest Sudan's President Omar Al-Bashir in Nairobi', 29 August 2010; and Gathii, 'Essays: Why Bashir Appeal Faces Uphill Task', Vol. 3 No. 1 *The Nairobi Law Monthly*, January 2012, p. 46.

86 See *The Prosecutor v. Omar Hassan Ahmad Al-Bashir*, Decision Pursuant to Article 87(7) of the Rome Statute on the Failure by the Republic of Malawi to Comply with the Cooperation Requests Issued by the Court with Respect to the Arrest and Surrender of Omar Hassan Ahmad Al-Bashir, ICC-02/05-01/09-139, 12 December 2011. It is quoted in Ssenyonjo 2013, p. 387.

87 See African Union Assembly/AU/Dec.397(XVIII), para. 7; Assembly/AU/Dec.334(XVI), para. 5.; and Assembly/AU/Dec.366(XVII), para. 5 of 2012.

African government before the Court's final order that Bashir be arrested. President Bashir is scheduled to return to South Africa in December. Meanwhile South Africa's ruling party, the ANC has voted to withdraw South Africa from the ICC. That is where we are with Al-Bashir, the President of the Sudan, who is still on the run. The question is until when?[88]

4.4.2. *The ICC and Gaddafi and Sons*

Another African Head of State who had had a brush with the ICC is the late Colonel Muammar Mohammed Abu Minyar Gaddafi of the Great Socialist People's Libyan Arab Jamahiriya (Libya). Three warrants of arrest were issued against him, his son Saif Al-Islam Gaddafi and Abdullah Al-Sanussi, his former intelligence chief for crimes against humanity alleged to have been committed in the country between 15 and 28 February 2011 when there were demonstrations and general civil disorder in the country.

In this case too, the African Union backed Colonel Gaddafi and urged member states not to cooperate with the ICC in the execution of the warrant against him. The African Union Assembly of Heads of State and Government intimated that it:

> EXPRESSES DEEP CONCERN at the manner in which the ICC Prosecutor handles the situation in Libya which was referred to the ICC by the UN Security Council through Resolution 1970 (2011). The Assembly NOTES that the warrant of arrest issued by the Pre-Trial Chamber concerning Gaddafi, seriously complicates the efforts aimed at finding a negotiated political solution to the crisis in Libya, which will also address, in a mutually reinforcing way, issues relating to impunity and reconciliation. In this regard, the Assembly DECIDES that *Member States shall not cooperate in the execution of the arrest warrant*, and REQUESTS the UN Security Council to activate the provisions of Article 16 of the Rome Statute with a view to deferring the ICC process on Libya, in the interest of Justice as well as peace in the country.[89]

---

88 The former Chief Prosecutor of the ICC Luis Moreno-Ocampo warns that: 'The destiny of the individuals sought by the Court [ICC] is to end up in the dock, in our Court – within months, or within years. They will end up in the dock. We are a permanent court. We can wait for those individuals to be arrested.' He however regrets that victims cannot wait. As long as the sought after individuals remain at large, the victims are exposed because they have told their stories and assisted in unveiling the truth and thus face the risk of reprisals by the alleged perpetrators. That is why enforcing the arrest warrants is such an important and urgent responsibility, he argues. See Moreno-Ocampo 2009, p. xix.

89 See African Union, Assembly/AU/Dec.366(XVII), para. 6, Decision on the Implementation of the Assembly Decision on the International Criminal Court Doc. Ex.CL/670(XIX) made at the 17th Ordinary Session of the Assembly of the Union meeting in Malabo, Equatorial Guinea on 30 June and 1 July 2011.

The Court terminated all the proceedings against Colonel Gaddafi following his killing on 20 October 2011 when his convoy was attacked by North Atlantic Treaty Organisation (NATO) air force working closely with planes from the United States and France.[90]

5. KENYA AND THE ICC

The prosecution of the President of Kenya and his Deputy before the International Criminal Court seems to trouble many African rulers. This is because the Court was putting on the dock a president who was in the office and his deputy. This was historical and unprecedented.[91] Without taking sides, we only need to refresh our memories about this case.

5.1. DEATHS AND DISPLACEMENT

Following the controversial general elections in Kenya of 27 December 2007 in which former President Mwai Kibaki was declared winner there was a crisis; violent ethnic clashes erupted which resulted in the deaths of over 1,200 innocent human beings with many injured[92] and over 500,000 displaced.[93]

Some of those displaced were to stay in Internally Displaced Persons (IDPs) Camps for over five years until early 2013 when they were given a token sum of money as compensation – but not their farms and houses destroyed during the 2007–2008 post-election violence. The violence changed their lives forever.[94]

5.2. THE WAKI COMMISSION AND THE ENVELOPE

In February 2008 the Government of Kenya established an International Commission to investigate the clashes in Kenya following the disputed Kenyan

---

90 See *In the Case of the Prosecutor v. Muammar Mohammed Abu Minyar Gaddafi, Saif Al-Islam Gaddafi and Abdullah Al-Senussi:* Decision to Terminate the Case Against Muammar Mohammed Abu Minyar Gaddafi, ICC-01/11-01/11, 22 November 2011. Later on, the ICC ruled that Abdullah Al-Senussi, former Intelligence Chief of Libya could be tried in Libya. His lawyer criticised this decision characterising it as condemning his client to 'mob justice' and an 'inevitable death penalty.' See 'ICC Defers Trial of Gaddafi Spy Chief to Libya in a Historic First', *Saturday Nation* (Nairobi), 12 October 2013, p. 31.

91 See Kegoro 2012, p. 153.

92 See Chege 2010, p. 3; 'The Lords of Ethnicity: Kibaki and Raila Perfect Culture of Tribalism in Public Appointments Started by Kenyatta and Moi', Vol. 2 No. 1 *The Nairobi Law Monthly*, January 2011, p. 34; and Mungai, 'Mungiki and the Media', *Expression Today* (Nairobi), June 2008, p. 10. Also important is Chaitidou 2014, p. 74.

93 See Njogu 2009; Ishiyama and Backstrom 2011, p. 366; and Nmaju 2009, p. 78.

94 The Kenyan Situation is analysed elaborately in Materu 2015 and Nichols 2015.

presidential election of 2007. This Commission, called the Commission of Inquiry on Post-Election Violence (CIPEV), was chaired by a Judge of the Court of Appeal of Kenya, Hon. Mr Justice Philip Waki. Other members of this Commission were Gavin Alistair McFadyen, a former Police Assistant Commissioner in New Zealand and Pascal K. Kambale, a lawyer from the Democratic Republic of the Congo. The Secretary to the Commission was George Kegoro and David Majanja was the Assisting Counsel.

The Waki Commission in its Report was very bold. It said that there must be an end to this cowardice and pious sense of self-preservation in public service if impunity will be eradicated in this country![95] It went on to recommend that persons bearing the greatest responsibility for crimes committed during post 2007 violence and particularly crimes against humanity should be held accountable. To this end, the Commission recommended further that a local court should be established to ensure that this is done. If this initiative failed, the matter should then be forwarded to the Prosecutor of the International Criminal Court.

What is important to note is the fact that it is this Commission which identified the masterminds of the 2007–2008 post-election violence, and not the International Criminal Court.[96]

Out of this investigation, six persons were identified as the ringleaders of the whole ethnic fracas. Their names were placed in an envelope which was given – not to President Mwai Kibaki, but to Kofi Annan, former United Nations Secretary General, the mediator in the crisis. In turn, Annan handed over the envelope to Mr Luis Moreno-Ocampo, the then ICC prosecutor.[97] The Government of Kenya was then given one year (July 2009 to August 2010) to set up a tribunal to deal with serious crimes committed during the post-election violence. However, the government of Kenya proved unable or unwilling to act.[98]

The government did not set up a tribunal, as requested, capable of conducting an effective and credible prosecution. Opinions were divided between The Hague and local mechanism. On two occasions the Parliament of Kenya voted in favour of taking the matter to the ICC in The Hague, The Netherlands. Interestingly, some of those voting for The Hague have now changed their minds and condemn the ICC.

---

95 See Government of the Republic of Kenya, *The Commission of Inquiry on Post-Election Violence (CIPEV) Report, 2008*, p. 460.

96 Interestingly, today some people are in court demanding for publication of the contents of the whole Commission's Report. See Ndurya, 'Court: I Don't Have PEV Report – Says Waki', *Daily Nation* (Nairobi), 20 March 2015, p. 10.

97 It is this seemingly harmless envelope that opened the way to The Hague. See 'In Focus: Annan's Finest Hour', Vol. 3 No. 2 *The Nairobi Law Monthly*, February 2012, p. 34; and Kabukuru, 'Kenya: Ocampo's Bombshell Leaves ICC Flat on Its Face', Vol. 48 No. 537 *New African*, March 2014, p. 70.

98 Notwithstanding several promises to investigate the post-election violence for purposes of prosecution by the politicians, nothing has been done over the years. See Maundu, 'Kibaki is Right on Local Trial of ICC Suspects', Vol. 3 No. 6, *The Nairobi Law Monthly*, 2012, p. 22.

Problems began when Mr Luis Moreno-Ocampo, eventually opened the envelope given to him by Dr Kofi Annan.[99] The names in the envelope were: Uhuru Muigai Kenyatta the then Deputy Prime Minister and Finance Minister; Mr Francis Kirimi Muthaura, the then Secretary to the Cabinet; Mr Mohammed Hussein Ali, former Police Chief; Mr Henry Kosgey, the then Minister for Industrialisation; Mr William Ruto, the then Suspended Minister for Education; and Mr Joshua Arap Sang, private Radio Executive.

These were indicted and went to The Hague for preliminary hearings.[100] Eventually, charges against two of the suspects, Ali and Kosgey, were dropped, while the remaining four had charges against them confirmed.[101] The confirmation of the charges against the four has rocked politics in Kenya.[102]The country, knowing the provisions of the Rome Statute, 1998,[103]did not attempt to argue for the immunity of its senior politicians.[104]

However, in order not to embarrass the coalition government, Kenyatta resigned as Minister for Finance, but he remained Deputy Prime Minister. Francis Muthaura resigned as head of the civil service.[105] William Ruto had earlier on been relieved of his public office as Minister of Education. Later on, due to the withdrawal of vital witnesses, the Office of the Prosecutor dropped

---

99 On the profile of Mr Ocampo and his work see Kimani and Owuor, 'Ocampo: The Good, the Bad and the Ugly', Vol. 2 No. 5 *The Nairobi Law Monthly*, May 2011, p. 32; and Rozenberg, Prosecutor Luis Moreno-Ocampo is the Best Asset of those Opposed to the International Criminal Court', Vol. 2 No. 5 *The Nairobi Law Monthly*, May 2011, p. 39. See also Khaminwa, 'Ocampo Should Listen to Wako', Vol. 2 No. 1 *The Nairobi Law Monthly*, January 2011, p. 18.

100 See 'International Justice: Italian Judge Holds Fate of 'Ocampo Six'', Vol. 3 No. 1 *The Nairobi Law Monthly*, January 2012, p. 8. See also Abdullah, 'Pressing the Panic Button Won't Change the Course on ICC Trials', Vol. 2 No. 4 *The Nairobi Law Monthly*, November 2011, p. 4; and Kimani and Owour, '2012: The ICC Elections', Vol. 2 No. 4 *The Nairobi Law Monthly*, November 2011, p. 50. Also important is Mathenge, 'Bensouda to Use '92 Clash Report', *The Star* (Nairobi), 12 June 2014, p. 2.

101 See the cases of *The Prosecutor v. Francis Kirimi Muthaura and Uhuru Muigai Kenyatta*, ICC-01/09-02/11 and *The Prosecutor v. William Samoei Ruto and Joshua Arap Sang*, ICC-01/09-01/11.

102 See Hansen 2011, p. 1.

103 Article 27 of the Rome Statute clearly provides that: "This Statute shall apply equally to all persons without any distinction based on official capacity. In particular, official capacity as a Head of State or Government, a member of a government or parliament, an elected representative or a government official shall in no case exempt a person from criminal responsibility under this Statute, nor shall it, in and of itself, constitute a ground for reduction of sentence."

104 The Government in Nairobi is having second thoughts about The Hague trials and has been fighting and seeking the support of both the African Union and members of the East African Community to have the two cases withdrawn and handled locally. However, this comes rather late in the day in the view of the court. See the decision of the ICC Appeal Chamber in Decision on the appeal of Mr Francis Kirimi Muthaura and Mr Uhuru Muigai Kenyatta against the decision of Pre-Trial Chamber II of 23 January 2012 entitled 'Decision on the Confirmation of Charges Pursuant to Article 61(7)(a) and (b) of the Rome Statute' ICC-01/09-02/11-425 delivered on 24 May 2012.

105 See Mungai, 'A Preliminary Commentary on the Decision of the Pre-Trial Chamber II in the Case of Prosecutor vs Francis Kirimi Muthaura & 2 Others and Its Implications', Vol. 3 No. 2 *The Nairobi Law Monthly*, February 2012, p. 24.

charges against Mr Muthaura and thus reducing the number of those charged to three. Two of those charged, Mr Kenyatta and Ruto vied for the Presidency and Deputy Presidency and campaigned under a coalition called Jubilee.[106] They won the elections and became president and deputy president, respectively.[107] Since then, the situation has fundamentally changed.[108] There have been campaigns by the Government of Kenya to have all these cases tried locally in Kenya or at least somewhere in Africa.[109] While the case against Mr Ruto is proceeding on smoothly,[110] that of Mr Kenyatta stalled for some time due to witnesses recanting their testimonies,[111] the Prosecutor requested for time to re-organise her case[112] but eventually she withdrew the charges.[113]

5.3. TAMPERING WITH WITNESSES

The biggest headache to any prosecutor in an international tribunal is to protect the witnesses. There are multi-interests in the witnesses scheduled to appear before the tribunal. Relatives and persons associated to those the witness is expected to testify against are on high alert and will use all means possible to identify and access the witness. In situations where the accused is free it is even more complicated. One can then imagine a situation where the accused is a Head of State or the Deputy Head of State. The pressure on the witnesses can be immense.

---

106 See Kabukuru, 'ICC's Long Shadow over Impending Elections', Vol. 47 No. 524 *New African*, January 2013, p. 30.

107 See Kabukuru, 'The Return of President Kenyatta', Vol. 47 No. 527 *New African*, April 2013; and Thatiah 2014, p. 201. It was not easy for the duo to be accepted as leaders in the local politics with some referring to them as fugitives. See Kajwang, 'We Cannot Allow Ourselves to be Ruled by Two Fugitives', No. 63 *The Africa Report*, August–September 2014, p. 12.

108 With two indictees as president and deputy president the matters before the ICC became more complex as well as international relations of the country. See Otiento, 'The ICC Tested the Strength of the EU-Kenya Relationship but we Survived', *The East African* (Nairobi), 14–20 March 2015.

109 With time, this campaign is losing support within the continent. See 'Kenya's anti-ICC Protocol Fails to Find AU Backers', *The East African* (Nairobi), 31 January 2015.

110 See for instance 'Ruto's Six-Hour Drama in Court', *Saturday Nation* (Nairobi), 26 October 2013, p. 1; Menya, 'ICC – Deputy President Lauded for his Patience: Keter's Experience at Ruto's Side – It's Boring and Calls for Lots of Patience', *Sunday Nation* (Nairobi), 27 October 2013, p. 19; and Menya, 'Ruto Defied Africa(n) Union Resolution for Which Uhuru Lobbied, while his Defence has Accused PNU for Fixing Him', *Sunday Nation* (Nairobi), 20 October 2013, p. 4.

111 See Menya, 'ICC Cases: Will Shifty Witnesses be Bensouda's Undoing?', *Sunday Nation* (Nairobi), 27 October 2013, p. 18.

112 See Mariam, 'Kenyatta at the ICC: Is Justice Deferred Justice Denied?', No. 664 *Pambazuka*, 5 February 2014 (available at: http://pambazuka.org/en/category/comment/90437).

113 Menya, 'ICC: Uhuru Wins Big as Bensouda Drops Charges', *Saturday Nation* (Nairobi), 6 December 2015, p. 2; and 'Uhuru Kenyatta is Free as ICC Drops Case', *The Guardian* (Tanzania), 6 December 2014, p. 1.

That is the situation in Kenya. It is the President and Deputy President and one other person who were arraigned in Court. While the ICC has witnesses but one witness after another withdrew.[114] While some witnesses have disappeared or died in unexplained circumstances,[115] at least, the Court has managed to identify one person who has been actively going around trying to influence witnesses through various means. This person has been identified as Mr Walter Osapiri Barasa, a journalist. The Court has issued a warrant of arrest against him and the government of Kenya appears to be cooperating and has handed the matter over to the judiciary as the law provides.[116]

5.4. CHALLENGE AND CRITICISM TO AFRICAN RULERS' SOLIDARITY

This solidarity of African rulers has been challenged by many, particularly from the continent. One writer calls the attempt by the Africa Union to get the affected rulers out of the hook as moral abdication. He questions the moral basis of their demand for respect:

> The irony is lost on our rulers that they are demanding the world's respect while they disrespect their citizens. What respect do African leaders have for the more than 1,000 Kenyans who perished in the post-election violence? Or for the tens of thousands that have fallen victim to Omar Al-Bashir's goons and killer squads in Darfur? Or the 3,000 or more Ivoirian citizens that perished when Gbagbo elected to defy the expressed will of the plurality of Ivoirian voters?[117]

Another writer has declared that enough is enough with the empty threats from the African Union:

---

114 Among witnesses said to have changed their positions after being compromised include Witnesses 487, 189 and 376. See Menya, 'Will Shifty Witnesses be Bensouda's Undoing?', *Sunday Nation* (Nairobi), 27 October 2013, p. 18.

115 An example is the controversial issue of witness Meshack Yebei who disappeared and was later found dead. See Thuku, 'The Big Puzzle – Ruto: Murdered Witness was on our Side', *The Standard* (Nairobi), 7 January 2015, p. 1 and 3; and Thuku, 'Ruto Clashes with Bensouda over Witness who was Killed', *The Standard* (Nairobi), 14 January 2015, p. 1 and 2. Also relevant is Lubanga, 'No Show: Politicians Snub Yebei Burial', *Sunday Nation* (Nairobi), 22 March 2015, p. 8; and Wafula, 'Ruto ICC Witness: Murdered by the State?', No. 719 *Pambazuka*, 26 March 2015.

116 On 5 October 2013 the Kenyan Interior Secretary Joseph Ole Lenku acknowledged receipt of the request for Barasa's arrest which he forwarded to the Chief Justice two days later for action. See Ogemba, 'Judge Declines to Rule on Barasa's Petition', *Saturday Nation* (Nairobi), 12 October 2013. Relevant also is 'Rome Statute Allows for Journalist Barasa to be Tried in Kenya', Vol. 4 No. 20 *The Nairobi Law Monthly*, November 2013, p. 35; and 'Judge Sets Date for Barasa's ICC Case', *Saturday Nation* (Nairobi), 19 October 2013, p. 5.

117 See Taiwo, 'The African Union and Moral Abdication', Issue 655 *Pambazuka*, 20 November 2013 (available at: http://pambazuka.org/en/category/comment/89685).

> The now-hot-now-cold attitude by the AU towards the ICC is ultimately unhelpful. Those countries that want to walk out of the membership of the Rome Statute should, as a matter of sovereignty, find the courage to do so … this will be a hard knock for the ICC, from which it might not recover. However, the benefit is that African people will be able to separate the sheep from the wolves in sheepskins.[118]

The African Union has a duty to react to these views and questions being directed at it. Particularly why it is so myopic that it cannot even address the fate of civilians charged together with the rulers they seek to protect by all means possible. For instance, in all resolutions, decisions etc. relating to Kenya, Radio Journalist Joshua Arap Sang, who is jointly charged with Deputy President William Ruto is never mentioned. Should he continue with the charge alone or can he ride on the immunity being sought for his co-accused?

6. IS THE ICC AN INSTRUMENT OF DECLINING IMPERIALISM?

A big portion of mankind hates impunity. That makes the Rome Statute of 1998 to some extent a popular international legal instrument. Currently, 123 members of the United Nations are party to the Statute. Staunchly, behind the Rome Statute are members of the European Union.

It is interesting to note states in Africa who are not members. They include Equatorial Guinea, Ethiopia, Libya, Mauritania, Rwanda, Somalia, South Sudan, Swaziland and Togo. Some of these are semi-failed states; others are not known to be democratic. It is not idle speculation to say that the rulers in these countries watch the ICC with suspicion for the likelihood of becoming clients of the Court one day.

Interestingly, the United States of America having participated spiritedly and having signed the Rome Statute, in May 2002 took the unusual step of un-signing the Statute.[119] There were also threats of withdrawing military aid to friendly countries which supported the Rome Statute. Like the US, China also opposes the Rome Statute. Israel and Russia are signatories but have not ratified the Statute. With these facts in place one doubts the charge that the ICC is a tool of imperialism.[120]

---

118 See Kegoro, 'Enough is Enough of Empty Threats from the AU', Vol. 2 No. 4 *The Nairobi Law Monthly*, 2011, p. 114.

119 On US rejection of the ICC and its reasoning see Forsythe 2004, p. 477.

120 Even former US diplomats still support Kenya against ICC. See Munene, 'ICC Process Will End in Empty Justice, Says Frazer', *Sunday Nation* (Nairobi), 27 October 2013, p. 19.

6.1. KENYA AND THE EXTRAORDINARY SUMMIT OF THE AFRICAN UNION

The African Union called an Extraordinary Summit in Addis Ababa specifically to discuss Mr Kenyatta's case and that of his Deputy. The main line of argument was that the ICC was a foreign institution established specifically to target and humiliate Africa and Africans.[121] Addressing his colleagues at this meeting, the President Kenyatta asserted that the ICC is a racist tool of imperialists who have ganged up to humiliate African leaders. Kenyatta said:

> The ICC has been reduced into a painfully farcical pantomime, a travesty that adds insult to the injury of victims. It stopped being the home of justice the day it became the toy of declining imperial powers ... It is a fact that this court performs on the cue of European and American governments against the sovereignty of African States and peoples that should outrage us. People have termed this situation 'race hunting', I find great difficulty adjudging them wrong.

He continued:

> We would love nothing more than to have an international forum for justice and accountability, but what choice do we have when we get only bias and race-hunting at ICC? ... If so, what justice can be rendered by a court which disregards our views? ... Like other African countries Kenya did not achieve its independence with ease. Blood was shed for it.[122]

President Kenyatta's speech, received in Nairobi with excitement in political circles,[123] was described by others as not being wise and well-chosen coming from a person seeking relief from the United Nations Security Council[124] and

121 This line of thinking has been gaining support even from those with no idea of what the ICC does and what its mandate is. See for instance 'The ICC Indictees – All African', Vol. 46 No. 516 *New African*, April 2012, p. 26. It has been pointed out that even the very first convict of the Court – Thomas Lubanga Dyilo of the Democratic Republic of the Congo – is also African! See Mbakwe, 'ICC Gets First Conviction after 10 Years in Existence', Vol. 46 No. 516 *New African*, April 2012, p. 18. See also Engle 2013, p. 161.

122 See Gekara and Opiyo, 'Uhuru's Stinging Attack on ICC and Europe', *Sunday Nation* (Nairobi), 13 October 2013, p. 3.

123 It was said that the President has pulled a masterstroke in diplomacy by converting 'small personal issue' into an international agenda, a rallying call for Africa's sovereignty. Now, international justice was on trial and so was the continent's engagement with the so-called Big Brother. See Special Correspondent, 'In the Eye of the Storm', Vol. 4 No. 10 *The Nairobi Law Monthly*, November 2013, p. 22.

124 See Kiai, 'Of Uhuru's Rattling AU Speech and Paradox of Stopping Hague Trials', *Saturday Nation* (Nairobi), 19 October 2013, p. 13.

later from the Court itself.[125] In fact this statement was to haunt Mr Kenyatta a lot later in his dealings with the Court.[126]

Wise counsel by former mediator in the Kenyan post-election crisis Kofi Annan that Kenya should not threaten to pull out of the ICC was dismissed by the combative Foreign Minister Amina Mohamed who responded referring to Annan:

> He lives in Switzerland and no longer speaks for the African Union. He is entitled to his opinion as a private citizen but I hope he is not disconnected from the rest of Africa.[127]

At the end of the meeting the Summit came out with the decision that no charges shall be commenced or continued before any international court or tribunal against any serving AU Head of State or Government or anybody acting or entitled to act in such capacity during their term of office.[128] In relation to Kenya, the Summit recommended for the suspension of the trials of President Uhuru Kenyatta and Deputy President William Samoei Ruto and deferral of this case by the UN Security Council under Article 16 of the Rome Statute.[129] At the same time, the African Union Commission was instructed to fast track the process of expanding the mandate of the African Court on Human and Peoples' Rights so as to be able to try international crimes, such as genocide, crimes against humanity and war crimes which are currently being handled by the ICC.[130] The Commission was further requested to follow up and report on the implementation of this decision in the next Ordinary Session of the Assembly.[131]

---

125 It has been observed that: 'You cannot accuse a court of being biased and of finding you guilty before trying you and then appear before it to face crimes against humanity.' See Opanga, 'The Hague: Will the Big Stick Diplomacy Deliver?', *Sunday Nation* (Nairobi), 20 October 2013, p. 32.

126 See Menya, 'Reprimand: ICC Critique Haunts Uhuru', *Sunday Nation* (Nairobi), 6 April 2014, p. 30.

127 See 'Briefing: Politics & News', Vol. 4 No. 10 *The Nairobi Law Monthly*, November 2013, p. 8.

128 See The African Union, *Decision on Africa's Relationship with the International Criminal Court*, Ext/Assembly/AU/Dec.1 (October 2013).

129 It has been noted that with this decision, Mr Kenyatta had succeeded in converting a 'small personal issue' into an international agenda – a rallying call for Africa's sovereignty. See 'In the Eye of the Storm', Vol. 4 No. 10 *The Nairobi Law Monthly*, November 2013, p. 23.

130 See Namunane, 'Uhuru Will not Appear at the ICC Until our Demands are Met: AU', *Sunday Nation* (Nairobi), 13 October 2013, p. 5; and Namunane and Oluoch, 'Africa vs Hague: Final Assault on ICC as Continent Asserts Itself and Demands a New Relationship', *The East African* (Nairobi), 12–18 October 2013, p. 12.

131 Not many are convinced that the African Union is doing itself any good in pursuit of this case. See Serumaga, 'Tantrums at Addis Ababa: Why Servants Don't Win Arguments with their Masters', *The East African* (Nairobi), 19–25 October 2013, p. 17; Onyango-Obbo, 'Kenya Being Duped by Neighbours on ICC', *The East African* (Nairobi), 19–25 October 2013, p. 18; and Wanyeki, 'An Africa-Wide Coup at Addis Ababa? 14 Out of 53', *The East African* (Nairobi), 19–25 October 2013, p. 18.

In total anger, the AU decided to deny the ICC to open a liaison office in Addis Ababa. This was rather awkward because such an office would have been the bridge between the organisation and the Court. As others have correctly noted, such an office would have helped to demystify the work of the Court in the continent and 'keep open the lines of communication between the two institutions'.[132]

In a bid to implement part of the decision by the Summit, the Commission commenced the process of preparing a Protocol to amend the Protocol on the Statute of the African Court of Justice and Human Rights to give it jurisdiction over serious violations of human rights.[133] In this amendment, the Protocol on the Statute of the African Court of Justice and Human and Peoples' Rights will be revised to add a criminal jurisdiction.[134] Draft Article 28A gives the Court powers to try persons charged with grave crimes.[135] Article 28B to 28M elaborates these crimes at length. What is interesting is the fact that the main offences provided here are those currently being handled by the ICC. It is therefore a political point being made that Africa can handle its own affairs and it does not need the ICC.[136] It is worth noting that the Protocol is yet to be adopted and this will take time.

Copying from the African Union, the members of the East African Community, though not tightly united,[137] decided in their recent Summit to give their own court, the East African Court of Justice jurisdiction over serious crimes, similar to those handled by the ICC.[138] This was a strange

---

132 See Kuwali, 'Friend or Foe of Africans: Will the Real ICC Please Stand Up?', *The East African* (Nairobi), 26 October–1 November 2013, p. 17.

133 See the Draft Protocol on Amendments to the Protocol on the Statute of the African Court of Justice and Human Rights, Exp/Min/IV/Rev.7 of 15 May 2012. This document was prepared by experts and approved by Ministers of Justice/Attorneys General and endorsed by the Heads of State and Government of the African Union.

134 Adopted on 1 July 2008, the Protocol merges the African Court on Human and Peoples' Rights and the Court of Justice of the African Union into one single court (Article 2). The Protocol, thus, replaces the Protocol to the African Charter on Human and Peoples' Rights on the Establishment of an African Court on Human and Peoples' Rights (adopted in 1998) and the Protocol of the Court of Justice of the African Union (adopted in 2003) (Article 1). The Statute of the African Court of Justice and Human Rights is contained in the annex to the Protocol. On this see Nkwame, 'Arusha Rights Court Granted Powers over War Crimes', *Daily News* (Tanzania), 13 March 2015, p. 1.

135 These crimes are: Genocide; Crimes Against Humanity; War Crimes; the Crime of Unconstitutional Change of Government; Piracy; Terrorism; Mercenarism; Corruption; Money Laundering; Trafficking in Persons; Trafficking in Drugs; Trafficking in Hazardous Wastes; Illicit Exploitation of Natural Resources; and the Crime of Aggression.

136 See 'Africa vs Hague: Final Assault on ICC as Continent Asserts itself and Demands a New Relationship', *The East African* (Nairobi), 12–18 October 2013, p. 12. Also see Oluoch, 'Getting Away with International Crimes? Presidents' Immunity Undermines Africa Court', *The East African* (Nairobi), 18–24 October 2014, p. 14.

137 Though not openly admitted, the rift between the five East African Community members over the pace of integration efforts is linked to the ICC cases. In the process Kenya, Uganda and Rwanda are on one side forming the so-called Coalition of the Willing (COW) and Tanzania and Burundi are on their own outside this arrangement. See Kituku 2014, p. 43.

138 See Kuria, 'Is the Urgency for an Expanded EAC Judiciary Justified?' *Africa Review*, 3 May 2012; Hansen, 'Masters of Manipulation: How Kenya Plans to Scuttle International Scrutiny

decision because the same rulers have for years denied this court human rights jurisdiction which is envisaged under the treaty establishing the Community.[139] It has been argued that this initiative was aimed at saving Kenya's 'Hague Four' from the ICC.[140]

6.2. THE UN SECURITY COUNCIL'S REACTION TO THE AU'S DEFERRAL REQUEST

At the United Nations level the request for deferral by the African Union was presented by Kenya and its friends to the Security Council.[141] However, this request was contested strongly by members of civil society and rights groups in particular.[142] The request for deferral did not go through due to insufficient support particularly to defer the cases of the two Kenyan rulers facing charges before the ICC.[143] The African Union was upset and disappointed but that is as far as they could go.[144]

---

of Post-Election Violence', *Wikimedia Commons*, 31 May 2012; Ubwani, 'Ministers Seek Wider Scope for EAC Court', *The Citizen* (Tanzania), 2 July 2012.

139 See Bossa 2010, p. 333; Nsekela 2011, p. 129; and Ruhangisa 2005, pp. 95–110.

140 As indicated earlier, the 'Hague Four' are the four Kenyans found with cases to answer after the preliminary hearings in The Hague. These are Mr Uhuru Muigai Kenyatta; Mr Francis Kirimi Muthaura; Mr William Samoei Ruto; and Mr Julius Arap Sang.

141 See identical letters of 21 October 2013 from the Permanent Representative of Kenya to the United Nations Macharia Kamau addressed to the UN Secretary General and President of the Security Council (United Nations Doc. S/2013/624); and the letter dated 31 October 2013 from Permanent Observer of the African Union to the United Nations Ambassador Tete Antonio to the President of the Security Council (United Nations Doc S/2013/639). The letter by Ambassador Kamau included a letter to the President of the Security Council from the Chair of the AU Commission Dr Nkosazana Dlamini Zuma of 16 October 2013 (Ref. BC/U/1814.10.13) and attaching AU Decision on Africa's Relationship with the International Criminal Court (ICC) Document Ext/Assembly/AU/Dec.1 (October 2013). See also Oduor and Oluoch, 'The Country has applied to the UN Security Council for Deferral of the Case', *The East African* (Nairobi), 19–25 October 2013, p. 14; and Kegoro, 'Kenya Pulls Out All Stops to Have President's Case Deferred', *Sunday Nation* (Nairobi), 13 October 2013, p. 5.

142 Human Rights Watch for instance made their objection to this request for deferral public arguing that there were simply no facts on the table that would warrant the extraordinary measure of suspending the ICC's Kenya Proceedings. See Kelley, 'Kenya and Rights Groups Set to Clash on Deferral of Cases', *Sunday Nation* (Nairobi), 20 October 2013, p. 5. The position taken by civil society – both international and national has not been taken well by the regime in Nairobi. Measures are being taken, at times legislative, to reign in the civil society. See Odunga, 'Amendment: We are Being Targeted over Hague Cases, NGOs Claim', *Sunday Nation* (Nairobi), 10 November 2013, p. 1 & 6.

143 The Draft Resolution before the UN Security Council was submitted by Azerbaijan, Burundi, Ethiopia, Gabon, Ghana, Kenya, Mauritania, Mauritius, Morocco, Namibia, Rwanda, Senegal, Togo and Uganda. Upon voting, there were 7 votes in favour and 8 abstentions and thus it did not obtain the required votes for adoption. See United Nations Security Council 7060th Meeting held on Friday, 15 November 2013 (United Nations Doc. S/PV.7060).

144 There was a lot of expectation that the Kenyan issue will divide the permanent members of the Security Council and thus be able to sail through but this did not happen. See Oluoch, 'A Friend in Need: Who among Big Five Will Support Kenya's ICC Deferral Quest?', *The East African* (Nairobi), 26 October–1 November 2013, p. 10.

In the meantime, due to allegedly withdrawal of witnesses, the Office of the Prosecutor applied to the Court to push the case of Uhuru Kenyatta forward in order to organise its trial strategy properly. Eventually the Kenyatta case collapsed. The case against Deputy President William Ruto and journalist Arap Sang, who was completely ignored in the various attempts to salvage Kenyatta and Ruto by the African Union, continues.

There was concern whether with that attitude Kenyatta would honour his Court appointments with the Judges at The Hague. Non-appearance at The Hague, with or without the blessings of the African Union, might have serious consequences, many had warned.[145]

7. THE ICC REPLIES TO CRITICS

Carefully and only when opportunity occurs, the ICC has been replying to its critics in a sober and very professional manner. Replying to critics that the Court was targeting African countries, Judge Sang-Hyun Song, then President of the Court had this to say:

> We never chased any African country, we didn't do anything in this respect, they brought their own situation to us. The Kenyan Parliament voted down twice the idea that was recommended that they should introduce a special criminal tribunal ... there was no option but for the ICC prosecutor to intervene.[146]

ICC Prosecutor Ms Fatou Bensouda underlines professionalism in the work of the Court[147] and refutes allegations that the Court is against Africa.[148] She takes a strong pro-victims position and calls for those critical of the Court to think of the victims of massive human rights violation and their plight.[149] She points out that:

> The decade-old court has sought justice for millions of victims in the Democratic Republic of the Congo, Uganda, the Central African Republic, Darfur in Sudan, Kenya, Libya and Ivory Coast ... We have done it with strong co-operation of African State Parties and we have benefited from the commitment and support of our partners within African civil society.[150]

---

145 See Opanga, 'Is there an Attempt to have the President Snub ICC?', *Sunday Nation* (Nairobi), 13 October 2013, p. 18. See also the poem titled 'The AU and the ICC', by Stephen Partington in *The East African* (Nairobi), 19–5 October 2013, p. 19.

146 See *Sunday Nation* (Nairobi), 20 October 2013, p. 13.

147 See Eze, 'Politics has no Place in ICC Decisions ... Says Chief Prosecutor Fatou Bensouda', Vol. 48 No. 536 *New African*, February 2014, p. 74.

148 See Eze, 'Fatou Bensouda: We are not Against Africa', Vol. 46 No. 520 *New African*, August/September 2012, p. 12.

149 For another pro-victim approach see Ferstman 2009, p. 286.

150 See Smith, 'New Chief Prosecutor Defends International Criminal Court', *The Guardian* (UK), 23 May 2012.

She therefore regrets that much of the attention about the Court is focused on wrong perceptions. It is this negative coverage which goes to the media, she argues:

> Again and again we hear criticisms about our so-called focus on Africa and about the court being an African court, having an African bias. Anti-ICC elements have been working very hard to discredit the court and to lobby for non-support and they are doing this, unfortunately, with complete disregard for legal arguments ...[151]

ICC Prosecutor Bensouda continues:

> With due respect, what offends me most when I hear criticisms about the so-called African bias is how quick we are to focus on the words and propaganda of a few powerful, influential individuals and to forget about the millions of anonymous people that suffer from these crimes ... because all the victims are African victims. Indeed, the greatest affront to victims of these brutal and unimaginable crimes ... women and young girls raped, families brutalised, robbed of everything, entire communities terrorised and shattered ... is to see those powerful individuals responsible for their sufferings trying to portray themselves as the victims of a pro-western, anti-African court.[152]

The ICC Prosecutor concludes:

> I don't think about the leaders we are pursuing. I am working for the victims of Africa; they are African like me. That is where I get my inspiration and my pride.[153]

In a lengthy interview with the media, Judge David Ntanda Nsereko of the Appeals Division of the Special Tribunal for Lebanon and a former Judge of the ICC strongly denied the allegation that the Court was witch-hunting Africans and the African continent. He provided a lengthy explanation:

> That is not true. [The] eight cases are from Uganda, DR Congo, Central African Republic, Sudan, Kenya, Ivory Coast, Mali and Libya.

---

151 This criticism is not entirely empty. Sometime back when the ICC's prosecutor decided to investigate alleged UK crimes in Iraq, there was strong criticism of the Court from British politicians and military. See Davis, 'Is the ICC Heading for a Fall?', Vol. 48 No. 542 *New African*, August/September 2014, p. 28. Also relevant is Mwale, 'Black Groups Challenge the ICC', Vol. 46 No. 520 *New African*, August/September 2012, p. 20.

152 See Smith, 'New Chief Prosecutor Defends International Criminal Court', *The Guardian* (UK), 23 May 2012. The plight of victims of serious human rights violations is also discussed passionately in Francioni 2008, p. 140. On the sufferings of the victims in the Kenyan situation context see Kiai, 'Think Again: Victims of Post-Poll Chaos Suffer as ICC, Jubilee and all Watch in Silence', *Saturday Nation* (Nairobi), 18 October 2014, p. 13.

153 See 'Quote Me', Vol. 3 No. 7 *The Nairobi Law Monthly*, July 2012, p. 9. See also Barigaba, 'ICC is not Targeting Africa, It is Responding to Calls from Africa', *The East African* (Nairobi), 21 March 2015.

Out of these eight cases four were referred to the court by African States themselves. First by Uganda, second by DR Congo, third the Central African Republic and fourth Mali; the fifth is Kenya.

After the election violence, under the mediation of Kofi Annan, former Secretary-General of the United Nations, Kenyan politicians agreed to set up a local court to prosecute and punish individuals in Kenya who were responsible for the violence. And it was agreed that if the Kenyan government failed to set up that special court, the matter would be referred to the ICC. Referral to the ICC would at least bring justice to the victims of the violence and their survivors.

The Kenyan government had two years to set up this special court but they failed. And in accordance with the settlement that was agreed on, Kofi Annan handed over the matter to the ICC and then the prosecutor sought permission from the Pre-Trial Chamber to investigate.

That investigation resulted in filing of charges against what they call the Ocampo Six. So, in these cases, you can't say that the ICC was targeting Africa. Rather, it was Africa that sought the assistance of the court to get justice for its people.

In the case of Ivory Coast, the president of that country invited the ICC to handle the case. First it was Laurent Gbagbo who called for the ICC and then Allassane Outtara reaffirmed this commitment. In the case of Sudan, all African States on the Security Council including Tanzania supported the referral to the ICC. Only the United States objected.

On the Libyan situation, the Security Council passed a unanimous resolution, two African members of the Security Council, South Africa and Nigeria, co-sponsored that resolution and the Arab League, which is a sister organisation of the African Union, actively encouraged the referral. In light of all this evidence it's clearly not fair to say that the ICC is witch-hunting African States.[154]

Support to the ICC also came from the UN Deputy Secretary General Jan Eliasson. Asked by a journalist whether ICC was a racist court out to get Africans, he replied:

> No, I wouldn't accept that. We have an African prosecutor, African judges, cases have been brought by African States to the court; I hope we can avoid seeing this in the context of racism. I think there are legitimate questions raised as to why other situations in the world are not being brought up. That is something we all should think about. There are several situations where serious crimes have been committed and should be taken into account by the ICC.[155]

---

154 See Nsereko, 'ICC is not after Africans – Most Cases were Referred to the Court', *The East African* (Nairobi), 19–25 October 2013, p. 31.

155 See 'UN Hopeful of a Workable Formula on Kenya and ICC', *The East African* (Nairobi), 26 October–1 November 2013, p. 12. Some of these ideas are also aired in Warigi, 'Kenyan Cases Have Prompted a Possible ICC Procedures Reform', *Sunday Nation* (Nairobi), 27 October 2013, p. 13.

Indeed, the Court has been very accommodative of the needs of both the President and his Deputy by allowing them time out to travel back home[156] and also to skip some of the sessions of the Court.[157] This attitude of the Court has also attracted sympathy from members of the public and the international community.

Commentators thus see the ICC as an institution just doing its work and in no way targeting the continent of Africa. Veteran journalist and lawyer Jenerali Ulimwengu asserts that given the crimes committed by African rulers on their population, there was a need of arraigning more at The Hague. In his own words:

> Talk of Africa being targeted! Not enough African rulers are summoned to The Hague, if we go by the crimes they have committed against their own peoples. I personally know at least seven who should be packing their bags to answer for hideous crimes, including murder and armed robbery. Yes, armed robbery. One who steals money and other properties that belong to other people (the citizens) commits the crime of theft. If the people protest and he uses armed police or soldiers to shoot unarmed citizens in order to suppress the protest and to help him to effect his theft that is armed robbery. It may not be on the statute books, but it would be if the law were not such an ass.[158]

Ulimwengu has elsewhere argued that if actually the ICC were targeting the continent, then it was doing its work and thus it should be commended:

> Targeting Africa? I'm sorry, but Africa has not been indicted at The Hague, only suspected wrongdoers, who happen to be African. We may also want to remember that a couple of Serbs and Cambodians have made their appearances before the appropriate tribunals. But also, let's face it Africa is where impunity is King, and the place most in need of a remedy.[159]

This is due to the performance of the rulers in the continent and their total disregard for human rights of their people.

---

156 For instance see 'Court Allows Ruto to Return Home for Three Days', *Saturday Nation* (Nairobi), 26 October 2013, p. 7.

157 See Shimoli, 'ICC Allows Uhuru to Skip Sittings: Judges Warn they May Issue Warrant of Arrest if Conditions are Violated', *Saturday Nation* (Nairobi), 19 October 2013, p. 4. See also Menya, 'Prosecutor Wants Uhuru Ruling Reversed', *Sunday Nation* (Nairobi), 27 October 2013, p. 3.

158 See Ulimwengu, 'Are we being Targeted? If so, Someone's Got very Poor Aim …', *The East African* (Nairobi), 19–25 October 2013, p. 19. His position is supported by Vlavonou, 'ICC: Does Politics Win over Justice?', Vol. 650 *Pambazuka*, 17 October 2013.

159 See Ulimwengu, 'ICC is targeting Africa, Continent of Impunity? Then it's Doing Its Job', *The East African* (Nairobi), 5 October 2013.

8. IS OPTING OUT OF THE ROME STATUTE THE SOLUTION?

African states through the 'trade union' of its rulers – the African Union, are threatening to leave the Rome Statute. They are wrongly talking of leaving the ICC *en masse*.[160] This is an embarrassing course of action to take. Firstly, it will be seen in Africa and beyond as an endorsement of impunity by the continent. According to Desmond Mpilo Tutu, the Archbishop Emeritus of Cape Town, South Africa, that decision will be a tragedy for the continent and he gives three reasons. One, without justice countries can attack neighbours or minorities in their own countries with immunity; two, without justice there can be no peace with grievances being harboured and thus leaving violence and hatred ticking like a time bomb in the corner; three, Africa will be undermining its voice in world affairs – voice which can only be strengthened through justice and rule of law.[161] Many sober commentators have identified themselves with similar views, arguing that countries in the continent should consider their long term needs and interests, and that they gain nothing by severing links with the world.[162] Of course, there are those who are encouraging the continent to proceed with this mischief because of narrow and at times immediate personal interests.[163]

---

160 See Namunane, 'Parting Ways: AU Chiefs Set to Endorse Exit from The Hague Court', *Saturday Nation* (Nairobi), 12 October 2013, p. 3.

161 See Tutu, 'Pulling out of the ICC would be Tragic for Africa', *The East Africa* (Nairobi), 12–18 October 2013, p. 13. He is supported by the former United Nations Secretary General Kofi Annan who argues that in event of such a walk-out there could be far-reaching implications for the scourge of impunity that has over the years become a salient feature of the African continent's governance. He adds that African departure from the ICC is also likely to have major impacts on the world's geo-political map as Africans are exposed to abuse, misrule and war crimes. See Mwagiru, 'Fears of Impunity as the AU Pushes for Africa's ICC Exit', *Sunday Nation* (Nairobi), 13 October 2013, p. 46. See also 'Siege Mentality against the ICC Unfortunate', *Sunday Nation* (Nairobi), 13 October 2013, p. 12; Ngwiri, 'Loss of Face or Not, Uhuru's Best Shot is to Attend Trial at the ICC', *Saturday Nation* (Nairobi), 12 October 2013, p. 12; and Ochieng, 'Arguments Against ICC is Sound, But Uhuru Should Oblige', *Sunday Nation* (Nairobi), 13 October 2013, p. 13.

162 Ochieng, 'It is not in Our Interest to Quit Rome Statute', *Sunday Nation* (Nairobi), 20 October 2013, p. 13; Ochieng, 'You Gain Nothing by Severing Links with the World', *Sunday Nation* (Nairobi), 27 October 2013, p. 13; Obegi, 'Do African Leaders Believe in Power Without Accountability?', *Sunday Nation* (Nairobi), 20 October 2013, p. 14; 'Is Africa Really Prepared to Leave the ICC?', *The East African* (Nairobi), 12–18 October 2013, p. 18; 'Withdrawal from ICC: Push to Remove Kenya from ICC is Ill-Advised', Vol. 4 No. 20 *The Nairobi Law Monthly*, November 2013, p. 3; and Branch, 'Reforms: Spare Baby and throw Bath Water', *Saturday Nation* (Nairobi), 19 October 2013, p. 19.

163 See Mungai, 'It is in Kenya's National Interest to Withdraw from Rome Statute', *The East Africa* (Nairobi), 12–18 October 2013, p. 12; Kamau, 'Kenya's Interests and the ICC', Vol. 47 No. 529 *New African*, June 2013, p. 6; Kagwanja, 'Kenyan ICC Cases and Doctrine of Sovereign Immunity', *Sunday Nation* (Nairobi), 20 October 2013, p. 33; Kimenyi, 'How World Politics, Funding Shape the Operations of ICC', *Saturday Nation* (Nairobi), 19 October

Secondly, the decision to withdraw from the Rome Statute will not meet or assist their immediate purpose of salvaging the rulers already under the radar of the Court – those charged and those with warrants in their names issued by the Court.[164] In addition, it is a decision that will take one full year to come into effect and the withdrawal does not discharge the state from its obligations arising from the Rome Statute while it was a party, including the duty to cooperate with the Court.[165]

Definitely, a state does not gain much by withdrawal. In the Kenyan situation for instance, the cases would go on undisturbed and the country, as long as it remains a UN member, should continue providing cooperation to the ICC.[166]

Thirdly, being a party to the Rome Statute or not does not affect the possibility of the ICC pursuing those violating the Statute anywhere on the globe. This is because assumption of jurisdiction by the Court is not dependent on membership to the Rome Statute. There are other avenues. Sudan for instance is not a member of the Rome Statute, but its President, Omar Hassan Ahmad Al-Bashir is being sought and warrants of arrest have been issued against him. He is a President of a country that is not a party to the Rome Statute and a fugitive as well.

The issue is whether the continent is capable of carrying out their threat to the logical conclusion. Many doubt it. The African Union is not a coherent body but a union of convenience. It has been pointed out that the very building they meet in is a donation by China. And to add insult to injury, the majority of the members have not paid their annual subscriptions and thus forcing the organisation to run at a budgetary deficit of 75% in 2013.[167] Therefore there is a lot of talk with very little in terms of action in the AU.[168]

2013, p. 18; Makokha, 'Why President Uhuru Must Not Go to The Hague', *Saturday Nation* (Nairobi), 12 October 2013, p. 13; and Mbiuki, 'ICC Supporters Hiding their Heads in the Sand', *The East African* (Nairobi), 26 October–1 November 2013, p. 22. Interesting also is Eyakuze, 'ICC Targets Africans, While Zuma Despises them; So What is the Big Deal?', *The East African* (Nairobi), 26 October–1 November 2013, p. 21.

164 See Mariam, 'The AU's Mass Treaty-cide Brinksmanship', Vol. 650 *Pambazuka*, 15 October 2013.

165 See Article 127 of the Rome Statute.

166 While encouraging Kenya to withdraw from the Rome Statute, one writer nonetheless warns: 'Kenya's withdrawal will not necessarily herald paradise for the lords of impunity.' See Mungai, 'It is in Kenya's National Interest to Withdraw from the Rome Statute', *The East African* (Nairobi), 12–18 October 2014, p. 12 – 13.

167 According to its 2014 Budget, the African Union needs donors to inject US $170 million (about 96% of total programmes Budget). See Mwanga, 'Why I'm Convinced that African Union is all Bark and no Bite', *Sunday Nation* (Nairobi), 20 October 2013, p. 13.

168 See 'The African Union: Short of Cash and Teeth – Africa's Paramount Body has Improved but it is Still Weak', *The Economist* (London), 27 January 2011.

9. WITHDRAWAL OF THE CHARGES AGAINST UHURU KENYATTA AND ITS IMPACT ON THE WORK OF THE ICC

The Kenya case is a major lesson for the International Criminal Court. As Mr Uhuru Kenyatta entrenched himself in office, it was gradually becoming hard for the Office of the Prosecutor to get evidence from within the country.[169] Several trips to Kenya and appeals to the Attorney General of Kenya Githu Muigai did not yield any results.[170] To underline the importance of cooperation, the Court summoned Mr Kenyatta to appear in person before it. This was a major challenge to Mr Kenyatta.[171] He was in a Catch-22 situation.[172] By appearing before the Court he was going to make history as the first sitting President to appear before the Court. This would undermine his authority as a Head of State and as an elected leader; he would be seen as dragging the whole Republic of Kenya to court with him. On the other hand, if he declined the summons, then logically a warrant of arrest would follow and thus making him a fugitive. This would have put him in the same league with Omar Hassan Ahmad Al-Bashir, the President of Sudan. Mr Kenyatta was well advised and chose to respect the summons. He however did that as a private citizen having delegated all his powers to his deputy, Mr William Ruto.[173]

A few weeks after this historical appearance, the Office of the ICC Prosecutor withdrew charges against Mr Kenyatta.[174] The reason given for this serious decision was that Kenya as a country and a state party to the Rome Statute was not cooperating and providing the information required by the Office of the ICC

---

169 The result was several postponements of the case. See Menya, 'Uhuru Trial: D-Day Set for Bensouda', *Daily Nation* (Nairobi), 29 August 2014, p. 1 & 5; Wanjala, 'ICC: Uhuru not yet off the Hook', Vol. 5 No. 10 *The Nairobi Law Monthly*, October 2014, p. 38; and 'ICC: 0 – Uhuru: 1 – Kenya:?', Vol. 48 No. 544 *New African*, November 2014, p. 42.

170 See Oluoch, 'The Hague: ICC Asks UN to Help Enforce Co-operation', *The East African* (Nairobi), 1–7 November 2014, p. 12; and 'Kenyatta Case: Will Collapse of Muthaura Case have Impact on Uhuru Ruling?', *Sunday Nation* (Nairobi), 2 November 2014, p. 10.

171 See Menya, 'History in the Making: ICC Summons Uhuru', *Saturday Nation* (Nairobi), 20 September 2014, p. 1 & 6; and Menya, 'Uhuru's Dilemma over Summons: Whom Will Uhuru Disregard, ICC or the African Union?', *Sunday Nation* (Nairobi), 21 September 2014, p. 1 & 2.

172 See 'Implication of Uhuru's Defiance of ICC on Kenya', Vol. 4 No. 10 *The Nairobi Law Monthly*, November 2013, p. 30. See also Makokha, 'ICC Must Rethink Decision Requiring Uhuru in the Dock', *Saturday Nation* (Nairobi), 27 September 2014, p. 13.

173 See Munene and Ndirachu, 'Hasty Summons: How Uhuru Confounded Allies with Ruto Take-over Game Plan', *Sunday Nation* (Nairobi), 12 October 2014, p. 1 & 2.

174 See Menya, 'ICC: Uhuru Wins Big as Bensouda Drops Charges', *Saturday Nation* (Nairobi), 6 December 2015, p. 2; 'Uhuru: I've Waited Six Years for This', *Saturday Nation* (Nairobi), 6 December 2015, p. 3; 'Kenyan President Says "vindicated" After ICC Drops Charges', *Daily News* (Tanzania), 6 December 2014; and 'Uhuru Kenyatta is Free as ICC Drops Case', *The Guardian* (Tanzania), 6 December 2014, p. 1. See also Kabukuru, 'Al-Shabaab Dampens Kenyatta's ICC Victory', Vol. 49 No. 546 *New African*, January 2015, p. 32.

Prosecutor.[175] The Prosecution was telling the world that Mr Kenyatta is not innocent but it could not get the information from within the country that would help it establish its case to the level required for serious cases of this nature.[176]

While the news of the withdrawal of case against the President was received with celebrations in Nairobi, at the expense of the victims,[177] the Office of the Prosecutor decided to do two things. One, to make public all the evidence it was holding against Mr Kenyatta;[178] and two, to report Kenya to the Assembly of States Parties to the Rome Statute. This course of action was not well received in Kenya and it was said to be malicious to make the existing evidence public. This was rather odd as at the end of the day, if the case had proceeded, this evidence would have been put in public sphere anyway.

While the President can sigh with relief for the time being,[179] the case against his deputy[180] and radio journalist Arap Sang continue at The

175 In the words of the Prosecutor: the 'Government of Kenya has prevented the Judges from carrying out their function of determining the truth.' See Bensouda, 'Unco-operative Government Killed Kenyatta Case', *The East African* (Nairobi), 6–12 December 2014, p. 10. See also 'Bensouda: It is Justice Denied', *Saturday Nation* (Nairobi), 6 December 2014, p. 3. Also relevant is Bensouda, 'Kenya Frustrated ICC Prosecutor by Non-Cooperation', No. 706 *Pambazuka*, 11 December 2014; Bensouda, 'Cry for Justice: I Feel Deeply for the Victims – I Will Appeal the Judges' Decision', *Sunday Nation* (Nairobi), 14 December 2014, p. 18. See also Simons, 'International Criminal Court Formally Ends Case against Kenya's President', *The New York Times* (USA), 13 March 2015.

176 See Kegoro, 'Justice: Why Headache May Linger for Uhuru Despite Win', *Saturday Nation* (Nairobi), 6 December 2015, p. 4. See Also Gaynor, 'Statement on Behalf of the Victims Following the Withdrawal of the Charges against Uhuru Kenyatta', No. 706 *Pambazuka*, 11 December 2014; Kenyans for Peace with Truth and Justice (KPTJ), 'KPTJ Statement Following the ICC Prosecutor's Notice of Withdrawal of Charges against Uhuru Kenyatta', No. 706 *Pambazuka*, 11 December 2014; and Redress, 'Kenyatta's ICC Case: Kenya Should Account for Impeding Access to Justice and Truth', No. 706 *Pambazuka*, 11 December 2014. See also Makokha, 'State-NGOs Rivalry Plays Out at New York ICC Meeting', *Sunday Nation* (Nairobi), 14 December 2014, p. 19.

177 With the cases in The Hague, the victims had been very hopeful that justice will at least be done. See Ombuor, 'ICC Victims' Lawyer: It is Daunting Task, but we shall Prevail', Vol. 5 No. 3 *The Nairobi Law Monthly*, March 2014, p. 66. Incidentally, people were gaining confidence and thus kept on joining the victims' list in the case against President Kenyatta. See Sum, '154 New Victims Join Hague Against Uhuru', *The Standard* (Nairobi), 25 September 2014, p. 4.

178 See Menya, 'Disclosure: Secrets of ICC Evidence Return to Haunt Uhuru', *Sunday Nation* (Nairobi), 18 January 2015, p. 1. See also 'Spilling the Beans: Bensouda Set to Reveal Secrets of Uhuru Charges', *Sunday Nation* (Nairobi), 18 January 2015, p. 4; and Kegoro, 'Release of Evidence Gives Prosecutor Chance to Tell Her Version of the Story', *Sunday Nation* (Nairobi), 18 January 2015, p. 5.

179 The ICC judges have officially terminated the case against Mr Uhuru Kenyatta with a lot of conditions. Judges Kuniko Ozaki, Robert Fremr, and Geoffrey Henderson warned Mr Kenyatta against interfering with witnesses or collection of evidence. In addition, the Court retained limited residue jurisdiction to consider certain procedural matters, including any review and possible reclassification of confidential filings in the case record, which shall remain confidential. See Njagi, 'Uhuru ICC Case Terminated', *Saturday Nation* (Nairobi), 14 March 2015, p. 2; and 'Kenyatta's ICC Case Terminated', *The Citizen* (Tanzania), 15 March 2015, p. 32.

180 On the evaluation of the evidence adduced so far against Mr William Ruto see Abdullahi, 'Why Ruto Should be Happy … and Worried', *Sunday Nation* (Nairobi), 27 October 2013, p. 20.

Hague.[181] One cannot rule out that this might have serious repercussions on their joint rule of Kenya.[182]

This case is interesting in two ways. Firstly, it indicates how difficult it is to prosecute a sitting president.[183] Secondly, it allows the Court and particularly the Office of the Prosecutor to think of its own procedures and avoidance of double standards when it comes to dealing with suspects. Why should some suspects stay at home while others are held in custody?[184] The Court is relatively new and there is a lot to learn both from practice and theory. More and more literature is coming out from our citadels of learning.[185]

10. CONCLUSION

The Rome Statute is extremely important and relevant to the African continent and its people. The majority of Africans support the existence of the Court as a threat against those violating their rights with total impunity in the name of 'sovereignty.' The possibility of being dragged to The Hague makes an African ruler think twice before acting or contemplating doing something against the people. This was not the case before. In the 1960s and 1970s Africa produced some of the most feared and unpredictable dictators in the world. Names like Idi Amin, Jean Badel Bokassa, Macias Nguema caused fear and awe to innocent people for no apparent reasons.

---

181 See Oluoch, 'ICC Focus Shifts as it Drops Rape, Murder Charges Against Uhuru – Spotlight now on Deputy President William Ruto and Journalist Sang', *The East African* (Nairobi), 6–12 December 2014, p. 8.

182 See Gaitho, 'Could Bensouda have Broken Chain that Held Jubilee Camps Together?', *Saturday Nation* (Nairobi), 6 December 2015, p. 5; Menya and Wanga, 'What Next? Anxiety in URP over the Ruto Question', *Sunday Nation* (Nairobi), 7 March 2015, p. 2. See also Wanyeki, 'AU Moves on as Jubilee Partners Start Falling Out', *The East African* (Nairobi), 7 February 2015; Sigei and Wanga, 'ICC Factor Fuels Ruto's Fights in the Rift Valley', *Saturday Nation* (Nairobi), 28 March 2015, p. 1; and Menya, 'Precarious: Will Graft Purge, ICC Load Undo UhuRuto?', *Sunday Nation* (Nairobi), 29 March 2015, p. 8.

183 See Kegoro, 'Hague Aftermath: Uhuru Used the state as a Shield Against his Trial', *Sunday Nation* (Nairobi), 7 December 2015, p. 4; and Shimoli, 'President's Strategy Took him to World Capitals', *Sunday Nation* (Nairobi), 7 December 2015, p. 5. Some citizens who would have been helpful to the Court just develop cold feet – at times expecting some favours from the state. See Munene, 'Me to Go Record Statement in The Hague? Never', *Sunday Nation* (Nairobi), 1 March 2015, p. 6 (Life Style).

184 There were times when the Office of the Prosecutor was beginning to re-think about the unfettered freedom given to some accused before the Court while others were in custody. See Menya, 'Hague Trial: Prosecutor Wants Uhuru Ruling Reversed', *Sunday Nation* (Nairobi), 27 October 2013, p. 3. On the thoughts of Luis Moreno-Ocampo the Prosecutor who allowed this double standard see Mutiga, 'ICC Not the International Body Needed to Keep Warlords in Check', *Sunday Nation* (Nairobi), 7 December 2014, p. 9.

185 More and more profound treatises are coming from universities where studies are being carried out on the Rome Statute and its practice. See for instance Werle et al. 2014; and Materu 2015.

The adoption of the African Charter on Human and Peoples' Rights in 1981 by the then Organisation of African Unity (OAU) was anticipated to curb human rights abuse in the continent. However, that was not to be. The Charter allotted the final word on investigations of human rights abuse to the very suspects of the crimes and their brethren – the Heads of State and Government of the OAU. That checked the capacity of the African Commission on Human and Peoples' Rights in its bid to stamp out abuse through its protective and promotion mandate. In an alleged true 'African' spirit which preferred conciliation to confrontation, establishment of a court was ruled out as a means of dealing with human rights abuse in the continent. When eventually one was allowed in 1998 it was a stillbirth, with so many restrictions including denying individuals and civil society organisations *locus standi*. In such a situation human rights in Africa remained a pipe dream.

The entry into force of the Rome Statute of the International Criminal Court was a welcome relief to millions of Africans. This explains the massive initial support in the continent from both official circles to the common man on the street. The Court was going to address serious crimes against the African people – crimes against humanity, genocide, war crimes and later the crime of aggression. The Court was established in such a way that it could only intervene when a state failed to deal with its human rights problem at home on its own. Under the principle of complementarity, the Court was an institution of last resort.

The frantic efforts now being undertaken in a disorganised way by the African Union, of attacking and condemning the ICC for 'targeting' the continent and being racist lack both sincerity and honesty. Equally, the attempts to give the African Court of Justice and Human Rights, which is yet to be formally established due to lack of support from within the continental body, mandate to address serious human rights violations in the continent is yet a non-starter. African rulers want accountability – to others but not to them. As Archbishop Emeritus Desmond Tutu correctly notes, those campaigning against the ICC, just because it is prosecuting one of them, want to take the continent back to 1970s. They are seeking a 'licence to kill and maim and oppress their people without consequences.' Right-minded Africans should shout loudest against this course of action. It should not be allowed – in their name – not in the name of sovereignty. Politicising a purely legal matter casts doubts on the genuineness of those involved. Like all democrats who believe in the rule of law, those arraigned before the ICC should make themselves available so that justice is done, and also seen to be done by all![186]

The ICC's move into its brand new and permanent headquarters within the city of The Hague, the Netherlands, underlines the obvious point that this court is here to stay. It is a clear statement of the resolve by a large section of the international community to totally eradicate impunity. It therefore goes

---

186 See Tutu, 'Pulling out of the ICC would be Tragic for Africa', *The East African* (Nairobi), 12–18 October 2014, p. 13.

without saying that no amount of politicking is going to seriously affect the existence of this important institution. Therefore, days when serious violations of human rights were handled with kid gloves by ad hoc tribunals are gone. The prosecution of core crimes facing humanity today has eventually found a home. Therefore victims of the offences of genocide, crimes against humanity, war crimes, aggression, and related crimes have a place to go, and expect a fair hearing. It is important for states to understand and appreciate this fact as a reality. From whichever angle one looks at the situation, there is no doubt that the African people need the ICC – as long as pockets of rights violations exist on the continent.

BIBLIOGRAPHY

BOOKS AND JOURNAL ARTICLES

Abbi-Saab 2003
Abbi-Saab, G., 'The Proper Role of Universal Jurisdiction', 1 Journal of International Criminal Justice, 2003.

Abegunrin 2009
Abegunrin, O., 'Africa in Global Politics in the Twenty-First Century; A Pan-African Perspective', Palgrave Macmillan, 2009.

Africa Legal Aid 2002
Africa Legal Aid, 'The Cairo-Arusha Principles on Universal Jurisdiction in Respect of Gross Human Rights Offences: An African Perspective', 7(1) AFLA Quarterly, 2002.

Africa Legal Aid 2001
Africa Legal Aid, 'Experts Meeting: African Perspectives on Universal Jurisdiction for International Crimes', 6(3) AFLA Quarterly, 2001.

Akande 2004
Akande, D., 'International Law Immunities and the International Criminal Court', 98 The American Journal of International Law, 2004.

Akhavan 2005
Akhavan, P., 'The Lord's Resistance Army Case: Uganda's Submission of the First State Referral to the International Criminal Court', 99 American Journal of International Law, 2005.

Ankumah 1996
Ankumah, E.A., 'The African Commission on Human and Peoples' Rights: Practice and Procedures', Martinus Nijhoff Publishers, 1996.

Ankumah and Kwakwa 2005
Ankumah, E.A. and Kwakwa, E. (eds.), 'African Perspectives on International Criminal Justice', Africa Legal Aid Book Series 3, 2005.

Arbour 2003
Arbour, L., 'Will the ICC Have an Impact on Universal Jurisdiction?', 1 Journal of International Criminal Justice, 2003.

Arsanjani 2005
Arsanjani, M.H. and Reisman, W.M., 'The Law in Action of International Criminal Court', 99 American Journal of International Law, 2005.
Baker 2004
Baker, B., 'Twilight of Impunity for Africa's Presidential Criminals', 25 Third World Quarterly, 2004.
Beauvais 2001
Beauvais, J., 'Benevolent Despotism: A Critique of UN State-building in East Timor', New York University Journal of International Law and Politics, 2001.
Bekker 2007
Bekker, G., 'The African Court on Human and Peoples' Rights: Safeguarding the Interests of African States', 51(1) Journal of African Law, 2007.
Bianchi 1994
Bianchi, A., 'Denying State Immunity to Violators of Human Rights', 46 Austrian Journal of Public and International Law, 1994.
Biswaro 2012
Biswaro, J.M., 'The Quest for Regional Integration in the Twenty First Century: Rhetoric Versus Reality – A Comparative Study', Mkuki na Nyota Publishers, 2012.
Bossa 2010
Bossa, S.B., 'A Critique of the East African Court of Justice as a Human Rights Court', in Eboe-Osuji, C. (ed.), 'Protecting Humanity: Essays in International Law and Policy in the Honour of Navanethem Pillay', Martinus Nijhoff Publishers, 2010.
Brown 2012
Brown, S. and Sriram, C.L., 'The Big Fish Won't Fry Themselves: Criminal Accountability for Post-Election Violence in Kenya', 111(443) African Affairs, 2012.
Burbach 2003
Burbach, R., 'The Pinochet Affair: State Terrorism and Global Justice', Zed Books, 2003.
Cahill 2007
Cahill, J., 'Blackwater: The Rise of the World's Most Powerful Mercenary Army', Serpent's Tail, 2007.
Cassese 2002
Cassese, A., 'When May Senior State Officials be Tried for International Crimes? Some Comments on The Congo v. Belgium Case', 13 European Journal of International Law, 2002.
Cassese 1996
Cassese, A. (ed.), 'The Path to The Hague: Selected Documents on the Origins of the ICTY', ICTY, 1996.
Chaitidou 2014
Chaitidou, E., 'The ICC Case Law on the Contextual Elements of Crimes Against Humanity', in Bergsmo, M. and Song, T. (eds.), 'On the Proposed Crimes Against Humanity Convention', Torkel Opsahl Academic EPublishers, 2014.
Chege 2010
Chege, M., 'Ethnic Pluralism and National Governance in Africa: A Survey', in Njogu, K. et al. (eds.), 'Ethnic Diversity in Eastern Africa: Opportunities and Challenges', Kolbe Press, 2010.
Chon and Thet 2010

Chon, G. And Thet, S., 'Behind the Killing Fields: A Khmer Rouge Leader and One of His Victims', University of Pennsylvania Press, 2010.

Dagash 2006

Dagash, I., 'The OAU: Reality or Fiction?', 2006.

Dawson 2010

Dawson, G., 'The 'Other' Milošević Case: The Prosecutor versus Serbia and Montenegro in re Production of Documents in Prosecutor v. Slobodan Milošević', in Eboe-Osuji, C. (ed.), 'Protecting Humanity: Essays in International Law and Policy in Honour of Navanethem Pillay', Martinus Nijhoff Publishers, 2010.

De Bertodano 2003

De Bertodano, S., 'Current Developments in Internationalized Courts', Journal of International Criminal Justice, 2003.

De Witte 2001

De Witte, L., 'The Assassination of Lumumba', Verso, 2001.

Deen-Racsmany 2005

Deen-Racsmany, Z., 'Prosecutor v. Taylor: The Status of the Special Court for Sierra Leone and its Implications for Immunity', 18 Leiden Journal of International Law, 2005.

Deguefe 2006

Deguefe, T., 'Minutes of An Ethiopian Century', Shama Books, 2006.

Desta 2007

Desta, M., 'Ethiopia's Role in African History', Shama Books, 2007.

Doria et al. 2009

Doria, J. et al. (eds.), 'The Legal Regime of the International Criminal Court', Martinus Nijhoff Publishers, 2009.

Driscoll et al. 2004

Driscoll, W., et al. (eds.), 'The International Criminal Court: Global Politics and the Quest for Justice', International Debate Education Association, 2004.

Eberechi 2011

Eberechi, I., '"Rounding Up the Usual Suspects:" Exclusion, Selectivity, and Impunity in the Enforcement of International Criminal Justice and the African Union's Emerging Resistance', 4(1) African Journal of Legal Studies, 2011.

Eberechi 2009

Eberechi, I., 'Armed Conflicts in Africa and Western Complicity: A Disincentive for African Union's Cooperation with ICC', 3 African Journal of Legal Studies, 2009.

El Zeidy 2011

El Zeidy, M.M., 'The Genesis of Complementarity', in Stahn, C. and El Zeidy, M.M., 'The International Criminal Court and Complementarity: From Theory to Practice (Volume I)', Cambridge University Press, 2011.

El Zeidy 2008

El Zeidy, M.M., 'From Primacy to Complementarity and Backwards: (Re) Visiting Rule 11 bis of the Ad Hoc Tribunals', 57 International and Comparative Law Quarterly, 2008.

El Zeidy 2005
El Zeidy, M.M., 'The Ugandan Government Triggers the First Test of the Complementarity Principle: An Assessment of the First State's Party Referral to the ICC', 5 International Criminal Law Review, 2005.
El Zeidy 2002
El Zeidy, M.M., 'The Principle of Complementarity: A New Machinery to Implement International Criminal Law', 23 Michigan Journal of International Law, 2002.
Engle 2013
Engle, E.A., 'The International Criminal Court and Lubanga: A Feminist Critique and Jus Gogens', 19(2) East African Journal of Peace & Human Rights, 2013.
Ferstman 2009
Ferstman, C., 'The ICC as a Tool for Social Transformation? Challenges and Prospects for Addressing Victims', in Van Genugten, W.J.M. et al. (eds.), 'Criminal Jurisdiction 100 Years after the 1907 Hague Peace Conference', TMC Asser Press, 2009.
Forsythe 2004
Forsythe, D.P., 'The United States and International Criminal Justice', in Bekou, O. and Cryer, R. (eds.), 'The International Criminal Court', Dartmouth Publishing Company and Ashgate Publishing Company, 2004.
Fox 2012
Fox, H., 'Functions of State Officials and the Restrictive Rule of State Immunity', in Kohen, M. et al. (eds.), 'Perspectives of International Law in the 21st Century: Liber Amicorum Professor Christian Dominice in Honour of his 80th Birthday', Martinus Nijhoff Publishers, 2012.
Fox 2008
Fox, H., 'The Law of State Immunity', 2nd ed., Oxford University Press, 2008.
Fox 2003
Fox, H., 'Some Aspects of Immunity from Criminal Jurisdiction of the State Officials', in Vohrah, L.C. et al. (eds.), 'Man's Inhumanity to Man: Essays on International Law in Honour of Antonio Cassese', Kluwer Law International, 2003.
Francioni 2008
Francioni, F., 'Reflections on Victims' Reparations and on Universal Jurisdiction', in Politi, M. and Gioia, F. (eds.), 'The International Criminal Court and National Jurisdictions', Ashgate Publishing, 2008.
Ginaburgs and Kudriavstev 1990
Ginaburgs, G. and Kudriavstev, V.N. (eds.), 'The Nuremberg Trial and International Law', Martinus Nijhoff, 1990.
Goy 2012
Goy, B., 'Individual Criminal Responsibility before the International Criminal Court: A Comparison with the Ad Hoc Tribunals', 12(1) International Criminal Law, 2012.
Hamalengwa et al. 1988
Hamalengwa, M. et al. (eds.), 'The International Law of Human Rights in Africa: Basic Documents and Annotated Bibliography', Martinus Nijhoff Publishers, 1988.
Hansen 2011
Hansen, T.O., 'The Policy Requirement in Crimes Against Humanity: Lessons from and for the Case of Kenya', 43 George Washington International Law Review, 2011.

Happold 2008
Happold, M., 'Darfur, the Security Council, and the International Criminal Court', 55 International & Comparative Law Quarterly, 2008.
Happold 2007
Happold, M., 'The International Criminal Court and the Lord's Resistance Army', 8 Melbourne Journal of International Law, 2007.
Harding and Hatchard 1993
Harding, A. and Hatchard, J. (eds.), 'Preventive Detention and Security Law: A Comparative Survey', Martinus Nijhoff Publishers, 1993.
Hawthorn 1999
Hawthorn, G., 'Pinochet: The Politics', 75(2) International Affairs, 1999, pp. 253-258.
Hoare 1968
Hoare, M., 'Mercenary', Corgi Books, 1968.
Howard 1986
Howard, R.E., 'Human Rights in Commonwealth Africa', Rowman & Littlefield Publishers, 1986.
Ishiyama and Backstrom 2011
Ishiyama, J. and Backstrom, J., 'Reconciliation and Conceptual Complexity: The Case of Post Conflict Kenya', 10 African and Asian Studies, 2011.
Jalloh et al. 2011
Jalloh, C.C. et al., 'Assessing the African Union Concerns About Article 16 of the Rome Statute of the International Criminal Court', 4(1) African Journal of Legal Studies, 2011.
Jalloh 2007
Jalloh, C., 'Consolidated Legal Texts for the Special Court for Sierra Leone', Martinus Nijhoff Publishers, 2007.
Jones 2009-2010
Jones, S., 'In the Pursuit of Justice: A Comment on the Arrest Warrant for President Al-Bashir of Sudan', 6 Eyes on the ICC, 2009-2010.
Jurdi 2011
Jurdi, N.N., 'The International Criminal Court and National Courts: A Contentious Relationship', Ashgate Publishing, 2011.
Kaleck 2008-2009
Kaleck, W., 'From Pinochet to Rumsfeld: Universal Jurisdiction in Europe 1998-2008', 30 Michigan Journal of International Law, 2008-2009.
Kalunga 1978-1981
Kalunga, L.T., 'Human Rights and Preventive Detention Act 1962 of the United Republic of Tanzania: Some Operative Aspects', 11-14 Eastern Africa Law Review, 1978-1981.
Katzenstein 2003
Katzenstein, S., 'Hybrid Tribunals: Searching for Justice in East Timor', 16 Harvard Human Rights Journal, 2003.
Kegoro 2012
Kegoro, G., 'Justice Versus Democracy: The Implications of ICC Charges for the Kenyatta Presidency', 2 Zanzibar Yearbook of Law, 2012.

Kerr 2004
Kerr, R., 'The International Criminal Tribunal for the Former Yugoslavia: An Exercise in Law, Politics, and Diplomacy', Oxford University Press, 2004.
Kioko 1998
Kioko, B., 'The Road to the African Court on Human and Peoples' Rights', 10 African Society of International and Comparative Law - Proceedings of the Tenth Annual Conference, 1998.
Kissinger 2001
Kissinger, H., 'The Pitfalls of Universal Jurisdiction', 80(4) Foreign Affairs, 2001.
Kituku 2014
Kituku, W., 'The State of Constitutionalism in Kenya – 2013', in Murangira, T.B. (ed.), 'The Annual State of Constitutionalism in East Africa 2013', Fountain Publishers, 2014.
Kleffner 2008
Kleffner, J.K., 'Complementarity in the Rome Statute and National Criminal Jurisdictions', Oxford University Press, 2008.
Koivu 2001
Koivu, V., 'Head-of-State Immunity v. Individual Criminal Responsibility under International Law', XII Finnish Yearbook of International Law, 2001.
Kufour 2010
Kufour, K.O., 'The African Human Rights System: Origin and Evolution', Palgrave Macmillan, 2010.
Kuosmanen 2007
Kuosmanen, T., 'Bringing Justice Closer: Hybrid Courts in Post-Conflict Societies', The Erik Castren Institute, 2007.
Lescure and Trintignac 1996
Lescure, K. and Trintignac, F., 'International Justice for Former Yugoslavia: The Working of the International Criminal Tribunal of The Hague', Kluwer Law International, 1996.
Lugakingira 2008
Lugakingira, K.S.K. and Peter, C.M., 'Victims Compensation and Aspects of Law and Justice in Tanzania', 18(3) International Criminal Justice Review, 2008.
Macedo 2004
Macedo, S. (ed.), 'Universal Jurisdiction: National Courts and the Prosecution of Serious Crimes under International Law', University of Pennsylvania Press, 2004.
Maier 2000
Maier, K., 'This House Has Fallen: Nigeria in Crisis', Penguin Books, 2000.
Malila 2011
Malila, M., 'Promising Siblings: The African Commission on Human and Peoples' Rights and the African Court on Human and Peoples' Rights', 17(2) East African Journal of Peace & Human Rights, 2011.
Mallory 1986
Mallory, J.L., 'Resolving the Confusion Over Head of State Immunity: The Defined Rights of Kings', 86 Columbia Law Review, 1986.

Mamdani 2009
Mamdani, M., 'The International Criminal Court's Case against the President of Sudan: A Critical Look', 62(2) Journal of International Affairs, 2009.
Martin 1974
Martin, R., 'Personal Freedom and the Law in Tanzania: A Study of Socialist State Administration', Oxford University Press, 1974.
Materu 2015
Materu, S.F., 'The Post-Election Violence in Kenya: Domestic and International Legal Responses', Asser Press, 2015.
Mayfield 1995
Mayfield, J.V., 'The Prosecution of War Crimes and Respect for Human Rights: Ethiopia's Balancing Act', 9 Emory International Law Review, 1995.
McCausland 2010
McCausland, J.S. and Rojo, E.C., 'Developments at the International Criminal Court', 10(3) The Law and Practice of International Courts and Tribunals, 2010.
Meng-Try and Sim 2001
Meng-Try, E.A. and Sim, S., 'Victims and Perpetrators? Testimony of Young Khmer Rouge Comrades', Documentation Center of Cambodia, 2001.
Minear 1971
Minear, R., 'Victor's Justice: Tokyo War Crimes Trial', Princeton University Press, 1971.
Moreno-Ocampo 2011
Moreno-Ocampo, L., 'A Positive Approach to Complementarity: The Impact of the Office of the Prosecutor', in Stahn, C. and El Zeidy, M.M., 'The International Criminal Court and Complementarity: From Theory to Practice (Volume I)', Cambridge University Press, 2011.
Moreno-Ocampo 2009
Moreno-Ocampo, L., 'Four Years of Action by the ICC Prosecutors' Office: Problems and Challenges', in Van Genugten, W.J.M. et al. (eds.), 'Criminal Jurisdiction 100 Years after the 1907 Hague Peace Conference', TMC Asser Press, 2009.
Morris and Scharf 1995
Morris, V. and Scharf, M.P., 'An Insider's Guide to the International Criminal Tribunal for Former Yugoslavia: A Documentary History and Analysis', Transnational Publishers, 1995.
Mullins 1921
Mullins, C., 'The Leipzig Trials: An Account of the War Criminals' Trials and Study of German Mentality', Witherby, 1921.
Munoz 2008
Munoz, H., 'The Dictator's Shadow: Life under Augusto Pinochet', Basic Books, 2008.
Naldi 1989
Naldi, G.J., 'The Organization of African Unity: An Analysis of its Role', Mansell, 1989.
Newton 2001
Newton, M., 'Comparative Complementary: Domestic Jurisdiction Consistent with the Rome Statute of the International Criminal Court', 167 Military Law Review, 2001.

Nichols 2015
Nichols, L., 'The International Criminal Court and the End of Impunity in Kenya', Springer International Publishing, 2015.
Njogu 2009
Njogu, K. (ed.), 'Healing the Wound: Personal Narratives About the 2007 Post-Election Violence in Kenya', Twaweza Communications, 2009.
Nmaju 2009
Nmaju, M.C., 'Violence in Kenya: Any Role for the ICC in the Quest for Accountability?', 3 African Journal of Legal Studies, 2009.
Nmehielle 2011
Nmehielle, V.O., 'Preventing and Responding to Atrocity Crimes in Africa: Interrogating the African Response in Darfur', 4(2) African Journal of Legal Studies, 2011.
Nouwen 2005
Nouwen, S., 'The Special Court for Sierra Leone and the Immunity of Taylor: The Arrest Warrant Case Continued', 18 Leiden Journal of International Law, 2005.
Nsekela 2011
Nsekela, H.R., 'The Performance of the East African Court of Justice in Respect of Achieving Regional Integration', in Gastorn, K. et al. (eds.), 'Processes of Legal Integration in the East African Community', Dar es Salaam University Press, 2011.
Odero 2011
Odero, S., 'Politics of International Criminal Justice, the ICC's Arrest Warrant for Al-Bashir and the African Union's Neo-Colonial Conspirator Thesis', in Murungu, C. and Biegon, J. (eds.), 'Prosecuting International Crimes in Africa', Pretoria University Press, 2011.
Odete 2013
Odete, A., 'The State of Constitutionalism Report for Kenya, 2011', in Makulilo, A.B. (ed.), 'Annual State of Constitutionalism in East Africa 2011', Fountain Publishers, 2013.
Ontiti 2005
Ontiti, K., 'Private Military Companies: The Challenges they Pose in Contemporary Armed Conflicts', 2 The East African Law Journal, 2005.
Othman 2000
Othman, H. (ed.), 'Reflections on Leadership in Africa: Forty Years after Independence – Essays in Honour of Mwalimu Julius K. Nyerere on the Occasion of his 75th Birthday', Institute of Development Studies and VUB University Press, 2000.
Ouguergouz 2003
Ouguergouz, F., 'The Establishment of an African Court of Human and Peoples' Rights: A Judicial Premiere for the African Union', 11 African Yearbook of International Law, 2003.
Penrose 2000
Penrose, M.M., 'It's Good to Be the King!: Prosecuting Heads of State and Former Heads of State Under International Law', 39 Columbia Journal of Transnational Law, 2000.

Perez 1999–2000
Perez, A.F., 'The Perils of Pinochet: Problems for Transitional Justice and a Supranational Governance Solution', 28(2) Denver Journal of International Law and Policy, 1999–2000.
Peter 1997
Peter, C.M., 'Incarcerating the Innocent: Preventive Detention in Tanzania', 19(1) Human Rights Quarterly, 1997.
Peter 1997
Peter, C.M., 'The International Criminal Tribunal for Rwanda', 37 International Review of the Red Cross, 1997.
Peter 1984
Peter, C.M., 'Mercenaries and International Humanitarian Law', 24(3) Indian Journal of International Law, 1984.
Pityana 2003
Pityana, N.B., 'Hurdles and Pitfalls in International Human Rights Law: Ratification Process of the Protocol to the African Charter on the Establishment of the African Court on Human and Peoples' Rights', 28 South African Yearbook of International Law, 2003.
Quigley 1978–1981
Quigley, J., 'Cases on Preventive Detention Act', 11–14 Eastern Africa Law Review, 1978–1981.
Roht-Arriaza 2009
Roht-Arriaza, N., 'The Multiple Prosecutions of Augusto Pinochet', in Lutz, E.L. and Reiger, C. (eds.), 'Prosecuting Heads of State', Cambridge University Press, 2009.
Roht-Arriaza 2005
Roht-Arriaza, N., 'The Pinochet Effect: Transitional Justice in the Age of Human Rights', University of Pennsylvania Press, 2005.
Rolling and Cassese 1993
Rolling, B.V.A. and Cassese, A., 'The Tokyo Trial and Beyond: Reflections of a Peacemonger', Polity Press, 1993.
Ruhangisa 2005
Ruhangisa, J.E., 'The East African Court of Justice', in Ajulu, R. (ed.), 'The Making of A Region: The Revival of the East African Community', Institute for Global Dialogue, 2005, pp. 95–110.
Saxum 2009–2010
Saxum, E.J., 'The ICC Versus Sudan: How Does the Darfur Case Impact the Principle of Complementarity?', 6 Eyes on the ICC, 2009–2010.
Schabas 2008
Schabas, W.A., 'Complementarity in Practice: Some Uncomplimentary Thoughts', 19 Criminal Law Forum, 2008.
Schabas 2004
Schabas, W.A., 'International Criminal Court: The Secret of its Success', in Bekou, O. and Cryer, R. (eds.), 'The International Criminal Court', Dartmouth Publishing Company and Ashgate Publishing Company, 2004.

Shelton 1999
Shelton, D., 'Remedies in International Human Rights Law', Oxford University Press, 1999.
Simbeye 2004
Simbeye, Y., 'Immunity and International Criminal Law', Ashgate Publishing, 2004.
Smeulers 2011
Smeulers, A. and Grunfeld, F., 'International Crimes and Other Gross Human Rights Violations: A Multi and Interdisciplinary Textbook', Martinus Nijhoff, 2011.
Solera 2002
Solera, O., 'Complementary Jurisdiction and International Criminal Justice', 84 International Review of the Red Cross, 2002.
Ssenyonjo 2013
Ssenyonjo, M., 'The Rise of the African Union to the International Criminal Court's Investigations and Prosecutions of African Leaders', 13 International Criminal Law Review, 2013.
Ssenyonjo 2012
Ssenyonjo, M. (ed.), 'The African Regional Human Rights System: 30 Years after the African Charter on Human and Peoples' Rights', Martinus Nijhoff, 2012.
Stahn 2011
Stahn, C. and El Zeidy, M.M (eds.), 'The International Criminal Court and Complementarity', Cambridge University Press, 2011.
Stranton 2011
Stranton, G.H., 'Why the World Needs an International Convention on Crimes against Humanity', in Sadat, L.N. (ed.), 'Forging a Convention for Crimes Against Humanity', Cambridge University Press, 2011.
Summers 2003
Summers, M.A., 'The International Court of Justice's Decision in Congo v. Belgium: How Has It Affected the Development of a Principle of Universal Jurisdiction that Would Obligate All States to Prosecute War Criminals?', 21 Boston University International Law Journal, 2003.
Tallgren 1998
Tallgren, I., 'International Criminal Order: The Rhetoric of International Repression and the Notion of Complementary in the Draft Statute for an International Criminal Court', 68 Nordic Journal of International Law, 1998.
Taylor 1993
Taylor, T., 'The Anatomy of the Nuremberg Trials', Bloomsbury, 1993.
Tehindrazanarivelo 2012
Tehindrazanarivelo, D.L., 'The African Union Principle on the Fight against Impunity and the Arrest Warrants for Omar Hassan El-Bashir', in Kohen, M. et al. (eds.), 'Perspectives of International Law in the 21st Century: Liber Amicorum Professor Christian Dominice in Honour of his 80th Birthday', Martinus Nijhoff Publishers, 2012.
Tejan-Cole 2009
Tejan-Cole, A., 'A Big Man in a Small Cell: Charles Taylor and the Special Court for Sierra Leone', in Lutz, E.L. and Reiger, C. (eds.), 'Prosecuting Heads of State', Cambridge University Press, 2009.

Thatiah 2014
Thatiah, I., 'Hard Tackle: The Life of Uhuru Kenyatta', Rizzan Media, 2014.
Tiba 2007
Tiba, F.K., 'The Mengistu Genocide Trial in Ethiopia', 5 Journal of International Criminal Justice, 2007.
Tladi 2009
Tladi, D., 'The African Union and the International Criminal Court: The Battle for the Soul of International Law', 34 South African Yearbook of International Law, 2009.
Trahan 2011
Trahan, J., 'The Rome Statute's Amendment on the Crime of Aggression: Negotiations at the Kampala Review Conference', 11(1) International Criminal Review, 2011.
Traylor 2009–2010
Traylor, A., 'Uganda and the ICC: Difficulties in Bringing the Lord's Resistance Army Leadership before the ICC', 6(1) Eyes on the ICC, 2009–2010.
Triffterer 1999
Triffterer, Otto (ed.), 'Commentary on the Rome Statute of the International Criminal Court: Observer's Notes, Article by Article', Nomos, 1999.
United Nations 2004
United Nations, 'Overview of the International Criminal Court', in Driscoll, W., et al. (eds.), 'The International Criminal Court: Global Politics and the Quest for Justice', International Debate Education Association, 2004.
Van den Herik 2005
Van den Herik, L.J., 'The Contribution of the Rwanda Tribunal to the Development of International Law', Martinus Njihoff Publishers, 2005.
Van der Mei 2003
Van der Mei, A.P., 'The International Criminal Court: Establishment, Jurisdiction and Composition', Africa Legal Aid Quarterly, 2003.
Van der Wolf 2011
Van der Wolf, W.J., 'Crimes Against Humanity and International Criminal Law', International Courts Association, 2011.
Van Heughten and Verhoeven 2011
Van Heughten, E. and Verhoeven, I. (eds.), 'Cambodia Tribunal: Selected Documents', International Courts Association, 2011.
Viljoen and Odinkalu 2006
Viljoen, F. and Odinkalu, C., 'The Prohibition of Torture and Ill-treatment in the African Human Rights System: A Handbook for Victims and their Advocates', World Organisation Against Torture (OMCT), 2006.
Waugh 2012
Waugh, C.M., 'Charles Taylor and Liberia: Ambition and Atrocity in Africa's Lone Star State', Zed Books, 2012.
Weldehaimanot 2011
Weldehaimanot, S., 'Arresting Al-Bashir: The African Union's Opposition and the Legalities', 19(2) African Journal of International and Comparative Law, 2011, pp. 208–235.

Weller 1999
Weller, M., 'On the Hazards of Foreign Travel for Dictators and Other International Criminals', 75 International Affairs, 1999.
Werle et al. 2014
Werle, G., Fernandez, L. and Vormbaum, M. (eds.), 'Africa and the International Criminal Court', Asser Press, 2014.
Wharton 2011
Wharton, S., 'The Evolution of International Criminal Law: Prosecuting 'New' Crimes before the Special Court for Sierra Leone', 11(2) International Criminal Law Review, 2011.
Williams 2012
Williams, S., 'Hybrid and Internalised Criminal Tribunals: Selected Jurisdictional Issues', Hart Publishing, 2012.
Williams and Sherif 2009
Williams, S. and Sherif, L., 'The Arrest Warrant for President Al-Bashir: Immunities of Incumbent Heads of State and the International Criminal Court', 14(1) Journal of Conflict & Security Law, 2009.
Wilson 2011
Wilson, T.Y.N., 'Procedural Developments at the International Criminal Tribunal for Rwanda (ICTR)', 10(2) The Law and Practice of International Courts and Tribunals, 2011.
Wilson 1999
Wilson, R., 'Prosecuting Pinochet: International Crimes in Spanish Domestic Law', 21 Human Rights Quarterly, 1999.
Woetzel 1962
Woetzel, R.K., 'The Nuremberg Trials in International Law', Stevens & Sons, 1962.
Yang 2005
Yang, L., 'On the Principle of Complementarity in the Rome Statute of the International Criminal Court', 4(1) Chinese Journal of International Law, 2005.
Yarnall 2011
Yarnall, J., 'Barbed Wire Disease: British & German Prisoners of War, 1914–19', Spellmount, 2011.

JURISPRUDENCE

High Court of Kenya at Nairobi 2011
High Court of Kenya at Nairobi, Kenya Section of the International Commission of Jurists v. Attorney General of Kenya and Another, Miscellaneous Criminal Application No. 685 of 2010, 28 November 2011.
House of Lords 1999
House of Lords, Regina v. Bow Street Magistrate, ex parte Pinochet Ugarte [1999] 2 All ER 97.
House of Lords 1999
House of Lords, Regina v. Bow Street Metropolitan Stipendiary Magistrate & Others, ex parte Pinochet Ugarte (3) [1999] 2 WLR 827.

House of Lords 1998
House of Lords, Regina v. Bow Street Metropolitan Stipendiary Magistrate & Others, ex parte Pinochet Ugarte (1) [1998] 4 All ER 897.
ICC 2012
ICC, Prosecutor v. Francis Kirimimuthaura, Uhuru Müigai Kenyatta and Mohammed Hussein Ali, ICC-01/09-02/11-425, 24 May 2012.
ICC 2012
ICC, Prosecutor v. Francis Kirimi Muthaura and Uhuru Muigai Kenyatta, ICC-01/09-02/11, 23 January 2012.
ICC 2012
ICC, Prosecutor v. William Samoei Ruto and Joshua Arap Sang, ICC-01/09-01/11, 23 January 2012.
ICC 2011
ICC, Prosecutor v. Omar Hassan Ahmad Al-Bashir, ICC-02/05-01/09-139, 12 December 2011.
ICC 2011
ICC, Prosecutor v. Muammar Mohammed Abu Minyar Gaddafi, Saif Al-Islam Gaddafi and Abdullah Al-Senussi, ICC-01/11-01/11-28, 22 November 2011.
ICC 2010
ICC, Prosecutor v. Omar Hassan Ahmad Al-Bashir, ICC-02/05-01/09-94, 12 July 2010.
ICC 2009
ICC, Prosecutor v. Omar Hassan Ahmad Al-Bashir, ICC-02/05-01/09-3, 4 March 2009.
ICC 2005
ICC, Situation in Uganda, ICC-02/04-01/05-53, 27 September 2005.
ICJ 2012
ICJ, Questions Relating to the Obligation to Prosecute or Extradite (Belgium v. Senegal), 20 July 2012.
ICTY 1997
ICTY, Prosecutor v. Blaskic, IT-95-14-AR 108, 29 October 1997.
SCSL 2013
SCSL, Prosecutor v. Charles Ghankay Taylor, SCSL-2003-01-I, 26 September 2013.

TREATIES, LEGISLATION AND AGREEMENTS

African (Banjul) Charter on Human and Peoples' Rights, OAU Doc. CAB/LEG/67/3 rev. 5, 27 June 1981.
AU, Decision on Africa's Relationship with the International Criminal Court (ICC), Ext/Assembly/AU/Dec.1(Oct.2013), October 2013.
AU, Decision on the Implementation of the Assembly Decision on the International Criminal Court Doc. Ex.CL/670(XIX), Assembly/AU/Dec.366(XVII), 30 June–1 July 2011.
AU, Decision on the Implementation of the Decisions on the International Criminal Court (ICC) Doc. EX.CL/639(XVIII), Assembly/AU/Dec.334(XVI), January 2011.

AU, Decision on the Progress Report of the Commission on the Implementation of the Assembly Decisions on the International Criminal Court (ICC) Doc. EX.CL/710(XX), Assembly/AU/Dec.397(XVIII), January 2012.
AU, Decision on the Report of the Commission on the Meeting of African States Parties to the Rome Statute of the International Criminal Tribunal (ICC) Doc. Assembly/AU/13 (XIII), Assembly/AU/Dec.245(XIII) Rev.1, July 2009.
AU, Draft Protocol on Amendments to the Protocol on the Statute of the African Court of Justice and Human Rights, Exp/Min/IV/Rev.7, 15 May 2012.
Charter of the Organisation of African Unity, 25 May 1963.
Kenya, Preservation of Public Security Act, Cap 57, 1966.
Protocol on the Establishment of an African Court on Human and Peoples' Rights, 9 June 1998.
Protocol on the Statute of the African Court of Justice and Human Rights, 1 July 2008.
Rome Statute of the International Criminal Court, 2187 UNTS 90/37, 17 July 1998.
Statute of the International Criminal Tribunal for the Former Yugoslavia, SC Res. 827, UN Doc. S/RES/827, 25 May 1993.
Tanzania, Preventive Detention Act, 1962 (No. 60 of 1962), 5 October 1962.

OTHERS

Abdullahi, A., 'Pressing the Panic Button Won't Change the Course on ICC Trials', Volume 2 No. 4 The Nairobi Law Monthly, November 2011.
Abdullahi, A., 'Why Ruto Should be Happy … and Worried', Sunday Nation (Nairobi), 27 October 2013.
African Union and European Union, 'AU-EU Technical Ad hoc Expert Group on the Principle of Universal Jurisdiction Report', 2009.
African Union, Report of the Commission on the Use of the Principle of Universal Jurisdiction by Some Non-African States as Recommended by the Conference of Ministers of Justice/Attorneys General, EX.CL/411(XIII), 2008.
Anangwe, A., 'Kenyatta's Case at the ICC Re-ignites Neo-colonial Debate', Volume 4 No. 10 The Nairobi Law Monthly, November 2013.
Barigaba, J., 'ICC is not Targeting Africa, It is Responding to Calls from Africa', The East African (Nairobi), 21 March 2015.
Bensouda, F., 'Cry for Justice: I Feel Deeply for the Victims – I Will Appeal the Judges' Decision', Sunday Nation (Nairobi), 14 December 2014.
Bensouda, F., 'Kenya Frustrated ICC Prosecutor by Non-Cooperation', No. 706 Pambazuka, 11 December 2014.
Bensouda, F., 'Uncooperative Government Killed Kenyatta Case', The East African (Nairobi), 6 December 2014.
Bojic, M., 'Immunity of High State Representatives with regard to International Crimes: are Heads of State, Heads of Government and Foreign Ministers still Untouchable?', Master's thesis, Faculty of Law, University of Lund, 2005.
Branch, D., 'Reforms: Spare Baby and throw Bath Water', Saturday Nation (Nairobi), 19 October 2013.

Chatham House, 'Universal Jurisdiction for International Crimes, A Summary of the Chatham House International Law Discussion Group Meeting held on 9 October 2008'.

Daily News (Tanzania), 'Kenyan President Says "vindicated" After ICC Drops Charges', 6 December 2014.

Davies, D., 'Is the ICC Heading for a Fall?', Volume 48 No. 542 New African, 5 September 2014.

Davies, D., 'Unfinished Business', Volume 46 No. 518 New African, June 2012.

De Lavarene, C., 'President Alassane Ouattara: We are Regaining our Former Glory', Volume 47 No. 533 New African, November 2013.

Dworkin, A. and Iliopous, K., 'The ICC, Bashir, and the Immunity of Heads of State', Crimes of War Education Project, 2011.

Eyakuze, E., 'ICC Targets Africans, While Zuma Despises them; So What is the Big Deal?', The East African (Nairobi), 26 October 2013.

Eze, M., 'Fatou Bensouda: We are not Against Africa', Volume 46 No. 520 New African, August/September 2012.

Eze, M., 'Politics has no Place in ICC Decisions ... Says Chief Prosecutor Fatou Bensouda', Volume 48 No. 536 New African, February 2014.

Gaitho, M., 'Could Bensouda have Broken Chain that Held Jubilee Camps Together?', Saturday Nation (Nairobi), 6 December 2015.

Gathii, J., 'Essays: Why Bashir Appeal Faces Uphill Task', Volume 3 No. 1 The Nairobi Law Monthly, January 2012.

Gathii, J., 'Why Bashir Appeal Faces Uphill Task', Volume 3 No. 1 The Nairobi Law Monthly, January 2012.

Gaynor, F., 'Statement on Behalf of the Victims Following the Withdrawal of the Charges against Uhuru Kenyatta', No. 706 Pambazuka, 11 December 2014.

Gekara, E.-M. and Opiyo, D., 'Uhuru's Stinging Attack on ICC and Europe', Sunday Nation (Nairobi), 13 October 2013.

Hansen, T.O., 'Masters of Manipulation: How Kenya Plans to Scuttle International Scrutiny of Post-Election Violence', Wikimedia Commons, 31 May 2012.

Hoile, D., 'Is the ICC fit for Purpose?', Volume 46 No. 515 New African, March 2012.

ICC, 'Statement of the Prosecutor of the International Criminal Court, Fatou Bensouda, on the withdrawal of charges against Mr Uhuru Muigai Kenyatta', Press Release, 5 December 2014.

International Law Commission, 'Third Report on the Immunity of State Officials from Foreign Criminal Jurisdiction – By Concepción Escobar Hernández, Special Rapporteur', UN Doc. A/CN.4/673, 2 June 2014.

Jabre, L. and Moni, J., 'Is Africa on Trial? ... the Role of ICC Examined', Volume 46 No. 519 New African, July 2012.

Kabukuru, W., 'Al-Shabaab Dampens Kenyatta's ICC Victory', Volume 49 No. 546 New African, January 2015.

Kabukuru, W., 'ICC's Long Shadow over Impending Elections', Volume 47 No. 524 New African, January 2013.

Kabukuru, W., 'Kenya: Ocampo's Bombshell Leaves ICC Flat on Its Face', Volume 48 No. 537 New African, March 2014.

Kabukuru, W., 'The Return of President Kenyatta', Volume 47 No. 527 New African, April 2013.

Kagwanja, P., 'Kenyan ICC Cases and Doctrine of Sovereign Immunity', Sunday Nation (Nairobi), 20 October 2013.

Kajwang, O., 'We Cannot Allow Ourselves to be Ruled by Two Fugitives', No. 63 The Africa Report, August–September 2014.

Kamau, M., 'Kenya's Interests and the ICC', Volume 47 No. 529 New African, June 2013.

Kegoro, G., 'African Human Rights Court Needs More than Just a Secretariat to Deliver', Volume 2 No. 11 The Nairobi Law Monthly, 2011.

Kegoro, G., 'Enough is Enough of Empty Threats from the AU', Volume 2 No. 4 The Nairobi Law Monthly, 2011.

Kegoro, G., 'Hague Aftermath: Uhuru Used the state as a Shield Against his Trial', Sunday Nation (Nairobi), 7 December 2015.

Kegoro, G., 'Justice: Why Headache May Linger for Uhuru Despite Win', Saturday Nation (Nairobi), 6 December 2015.

Kegoro, G., 'Kenya Pulls Out All Stops to Have President's Case Deferred', Sunday Nation (Nairobi), 13 October 2013.

Kegoro, G., 'Release of Evidence Gives Prosecutor Chance to Tell her Version of the Story', Sunday Nation (Nairobi), 18 January 2015.

Kelley, K.J., 'Kenya and Rights Groups Set to Clash on Deferral of Cases', Sunday Nation (Nairobi), 20 October 2013.

Kenya, Commission of Inquiry into the Post-Election Violence (CIPEV) Report, October 2008.

Kenyans for Peace with Truth and Justice (KPTJ), 'KPTJ Statement Following the ICC Prosecutor's Notice of Withdrawal of Charges against Uhuru Kenyatta', No. 706 Pambazuka, 11 December 2014.

Khaminwa, J., 'Ocampo Should Listen to Wako', Volume 2 No. 1 The Nairobi Law Monthly, January 2011.

Kiai, M., 'Of Uhuru's Rattling AU Speech and Paradox of Stopping Hague Trials', Saturday Nation (Nairobi), 19 October 2013.

Kiai, M., 'Think Again: Victims of Post-Poll Chaos Suffer as ICC, Jubilee and all Watch in Silence', Saturday Nation (Nairobi), 18 October 2014.

Kimani, E. and Owour, M., '2012: The ICC Elections', Volume 2 No. 4 The Nairobi Law Monthly, November 2011.

Kimani, E. and Owuor, M., 'Ocampo: The Good, the Bad and the Ugly', Volume 2 No. 5 The Nairobi Law Monthly, May 2011.

Kimenyi, M., 'How World Politics, Funding Shape the Operations of ICC', Saturday Nation (Nairobi), 19 October 2013.

Kuria, G.K., 'Is the Urgency for an Expanded EAC Judiciary Justified?', Africa Review, 3 May 2012.

Kuwali, D., 'Friend or Foe of Africans: Will the Real ICC Please Stand Up?', The East African (Nairobi), 26 October 2013.

Lubanga, D., 'No Show: Politicians Snub Yebei Burial', Sunday Nation (Nairobi), 22 March 2015.

Makokha, K., 'ICC Must Rethink Decision Requiring Uhuru in the Dock', Saturday Nation (Nairobi), 27 September 2014.

Makokha, K., 'State-NGOs Rivalry Plays Out at New York ICC Meeting', Sunday Nation (Nairobi), 14 December 2014.

Makokha, K., 'Why President Uhuru Must Not Go to The Hague', Saturday Nation (Nairobi), 12 October 2013.

Mariam, A.G., 'Kenyatta at the ICC: Is Justice Deferred Justice Denied?, No. 664 Pambazuka, 5 February 2014.

Mariam, A.G., 'The AU's Mass Treaty-cide Brinksmanship', Volume 650 Pambazuka, 15 October 2013.

Mathenge, O., 'Bensouda to Use '92 Clash Report', The Star (Nairobi), 12 June 2014.

Maundu, S.D., 'Kibaki is Right on Local Trial of ICC Suspects', Volume 3 No. 6 The Nairobi Law Monthly, 2012.

Mbakwe, T., 'ICC Gets First Conviction after 10 Years in Existence', Volume 46 No. 516 New African, April 2012.

Mbiuki, J., 'ICC Supporters Hiding their Heads in the Sand', The East African (Nairobi), 26 October 2013.

McGreal, C., 'Top Rwandan Aide Chooses French Terror Trial', The Guardian (UK), 10 November 2008.

Menya, W. and Wanga, J., 'What Next? Anxiety in URP over the Ruto Question', Sunday Nation (Nairobi), 7 March 2015.

Menya, W., 'Disclosure: Secrets of ICC Evidence Return to Haunt Uhuru', Sunday Nation (Nairobi), 18 January 2015.

Menya, W., 'Hague Trial: Prosecutor Wants Uhuru Ruling Reversed', Sunday Nation (Nairobi), 27 October 2013.

Menya, W., 'History in the Making: ICC Summons Uhuru', Saturday Nation (Nairobi), 20 September 2014.

Menya, W., 'ICC – Deputy President Lauded for his Patience: Keter's Experience at Ruto's Side – It's Boring and Calls for Lots of Patience', Sunday Nation (Nairobi), 27 October 2013.

Menya, W., 'ICC Cases: Will Shifty Witnesses be Bensouda's Undoing?', Sunday Nation (Nairobi), 27 October 2013.

Menya, W., 'ICC: Uhuru Wins Big as Bensouda Drops Charges', Saturday Nation (Nairobi), 6 December 2015.

Menya, W., 'Precarious: Will Graft Purge, ICC Load Undo UhuRuto?', Sunday Nation (Nairobi), 29 March 2015.

Menya, W., 'Prosecutor Wants Uhuru Ruling Reversed', Sunday Nation (Nairobi), 27 October 2013.

Menya, W., 'Reprimand: ICC Critique Haunts Uhuru', Sunday Nation (Nairobi), 6 April 2014.

Menya, W., 'Ruto Defied Africa(n) Union Resolution for Which Uhuru Lobbied, while his Defence has Accused PNU for Fixing Him', Sunday Nation (Nairobi), 20 October 2013.

Menya, W., 'Uhuru Trial: D-Day Set for Bensouda', Daily Nation (Nairobi), 29 August 2014.

Menya, W., 'Uhuru's Dilemma over Summons: Whom Will Uhuru Disregard, ICC or the African Union?', Sunday Nation (Nairobi), 21 September 2014.

Menya, W., 'Will Shifty Witnesses be Bensouda's Undoing?', Sunday Nation (Nairobi), 27 October 2013.
Munene, M. and Ndirachu, J. 'Hasty Summons: How Uhuru Confounded Allies with Ruto Take-over Game Plan', Sunday Nation (Nairobi), 12 October 2014.
Munene, M., 'ICC Process Will End in Empty Justice, Says Frazer', Sunday Nation (Nairobi), 27 October 2013.
Munene, M., 'Me to Go Record Statement in The Hague? Never', Sunday Nation (Nairobi), 1 March 2015.
Mungai, K., 'A Preliminary Commentary on the Decision of the Pre-Trial Chamber II in the Case of Prosecutor vs Francis Kirimi Muthaura & 2 Others and Its Implications', Volume 3 No. 2 The Nairobi Law Monthly, February 2012.
Mungai, K., 'It is in Kenya's National Interest to Withdraw from Rome Statute', The East African (Nairobi), 12 October 2013.
Mungai, K., 'Mungiki and the Media', Expression Today (Nairobi), June 2008.
Mutambo, A., 'What AU Positions on Kenya Mean', Sunday Nation, 20 October 2013.
Mutiga, M., 'ICC Not the International Body Needed to Keep Warlords in Check', Sunday Nation (Nairobi), 7 December 2014.
Mwagiru, C., 'Fears of Impunity as the AU Pushes for Africa's ICC Exit', Sunday Nation (Nairobi), 13 October 2013.
Mwale, M., 'Black Groups Challenge the ICC', Volume 46 No. 520 New African, August/September 2012.
Mwanga, P., 'Why I'm Convinced that African Union is all Bark and no Bite', Sunday Nation (Nairobi), 20 October 2013.
Namunane, B. and Oluoch, F., 'Africa vs Hague: Final Assault on ICC as Continent Asserts Itself and Demands a New Relationship', The East African (Nairobi), 12 October 2013.
Namunane, B., 'Parting Ways: AU Chiefs Set to Endorse Exit from The Hague Court', Saturday Nation (Nairobi), 12 October 2013.
Namunane, B., 'Uhuru Will not Appear at the ICC Until our Demands are Met: AU', Sunday Nation (Nairobi), 13 October 2013.
Ndurya, M., 'Court: I Don't Have PEV Report – Says Waki', Daily Nation (Nairobi), 20 March 2015.
New African, 'ICC: 0 – Uhuru: 1 – Kenya:?', Volume 48 No. 544, November 2014.
New African, 'The ICC Indictees – All African', Volume 46 No. 516, April 2012.
Ngwiri, M., 'Loss of Face or Not, Uhuru's Best Shot is to Attend Trial at the ICC', Saturday Nation (Nairobi), 12 October 2013.
Njagi, J., 'Uhuru ICC Case Terminated', Saturday Nation (Nairobi), 14 March 2015.
Njiru, B., 'Fumbling over the Head of State Immunity', No. 1 The Platform (Nairobi), December 2014.
Nkwame, M., 'Arusha Rights Court Granted Powers over War Crimes', Daily News (Tanzania), 13 March 2015.
Nsereko, D.N., 'ICC is not after Africans – Most Cases were Referred to the Court', The East African (Nairobi), 19 October 2013.
Obegi, B., 'Do African Leaders Believe in Power Without Accountability?', Sunday Nation (Nairobi), 20 October 2013.

Ochieng, P., 'Arguments Against ICC is Sound, But Uhuru Should Oblige', Sunday Nation (Nairobi), 13 October 2013.
Ochieng, P., 'You Gain Nothing by Severing Links with the World', Sunday Nation (Nairobi), 27 October 2013.
Ochieng, P., 'It is not in Our Interest to Quit Rome Statute', Sunday Nation (Nairobi), 20 October 2013.
Odinkalu, C.A., 'Saving international justice in Africa', No. 445 Pambazuka, 6 August 2009.
Odunga, D., 'Amendment: We are Being Targeted over Hague Cases, NGOs Claim', Sunday Nation (Nairobi), 10 November 2013.
Oduor, E. and Oluoch, F., 'The Country has applied to the UN Security Council for Deferral of the Case', The East African (Nairobi), 19 – 25 October 2013.
Ogemba, P., 'Judge Declines to Rule on Barasa's Petition', Saturday Nation (Nairobi), 12 October 2013.
Oluoch, F., 'A Friend in Need: Who among Big Five Will Support Kenya's ICC Deferral Quest?', The East African (Nairobi), 26 October – 1 November 2013.
Oluoch, F., 'Getting Away with International Crimes? Presidents' Immunity undermines Africa Court', The East African (Nairobi), 18 October 2014.
Oluoch, F., 'ICC Focus Shifts as it Drops Rape, Murder Charges Against Uhuru – Spotlight now on Deputy President William Ruto and Journalist Sang', The East African (Nairobi), 6 December 2014.
Oluoch, F., 'The Hague: ICC Asks UN to Help Enforce Co-operation', The East African (Nairobi), 1 – 7 November 2014.
Ombuor, J., 'ICC Victims' Lawyer: It is Daunting Task, but we shall Prevail', Volume 5 No. 3 The Nairobi Law Monthly, March 2014.
Onyango-Obbo, C., 'Kenya Being Duped by Neighbours on ICC', The East African (Nairobi), 19 October 2013.
Opanga, K., 'Is there an Attempt to have the President Snub ICC?', Sunday Nation (Nairobi), 13 October 2013.
Opanga, K., 'The Hague: Will the Big Stick Diplomacy Deliver?', Sunday Nation (Nairobi), 20 October 2013.
Otieno, J., 'The ICC Tested the Strength of the EU-Kenya Relationship but we Survived', The East African (Nairobi), 14 March 2015.
Partington, S., 'The AU and the ICC', The East African (Nairobi), 19–25 October 2013.
Peter, C.M., 'The AU, African States and the International Criminal Court', Guardian on Sunday (Tanzania), 20 October 2013.
Princeton Project On Universal Jurisdiction, 'The Princeton Principles on Universal Jurisdiction', Princeton University, 2001.
Ratemo, F.M., 'Immunity of President', Volume 50 No. 6 The Nairobi Law Monthly, June 2014.
Redress, 'Kenyatta's ICC Case: Kenya Should Account for Impeding Access to Justice and Truth', No. 706 Pambazuka, 11 December 2014.
Rozenberg, J., 'Prosecutor Luis Moreno-Ocampo is the Best Asset of those Opposed to the International Criminal Court', Volume 2 No. 5 The Nairobi Law Monthly, May 2011.
Saturday Nation (Nairobi), 'Bensouda: It is Justice Denied', 6 December 2014.

Saturday Nation (Nairobi), 'Court Allows Ruto to Return Home for Three Days', 26 October 2013.
Saturday Nation (Nairobi), 'ICC Defers Trial of Gaddafi Spy Chief to Libya in a Historic First', 12 October 2013.
Saturday Nation (Nairobi), 'Judge Sets Date for Barasa's ICC Case', 19 October 2013.
Saturday Nation (Nairobi), 'Ruto's Six-Hour Drama in Court', 26 October 2013.
Saturday Nation (Nairobi), 'Uhuru: I've Waited Six Years for This', 6 December 2015.
Serumaga, K., 'Tantrums at Addis Ababa: Why Servants Don't Win Arguments with their Masters', The East African (Nairobi), 19 October 2013.
Sesay, A. and Mahony, C., 'Has International Justice been Served by the Verdict?', 23(3) BBC Focus on Africa, July–September 2012.
Shimoli, E., 'ICC Allows Uhuru to Skip Sittings: Judges Warn they May Issue Warrant of Arrest if Conditions are Violated', Saturday Nation (Nairobi), 19 October 2013.
Shimoli, E., 'President's Strategy Took him to World Capitals', Sunday Nation (Nairobi), 7 December 2015.
Sigei, J. and Wanga, J., 'ICC Factor Fuels Ruto's Fights in the Rift Valley', Saturday Nation (Nairobi), 28 March 2015.
Simons, M., 'International Criminal Court Formally Ends Case against Kenya's President', The New York Times (USA), 13 March 2015.
Smith, D., 'New Chief Prosecutor Defends International Criminal Court', The Guardian (UK), 23 May 2012.
Sum, A., '154 New Victims Join Hague Against Uhuru', The Standard (Nairobi), 25 September 2014.
Sunday Nation (Nairobi), 'Kenyatta Case: Will Collapse of Muthaura Case have Impact on Uhuru Ruling?', 2 November 2014.
Sunday Nation (Nairobi), 'Siege Mentality against the ICC Unfortunate', 13 October 2013.
Sunday Nation (Nairobi), 'Spilling the Beans: Bensouda Set to Reveal Secrets of Uhuru Charges', 18 January 2015.
Taiwo, O., 'The African Union and Moral Abdication', No. 655 Pambazuka, 20 November 2013.
The Citizen (Tanzania), 'Kenyatta's ICC Case Terminated', 15 March 2015.
The East African (Nairobi), 'Is Africa Really Prepared to Leave the ICC?', 12 October 2013.
The East African (Nairobi), 'Kenya's anti-ICC Protocol Fails to Find AU Backers', 31 January 2015.
The East African (Nairobi), 'UN Hopeful of a Workable Formula on Kenya and ICC', 29 October 2013.
The Economist (London), 'The African Union: Short of Cash and Teeth – Africa's Paramount Body has Improved but it is Still Weak', 27 January 2011.
The Guardian (Tanzania), 'Uhuru Kenyatta is Free as ICC Drops Case', 6 December 2014.
The Guardian (UK), 'Kenya defends failure to arrest Sudan's President Omar Al-Bashir in Nairobi', 29 August 2010.
The Nairobi Law Monthly, 'Briefing: Politics & News', Volume 4 No. 10, November 2013.
The Nairobi Law Monthly, 'Implication of Uhuru's Defiance of ICC on Kenya', Volume 4 No. 10, November 2013.

The Nairobi Law Monthly, 'In Focus: Annan's Finest Hour', Volume 3 No. 2, February 2012.
The Nairobi Law Monthly, 'In the Eye of the Storm', Volume 4 No. 10, November 2013.
The Nairobi Law Monthly, 'Quote Me', Volume 3 No. 7, July 2012.
The Nairobi Law Monthly, 'Rome Statute Allows for Journalist Barasa to be Tried in Kenya', Volume 4 No. 20, November 2013.
The Nairobi Law Monthly, 'The Lords of Ethnicity: Kibaki and Raila Perfect Culture of Tribalism in Public Appointments Started by Kenyatta and Moi', Volume 2 No. 1, January 2011.
The Nairobi Law Monthly, 'Withdrawal from ICC: Push to Remove Kenya from ICC is Ill-Advised', Volume 4 No. 20, November 2013.
The Nairobi Law Monthly, 'International Justice: Italian Judge Holds Fate of "Ocampo Six"', Volume 3 No. 1, January 2012.
The Standard (Nairobi), 'President Kenyatta cannot be prosecuted while in office, AU says', 14 October 2014.
The Sunday Times (Kigali), 'Lifting of Judicial Restriction on Kabuye, We Remain Vindicated', 27 September 2009.
Thuku, W., 'Ruto Clashes with Bensouda over Witness who was Killed', The Standard (Nairobi), 14 January 2015.
Thuku, W., 'The Big Puzzle – Ruto: Murdered Witness was on our Side', The Standard (Nairobi), 7 January 2015.
Tutu, D., 'Pulling out of the ICC would be Tragic for Africa', The East African (Nairobi), 12 October 2014.
Ubwani, Z., 'Ministers Seek Wider Scope for EAC Court', The Citizen (Tanzania), 2 July 2012.
Ulimwengu, J., 'Are we being Targeted? If so, Someone's Got very Poor Aim …', The East African (Nairobi), 19 October 2013.
Ulimwengu, J., 'ICC is targeting Africa, Continent of Impunity? Then it's Doing Its Job', The East African (Nairobi), 5 October 2013.
UN Security Council, Letter to the President of the Security Council from the Chair of the AU Commission Dr Nkosazana Dlamini Zuma of 16 October 2013 (Ref. BC/U/1814.10.13), Annex to UN Doc. S/2013/624.
UN Security Council, '7060th Meeting held on Friday, 15 November 2013, 10 a.m. New York', UN Doc. S/PV.706015, 15 November 2013.
UN Security Council, 'Identical letters of 21 October 2013 from the Permanent Representative of Kenya to the United Nations addressed to the UN Secretary-General and President of the Security Council', UN Doc. S/2013/624, 22 October 2013.
UN Security Council, 'Letter dated 31 October 2013 from Permanent Observer of the African Union addressed to the President of the Security Council', UN Doc. S/2013/639, 1 November 2013.
Vlavonou, G., 'ICC: Does Politics Win over Justice?', Volume 650 Pambazuka, 17 October 2013.
Wafula, K., 'Ruto ICC Witness: Murdered by the State?', No. 719 Pambazuka, 26 March 2015.

Wanjala, D., 'ICC: Uhuru not yet off the Hook', Volume 5 No. 10 The Nairobi Law Monthly, October 2014.

Wanyeki, L.M., 'An Africa-Wide Coup at Addis Ababa? 14 Out of 53', The East African (Nairobi), 19–25 October 2013.

Wanyeki, L.M., 'AU Moves on as Jubilee Partners Start Falling Out', The East African (Nairobi), 7 February 2015.

Warigi, G., 'Kenyan Cases Have Prompted a Possible ICC Procedures Reform', Sunday Nation (Nairobi), 27 October 2013.

Y'gihanga, I., 'Reflections: France, Truth Passes Through Fire Without Getting Scathed', The Sunday Times (Kigali), 4 October 2009.

THE ROME STATUTE AND UNIVERSAL HUMAN RIGHTS

Sanji Mmasenono Monageng
and Alexander Heinze

1. INTRODUCTION

When the International Criminal Court was established in 1998, the former Secretary-General of the United Nations, Kofi Annan noted that it was 'a historic moment and certainly one of the finest moments in the history of the United Nations, when, finally, the Rome Statute, creating ... a permanent International Criminal Court was adopted ... Its creation represents a giant step forward in the march towards universal human rights and the rule of law.'[1]

Accordingly, the International Criminal Court, established 'to guarantee lasting respect for and the enforcement of international justice' and to 'put an end to impunity' for the perpetrators of 'the most serious crimes of concern to the international community as a whole',[2] ultimately raises the recurring questions of what universal human rights are and what the purpose and role of international criminal law in human rights is.[3]

2. THE HISTORY OF UNIVERSAL HUMAN RIGHTS

2.1. THE HUMAN RIGHTS MOVEMENT

The beginning of the modern international human rights movement occurred in the post war period, with the promulgation of the Universal Declaration of Human Rights,[4] shortly after the establishment of the International Military

1 Lee 1999, p. ix; Triponel and Pearson 2010, p. 66.
2 See Preamble to the Rome Statute of the International Criminal Court, A/CONF.183/9.
3 See Teitel 1998–1999, p. 302.
4 Universal Declaration of Human Rights, Dec. 10, 1948, GA Res. 217A, UN GAOR, 3d Sess., 67th plen. mtg., UN Doc. A/810 (1948). See also Bos 1998–1999, p. 231; Greenstock 1999, p. 398.

Tribunal at Nuremberg (IMT).[5] The movement embraced the idea that there is a correlation between peace and human rights, that there could be no peace without justice, that universal values and morality exist in human life and that 'it is not reasonable to allow this value to be diluted by the mere boundaries which human beings happen to have constructed against each other'.[6]

The International Military Tribunal at Nuremberg has long been an important symbol of the universality of law.[7] Individuals could be held accountable for crimes against international law,[8] in particular 'crimes against humanity' as defined in the Nuremberg Charter.[9] The IMT, and its subsequent trials, 'provided a springboard for the development of international human rights law'.[10]

2.2. HUMAN RIGHTS GLOBALISATION

International human rights norms have now 'gone global'.[11] Their protection is a collective goal of the international community[12] as evidenced by the establishment of the International Criminal Tribunal for the former Yugoslavia and that for Rwanda and not least the creation of the world's first permanent International Criminal Court,[13] created by the Rome Statute.[14] In this respect, the ICC is vested with jurisdiction over the most serious crimes of concern to the international community as a whole and is entrusted with putting an end to impunity for the perpetrators of such crimes.[15]

Further evidence of the globalisation of human rights protection is also seen in the Rome Statute's heightened protection of women from sexual violence,

---

5 The IMT at Nuremberg was established by the 'Declaration of London' of 8 August 1945, concluded by the governments of Britain, the USA, France, and the Soviet Union (USSR), see http://avalon.law.yale.edu/imt/imtchart.asp (last visited 31 July 2015). See also Ambos 2013, p. 4.

6 Futamura 2008, p. 39; Vincent 1986, p. 125; Steiner, Alston and Goodman 2007, p. 134; Cassel 2001, p. 134.

7 Steiner, Alston and Goodman 2007, p. 134; Teitel 1998–1999, p. 287.

8 See generally Triggs 1999, p. 176; Jensen 2004, p. 172.

9 Teitel 1998–1999, p. 287.

10 Jensen 2004, p. 172; Teitel 1998–1999, p. 287.

11 Teitel 1998–1999, p. 294. About the definition of globalization see in detail Jensen 2004 p. 159, 166.

12 Alston 2014, p. 208; Donnelly 2014, p. 233.

13 Grover 2014, pp. 113–114, pointing out that the international human rights movement provided 'the necessary political momentum for the creation of the Court'.

14 Bos 1998–1999, pp. 232–233: 'The content of the Rome Statute is taken from the Hague Conventions, the Geneva Conventions, and the Additional Protocols. Compared to the Protocol Additional to the Geneva Conventions of 12 August 1949, and Relating to the Protection of Victims of Non-International Armed Conflicts ('Additional Protocol II'), dealing with internal armed conflicts, the threshold in the Rome Statute is lower.'

15 See the Preamble to the Rome Statute.

with the codification of rape as a 'war crime'[16] as a 'crime against humanity',[17] or as 'genocide.'[18] Where rape is prosecuted as a 'war crime', the offence constitutes 'a limit on the waging of war'.[19] Where rape is prosecuted as a 'crime against humanity', it emphasises that during war or peace, rape is an 'outrage to personal dignity',[20] and where rape is prosecuted as 'genocide', it emphasises the intersectionality of gender-based violence with ethnic-based violence, and shows how sexual violence can destroy a group.[21] Thus, rape would be prosecuted as genocide if the intent to destroy the particular group was present.[22]

3. THE HEART OF THE ROME STATUTE: ARTICLE 21(3)

For purposes of this short paper, it will be highlighted how Article 21(3) is at the heart of the Rome Statute when it comes to the promotion of universal human rights.

3.1. THE CONTEXT OF ARTICLE 21(3)

Article 21(3) of the Rome Statute forms part of the provisions that identify the applicable law of the Court. It states that the 'application and interpretation of law ... must be consistent with internationally recognized human rights, and be without any adverse distinction founded on grounds such as gender ...,[23] age, race, colour, language, religion or belief, political or other opinion, national, ethnic or social origin, wealth, birth or other status'.[24] ICC judges therefore draw from a large body of human rights law with ample discretion to guarantee

16 Article 8(2)(b)(xxii) and (e)(vi) Rome Statute.

17 Article 7(1)(g) Rome Statute.

18 See the footnote to para. 1 of the Elements of Crimes to Article 6(b) Rome Statute: 'This conduct may include, but is not necessarily restricted to, acts of torture, rape, sexual violence or inhuman or degrading treatment.' About rape as part of Article 6(d) of the Rome Statute see Schabas 2016; Schabas 2009, pp. 188 *et seq.* On the Rome Statute's heightened protection of women from sexual violence see also ICC Pre-Trial Chamber I, *Prosecutor v. Germain Katanga*, Warrant of Arrest for Germain Katanga, ICC-01/04-01/07-1-tENG, 2 July 2007, pp. 4–5; *Prosecutor v. Germain Katanga and Mathieu Ngudjolo Chui*, Decision on the Confirmation of Charges, ICC-01/04-01/07-717, 30 September 2008, paras. 354, 436, 444.

19 Teitel 1998–1999, p. 301.

20 ICTR Trial Chamber I, *Prosecutor v. Jean-Paul Akayesu*, Judgement, ICTR-96-4-T, 2 September 1998, para. 638.

21 De Brouwer 2005, p. 47.

22 *Ibid*, p. 80.

23 As defined in Article 7(3), the term 'gender' 'refers to the two sexes, male and female, within the context of society' (fn. added).

24 Article 21(3).

the most basic and important protections.[25] Article 21(3) thus reflects support for the view 'that the nature of human rights is such that they may have a certain special status or, at a minimum, a permeating role within international law'.[26]

The Appeals Chamber of the ICC has ruled, with regard to the role of human rights in the interpretation of the Statute, that '[h]uman rights underpin the Statute; every aspect of it ... Its provisions must be interpreted, and more importantly applied in accordance with internationally recognized human rights; first and foremost, in the context of the Statute, the right to a fair trial, a concept broadly perceived and applied, embracing the judicial process in its entirety'.[27] In other words, human rights can certainly be seen as the mainstay of the Rome Statute.[28]

Of course, Article 21(3) of the Statute speaks of 'internationally recognized human rights' as opposed to 'universal human rights', indeed an important distinction.[29]

The term 'universal' in the context of human rights incorporates geographic, cultural, historic and political dimensions – it pertains to the whole world and is relevant in all societies of the world.[30] On the other hand, the term 'international' suggests the recognition of rights by a subset of the world thus not necessarily relevant in all societies of the world.[31] It follows therefore that all 'universally recognized human rights' would necessarily be 'internationally recognized', whilst not all 'internationally recognized human rights' may be 'universally recognized.'[32]

---

25 See also Bos 1998–1999, p. 234.

26 Young 2011, p. 190; Reisman 1990, p. 872: 'The international human rights program is more than a piecemeal addition to the traditional corpus of international law, more than another chapter sandwiched into traditional textbooks of international law. By shifting the fulcrum of the system from the protection of sovereigns to the protection of people, it works qualitative changes in virtually every component'; Fry 2007–2008, p. 123: 'The possibility exists that the field of human rights is an extra-special type of specialized regime that impacts all aspects of international law, and should not be seen as just another specialized body of law that other specialized bodies might use to reinterpret their own rules in its light, but is one that requires other specialized bodies to be reinterpreted in its light'; Shelton 2006, p. 294.

27 ICC Appeals Chamber, *Prosecutor v. Thomas Lubanga Dyilo*, Judgment on the Appeal of Mr Thomas Lubanga Dyilo against the Decision on the Defence Challenge to the Jurisdiction of the Court Pursuant to Article 19(2)(a) of the Statute of 3 October 2006, ICC-01/04-01/06-772, 14 December 2006, para. 37 (fn. omitted). The ICC Pre-Trial Chamber I referred to that Judgment in *Prosecutor v. Laurent Gbagbo*, Decision on the fitness of Laurent Gbagbo to take part in the proceedings before this Court, ICC-02/11-01/11-286-Red, 2 November 2012, para. 45.

28 Perrin 2007–2008, p. 398.

29 Sheppard 2010, p. 44. About the different terminology used during the negotiations of the Rome Statute see Grover 2014, p. 117.

30 Edwards 2001, p. 378. About the term in detail see Donnelly 2007, p. 283.

31 *Ibid.*

32 *Ibid.*

Thus, generally speaking, the phrase 'internationally recognized human rights' appears to denote something less than universal acceptance.[33] In this regard, it will be important how the Court distinguishes between the two concepts.

Universal human rights movements have been labelled as 'human rights crusades' of the West against non-Western states[34] and as an expression of a particular European-American culture.[35] This accusation stems from international law's failure to engage with and adapt to local cultural settings.

Some countries, for instance, generally resist the idea of universal human rights, arguing that Western nations, in particular, use the idea of universal human rights as a pretext for illegitimate political interference in the internal affairs of other states with very unique value systems and challenges.[36] The voices from some African states, arguing that the ICC is a patently 'political' institution, which has been created to further Western imperialism, are still present and resonating. Yet it is African states which participated in the drafting of the Rome Statute and to this day constitute the largest regional block amongst states which have voluntarily signed up to the Rome Statute system.

The human rights regime in African states is still developing and faces difficult challenges.[37] While it strives to match international human rights norms, it needs to take into account African cultural norms at the same time.[38] Furthermore, although the African Court on Human and Peoples' Rights certainly contributes to the universalisation of human rights, access of individuals and non-governmental organisations to this Court is still a sensitive matter.[39] More needs to be done on the continent to fortify civil society and to

---

33 Edwards 2001, pp. 375–377; Bailey 2014, p. 524 with n. 43.

34 Mutua 2007, p. 555 *et seq.*, 610, 573; Mutua 1995–1996, p. 592. See also Osiatyński 2009, p. 153 with further references; Sainati 2012, p. 170; Donnelly 2007, p. 287: 'The social-structural 'modernity' of these ideas and practices, however, not their cultural "Westernness", deserves emphasis. Human rights ideas and practices arose not from any deep Western cultural roots but from the social, economic, and political transformations of modernity. They thus have relevance wherever those transformations have occurred, irrespective of the pre-existing culture of the place.'

35 Mutua 2002, p. 5: 'The human rights corpus is driven – normatively and descriptively – by what I have called the savage-victim-savior metaphor, in which human rights is a grand narrative of an epochal contest that pits savages against victims and saviors. In this script of human rights, democracy and western [*sic*] liberalism are internationalized to redeem savage non-Western cultures from themselves, and to alleviate the suffering of victims, who are generally non-western [*sic*] and non-European' (fn. omitted); Mutua 1995–1996, pp. 592–593. Crit. Goldman 2007, p. 233; Sen 2004, p. 320.

36 World Conference on Human Rights, Regional Meeting for Asia, Bangkok, Thai., March 29-April 2 1993, Final Declaration, UN Doc. A/CONF.157/ASRM/8, A/CONF. 157/PC/59 (7 April 1993). See also the description in Goldman 2007, p. 233.

37 Heyns 2001, pp. 173–174.

38 Baderin 2005, p. 148; Juma 2009, p. 270: '[T]he development of the African human rights system, as indeed other human rights systems, is "work in progress"'.

39 Heyns 2001, p. 170; Eno 2002, pp. 229–231, 233: 'Should the Court ... interpret articles 34(6) and 5(3) of the Protocol narrowly, it could effectively foreclose NGO and individual access to

ensure that a universal standard of adherence to human rights norms is fostered throughout the continent.

3.2. THE ROLE OF THE ICC

The ICC plays a critical role as both a tribunal of individual criminal responsibility and as a human rights institution, both in the application and development of existing law.

Specifically, its establishment:

1. develops the relationship between human rights and humanitarian law;[40]
2. builds on an existing regime of international human rights guarantees; and
3. creates the possibility for cooperation with international human rights bodies.[41]

While the ICC is primarily a judicial institution and 'was not established to be an international court of human rights, sitting in judgment over domestic legal systems to ensure that they are compliant with international standards of human rights',[42] its mere existence and work help to promote human rights by: creating a historical record for past wrongs;[43] offering a forum for victims to voice their opinions and receive satisfaction and compensation for past violations;[44]

the Court'; Baderin 2005, pp. 144–146; Mohamed 1999, pp. 377 *et seq.*; Viljoen 2004–2005, pp. 22 *et seq.*; Ssenyonjo 2013 pp. 17–56. About access of individuals and Non Governmental Organisations to the new African Court of Justice and Human Rights see also Juma 2009, pp. 267, 269, 287 *et seq.*

40 Young 2011, pp. 190–191; Perrin 2007–2008, pp. 367, 369. Crit. Robinson 2008, pp. 928–929: 'Human rights and humanitarian law focus more simply on broad and liberal construction to maximise protection for beneficiaries, and are not accustomed to the special moral restraints which arise when fixing guilt upon an individual actor.'

41 Pocar 2001, p. 67.

42 ICC Appeals Chamber, *Prosecutor v. Saif-Al-Islam Gaddafi and Abdullah Al-Senussi*, Judgment on the appeal of Mr Abdullah Al-Senussi against the decision of Pre-Trial Chamber I of 11 October 2013 entitled 'Decision on the admissibility of the case against Abdullah Al-Senussi', ICC-01/11-01/11-565, 24 July 2014, para. 219, citing Benzing 2003, p. 598: '... international law provides other, more suitable remedies to address breaches of human rights of the accused in the context of other instruments and institutions. Were the protection of human rights of the accused in national jurisdictions added to the mandate of the Court, this would indeed add a dimension entirely different from the initial idea for its establishment'. In another Judgment, the ICC Appeals Chamber recognised 'the different mandate of human rights courts', see *Prosecutor v. Thomas Lubanga Dyilo*, Judgment on the appeals against the 'Decision establishing the principles and procedures to be applied to reparations' of 7 August 2012, ICC-01/04-01/06-3129, 3 March 2015, para. 128.

43 Statement of Judge Claude Jorda, UN SCOR, 55th Sess., 4161st mtg. at 3, UN Doc. S/PV.4161, 20 June 2000; Ohlin 2009, pp. 86 *et seq.*; McClelland 2002, p. 2; Wilson 2005, p. 908. In more detail Heinze 2014, pp. 218 *et seq.*

44 Swart 2008, p. 100; Schrag 2004, p. 428; Wiessner and Willard 1999, pp. 316, 330.

creating judicial precedent; and deterring potential violators of the gravest crimes[45] while punishing past offenders.[46]

It has been suggested that too much attention is focused on the ICC bringing justice to so few at a high cost compared to other types of human rights work.[47] First, it is not true that the Court is bringing justice to only a few people. The victims of the mass crimes with which it deals are in thousands. To date, the Trust Fund for Victims has assisted over 100,000 victims in Northern Uganda and other places.[48] Second, it should be noted that the ICC is just one part of a larger effort to guarantee human rights to all. International justice holds a different place in the spectrum of human rights programmes, just as its source of funding varies from human rights advocacy organisations and humanitarian missions. Compared to peacekeeping, the price of justice is quite low.[49] Furthermore, it is difficult to measure the success of future proceedings and prevented crimes. By drawing attention to the worst crimes and prosecuting the worst offenders, the ICC is setting an example for the prosecution of other, perhaps, less serious human rights violations and offenders. Even though the creation of the Court has raised excitement and controversy in the international community, the ICC, like national courts, is meant to complement existing and future human rights efforts.

---

45 Ambos 2013, p. 71.

46 *Prosecutor v. Omar Serushago*, Sentence, ICTR 98-39-S, 5 February 1999, para. 20; *Prosecutor v. Rutaganda*, Judgement, ICTR-96-3-T, 6 December 1999, para. 455; *Prosecutor v. Ndindabahizi*, Judgement, ICTR-2001-71-I, 15 July 2004, para. 498; *Prosecutor v. Karera*, Judgement, ICTR-01-74-T, 7 December 2007, para. 571. See generally Heinze 2014, pp. 216 *et seq.*

47 See Higgins 2007, pp. 394 *et seq.* Similar accusations have been brought forward against the ad hoc Tribunals, see Zacklin 2004, pp. 543–545; Swoboda 2013, pp. 235, 343 *et seq.*; Kwon 2007, pp. 360 *et seq.*

48 See Trust Fund for Victims, Strategic Plan 2014–2017, August 2014, pp. 6 *et seq.*, available at: www.trustfundforvictims.org/sites/default/files/media_library/documents/pdf/TFV_Strategic_Plan_2014_2017__approved.pdf (last visited 28 October 2015).

49 Statement by Prince Zeid al-Hussein before the UN Security Council, from Edith M. Lederer, Security Council Told to Stop Complaining About High Cost of War Crimes Tribunals, Associated Press, 7 October 2004, available at: https://www.globalpolicy.org/component/content/article/163/28289.html (last visited 28 October 2015). 'He criticized the council for repeatedly complaining about the high cost of the tribunals, saying the $175 million spent annually to prosecute those responsible for war crimes in former Yugoslavia 'is less than one-twentieth' of what the United Nations paid annually during the war for peacekeeping operations.' He is also quoted as saying: 'With an international community prepared to spend almost one trillion U.S. dollars a year on weapons that historic companion of war how can we say that anything we have spent thus far on justice, the surest companion of peace, is too expensive?' The Court's approved budget for 2015 is a total of €130,665,600, see Resolution ICC-ASP/13/Res.1 of the Assembly of States Parties (ASP), Programme budget for 2015, adopted at the 12th plenary meeting, on 17 December 2014, available at: www.icc-cpi.int/iccdocs/asp_docs/Resolutions/ASP13/ICC-ASP-13-Res1-ENG.pdf (last visited 28 October 2015). For an overview of the ICC's budget over the past years see O'Donohue 2013, pp. 269, 278. For further examples that the costs of the ICC are relatively low in comparison to the costs of other institutions and other trials, see Heinze 2014, p. 42 with further references in n. 11.

To have regard to the universality of human rights, the ICC has always looked to human rights norms and their related jurisprudence from a geographically broad spectrum, including references to the Universal Declaration of Human Rights, the International Covenant on Civil and Political Rights (ICCPR), the Convention on the Rights of the Child (CRC), and the regional European Convention on Human Rights (ECHR) and the Inter-American Convention on Human Rights (IACHR).[50] Even the Presidency of the ICC in a decision concerning the right to funded family visits, has relied on these, including the African Charter on Human and Peoples' Rights, the African Charter on the Rights and Welfare of the Child and the Arab Charter on Human Rights.[51] This puts pressure on judges, parties and participants to be human rights compliant.

The Court has never been busier, and the workload continues to increase exponentially.

4. CONCLUSION

Human rights provide the platform for the imputation of legal rights and duties to individuals under international law.[52] These rights should be accorded to all people, not only those who happen to live in certain parts of the world.[53] Despite

50 In ICC Appeals Chamber, Situation in the Democratic Republic of the Congo, Judgment on the Prosecutor's Application for Extraordinary Review of Pre-Trial Chamber I's 31 March 2006 Decision Denying Leave to Appeal, ICC-01/04-168, 13 July 2006, para. 11, the Appeals Chamber referred to the ICCPR, ECHR, IACHR and African Charter on Human and Peoples' Rights. See also ICC Pre-Trial Chamber I, Situation in the Democratic Republic of the Congo, Decision on the Prosecution's Application for Leave to Appeal the Chamber's Decision of 17 January 2006 on the Applications for Participation in the Proceedings of VPRS 1, VPRS 2, VPRS 3, VPRS 4, VPRS 5 and VPRS 6, ICC-01/04-135-tEN, 31 March 2006, para. 34: 'Many international instruments guarantee the right to a fair trial. In this respect one could cite article 10 of the Universal Declaration of Human Rights, article 14 (1) of the International Covenant on Civil and Political Rights, article 6 (1) of the European Convention for the Protection of Human Rights and Fundamental Freedoms, article 8 (1) of the American Convention on Human Rights, or indeed article 7 (1) of the African Charter on Human and Peoples' Rights' (fn. omitted); ICC Appeals Chamber, *Prosecutor v. Thomas Lubanga Dyilo*, Reasons for 'Decision of the Appeals Chamber on the Defence application 'Demande de suspension de toute action ou procédure afin de permettre la désignation d'un nouveau Conseil de la Défense' filed on 20 February 2007' issued on 23 February 2007, ICC-01/04-01/06-844, 9 March 2007, para. 12. For further references, see Young 2011, p. 203 with n. 67.

51 ICC Presidency, *Prosecutor v. Germain Katanga and Mathieu Ngudjolo Chui*, Decision on 'Mr Mathieu Ngudjolo's Complaint Under Regulation 221(1) of the Regulations of the Registry Against the Registrar's Decision of 18 November 2008', ICC-RoR217-02/08-8, para. 44 with n. 112. See also Young 2011, p. 203.

52 Engle 2006, p. 236.

53 Bagaric and Morss 2005-2006, p. 204; Donnelly 2007, p. 306: 'International legal universality is one of the great achievements of the international human rights movement, both intrinsically and because it has facilitated a deepening overlapping consensus.'

terminological nuances[54] and cultural conflicts,[55] which result in differences about the scope, content and philosophical bases of human rights:[56] human rights are universal![57]

International law increasingly plays a role in shaping state policy and domestic law in advancing protection of human rights. If we add to this trend, the growth of international criminal law and its emphasis on the criminal responsibility of the individual, the picture is clear: the role of the individual as a subject and object of international law is unassailable. Serious crimes have been brought within the reach of international law along with an acceptance of the notion that individual accountability is integral to the maintenance of international peace. The legal and political considerations that led to this development are instructive to see where the process will take us next.

As mentioned at the beginning, repeating the words of Kofi Annan: the creation of the ICC represents a giant step forward in the march towards universal human rights. This step forward must be engaged in with all confidence and all awareness of the Court's role for the protection of human rights. Only then can the step forward actually leave some footprints in the rocky soil of impunity and human rights violations.

BIBLIOGRAPHY

BOOKS AND JOURNAL ARTICLES

Abdelsalam 1999

Abdelsalam, A.M., 'Individual and NGO Participation in Human Rights Litigation Before the African Court of Human and Peoples' Rights: Lessons from the European and Inter-American Courts of Human Rights', 8 Mich. St. U.-DCL J. Int'l L., 1999.

Alston 2014

Alston, P., 'Against a World Court for Human Rights', 28 Ethics & International Affairs, 2014.

Ambos 2013

Ambos, K., 'Treatise on International Criminal Law, Volume I: Foundations and General Part', Oxford University Press, 2013.

---

54 Tay 1999, p. 5; Goldman 2007, p. 230; Bix 2010, pp. 211, 215; Donnelly 2007, pp. 281, 282, 283.

55 Nedelsky 2000, p. 245: 'The debates over "universal" human rights versus alleged abuses in the name of culture and tradition are best understood as conflicts between different communities of judgment'; Goldman 2007, p. 233.

56 Mutua 1995–1996, p. 590; Gamble, Bailey, Hawk and McCurdy 2001, pp. 33, 34: 'Put metaphorically, there has been such rapid cultivation of human rights trees in many and varied environments that scant attention has been paid to the forest of international human rights law.'

57 Engle 2006, p. 236.

Baderin 2005
Baderin, M.A., 'Recent Developments in the African Regional Human Rights System', 5 Hum. Rts. L. Rev., 2005.
Bagaric and Morss 2005–2006
Bagaric, M. and Morss, J., 'In Search of a Coherent Jurisprudence for International Criminal Law: Correlating Universal Human Responsibilities with Universal Human Rights', 29 Suffolk Transnat'l L. Rev., 2005–2006.
Bailey 2014
Bailey, S., 'Article 21(3) of the Rome Statute: A Plea for Clarity', 14 ICLR, 2014.
Benzing 2003
Benzing, M., 'The Complementarity Regime of the International Criminal Court: International Criminal Justice between State Sovereignty and the Fight against Impunity', 7 Max Planck Y.B. U.N. L., 2003.
Bix 2010
Bix, B., 'Natural Law Theory', in Patterson, D. (ed.), 'A Companion to Philosophy of Law and Legal Theory', 2nd ed., John Wiley & Sons, 2010.
Bos 1998–1999
Bos, A., '1948–1998: The Universal Declaration of Human Rights and the Statute of the International Criminal Court', 22 Fordham Int'l L.J., 1998–1999.
Cassel 2001
Cassel, D., 'Does International Human Rights Law Make a Difference?', 2 Chi. J. Int'l L., 2001.
De Brouwer 2005
De Brouwer, A.M, 'Supranational Criminal Prosecution of Sexual Violence: the ICC and the Practice of the ICTY and the ICTR', Intersentia, 2005.
Donnelly 2014
Donnelly, J., 'State Sovereignty and International Human Rights', 28 Ethics & International Affairs, 2014.
Donnelly 2007
Donnelly, J., 'The Relative Universality of Human Rights', 29 Hum. Rts. Q., 2007.
Edwards 2001
Edwards, G.E., 'International Human Rights Law Challenges to the New International Criminal Court: The Search and Seizure Right to Privacy', 26 Yale J. Int'l L., 2001.
Engle 2006
Engle, E., 'Universal Human Rights: A Generational History', 12 Annual Survey of International and Comparative Law, 2006.
Eno 2002
Eno, R.W., 'The jurisdiction of the African Court on Human and Peoples' Rights', 2 Afr. Hum. Rts. L.J., 2002.
Fry 2007–2008
Fry, J.D, 'International Human Rights Law in Investment Arbitration: Evidence of International Law's Unity', 18 Duke J. Comp. & Int'l L., 2007–2008.
Futamura 2008
Futamura, M., 'War Crimes Tribunals and Transitional Justice', Routledge, 2008.

Gamble, Bailey, Hawk, and McCurdy 2001
Gamble, J.K., Bailey, T.A., Hawk, J.S., and McCurdy, E.E., 'Human Rights Treaties: A Suggested Typology, An Historical Perspective', 7 Buff. Hum. Rts. L. Rev., 2001.
Goldman 2007
Goldman, D.B., 'Globalisation and the Western Legal Tradition', Cambridge University Press, 2007.
Greenstock 1999
Greenstock, J., 'International Human Rights and Standards', 23 Fordham Int'l L.J., 1999.
Grover 2014
Grover, L., 'Interpreting Crimes in the Rome Statute of the International Criminal Court', Cambridge University Press, 2014.
Heinze 2014
Heinze, A., 'International Criminal Procedure and Disclosure', Duncker & Humblot, 2014.
Heyns 2001
Heyns, C., 'The African Regional Human Rights System: In need of Reform?', 1 Afr. Hum. Rts. L.J., 2001.
Higgins 2007
Higgins, G., 'Fair and Expeditious Pre-Trial Proceedings', 5 JICJ, 2007.
Jensen 2004
Jensen, R., 'Globalization and the International Criminal Court: Accountability and a New Conception of State', in Dekker, I.F. and Werner, W.G. (eds.), 'Governance and International Legal Theory', Brill, 2004.
Juma 2009
Juma, D., 'Lost (or Found) in Transition? The Anatomy of the New African Court of Justice and Human Rights', 13 Max Planck Y.B. U.N. L., 2009.
Kwon 2007
Kwon, O.G., 'The Challenge of an International Criminal Trial as Seen from the Bench', 5 JICJ, 2007.
Lee 1999
Lee, R.S. (ed.), 'The International Criminal Court: The Making of the Rome Statute; Issues, Negotiations, Results', Kluwer Law International, 1999.
McClelland 2002
McClelland, G.A., 'A Non Adversary Approach to International Criminal Tribunals', 26 Suffolk Transnat'l L. Rev., 2002.
Mutua 2007
Mutua, M.W., 'Standard Setting in Human Rights: Critique and Prognosis', 29 Hum. Rts. Q., 2007.
Mutua 2002
Mutua, M.W., 'Terrorism and Human Rights: Power, Culture, and Subordination', 8 Buff. Hum. Rts. L. Rev., 2002.
Mutua 1995–1996
Mutua, M.W., 'The Ideology of Human Rights', 36 Va. J. Int'l L., 1995–1996.
Nedelsky 2000
Nedelsky, J., 'Communities of Judgment and Human Rights', 1 Theoretical Inq. L., 2000.

O'Donohue 2013
O'Donohue, J., 'Financing the International Criminal Court', 13 ICLR, 2013.
Ohlin 2009
Ohlin, J.D., 'A Meta-Theory of International Criminal Procedure: Vindicating the Rule of Law', 14 UCLA J. Int'l L. & Foreign Aff., 2009.
Osiatyński 2009
Osiatyński, W., 'Human Rights and Their Limits', Cambridge University Press, 2009.
Perrin 2007–2008
Perrin, B., 'Searching for Law While Seeking Justice: The Difficulties of Enforcing International Humanitarian Law in International Criminal Trials', 39 Ottawa L. Rev, 2007–2008.
Pocar 2001
Pocar, F., 'The Rome Statute of the International Criminal Court and Human Rights', in Politi, M., et al. (eds.), 'The Rome Statute of the International Criminal Court: A Challenge to Impunity', Ashgate, 2001.
Reisman 1990
Reisman, W.M., 'Sovereignty and Human Rights in Contemporary International Law', 84 Am. J. Int'l L., 1990.
Robinson 2008
Robinson, D., 'The Identity Crisis of International Criminal Law', 21 LJIL, 2008.
Sainati 2012
Sainati, T.E, 'Toward a Comparative Approach to the Crime of Genocide', 62 Duke L.J., 2012.
Schabas 2016
Schabas, W.A., 'Article 6', in Triffterer, O. and Ambos, K. (eds.), 'Commentary on the Rome Statute of the International Criminal Court', 3rd ed., Beck et al., 2016.
Schabas 2009
Schabas, W.A., 'Genocide in International Law', 2nd ed., Cambridge University Press, 2009.
Schrag 2004
Schrag, M., 'Lessons Learned from ICTY Experience', 2 JICJ, 2004.
Sen 2004
Sen, A., 'Elements of a Theory of Human Rights', 32 Philosophy & Public Affairs, 2004.
Shelton 2006
Shelton, D., 'Normative Hierarchy in International Law', 100 Am. J. Int'l L., 2006.
Sheppard 2010
Sheppard, D., 'The International Criminal Court and 'Internationally Recognized Human Rights': Understanding Article 21(3) of the Rome Statute', 10 ICLR, 2010.
Ssenyonjo 2013
Ssenyonjo, M., 'Direct Access to the African Court on Human and Peoples' Rights by Individuals and Non-Governmental Organisations: An Overview of the Emerging Jurisprudence of the African Court 2008–2012', 2 Int'l Hum. Rts. L. Rev., 2013.
Steiner, Alston, and Goodman 2007
Steiner, H.J., Alston, P. and Goodman R., 'International Human Rights in Context', 3rd ed., Oxford University Press, 2007.

Swart 2008
Swart, B., 'Damaska and the Faces of International Criminal Justice', 6 JICJ, 2008.
Swoboda 2013
Swoboda, S., 'Verfahrens- und Beweisstrategien vor den UN-ad hoc Tribunalen', Nomos, 2013.
Tay 1999
Tay, A., 'Human Rights and Human Wrongs', 21 Adelaide L. Rev., 1999.
Teitel 1998–1999
Teitel, R., 'The Universal and the Particular in International Criminal Justice', 30 Colum. Hum. Rts. L. Rev., 1998–1999.
Triggs 1999
Triggs, G., 'National Prosecutions of War Crimes and the Rule of Law', in Durham, H. and McCormack, T.H. (eds.), 'The Changing Face of Conflict and the Efficacy of International Humanitarian Law', Kluwer Law International, 1999.
Triponel and Pearson 2010
Triponel, A. and Pearson, S., 'African States and the International Criminal Court', 12 U.S.F. J.L. & Soc. Challenges, 2010.
Viljoen 2004–2005
Viljoen, F., 'A Human Rights Court for Africa, and Africans', 30 Brook. J. Int'l L., 2004–2005.
Vincent 1986
Vincent, J., 'Human Rights and International Relations', Cambridge University Press, 1986.
Wiessner and Willard 1999
Wiessner, S. and Willard, A.R., 'Policy-Oriented Jurisprudence and Human Rights Abuses in Internal Conflict: Toward a World Public Order of Human Dignity', in 'Symposium on Method in International Law', 93 Am. J. Int'l L., 1999.
Wilson 2005
Wilson, R.A., 'Judging History: The Historical Record of the International Criminal Tribunal for the Former Yugoslavia', 27 Hum. Rts. Q., 2005.
Young 2011
Young, R., "Internationally Recognized Human Rights' Before the International Criminal Court', 60 ICLQ, 2011.
Zacklin 2004
Zacklin, R., 'The Failings of Ad Hoc International Tribunals', 2 JICJ, 2004.

JURISPRUDENCE

ICC 2015
ICC, Prosecutor v. Thomas Lubanga Dyilo, ICC-01/04–01/06–3129, 3 March 2015.
ICC 2014
ICC, Prosecutor v. Saif-Al-Islam Gaddafi and Abdullah Al-Senussi, ICC-01/11-01/11–565, 24 July 2014.
ICC 2012
ICC, Prosecutor v. Laurent Gbagbo, ICC-02/11–01/11–286-Red, 2 November 2012.

ICC 2009
ICC, Prosecutor v. Germain Katanga and Mathieu Ngudjolo Chui, ICC-RoR217–02/08–8, 23 March 2009.
ICC 2008
ICC, Prosecutor v. Germain Katanga and Mathieu Ngudjolo Chui, ICC-01/04–01/07–717, 30 September 2008.
ICC 2007
ICC, Prosecutor v. Germain Katanga, ICC-01/04–01/07–1-tENG, 2 July 2007.
ICC 2007
ICC, Prosecutor v. Thomas Lubanga Dyilo, ICC-01/04–01/06–844, 9 March 2007.
ICC 2006
ICC, Prosecutor v. Thomas Lubanga Dyilo, ICC-01/04–01/06, 14 December 2006.
ICC 2006
ICC, Judgment on the Prosecutor's Application for Extraordinary Review of Pre-Trial Chamber I's 31 March 2006 Decision Denying Leave to Appeal, ICC-01/04–168, 13 July 2006.
ICC 2006
ICC, Decision on the Prosecution's Application for Leave to Appeal the Chamber's Decision of 17 January 2006 on the Applications for Participation in the Proceedings of VPRS 1, VPRS 2, VPRS 3, VPRS 4, VPRS 5 and VPRS 6, ICC-01/04–135-tEN, 31 March 2006.
ICTR 2007
ICTR, Prosecutor v. Karera, Judgement, ICTR-01–74-T, 7 December 2007.
ICTR 2004
ICTR, Prosecutor v. Ndindabahizi, ICTR-2001–71-I, 15 July 2004.
ICTR 1999
ICTR, Prosecutor v. Rutaganda, ICTR-96–3-T, 6 December 1999.
ICTR 1999
ICTR, Prosecutor v. Omar Serushago, ICTR 98–39-S, 5 February 1999.
ICTR 1998
ICTR, Prosecutor v. Jean-Paul Akayesu, ICTR-96–4-T, 2 September 1998.

TREATIES, LEGISLATION AND AGREEMENTS

Charter of the International Military Tribunal, August 1945.
Rome Statute of the International Criminal Court, 2187 UNTS 90/37, 17 July 1998.
Universal Declaration of Human Rights, GA Res. 217A (III), UN Doc. A/810, 10 December 1948.

OTHERS

Assembly of State Parties to the Rome Statute of the ICC, Resolution ICC-ASP/13/Res.1, Programme budget for 2015, 17 December 2014.

Statement by Prince Zeid al-Hussein before the UN Security Council, from Edith M. Lederer, Associated Press, 7 October 2004.
Statement of Judge Claude Jorda, UN SCOR, 55th Sess., 4161st mtg. at 3, UN Doc. S/PV.4161, 20 June 2000.
Trust Fund for Victims, Strategic Plan 2014–2017, August 2014.
World Conference on Human Rights, Regional Meeting for Asia, Bangkok, Thai., Mar. 29-Apr.2, 1993, Final Declaration, UN Doc. A/CONF.157/ASRM/8, A/CONF. 157/PC/59, 7 April 1993.

CHALLENGING THE CULTURE OF IMPUNITY FOR SEXUAL AND GENDER-BASED CRIMES

Fatou BENSOUDA

1. INTRODUCTION

In Greek mythology, the rape of Helen sparked the Trojan War. Sixteenth-century theologian Francisco de Vitoria is said to have considered sacking a city, with the attendant horrors of rape to be permissible if it would act as a 'spur to the courage of the troops.'[1] But such thinking ought not be easily forgivable. Just as atrocity crimes of sexual violence ought not be easily forgotten from the global consciousness.

And yet the tragedy of our modern times is that these heinous crimes continue to be shrouded in a culture of silence and impunity. Sexual violence of a massive scale occurred in the infamous Foca rape camps of Republika Srpska,[2] sexual and gender-based violence were an almost routine occurrence during the Rwandan genocide,[3] and rapes also featured in the Khmer Rogue's Tuol Sleng prison.[4] At the time of writing, numerous non-governmental organisations (NGOs) have documented horrific acts of sexual violence in conflict-zones around the world – in Iraq[5], the DR Congo,[6] and Nigeria.[7]

---

1 De Vitoria 2015, p. 133.

2 See ICTY, *Prosecutor v. Kunerac et al.*, Judgement, Trial Chamber, IT-96-23, 22 February 2001, p. 302.

3 See generally ICTR, *Prosecutor v. Akayesu*, Judgment, Chamber, IT-96-4-T, 2 September 1998.

4 See ECCC, 0001/18-07-2007-ECCC/SC, Appeal Judgement, Supreme Court Chamber, 3 February 2012, para. 86.

5 Human Rights Watch, 'Iraq: ISIS Escapees Describe Systematic Rape' 14 April 2015: https://www.hrw.org/news/2015/04/14/iraq-isis-escapees-describe-systematic-rape (last visited 16 September 2015).

6 Human Rights Watch, 'Democratic Republic of Congo: Ending Impunity for Sexual Violence' 10 June 2014: https://www.hrw.org/news/2014/06/10/democratic-republic-congo-ending-impunity-sexual-violence (last accessed 16 September 2015).

7 Human Rights Watch, 'Those Terrible Weeks in their Camp: Boko Haram Violence against Women and Girls in Northeast Nigeria', 2014.

The presence of these crimes perpetuates the narrative that sexual violence is an inevitable consequence; or worse, simply an unfortunate 'side-effect' of war. The lack of justice for victims, and the corresponding lack of accountability for perpetrators have emboldened those whose interests lie in waging and continuing wars. In the course of which, sexual and gender-based crimes, as well as the recruitment of child soldiers, and other crimes, with sexual and gender elements, have become the norm.

But there is a competing narrative. One that says that rape and other forms of sexual violence are not inevitable; that they are not mere trophies to be won in a war. That sexual violence is an odious practice that must be exposed for what it really is: a heinous crime deserving of global condemnation and action.

This article seeks to shed light on both narratives. With regard to the former, I discuss why a culture of impunity for sexual and gender-based crimes continues to exist at the national and international level. With regard to the latter, I argue for a criminal justice approach that focuses on the effective investigation and prosecution of sexual and gender-based crimes at the national and international levels. Concomitantly, I illustrate the steps taken by the international community, and specifically, the steps I have initiated at the Office of the Prosecutor (OTP) at the ICC, to address this pressing need for accountability.

2. CHALLENGES AT THE NATIONAL LEVEL

2.1. RESOURCE CHALLENGES

Sexual violence and gender-based crimes are often not adequately addressed at the national level, but this shortfall is greatly exacerbated in countries with conflicts, or emerging from conflicts.

There are a number of difficulties faced by countries embroiled in conflicts, or in post-conflict situations. National proceedings are often stymied by a lack of, or ineffective, judicial infrastructure such as courts,[8] insufficient prosecutorial or investigative resources, a resort to informal mediation, or in many cases, inadequate legislation that severely limits access to justice for victims of sexual violence crimes.

---

[8] Afghanistan ranks second-to-last in the Rule of Law Index; see World Justice Project, 'Rule of Law Index: Rule of Law Around the World 2015': http://worldjusticeproject.org/rule-law-around-world (last accessed 16 September 2015).

2.2. A CULTURE OF INDIFFERENCE LEADS TO A CULTURE OF IMPUNITY

In some cases, the lack of political will, official attitudes of trivialisation, or denial of these crimes, and other discriminatory attitudes further compound the challenges of seeking accountability. Governments need to take firm steps to enact legislation to protect women against sexual and gender-based crimes, especially against the systemic perpetuation of such crimes. They also need to prioritise resources to the police and courts such that enough is being done to investigate and prosecute.

In addition, in many cases, sexual violence crimes remain severely under-reported due to societal taboos and the social stigma that accompanies the sensitive nature of these offences. A survivor from the Rwandan genocide describes the horrific experience of being raped multiple times, on multiple occasions, but still feeling induced by shame to cover her wounds:

> [Two *Interhamwe*] sharpened the end of a stick of a hoe. They held open my legs and pushed the stick into me. I was screaming ... One *Interhamwe* saw me and took me aside along with four other women ... There, he raped me. I cried out because I was still wounded from before and he was opening all the wounds again ...
>
> After the rape, I was left alone and naked. I decided to try and escape. I couldn't walk properly and so I was on all fours. When people passed me, I sat down and stopped walking so they wouldn't know that I had been raped because I was ashamed. I crawled like that for two days in the bush.[9]

United Nations (UN) agencies have estimated as many as 100,000–250,000 women were raped during the Rwandan genocide.[10] But there, as in many conflict areas, underreporting and non-reporting of sexual violence remained the norm due to the stigmatisation of rape victims.

The confluence of the above factors – a lack of adequate capability or willingness by governments and stigmatisation of victims of sexual violence – can lead to severely pernicious outcomes for survivors of these atrocity crimes. Investigative opportunities become severely reduced where the evidence cannot be collected or preserved in a timely or proper manner, whether it is due to stigmatisation, ongoing conflict, or the lack of capacity or trust in the relevant judicial system. All these difficulties contribute to a continuing reign of impunity that simply must change.

---

9 Nowrojee 1996, pp. 57–60; cited by de Brouwer 2005, pp. 1–2.

10 USIP, 'Ending Sexual Violence in Conflict? First, Understanding It' 10 June 2014: www.usip.org/publications/ending-sexual-violence-in-conflict-first-understanding-it (last accessed 16 September 2015).

3. CHALLENGES AT THE INTERNATIONAL LEVEL

Although rape and sexual violence were pervasive during WWII, the Nuremberg Tribunal did not adequately prosecute these crimes.[11] Undoubtedly, this nonchalance had to do with the prevailing attitudes of political leaders at the time. Stalin is infamously known to have remarked off-handedly that '[it is understandable] if a soldier who has crossed thousands of kilometres through blood and fire and death has fun with a wench or takes some trifle.'[12]

It was not until the UN International Criminal Tribunal for the Former Yugoslavia (ICTY) and International Criminal Tribunal for Rwanda (ICTR) that rape was formally considered as a crime against humanity. The ICTR Statute also included rape as a war crime.[13] Whilst the ICTY Statute did not include rape as a war crime, incidents of sexual violence as war crimes were prosecuted as outrages upon personal dignity, as in *Furundzija*.[14] The hybrid tribunal of the Dili district court with Exclusive Jurisdiction over Serious Offences in East Timor, created in 2000, was also vested with the authority to try sexual offences.[15]

As this article will go on to elaborate, the international tribunals, including the Special Court for Sierra Leone (SCSL) and the Extraordinary Chambers in the Courts of Cambodia (ECCC) have made impressive strides in the field of international justice toward the prosecution of sexual and gender-based crimes. However, particular problems remain extant.

3.1. RESOURCE CHALLENGES AND SOCIAL STIGMATISATION

One of these problems has to do with difficulties at the national level, but magnified when transposed to the international plane. To some extent, this is not surprising; it is only when national systems are incapable of successfully investigating and prosecuting that cases of sexual and gender-based violence then come before an international tribunal; and sometimes, not even then. The paradox of international justice is that the conflict areas with the greatest need for justice are often places where victims have the least access to accountability mechanisms.

11 See Green et al. 1994, p. 173, 'Rape and forced prostitution were not recognized as offences by the Nuremberg Tribunal. Rape was recognized as a crime against humanity in Local Council Law No. 10, which governed the subsequent trials of lower-level Nazis held by the Allied military powers; however, none of the accused [were] charged with rape.'

12 Djilas 1990, p. 95; cited also by McDonald 2000, p. 16.

13 See Articles 3(g) and 4(e) of the ICTR Statute; Article 5(g) of the ICTY Statute.

14 See ICTY, *Prosecutor v. Furindzija*, Judgement, Trial Chamber, IT-95-17/1-T, 10 December 1998; See also Bensouda, *The Sexual and Gender-based Crimes Policy Paper of the Office of the Prosecutor.*

15 United Nations Security Council Resolutions 1272 (1999) cited in Bensouda and Jallow 2008, p. 37.

In Darfur, UN aid workers have suggested that there is significant underreporting of sexual violence crimes in the Sudan because they were prevented access to conflict-riddled areas by government officials.[16] In Syria, the UN has similarly been unable to solicit accounts of sexual violence, or verify allegations, due to the 'fear of reprisals, social stigmatisation and a lack of safe and confidential response services for survivors.'[17] These examples demonstrate that many of these traumatic experiences (and their survivors) are being silenced even before judicial systems have had the chance to examine, much less investigate and prosecute these crimes.

In Rwanda, the social stigmatisation experienced by rape victims was compounded by the conflict and its aftermath. ICTR reported that 'it was sometimes said that a rape victim must have collaborated with the enemy, or traded sexual relations to survive the widespread killings. Allegations like [these] not only silence victims but place them at the risk of reprisals.'[18] There is a clear link between societal stigmatisation and the difficulty in collecting crucial witness testimony. How can justice begin to be seen to be done if the voices of victims are not even heard?

Moreover, the problems of weak national judicial mechanisms, ongoing conflicts and social stigmatisation represent only one layer of obstacles. International tribunals may also be hampered by resource constraints. As the ICTR's *Best Practices Manual* for Sexual Violence Crimes has noted, effective investigations and prosecutions of sexual and gender-based violence will require, *inter alia*, diverse staff, comprehensive witness protection and medical programmes, integrated investigative and prosecution teams and counselling units for both victims, witnesses and staff members who may suffer from secondary trauma.[19] These are required from institutions that are already stretched thin from pursuing other grave violations of international law.

3.2. JUDICIAL LIMITS – PROSECUTION AND CODIFICATION OF SEXUAL AND GENDER-BASED CRIMES

Despite the significant advancements by international tribunals, it must be acknowledged that they were operating in a new judicial environment. In some cases, judges had to make sure that the gravity of sexual offences was accurately

16 United Nations Security Council, *Conflict-related Sexual Violence: Report of the Secretary General*, S/2014/181, 13 March 2014, p. 15.

17 *Ibid*, p. 17.

18 ICTR, *Best Practices Manual for the Investigation and Prosecution of Sexual Violence Crimes in Post-Conflict Regions: Lessons Learned from the Office of the Prosecutor for the International Criminal Tribunal for Rwanda* ('*Best Practices*'), 30 January 2014, p. 18.

19 *Ibid*, pp. 11–24.

reflected. The landmark *Akayesu* judgment simultaneously defined rape in international law and convicted the accused of using rape to further genocide.[20] The President of the ICTY, Judge Gabrielle Kirk McDonald, intervened to ensure that the prosecution accurately reflected the accounts of rape in its indictments.[21]

The Rome Statute of the ICC has benefitted from the experience of these tribunals and includes an expansive list of sexual and gender-based crimes as crimes against humanity and war crimes in both international and non-international armed conflicts. These include rape, sexual slavery, enforced prostitution, forced pregnancy, forced marriage, enforced sterilisation, and other forms of sexual violence. It also criminalises persecution on the basis of gender as a crime against humanity. The jurisprudence of international criminal law therefore has developed over time, but there is still room for further advancements.

3.3. SEXUAL VIOLENCE AGAINST BOYS AND MEN IN CONFLICT

One of these novel legal areas includes sexual violence against boys and men. Although the issue of sexual violence against males during conflict has only recently been given due attention by the international community, it is certainly not a novel practice.

In the ICTR case of *Niyitegeka*, the accused was convicted of castrating a Tutsi man.[22] A particularly egregious instance was in the first ICTY case of *Tadic*. In that case the accused was convicted of inhumane treatment for forcing one victim to perform fellatio on another victim, and cannibalise his sexual organs.[23] Sexual violence against men was also observed in *Delic*, *Mucic*, and *Simic*. The Organisation for Security and Cooperation in Europe (OSCE) reported multiple instances of forced nudity amongst males in Kosovo.[24] Sexual crimes would encompass both physical and non-physical violence directed toward a victim's sexual characteristics, with forced nudity a clear example of the latter.[25]

---

20 ICTR, *Prosecuor v. Akayesu*, para. 731.

21 'As soon as I looked at the Indictment, I called the prosecutor assigned to the case and asked him about it [rape accounts] and he said "We do not have any statements. There is no support for it." So I said, "You know me. I am going to go through every single page, every single page of this material, and if I find something, I am going to tell you. I worked through it all and I found numerous statements referring to rape."' McDonald 1999, p. 30.

22 ICTR, *Prosecutor v. Niyitegeka*, Trial Judgement, Trial Chamber, ICTR-96-14-T, 16 May 2003, paras. 303, 312, 462, 467.

23 ICTY, *Prosecutor v. Tadic*, Sentencing Judgment, Trial Chamber, IT-94-1-T, 14 July 1997, para. 21.

24 OSCE, *Kosovo/Kosova: As Seen, As Told* (1999); Chapter 7 cited in Sivakumaran 2007, p. 266.

25 ICC, Office of the Prosecutor, *Policy Paper on Sexual and Gender-Based Violence*, June 2014, para. 17.

Under the Rome Statute, Article 7(3) defines 'gender' as 'referring to the two sexes, male and female, within the context of society. The term 'gender' does not indicate any meaning different from the above.' My Office interprets this definition in accordance with internationally recognised human rights pursuant to Article 21(3). It considers gender-based-crimes as those committed against persons, whether male or female, because of their sex, or because of their socially constructed gender roles.[26]

Of course, women bear the brunt of sexual violence crimes during conflict. But this should not obscure the fact that men can also be victims. Many of the practical and psychological challenges mirror those faced by female victims, such as stigmatisation and lasting damage to physical and mental health. Some of the difficulties reflect the victim's gendered role within their societies – such as underreporting due to the victim's fear that he will lose masculine status within his family and society.[27] All these are thorny issues that the international community must begin to grapple with, whilst taking care not to reinforce pre-existing structures of gender inequality.

4. FOCUSING ON SEXUAL AND GENDER-BASED CRIMES

There is no hierarchy of offences within international criminal law, or within the Rome Statute. However, sexual offences should rank amongst the gravest.[28] Correspondingly, they should also be one of the foremost priorities in the international community for prosecution.[29] In this section, I highlight a number concerns that national and international authorities may consider when combating the menace of sexual and gender-based violence.

4.1. THE HARMS TO THE VICTIM

The very reasons underlying the difficulties in prosecuting sexual and gender-based crimes are also the very same harms that are inflicted upon the victim. Among these are the unique physical harms perpetuated on the victim, such as the damage to sexual organs, sexual mutilation, castration and infertility. In many cases, despite suffering grievous injuries, victims remain reluctant to come forward to seek treatment because of the associated stigma.

---

26 *Ibid*, para. 15.

27 See Sivakumaran 2007, p. 270.

28 *Policy Paper on Sexual and Gender-Based Crimes*, p. 5.

29 See Jallow 2005, p. 153, 'Whilst the offences triable at the ICTR are broadly defined to include non-loss of life, cases involving the killing of children and sexual offences rank in priority for prosecution.'

Equally horrific is the psychological damage. There is, on the one hand, the trauma of the sexual violence itself. But this is also accompanied by the fact that the victim is selected on the basis of his or her gender and/or sex. The knowledge that the perpetrator has targeted the victim on this basis *objectifies* the victim, further removing their autonomy beyond the immediate commission of the crime.

On the other hand, the victim suffers extensive social disapprobation. It is a continuing psychic scar. The wounds are unfairly inflicted by his or her own community, but initiated by the perpetrator. As the ICTY Trial Chamber in *Stakic* observed, '[f]or a woman, rape is by far the ultimate offense, sometimes even worse than death because it brings shame on her.'[30]

4.2. THE HARMS TO SOCIETY

Crimes of sexual and gender-based violence can also rend apart the fabric of family. The ICTR *Best Practices* mentions several cases of rape victims, who had heretofore not revealed their assault to their partners and spouses, testifying in public proceedings. They were subsequently 'ostracized and abandoned' by their partners and spouses.[31] These harms can happen to male victims as well. A male victim in the Central African Republic alleged that after being raped, '[my wife] said to me, 'You are no longer a man. You are a woman like myself, so I cannot live with you. I have to leave you.'[32]

In some cases, perpetrators commit, facilitate, or organise sexual crimes with the very intention of destabilising society. In *Akayesu*, the convicted person declared '[n]ever ask me again what a Tutsi woman tastes like.'[33] In *Nyiramasuhuko*, the convicted person was the Minister for Family and Women's Affairs, but instead used her position of power to perpetuate rape as a crime against humanity.[34] She had 'ordered that the women be raped because they refused to marry Hutus'.[35] Perpetrators of crimes of sexual violence tend to caricature women on the basis of their ethnicity, reinforcing their view that these women are 'other', that is to say, different and unworthy of the same consideration as they are.

During the Bosnian war, one victim recounted that her captors told her that 'they wanted to plant the seeds of Serbs in Bosnia'. Another woman reported that

30 ICTY, *Prosecutor v. Stakic*, Trial Chamber, Judgement, IT-97-24-T, 31 July 2003, para. 803 cited in DeGuzman 2012, p. 23.
31 ICTR, *Best Practices*, para. 66.
32 ICC, *Prosecutor v. Bemba*, Trial Transcript, ICC-01/05-01/08-T-51-Red-ENG CT2 WT, Trial Chamber III, 21 January 2011, pp. 41–42.
33 *Akayesu*, para. 422.
34 ICTR, *Prosecutor v. Nyiramasuhuko*, Judgement and Sentencing, Trial Chamber, ICTR-98-42-T, para. 6022.
35 *Ibid*, para. 2254.

she was raped almost daily by three or four soldiers and was told that she would give birth to a 'chetnik' [Serbian nationalist] boy who would then kill Muslims when he grew up.[36] Since then, this reprehensible intent to 'ethnicise' through rape has been captured in the inclusion of forced pregnancy as a crime against humanity or as a war crime in the Rome Statute.

Sexual and gender-based violence upends societal structures. As my Office's *Policy Paper on Sexual and Gender-Based Crimes* has pointed out, particularly when sexual violence is committed as genocide, it can 'cause significant and irreversible harm to individual victims and to their communities.'[37] As far as possible, pursuant to Article 21(3) of the Rome Statute, my Office applies a gender analysis to every stage of the proceedings. My Office will seek to analyse the intersection of various personal characteristics and socially-constructed attributes, such as gender, age, race, disability, religion, ethnicity, sex, sexual orientation. The matrix in which these status identities interact will be given consideration, with particular attention paid to how sexual violence might be used to diminish gender, ethnic, racial or other identities.[38]

4.3. SEXUAL CRIMES AS A VICIOUS CYCLE

One of the destructive myths of sexual violence in conflict is that sex-based violence ends when the conflict draws to a close. But when rape and sexual violence are pursued on a widespread and systematic basis, or in relation to an armed conflict, societal norms may become shattered.[39] Drastically changed attitudes towards the sanctity of the body mean that sexual violence will remain endemic. The bodies of children, women, and men continue to be battlefields upon which sexual violence is re-enacted long after the conflict has ceased.

Moreover, sexual and gender-based violence can serve as a root cause of conflicts, and the seeming intractability of continuing conflicts. As it has been stated, sexual violence in conflict may well be a 'national security imperative.' This is because sexual and gender-based violence 'traps survivors in conflict, poverty and insecurity' and 'undermines reconciliation.'[40]

---

36 Final Report of the Commission of Experts Established Pursuant to Security Council Resolution 780 (1992), S/1994/674, para.248 cited in Fisher 1996, p. 111.

37 *Policy Paper on Sexual and Gender-Based Crimes*, para. 31.

38 *Ibid*, para. 27.

39 See 'After Wars, Mass Rapes Persist', 20 May 2009, *New York Times*, available at: www.nytimes.com/2009/05/21/opinion/21kristof.html?_r=0 (last visited 16 September 2015).

40 See 'Preventing Sexual Violence Is a National Security Imperative' 25 February 2014, *Huffington Post*, available at: www.huffingtonpost.com/johnkerry/preventing-sexual-violenc_b_4856070.html (last visited 16 September 2015).

4.4. SEXUAL CRIMES AS UNDER-PROSECUTED CRIMES

For the reasons elucidated above, sexual and gender-based violence have traditionally been under-prosecuted. This is despite the fact that these crimes wreak devastating effects on individuals, their families and their societies. In order to successfully combat these crimes, it may require a substantial outlay of legal and political resources. Countries and international institutions will need to buttress investigative and policing resources, enact new legislation and develop the required jurisprudence – all these make combating sexual violence in conflict uncertain territory. It may also seem an unwise use of limited resources, particularly for post-conflict countries or international institutions that already are stretched to capacity.

But the converse could well be true. Because sexual crimes are often overlooked, each successful investigation and prosecution sends a powerful message that sexual and gender-based violence will not be condoned. The initial investment in enforcement and judicial resources has a more than proportionate return in terms of impact. In this regard, the law serves as a powerful practical tool (through arrests and convictions) and normative tool (through judgments and precedents) to shape behaviours.[41]

5. CHALLENGING THE NARRATIVE INTERNATIONALLY

Over the past few decades, the international community has taken many concrete and progressive steps in response to the increasing calls to recognise sexual and gender-based crimes as serious crimes nationally and internationally. In the following, I illustrate the steps taken at the international level, particularly by my Office to reshape the dialogue surrounding sexual violence and to end the culture of impunity for its perpetrators.

5.1. THE DEVELOPING JURISPRUDENCE OF THE INTERNATIONAL CRIMINAL COURT

As analysed earlier, the statutes and case law of the UN ad hoc tribunals began by including rape as a crime against humanity, and convicting rape as a form of genocide. The Rome Statute establishing the ICC has consolidated these jurisprudential developments. My Office acts within its mandate and statutory duties in Article 54(1)(a) to 'establish the truth' within an investigation.

---

41 See generally, deGuzman 2012, pp. 11–44.

Accordingly, when supported by the necessary evidence, my Office will charge acts of sexual and gender-based crimes as different categories of crimes in the Court's subject-matter jurisdiction, such as genocide, war crimes, or crimes against humanity, so as to properly and fully reflect, *inter alia*, the nature and manner of commission of the crime.[42]

In *Ntaganda*, the Pre-Trial Chamber confirmed the charges brought by my Office against the accused with regard to rape as a crime against humanity under Article 7(1)(g), and rape as a war crime under Article 8(2)(e)(vi). It also confirmed charges against the accused in relation to sexual slavery as a crime against humanity under Article 7(1)(g), and sexual slavery as a war crime under Article 8(2)(e)(vi)[43] for actions committed by the troops under his command in Ituri Province in the DR Congo.

In *Gbagbo*, the Pre-Trial Chamber found substantial grounds to believe that the pro-Gbagbo forces raped at least 38 persons during the conflict in Côte d'Ivoire and accordingly confirmed the charge of rape as a crime against humanity.[44] In *Al-Bashir*, the Appeals Chamber granted the Prosecution's request to issue an arrest warrant against the accused, finding that there are reasonable grounds to believe that acts of rape had been committed in furtherance of genocide under Article 6(b) of the Rome Statute.[45]

The jurisprudence of the ICC on sexual and gender-based crimes is slowly but surely being built up. I believe that the law serves as a powerful symbolic tool. By seeking to accurately describe the crimes that have occurred, not only does the law highlight the brutal and barbaric nature of these crimes, but it also gives a voice to the far too often voiceless victims, and to hold perpetrators accountable. I am confident that in time, through its deterrent and disciplining effect, the law will help to change behaviours and will establish new norms of acceptable conduct.

5.2. THE OTP'S POLICY ON SEXUAL AND GENDER-BASED CRIMES

The ad hoc tribunals have done notable work in ensuring their experiences remain alive and current. The *Best Practices* Manual of the ICTR is one example, as is the ICTY's recently launched *Prosecuting Sexual Violence* Legacy Project.

---

42 *Policy Paper on Sexual and Gender-Based Crimes*, para. 73.

43 ICC, *Prosecutor v. Ntaganda*, Decision Pursuant to Article 61(7)(a) and (b) of the Rome Statute on the Charges of the Prosecutor Against Bosco Ntaganda, ICC-01/04–02/06, 9 June 2014, para. 36.

44 ICC, *Prosecutor v. Gbagbo*, Decision on the confirmation of charges against Laurent Gbagbo, ICC-02/11–01/11, 12 June 2014, para. 197.

45 ICC, *Prosecutor v. Al-Bashir*, Second Decision on the Prosecutor's Application for a Warrant of Arrest, ICC-02/05–01/09, 12 July 2010, para. 30.

Through these and various colloquiums for international prosecutors, the ICC has sought to learn from their insights. The *Policy Paper on Sexual and Gender-Based Crimes* by my Office is the first such comprehensive policy to be adopted by an International Court or Tribunal.[46]

In recognising that the OTP has a statutory duty in relation to the investigation and prosecution of sexual and gender-based crimes, and the numerous obstacles and challenges I have earlier elaborated upon, I have elevated the issue to one of my Office's key strategic goals.[47]

The threads running through the OTP's policy are in its application of a 'gender perspective' – the understanding of status and power differences between males and females, and the impact of gender on opportunities and interactions – and an application of a 'gender analysis' – the understanding of how status differences and inequalities between the genders and sexes give rise to assumptions and stereotypes, and considering how crimes are related to gender and sexual norms and inequalities at every stage of our work. The policy enables us to approach the investigation and prosecution of such crimes in a systematic and methodological manner.

Among other things, the application of a gender analysis and a gender perspective will guide the general policy in three concrete ways. Firstly, my Office will move toward a victim-responsive approach within the ambit of Article 54(1)(b) that requires the Prosecutor to effectively investigate and prosecute crimes while respecting the interests and personal circumstances of the victims and witnesses. It will attempt to engage and consult victim groups and representatives to the extent possible, with the consideration that the OTP must manage expectations, since not all victims have the same interests or concerns.[48]

Secondly, under Regulation 34 of the Regulations of the Office of the Prosecutor, the Prosecutor will generally investigate and prosecute those most responsible for the most serious crimes, where supported by the evidence. This may mean that the OTP will prosecute officers or individuals that are mid or even low-ranking as long as they have participated in, or are responsible for, particularly serious or notorious crimes.[49] Regulation 34(2) further emphasises that sexual and gender violence may represent particularly grievous forms of victimisation.

Thirdly, my Office is committed toward investing in our staff, so that they have the requisite skills and sensitivity in relation to sexual and gender-based crimes. This might mean amongst other things, a thorough knowledge of the statutory provisions relating to sexual and gender-based crimes, well-developed skills in

---

46 See generally, ICC, Office of the Prosecutor, *Policy Paper on Sexual and Gender-Based Crimes*, June 2014.

47 *Ibid*, para. 5.

48 *Ibid*, para. 22.

49 *Ibid*, para. 23.

observing victims who are suffering from possible post-event traumas, taking active steps to prevent re-traumatisation, and addressing any secondary trauma.[50]

All of this takes place within the sphere of close coordination between the OTP's own Gender and Children Unit (GCU) and the Prosecutor's Special Gender Advisor. It also involves liaising with the Registry's Victims and Witnesses Unit (VWU) and Victims Participation and Reparations Section (VPRS).[51]

5.3. PRELIMINARY EXAMINATIONS

On the basis of available information, the OTP will conduct (in situations not manifestly outside of the Court's jurisdiction) a preliminary examination of crimes. It will pay attention to the context in which sexual and gender-based crimes are alleged to have been committed, and to the existence of genuine and relevant national proceedings.[52] In this regard, my Office makes its assessment of complementarity – whether or not national proceedings are vitiated by an unwillingness or inability using indicators contained in the *Policy Paper on Preliminary Examination*.[53]

The overall admissibility assessment will evaluate, *inter alia*, the presence of discriminatory attitudes and gender stereotypes in substantive law, official attitudes of trivialisation and minimisation or denial of crimes of a sexual and gender-based nature and manifestly insufficient steps in the investigation and prosecution of said crimes. It will also include a gravity assessment, such as the nature, scale, manner of commission, and impact of these crimes.[54] The OTP considers that, implicit in the gravity assessment on the factor of the 'nature of the crime', a sexual and gender-based crime is one of the gravest offences under the Rome Statute.[55]

5.4. INVESTIGATIONS

The Prosecutor has a duty under Article 54 of the Rome Statute to fairly and impartially establish the truth by investigating both incriminating and exonerating circumstances. Cognisant of this duty, it must be noted that investigating sexual and gender-based crimes present additional hurdles that have been highlighted earlier, such as the under-reporting, or even non-reporting of crimes due to stigmatisation, the lack of cooperation or investigations by

50 *Ibid*, paras. 21 and 37.
51 *Ibid*, paras. 70, 111 and 112.
52 *Ibid*, paras. 38, 40 and 41.
53 ICC, Office of the Prosecutor, *Policy Paper on Preliminary Examination*, 2013, paras. 48–56.
54 *Policy Paper on Sexual and Gender-Based Crimes*, paras. 41, 44 and 45.
55 *Ibid*.

domestic actors, the lack of forensic or documentary evidence and the lack of health services.[56]

To ameliorate these difficulties, the OTP adopts a holistic approach in investigations. On the one hand, at the preparation stage of investigations, my Office will use an integrated approach, carefully considering the report produced during the preliminary examination to develop its case hypotheses. During the investigation stage proper, my Office will seek to maximise efficiency using investigative strategies that take advantage of the fact that victims and witnesses of sexual and gender-based crimes may also have witnessed other crimes.[57]

On the other hand, the OTP is guided by Article 68(1), such that it must take 'appropriate measures to protect the safety, physical and psychological well-being, dignity and privacy of victims and witnesses.' This is especially so when 'the crime involves sexual or gender violence or violence against children.' From interviews to sourcing intermediaries, the OTP will ensure that staff members possess the appropriate cultural sensitivities and due regard to the effects of potential traumatisation arising from sexual and gender-based violence.[58] Potential victim-witnesses in respect to these crimes will mandatorily undergo preliminary psychosocial screenings, conducted by a psychosocial expert. The expert may be present at interviews, and may provide support to the witness if requested.[59]

Contextually, staff members will require familiarity with euphemisms and other non-verbal communications used by witnesses to refer to sexual violence.[60] Euphemisms may stem from a different cultural context, but also from the difficulties faced by victims in reliving their traumas. Prior to contact with witnesses, interview teams receive briefings and glossaries to familiarise themselves with appropriate terms to describe these acts.[61]

5.5. PROSECUTIONS

In addition to jurisdictional, admissibility and policy considerations, my Office also faces resource constraints. We will therefore be able to prosecute only a limited number of perpetrators responsible for crimes of a sexual and gendered nature. However, an integrated approach to trials and an application of a gender analysis and perspective will assist my Office in a number of dimensions:

Firstly, in line with my Office's Strategic Plan (2012–2015), we have adopted an approach for more in-depth, open-ended investigations while maintaining

56 *Ibid*, paras. 48, 49 and 50.
57 *Ibid*, paras. 54 and 66.
58 *Ibid*, paras. 56, 57 and 58.
59 *Ibid*, para. 61.
60 *Ibid*, para. 58.
61 *Policy Paper on Sexual and Gender-Based Crimes*, para. 58.

focus so that more evidence from diversified sources will be collected.[62] By building upon this new approach used by investigative teams, my Office will now aim to have cases as trial-ready as possible. If possible, as early as the confirmation of hearings stage. This has the benefit of proceeding with our cases on a more solid footing early in the proceedings, enhancing the prospects of successful prosecutions. It also has the additional benefit of time and cost-savings. I hope that this will help in ensuring that our prosecutions are effective *and* efficient *vis-à-vis* sexual and gender-based crimes.

Secondly, not only will the OTP seek to charge sexual and gender-based crimes within the different categories, it will also seek to explore the full potential of charging under the full range of the modes of liability and mental elements. In *Bemba*, the Pre-Trial Chamber confirmed the charges brought by the OTP against the accused with regard to acts of rape committed by the *Mouvement de libération du Congo* (MLC) as both a crime against humanity and a war crime in the Central African Republic.[63] Simultaneously, the Pre-Trial Chamber declined to establish the accused's responsibility as a co-perpetrator under Article 25(3), but found that there were substantial grounds to believe that the accused was responsible as a commander with effective authority and control over MLC troops under Article 28.[64]

The prior case law and experience at international tribunals and this Court has shown there is often no explicit evidence of orders to commit sexual or gender-based crimes. However, under Article 30(2)(b), the mental element may be established through evidence of patterns of prior or subsequent conduct, or specific notice, in order to prove an awareness on the part of the accused that sexual and gender-based crimes would occur in the ordinary course of events. My Office will also fully explore the potential of this provision.[65]

To date, 18 individuals have been charged with gender-related crimes in 13 cases; specific sexual violence charges were made in 68 percent of the ICC's cases and with respect to 58 percent of its suspects. We are seeking to add charges of sexual and gender-based crimes in other cases on the strength of our evidence.

Thirdly, my Office has established its own Protection Strategies Unit (PSU) and Operations Support Unit (OSU) to offer protection and support to witnesses, families and other persons at risk by virtue of their interaction with the Office.[66] In relation to sexual and gender-based crimes, my Office will take into account victims' and witnesses' needs at every stage of the proceedings.

---

62 ICC, Office of the Prosecutor, *Strategic Plan 2012–2015*, 2013, 11 October 2013, p. 6.

63 ICC, *Prosecutor v. Bemba*, Decision Pursuant to Article 61(7)(a) and (b) of the Rome Statute on the Charges of the Prosecutor Against Jean-Pierre Bemba Gombo, ICC-01/05-01/08, 15 June 2009, paras. 188 and 288.

64 *Ibid*, paras. 403 and 444.

65 *Policy Paper on Sexual and Gender-Based Crimes*, para. 81.

66 *Ibid*, para. 85.

For instance, during the disclosure of evidence, it will inform witnesses of disclosure obligations with due regard to particularly vulnerable witnesses. It may opt for the use of witness statement summaries prior to trial as per Articles 61(5) and 68(5). Whilst in Court, the Chambers may also decide, according to Article 68(2) of the Statute, to conduct *in camera* proceedings. As a matter of policy, the Prosecutor will also request the Chamber to redact important identifying information for victims or witnesses of sexual and gender-based crimes, pursuant to Rule 87 of the Rules of Procedure and Evidence.[67]

Significantly, my Office will also utilise the protections of Rule 70 of the Rules of Procedure and Evidence that the victim's consent cannot be inferred where he or she was taken advantage of in a coercive environment; and Rule 70(d) that the credibility, character or predisposition to sexual availability of a victim or witness cannot be inferred by reason of the sexual nature of the prior or subsequent conduct of the victim or witness.[68]

Finally, at the sentencing stage, the OTP takes note of Rule 145(2)(b) where the discriminatory motives of the perpetrators, particularly toward vulnerable victims, and on grounds on gender, constitute aggravating circumstances. It will, where appropriate, propose sentences that fully reflect the devastation of the convicted person's crimes on victims, their families, and their communities, and that fully account for the gravity of the crime.[69]

5.6. REPARATIONS

Although the Statute does not confer an explicit role to the Prosecutor for reparations, the Chamber may invite observations from the OTP.[70] The Prosecution has taken due notice of this provision. In *Katanga*, although the convicted person was not ultimately convicted of rape and sexual slavery as crimes against humanity or a war crime, he was convicted of intentionally directing attacks toward civilians under Article 8(2)(e)(i). Accordingly the Prosecution has submitted to the Chamber that victims of 'acts of rape committed during the attack' are entitled to reparations.[71] It has also observed that any 'award of reparations should avoid reinforcing previous structural inequalities between victims, or between victims and the communities in which they live, and avoid perpetuating previous discriminatory practices.'[72]

---

67 *Ibid*, paras. 87–90.
68 *Ibid*, paras. 94–95.
69 *Ibid*, paras. 99 and 100.
70 Article 75 of the Rome Statute.
71 ICC, *Prosecutor v. Katanga*, Prosecution's Observations on the Procedure for Reparations, ICC-01/04-01/07-3544, 30 April 2015, para. 13.
72 *Ibid*, para. 27.

6. CHALLENGING THE NARRATIVE NATIONALLY

6.1. SUPPORT BY STATES AND INSTITUTIONS AT THE INTERNATIONAL LEVEL

While the ICC is a key pillar of the emerging international criminal justice system, ending impunity for sexual and gender-based crimes requires collective action and resolve. We should begin giving thought to establishing an organised network that enables civil society, UN agencies, international courts and other stakeholders to draw upon each other's expertise. A most important development has been the creation of the UN Office of the Special Representative of the Secretary-General on Sexual Violence in Conflict (SRSG-SVC); a landmark in our quest to end sexual and gender-based atrocity crimes. States should consult with the Office of the SRSG-SVC, drawing upon its broad expertise.

In particular, states parties should also adhere to their obligations under the Rome Statute to effectively investigate and prosecute crimes within the Statute's subject-matter jurisdiction. Non-states parties have a similar obligation. A key contribution can be made by states parties to advance universal ratification and accession to the Rome Statute. The OTP welcomes states parties who assist in cooperation with the Court, adopt domestic legislation prohibiting the sexual and gender-based crimes listed within the Statute and enhancing the execution of ICC arrest warrants against perpetrators of these, and other, crimes.

Specifically, the OTP welcomes the United Kingdom's push for strong international action and condemnation of sexual and gender-based crimes. These include valuable correction of misperceptions regarding the inevitable scourge of rape as a result of armed conflict; its advocacy through the Global Summit to End Sexual Violence in Conflict;[73] and its role in spearheading, in tandem with other international actors, the International Protocol on the Documentation and Investigation of Sexual Violence in Conflict.[74]

6.2. COORDINATION AND COOPERATION AT THE NATIONAL LEVEL

I hope that the *Policy Paper on Sexual and Gender-Based Crimes* will serve as a valuable 'template' for states and other relevant actors as they work towards combatting sexual and gender-based crimes more effectively. Our policy may

---

73 Government of UK, 'Global Summit to End Sexual Violence in Conflict', June 2014, available at: https://www.gov.uk/government/topical-events/sexual-violence-in-conflict (last visited 16 September 2015).

74 Government of UK, 'International Protocol on the Documentation and Investigation of Sexual Violence in Conflict', June 2014.

assist national jurisdictions by being a useful reference document in their efforts to formulate, adopt, or amend domestic legislation and refine their practices.

But no organisation, or state, can go it alone in this fight against impunity for perpetrators of sexual violence. It is therefore imperative to continue to work to support and enhance domestic capacities, for instance through training activities and secondments of judicial and law enforcement officials to countries where judicial systems have a proven track record of success and effectiveness in dealing with these crimes.

The cornerstone of any collaboration between the OTP and national authorities is our positive approach to complementarity. In Guinea, for example, our cooperation with the national authorities has thus far proved fruitful. The OTP has continuously supported the efforts of the authorities which have the primary responsibility to deliver justice and accountability to the victims of the 28 September 2009 massacre, including the numerous victims of sexual and gender-based crimes.[75]

My Office stands ready to assist national jurisdictions seeking to investigate and prosecute those most responsible for atrocity crimes of a sexual and gender-based nature. We will seek to combine our efforts with national authorities in conducting proceedings against perpetrators. At the same time, we stand ready to consult with states parties and non-governmental organisations (NGOs) in best practices and innovative approaches to deterring the commission of sexual violence crimes.

7. CONCLUSION

We have come a long way, but we cannot underestimate the challenges present. The ICC alone cannot end impunity for sexual and gender-based crimes. It is my firm and unyielding belief that our collective efforts and dedication is the only way to achieve the goal of breaking the cycle of impunity and ending the scourge of sexual and gender-based crimes. These crimes are an affront to our most basic notions of decency. They degrade humanity's good name.

I close this article by paraphrasing a judgment by the learned Judge Odio Benito, invisibility of sexual violence leads to further discrimination against the victims who suffer from crimes of sexual and gender-based violence.[76]

Their voices – the voices of victims – are only just beginning to be heard. We must strengthen their voices and declare that the horrors they have experienced will not be tolerated and that we will relentlessly pursue those who deign to

[75] See ICC, 'Statement to the press by Mrs Fatou Bensouda, Prosecutor of the International Criminal Court', Conakry, Guinea, 4 July 2015.

[76] ICC, *Prosecutor v. Lubanga*, Separate and Dissenting Opinion of Judge Odio Benito, Trial Chamber, ICC-01/04–01/06–2842, 14 March 2012, para. 16.

commit such egregious crimes. We have only just begun to turn the page on the traditional narrative of sexual violence and gender-based crimes in times of conflict. While we should celebrate the gains made, 'we have miles to go still before we sleep.'

BIBLIOGRAPHY

BOOKS AND JOURNAL ARTICLES

Bensouda and Jallow 2008
Bensouda, F. and Jallow, H.B., 'International Criminal Law in an African Context', Institute for Security Studies, 2008.

De Brouwer 2005
De Brouwer, A.M., 'Supranational Criminal Prosecution of Sexual Violence: The ICC and the Practice of the ICTY and the ICTR', Intersentia, 2005.

De Vitoria 2015
De Vitoria, F., 'On the Law of War, Just and Unjust Wars: A Moral Argument with Historical Illustrations', Basic Books, 2015.

DeGuzman 2012
DeGuzman, M.M., 'An Expressive Rationale for the Thematic Prosecution of Sex Crimes', FICHL Publication Series 13, 2012, pp. 11–44.

Djilas 1990
Djilas, M., 'Conversations with Stalin', Harcourt Brace & Company, 1990.

Fisher 1996
Fisher, S.K., 'Occupation of the Womb: Forced Impregnation as Genocide', Duke Law Journal, 1996.

Green et al. 1994
Green, J. et al., 'Affecting the Rules of the Prosecution of Rape and Other Gender-Based Violence Before the International Criminal Tribunal for the Former Yugoslavia: A Feminist Critique and Proposal', 5(2) Hastings Women's Law Journal, 1994.

Jallow 2005
Jallow, H.B., 'Prosecutorial Discretion and International Criminal Justice', 3 Journal of International Criminal Justice, 2005.

McDonald 2000
McDonald, G.K., 'Crimes of Sexual Violence: The Experience of the International Criminal Tribunal', 39(1) Columbia Journal of Transnational Law, 2000.

Nowrojee 1996
Nowrojee, B., 'Shattered Lives: Sexual Violence during the Rwandan Genocide and its Aftermath', Human Rights Watch Africa, 1996.

Sharratt and Kaschak 1999
Sharratt, S. and Kaschak, E. (Eds.), 'Assault on the Soul: Women in Former Yugoslavia', Routledge, 1999.

Sivakumaran 2007
Sivakumaran, S., 'Sexual Violence Against Men in Armed Conflict', 18(2) European Journal of International Law, 2007.

JURISPRUDENCE

ECCC 2012
ECCC, No. 0001/18-07-2007-ECCC/SC, 3 February 2012.
ICC 2015
ICC, Prosecutor v. Katanga, ICC-01/04-01/07-3544, 30 April 2015.
ICC 2014
ICC, Prosecutor v. Gbagbo, ICC-02/11-01/11, 12 June 2014.
ICC 2014
ICC, Prosecutor v. Ntaganda, ICC-01/04-02/06, 9 June 2014.
ICC 2012
ICC, Prosecutor v. Lubanga, ICC-01/04-01/06-2842, 14 March 2012.
ICC 2011
ICC, Prosecutor v. Bemba, ICC-01/05-01/08-T-51-Red-ENG CT2 WT, 21 January 2011.
ICC 2010
ICC, Prosecutor v. Al-Bashir, ICC-02/05-01/09, 12 July 2010.
ICC 2009
ICC, Prosecutor v. Bemba, ICC-01/05-01/08, 15 June 2009.
ICTR 2011
ICTR, Prosecutor v. Nyiramasuhuko, ICTR-98-42-T, 24 June 2011.
ICTR 2003
ICTR, Prosecutor v. Niyitegeka, ICTR-96-14-T, 16 May 2003.
ICTR 1998
ICTR, Prosecutor v. Akayesu, ICTR-96-4-T, 2 September 1998.
ICTY 2003
ICTY, Prosecutor v. Stakic, IT-97-24-T, 31 July 2003.
ICTY 2001
ICTY, Prosecutor v. Kunerac et al., IT-96-23, 22 February 2001.
ICTY 1998
ICTY, Prosecutor v. Furindzija, IT-95-17/1-T, 10 December 1998.
ICTY 1997
ICTY, Prosecutor v. Tadic, IT-94-1-T, 14 July 1997.

TREATIES, LEGISLATION AND AGREEMENTS

Rome Statute of the International Criminal Court, 2187 UNTS 90/37, 17 July 1998.
Statute of the International Criminal Tribunal for Rwanda, SC Res. 955, UN Doc. S/RES/955, 8 November 1994.

Statute of the International Criminal Tribunal for the Former Yugoslavia, SC Res. 827, UN Doc. S/RES/827, 25 May 1993.
UN Security Council, Resolution 1272 (1999), UN Doc. S/RES/1272, 25 October 1999.

OTHERS

Final Report of the Commission of Experts Established Pursuant to Security Council Resolution 780 (1992), UN Doc. S/1994/674, 27 May 1994.
Government UK, 'Global Summit to End Sexual Violence in Conflict', June 2014.
Government UK, 'International Protocol on the Documentation and Investigation of Sexual Violence in Conflict', June 2014.
Huffington Post, 'Preventing Sexual Violence Is a National Security Imperative', 25 February 2014.
Human Rights Watch, 'Democratic Republic of Congo: Ending Impunity for Sexual Violence', 10 June 2014.
Human Rights Watch, 'Iraq: ISIS Escapees Describe Systematic Rape', 14 April 2015.
Human Rights Watch, 'Those Terrible Weeks in their Camp': Boko Haram Violence against Women and Girls in Northeast Nigeria', 27 October 2014.
ICC, Office of the Prosecutor, 'Policy Paper on Preliminary Examination', ICC-OTP 2013, November 2013.
ICC, Office of the Prosecutor, 'Policy Paper on Sexual and Gender-Based Crimes', June 2014.
ICC, Office of the Prosecutor, 'Strategic Plan 2012–2015', ICC-OTP 2013, 11 October 2013.
ICC, Statement to the press by Mrs Fatou Bensouda, Prosecutor of the International Criminal Court, Conakry, Guinea, 4 July 2015.
ICTR, 'Best Practices Manual for the Investigation and Prosecution of Sexual Violence Crimes in Post-Conflict Regions: Lessons Learned from the Office of the Prosecutor for the International Criminal Tribunal for Rwanda ('Best Practices')', 30 January 2014.
New York Times, 'After Wars, Mass Rapes Persist', 20 May 2009.
OSCE, 'Kosovo/Kosova: As Seen, As Told, An analysis of the human rights findings of the OSCE Kosovo Verification Mission', 1999.
UN Security Council, 'Conflict-related sexual violence: Report of the Secretary General', UN Doc. S/2014/181, 13 March 2014.
United States Institute of Peace, 'Ending Sexual Violence in Conflict? First, Understanding It', 10 June 2014.
World Justice Project, 'Rule of Law Index: Rule of Law Around the World', 2015.

IMPUNITY THROUGH IMMUNITY

The Kenya Situation and the International Criminal Court

Leila Nadya SADAT* and Benjamin COHEN

1. INTRODUCTION

The International Criminal Court has faced a number of challenges to its legitimacy and effectiveness. One recent struggle stems from the *Kenyatta* case, which was confirmed in 2012, and became increasingly fractious and politically charged when Uhuru Muigai Kenyatta was elected President of Kenya in 2013. The ICC faces similar difficulties with the trial of William Samoei Ruto, Kenyatta's running mate, who is currently serving as Kenya's Deputy President. With the possible exception of the situation in Darfur, no other situation has posed as grave a challenge to the Court, and particularly the Prosecutor, than the investigation and prosecution undertaken by it in the wake of the brutal post-election violence which shook Kenya in 2007. The Kenya Situation is the only one referred to the Court by the Prosecutor acting truly *proprio motu*, and has been objected to by the territorial state from the start, which has refused to cooperate with the Court in some respects. Perhaps most problematic, however, is that the accused in the Kenyatta and Ruto cases have argued that they are not required to appear before the Court because of their high-ranking office. Their insistence on special privileges and prerogatives flowing from their high office is reminiscent of arguments made by the Kaiser following World War I, and the accused before the Nuremberg Tribunal following World War II.

The accused have challenged a foundational premise of the Rome Statute – that it applies 'equally to all persons without any distinction based on official capacity'[1] – a principle codified by the International Law Commission as one of

* This essay represents the personal views of the author and does not represent the official views of any organ of the International Criminal Court.

1 Rome Statute of the International Criminal Court, Article 27(1), 17 July 1998, 2187 UNTS 90/37 (hereinafter Rome Statute).

the seven 'Nuremberg Principles' in 1950,[2] and found in countless international instruments, including the Genocide Convention, amongst others.[3] Were Kenyatta and Ruto the only accused to raise this argument, it might be seen simply as aggressive defence tactics.

However, there has been a renewed push from African states and the African Union to prevent the trials of sitting Heads of State, a push that has caused the ICC Assembly of States Parties to adopt a special exception for Heads of State on trial (Rule 134*quarter*), and has led to blistering attacks upon the Court from partisans of Kenyatta's position.[4]

This article discusses the *Kenyatta* case and the issue of Head of State immunity under international criminal law. Additionally, it analyses the new rules adopted by the Assembly of States Parties to excuse presence from trial and their application in *Ruto*. We conclude that the Trial Chamber's application of Rule 134*quarter* is incompatible with Articles 63(1) and 27(1) of the Rome Statute. For the ICC to work effectively, Heads of State and other high ranking government officials cannot be cloaked with immunities or special privileges that exempt them from appearance at trial.

2. THE KENYA SITUATION'S REFERRAL TO THE INTERNATIONAL CRIMINAL COURT AND LITIGATION IN THE *KENYATTA* AND *RUTO* CASES REGARDING THE OBLIGATION OF THE ACCUSED TO APPEAR BEFORE THE COURT

To understand the *Kenyatta* case and its implications for the ICC and international justice more generally, some background is required. Following the results of the 2007 Kenyan presidential election, violence erupted on both sides of the political contest.[5] In the election, two coalitions vied for the government,

2 The seven Nuremberg principles can be found in a 1946 Resolution by the United Nations General Assembly, 1 UN GAOR (Part II) at 188, UN Doc. A/61/Add.1 (1946). See also Report of the International Law Commission to the General Assembly, 4 UN GAOR Supp. No. 10, at 1, UN Doc. A/925 (1949).

3 Convention on the Prevention and Punishment of the Crime of Genocide, opened for signature 9 December 1948, 78 UNTS 278.

4 Kenneth Roth, *Africa Attacks the International Criminal Court*, Human Rights Watch, 14 January 2014, available at: www.hrw.org/news/2014/01/14/africa-attacks-international-criminal-court; 'African Leaders Accuse ICC of 'Race Hunt', *Al Jazeera*, 28 May 2013, available at: www.aljazeera.com/news/africa/2013/05/201352722331270466.html. President Yoweri Museveni of Uganda, President Alassane Ourttara of the Ivory Coast, and Prime Minister Hailemariam Desalegn of Ethiopia and then AU Chairman vocalised support for Kenyatta's campaign against the ICC.

5 *Prosecutor v. Francis Kirimi Muthaura, Uhuru Muigai Kenyatta and Mohammed Hussein Ali*, Decision on the Confirmation of Charges Pursuant to Article 61(7)(a) and (b) of the Rome

the Orange Democratic Movement led by Raila Odinga and the Party of National Unity led by Mwai Kibaki. The Orange Democratic Movement was largely 'backed by Luo, Luhya and Kalenjin ... in the Nyanza and Western Provinces and Rift Valley.'[6] The Party of National Unity 'was supported by Kikuyu, based in the Central and Eastern Provinces, and strongly represented in Nairobi, the Coast Province, and Rift Valley.'[7]

The turnout for the 2007 election was the highest on record; approximately 70% of voters participated. Opinion polls published prior to the election showed that Odinga had a narrow lead; however, Kenya's Electoral Commission chairman declared Kibaki the winner.[8] While Kibaki was hastily sworn in, Odinga rejected the results. The announcement triggered widespread and systematic violence resulting in over 1,000 deaths and more than 500,000 displaced civilians. Clashes were characterised by ethnically-targeted killings based on party affiliation, and violence was particularly endemic in the Kikuyu-dominated region of the Rift Valley.[9] The violence was brutal and terrifying in its ferocity.[10]

The violence was investigated by the Commission of Inquiry into Post Election Violence, which published its final report, known as the Waki Commission Report, in February 2008.[11] The Waki Commission handed the report to the President and the Prime Minister in October 2008, but did not publicly disclose the names of alleged perpetrators. Separately, the Waki Commission compiled a list of alleged perpetrators, which was ultimately to be turned over to former ICC Chief Prosecutor Luis Moreno-Ocampo with instructions to address the matter only if the Kenyan Government failed to set up a tribunal within one year. After the Kenyan Parliament refused twice to establish a tribunal,[12] Prosecutor Ocampo used his *proprio motu* power under Article 15 of the ICC Statute and requested permission to open an investigation into the Republic of Kenya based on the names provided by Kofi Annan.[13] Despite Kenya's repeated claims that it was opening investigations, in February 2014, Keriako Tobiko, Kenya's Director of Public Prosecutions said of the more

Statute, ICC-01/09–02/11, para. 117 (23 January 2012) (hereinafter 'Kenyatta Confirmation Decision').

6 *The Crisis in Kenya*, International Coalition for the Responsibility to Protect, available at: www.responsibilitytoprotect.org/index.php/crises/crisis-in-kenya#1.

7 *Ibid.* Kenya has over 70 distinct ethnic groups with the 'five largest being Kikuyu (20%), Luhya (14%), Luo (13%), Kalenjin (11%), and Kamba (11%).'

8 *Ibid.*

9 *Ibid.*

10 See Commission of Inquiry on Post-Election Violence, *Report of the Commission of Inquiry on Post-Election Violence*, p. 102, 15 October 2008, available at: www.kenyalaw.org/Downloads/Reports/Commission_of_Inquiry_into_Post_Election_Violence.pdf.

11 *Ibid.*

12 Mueller 2014.

13 Situation in the Republic of Kenya, Decision Pursuant to Article 15 of the Rome Statute on the Authorization of an Investigation, ICC. 10/09, para. 70 (31 March 2010) (hereinafter 'Kenya Investigation').

than 4,576 cases Kenya opened after the post-election violence not a single one was deemed prosecutable.[14]

In 2010, Prosecutor Ocampo sought summons for six individuals in the Kenya case: Deputy Prime Minister Uhuru Kenyatta, Industrialisation Minister Henry Kosgey, Education Minister William Ruto, Cabinet Secretary Francis Muthaura, radio executive Joshua Arap Sang and former police commissioner Mohammed Hussein Ali.[15]

Known colloquially as the 'Ocampo Six',[16] they were charged with crimes against humanity based on the information provided by numerous human rights investigations. Three of the accused were members of the PNU party; three were ODM members.[17]

Pre-Trial Chamber II confirmed charges against Ruto, Kosgey, Kenyatta and Muthaura. Following the confirmation of the charges, Kenyatta launched a campaign both externally and through his defence counsel to prevent the Court from treating him like any other defendant.[18] He attempted to move his trial to Kenya for 'reasons of judicial economy and to ensure that the judicial process takes place within the territory affected.'[19] This request was rejected. He also requested excusal from continuous presence at trial in order to attend to affairs of State in Kenya, following the defence strategy in *Ruto*, described below.

Ruto also mounted a vigorous defence, and on 17 April 2013 applied for excusal from continuous presence at trial in order to 'enable him to perform his duties as the Deputy President of Kenya.'[20] Two months later, Trial Chamber V(A) largely granted his request. In dispute was whether or not Article 63(1) of the Rome Statute, which states 'the accused shall be present during the trial', prohibited the Court from exercising discretion to allow Ruto to be excused

14 McConnell, 'How Kenya Took on the International Criminal Court', *Global Post*, 25 March 2014, available at: www.globalpost.com/dispatch/news/regions/africa/kenya/140325/how-kenya-beat-the-international-criminal-court.

15 Situation in the Republic of Kenya, Prosecutor's Application Pursuant to Article 58 as to William Samoei Ruto, Henry Kiprono Kosgey and Joshua Arap Sang, ICC-01/09, 15 December 2010 (hereinafter 'Ruto et al Summons'); Situation in the Republic of Kenya, Prosecutor's Application Pursuant to Article 58 as to Francis Kirimi Muthaura, Uhuru Muigai Kenyatta and Mohammed Hussein Ali, ICC-01/09, 15 December 2010 (hereinafter 'Kenyatta et al Summons').

16 ICC Judges Summon 'Ocampo Six', 8 March 2011, *Al Jazeera*, available at: www.aljazeera.com/news/europe/2011/03/201138194041369272.html.

17 Ruto et al Summons, para. 5.

18 On 5 April 2011, the Pre-Trial chamber ordered the Registrar to transmit a request for cooperation to the Kenyan government in order to identify, trace, and freeze or seize property and assets belonging to or under the control of Kenyatta. Pre-Trial Chamber's Order, ICC-01/09–02/11–42-Conf, p. 5. The Kenyan Government failed to comply with the Order for three years before finally challenging its legality.

19 *Prosecutor v. Francis Kirimi Muthaura and Uhuru Muigai Kenyatta*, Decision on the Defence Request to Change the Place of the Proceedings, ICC-01/09–02/11, para. 2 (7 November 2012).

20 *Ibid*, para. 13.

from continuous presence during the trial.[21] Influenced heavily by the terrorist attack on the Westgate Mall incident in Nairobi,[22] the Trial Chamber read a measure of judicial discretion into Article 63(1) and gave Ruto leave to return to Kenya during the trial.[23] The Trial Chamber noted that Ruto had 'duties of state to perform' and that those 'facts and circumstances [made the] case different from the average case.'[24]

Trial Chamber V(B) essentially agreed with Trial Chamber V(A) in its decision on a similar request from *Kenyatta*. It also cited the Westgate Mall incident and the 'damaging possibilities of the refusal to grant relief.'[25] The majority called it a 'veritable "early warning sign" not ... to be ignored',[26] over a stinging dissent from Judge Ozaki.[27] It also noted the negative practical consequences of having to constantly suspend trial in order to allow Kenyatta to return home to address matters of state. Looking to Article 63(1) of the Rome Statute, the majority determined that the Court had, through Article 64(6)(f),[28] an '*ex aequo et bono* power ... to prevent the generally accepted rule of presence of accused at trial from being something that unwittingly produces injustice, unfairness or inefficiencies in the administration of justice.'[29] Therefore, according to the majority, it was legally correct for it to make a 'public policy choice in finding workable legal solutions.'[30]

One week after Trial Chamber V(B) permitted Kenyatta's excusal from continuous presence, the Appeals Chamber released its decision on Ruto's relief, holding that while Article 63(1) allowed for some measure of judicial discretion, the Trial Chamber had abused this discretion in granting Ruto excusal from continuous presence at his trial.[31] The Appeals Chamber rejected the *ex aequo*

21 *Prosecutor v. William Samoei Ruto and Joshua Arap Sang*, Decision on Mr Ruto's Request for Excusal from Continuous Presence at Trial, ICC-01/09-01/11, para. 43, 18 June 2013 (hereinafter 'Ruto Trial Chamber Excusal').

22 National Consortium for the Study of Terrorism and Responses to Terrorism, *Al-Shabaab Attack on Westgate Mall in Kenya: Background Report*, September 2013.

23 Ruto Trial Chamber Excusal, para. 110.

24 *Ibid*, para. 27. This opinion better reflected Judge Fremr's opinion on the case whereas Judge Eboe-Osuji's opinion became clearer in his separate opinion in the *Kenyatta* request for excusal.

25 *Prosecutor v. Uhuru Muigai Kenyatta*, Decision on Defence Request for Conditional Excusal from Continuous Presence at Trial, ICC-01/09/02/11, para. 62, 18 October 2013 (hereinafter 'Kenyatta Trial Chamber Excusal').

26 *Ibid.*

27 *Prosecutor v. Uhuru Muigai Kenyatta*, Decision on Defence Request for Conditional Excusal from Continuous Presence at Trial, ICC-01/09/02/11, partially dissenting Opinion of Judge Ozaki, 18 October 2013.

28 'In performing its functions prior to trial or during the course of trial, the Chamber may, as necessary ... rule on any other relevant matters.' Rome Statute of the International Criminal Court, Art. 64(6)(f), 17 July 1998, 2187 UNTS 90/37.

29 Kenyatta Trial Chamber Excusal, para. 86.

30 *Ibid*, para. 94.

31 *Prosecutor v. William Samoei Ruto and Joshua Arap Sang*, Judgment on the Appeal of the Prosecutor Against the Decision of Trial Chamber V(A) of 18 June 2013 Entitled 'Decision

et bono argument stemming from discretion permitted in Article 64(6)(f) of the Rome Statute.[32] Instead, it held that the limits of the Chamber's discretionary power are derived from 63(2) which allows for the accused's removal in the event of disruptive behavior.[33] In order for the Trial Chamber to excuse an accused person from presence during trial, a series of requirements must be met:

> (i) the absence of the accused can only take place in exceptional circumstances and must not become the rule; (ii) the possibility of alternative measures must have been considered, including, but not limited to, changes to the trial schedule or a short adjournment of the trial; (iii) any absence must be limited to that which is strictly necessary; (iv) the accused must have explicitly waived his or her right to be present at trial; (v) the rights of the accused must be fully ensured in his or her absence, in particular through representation by counsel; and (vi) the decision as to whether the accused may be excused from attending part of his or her trial must be taken on a case-by-case basis, with due regard to the subject matter of the specific hearings that the accused would not attend during the period for which excusal has been requested.[34]

Trial Chamber V(B) then reconsidered and rejected Kenyatta's request for excusal, holding that, 'as a general rule, [Kenyatta would] have to be present for his trial.'[35]

Unfortunately, facing unrelenting pressure from many African states, the day after this decision the ICC Assembly of States Parties amended Rule 134 to add a new provision, Rule 134*quarter*, covering 'excusal from presence at trial due to extraordinary public duties.'[36] Trial Chamber V(A) then issued an oral ruling excusing Ruto from trial except for the closing statements of all parties, the victims' presentations of their views and concerns, the judgment, the sentencing hearing, sentencing, victim impact hearings, and the first five days after a judicial recess.[37] On 18 February 2014, Trial Chamber V(A) released its reasons for excusing Ruto from trial again, this time citing the new Rule 134*quarter*, and holding that:

on Mr Ruto's Request for Excusal from Continuous Presence at Trial, ICC-01/09–01/11 OA 5, para. 61, 25 October 2013 (hereinafter 'Ruto Appeals Chamber Excusal').

32 *Ibid*, para. 56.

33 *Ibid*, para. 61.

34 *Ibid*, para. 62.

35 *Prosecutor v. Uhuru Muigai Kenyatta*, Decision on the Prosecution's Motion for Reconsideration of the Decision Excusing Mr Kenyatta from Continuous Presence at Trial, ICC-01/09–02/11, para. 16, 26 November 2013 (hereinafter 'Kenyatta Excusal Reconsideration').

36 *Prosecutor v. William Samoei Ruto and Joshua Arap Sang*, Reasons for the Decision on Excusal from Presence of Trial Under Rule 134quarter, ICC-01/09–01/11, para. 45, 18 February 2014 (hereinafter 'Ruto 134quarter Decision').

37 *Ibid*, para. 10.

> [W]hen it is reasonably expected, based on the Constitution of Kenya, that the accused is highly likely to be frequently required to fulfill extraordinary duties at the highest national level, the proper accommodation of these duties is to excuse him from presence at trial, with limitations.[38]

Trial Chamber V(A) rejected the Prosecution's request to appeal its decision, preventing the Appeals Chamber from addressing its ruling.[39]

Back in *Kenyatta*, the Kenyan Government challenged the Pre-Trial Chamber's Order to seize and provide information on Kenyatta's assets and bank records on 3 March 2014. Due to both the lack of cooperation from the Kenyan Government and recanted testimony from witnesses, the Prosecution filed to adjourn the case and for a finding of non-compliance pursuant to Article 87(7) of the Rome Statute for Kenya's unwillingness to cooperate by turning over financial information promised two years earlier. Trial Chamber V(B) granted a limited adjournment for six months and delayed a ruling on non-compliance to give Kenya an opportunity to hand over required financial information relating to Kenyatta.[40] The Chamber noted that there was a 'substantial unexplained delay' by the Kenyan Government in relation to the Prosecution's records request,[41] but also cautioned the Prosecution, stating that the 'primary obligation to produce a case ready for trial is on the Prosecution.'[42] The Chamber further stated that 'it had serious concerns regarding the timeliness and the thoroughness of Prosecution investigations in this case – including ... verifying the credibility and reliability of the evidence upon which it intended to rely at trial.'[43]

On 3 December 2014, the Trial Chamber held that the Kenyan Government's failure to cooperate with the Court and the Prosecution by providing requested records 'reached the threshold of non-compliance.'[44] The Chamber found that the 'Kenyan Government's non-compliance ... not only compromised the Prosecution's ability to thoroughly investigate the charges, but ... ultimately impinged upon the Chamber's ability to fulfill its mandate'.[45] Curiously, the

38 *Ibid*, para. 55.
39 *Prosecutor v. William Samoei Ruto and Joshua Arap Sang*, Decision on Prosecution's Application for Leave to Appeal the Decision on Excusal from Presence at Trial Under Rule 134quarter, ICC-01/09-01/11, para. 6, 2 April 2014 (hereinafter 'Ruto 134*quarter* Leave for Appeal Decision').
40 *Prosecutor v. Uhuru Muigai Kenyatta*, Decision on Prosecution's Applications for a Finding of Non-Compliance Pursuant to Article 87(7) and for an Adjournment of the Provisional Trial Date, ICC-01/09-02/11, para. 100, 31 March 2014.
41 *Ibid*, para. 83.
42 *Ibid*, para. 88.
43 *Ibid.*
44 *Prosecutor v. Uhuru Muigai Kenyatta*, Decision on Prosecution's Application for a Finding of Non-Compliance under Article 87(7) of the Statute, ICC-01/09-02/11, para. 78, 3 December 2014.
45 *Ibid*, para. 79.

Chamber chose not to refer the Kenyan Government to the Assembly of States Parties for its non-compliance.[46] On the same day, the Trial Chamber rejected the Prosecution's request to further adjourn the case, and also rejected the defence's request for termination in order to give the Prosecution an opportunity to withdraw the charges against Kenyatta,[47] which it did on 5 December 2014.[48] Parallel to the ICC cases, the Kenya National Dialogue and Reconciliation process, which followed the post-election violence, led to the establishment of a Truth, Justice and Reconciliation Commission.[49] The Commission was tasked with investigating 'gross violations of human rights and historical injustices that occurred in Kenya between' its independence 12 December 1963 and 28 February 2008.[50]

In its final report, submitted to President Kenyatta on 21 May 2013,[51] the Commission made several recommendations to address injustices resulting from the post-election violence. First, the Commission recommended that the president, among others, publicly apologise and establish a system of reparations.[52] Second, the Commission recommended that 'alleged perpetrators of ethnic incitement to violence be investigated and prosecuted accordingly, notwithstanding their official or other status.'[53] Third, the Commission tasked the Director of Public Prosecutions to investigate and prosecute ethnic and political violence as recommended by the Kenya National Commission on Human Rights in its report on the post-election violence.[54] Finally, the Commission tasked the Director of Public Prosecutions with 'publicly reporting its progress on investigating and prosecuting' the post-election violence-related cases.[55]

While the Commission's recommendations were intended to be implemented within months of the report's publication, the report was instead ignored for nearly two years. Finally, on 26 March 2015, President Kenyatta apologised during his State of the Nation address. Kenyatta noted that, moving forward the government would focus on 'restorative justice and creating a new

46 *Ibid*, para. 82.
47 *Ibid*, para. 62.
48 Statement of the Prosecutor of the International Criminal Court, Fatou Bensouda, on the Withdrawal of Charges Against Mr Uhuru Muigai Kenyatta, 5 December 2014, available at: www.icc-cpi.int/en_menus/icc/press%20and%20media/press%20releases/Pages/otp-statement-05-12-2014-2.aspx.
49 Ndungú, 'Lessons to Be Learned: An Analysis of the Final Report of Kenya's Truth, Justice and Reconciliation Commission', International Center for Transitional Justice, 2 May 2014 (hereinafter 'TJRC Analysis').
50 Sheria, 'Summary of Truth, Justice, and Reconciliation Commission (TJRC) Report', Legal Advice Centre, 2014.
51 TJRC Analysis, p. 2.
52 *Final Report of the Truth, Justice and Reconciliation Commission*, Vol. IV, 29, 3 May 2013.
53 *Ibid*, p. 62.
54 *Ibid.*
55 *Ibid.*

government department to pay more attention to the more marginalized parts of Kenya.'[56] In addition to the new department, Kenyatta announced a plan to set aside 10 billion shillings to be disbursed to the victims over three years.[57] However, citing a report from the Director of Public Prosecutions on cases related to the post-election violence, Kenyatta declared that it would be difficult to prosecute *any* cases due to 'weak evidence, inability to identify perpetrators, and witnesses' fear of reprisals.'[58] In response to this speech, victims of the violence and human rights organisations criticised the president's evasion of criminal justice, noting that 'a reparations fund is complementary to criminal justice, not a replacement for it.'[59]

3. CHALLENGES TO KENYATTA'S TRIAL AND THE LAW ON HEAD OF STATE IMMUNITY

Kenyatta's request to be recused from trial must be seen in light of the ongoing efforts by Kenya and the African Union to recognise immunity for incumbent Heads of State. Following the ICC's indictment of Sudanese President, Omar Al-Bashir, the African Union began a campaign to limit prosecutions against Heads of State.[60] In a resolution in 2009, the African Union requested a 'comparative analysis of the practical application of Articles 27 and 98 of the Rome Statute.'[61] The purpose of undergoing this analysis was to move the Court toward assessing 'regional input ... in determining whether or not to proceed with prosecution; particularly against senior state officials.'[62] At the eighth session of the ASP, South Africa put forward a proposal on behalf of all African parties to the Rome Statute to extend the power to defer ICC cases to the General Assembly.[63]

56 Maliti, 'Kenyan President and Chief Justice Apologize for Past Injustices', International Justice Monitor, 9 April 2015, available at: www.ijmonitor.org/2015/04/kenyan-president-and-chief-justice-apologize-for-past-injustices/.

57 *Ibid.*

58 *Ibid.*

59 *Prosecutor v. Uhuru Muigai Kenyatta*, Decision on the Victims' Request to Participate in the Appeal Proceedings, ICC-01/09-02/11, para. 36, 27 March 2015; Amnesty International, Kenya: Amnesty International Calls for Justice as well as Reparations for Victims of the 2007–8 Post-Election Violence, AFR 32/1446/2015, 14 April 2015, available at: www.iccnow.org/documents/AFR3214462015ENGLISH.pdf.

60 *Prosecutor v. Omar Al Hassan Ahmad Al-Bashir (Omar Al-Bashir)*, Warrant of Arrest for Omar Hassan Ahmad Al-Bashir, ICC-02/05-01/09, 4 March 2009.

61 Decision on the Meeting of African States Parties to the Rome Statute of the International Criminal Court, Assembly/AU/Dec.245 (XIII) Rev.1.

62 *Ibid.*

63 African Union States Parties to the Rome Statute, Annex VI of the 8th Session of the Assembly of States Parties to the Rome Statute, 18 November 2009. There was very little support voiced for this proposal at the ASP.

Following the Prosecutor's investigation into the post-election violence in Kenya, the African Union adopted Resolution 296 in 2010 reiterating their request in regard to Bashir and urging that the UN General Assembly should gain the power to defer cases before the ICC for one year.[64] The following year, in Resolution 334, the African Union once again reiterated its criticism of the Bashir indictment and specifically supported Kenya's request for deferral of the ICC investigation and prosecution in cases arising out of the 2008 post-election violence.[65] The African Union further pushed for African states to vote for an amendment to Article 16 of the Rome Statute to allow for the UN General Assembly to defer cases for a year.[66] The AU reiterated this position in Resolutions 366,[67] 397[68] and 419.[69]

Civil society organisations in Kenya and across Africa objected to Kenya's intransigence in pursuing justice for the post-election violence and the African Union's push for immunity, arguing that immunity inherently leads to impunity. In early 2011, several civil society organisations condemned the Kenyan Parliament's vote supporting a withdrawal from the Rome Statute and called on the Kenyan Government to 'cooperate fully with the International Criminal Court in ... its investigation and prosecution of any crimes committed within its jurisdiction.'[70] Kenyans for Peace with Truth and Justice, a civil society 'coalition of over thirty Kenyan and East African legal, human rights, and governance organizations ... convened in the immediate aftermath of the disputed 2007 presidential election',[71] urged the government to cooperate with the ICC.[72]

In 2013, however, the declarations in the African Union Resolutions grew more demanding following the election of Kenyatta and Ruto as President and Deputy President of Kenya. In Resolution 482, the African Union stressed

---

64 Decision on the Progress Report of the Commission on the Implementation of Decision Assembly/AU/DEC.270 (XIV) on the Rome Statute of the International Criminal Court, Assembly/AU/Dec.296 (XV).

65 Decision on the Implementation of the Decisions on the International Criminal Court, Assembly/AU/Dec.334 (XVI).

66 *Ibid.*

67 Decision on the Implementation of the Assembly Decisions on the International Criminal Court, Assembly/AU/Dec.366 (XVII).

68 Decision on the Progress Report of the Commission on the Implementation of the Assembly Decisions on the International Criminal Court, Assembly/AU/Dec.397 (XVIII).

69 Decision on the Progress Report of the Commission on the Implementation of the Assembly Decisions on the International Criminal Court, Assembly/AU/Dec.419 (XIX).

70 Kapinga, Statement on the Application for Summons by the International Criminal Court Chief Prosecutor Against 6 Persons for Their Alleged Complicity in Crimes Against Humanity Arising out of the 2007 Kenyan Post Election Violence, 2 January 2011.

71 Kenyans for Peace with Truth and Justice, Memo Responding to Kenyan Ambassador's Letter to the UNSC on ICC Cases, 17 May 2013.

72 Kenyans for Peace with Truth and Justice, Press Statement on the Confirmation of Charges, 20 January 2012.

that the ICC should withdraw the indictments against them, as they could pose a threat to the ongoing efforts to promote peace and reconciliation as well as the rule of law and stability in the region.[73] They also contended that the principle of complementarity meant that Kenya had primary jurisdiction over the crimes.[74] In an Extraordinary Session held in October of 2013, the African Union complained of the 'unprecedented' indictments and proceedings against the sitting President and Deputy President of Kenya.[75] Arguing that Kenya was an essential state to the fight against terrorism and that the proceedings in the ICC would prevent Kenyatta and Ruto from being able to fulfil their duties, the African Union decided that 'no charges shall be commenced or continued before any International Court or Tribunal against any serving African Union Head of State or Government, or anybody acting or entitled to act in such capacity during their term of office.'[76] In respect of this, the African Union declared that the ICC trials of Kenyatta and Ruto should be suspended.[77]

Civil society organisations continued to protest against the actions of the Kenyan Government and the African Union. In May 2013, Kenyans for Peace with Truth and Justice wrote a memo in response to the Kenyan Ambassador's letter to the UN Security Council to defer the Kenyan cases before the ICC, arguing that Kenyatta had insisted while running for President that he could manage his professional duties and his personal obligations to cooperate with the ICC.[78] Following Trial Chamber V(A)'s initial decision to excuse Ruto from trial, Kenyans for Peace with Truth and Justice wrote an open letter to the President of the ICC complaining that:

> Allowing Mr Ruto to miss sections of his trial owing to his ascendancy to the Deputy Presidency panders to the whims of the accused and accords him preferential treatment purely on the basis of his position as a state officer. This creates a distinction in treatment of state and non-state officers by the Court. The decision contradicts the essence of Article 27 on equal application of the statute without distinction based on official capacity.[79]

---

73 Decision on International Jurisdiction and the International Criminal Court, Assembly/AU/Dec.482 (XXI).

74 *Ibid.*

75 Decision on Africa's Relationship with the International Criminal Court, Ext/Assembly/AU/Dec.1, October 2013.

76 *Ibid.*

77 *Ibid.*

78 Kenyans for Peace with Truth and Justice, Memo Responding to Kenyan Ambassador's Letter to the UNSC on ICC Cases, 17 May 2013.

79 Kenyans for Peace with Truth and Justice, Open Letter to the President of the ICC on the Decision on William Ruto's Excusal from Continuous Presence at his Trial, 9 July 2013.

Ultimately, the Security Council vote was seven States[80] in favour of deferral with eight States[81] abstaining.[82] No state voted 'no'. Addressing the Assembly of States Parties directly, Kenyans for Peace with Truth and Justice stated: 'Allowing certain individuals to absent themselves from the trials on the basis of their status violates the principle of equality before the law.'[83] This perspective appears to be consistent with the views of other civil society organisations and a large percentage of the Kenyan public at the time. One independent public opinion poll designed to gauge attitudes towards the ICC cases from November 2013 showed 'that 42% of those polled support[ed] the trial of the cases before the ICC as opposed to 30% who prefer[ed] the cases to be dropped. Also in the same poll, 67% of those polled would want the president and deputy to attend their trials before the ICC.'[84]

On 27 November 2013, the Assembly of States Parties amended Rule 134 to add three new provisions to the ICC's trial procedure.[85] Rule 134*bis* permitted an accused to request 'presence through the use of video technology.'[86] Rule 134*ter* followed the decision by the Appeals Chamber in *Ruto* and permitted the Trial Chamber to grant a request to be excused from trial if satisfied that there are 'exceptional circumstances ... to justify such an absence, alternative measures, including changes to the trial schedule or adjournment ... would be inadequate, the accused has explicitly waived his or her right to be present at the trial, and the rights of the accused will be fully ensured in his or her absence.'[87]

Rule 134*quater* stated that in the event of a summons to appear, '[a]n accused ... who is mandated to fulfill extraordinary public duties at the highest national level may ... request to the Trial Chamber to be excused and to be represented by counsel only; the request must specify that the accused explicitly waives the right to be present at the trial.'[88]

The African Union also adopted an amendment to the proposed Statute of the African Court of Justice and Human Rights at a summit on 26 June 2014 providing:

> No charges shall be commenced or continued before the court against any Serving Head of State or Government, or anybody acting or entitled to act in such capacity,

---

80 Azerbaijan, China, Morocco, Pakistan, Russian Federation, Rwanda, and Togo are all ICC non-party states.

81 Argentina, Australia, France, Guatemala, Luxembourg, Republic of Korea, United Kingdom, and the United States, are all, with the exception of the United States, ICC states.

82 SC Press Statement 2013/S/RES/11176, 15 November 2013, available at: www.un.org/News/Press/docs/2013/sc11176.doc.htm.

83 Kenyans for Peace with Truth and Justice, Statement at the Assembly of States Parties, 21 November 2013.

84 *Ibid.*

85 Resolution on the Amendments to the Rules, ICC-ASP/12/Res.7, 27 November 2013.

86 *Ibid.*

87 *Ibid.*

88 *Ibid.*

or other senior state officials based on their functions, during their tenure in office.[89]

Kenyan civil society organisations rejected the amendment when it was proposed. Kenyans for Peace with Truth and Justice wrote: 'The amendment to give immunity to [H]eads of [S]tate and senior officials … purports to ignore over half a century of developments in international human rights and criminal justice law.'[90] They argued further: 'It is obvious to even the most casual observer that what they are doing is creating a court whose primary purpose is to shield powerful individuals from justice at the expense of victims.'[91]

Despite repeated outcries from civil society organisations, some African states have continued to defy their obligations under the Rome Statute. In June 2015, the South African government permitted Omar Al-Bashir to attend an African Union summit in South Africa, further inflaming tensions between the ICC and some African states. As a party to the Rome Statute, South Africa was obligated to comply with the Court's outstanding warrants for Bashir's arrest. South Africa's high court issued an interim order barring Bashir from leaving the country in order to hear an application by the Southern African Litigation Centre to force authorities to arrest him.[92] The ICC called upon South Africa to detain Bashir and 'spare no effort in ensuring the execution of the arrest warrants.'[93] In response to the interim order issued by the high court, the South African government permitted Bashir to fly out of the country while the high court was hearing the application to arrest Bashir. Following the hearing, the high court held that Bashir should have been detained.[94] The government's actions were condemned by the high court judges,[95] over 100 civil society organisations,[96] and the international community.[97]

89 Draft Protocol on Amendments to the Protocol on the Statute of the African Court of Justice and Human Rights, Article 46A *bis*, EX.CL/846(XXV), May 2014.

90 Njonjo Mue, 'Granting Presidents Immunity is Wrong', *The Star*, 9 June 2014, available at: www.the-star.co.ke/news/article-170300/granting-presidents-immunity-wrong.

91 *Ibid.*

92 Bowcott & Grierson, 'Sudan President Barred From Leaving South Africa', *The Guardian*, 15 June 2015, available at: www.theguardian.com/world/2015/jun/14/sudan-president-omar-al-bashir-south-africa-icc.

93 *Ibid.*

94 Bowcott, 'Sudan President Omar Al-Bashir Leaves South Africa as Court Considers Arrest', *The Guardian*, 15 June 2015, available at: www.theguardian.com/world/2015/jun/15/south-africa-to-fight-omar-al-bashirs-arrest-warrant-sudan.

95 Onishi, 'Omar Al-Bashir, Leaving South Africa, Eludes Arrest Again', *New York Times*, 15 June 2015, available at: www.nytimes.com/2015/06/16/world/africa/omar-hassan-al-bashir-sudan-south-africa.html?_r=0.

96 Human Rights Watch, 'Civil Society Declaration on Sudanese President Omar Al-Bashir's Visit to South Africa Without Arrest', 1 July 2015, available at: https://www.hrw.org/news/2015/07/01/civil-society-declaration-sudanese-president-omar-al-bashirs-visit-south-africa.

97 Bowcott & Grierson, 'Sudan President Barred From Leaving South Africa', *The Guardian*, 15 June 2015, available at: www.theguardian.com/world/2015/jun/14/sudan-president-omar-al-bashir-south-africa-icc.

4. HEAD OF STATE IMMUNITY IN INTERNATIONAL LAW

The question remains whether Kenyatta and the AU's argument is founded either in the Rome Statute, or, more generally, in customary international law. As a matter of customary international law, Head of State immunity has been rejected in international criminal proceedings since Nuremberg. Article 7 of the Nuremberg Charter states that the official position of an accused person *shall* not free that person from responsibility for any of the crimes charged under the Charter.[98] Indeed, the International Military Tribunal at Nuremberg tried, without issue, Karl Dönitz, then Germany's Head of State.[99] Likewise, Article 6 of the Statute of the International Criminal Tribunal for Rwanda (ICTR) and Article 7 of the ICTY Statute states that the official position of an accused 'shall not relieve such person of criminal responsibility.'[100] The ICTY tried Slobodan Milosevic as well as other high-ranking government officials,[101] and the ICTR tried Jean Kambanda, Rwanda's Prime Minister.[102]

Diplomatic immunity in national proceedings was raised as an issue in the *Case Concerning the Arrest Warrant of 11 April 2000* ('The Yerodia Case') before the International Court of Justice (ICJ) in 2002. The Yerodia Case concerned an arrest warrant issued by Belgium against the incumbent Minister for Foreign Affairs of the Democratic Republic of Congo, Abdulaye Yerodia Ndombasi, for war crimes and crimes against humanity.[103] Yerodia was accused of making various speeches to incite 'racial hatred' which allegedly incited attacks against Tutsi populations in Kinshasa.[104]

---

98 Charter of the International Military Tribunal, Article 7, 8 August 1945, 82 UNTS 279; Bassiouni 1992.

99 The Trial of German Major War Criminals by the International Military Tribunal Sitting at Nuremberg, Germany, Indictment, Appendix A: Statement of Individual Responsibility for Crimes Set Out in Counts One, Two, Three and Four (1946). Technically, Admiral Donitz could be considered a former Head of State, rather than an incumbent Head of State, as the Allied forces dissolved the German government on 23 May 1945 and the trials did not begin until 19 November 1945. See Wolfe 2014.

100 Statute of the International Criminal Tribunal for the Former Yugoslavia, SC Res. 827, art. 7, UN Doc. S/RES/827 (1993) (hereinafter 'ICTY Statute'); Statute of the International Criminal Tribunal for Rwanda, SC Res.955, art. 6, UN SCOR, 49th Sess., UN Doc. S/RES/955 (1994) (hereinafter 'ICTR Statute').

101 *Prosecutor v. Slobodan Milosevic, Milan Milutinovic, Nokola Sainovic, Dragoljub Ojdanic, Vlajko Stojiljkovic*, Indictment, IT-99-37, 22 May 1999. While Slobodan Milosevic was not an incumbent Head of State when he was tried before the ICTY, he was when he was indicted. See Bassiouni 2008.

102 *Prosecutor v. Jean Kambanda*, Judgment and Sentence, ICTR 97-23-S, 4 September 1988. Technically, like Donitz, Kambanda was also a former Head of State, not an incumbent Head of State, when tried and convicted of genocide by the ICTR. See Alvarez 2010.

103 Case Concerning the Arrest Warrant of 11 April 2000, *Democratic Republic of Congo v. Belgium*, 2002 ICJ 3 para. 13, 14 February 2002 (also known as 'The Yerodia Case').

104 *Ibid*, para. 67.

The ICJ rejected the application of universal jurisdiction by national courts over an incumbent Minister for Foreign Affairs; however, in doing so, it rationalised its decision, in part, based on the fact that no immunity would be present before international tribunals:

> An incumbent or former Minister for Foreign Affairs may be subject to criminal proceedings before certain international criminal courts, where they have jurisdiction. Examples include ... the future International Criminal Court created by the 1998 Rome Convention (citing Article 27(2) of the Rome Statute).[105]

The Special Court for Sierra Leone (SCSL) rejected Head of State immunity in the trial of Charles Taylor for war crimes and crimes against humanity. The Court's statute had a similar provision to Article 27 of the Rome Statute in Article 6(2), which stated that 'the official position (including as Head of State) of such persons shall not relieve them of criminal responsibility nor mitigate punishment.'[106] The SCSL recognised the limitations placed on domestic courts for trying Heads of State in *Taylor*, but cited *Yerodia* as creating the distinction permitting competent international courts and tribunals to try sitting Heads of State.[107] According to the Chamber, 'sovereign equality does not prevent a Head of State from being prosecuted before an international tribunal or court.'[108] This view has been uniformly accepted by well-known publicists, who have treated this as a rule of customary international law.[109]

Of course, it is possible to argue that the presence of Article 27 means that the abolition of Head of State immunity in the ICC Statute is simply a matter of waiver;[110] but, that view would not be consistent with the inclusion of Articles 6 and 7 in the ICTR and ICTY Statute, which are clearly thought to articulate already existing rules of customary international law.[111] The Rome Statute codified this custom in Article 27, thereby depriving Kenyatta (and Al-Bashir of Sudan), a defence based upon their formal status.

---

105 *Ibid*, para. 61.

106 *Prosecutor v. Charles Ghankay Taylor*, Decision on Immunity from Jurisdiction, SCSL-2003-01-I, para. 28, 31 May 2004.

107 *Ibid.* para. 50, Sriram 2005.

108 *Ibid.* para. 52.

109 See e.g. Cassese 2005; Crawford 2008; Naqvi 2010.

110 *Ibid.*

111 UN Secretary-General, *Report of the Secretary-General Pursuant to Paragraph 2 of Security Council Resolution 808 (1993)*, 14–15, S/25704, 3 May 1993; UN Secretary-General, *The Charter and Judgment of the Nürnberg Tribunal – History and Analysis: Memorandum submitted by the Secretary-General*, A/CN.4/5 (1949).

5. CONCLUSION

The *Kenyatta* case reintroduced claims to Head of State immunity similar to those advanced by the European powers in the wake of World War I, created new rules of presence of the accused at trial, and ultimately through both the lack of cooperation by the Kenyan Government and recanted testimony has been unable to produce a just outcome for the victims of the post-election violence. Recent attempts by the African Union to establish immunity for incumbent Heads of State threatens one of the core principles of international justice, and provides a perverse incentive for leaders who will face investigation by the Court to remain in power for as long as possible to avoid the Court's jurisdiction. Although there may be real concerns about the fact that, thus far, the Court is not yet pursuing justice in situations outside of Africa, and it cannot be denied that five of the world's Heads of State are permanently protected – as a political matter – by virtue of their countries veto power in the Security Council, this cannot be used to protect those who commit crimes at the expense of justice for victims. Indeed, it is worth recalling that at least one of the P5, France, recognised the importance of lifting immunities to promote international criminal justice and amended its Constitution as part of the ICC ratification process to remove immunity for its President and other government leaders.[112]

Six of the ICC's current situations were referred to the Court by the 'states where the crimes were committed (Uganda, Democratic Republic of Congo, Central African Republic, Côte d'Ivoire, and Mali).[113] Two of the other situations before the Court were referred by the UN Security Council (Libya and Darfur, Sudan) with the support of representatives of African States.[114] Kenya remains the only case brought *proprio motu* by the Office of the Prosecutor. While *Kenyatta* was not referred to the ICC by Kenya, Kenya had numerous opportunities to investigate the post-election violence, and it was only after its continued failure to do so that Kofi Annan submitted the sealed envelopes containing Kenyatta's and Ruto's names to the Prosecutor to bring charges.

The ICC Appeals Chamber attempted to reconcile legitimate concerns and dissent from the African members of the Court with the law of the Rome Statute. The Court admitted that there might be circumstances in which a state requires the presence of its leader, and in such extraordinary circumstances, the accused should be permitted to remain in state, but only for as long as necessary to establish some measure of stability. However, this restriction can and should only be limited to non-essential portions of a trial, must be limited in duration to only the amount of time absolutely necessary, and must always be tethered

112 Sadat 2010.

113 Human Rights Watch, Letter to Foreign Ministers on Support for the ICC in Advance of Extraordinary AU Summit, 10 October 2013.

114 *Ibid.*

to truly exceptional circumstances. These concerns must then be weighed very carefully against the rights of the victims. As judges Erkki Kourula and Anita Ušacka stated, 'it seems indisputable that the establishment of the presence of the accused as a requirement is consistent with the gravitas of the proceedings and their importance from the perspective of the victims of the alleged crimes and the international community as a whole.'[115]

The Appeals Chamber's interpretation of Rule 63(1) permitted excusal in exceptional circumstances and is therefore consistent with Articles 27 and 21 of the Statute. Rule 134*quarter*, however, is problematic and arguably *inconsistent* with Article 27(1) and Article 21(3) of the Rome Statute as it grants special treatment to individuals based on their official status.

Article 27(1) explicitly states that the Rome Statute applies equally to all persons regardless of official capacity. Similarly, Article 21(3) requires that the Rome Statute and the procedural rules without any 'adverse distinction founded on … status.'[116] As Judge Carbuccia argued, '[a]ll persons should be equal before courts and tribunals and no accused should be accorded privileged treatment, as equality under the law is a fundamental value of the administration of justice.'[117] This approach is most consistent with the drafting of the Rome Statute. During the drafting process, a separate proposal was put forward regarding the official capacity of the accused but lacking the language that the statute must apply without discrimination. This proposal was rejected in favour of one which required equal application.[118]

Conversely, 134*quarter* applies only to persons who have a mandate to fulfil extraordinary public duties at the highest national level. By definition, this creates two categories of persons before the Court, those mandated to fulfil extraordinary public duties and those not mandated to fulfil extraordinary public duties. As the amendments to Rule 134 are exceptions to Article 63(1), Rule 134*quarter* creates circumstances in which Article 63(1) of the Rome Statute may be applied differently depending on the official capacity of the accused. This seems clearly to violate the requirement that the Rome Statute be applied equally to all persons, regardless of official capacity.

Unfortunately, the Trial Chamber prevented the Prosecutor from appealing its 134*quarter* decision in Ruto, and therefore the Appeals Chamber will not have an opportunity to address the rule's compatibility with Article 27(1) and

---

115 *Prosecutor v. William Samoei Ruto and Joshua Arap Sang*, Judgment on the Appeal of the Prosecutor Against the Decision of Trial Chamber V(A) of 18 June 2013 Entitled 'Decision on Mr Ruto's Request for Excusal from Continuous Presence at Trial', Joint Separate Opinion of Judge Erkki Kourula and Judge Anita Ušacka, ICC-01/09-01/11 OA 5, para. 8, 25 October 2013.

116 Art. 23(1) Rome Statute.

117 *Prosecutor v. William Samoei Ruto And Joshua Arap Sang*, Decision on Mr Ruto's Request for Excusal from Continuous Presence at Trial, ICC-01/09-01/11, Dissenting Opinion of Judge Herrera Carbuccia, para. 7, 18 June 2013.

118 Bassiouni 1998.

Article 63(1). At the first available opportunity, however, this rule should be rejected as incompatible with the substantive provisions of the Rome Statute.

The Assembly of States Parties has the authority to amend the procedural applications of the Rome Statute, but not in a way inconsistent with the Rome Statute.[119] It is clear looking to the closing remarks of the President of the Assembly of States Parties that in its discussion on the '[i]ndictment of sitting Heads of State and Government and its consequences on peace and stability and reconciliation' led by Prince Zeid Ra'ad Hussein of Jordan, that states were not willing to change the substantive articles of the Rome Statute.[120] The main goal of the ASP in amending Rule 134 was to 'codify the 25 October 2013 Appeals Chambers decision in the case against Ruto and Sang' in regards to Article 63(1).[121] Rule 134*quarter* goes too far.

It is unclear what the outcome of the *Kenyatta* case will be. Emotions are running high on all sides. Certainly, the difficulties engendered will almost certainly affect the way that the Prosecutor approaches future cases against incumbent Heads of State and cases initiated *proprio motu* under Article 15 of the Rome Statute. Kenya's refusal to cooperate with the Court's orders underscores the difficulties faced by the ICC as *justice sans police*. The withdrawal of the charges against Kenyatta puts greater pressure on the success of the *Ruto* case, which may be the only opportunity for the victims of the post-election violence to achieve some measure of justice, unless the *Kenyatta* case is ultimately reopened.

BIBLIOGRAPHY

BOOKS AND JOURNAL ARTICLES

Alvarez 2010

Alvarez, A., 'Genocidal Crimes', Routledge, 2010.

Bassiouni 2008

Bassiouni, M.C., 'International Criminal Law, Volume 2: Multilateral and Bilateral Enforcement Mechanisms', 3rd ed., Martinus Nijhoff Publishers, 2008.

Bassiouni 1998

Bassiouni, M.C., 'The Statute of the International Criminal Court: A Documentary History, Report of the Preparatory Committee on the Establishment of an International Criminal Court', Transnational Publishers, 1998.

119 Article 51(4) Rome Statute.

120 Pace, Closing Remarks of the President of the Assembly of States Parties at the thirteenth meeting of the Assembly, 28 November 2013.

121 Coalition for the International Criminal Court, Report on the 12th Session of the Assembly of States Parties to the Rome Statute, 20–28 November 2013, pp. 19–20, available at: www.coalitionfortheicc.org/documents/asp12_report.pdf.

Bassiouni 1992
Bassiouni, M.C., 'Crimes against Humanity in International Law', Martinus Nijhoff Publishers, 1992.
Cassese 2005
Cassese, A., 'International Law', 2nd ed., Oxford University Press, 2005.
Crawford 2008
Crawford, J., 'Brownlie's Public International Law', 8th ed., Oxford University Press, 2008.
Mueller 2014
Mueller, S.D., 'Kenya and the International Criminal Court (ICC): Politics, the Election and the Law', 8 J. E. Afr. Stud., 2014.
Naqvi 2010
Naqvi, Y.Q., 'Impediments to Exercising Jurisdiction over International Crimes', T.M.C. Asser Press, 2010.
Sadat 2010
Sadat, L.N., 'The Nuremberg Paradox', 58 Am. J. Comp. L., 2010.
Sriram 2005
Sriram, C.J., 'Globalizing Justice For Mass Atrocities: A Revolution in Accountability', Routledge, 2005.
Wolfe 2014
Wolfe, S., 'The Politics of Reparations and Apologies', Springer Series in Transitional Justice Book 7, 2014.

JURISPRUDENCE

ICC 2015
ICC, Prosecutor v. Uhuru Muigai Kenyatta, ICC-01/09-02/11, 27 March 2015.
ICC 2014
ICC, Prosecutor v. Uhuru Muigai Kenyatta, ICC-01/09-02/11, 3 December 2014.
ICC 2014
ICC, Prosecutor v. William Samoei Ruto and Joshua Arap Sang, ICC-01/09-01/11, 2 April 2014.
ICC 2014
ICC, Prosecutor v. Uhuru Muigai Kenyatta, ICC-01/09-02/11, 31 March 2014.
ICC 2014
ICC, Prosecutor v. William Samoei Ruto and Joshua Arap Sang, ICC-01/09-01/11, 18 February 2014.
ICC 2013
ICC, Prosecutor v. Uhuru Muigai Kenyatta, ICC-01/09-02/11, 26 November 2013.
ICC 2013
ICC, Prosecutor v. William Samoei Ruto and Joshua Arap Sang, ICC-01/09-01/11, 25 October 2013.
ICC 2013
ICC, Prosecutor v. Uhuru Muigai Kenyatta, ICC-01/09/02/11, 18 October 2013.

ICC 2013
ICC, Prosecutor v. William Samoei Ruto And Joshua Arap Sang, ICC-01/09-01/11, 18 June 2013.
ICC 2012
ICC, Prosecutor v. Francis Kirimi Muthaura and Uhuru Muigai Kenyatta, ICC-01/09-02/11, 7 November 2012.
ICC 2012
ICC, Prosecutor v. Francis Kirimi Muthaura, Uhuru Muigai Kenyatta and Mohammed Hussein Ali, IC-01/09-02/11, 23 January 2012.
ICC 2011
ICC, Decision Ordering the Registrar to Prepare and Transmit a Request for Cooperation to the Republic of Kenya for the Purpose of Securing the Identification, Tracing and Freezing or Seizure of Property and Assets of Francis Kirimi Muthaura, Uhuru Muigai Kenyatta and Mohammed Hussein Ali, ICC-01/09-02/11-42-Conf, 5 April 2011.
ICC 2010
ICC, Prosecutor's Application Pursuant to Article 58 as to Francis Kirimi Muthaura, Uhuru Muigai Kenyatta and Mohammed Hussein Ali, ICC-01/09-31-Red2, 15 December 2010.
ICC 2010
ICC, Prosecutor's Application Pursuant to Article 58 as to William Samoei Ruto, Henry Kiprono Kosgey and Joshua Arap Sang, ICC-01/09, 15 December 2010.
ICC 2010
ICC, Decision Pursuant to Article 15 of the Rome Statute on the Authorization of an Investigation into the Situation in the Republic of Kenya, ICC-01/09-19, 31 March 2010.
ICC 2009
ICC, Prosecutor v. Omar Al Hassan Ahmad Al-Bashir (Omar Al-Bashir), ICC-02/05-01/09, 4 March 2009.
ICJ 2002
ICJ, Case Concerning the Arrest Warrant of 11 April 2000 (Democratic Republic of Congo v. Belgium), Judgment, 14 February 2002.
ICTR 1988
ICTR, Prosecutor v. Jean Kambanda, ICTR-97-23-S, 4 September 1988.
ICTY 1999
ICTY, Prosecutor v. Slobodan Milosevic, Nokola Sainovic, Dragoljub Ojdanic, Vlajko Stojiljkovic, IT-99-37, 22 May 1999.
SCSL 2004
Special Court for Sierra Leone, Prosecutor v. Charles Ghankay Taylor, SCSL-2003-01-I, 31 May 2004.

TREATIES, LEGISLATION AND AGREEMENTS

AU, Decision on Africa's Relationship with the International Criminal Court (ICC), Ext/Assembly/AU/Dec.1, October 2013.

AU, Decision on International Jurisdiction and the International Criminal Court (ICC), Assembly/AU/Dec.482 (XXI), 26–27 May 2013.
AU, Decision on the Implementation of the Assembly Decisions on the International Criminal Court, Assembly/AU/Dec.366 (XVII), 30 June-1 July 2011.
AU, Decision on the Implementation of the Decisions on the International Criminal Court, Assembly/AU/Dec.334 (XVI), 30–31 January 2011.
AU, Decision on the Meeting of African States Parties to the Rome Statute of the International Criminal Court (ICC), Assembly/AU/Dec.245 (XIII) Rev.1, 1–3 July 2009.
AU, Decision on the Progress Report of the Commission on the Implementation of Decision Assembly/AU/DEC.270 (XIV) on the Rome Statute of the International Criminal Court (ICC), Assembly/AU/Dec.296 (XV), 25–27 July 2010.
AU, Decision on the Progress Report of the Commission on the Implementation of the Assembly Decisions on the International Criminal Court (ICC), Assembly/AU/Dec.397 (XVIII), 29–30 January 2012.
AU, Decision on the Progress Report of the Commission on the Implementation of the Assembly Decisions on the International Criminal Court (ICC), Assembly/AU/Dec.419 (XIX), 15–16 July 2012.
AU, Draft Protocol on Amendments to the Protocol on the Statute of the African Court of Justice and Human Rights, EX.CL/846(XXV), May 2014.
Charter of the International Military Tribunal, 82 UNTS 279, 8 August 1945.
Convention on the Prevention and Punishment of the Crime of Genocide, GA Res. 260 (III), 78 UNTS. 278, 9 December 1948.
Resolution on the Amendments to the Rules, ICC-ASP/12/Res.7, 27 November 2013.
Rome Statute of the International Criminal Court, 2187 UNTS 90/37, 17 July 1998.
Statute of the International Criminal Tribunal for Rwanda, SC Res. 955, UN Doc. S/RES/955, 8 November 1994.
Statute of the International Criminal Tribunal for the Former Yugoslavia, SC Res. 827, UN Doc. S/RES/827, 25 May 1993.
UN General Assembly, Resolution by the United Nations General Assembly, UN GAOR (Part II) at 188, UN Doc. A/61/Add.1, 1946.

OTHERS

Assembly of States Party to the Rome Statute of the ICC, African Union States Parties to the Rome Statute, Annex VI of the 8th Session of the Assembly of States Parties to the Rome Statute, 18 November 2009.
Aljazeera, 'African Leaders Accuse ICC of 'Race Hunt'', 28 May 2013.
Aljazeera, 'ICC Judges Summon 'Ocampo Six'', 8 March 2011.
Amnesty International, 'Kenya: Amnesty International Calls for Justice as well as Reparations for Victims of the 2007–8 Post-Election Violence', AFR 32/1446/2015, 14 April 2015.
Bowcott, O. and Grierson, J., 'Sudan President Barred From Leaving South Africa', The Guardian, 15 June 2015.

Bowcott, O., 'Sudan President Omar Al-Bashir Leaves South Africa as Court Considers Arrest', The Guardian, 15 June 2015.
Coalition for the International Criminal Court, Report on the 12th Session of the Assembly of States Parties to the Rome Statute, 20–28 November 2013.
Commission of Inquiry on Post-Election Violence, Report of the Commission of Inquiry on Post-Election Violence, 15 October 2008.
Human Rights Watch, Civil Society Declaration on Sudanese President Omar Al-Bashir's, 1 July 2015.
Human Rights Watch, Letter to Foreign Ministers on Support for the ICC in Advance of Extraordinary AU Summit, 10 October 2013.
International Coalition for the Responsibility to Protect, 'The Crisis in Kenya'.
International Military Tribunal Indictment, Appendix A: Statement of Individual Responsibility for Crimes Set Out in Counts One, Two, Three, and Four, 1946.
Justice and Reconciliation Commission, Final Report of the Truth, Vol. IV, 29, 3 May 2013.
Kapinga, Dr W., Statement on the Application for Summons by the International Criminal Court Chief Prosecutor Against 6 Persons for Their Alleged Complicity in Crimes Against Humanity Arising out of the 2007 Kenyan Post Election Violence, 21 January 2011.
Kenyans for Peace with Truth and Justice, Kenyan Ambassador's Letter to the UNSC on ICC Cases, 17 May 2013.
Kenyans for Peace with Truth and Justice, Open Letter to the President of the ICC on the Decision on William Ruto's Excusal from Continuous Presence at his Trial, 9 July 2013.
Kenyans for Peace with Truth and Justice, Press Statement on the Confirmation of Charges, 20 January 2012.
Kenyans for Peace with Truth and Justice, Statement at the Assembly of States Parties, 21 November 2013.
Kituo Cha Sheria (Legal Advice Centre), Summary of Truth, Justice, and Reconciliation Commission (TJRC) Report, 2014.
Maliti, T., 'Kenyan President and Chief Justice Apologize for Past Injustices', International Justice Monitor, 9 April 2015.
McConnell, T., 'How Kenya Took on the International Criminal Court, Global Post, 25 March 2014.
Mue, N., 'Granting Presidents Immunity is Wrong', the Star, 9 June 2014.
National Consortium for the Study of Terrorism and Responses to Terrorism, Al-Shabaab Attack on Westgate Male in Kenya, Background Report, September 2013.
Ndungú, C.G., 'Lessons to Be Learned: An Analysis of the Final Report of Kenya's Truth', Justice and Reconciliation Commission, International Center for Transitional Justice, 2014.
Onishi, N., 'Omar Al-Bashir, Leaving South Africa, Eludes Arrest Again', The New York Times, 15 June 2015.
Pace, W.R., Closing Remarks of the President of the Assembly of States Parties at the thirteenth meeting of the Assembly, 28 November 2013.
Report of the International Law Commission to the General Assembly, 4 UN GAOR Supp. No. 10, at 1, UN Doc. A/925, 1949.

Roth, K., 'Africa Attacks the International Criminal Court', Human Rights Watch, 14 January 2014.
Statement of the Prosecutor of the International Criminal Court, Fatou Bensouda, on the Withdrawal of Charges Against Mr Uhuru Muigai Kenyatta, 5 December 2014.
UN Secretary-General, Report of the Secretary-General Pursuant to Paragraph 2 of Security Council Resolution 808 (1993), 14–15, S/25704, 3 May 1993.
UN Secretary-General, The Charter and Judgment of the Nürnberg Tribunal – History and Analysis: Memorandum submitted by the Secretary-General, A/CN.4/5, 1949.
UN Security Council, 'Security Council Resolution Seeking Deferral of Kenyan Leaders' Trial Fails to Win Adoption, with 7 Voting in Favour, 8 Abstaining', SC/11176, Press Statement, 15 November 2013.

DEFENCE PERSPECTIVES: STATE COOPERATION AND ICC DETENTION

A Decade Past an Arrest Warrant

Xavier-Jean KEÏTA*

1. INTRODUCTION

In 2014, twelve years into the life of the Court, the ICC welcomed its first Memorandum of Understanding (MoU) on Interim Release, signed by the ICC and the Belgian government, and effectuated on 10 April 2014. In doing so, Belgium became the first country to indicate a willingness to accept suspects and accused on provisional release. However, this signifies only the beginning of work to come in developing cooperation agreements related to the detention and release of the ICC's defendants.

The work of the Court on such framework agreements is essential to ensuring the human rights of accused and convicted persons as enshrined in Article 67 of the Rome Statute. In particular, state cooperation in post-conviction matters is of great importance as defendants whose proceedings have been finalised remain in The Hague, awaiting the final steps which will determine where they will serve the remainder of their sentences – Mr Lubanga having a total 15-year sentence and Mr Katanga with a 12-year sentence. For Mr Ngudjolo Chui, whose acquittal was upheld on appeal, the question of where he would be able to live the rest of his life in a free and safe manner was also of real concern with asylum proceedings undertaken in and rejected by The Netherlands. For these men, and all future individuals brought before the Court, there remains necessary action on the part of states and the Court to ensure that the legal processes set in motion against them do not deprive them of basic civil liberties or exacerbate the sentences properly doled out by the judicial proceedings. Matters of detention

* Special thanks to Marie O'Leary, OPCD Legal Adviser/Counsel, and Lucy Turner, OPCD Intern, for their exceptional contributions to the drafting of this work. The views expressed herein are those of the author alone and do not reflect the views of the International Criminal Court.

conditions, protection, citizenship and care are all responsibilities of a Court when it disrupts an individual's life by bringing charges.

2. 'DETENTION AS AN EXCEPTION'

As outlined by the ICCPR, pre-trial detention should be an exception to be justified, not a general rule.[1] This was later emphasised by the Single Judge sitting in the ICC case of *Prosecutor v. Bemba*, holding: 'when dealing with the right to liberty, one should be mindful of the fundamental principle that deprivation of liberty should be an exception and not a rule'.[2]

It is the right to a presumption of innocence that underpins the preference for non-custody – ensuring that defendants not be punished before a conviction. This is demonstrated by a 2006 'Recommendation on the use of remand in custody, the conditions in which it takes place and the provision of safeguards against abuse', in which the Council of Europe's Committee of Ministers found that:

> Remand prisoners shall be subject to conditions appropriate to their legal status; this entails the absence of restrictions other than those necessary for the administration of justice, the security of the institution, the safety of the prisoners and staff and the protection of rights of others and in particular the fulfilment of the requirements of the European Prison Rules and the other rules set out in Part III of the present text.[3]

Moreover, the Committee of Ministers accentuated the 'irreversible damage that remand in custody may cause to persons ultimately found to be innocent or discharged and of the detrimental mental impact that remand in custody may have on the maintenance of family relationships'.[4]

Deviation from the rule of pre-trial release, then, must express a legitimate aim and take full consideration of the panoply of rights afforded to a suspect or

---

1 Art. 9(3) International Covenant on Civil and Political Rights provides that: 'it shall not be the general rule that persons awaiting trial shall be detained in custody'.

2 *Prosecutor v. Bemba*, 'Decision on the Interim release of Jean-Pierre Bemba Gombo' and Convening Hearings with the Kingdom of Belgium, the Republic of Portugal, the Republic of France, the Federal Republic of Germany, the Italian Republic, and the Republic of South Africa, ICC-01/05-01/08-475, 14 August 2009, para. 36, citing Pre-Trial Chamber II, ICC-01/05-01/08-403, para. 36. See also Inter-American Court of Human Rights (the 'IACtHR'), *Case of Tibi v. Ecuador*, Judgment of 7 September 2004, Series C No. 114, para. 106; IACtHR, *Case of Acosta-Calderón v. Ecuador*, Judgment of 24 June 2005, para. 74; IACtHR, *Case of Children's Rehabilitation*, Judgment of 2 September 2004, Series C No. 112, para. 228; Human Rights Committee, Communication 526/1993, *Hill and Hill v. Spain*, 23 June 1997, para. 12.3; ECtHR, *Ilijkov v. Bulgaria*, Judgment of 26 July 2001, Application no. 33977/96, para. 85.

3 Council of Europe, Recommendation (2006) 13, on the use of remand in custody, the conditions in which it takes place and the provision of safeguards against abuse, adopted by the Committee of Ministers on 27 September 2006 at the 974th meeting of Ministers' Deputies, para. 5.

4 *Ibid.*

accused; not only the presumption of innocence, but also, *inter alia*, the right to an expeditious trial and the right to liberty.[5] For this, the Inter-American Court of Human Rights (IACtHR) has held that it must be demonstrated that pre-trial detention is 'absolutely essential to attain the desired objective, and that there is no measure that is less onerous in relation to the affected right, among all those that are similarly appropriate to achieve the proposed objective'. Equally, the ECtHR has held that '[a] person charged with an offence must always be released pending trial unless the State can show that there are 'relevant and sufficient' reasons to justify the continued detention'. They have gone on to hold that prolonged or unwarranted pre-trial detention can be regarded as a 'serious departure from the rules of respect for individual liberty and of the presumption of innocence'.[6] However it has been suggested that 'care should be taken that too great a reliance is not placed upon [the decisions of the ECtHR] as defining what is a reasonable length of pre-trial detention in an international criminal court or tribunal rather than in particular domestic jurisdictions in Europe'.[7]

Given that the presumption of innocence is fundamentally included in the texts of the relevant international courts,[8] what has developed are a series of procedures to allow for request of interim or provisional release by an in-custody defendant.[9] In fact, certain cases have made specific reference to the principle of provisional release in allowing such procedures. The ICTY has held that:

> [T]he rationale behind the institution of detention on remand is to ensure that the accused will be present for his/her trial. Detention on remand does not have a penal character, it is not a punishment as the accused, prior to his conviction, has the benefit of the presumption of innocence. This fundamental principle is enshrined

5 The Right to liberty is enshrined in: Art. 9 International Covenant on Civil and Political Rights; Art. 5 Convention on Human Rights and Fundamental Freedoms (1953) (ECHR); Art. 7 American Convention on Human Rights (1978) (ACHR); Art. 6 African Charter on Human and People's Rights (1986) (ACHPR); the right to be tried within a reasonable time is enshrined in: Art. 9(3) International Covenant on Civil and Political Rights: 'everyone ... shall be entitled to trial within a reasonable time or to release; Art. 5(3) ECHR: 'everyone ... shall be entitled to trial within a reasonable time or to release pending trial'; Art. 7(5) ACHR: 'everyone ... shall be entitled to trial within a reasonable time or to be released without prejudice to the continuation of the proceedings'; the ACHPR does not provide such a right; the presumption of innocence is enshrined in: Art. 14(2) International Covenant on Civil and Political Rights; Art. 6(2) ECHR; Art. 8(2) ACHR; and Art. 7(1)(b) ACHPR, cited in Zeegers 2013.

6 *Stogmuller v. Austria*, ECHR (1969) Appl. No. 1602/62, x 4.

7 *Prosecutor v. Brđanin & Talić*, IT-99-36-PT, Decision on Motion by Radoslav Brđanin for Provisional Release, 25 July 2000, paras. 26–27.

8 See ICC Statute, Article 66(1); ICTR Statute, Article 20(3); ICTY Statute, Article 21(3); SCSL Statute, Article 17(3).

9 See e.g. D. Abels 2012, p. 215 referencing *Prosecutor v. Aleksovski*, IT-95-14/1-T, Trial Chamber, 23 January 1998, para. 3; *Prosecutor v. Sesay, Kallon and Gbao*, SCSL-04-15-AR65, Appeals Chamber, 14 December 2004.

in Article 21, paragraph 3 of the [ICTY] Statute and applies at all stages of the proceeding, including the trial phase.[10]

As there is no guaranteed right to provisional release,[11] interim detention can be justified on a number of grounds. Firstly, it may be considered necessary to ensure the administration of justice, in instances where the defendant might be in a position to interfere with witnesses or evidence.[12] Detention may also be justified in instances where it could curtail the continued commission of offences,[13] and at the ICC the risk of commission of further crimes has been expressly referred to as a consideration.[14] Detention may also be justified, where there is a risk of a suspect absconding, to ensure their appearance at trial.[15] These three standard reasons mirror the jurisprudence of the European Court of Human Rights and many domestic jurisdictions.[16]

3. INTERIM RELEASE AT THE ICC

3.1. THE STANDARD OF REVIEW

Article 60(2) of the Rome Statute sets out the considerations for an accused's application for release. Primarily, this provision refers back to the conditions that have been established in issuance of the original arrest warrant inquiring whether the conditions set out in Article 58(1) continue to apply. If these conditions are met then the person's detention shall continue.[17] Article 58(1) requires the Pre-Trial Chamber to find that there are reasonable grounds to show that a person has committed a crime that falls within the jurisdiction of the Court, *and* that the arrest and detention of that person is necessary *either*:

10 *Prosecutor v. Brđanin & Talić*, IT-99-36-T, Decision on the Motion for Provisional Release of the Accused Momir Talić, 20 September 2002.

11 *Prosecutor v. Norman et al.*, SCSL-04-14-AR65, Appeal against Decision Refusing Bail, 11 March 2005, para. 32.

12 See ICC Rome Statute, Arts. 58(1)(b)(ii), 60(2).

13 See ICC Rome Statute, Arts. 58(1)(b)(iii), 60(2).

14 ICC Rome Statute, Arts. 58(1)(b)(iii).

15 See ICC Rome Statute, Arts. 58(1)(b)(i), 60(2).

16 ECHR, Art. 5(3); see also Trotter 2013, pp. 351–377 citing examples of Criminal Code (Canada) Section 515; Code of Criminal Procedure (Germany) Art. 112(2), (3); Code of Criminal Procedure (France) Art. 144; Criminal Procedure Code of the Russian Federation (Russia) Arts. 97(1), 108(1); Code of Criminal Procedure (Bulgaria) Arts 56–57; Code of Criminal Procedure (Estonia) Arts. 127(1), 130(2); Criminal Procedure Code of the Former Yugoslav Republic of Macedonia (Macedonia) Art. 419(1).

17 Khan 2008, marginal no. 7.

- to ensure their attendance at their trial;
- to ensure that the person does not obstruct or endanger the investigation or the court proceedings; or
- to prevent the person from continuing with the commission of that crime or a related crime.

If the Chamber finds that the above requirements will be protected, it shall release the suspect, with or without conditions.[18] It has been suggested that this is a peculiar arrangement, as if the Prosecutor cannot establish reasonable grounds that a person will either fail to appear at trial, commit further offences, or interfere or obstruct the course of justice, it is not exactly clear why their freedom ought to be inhibited at all.[19] Rather, the Prosecution should have to persuade the Court that the conditions imposed are required for one of the reasons stipulated in Article 58(1).[20] Furthermore, it is proposed that, as a manifestation of the presumption of innocence, the Court should impose as few limitations as possible to 'ensure the interests identified in Article 58(1) are protected', and that the Prosecution should be charged with demonstrating why either detention or release *with conditions* should be imposed.[21]

The real burden, then, is placed on the Prosecution in seeking an arrest warrant rather than a summons. As to what level of review is performed by the Judge in issuing the arrest warrant, it is one that he/she must be incredibly cautious of as it is shown that once the suspect has been transferred to the ICC, the ability to find any change of circumstances from the arrest warrant are slim. Furthermore, the onus of a willing state to host an interim release agreement has made release relatively impossible, owing to a sheer lack of states who have been willing to fulfil these cooperation requests.

---

18 *Ibid*, marginal no. 9.

19 *Ibid*.

20 *Ibid*.

21 *Ibid*, marginal no. 10. Article 59(4) (detention in the custodial state) more clearly constructs a presumption in favour of detention, by making it the default unless there are urgent and exceptional circumstances to justify interim release. However, this language does not appear in Article 60, and it is stated that the Pre-Trial Chamber need only deem that two components are met: the Chamber must be satisfied that there are 'reasonable grounds to believe' that the suspect has committed a crime; and, if it is satisfied of the first requirement, the Chamber must then determine that an arrest is 'necessary'. *Ibid*, marginal no. 8. In relation to Article 60(2), it is possible that the Pre-Trial Chamber could issue a warrant of arrest, pursuant to Article 58(1), and that the person could be arrested by the custodial state, but granted provisional release pending surrender, in accordance with Article 59(4). The relevant person could then be released, or, at least, not detained, whilst awaiting transfer to the ICC. *Ibid*, marginal no. 11.

3.2. THE DECISIONS

3.2.1. *Article 5 Cases*

Mr Jean-Pierre Bemba Gombo was the first person at the ICC who was granted provisional release by a Single Judge. Detained in July 2008, Mr Bemba was granted release on 14 August 2009, but remained in detention due to the lack of a state willing to host him.[22] The implementation of this decision was deferred pending the determination of which state Mr Bemba would be released to and which set of conditions would be imposed. The very same day, the Prosecutor appealed this decision. The appeal was granted suspensive effect.[23] Thereafter, the Appeals Chamber went on to hold that the Single Judge had erred in granting release given the lack of state cooperation, stating that:

> [T]he Pre-Trial Chamber erred in granting conditional release without specifying the appropriate conditions that make conditional release feasible, identifying the State to which Mr Bemba would be released and whether that State would be able to enforce the conditions imposed by the Court.[24]

Thus, the necessity of state cooperation in the matter of release was signalled as a consideration of critical impact to any such application. In fact, Mr Bemba still remains in the custody of the Court awaiting a Trial Judgement. His interim release was never effectuated.

In other cases where conditional release was considered, it was established that state cooperation and assurances are mandatory. Drawing on later Appeals Chamber jurisprudence in *Bemba*, the Single Judge in the *Ntaganda* case held an 'imperative' nature of a state's willingness to host a suspect/accused, recalling: as the Appeals Chamber explicitly stated, 'for conditional release to be granted, "a State willing to accept the person concerned as well as enforce related conditions is necessary".[25] The Court further held that the state needs not only indicate a willingness to host a suspect/accused, but must

---

22 See *Prosecutor v. Bemba*, Decision on the Interim Release of Jean-Pierre Bemba Gombo and Convening Hearings with the Kingdom of Belgium, the Republic of Portugal, the Republic of France, the Federal Republic of Germany, the Italian Republic, and the Republic of South Africa, ICC-01/05-01/08-475, 14 August 2009, para. 90.

23 *Prosecutor v. Bemba*, Decision on the Request of the Prosecutor for Suspensive Effect, ICC-01/05-01/08-499, 3 September 2009.

24 *Prosecutor v. Bemba*, Judgment on the appeal of the Prosecutor against Pre-Trial Chamber II's 'Decision on the Interim Release of Jean-Pierre Bemba Gombo and Convening Hearings with the Kingdom of Belgium, the Republic of Portugal, the Republic of France, the Federal Republic of Germany, the Italian Republic, and the Republic of South Africa', ICC-01/05-01/08-631-Red, 2 December 2009, para. 109.

25 *Prosecutor v. Ntaganda*, Decision on the Defence's Application for Interim Release, ICC-01/04-02/06-147, 18 November 2013, para. 62.

demonstrate its ability to enforce the specific conditions put in place by a Chamber.[26]

Mr Gbagbo has made several applications for conditional release including for medical reasons and to attend his mother's funeral. The Court has recalled that:

> In circumstances where a State has offered to accept a detained person and to enforce conditions, it is incumbent upon the chamber to consider conditional release. On the other hand, where no such proposals for conditional release are presented and none are self-evident, the chamber's discretion to consider conditional release is unfettered.[27]

While the Trial Chamber in the case against Mr Gbagbo did recognise that a defendant can be released 'when compelling humanitarian circumstances justify', they denied any such release as his release ran 'a risk of endangering the populace in Côte d'Ivoire, Court staff and Mr Gbagbo himself'.[28]

3.2.2. *Article 70 Cases*

In November 2013, four individuals (including members of Mr Bemba's Defence team) were arrested on charges pursuant to Article 70. Four of the suspects requested interim release. No less than five states were called upon to submit observations about hosting a specific suspect on provisional release. However, none of them came forward to indicate a willingness to host the suspects.

Nearly a year later, the Single Judge, *motu proprio*, ordered the release of the four suspects – after 11 months spent in detention. The Single Judge held that 'the reasonableness of the duration of the detention has to be balanced inter alia against the statutory penalties applicable to the offences at stake'. In this case, the Appeals Chamber rejected the Prosecution's request for suspensive effect, noting 'that the four suspects are alleged to have committed offences under Article 70 of the Statute, which carry a maximum penalty of five years imprisonment, and that they have already spent several months in pre-trial detention'. Three of the suspects were released on 23 October. However, the fourth suspect had to wait in custody for an additional week pending negotiations with the state to which he would be released regarding his visa.[29]

---

26 *See Prosecutor v. Bemba*, Judgment on the appeal of Mr Jean-Pierre Bemba Gombo against the decision of Trial Chamber III of 27 June 2011 entitled 'Decision on Applications for Provisional Release', ICC-01/05-01/08-1626-Red, 12 September 2011.

27 *Prosecutor v. Gbagbo*, Seventh decision on the review of Mr Laurent Gbagbo's detention pursuant to Article 60(3) of the Statute, ICC-02/11-01/11-718-Red, 11 November 2014, para. 31(h).

28 *Prosecutor v. Gbagbo*, Decision on the urgent request of the Defence for Mr Gbagbo to attend his mother's funeral, ICC-02/11-01/11-711-Red, 29 October 2014, paras. 25–27.

29 Mr Mangenda has also lodged an Article 85 request for compensation for his continued detention in the week following the release decision. *Prosecutor v. Bemba et al.*, Public Redacted Version of Request for Compensation for Unlawful Detention, ICC-01/05-01/13-921-Red, 1 May 2015.

It is notable that prior to releasing the four defendants the Pre-Trial Chamber had sought and received observations from five states – the Netherlands, Belgium, the United Kingdom, France and the Democratic Republic of the Congo.[30] These did not indicate any equivocated willingness to host one of the accused, even those who were their own citizens or nationals. Regardless, the Single Judge held that they could be released to the countries to which they are nationals or where they were residing at the time of arrest.[31]

Ultimately, the Decision went up on appeal to which the Appeals Chamber found error of the Single Judge and remanded the Decision back to the Trial Chamber; the Appeals Chamber held, *inter alia*:

> In these circumstances, the Appeals Chamber concludes that it is not apparent that the Pre-Trial Chamber conducted a proper assessment of the risks justifying detention that are listed in article 58 (1) (b) of the Statute. Moreover, without a proper assessment of the risks, it is unclear on what basis the Pre-Trial Chamber reached its conclusion that the imposition of one condition was sufficient to mitigate those risks. The Pre-Trial Chamber therefore erred in law in its review under article 60 (3) of the Statute.[32]

While these men were not taken back into custody pending the remand, it would seem from this Appeals Chamber Decision that there are still no successful grants of interim release – at least those surviving appellate review – in the history of the ICC.

4. COOPERATION

4.1. INTERIM/CONDITIONAL RELEASE

The agreement between the Government of the Kingdom of Belgium and the ICC on the interim release of detainees on the Belgian territory pursuant to

---

30 *Prosecutor v. Bemba et al.*, Decision requesting observations from States for the purposes of the review of the detention of the suspects pursuant to regulation 51 of the Regulations of the Court, ICC-01/05-01/13-683, 26 September 2014; *Prosecutor v. Bemba et al.*, Transmission of the observations submitted by the Belgian, Dutch, French and British authorities on the 'Decision requesting observations from States for the purpose of the review of the detention of the suspects pursuant to regulation 51 of the Regulations of the Court', ICC-01/05-01/13-691, 10 October 2014; *Prosecutor v. Bemba et al.*, Transmission of the observations submitted by the Congolese authorities on the 'Decision requesting observations from States for the purposes of the review of the detention of the suspects pursuant to regulation 51 of the Regulations of the Court', ICC-01/05-01/13-694, 15 October 2014.

31 *Prosecutor v. Bemba et al.*, Decision ordering the release of Aimé Kilolo Musamba, Jean-Jacques Mangenda Kabongo, Fidéle Babala Wandu and Narcisse Arido, ICC-01/05-01/13-703, 21 October 2014, pp. 5–7.

32 *Prosecutor v. Bemba et al.*, Judgment on the appeals against Pre-Trial Chamber II's decisions regarding interim release in relation to Aimé Kilolo Musamba, Jean-Jacques Mangenda, Fidèle Babala Wandu, and Narcisse Arido and order for reclassification, ICC-01/05-01/13-969, 29 May 2015, para. 55.

decisions of the Chambers of the Court entered in to force on 10 April 2014.[33] Belgium became the first country to agree to temporarily accept detainees of the Court on its territory under conditions established by the competent Chamber.[34] Original contemplation of such appears to have occurred in the *Bemba* case, when in 2011 the Trial Chamber stated that, despite no legal basis under Belgian law for the Court to order 'conditional detention' on Belgian territory, Belgium had left open the possibility that this problem could be solved through a formal agreement between Belgium and the Court regarding provisional release.[35] This agreement regulates the procedure for the interim release of an ICC detainee and formalises the necessary consultations with the Court's Registry with the Belgian authorities. It states that the Belgian authorities will examine the requests of the Courts on the merits of each case.[36]

In the ICC Press Release, the Registrar expressed that:

> This agreement represents a step forward in terms of cooperation with the ICC and we wish to express our gratitude to the Belgian authorities for their support', adding that '[the Court] also hope[s] that this advancement will encourage other States to sign such agreements with the Court.[37]

In this press release, the ICC stated that it relies on the cooperation of states and International Organisations to receive detainees after their interim release, to enforce sentences of imprisonment pronounced by the Court, and to relocate witnesses.[38]

To date, no other state has signed such an agreement with the Court. In instances where a suspect, who is otherwise entitled to release but prevented from so doing because no state will accommodate him/her, it could be asked to what extent state parties could be obliged to host. While there is a general obligation of cooperation on state parties, this is confined to the 'investigation and prosecution of crimes',[39] and it has been suggested that the phrasing of the decision in *Bemba* implies that this responsibility likely does not include acceptance to host a suspect/accused on provisional release.[40]

---

33 ICC Press Release: Belgium and ICC sign agreement on interim release of detainees, ICC-CPI-20140410-PR993, 10 April 2014.

34 *Ibid.*

35 *Prosecutor v. Bemba*, Public Redacted Version of the 'Decision on Applications for Provisional Release' of 27 June 2011, ICC-01/05-01/08-1565-Red, 16 August 2011, para. 39, n. 96.

36 ICC Press Release: Belgium and ICC sign agreement on interim release of detainees, ICC-CPI-20140410-PR993, 10 April 2014.

37 *Ibid.*

38 *Ibid.*

39 ICC Rome Statute, Article 86. See also Article 87(7) regarding consequences of non-compliance with requests for cooperation, cited in Trotter 2013, pp. 351–377.

40 Trotter 2013, p. 368.

However, at the same time, the Court has established that any application for release of a suspect/accused must include the following conditions that are wholly dependent on the availability of a state, including:

- a defendant must indicate the state to which he or she wishes to be released;[41]
- the Chamber must seek 'observations from the host State and from the State to which the person seeks to be released';[42] and
- the state to which a defendant wishes to be released should also be heard on the conditions that should be imposed in such a release order.[43]

Therefore, without agreements in place to signal such willingness, a suspect or accused is often relegated making such requests of his/her country of nationality or merely 'cold-calling' states seeking help. Essentially, it is up to a defendant to 'guess' which states may be supportive of hosting him/her after an interim release and, without the diplomatic channels of the Court as readily at their disposal, find a way to approach these states with these significant requests. This is an extremely narrow window for defendants, some of whom may have been involved in bitter civil wars and may be unable to seek recourse from a home country.

4.2. POST-CONVICTION/ACQUITTAL

It should be noted that the same cooperation issues that govern interim release are applicable to the early release of a convicted person, or to the residence/citizenship of an acquitted person. The latter need is highlighted by the case of Mr Ngudjolo Chui who was in asylum-seekers' custody for nearly five months following his acquittal on 18 December 2012. A Court such as this, founded on principles of fair trials with a presumption of innocence and requirement of findings of guilt beyond reasonable doubt, must be prepared for some acquittals. Just as states are called upon in the Rome Statute to assist in, *inter alia*, the surrender, arrest, and transfer of suspects/accused persons, these same states must assist in processes, as guided by the Chambers, which allow such persons to retain certain liberties until a case against them can be proven. To date, the Rome Statute, whilst imposing an obligation on states to assist in the arrest and investigation of defendants, does not contain a provision for assistance, such as accommodation, of those acquitted of the charges against them or for those who are released after serving their sentence.

---

41 *Prosecutor v. Lubanga*, Order on the application for release, ICC-01/04-01/06-128-tEN, 29 May 2006, citing ICC Regulations of the Court, Regulation 51.

42 *Ibid.*

43 ICC Rules of Procedure and Evidence, Rule 119(3); *Prosecutor v. Bemba*, Judgment on the appeal of Mr Jean-Pierre Bemba Gombo against the decision of Trial Chamber III of 27 June 2011 entitled 'Decision on Applications for Provisional Release', ICC-01/05-01/08-1626-Red, 19 August 2011, para. 55.

The Rome Statute does provide for the right to compensation for unlawful arrest or detention pursuant to its Article 85. Some commentators have suggested that international courts should consider providing compensation for lengthy detentions where the defendant is acquitted, and a strict liability should be imposed in international criminal courts so that acquitted detainees are compensated upon their release, as a matter of policy.[44] Mr Ngudjolo Chui has filed a claim for compensation pursuant to Article 85.[45] As there is not yet a ruling on his request, or any other publicly available jurisprudence on how Article 85 will be interpreted, it remains to be seen how such pleadings will be treated, especially when the request for relief involves a significant amount of money or to directing the action of a state and/or the Court. For example, Mr Ngudjolo Chui requests, *inter alia*, a sum of €906.346 for material and emotional damages, and an order from the Court to its officials to conduct public outreach in the DRC to better explain his case and acquittal, particularly in Bedu Ezekere, where Mr Ngudjolo asserts the Prosecution made comments as to his guilt in the involvement of the attack on Bogoro in February 2003.[46]

5. CONCLUSION

The signing of the provisional release agreement by Belgium was a long-time in the making[47] and serves as a positive development in this area of cooperation. At present, the Rome Statute does not outline specific duties of states with respect to hosting interim release, accepting convicted persons, or granting asylum to those who have been acquitted and require such. However, it cannot be ignored that Article 86 does impart a 'general obligation to cooperate' to the signatory states, at least in principle. Further, those who undertake to see the success of this institution – one that fully respects the rights of persons and the presumption of innocence – must promote the signing of interim release agreements as signed by the Kingdom of Belgium and assist in advancing policies for post-conviction and acquittal asylums. To ignore the reality or outcome of the 'investigations and prosecutions' for any human would be to ignore the very basis of the Rome Statute, which is 'Resolved to guarantee lasting respect for and the enforcement of international justice'.[48] Further, to turn a blind eye to the realities faced by the ICTR in this area of post-judgement – where statehood remains a problem for some of the acquitted persons even today – would deny the ICC the chance

44 Michels 2010, p. 408.
45 *Prosecutor v. Ngudjolo*, Requête en indemnisation sur pied de l'article 85 (1) et (3) du Statut de Rome, ICC-01/04-02/12-290, 14 August 2015.
46 *Ibid.*
47 In 2010, for example, the OPCD put forth draft Memoranda of Understanding on Provisional Release/Acquittal that could serve to foster such discussions and eventual agreements.
48 ICC Rome Statute, Preamble.

to anticipate and learn from issues that have been seen in the dynamics of international criminal proceedings.

Therefore, the ICC is called upon to develop framework agreements or arrangements, or any other means in areas such as interim release, final release, and sentence enforcement which may be essential to ensuring the rights of the suspects/accused as stipulated in Article 67 of the Rome Statute and guaranteeing the rights of convicted persons. The signing of such agreements would be a clear sign by states that they want a Court that is impartial and respectful of the rights of defendants. Further, this would indicate a willingness of cooperation by the states with both prosecution and defence, not only cooperation with the prosecution orders issued by the Chambers, such as arrest warrants or freezing of assets. Such a development would demonstrate the respect for the entirety of the process, which includes a presumption of innocence and the right to a fair trial. For this, it is important to recall that the upheld principle is that of detention being the exception.

BIBLIOGRAPHY

BOOKS AND JOURNAL ARTICLES

Abels 2012

Abels, D., 'Prisoners of the international community: The legal position of persons detained at International Criminal Tribunals', TMC Asser Press, 2012.

Khan 2008

Khan, K., 'Investigation and Prosecution: Initial Proceedings Before the Court - Article 60 (2)', in O. Triffterer (ed.), 'Commentary on the Rome Statute of the International Criminal Court', 2nd ed., Beck/Hart, 2008.

Michels 2010

Michels, J.D., 'Compensating Acquitted Defendants for Detention Before International Criminal Courts', Journal of International Criminal Justice, 2010.

Trotter 2013

Trotter, A., 'Pre-Conviction Detention in International Criminal Trials', 11(2) Journal of International Criminal Justice, 2013.

Zeegers 2013

Zeegers, K., 'Provisional Release Before the Ad Hoc Tribunals', Amsterdam Center for International Law of the University of Amsterdam, 2013.

JURISPRUDENCE

ECtHR 2001

ECtHR, Ilijkov v. Bulgaria, Application no. 33977/96, 26 July 2001.

ECtHR 1969

ECtHR, Stogmuller v. Austria, Application no. 1602/62, 10 November 1969.

HRC 1997
HRC, Hill and Hill v. Spain, Communication 526/1993, 23 June 1997.
IACtHR 2005
IACtHR, Acosta-Calderón v. Ecuador, (Ser. C) No. 129, 24 June 2005.
IACtHR 2004
IACtHR, Tibi v. Ecuador, (Ser. C) No. 114, 7 September 2004.
IACtHR 2004
IACtHR, Children's Rehabilitation v. Paraguay, (Ser. C) No. 112, 2 September 2004.
ICC 2015
ICC, Prosecutor v. Ngudjolo, ICC-01/04-02/12-290, 14 August 2015.
ICC 2015
ICC, Prosecutor v. Bemba et al., ICC-01/05-01/13-969, 29 May 2015.
ICC 2015
ICC, Prosecutor v. Bemba et al., ICC-01/05-01/13-921-Red, 1 May 2015.
ICC 2015
ICC, Prosecutor v. Ngudjolo, ICC-01/04-02/12-273, 26 March 2015.
ICC 2014
ICC, Prosecutor v. Gbagbo, ICC-02/11-01/11-718-Red, 11 November 2014.
ICC 2014
ICC, Prosecutor v. Gbagbo, ICC-02/11-01/11-711-Red, 29 October 2014.
ICC 2014
ICC, Prosecutor v. Bemba et al., ICC-01/05-01/13-703, 21 October 2014.
ICC 2014
ICC, Prosecutor v. Bemba et al., ICC-01/05-01/13-694, 15 October 2014.
ICC 2014
ICC, Prosecutor v. Bemba et al., ICC-01/05-01/13-691, 10 October 2014.
ICC 2014
ICC, Prosecutor v. Bemba et al., ICC-01/05-01/13-683, 26 September 2014.
ICC 2013
ICC, Prosecutor v. Bemba, ICC-01/04-02/06-147, 18 November 2013.
ICC 2011
ICC, Prosecutor v. Bemba, ICC-01/05-01/08-1626-Red, 12 September 2011.
ICC 2011
ICC, Prosecutor v. Bemba, ICC-01/05-01/08-1626-Red, 19 August 2011.
ICC 2011
ICC, Prosecutor v. Bemba, ICC-01/05-01/08-1565-Red, 16 August 2011.
ICC 2009
ICC, Prosecutor v. Jean-Pierre Bemba Gumbo, ICC-01/05-01/08-631-Red, 2 December 2009.
ICC 2009
ICC, Prosecutor v. Bemba, ICC-01/05-01/08-499, 3 September 2009.
ICC 2009
ICC, Prosecutor v. Bemba, ICC-01/05-01/08-475, 14 August 2009.
ICC 2006
ICC, Prosecutor v. Lubanga, ICC-01/04-01/06-128-tEN, 29 May 2006.

ICTY 2002
ICTY, Prosecutor v. Brđanin & Talić, IT-99-36-T, 20 September 2002.
ICTY 2000
ICTY, Prosecutor v. Brđanin & Talić, IT-99-36-PT, 25 July 2000.
ICTY 1998
ICTY, Prosecutor v. Aleksovski, IT-95-14/1-T, 23 January 1998.
SCSL 2005
SCSL, Prosecutor v. Norman et al., SCSL-04-14-AR65, 11 March 2005.
SCSL 2004
SCSL, Prosecutor v. Sesay, Kallon and Gbao, SCSL-04-15-AR65, 14 December 2004.

TREATIES, LEGISLATION AND AGREEMENTS

African (Banjul) Charter on Human and Peoples' Rights, OAU Doc. CAB/LEG/67/3 rev. 5, 27 June 1981.
American Convention on Human Rights 'Pact of San Jose, Costa Rica' (B-32), 22 November 1969.
European Convention on Human Rights, 4 November 1950.
International Covenant on Civil and Political Rights, GA Res. 2200A (XXI), 16 December 1966.
International Criminal Court Rules of Procedure and Evidence, ICC-ASP/1/3 (Part II-A), 9 September 2002.
Rome Statute of the International Criminal Court, 2187 UNTS 90/37, 17 July 1998.
Statute of the International Criminal Tribunal for Rwanda, SC Res. 955, 8 November 1994.
Statute of the Special Court for Sierra Leone, SC Res. 1315, 16 January 2002.
Statute of the International Criminal Tribunal for the former Yugoslavia, SC Res. 827, 25 May 1993.

OTHERS

Council of Europe, Recommendation on the use of remand in custody, 27 September 2006.
ICC Press Release, 'Belgium and ICC sign agreement on interim release of detainees', ICC-CPI-20140410-PR993, 10 April 2014.
ICC Regulations of the Court, Regulation 51 (Decision on Interim Release), ICC-BD/01-01-04, 26 May 2004.
Office of Public Counsel for the Defence (OPCD), Draft Memorandum of Understanding on Provisional Release/Acquittal.

TOWARDS A MULTI-LAYERED SYSTEM OF INTERNATIONAL CRIMINAL JUSTICE

Mia SWART*

1. INTRODUCTION

In the ongoing heated debates on the tension between Africa and the International Criminal Court (ICC) it is easy to lose sight of what is most fundamental: the ICC was established to prosecute the most serious international crimes. The court had to fulfil the enormous expectation of fighting impunity on a global scale. Whereas it is clear that international criminal law lies on the fault-line of law and politics, the *legal* should still prevail and the court should, first and foremost fulfil its independent legal mandate. The tensions between the African Union (AU) and the ICC have however taken centre stage in the way the court has been perceived. The debates on the ICC have become almost entirely political. It will be argued here that, whereas it is impossible to separate law and politics entirely, the court should not be diverted from its primary purpose and mandate. It will further be argued that the work of the ICC is not the preserve of the ICC alone and can feasibly be shared by domestic, sub-regional and regional courts. Although prosecution in these fora are still hampered by significant constraints, recent jurisprudence from Southern Africa shows that the potential exists for an effective multi-layered international criminal justice system.

The tension between the AU and the ICC has been simmering for many years. The tension intensified when the politically powerful in Africa were targeted for investigations. This is clearly illustrated by the fact that the relationship between the AU and the ICC started to deteriorate dramatically when the ICC issued an indictment to arrest the Sudanese President Al-Bashir in 2008. The issue of Head of State immunity has become the main point of contention between the two sides. Some believe the adversarial stance has been channelled through,

* With thanks to Deborah Mutemwa for research assistance.

and encouraged by, the African Union.[1] In 2013 the African Union asked its members to implement a policy of non-compliance and non-cooperation with the ICC.[2] Although African states have not formally adopted such a policy, the non-cooperation of the Kenyan government illustrates the power of the African Union's strategy.

This article will consider two alternatives to the ICC route of addressing international crimes that may be suitable for the African context and beyond. Such alternatives could assist in giving African countries a sense of ownership over their problems in the field of international criminal justice. The first alternative consists of national prosecutions of international crimes. The second is resorting to a regional African court with the mandate to adjudicate international crimes. These solutions should not merely be seen as alternatives to the ICC route of achieving justice but, in the spirit of the principle of complementarity, can complement and supplement the court's work.

The article will start by examining the mutual dependency that exists between the ICC and Africa. The question of how this relationship impacts on the legitimacy of the ICC will briefly be considered. The article will then focus on attempts of southern African states, in particular the states that belong to the Southern African Development Community (SADC) to prosecute foreign high-level state officials for international crimes.

The article will analyse three cases which form part of a package of cases that could provide hope for the successful prosecution of international crimes in Southern Africa. Two of the cases, the *Campbell*[3] and *Fick*[4] cases, were heard by the tribunal of the Southern African Development Community. The third case, the so-called *Zimbabwe Torture Docket Case*,[5] was a ground-breaking case heard by the Constitutional Court of South Africa that involved the prosecution of Zimbabwean officials for torture committed in Zimbabwe. This case represents the first successful attempt of South African courts to implement the Implementation of the Rome Statute Act extraterritorially. The positive development in the *Zimbabwe Torture Docket Case* was however followed by more negative developments in South Africa when the South African government refused to honour an arrest warrant for Sudanese President Omar Al-Bashir.

---

1 See Global Justice, 'Civil Society Defends ICC at African Union Summit', 25 March 2014, available at: http://ciccglobaljustice.wordpress.com/2014/03/25/civil-society-defends-icc-at-african-union-summit/.

2 Mbaku 2014.

3 *Mike Campbell (Pty) Ltd and Others v. Republic of Zimbabwe*, Case No. 2 of 2007.

4 *Fick and Others v. Government of the Republic of Zimbabwe*, Case No. 77880/2009, North Gauteng High Court, Pretoria, 13 January 2010, unreported.

5 *Southern African Litigation Centre and Another v. National Director of Public Prosecutions and Others* [2012].

Much of the dispute between the AU and the ICC revolved around the question of immunity. The sticking point of immunity can be viewed as part of a broader political backlash to the perceived double standards of the Court in selecting individuals for indictment. This is also indicated by the resurgence in Pan-Africanist rhetoric, emphasising the need to find 'African solutions to African problems' instead of turning to foreign institutions, which have so far yielded unsatisfactory results.

It is clear that disrespect for the principle of the irrelevance of official capacity for Heads of State (former or sitting) can do tremendous damage to the Rome Statute system. Although the question of immunity for Heads of State and senior government officials lays at the heart of the dispute, this article will not focus on the question of immunity since this issue has already been extensively discussed elsewhere.[6] The focus will be on the appropriate fora for prosecuting international crimes in Africa. The initiatives in Uganda and Senegal will be briefly discussed in this regard.

The article concludes with some remarks on the proposed expansion of the jurisdiction of the African Court of Justice and Human Rights and the feasibility of such a court succeeding in conducting successful prosecutions.

2. MUTUAL DEPENDENCY AND LEGITIMACY

The relationship between Africa and the International Criminal Court is a relationship of mutual dependency. The relationship is also a complex one. Simply put, Africa needs the ICC and the ICC needs Africa. For many African states, membership of the ICC presented an opportunity to show that they are part of the international community and share the values of the international community, most importantly ending impunity for international crimes. At the same time, the ICC was always in danger of eliciting the same criticism that other international courts, such as the ad hoc international criminal tribunals, elicited[7], namely that they are products of Western power politics and Western thinking and, by extension, neo-colonialist. Various African statesmen have commented that the ICC is a hegemonic tool of the West.[8] African countries further felt that their sovereignty was threatened by the court. For the first time

6 See for example Gaeta 2009; Tladi 2015; Swart and Krisch 2014.

7 See for example Chatham House Discussion Paper, 'The International Criminal Court-Taking Stock', 2008.

8 Ethiopia's Prime Minister Hailemariam Desalegn, stated for example that the decision of the AU to lambast the ICC was borne from the fact that: 'African leaders came to a consensus that the ICC process conducted in Africa has a flaw … [T]he process has degenerated to some kind of race-hunting rather than the fight against impunity'. See Dersso, 'The International Criminal Court's Africa problem', *Al Jazeera*, 2013, available at: www.aljazeera.com/indepth/opinion/2013/06/201369851918549.html (accessed 11 June 2013).

in history, African states delegated to the court and its independent prosecutor the ability to investigate, arrest, prosecute, and punish international crimes that would traditionally fall in the domain of domestic sovereignty.

When the ICC was created in 2002 it represented the fulfilment of the dream of creating an international criminal court that symbolised the shared intention of the international community to prosecute the gravest of crimes. When African states threatened to collectively withdraw from the ICC in 2013, the question arose: can the ICC survive without Africa? It is clear that the ICC needs Africa. The legitimacy of the ICC depends on the court being geographically representative.[9] The court needs to show that it is indeed not just an instrument of the West or developed countries but that it can at least make some claim to universality. The fact that almost two-thirds of states on the African continent ratified the Rome Statute was a great achievement for the court. With 34 ratifications, Africa remains the most represented region in the Assembly of States Parties.[10] What was particularly surprising and encouraging was the fact that the ICC Statute was widely ratified by many states that had an unsavoury human rights record.[11]

However, the court further needs Africa since Africa is the site of many international crimes and the continent suffers from large-scale impunity. As David Bosco stated in the context of the possible withdrawal of African states from the ICC, '[i]t would be a really dramatic step. In many ways, it would put the whole ICC project into jeopardy.'[12]

The legitimacy argument is circular. The ICC needs Africa to bolster the court's legitimacy, and Africa is more likely to participate in a legitimate court. Legitimacy in this context can be understood as justification for the exercise of authority.[13] Like many international courts and institutions, the ICC lacks democratic legitimacy. As Marston Danner writes, international institutions, almost by definition, have to rely on alternative bases for legitimacy.[14] As suggested, geographical representation can lend legitimacy to an international body. The fact that the ICC is based on voluntary participation certainly lends legitimacy to the court. The court's predecessors, the International Criminal Tribunals for Yugoslavia and Rwanda, were established by Security Council resolutions,[15] which meant that states were bound to cooperate with the court.

---

9 See Danner 2003.

10 Website of the ICC available at: www.icccpi.int/en_menus/asp/states%20parties/Pages/the%20states%20parties%20to%20the%20rome%20statute.aspx.

11 Yvonne Dutton writes that 'bad States' may either commit to a regime such as the ICC for noble self-improvement reasons or because such states were pressurised by powerful states or NGOs. See Dutton 2013.

12 See http://thinkprogress.org/security/2013/09/20/2657051/african-union-icc/.

13 Bodansky 1999.

14 Danner 2003, p. 535.

15 The ICTY was established by Security Council Resolution 827. The ICTR was established by SC Resolution 995, 8 November 1994.

The voluntary nature of ICC membership gives states unintended power: the power to withdraw from the Court.

Only a dozen years after it started its work, the ICC is experiencing a crisis of legitimacy.[16] The dropping of charges against Uhuru Kenyatta only compounds the problems created by the ongoing dispute over what Geoffrey Dancy describes as the ICC's 'geography of justice.' African state officials who participated at a 2014 'high-level seminar meeting' in Addis Ababa issued a number of incendiary statements about the Court, arguing that 'the ICC has become the greatest threat to Africa's sovereignty, peace and stability', and that 'the ICC is a colonial institution under the guise of international justice.'[17] Dancy writes that these claims are perhaps evidence of a greater concern: international courts face terrific obstacles in building 'diffuse support' because global judicial institutions, compared to national courts, have to appeal to a much wider and more diverse audience.[18] The ICC must please many masters, very few of whom are going to be satisfied with its activities.

Another challenge to the legitimacy of the ICC comes from scholars, who have produced a number of articles that are highly critical of ICC action. For example, conflict experts blame untimely ICC indictments against perpetrators of rights violations like Ugandan rebel leader Joseph Kony and Sudan's President Omar Al-Bashir for ruining peace negotiations that might have ended civil wars.[19] Some even surmise that Libyan President Muammar Gaddafi may have accepted exile were it not for his indictment by the ICC on 26 February 2011; instead, he dug in his heels and fought a bloody war against rebels.[20] Critics also claim that the ICC lacks deterrent abilities, which could mean that its decisions will not advance the effort to promote peace or prevent violations of international human rights and humanitarian law.[21]

From early in the life of the court, the ICC has treated Africa as if it is the only site of impunity. The fact that all thirty-two of the court's indictees have been African has understandably caused outrage. The tension between the ICC and African states has obstructed the work of the ICC. This was most clearly illustrated in the Kenyan case.[22] The Kenyan government's resistance to cooperating with the ICC meant that the Prosecutor had to withdraw the charges. The ongoing tension between the AU and ICC has also given rise to the search for alternatives to a forum such as the ICC. Even if African states remain part of the ICC project, in light of the lateness of justice achieved by the ICC (only four cases have been completed in 12 years), African states need to search

16 Dancy, 'Sections from 'Unintended Positive Complementarity', Post-Conflict Justice.
17 Fabricius, 'Geography of Justice riles Africa', *Cape Times*, 10 April 2014.
18 Dancy, 'Sections from 'Unintended Positive Complementarity', Post-Conflict Justice.
19 See for example Branch 2007, pp. 179–198.
20 Diehl, 'After the Dictators Fall', *Washington Post*, 5 June 2011.
21 See for example Cronin-Furman 2013.
22 *The Prosecutor v. Uhuru Muigai Kenyatta*, ICC 01/09–02/11.

for alternative ways of prosecuting international crimes. One reason for this is that the doctrine of complementarity applies to states regardless of whether a state ratified the Rome Statute. This is in line with the notion of complementarity as a 'big idea'.[23] Complementarity can be severed from the admissibility context of the ICC and can be interpreted as requiring states to take the initiative to investigate or prosecute international crimes. This means that even if African states withdraw from the ICC they cannot withdraw from their responsibilities under complementarity if they want to be perceived as responsible and 'full' members of the international community.

Having described some of the crucial reasons why the relationship between Africa and the ICC is of crucial importance to the legitimacy of the court, one can ask: what avenues exist for states to fight impunity outside the framework of the ICC? One potentially powerful alternative would be prosecuting those accused of international crimes in African domestic courts. This is not an avenue that has often been pursued in Africa. Very recently, however, there has been a flickering of hope in this regard.

On 30 October 2014, the Constitutional Court of South Africa issued a landmark decision on the duty of the South African Police Services to investigate the allegations of international crimes committed by foreign officials in Zimbabwe.[24] This judgment constitutes an unprecedented move on the African continent to apply principles in the fight against impunity for international crimes, and has been welcomed by many commentators as a significant step towards ending impunity.

This case has been described as representing a beacon of hope for the continent and a great example of how the Rome Statute and the International Criminal Court can serve as powerful tools in combating, and possibly bringing to justice, perpetrators of international crimes. This raises some interesting questions in relation to the application of principles such as complementarity, universal jurisdiction, and sovereign immunity. It also brings to light a host of other considerations in relation to the geopolitical landscape, including considerations that arise in light of recent developments in the relationship between the African Union and the International Criminal Court.

3. A PACKAGE OF CASES: CAMPBELL, FICK, AND ZIMBABWE TORTURE DOCKET CASE

The *Zimbabwe Torture Docket Case* represents the most exciting recent example of a domestic African court exercising extraterritorial jurisdiction under its domestic legislation and implementing the Rome Statute. To understand the

23 Nouwen 2013.

24 *National Commissioner of The South African Police Service v. Southern African Human Rights Litigation Centre and Another*, CCT 02/14 [2014] ZACC 30.

Zimbabwe Torture Docket Case, it is vital to understand the prior attempts that were made by the Southern African sub-regional court, the Southern African Development Community (SADC) Tribunal, as well as South African domestic courts, to hold Zimbabwe accountable for gross human rights violations such as torture.

Oppong observes that the *Campbell* case was possibly the most controversial case to be decided by a regional economic community in Africa.[25] In *Campbell*, the SADC Tribunal confronted the question of land redistribution and so-called 'land grabs' in Zimbabwe.[26] The subsequent *Fick* case was concerned with enforcing the decision made by the SADC Tribunal in the *Campbell* case. In *Fick*, Constitutional Court of South Africa dealt a blow to the Zimbabwean government when it unanimously ruled that property owned by the Zimbabwean government in South Africa could be sold to defray legal expenses in a human rights case.

The *Campbell*, *Fick*, and *Torture Docket* cases can be described as a package of cases. All three of these cases represented attempts to hold the Zimbabwean government accountable. In all three cases, the judges took innovative and activist decisions. These cases represent a step forward for prosecutions of international crimes in Southern Africa. It shows that the judiciary is willing to take their obligations under domestic, regional, and international law seriously.

3.1. THE *CAMPBELL* CASE

In essence, the *Campbell* case concerned 79 white Zimbabwean commercial farmers who took the Zimbabwean government to the SADC Tribunal to stop the compulsory acquisition of their farms by the Mugabe government. Such acquisition is colloquially referred to as 'land-grabbing'.[27]

The government of Zimbabwe, despite being a member of SADC, amended its Constitution to cater for compulsory acquisition by the state of all agricultural land identified by the State's acquiring authority – without compensation. Because of the lack of domestic remedies afforded to the farmers affected by this, the agrarian reform policy was challenged before the SADC Tribunal.

The first applicant, Mike Campbell, filed his case in October 2007 contesting the seizure of his mango and citrus farm by the government.[28] In 2008, Campbell and members of his family were allegedly tortured for nine hours by the ruling Zimbabwe African National Union Patriotic Front (ZANU-PF), and

---

25 Oppong 2010.

26 Swart 2013.

27 See the description available at: www.hrw.org/news/2011/08/11/sadc-qa-tribunal.

28 *Mike Campbell (Pty) Ltd and Others v. Republic of Zimbabwe*, Case No. 2 of 2007. Campbell simultaneously asked for interim measures to protect him and his property. The SADC Tribunal granted the interim measures in a decision on 13 December 2007.

he eventually died from the injuries he sustained. He contended that the seizure was illegal and racist and that it violated the SADC Treaty.[29] He approached the Tribunal after having exhausted all domestic remedies. The Zimbabwean Supreme Court made an unfavourable ruling against him in January 2008. The Court came to the conclusion that the compulsory acquisition of farmland in Zimbabwe did not constitute 'racial discrimination' as the text of applicable law made no reference to race or colour.[30]

The SADC Tribunal assumed jurisdiction over the case. The Tribunal stated that the basis for assuming jurisdiction was that the dispute concerned human rights, democracy, and the rule of law, which are binding principles for members of SADC.[31] This corresponded with substantive provisions invoked by the applicant which were found in Article 4 (headed 'Principles') in the SADC Treaty.[32] In its final decision, the Tribunal also referred to Article 6 of the Treaty, which states that member states shall not discriminate on the grounds of race or political views, among others.[33] The Tribunal interpreted Article 4 as importing the right to property into the SADC Treaty since they considered it a natural element of 'human rights, democracy, and the rule of law' as referred to in Article 4 of the Treaty.[34] This 'human rights role' was not explicitly stated in the SADC Treaty or the Protocol establishing the Tribunal. In its final judgment, the Tribunal made references to the Statutes and Decisions of other regional human rights courts as well as international human rights instruments.[35]

As was expected, Zimbabwe disputed the Tribunal's interpretation of the SADC Treaty. Zimbabwe argued that the SADC Treaty 'only sets out the principles and objectives of SADC. It does not set out the standards against which actions of Member States can be assessed.' Since there was no implementing Protocol with regard to Article 4 of the SADC Treaty, Zimbabwe regarded the statement of the SADC Tribunal that it had jurisdiction to hear a case that involved human rights violations as *ultra vires*.[36]

---

29 *Ibid*, at IV.

30 Supreme Court of Zimbabwe, *Mike Campbell (Pty) Ltd and Another v. Minister of National Security Responsible for Land, Land Reform and Resettlement*,124/060 [2008] ZWSC 1, 22 January 2008; decision made by the Southern African Legal Information Institute, available at: www.saflii.org/zw/cases//ZWSc/2008/1.html.

31 *Ibid* at IV.

32 Article 4(c) states that SADC and its member states shall act in accordance with the following principles: human rights, democracy and the rule of law.

33 Article 6(2).

34 See the discussion by Ziegler 2011, p. 8.

35 The Tribunal referred *inter alia* to Article 26 of the European Convention on Human rights and Article 50 of the African Charter. With regard to the prohibition of discrimination on the ground of race the Tribunal referred to Article 1(2) of the UN Charter, Article 2 of the UN Declaration of Human Rights and Article 2(1) of the International Covenant on Economic, Social and Cultural Rights and the Convention on the Elimination of all Forms of Racial Discrimination. See Main Decision of 28 November 2008 in *Mike Campbell (Pty) Ltd and Others v. Republic of Zimbabwe*, Case No. 2 of 2007, p. 17 ff.

36 *Ibid*.

The Tribunal held that according to Article 21(b) of the Protocol of the Tribunal and the Rules of Procedure thereof, it was enjoined to develop its jurisprudence and also to do so 'having regard to applicable treaties, general principles and rules of public international law'.[37] The Tribunal held that it can 'look elsewhere' to find answers when the Treaty is silent.[38]The Tribunal concluded that the applicants 'have been deprived of their lands without having the right to access to the courts and the right to a fair hearing, which are essential elements of the rule of law', and that, accordingly, Article 4(c) of the SADC treaty had been breached.[39]

Subsequent to the SADC Tribunal's ruling in Mike Campbell's favour, the Zimbabwean government refused to enforce the ruling. The Zimbabwean government subsequently challenged the validity of the Tribunal.[40]

The controversy triggered by the *Campbell* case led to the suspension of the SADC Tribunal. The SADC summit announced in 2012 that a protocol for a new tribunal would be negotiated and its jurisdiction would be limited to the adjudication of disputes between member states. The decision made in 2012 to shut down the SADC Tribunal raised a fundamental question as to whether the decisions of the SADC Tribunal were binding and enforceable, since the SADC Tribunal was the only avenue to access justice for many Zimbabweans and individuals from other countries whose domestic justice system failed them.

As a result of the *Campbell* decision, Zimbabwe was ordered to protect the ownership, occupation, and possession rights of the farmers who had not yet been evicted, and to compensate those who had been.[41] This was met with a complete lack of compliance from Zimbabwe, which was then referred back to the Tribunal by the farmers.

3.2. THE *FICK* CASE

The *Fick* case involved the enforceability of the decisions of the SADC Tribunal according to the terms of its Protocol, which was binding on South Africa by way of the SADC Treaty. It was the first time the Constitutional Court was confronted with the question of the status of an international decision by a domestic court.[42]

The North Gauteng High Court was approached. Zimbabwe argued that it was immune from the jurisdiction of civil courts in South Africa. In a

37 *Ibid*, p. 25.
38 *Ibid.*
39 *Ibid*, p. 24.
40 Danner 2003.
41 *National Commissioner of The South African Police Service v. Southern African Human Rights Litigation Centre and Another*, CCT 02/14 [2014] ZACC 30 at 14.
42 De Wet 2014.

progressive judgment, the High Court considered that the Immunity Act must be interpreted to promote the spirit, purport, and objects of the Bill of Rights, and that it is required to consider international law in terms of section 39(1)(b) of the Constitution. The Court stated that the old doctrine of absolute immunity had yielded to a restrictive doctrine, including in relation to human rights issues, but the Court did not elaborate on the significance of this for the present case. The Court found that section 3(2) of the Immunity Act provides for a waiver of immunity 'by prior written agreement', and that a treaty is indeed an agreement.

Tuchten AJ subsequently made a service order against Zimbabwe,[43] and a registration order,[44] which then led to the authorisation of the attachment and sale of certain Zimbabwean-owned properties in Cape Town in execution of the costs order made by the Tribunal. This progressive judgment set the tone for the subsequent litigation.

The decision of the High Court was challenged by Zimbabwe in the Supreme Court of Appeal (SCA). The service order was challenged on the basis of Zimbabwe's immunity from civil prosecution in South Africa.[45] The registration order was challenged on the basis that the Tribunal did not have jurisdiction over land reform policy, and that the High Court did not have jurisdiction to enforce the costs order because the Treaty and Tribunal Protocol had not been approved by the South African Parliament.

The SCA found that Zimbabwe had waived its purported immunity by becoming a party to the Treaty, and that the Amending Agreement was adopted by the prescribed majority.[46] In effect, the Tribunal's jurisdiction over the matter was held to be sufficient for South Africa to enforce its costs order. The SCA stated that South Africa's common law on the enforcement of foreign judgments also applied to international tribunals, and as such the costs order was enforceable. The decision was challenged in the Constitutional Court.

When the Constitutional Court found that all of the requirements for the recognition of a foreign judgment (the definition of which the Court extended to include international tribunals) had been met, Zimbabwe further argued that it enjoys immunity from civil suits in South Africa under section 2 of the Immunities Act.

The Constitutional Court, however, found that Zimbabwe has waived its immunity under the Act. It pointed to Article 32 of the Tribunal Protocol (to which Zimbabwe had agreed to be bound) that obliges member states to facilitate the enforcement of judgments of the Tribunal, and that decisions of the Tribunal are binding and enforceable 'within the Territories of the States concerned'.

---

43 *Fick and Others v. Government of the Republic of Zimbabwe*, Case No. 77880/2009, North Gauteng High Court, Pretoria, 13 January 2010, unreported.

44 *Fick and Others v. Government of the Republic of Zimbabwe*, Case No. 77881/2009, North Gauteng High Court, Pretoria, 25 February 2010, unreported.

45 In terms of the Foreign States Immunities Act 87 of 1981.

46 *Government of the Republic of Zimbabwe v. Fick and Others*, 2012 ZASCA 122 at 40.

The Constitutional Court emphasised that South Africa, in accordance with section 231 of the Constitution (which regulates the ratification of treaties), had become a party to those SADC instruments, which obliged the country to give effect to decisions of the SADC Tribunal.

In a majority judgment, written by Mogoeng Mogoeng CJ, the Constitutional Court developed the common law on the enforcement of foreign judgments and orders to apply to those of the Tribunal. The majority held that the High Court correctly ordered that the costs order be enforced in South Africa.

A central question was whether the common law allowed for the enforcement of an international Tribunal as a 'foreign judgment or order'.[47] In consideration of this, the Court affirmed that they do not provide for South African enforcement of the decisions of the Tribunal; as such, the common law would need to be developed accordingly.[48]

The Constitutional Court went on to develop the common law in a significant manner, finding that:

> [T]he basis for objecting to the jurisdiction of a foreign court or tribunal whose order is sought to be enforced in a South African court must, in my view, be materially similar to the objections previously raised before the foreign court or tribunal that made the order to be enforced. Otherwise the objection should be dismissed.[49]

The common law requirements for the enforcement of a foreign judgment were thus met, and the domestic South African courts were deemed to have the necessary jurisdiction to register the costs order of the Tribunal. The Constitutional Court dismissed the appeal with costs.

The fact that the SADC Tribunal was binding on South Africa and included the obligation to 'take forthwith all measures necessary to ensure execution of decisions of the Tribunal',[50] when considered in light of the constitutional right to access to courts,[51] was crucial to the court's decision that the spirit, purport, and object of the Bill of Rights required the common law to be developed in this manner.

It is commendable that the Constitutional Court of South Africa took sub-regional jurisprudence seriously enough to develop its common law to allow for the implementation of such decisions. The conclusions in *Fick* will also apply to the jurisprudence of other sub-regional courts in Africa, such as the ECOWAS Court of Justice and East African Court of Justice (EACJ). Whereas the EACJ

47 *National Commissioner of The South African Police Service v. Southern African Human Rights Litigation Centre and Another*, CCT 02/14 [2014] ZACC 30 at 54.
48 *Ibid*, at 53.
49 *Ibid*, at 44.
50 *Ibid*, at 59.
51 Section 34 of the Constitution of the Republic of South Africa 1996.

has only issued a handful of cases, the ECOWAS Court of Justice is a particularly active and productive court.[52]

The significance of the *Fick* case reaches far beyond the narrow legal question of whether decisions of the SADC Tribunal can be enforced in South Africa. It highlights the question of the enforcement of international decisions in domestic courts as well as the status of such decisions in domestic courts. Whereas SADC states currently have regimes for enforcing judgments from foreign national courts, they do not have regimes for enforcing judgments of international courts.[53] It is crucial that the progressive decisions issued by sub-regional and regional human rights courts should not merely have symbolic value, but should also be enforceable in domestic courts in Africa. By elevating the status of foreign decisions in South Africa, the *Fick* decision can potentially have exciting consequences. It can open the door for the recognition of foreign decisions in South African Courts.

The legal team in the *Fick* case, led by Jeremy Gauntlett SC, is currently challenging before the African Commission (as a means of access to the African Court at Arusha) the decision by SADC Heads of State to suspend access by individuals to the SADC Tribunal.

3.3. THE *ZIMBABWE TORTURE DOCKET* CASE

The genesis of the *Torture Docket* case was a docket submitted by the Southern Africa Litigation Centre (SALC) to the Priority Crimes Litigation Unit of the National Prosecuting Authority (NPA) of South Africa on 14 March 2008. The docket contained evidence of acts of torture committed in Zimbabwe following a raid on Harvest House – the headquarters of the opposition Movement for Democratic Change – on 28 March 2007. The docket further alleged that the torture was *systematic* and took place as part of *an attack against the civilian population, pursuant to a State policy.* This elevated the torture to the level of crimes against humanity. The docket named senior security and government officials that allegedly bore individual criminal responsibility for these crimes under the doctrine of command responsibility. According to the docket, these individuals regularly visited South Africa on both official and personal business. On this basis, SALC requested the authorities investigate, and if necessary prosecute, the crimes under section 4 of the Rome Statute Act, on the basis of universal jurisdiction.

More than a year later, in June 2009, the Acting National Director of Public Prosecutions informed SALC that it did not intend to investigate the alleged crimes. In light of this, SALC applied to the North Gauteng High Court for an order setting aside the decision not to investigate. SALC argued that the National Prosecuting Authority and the South African Police Services had a duty to

---

52 See Alter et al. 2013, pp. 737–779.

53 De Wet 2014; *cf* Article 32(1) of the Protocol on the SADC Tribunal.

investigate under the Implementation of the Rome Statute of the International Criminal Court and South Africa's international law obligations. The High Court granted the order. The National Commissioner of the South African Police Services and the Acting National Director of Public Prosecutions appealed to the SCA, which held that under the ICC Act, the South African Police Service Act, and the Constitution of the Republic of South Africa, the South African Police Services had a duty to investigate the allegations of torture.

The National Commissioner of the South African Police Services subsequently approached the Constitutional Court for leave to appeal against the Supreme Court of Appeal's decision. In 2014, the Constitutional Court granted the leave to appeal but dismissed the appeal. In a unanimous judgment, the Court concluded that the South African Police Services must investigate. It reasoned that they had a duty to do so under the Constitution, the ICC Act, and South Africa's international law obligations (in this regard the court made reference to the principle of universal jurisdiction and a number of international crimes, including those which exist even in the absence of binding international treaty law). The court further concluded that SAPS has a duty to investigate if Zimbabwe was either unwilling or unable to investigate and if, based on the facts and circumstances of the particular case, an investigation would be reasonable and practicable.

The court's explanation of why states should be able to conduct such investigations:

> This approach is to be followed for several valid reasons. Requiring presence for an investigation would render nugatory the object of combating crimes against humanity. If a suspect were to enter and remain briefly in the territory of a State party, without a certain level of prior investigation, it would not be practicable to initiate charges and prosecution. An anticipatory investigation does not violate fair trial rights of the suspect or accused person.[54]

The Court then proceeded to hold that SAPS not only had the right to open a universal-jurisdiction investigation into torture in Zimbabwe, it had an *obligation* to do so – a remarkable position for the Court to take.[55] The Court, however, imposed two limitations on that obligation. The first limitation is that the territorial state must have failed to prosecute the international crimes in question. The Court stated:

> This limitation arises from the principle of subsidiarity … [T]he principle of non-intervention in the affairs of another country must be observed; investigating

54 *National Commissioner of the South African Police Services v. Southern African Human Rights Litigation Centre* [2014] ZACC 30, para. 48.

55 Heller, 'Huge Win in the Zimbabwe Torture Docket Case', *Opinio Juris*, 30 October 2014.

> international crimes committed abroad is permissible only if the country with jurisdiction is unwilling or unable to prosecute and only if the investigation is confined to the territory of the investigating State. Simply put, we may not investigate or prosecute international crimes in breach of considerations of complementarity and subsidiarity.[56]

The second is that there must be 'anticipated presence' of the suspect in South Africa:

> The second limiting principle is practicability. Before South Africa assumes universal jurisdiction it must consider whether embarking on an investigation into an international crime committed elsewhere is reasonable and practicable in the circumstances of each case. That decision must be made in the light of all the relevant circumstances. None of these factors alone should be dispositive of the enquiry.

4. COMPLEMENTARITY AND JURISDICTION

Although the courts did not make any pronouncements on whether the National Prosecuting Authority would have the duty to prosecute Zimbabwean officials (including high level officials) should the SAPS find evidence of torture, this can clearly be construed from the judgments. For example, the courts ultimately based their decisions regarding the duty to investigate on various provisions of the Rome Statue and the ICC Act. In particular, the Supreme Court of Appeal stated the following:

> The Rome Statute's structures of international criminal justice are grounded in the core principle of complementarity. The statute devises a system of international criminal justice wherein the primary responsibility for the investigation and prosecution of those most responsible for serious violations of international law rests with domestic jurisdictions.[57]

Furthermore the Constitutional Court in its judgment stated that:

> parties may take the lead in investigating and prosecuting international crimes. The International Criminal Court will only undertake investigations and prosecutions as a court of last resort where States parties are unwilling or unable to do so. The primary responsibility to investigate and prosecute international crimes remains with states parties.[58]

---

56 *National Commissioner of the South African Police Services v. Southern African Human Rights Litigation Centre* [2014] ZACC 30 para. 61.

57 *Ibid*, para. 42.

58 Paras., 33–40.

The court held that 'torture, whether on the scale of crimes against humanity or not, is a crime in terms of section 232 of the Constitution because the customary international law prohibition against torture has the status of a peremptory norm.'[59]

Therefore, the consideration of whether South African courts have correctly applied the principle of complementarity and are competent to prosecute foreign state officials for crimes against humanity is a valid one.

The principle of complementarity forms a pillar of the Rome Statute system. Article 17 of the Rome Statute states that the International Criminal Court has jurisdiction over a matter only if state parties are unwilling or unable to investigate or prosecute the international crimes that fall within its jurisdiction. This principle places the primary burden of prosecution of international crimes on domestic courts. The principle is, however, not fully understood or uniformly applied by domestic courts.

In the *Torture Docket* case, however, the courts seem to have applied the principle of complementarity a little wider than described above. It is important to state that the courts' interpretation of complementarity should not be faulted if one has the view of ending impunity for international crimes and doing away with the havens that perpetrators have used since the advent of international criminal law to avoid accountability for their crimes. Indeed, it cannot be left to the International Criminal Court to combat all international crimes, especially in light of the obligations *erga omnes* that arise for all states to act in instances where certain international crimes are committed.

In terms of Article 27 of the Rome Statute, it is apparent that the International Criminal Court can prosecute even Heads of State for international crimes. Section 4(1) and (2) of South Africa's ICC Act also says something to that effect. However, the Rome Statute also limits the exercise of the court's jurisdiction to three preconditions in Article 12, all of which envision some form of consent or permissive act from non-state parties or the acceptance of the court's jurisdiction. Nonetheless, the ICC Act's only requirement for founding jurisdiction in similar instances is the presence of the accused person within South African territory.[60]

This can be construed as giving South Africa very wide powers to prosecute foreign officials, even Heads of State, in its domestic courts, powers that reach beyond even that of the International Criminal Court.

Therefore, although the judgment has been pronounced and the wheels have started turning, there will undoubtedly be various hurdles that may stop South African courts from bringing this issue to full completion. As it stands, the application of the principle of complementarity may be insufficient to found adequate jurisdiction to bring about justice in cases such as this.

---

59 Para. 42.

60 Section 4(3)(c).

The *Zimbabwe Torture Docket Case* was the first to flesh out the meaning of the Implementation Act's provisions. The case was remarkably progressive for a jurisdiction such as that of South Africa, which has a history of neglecting international law.

As observed by Werle and Bornkamm, the decision explores the limits of the universality principle under South African law and international law and emphasises the obligation to investigate serious human rights violations.[61] The judgment relies strongly on the ICC Act, which provides for universal jurisdiction in cases where a person suspected of committing a crime under international law does so abroad and is present on South African soil.[62]

It is to be hoped that the strong language the Constitutional Court used against torture, and the acknowledgment of the fact that torture is a *jus cogens* crime, will inspire South African lawyers to urgently litigate on the many instances of torture that occur *within* South Africa.

5. THE AL-BASHIR MATTER: A STEP BACKWARDS

The optimism following the progress made in the *Zimbabwe Torture Docket Case* was, however, swiftly dampened when the Sudanese president Omar Al-Bashir visited South Africa to attend an AU Summit in Johannesburg in June 2015. The ICC issued an arrest warrant for Al-Bashir in 2009 and has since struggled to secure his presence in The Hague. Upon his arrival in South Africa, the Southern Africa Litigation Centre (SALC) brought an urgent application for the South African authorities to arrest Al-Bashir. The South African government subsequently ignored an order of the Pretoria High Court by Judge Hans Fabricius stating that Al-Bashir be kept in South Africa and arrested.[63] The matter re-ignited the debate on the tensions between the AU and the ICC. The court order has created a backlash by the South African executive in the form of threats of withdrawal from the ICC.[64] The South African government has subsequently been held in contempt of court.

Had the South African government obeyed the court order to arrest Al-Bashir, South Africa would have made history. It would have been the first country to arrest a sitting head of state accused of international crimes. This would have been a dramatic step forward for the fight against impunity and for

---

61 Werle & Bornkamm 2013.

62 Implementation of the Rome Statute of the International Criminal Court Act No. 27 of 2002 (hereafter 'ICC Act').

63 *Southern Africa Litigation Centre v. The Minister of Justice and Constitutional Development and Others*, Case No. 27740/2015.

64 Journalists for Justice, 'South Africa threatens to withdraw from ICC as last resort', June 2015, available at: www.jfjustice.net/south-africa-threatens-to-withdraw-from-the-icc-as-a-last-resort/.

the recognition of the obligations under the Rome Statute.[65] The decision of the Pretoria High Court can nevertheless be considered a step forward from a legal point of view since it is the first South African judgment urging the government to give effect to its obligations under the Rome Statute. The outcry over the decision has also helped raise awareness of the Rome Statute system in South Africa.

Responding to the failure to arrest Al-Bashir, the President of the Assembly of States Parties expressed his deep concern about the negative consequences for the Court in case of non-execution of the warrants by states parties. It is clear that the ICC cannot function effectively without the cooperation of states.

The *Zimbabwe Torture Docket Case* gave the South African authorities wide powers to prosecute international crimes. However, the behaviour of the South African government in the Al-Bashir matter illustrates vividly that such power can remain merely theoretical if it is not backed up by political will. The South African government acted as it did because it wanted to show its loyalty to regional African interests. The broad conception of complementarity that this article supports can only exist if African leaders realise that it is in their interest not to protect other African leaders who are accused of international crimes.

6. PROMISING COMPLEMENTARITY INITIATIVES IN UGANDA AND SENEGAL

In 2008, under the third schedule of Accountability and Reconciliation of the Juba Peace Agreement, a War Crimes Division (WCD) was set up by the Ugandan government. In 2011, the WCD was renamed and became the International Crimes Division (ICD). The initiative taken by Uganda to create an ICD within its High Court with a mandate to prosecute genocide, war crimes, and crimes against humanity, in addition to crimes such as terrorism, should be closely watched. If the ICD executes its mandate effectively, it could have the effect of triggering other complementarity initiatives in domestic jurisdictions in Africa. The first case decided by the ICD, the case of Thomas Kwoyelo, was particularly controversial and highlighted some of the serious obstacles the ICD still needs to overcome.[66]

The Senegalese trial of the former dictator of Chad, Hissène Habré, is set to start in the Extraordinary African Chambers of the Court of Senegal in 2015. After decades of unsuccessful attempts to prosecute Habré, the Senegalese courts

65 See Swart, 'Opportunity lost to make history by arresting Al-Bashir', *Business Day*, 19 June 2015.

66 Kihika & Regue, 'Pursuing Accountability for Serious Crimes in Uganda's Courts', available at: https://www.ictj.org/sites/default/files/ICTJ-Briefing-Uganda-Kwoyelo-2015.pdf.

will have to face this challenge.[67] Habré will finally be facing the charges of war crimes, crimes against humanity, and torture.[68] Habré's trial will be significant on many levels. It will be the first trial in the world in which the courts of one country prosecute the former ruler of another for alleged human rights crimes. According to Human Rights Watch, it will also be the first universal jurisdiction case to proceed to trial in Africa.[69]

7. THE AFRICAN COURT OF JUSTICE AND HUMAN RIGHTS: A VIABLE ALTERNATIVE?

The ICC is currently the only international institution capable of effectively prosecuting international crimes on an international scale. For quite a few years, it has been suggested that an African regional court should acquire jurisdiction over international crimes. The track record of the judicial institutions of the African Union is disappointing. The record of the African Court on Human and Peoples' Rights (African Court or AfCHPR) has been particularly uninspiring. The African Court has only heard a handful of cases and, as an ad hoc court, is not currently equipped to take prosecutions of this kind on.[70] In addition, sub-regional courts such as the East African Court of Justice and the now defunct SADC Tribunal have, so far, only decided a handful of cases and are widely regarded as ineffective. It is highly unlikely that a newly created African Court of Justice and Human Rights would be more effective. Kenya's suggestion that it extend its jurisdiction to hear international criminal cases will not only stretch the court's mandate beyond its capacity but is simply unrealistic in light of the general inefficiency of this court. The ICC represents much more than a court.

Both the AU and the ICC share the mandate and responsibility to address impunity on the African continent and to ensure accountability for gross violations of human rights and international crimes. In discussing the AU's budding peace and security architecture, Jalloh emphasises that African governments undertook to engage other governments and civil society, international organisations such as the UN, and other external entities that could assist it to realise its human security objectives, in the Constitutive Act of

---

67 For background to this case see Sriram, 'Trying Habré in Senegal: An African Solution to an African Problem?', Jurist – Legal News and Research, 2006, available at: ww.jurist.org.

68 Human Rights Watch',Senegal: Hissène Habré Trial', 27 April 2015, available at: www.hrw.org/news/2015/04/27/senegal-hissene-habre-trial.

69 *Ibid.*

70 Trying individuals for serious crimes is distinct from the African Court's present work and will place unique burdens and expenses on the court, such as the need for systems of witness protection, evidence collection, and detention of accused.

the AU as well as in the Peace and Security Protocol. He writes: 'In relation to the Court, these instruments open up an avenue for mutually beneficial AU-ICC cooperation on issues ranging from technical cooperation to concrete measures combating impunity'.[71]

It seems clear that no African court of this kind can replace the ICC.[72] Setting up a court with the ability to prosecute effectively will be an enormously ambitious and costly undertaking. For such a new court to function effectively it would need strong Prosecution and Defence offices. It would need the equivalent of a police force or very strong state cooperation for purposes of enforcement and it would need facilities such as detention centres. The enforcement of the decision of the court will need political will and it is unlikely that African governments will all be equally supportive of the criminal jurisdiction of the court. Since enforcement of court orders is already a problem in Africa, there is good reason to believe that it will be a major problem in the context of the new court. Some of the same political considerations that obstruct the working of the ICC might creep into the working of a new court. The issue of the selectivity of prosecutions in international criminal courts, an inevitable feature of dispensing international criminal justice, will certainly raise its head again. Ngoepe also makes the point that there is a difference between the valid creation of an institution and the credibility of an institution.[73] The court will certainly struggle to attain legitimacy.

8. CONCLUSION

Under a broad conception of complementarity, one should not only encourage and support the prosecution of international crimes by domestic courts, but also support prosecutions by sub-regional and regional courts. In spite of the abovementioned reservations about the effectiveness of awarding criminal jurisdiction to the African Court of Justice and Human Rights, one has to be idealistic about the potential for effective prosecution by sub-regional and regional courts. The fact that the judges in the cases of *Campbell*, *Fick*, and *Zimbabwe Torture Docket* were prepared to be innovative and courageous in applying international law gives one reason for hope.

Institutions such as the SADC Tribunal and other African sub-regional courts are of the very few institutions in Africa that create a window of opportunity for citizens of African states to be heard, and for their rights to

71 Jalloh 2009.

72 Remarks made by Judge Bernard Ngoepe, 'Universalizing the Rome Statute of the International Criminal Court', Conference; Africa Legal Aid, 19 May 2015, Johannesburg.

73 *Ibid.*

be vindicated especially in the absence of meaningful domestic human rights protection. The closing down of the individual application procedure at the SADC Tribunal is therefore a particularly serious blow to international criminal justice. Furthermore, following from the Al-Bashir crisis in South Africa, there are currently strong indications that South Africa might withdraw from the ICC.[74] This deeply unfortunate prospect fortifies the argument for regional and sub-regional alternatives to the ICC.

If the rule of law protects the vulnerable rather than the powerful, the optimal functioning and development of sub-regional and regional courts is of pressing concern for the rule of law in Africa. One reason why the existence and optional functioning of sub-regional and national alternatives for prosecuting international crimes is crucial is that the gravity and extent of human rights violations and international crimes in Africa far surpasses what the ICC could ever deal with.

One of the most serious concerns is that of enforcement of decisions such as the court orders obtained in the *Zimbabwe Torture Docket Case* and in the subsequent Al-Bashir matter. The South African National Prosecuting Authority (NPA) has let South Africans down before in deciding not to prosecute. Examples of this would be the *Wouter Basson* case[75] of the Constitutional Court of South Africa in which the NPA decided not to prosecute Basson after the court gave the NPA the go-ahead to do so. The fact that the NPA failed to prosecute the alleged perpetrators of international crimes who failed to apply for amnesty in terms of the Truth and Reconciliation Commission process is another example.

It is unfortunate that the ICC has become mired in politics. Although politics is an inescapable reality of international criminal justice, the tension between the ICC and Africa has led to the obstruction of the court's work. The notion of *jus cogens* crimes transcends the political.

Mahmood Mamdani famously wrote of the popular outrage 'throughout Africa, against the impunity with which a growing number of regimes have been resorting to slaughter to brutalise their populations into silence'.[76] When perceived through the lens of the victims of international crimes, the AU's position vis a vis the ICC does not acknowledge this outrage and the need to fight impunity. However, this does not mean that the ICC should be the foremost forum and champion for the realisation of international criminal justice.

---

74 See Mustgrave, 'NGC: SA must withdraw from ICC', IOL News, 11 October 2015, available at: www.iol.co.za/news/politics/ngc-sa-must-withdraw-from-icc-1.1928057#.ViHWhbcaJD8.

75 *S v. Basson* 2005 (12) BCLR 1192 (CC).

76 Mamdani, 'The New Humanitarian Order', *The Nation*, 10 September 2008.

BIBLIOGRAPHY

BOOKS AND JOURNAL ARTICLES

Alter et al. 2013
Alter, K.J. et al., 'A New International Human rights Court for West Africa: The ECOWAS Community Court of Justice', 107 American Journal of International Law, 2013, pp. 737–779.

Bodansky 1999
Bodansky, D., 'The Legitimacy of International Governance: A Coming Challenge for International Environmental Law?', 93 AJIL, 1999.

Branch 2007
Branch, A., 'Uganda's Civil War and the Politics of ICC Intervention', 21(2) Ethics and International Affairs, 2007.

Cronin-Furman 2013
Cronin-Furman, K., 'Managing Expectations: International Criminal Trials and the Prospects for Deterrence of Mass Atrocities', International Journal of Transitional Justice, 2013, pp. 10–25.

Danner 2003
Danner, A.M., 'Accountability and Legitimacy of Prosecutorial Discretion at the ICC', American Journal of International Law, 2003.

De Wet 2014
De Wet, E., 'The Case of Government of the Republic of Zimbabwe v Louis Karel Fick: A First Step Towards Developing a Doctrine on the Status of International Judgements within the Domestic Legal Order', 17 Potchefstroom Electronic Law Journal, 2014.

Dutton 2013
Dutton, Y., 'Rules, Politics and the International Criminal Court: Committing to the Court: Committing to the Court', Routledge, 2013.

Gaeta 2009
Gaeta, P., 'Does President Al-Bashir Enjoy Immunity from Arrest?', 7 Journal of International Criminal Justice, 2009.

Jalloh 2009
Jalloh, C., 'Regionalising International Criminal Law', 9 International Criminal Law Review, 2009.

Nouwen 2013
Nouwen, S. 'Complementarity in the Line of Fire', Cambridge University Press, 2013.

Oppong 2010
Oppong, R.F., 'Enforcing Judgments of the SADC Tribunal in the Domestic Courts of Members States', 10 Monitoring Regional Integration in Southern Africa Yearbook, 2010, pp. 115–142.

Swart and Krisch 2014
Swart, M. and Krisch, K., 'Irreconcilable Differences? An Analysis of the Standoff between the African Union and the International Criminal Court', African Journal of International Criminal Justice, 2014.

Swart 2013
Swart, M., 'Alternative fora for human rights protection? An evaluation of the human rights standards of the African sub-regional courts', 3 Journal of South African Law, 2013.
Tladi 2015
Tladi, D., 'The Immunity Provision in the AU Amendment Protocol: Separating the (Doctrinal) Wheat from the (Normative) Chaff', 3 Journal of International Criminal Justice, 2015.
Werle and Bornkamm 2013
Werle, G. and Bornkamm, P., 'Torture in Zimbabwe under Scrutiny in South Africa', Journal of International Criminal Justice, 2013.

JURISPRUDENCE

Constitutional Court of South Africa 2014
SACC, National Commissioner of The South African Police Service v. Southern African Human Rights Litigation Centre and Another, CCT 02/14, ZACC 30, 30 October 2014.
Constitutional Court of South Africa 2005
SACC, S v. Basson, CCT 30/03A, ZACC 10, 9 September 2005.
ICC 2014
ICC, Prosecutor v. Uhuru Muigai Kenyatta, ICC 01/09–02/11, 5 December 2014.
North Gauteng High Court 2015
NGHC, Southern Africa Litigation Centre v. The Minister of Justice and Constitutional Development and Others, Case no. 27740/2015, ZAGPPHC 402, 24 June 2015.
North Gauteng High Court 2012
NGHC, Southern African Litigation Centre and Another v. National Director of Public Prosecutions and Others, 77150/09, ZAGPPHC 61, 8 May 2012.
North Gauteng High Court 2010
NGHC, Fick and Others v. Government of the Republic of Zimbabwe, Case no. 77881/2009, 25 February 2010.
North Gauteng High Court 2010
NGHC, Fick and Others v. Government of the Republic of Zimbabwe, Case no. 77880/2009, 13 January 2010.
SADC Tribunal 2008
SADC Tribunal, Mike Campbell (Pty) Ltd and Others v. Republic of Zimbabwe, Case no. 2/2007, SADCT 2, 28 November 2008.
Supreme Court of Appeal of South Africa 2012
SCA, Government of the Republic of Zimbabwe v. Fick and Others, Case no. 657/11, ZASCA 122, 20 September 2012.
Zimbabwe Supreme Court 2008
ZSC, Mike Campbell (Pty) Ltd and Another v. Minister of National Security Responsible for Land, Land Reform and Resettlement, Case no. 124/060, ZWSC 1, 22 January 2008.

TREATIES, LEGISLATION AND AGREEMENTS

Protocol on Tribunal in the Southern African Development Community, 7 August 2000.
Rome Statute of the International Criminal Court, 17 July 1998.
South Africa, Constitution of the Republic of South Africa, 4 December 1996.
South Africa, Foreign States Immunities Act 87 of 1981, 6 October 1981.
South Africa, Implementation of the Rome Statute of the International Criminal Court Act, Act No. 27 of 2002, 12 July 2002.
Statute of the International Criminal Tribunal for Rwanda, SC Res. 955, UN Doc. S/RES/955, 8 November 1994.
Statute of the International Criminal Tribunal for the Former Yugoslavia, SC Res. 827, UN Doc. S/RES/827, 25 May 1993.
Treaty of the Southern African Development Community, 17 August 1992.

OTHERS

Beauchamp, Z., 'Are African Countries About To Destroy The ICC?', Think Progress, 20 September 2013.
Chatham House, 'The International Criminal Court – Taking Stock', Discussion Paper, 12 June 2008.
Dancy, G., 'Selections from 'Unintended positive Complementarity: Why ICC Investigations Increase Domestic Human Rights Prosecutions', Post-Conflict Justice, 2014.
Dersso, S., 'The International Criminal Court's Africa problem', Aljazeera, 11 June 2013.
Diehl, J. 'After the Dictators Fall', Washington Post, 5 June 2011.
Fabricius, P., 'Geography of Justice riles Africa', Cape Times, 10 April 2014.
Global Justice, 'Civil society defends ICC at African Union summit', 25 March 2014.
Heller, K., 'Huge Win in the Zimbabwe Torture Docket Case', Opinio Juris, 30 October 2014.
Journalists for Justice, 'South Africa threatens to withdraw from ICC as last resort', 25 June 2015.
Judge B. Ngoepe's remarks at the 'Universalizing the Rome Statute of the International Criminal Court' Conference in Johannesburg, Africa Legal Aid, 19 May 2015.
Kihika, K.S. and Regue, M., 'Pursuing Accountability for Serious Crimes in Uganda's Courts', International Center for Transitional Justice Briefing Paper, January 2015.
Mamdani, M., 'The New Humanitarian Order', The Nation, 10 September 2008.
Mbaku, J., 'International Justice: The International Criminal Court and Africa', Brookings Institution Report, January 2014.
Mustgrave, A., 'NGC: SA must withdraw from ICC', IOL News, 11 October 2015.
Sriram, C., 'Trying Habré in Senegal: An African Solution to an African Problem?', JURIST, 6 July 2006.
Swart, M., 'Opportunity lost to make history by arresting Al-Bashir', Business Day, 19 June 2015.

Ziegler, A., 'Regional Economic Integration Agreements and Investor Protection in Africa – The Case of SADC: Why Institutional Overlap may be necessary in certain cases', NCCR Trade Working Paper No. 2011/59, May 2011.

COMPLEMENTARITY IN PRACTICE AND ICC IMPLEMENTING LEGISLATION

Lessons from Uganda

Elizabeth Ibanda-Nahamya

1. INTRODUCTION

I will begin by quoting from Katharine A. Marshall's Article entitled 'Prevention and Complementarity in the International Criminal Court: A Positive Approach' in which she stated that:

> Complementarity … presents a way by which the ICC can increase its potential positive impact on both domestic and international criminal justice and, in the long term, prevention. By proactively engaging with and assisting domestic legal Institutions, the ICC will be able to strengthen the rule of law in nations suffering from violent conflict and instability … A society that has, on the other hand, strong legal institutions and a strong sense of the rule of law, may be less likely to come to the brink [of war and conflict which creates an environment in which crimes such as genocide, crimes against humanity and war crimes are likely to be committed with impunity.][1]

Uganda has had its share of wars, and its internal conflict has lasted for over twenty years, closer to three decades. The consequences of the conflict have been far-reaching and include destabilisation of the region, the displacement of up to 1.8 million people, the killing and mutilation of tens of thousands of civilians, and the abduction of even more, mainly children, for recruitment in the LRA forces. The prosecution of these alleged crimes committed in Uganda is long overdue. Uganda has endeavoured – by way of negotiations, treaties, enacting legislation, working with international courts and creating courts – a myriad of ways to resolve, adjudicate, reconcile and evolve from this conflict. Uganda

1 Marshall, 'Prevention and Complementarity in the International Criminal Court: A Positive Approach', 17 Human Rights Brief (Winter 2010).

is finally at a point in its history where there are strengthened national courts to deal with adjudicating alleged perpetrators of international crimes. With related but separate cases ongoing at the ICC, Uganda and also the international community are finally at a new point in history in international criminal law. This is at a time when complementarity is the main principle in which its premises, boundaries, definitions, failures and successes are yet to be determined but which will soon be tested.

From the beginning, the idea of complementarity was intended to balance the competing interests of a court with universal jurisdiction and the principle of state sovereignty. The concept of complementarity began not with the Rome Statute but, rather, in 1937 with the League of Nations Draft Convention for an international criminal court.

This status still pertains with the concession that the ICC would deal with cases of such gravity that national jurisdictions may not be able to prosecute or may not be willing to prosecute. According to the preamble of the Rome Statute and Article 1 of the Statute, this International Criminal Court was meant to be 'complementary to national criminal jurisdictions' and the ICC will have jurisdiction only where a state is unable or unwilling to investigate or prosecute those most responsible, pursuant to Article 17.

Positive complementarity is the idea that the ICC should encourage genuine national proceedings where possible. This entails, *inter alia*, the Court's cooperation with states to build capacity and put up structures to ensure domestic prosecutions. Strong judicial institutions will foster respect for government institutions thus promoting the rule of law and democracy which reduces future atrocities.

I will discuss complementarity in the context of the perspective of the International Crimes Division (ICD) of the High Court of Uganda and the solutions and also challenges that complementarity brings. The paper will be demarcated in two parts. While the first part is more informative, the second part captures the current status of the ICD, the challenges confronting the ICD and their solutions.

2. BACKGROUND: THE HISTORY AND ORIGINS OF THE WAR CRIMES DIVISION AND THE CONFLICT PROPAGATED BY THE LORD'S RESISTANCE ARMY

The ICD (formerly known as the War Crimes Division) had its genesis in Uganda's internal conflict, which involved the national Uganda government and Joseph Kony's rebellion, the Lord's Resistance Army (LRA), which originated in Northern Uganda in 1986.

The LRA has unleashed violence in Northern Uganda, 'which has resulted in human tragedy, chronic insecurity, lawlessness, serious human rights violations, marginalisation and the impoverishment of vast segments of the population.'[2] The LRA's crimes have been well documented over the years. LRA violence includes attacks against the civilian population, abductions of children, extrajudicial killings, and gender-based violence.

The group has committed egregious offences that include crimes against humanity, particularly murder and torture. LRA also committed war crimes in violation of the Geneva Conventions such as violence to life and person, in particular murder of all kinds, mutilation, cruel treatment and torture; pillaging of towns or places; committing rape, sexual slavery, forced pregnancy, forced marriage and other forms of sexual violence also constituting serious violations of Common Article 3 of the Geneva Conventions; and conscripting or enlisting children under the age of fifteen years into armed forces or groups or using them to participate actively in hostilities.

2.1. THE UGANDAN AMNESTY ACT OF 2000

The Amnesty Act was enacted in 2000 for the purposes of restoring peace in conflict areas of Uganda. Hitherto, the Statute has been considered as one that provides for blanket amnesty to Ugandans who had been involved in rebellion against the Government of Uganda since 1986. The Amnesty Act has implications on Uganda's ability to fulfil the principle of complementarity. Initially, the Amnesty Act was to remain in force for a period not exceeding six months with a possibility of extension of the period by the relevant Minister. In the Amnesty (Amendment) Act of 2006, it was stipulated that it could remain in force for two years from 19 July 2006. The Amended Amnesty Act of 2006 also stipulates that the Minister may declare the lapse of the operation of Part II of the Act, which relates to declaration, qualification and the grant of amnesty. Under the same amended Act, a person shall not be eligible for grant of amnesty if he or she is declared not to be eligible by the Minister of Internal Affairs by virtue of a statutory instrument approved by Parliament. The provision is silent on the criteria by which individuals may be considered to be ineligible for amnesty. It does not also make the designation of ineligibility of amnesty under certain circumstances mandatory by law.

The Act has been extended several times and The Act does not indicate the criteria for renewal. On 25 May 2012, the Amnesty Act lapsed but upon consultation with the leaders of the Justice, Law and Order Sector (JLOS), Part II

---

2 UN Secretary-General, *Report of the Secretary-General Pursuant to Resolutions 1653(2006) and 1663 (2006)*, UN Doc. S/2006/478, para. 2, 29 June 2006, available at: www.un.org/en/ga/search/view_doc.asp?symbol=S/2006/478.

of the Amnesty Act (the Declaration of Amnesty) was removed by the then Minister of Internal Affairs, Hon. Hillary Onek, for 12 months. It continued to operate until 25 May 2013, when again Part II was reinstated by the mentioned Minister to run until May 2015. This may have been influenced by the uproar of the citizens in the conflict areas who feared that the removal of amnesty would affect the ease of renunciation of the rebellion.[3] On 26 May 2015, it lapsed and was recently extended by the Minister for another two years until May 2017. This was surprising considering the expectation by human rights activists and other stakeholders that it was unlikely that the Amnesty Act would be renewed in its current form. This view was expressed in a Stakeholders Workshop organised by JLOS attended by the Attorney General, MPs and Judicial Officers in February 2015. In that forum, members raised issues relating to the relevance of the Amnesty Act fifteen years after its inception. It was resolved that the Amnesty law is still relevant as a tool of championing peace but must be amended to make it conditional. The Draft Transitional Justice Policy provides for the removal of blanket amnesty and proposes truth telling and traditional justice processes for those that have been amnestied. The Policy is currently before the Cabinet awaiting discussion and approval.

2.2. THE REFERRAL OF THE UGANDAN SITUATION TO THE ICC

Uganda became a signatory to the ICC Statute on 17 March 1999 and ratified it on 14 June 2002. President Yoweri Museveni referred the Northern Uganda situation to the ICC in December 2003. The ICC Prosecutor Luis Moreno Ocampo commenced investigations on 29 July 2004. On 14 October 2005, arrest warrants were unsealed for Joseph Kony, Vincent Otti, Okot Odhiambo, Raska Lukwiya and Dominic Ongwen. Out of the five, only Ongwen has been captured and transferred to the ICC. On 26 January 2015, Ongwen was the first LRA leader to appear before the ICC, and the hearing in respect of the confirmation of charges against him took place as scheduled on 21 January 2016.

2.3. THE JUBA AGREEMENT ON ACCOUNTABILITY AND RECONCILIATION

In 2007, at Juba, the Government of Uganda and the Lord's Resistance Army entered several agreements. The Juba Accountability and Reconciliation Agreement and its annexure is one of the Agreements and was signed on

3 The End of Amnesty in Uganda: Implications of the LRA Defections by Kasper Agger, August 2012, Enough Project, available at: www.enoughproject.org/files/GuluDispatch.pdf (last accessed on 14 January 2016).

29 June 2007 (Juba Agreement).[4] Although it was never signed by Joseph Kony, it contained several notable provisions, one requirement being that the LRA Commanders be tried in Uganda within the national legal framework. Amongst the legal and institutional framework changes envisaged was the establishment of a Special Division of the High Court.[5] The Juba Agreement stipulated for the establishment of a Special Court to try those who committed serious crimes and human rights violations.[6] These provisions acted as catalysts to the expedited establishment of the Special War Crimes Division, now known as the ICD.

3. THE CREATION OF THE ICD AND THE LAWS APPLICABLE

The creation of the ICD in 2008 fulfilled both the ICC's requirement of a competent court under Article 17 and the Government of Uganda's commitment to the actualisation of The Juba Agreement.

3.1. UGANDAN LAWS

The substantive laws include the Geneva Conventions Act, Cap 363, the Penal Code, Cap 120, the ICC Act, No. 11 of 2010 and the Magistrates' Courts' Act, Cap 16. Other procedural and evidential laws include: the Criminal Procedure Act, Cap 116: Trial on Indictment Act, Cap 23, the Evidence Act, Cap 6: the Constitution of the Republic of Uganda, 1995; the Judicature Act, Cap 13; the Amnesty Act, Cap 59; and the Children's Act, Cap 59.

3.2. THE INTERNATIONAL CRIMINAL COURT ACT 2010 (THE ICC ACT 2010)

Uganda is a dualist nation. Thus international law cannot be applied directly as a source of law but rather international law or treaty obligations have to be incorporated by enacting an Act of Parliament. Uganda is still grappling with the issue of applicability of customary international law. The question often posed is: can Uganda apply customary international law directly or does it also need Parliamentary ratification?

---

4 Clause 6.1 of the Accountability Agreement requires the establishment of formal courts to exercise jurisdiction over individuals alleged to bear particular responsibility for the most serious crimes, p. 7; See also clause 23 of the Annexure.

5 *Ibid*, clause 7 of the Annexure, p. 3.

6 See clause 4 of the Juba Agreement and the relevant parts of Annexure 3 thereto.

Uganda's 8th Parliament passed the International Criminal Court Act 2010 (ICC Act 2010) on 25 May 2010, which entered into force on 25 June 2010. This Act incorporates the precepts of the ICC's Rome Statute (Rome Statute) into Ugandan Law. The ICC Act 2010 does not specifically mention the International Crimes Division (ICD) of the High Court of Uganda (formerly the War Crime Division), which was established administratively in 2008. The ICC Act 2010 gives inherent jurisdiction to the High Court of Uganda to adjudicate upon cases of war crimes, crimes against humanity and genocide as a court of first instance and of which the ICD is part.[7] It is not a secret that ICC bills had existed in 2004 and 2006. Both were crafted along similar frameworks. It is the latter bill which was revised to birth the ICC Act 2010 of Uganda.

The law to be applied by the ICD comprises of, *inter alia*, the ICC Act 2010, the Geneva Conventions, Act, Cap 323, and the Penal Code Act, Cap 120. In this paper, I have considered the ICC Act 2010 of Uganda which is the implementing legislation for complementarity. The ICC Act 2010 is yet to be applied to any situation because the date of commencement is so current that it excludes most of the past war crimes in Uganda. Uganda hosted the first ICC Review Conference from 31 May to 11 June 2010.[8] Among the main stocktaking issues that were discussed was the principle of complementarity. The conference's theme 'Taking Stock of the Principle of Complementarity: Bridging the Gap.' Various issues emerged, but the most prominent one was the need to strengthen capacities of states to implement their own obligations under Article 17 of the Rome Statute in order to be able to investigate and prosecute crimes within the jurisdiction of the ICC.

3.2.1. Objective of the ICC Act

The ICC Act 2010 states its objectives as '[a]n Act to give effect to the Rome Statute of the International Criminal Court, to provide for offences under the Laws of Uganda corresponding to offences within the jurisdiction of that Court and for connected matters'.

Pursuant to Section 2 of the ICC Act 2010, the main purposes of the Act are twofold:

- to give the force of law in Uganda to the Rome Statute; and
- to implement obligations assumed by Uganda under the Rome Statute.

---

7 Open Society Justice Initiative, *Putting Complementarity into Practice, Domestic Justice for International Crimes in DRC, Uganda and Kenya*, 2011, p. 65.

8 Thanks to the tireless efforts of Uganda's Ambassador to the Benelux Countries and the European Union, Her Excellency MirjamBlaak.

The ICC Act 2010 does not cover crimes committed before July 2002 when the ICC Statute entered into force, yet most of the serious crimes in Northern Uganda occurred from 1986–2002. The Act specified the particular laws saved under the Act, including the 1964 Geneva Conventions Act, Cap 363. However, the ICC Act 2010 fell short of domesticating the Additional Protocols of 1977 which Uganda signed but never ratified nor domesticated. In order to synchronise the ICC Act 2010 with the existing criminal law, reference is made to the Penal Code Act, Cap 120.

3.2.2. Crimes within the Jurisdiction of the Court

Sections 7–9 of the ICC Act 2010 criminalise the offences of genocide, crimes against humanity and war crimes. A person convicted of any of these offences is liable to life imprisonment or a lesser term. This is in consonance with Articles 6–9 of the Rome Statute.

3.2.3. Retrospectivity

Retrospective rulemaking has a few supporters and those who defend retrospective law usually argue that it is a necessary evil in specific or limited circumstances for the most egregious and heinous international crimes and acts. For example, it is necessary to deal with terrorists or prosecute fallen tyrants who allegedly committed genocide or war crimes. The rationale for the presumption against retrospective application of criminal law is the need for certainty and predictability of actions with regards to punishment in the law. This is essential to enable those likely to be affected by a law to be capable of understanding it and regulate their conduct in order to avoid breaking it.[9] Whilst absolute certainty is not required, it is considered that individuals should at least be able to foresee, with a reasonable degree of accuracy, the consequences of their actions.[10]

Article 28(7) of the Constitution of Uganda 1995 stipulates that 'no person shall be charged with or convicted of a criminal offence which is on an act/omission that did not, at the time it occurred, constitute a criminal offence'. The ICC Act 2010 did not remove this prohibition. Hence, since all the crimes committed prior to 2002 were excluded, the ICC Act 2010 strictly applies to crimes that are committed after 25 June 2010. This eliminates the possibility of applying the ICC Act 2010 to crimes committed prior to its enactment and preventing the ICD from having jurisdiction over such crimes. It would therefore seem unlikely that the ICC Act 2010, which does not refer to the ICD specifically will have jurisdiction over crimes committed prior to 2002. Similarly, Uganda will not have a moral basis to put up a challenge on the admissibility of the

---

9 *Sunday Times v. UK* (1979–80) 2 EHRR 245.

10 *Ibid*, p. 271.

Lord's Resistance Army (LRA) cases under Article 19 of the Rome Statute. However, it is not clear whether there is a possibility of giving the ICC Act 2010 retroactive effect on the basis that some crimes within the ICD's jurisdiction – namely genocide, war crimes and crimes against humanity – previously existed as part customary international law. There is a need to test the judicial waters by filing a declaratory case before the Constitutional Court.

3.2.4. General Principles of Law in the ICC Act 2010

The ICC Act 2010 adopted the Principles set out in the Rome Statute. Pursuant to section 19 of the ICC Act 2010, certain provisions of the Rome Statute apply, but with non-fundamental modifications as may be required. It embodies the usual principles known to any criminal law scholar such as *ne bis in dem*, the *nullum crimen sine lege* or non-retroactivity *ratione personae*. The section also prohibits prosecution of persons below 18 years of age. It is interesting to note that in Uganda the age of criminal responsibility is 12 years. The Geneva Conventions Act does not preclude prosecution of persons below 18 years. There have been discussions in Uganda whether the age of criminal responsibility should be raised upwards to 16 years. One view has been that age should be linked to cultural conceptions relating to childhood, maturity and practical realities in Africa between the ages of 12–14 years. Nevertheless, these arguments will not affect the provisions in the Rome Statute as reflected in the ICC Act 2010. Section 19(3) of the ICC Act 2010 stipulates that where there are inconsistencies between the provisions falling under the ICC Act 2010 (domestic jurisdiction law) and the Rome Statute (international law), the provisions of the Rome Statute will prevail. The provision gives supremacy of international law over domestic law. This means that those who commit genocide, crimes against humanity and war crimes and are below 18 years of age will be spared from prosecution.

3.2.5. Defence

The available defences in section 19(1) of the ICC Act 2010 such as mistake of fact, mistake of law,[11] superior orders[12] or the fact that one has already been convicted or acquitted[13] are similar to what pertains in Uganda's criminal law.[14]

11 Article 32 of the Rome Statute.
12 Article 33 of the Rome Statute.
13 Article 20 of the Rome Statute.
14 The Penal Code Act of Uganda, Cap 120.

3.2.6. *Immunity Provisions under ICC Act 2010*

There are provisions relating to immunity in the ICC Act 2010. Pursuant to section 25 of the ICC Act, the existence of any immunity or special procedural rule attaching to the official capacity of a person is not a ground for refusing or postponing a request for surrender. Hence the ICC Act 2010, just like the Rome Statute, does not grant immunity to perpetrators. The limitation of this provision, however, is a disappointing factor because it only relates to persons to be surrendered to the ICC. In contrast, Article 98(4) of Uganda's Constitution of 1995 as amended grants the President immunity as long as he is still holding office. It is therefore not possible to surrender a sitting President in Uganda and hand him over to the ICC for prosecution. A similar logistical problem would ensue, if there were a provision permitting the prosecution of a sitting President because the national police force still has the responsibility of effecting the arrest of the President and this would complicate matters.

3.2.7. *Rules of Procedure*

There are no laid down rules in the ICC Act 2010. Pursuant to section 5(c) of ICC Act 2010, Uganda borrows from the Rome Statute,[15] the principles in respect of requests made by the ICC to the Uganda Government for surrender and other forms of assistance. Besides requests from the ICC pertaining to surrender and assistance, the normal procedure is that the general Rules of Procedure and Evidence will apply to criminal law cases. I will consider aspects of this later when I discuss the challenges faced by the ICD.

3.2.8. *Disclosure of Evidence*

The existing criminal justice lacks disclosure rules, yet in comparison, Article 67(2) of the Rome Statute is elaborate on this aspect. Under Ugandan law, the Evidence Act, the Criminal Procedure Code Act and the Trial on Indictments Act do not specify any rules governing disclosure. I posit that there must be pre-trial disclosure relating to Prosecution witnesses such as the names of the impending witnesses; their statements. All these disclosures are subject to protection of the witnesses and their privacy. Pursuant to Rule 77 of the Rome Statute, prosecution may avail to the Defence an opportunity to inspect any books, documents, photographs and other tangible objects in their possession but subject to Rules 81 and 82 which refer to the work product of the prosecuting Attorney. In Uganda, the Diary of Investigation should not be revealed. Also, exculpatory evidence must be disclosed.

---

15 See Articles 20, 32, 33, 51 and 52 of the Rome Statute and sections 9, 11, 12 and 18 of Uganda Penal Code Act.

Section 164 of the Evidence Act Cap 6 provides that a judge may order the production of any document or thing. The case of *Soon Yeon Kong Kim & Kwanga Mao v. Attorney General* (Constitutional Reference No. 6 of 2007) was a landmark case on disclosure in criminal trials in Uganda. In that case, the Accused persons sought to have copies of all statements made to the Police by the potential witnesses for Prosecution and the exhibits that the state would rely on at the trial. This was intended to assist the accused persons in the preparation of each of their defence. Prosecution objected and a Constitutional Reference was made to the Constitutional Court to determine whether the matter did not impinge the right to fair trial. The Constitutional Court held that Article 28 (1)(3)(a)(c)(d) and (e) of the Constitution of Uganda, in its plain, natural and practical meaning *prima facie* entitles the accused person in a Magistrate's Court to disclosure of the copies of statements made to the Police by would be witnesses for Prosecution as well as the documentary exhibits which Prosecution intends to produce at trial. It is incumbent upon Prosecution to establish the limitations of such disclosure through evidence. The Draft ICD Rules of Procedure encompass provisions on disclosure and attempts to stipulate the time period within which to disclose the requisite documents. It would be prudent to include reciprocal disclosure in respect of the Defence in order to bring about equality of arms and remove the element of surprise. The Rule on disclosure will be subjected to witness protection orders which the court would have issued in respect of the witnesses.

3.2.9. Military Trials

Section 18(b) of the ICC Act 2010 stipulates for acts committed by a person employed in his military capacity, if he/she does acts which amount to crimes under the ICC Act. It provides that a person who is employed by Uganda in a civilian or military capacity is subject to criminal proceedings, if it is established that the person in his/her capacity committed the specified crimes. The ICC Act does not specify which court would try a perpetrator, particularly in light of the UPDF Act Cap 307.[16] In practice, it is debatable whether military officials will be prosecuted before the ICD. In Uganda's criminal justice system, a latter Act supersedes the earlier one in case of conflict. It is noteworthy that, the ICD is empowered to handle war crimes, genocide, and crimes against humanity. This mandate does not fall within the jurisdiction of any other court in Uganda although generally, the High Court of Uganda has inherent jurisdiction. Hence, the ICD is competent and ready to prosecute any UPDF personnel who are alleged to have committed crimes that fall within its jurisdiction unless such persons are disqualified by reason of age. It remains to be seen if the DPP in

16 See sections 15 and 105 of the UPDF Act Cap 307.

exercise of his discretionary powers pursuant to Article 120 of the Constitution of Uganda 1995 will prosecute them before the ICD.

3.2.10. Rights of the Accused and Right to Counsel

Section 30 of the ICC Act 2010 recognises the rights of the Accused when the ICC has requested Uganda to surrender an indicted person to be tried by the ICC. Article 23(2) and (3) of the 1995 Constitution of Uganda enshrines similar rights. The right to legal representation is a core feature of a fair trial as there must be equality of arms.

Under the Rome Statute, the right to Counsel is open to all accused appearing before the Court. Under the Constitution of Uganda, the right to Counsel is available only to persons charged with an offence which carries a death sentence or life imprisonment.

In practice, in capital offences, Counsel is assigned by the registrars of the appropriate court to act for the accused on State brief. It is noteworthy that the offences, which fall within the jurisdiction of the ICD are serious offences for which an advocate must be assigned and paid for by the State. What is lacking is a system of supervision of the assigned Counsel to ensure that they provide effective representation to the accused. The judges are always on the watch to identify non-performing Counsel or unprofessional Counsel. Concerning the rights of the defence, the Draft ICD Rules will make it a requirement that the assigned Counsel should be conversant with International Criminal Law procedure.

3.2.11. Bail

Section 31 of the ICC Act 2010 makes provision for a person whose surrender has been requested by the ICC to apply for bail, if brought before a Registrar. This is in consonance with Article 23(6)(a) of the Constitution of Uganda 1995. The Constitution stipulates that an accused has the right to apply for bail and the court may admit him to bail subject to certain conditions as it deems fit. Consequently, grant of bail to an accused is not mandatory but discretionary depending on the circumstances of each case. Section 15(3) of the Trial on Indictment Act Cap 23 provides that bail may be granted, if exceptional circumstances exist to justify his/her release. The envisaged exceptional circumstances are: the infancy or advanced age of the accused; grave illness if certified by a medical officer of the holding institution or that the consent of the Director of Public Prosecutions has been issued. This restriction is included in the law as a guideline to the issuance of bail to Accused persons facing capital offences. In consonance with section 15(1) of the Trial on Indictment Act Cap 23, bail is not automatic for capital offences. However, the decision to grant or not to grant bail is discretionary and it depends on each presiding judge.

An interesting observation is that usually a convict who lodges an appeal could easily be granted bail pending his appeal. This is because the Supreme Court set a precedent on appeal in the case of *Arvind Patel v. Uganda*.[17] The Honourable Justices of the Supreme Court laid down the salient factors to be considered including, the fact that the Appeal is likely to succeed. Currently, the President of Uganda has been advocating for the amendment of the Constitution to bar those who demonstrate against Government from getting bail until after a certain period.[18] He reasons that such a constitutional amendment will discipline individuals undermining Uganda's economy. The Constitution of Uganda 1995 contains a mandatory release if someone spends a period of 180 days before appearing in the High Court.

3.2.12. Sentencing and the Aspect of Differential Sentencing

The Rome Statute provides in Article 80 that: 'Nothing in this part affects the application by States of penalties prescribed by neither their national Law nor the Law of States which do not provide penalties prescribed in this part.' The problem that arises is that for seemingly very grave offences like crimes against humanity, genocide, and war crimes one would get a life imprisonment as the maximum sentence, if convicted, yet under the Penal Code, the death penalty is still the maximum sentence for capital offenders. In Uganda there is a key decision on the death penalty. In the case of *Susan Kigula and 417 others v. Attorney General*, Constitutional Appeal No. 3 of 2006, the appellant and 417 others appealed to the Supreme Court, against a Constitutional Ruling pertaining to the death penalty. It was held that it is no longer mandatory to impose a death sentence on persons convicted of capital offences. It is now within the discretion of the presiding judge. Ugandans still await Parliamentary action to make the appropriate changes and perhaps abolish the death penalty.

4. THOMAS KWOYELO: TESTING THE WATERS AND THE INTERNATIONAL CRIMES DIVISION'S FIRST CASE

Kwoyelo was charged before the Buganda Chief Magistrates Court on 6 September 2010 with various offences under the Geneva Conventions Act. He was later committed to the ICD for trial. The Applicant appeared before the ICD on 11 July 2010 on an amended indictment containing over 53 counts. Kwoyelo's counsel made an application to the ICD in which he requested that the matter be

17 Supreme Court Criminal Application No. 1 of 2003.

18 Crispy Kaheru, 'Does the Bail Question Confirm Museveni's Mastery of the Political Law of Diversion?', available at: www.politicalarticles.net.

sent to the Constitutional Court for interpretation as a Constitutional Reference. The ICD sent the Constitutional Reference to the Constitutional Court,[19] pursuant to Article 137(5) of the Constitution of the Republic of Uganda 1995 and the Constitutional Court (Petitions and References) Rules SI No. 91/05. The Constitutional Court had to determine three issues, the pivotal one being:

(1) Whether failure by the Director of Public Prosecutions (DPP) and the Amnesty Commission to act on the application by the Accused person for grant of a certificate of Amnesty where such certificates were granted to other people in similar circumstances to that of the accused person is, discriminatory, in contravention of, and inconsistent with Articles 1, 2, 20(2), 21(1) and (3) of the 1995 Constitution of the Republic of Uganda.

On 12 August 2011, the applicant informed the Court that he had abandoned the second issue which dealt with the Geneva Conventions. On the other hand, the Senior Principal State Attorney, had no objection to the proposed amendments but she also put forward another issue which had not formed part of the framed issues: 'whether Sections 2, 3 and 4 of the Amnesty Act were inconsistent with Articles 120(3)(b) (c) and (d) (5) (6), 126 (1) and 287 of the 1995 Constitution of the Republic of Uganda.'

Kwoyelo's application was supported by his affidavit in which he gave the details of his capture by the LRA. He attested that this occurred in 1987 while he was going to school and at the time, he was aged 13. He narrated how he rose through the ranks to become one of the commanders of the LRA until his capture in 2008 in the DRC. In his Supporting Affidavit, which he deponed to during his detention at the Upper Prison Luzira, Thomas Kwoyelo renounced the rebellion and requested to be amnestied, pursuant to section 2 of the Amnesty Act.[20]

The thrust of his argument was that he had been discriminated against and had been deprived of equal protection of the law pursuant to Article 21 of the Constitution of the Republic of Uganda 1995. Kwoyelo's Defence Counsel submitted that the enactment of the Amnesty Act was meant to be an avenue for bringing the rebellion to an end. He further submitted that the Act was in line with the national objectives and principles of state policy. As such, the Act was constitutional.

On behalf of the Attorney General, the state Attorney's submissions were that the applicant did not have any protection under the Amnesty Act since it infringes upon the Constitutional independence of the DPP as guaranteed under Article 120(3)(b)–(d), (5) and (6) of the Constitution. Furthermore, she argued that the Amnesty Act infringes upon the independence of the Judiciary guaranteed by Article 126(2)(a) and Articles 128(1) and (2) of the 1995 Uganda Constitution. The State Attorney contended that the Amnesty Act is inconsistent with Article 287 of

---

19 A Constitutional Petition (Reference) vide No. 036 of 2011 arose from HCT-00-ICD-Case No. 02 of 2010.

20 Cap 294, Laws of Uganda.

the same Constitution because it grants amnesty to perpetrators of war crimes, which includes grave breaches under the Geneva Conventions. Consequently, the Amnesty Act violates the principles of international law. She asked the Court to order for the trial of the Applicant to proceed.

In his reply, Counsel for Kwoyelo vehemently opposed the contentions of the state. He contended that the Act was amended in 2006 and the Minister was given powers to declare rebels who were not eligible for amnesty. He argued that the Amnesty Act did not whittle down the Prosecutorial powers of the DPP nor did it interfere with his independence. The Defence Counsel contended that the DPP did not give any reasonable, objective explanation as to why he did not heed to the Applicant's request to be granted amnesty like other LRA Commanders who had renounced the rebellion.

The Justices of Appeal identified an additional issue and stated that they were at liberty to decline to hear it. However, based upon rule 20 of the Constitutional Court (Petitions and References) Rules SI No. 91/05, they agreed to hear it. The Rule stipulates that when the Constitutional Court is determining a Reference, it is exercising special and limited jurisdiction on matters and issues that have arisen in the proceedings before the Trial Court. Applying this rationale to the Kwoyelo Constitutional Reference, the Constitutional Court determined that the additional issue pertaining to the unconstitutionality of the Amnesty Act was vital. They held that it touched on the legality and constitutionality of an Act of Parliament. As such, the Justices of the Constitutional Court recognised that it was their duty to determine the allegation.

The Court had to review the provisions of the Constitution under which the Applicant alleged discrimination against him. The Court also considered the provisions under which the State Attorney alleged the unconstitutionality of the Amnesty Act. It was held that the Amnesty Commission and the Director of Public Prosecutions did not accord Thomas Kwoyelo equal treatment under the Amnesty Act. Therefore, he was entitled to a declaration that the Amnesty Commission and the DPP's acted inconsistently and breached Articles 21(1) and (2) of the Constitution. On 22 September 2011, the Constitutional Court ordered that the file be returned to the ICD for it to cease Kwoyelo's trial.

4.1. APPLICATION FOR A STAY OF EXECUTION

In the meantime, an application for stay of execution was filed in the Constitutional Court.[21] The application for stay of execution was necessitated by the fact that the criminal case against Kwoyelo had been scheduled to take place on 11 November 2011, when the Trial Court would cease his trial and

21 See Constitutional Application No. 050 of 2011 arising from Constitutional Reference No. 036 of 2011 pursuant to Rules 2(2), 6(2), (b), 43(1) and 44(1) Judicature (Court of Appeal) Rules.

release him. The outcome of the application for stay of execution was a Ruling by the Court of Appeal in which it held that the applicant/Attorney General had not made out a case to warrant the granting of an order for stay of execution. Hence, the application was duly dismissed. Following this development, the Attorney General's office filed an appeal. This appeal took over two years to be determined due to a lack of quorum in the Supreme Court.

Meanwhile, the ICD sat in Gulu on 11 November 2011 and implemented the Constitutional Court's Order of 22 September 2011 to cease the trial of Thomas Kwoyelo.

4.2. APPLICATION FOR JUDICIAL REVIEW

The application was filed to force the Director of Public Prosecutions and the Amnesty Commission to execute the orders of the Constitutional Court and issue or grant a Certificate of Amnesty to Kwoyelo. The DPP based his inactivity on the pending case before a Magistrate's Court in Gulu. It is against this backdrop that on 23 November 2011, Kwoyelo's Counsel applied for judicial review to the High Court of Uganda.[22] The purpose of the judicial review was to seek:

(a) an Order of Mandamus to compel the Chairman of the Amnesty Commission and the Director of Public Prosecutions to grant a Certificate of Amnesty to the Applicant;
(b) an Order of Certiorari to quash the decision of the Commissioner General of Prisons, detaining the Applicant without a valid remand warrant;
(c) an Order that the Applicant be set free;
(d) general damages for inconvenience suffered by the Applicant as a result of the failure of the Respondent's agents or servants failure to comply with the Directions and Ruling of the Constitutional Court.

The application for judicial review was heard on 8 December 2011. Counsel for Kwoyelo argued the case based upon the grounds and prayers listed above. On the other hand, the Attorney General, arguing on the first ground contended that the DPP had written to the Amnesty Commission informing it that the Applicant was not eligible for the grant of amnesty. The Amnesty Commission never responded to that letter. The Attorney General presented another argument that the Amnesty Commission could only grant the Certificate of Amnesty after the DPP had withdrawn the case. The State Attorney posited that the Constitutional

---

22 See Miscellaneous Cause No. 162 of 2011 brought under Articles 20, 23 and 28 of the 1995 Constitution of the Republic of Uganda and sections 2 and 3 of the Amnesty Act and Rules 3(1)(a), 5 and 6 of the (Judicature Review) Rules SI No. 11 of 2009; and sections 33, 36(1)(a) and 37(1)(2) Judicature Act, Cap 13 filed on 23 November 2011.

Court did not make any orders for the withdrawal of the case. In an effort to justify the continued detention of Kwoyelo, the Respondent also argued that the crimes with which Kwoyelo was charged are international crimes for which amnesty was not applicable. Additionally, the ICD never ordered Kwoyelo's release nor did it issue a remand warrant for his continued stay in detention. The Respondent's argument was that the continued remand was reasonable and justified in light of *Criminal Case No. 118 of 2009*. This case is still pending in the High Court of Gulu and it is a separate, independent case, which is different from the present case. It has not been heard at all due to challenges relating to the issue of amnesty, which had not been resolved until last year.

Concerning the issue of setting Kwoyelo free, the Respondent argued that the Constitutional Court did not order the ICD to release the Applicant. The Respondent contended that the orders sought by the Applicant were not concise enough to enable the Constitutional Court to make any specific orders.[23]

On 25 January 2012, Justice Vincent Zehurikirize rendered his Ruling on the Judicial Review Application. He stated that both the Director of Public Prosecutions, Richard Buteera, and the Amnesty Commission chairman, Justice Peter Onega, have the mandate to issue the certificate under sections 2 and 3 of the Amnesty Act 2000.

While giving his ruling, the Judge disagreed with the submission of the state denying Kwoyelo amnesty. Justice Zehurikirize ruled that the alleged crimes as by the DPP could have been committed when Kwoyelo was still a rebel. Hence, there was no way Kwoyelo could be denied amnesty based on such crimes. The Judge's opinion was that the former rebel commander, who was captured in 2009, had denounced rebellion during his detention in Luzira Prison.[24]

The Judge further held that even the Constitutional Court in its 22 September 2011 ruling had in mind such grave crimes as enumerated in the Geneva Conventions Act Cap 363. He held that Kwoyelo was entitled to amnesty just like other former rebels who had renounced rebellion. Judge Zehurikirize then ordered the Directorate of Public Prosecutions and the Amnesty Commission to process the Certificate of Amnesty for Thomas Kwoyelo.

4.3. THE LATEST SUPREME COURT DECISION ON KWOYELO

The implication of the existence of amnesty has been that, until recently, Uganda has been unable to prosecute those responsible for serious crimes, hence putting the principle of complementarity in abeyance. However, in April 2015, the Ugandan Supreme Court unanimously made a decision not to grant

---

23 See discussion about this application by Nouwen 2013, p. 221.

24 Cap 294, Laws of Uganda.

amnesty to Kwoyelo and deemed it proper for Kwoyelo to be tried before the ICD.

There were multifarious grounds of Appeal advanced by the Attorney General in the Supreme Court of Uganda. The Supreme Court opted to adopt the issues raised by the Respondent's Counsel. The issues were: whether the Amnesty Act violated Uganda's obligations under International Laws and Covenants; whether the Amnesty Act is unconstitutional and, whether the Respondent is entitled to Amnesty under Article 21 of the Constitution of the Republic of Uganda. In the main opinion, Hon. Bart Katureebe, the Chief Justice, who read the main Opinion, expressed the view that, 'when a country commits itself to international obligations, one must assume that it does so deliberately, lawfully and in its national interest ... Therefore, a State should not easily shun its obligation as and when it wishes to. The framers of the Constitution ... must have been convinced that all the international treaties were in the best interest of Uganda.'[25]

He held, *inter alia,* that the Amnesty Act was inconsistent with international crimes. The Amnesty Act did not foreclose on certain individuals, who might have committed these types of offences, from being made accountable for their actions. He opined that any crimes committed which were not necessitated by the 'furtherance of the war or rebellion' were not a subject of amnesty under the Amnesty Act.[26] He posited that these kind of crimes were not political offences but crimes committed on members of the society. He highlighted the offence of wilful murder of civilians as being tantamount to crimes against humanity. He stated that, in respect of crimes under the Geneva Conventions Act, an Offender cannot be granted amnesty. Additionally, the Amnesty Act does not purport to grant amnesty to such crimes. Resultantly, the Amnesty Act does not contravene the international treaties and obligations which Uganda signed and ratified.[27]

On whether or not Kwoyelo had been discriminated against, the Chief Justice Katureebe further held that the Respondent had to enunciate the sphere in which he had been treated unequally. For example, he had to demonstrate under which Constitutional ground he had been discriminated against: whether it was on sex, colour, race, tribalism, religious grounds, etc. Kwoyelo also had to show how he had been denied equal protection of the law. Katureebe JSC's opinion was that it is not, and cannot be unequal treatment under the law simply for one person to be charged with specific crimes and for another person not to have been charged when each one of them committed similar crimes.

---

25 Supreme Court Constitutional Appeal No. 01 of 2012, *Uganda v. Thomas Kwoyelo*, p. 35, line 17 to p. 36, line 5.

26 *Ibid*, p. 63, lines 15–19.

27 Supreme Court Ruling, p. 35, line 17 to p. 36, line 5; see also p. 43, lines 13–25, p. 55, lines 5–10.

He cited paragraph 8 of General Comment 18 of the Human Rights Committee on non-discrimination and underscored the fact that the enjoyment of rights and freedoms were on an equal footing. However, this did not translate into identical treatment in every incidence. Referring to paragraph 13 of General Comment 18, he further emphasised that not every differentiation or treatment would constitute discrimination, if the criteria for such differentiation are reasonable and objective and if the aim is to achieve a purpose which is legitimate under the Covenant.[28]

The implication of the Supreme Court Ruling is that the trial, which was halted in September 2011 by the International Crimes Division of the High Court, will resume. The Supreme Court Ruling overturned the Constitutional Court's Ruling of 22 September 2011 which had halted Kwoyelo's trial and pronounced that he should be granted amnesty.

5. THE CHALLENGES OF THE INTERNATIONAL CRIMES DIVISION (ICD)

For a proper discourse on the ICD's operation, I must raise the different challenges facing the ICD and how they are being addressed. Challenges are not unique to the ICD and exist in other national jurisdictions prosecuting war crimes. For example, during his address to the Security Council, Prosecutor Brammertz of the ICTY warned that 'national judiciaries continue to face significant legal obstacles and challenges with regards to the Prosecution of war crimes.'[29] In respect of the ICD, there are diverse challenges and I address them below.

5.1. INSTITUTIONAL CHALLENGES

The ICD exists, but it is lacking in various aspects because the authorities argue that the ICD is just a Division of the High Court like any other Division and not an international 'court'. The argument is that no priority should be accorded to it. It should be on a par with other Divisions in respect to budgetary or logistical necessities. The debate on whether the ICD is a Division or a Court overlooks the objectives and goals of the ICD.

---

28 *Ibid*, p. 49, lines 7–15; p. 53, lines 11, 14–16; and p. 54, lines 26–30.

29 Prosecutor Brammertz's Address before the Security Council, Press Release No. 3, December 2009, available at: www.icty.org/en/press/prosecutor-brammertz%E2%80%99s-address-security-council-0.

5.1.1. Response to Institutional Challenges

The best response to institutional challenges is for the staff of the ICD to recognise the importance of a primary court *vis-à-vis* the ICC, which is a court of complementarity and for staff to be committed to the implementation of the Rome Statute in order to achieve the expected results. Although the ICD is named as a 'Division', its function, form, laws and jurisdiction show that it is a domestic court applying both international and national law and it has the mandate to handle international crimes.[30] The ICD has four judges and a Registrar. The latter engages in outreach programmes, among his other responsibilities. The ICD is currently dealing with issues pertaining to witness protection mechanisms. The ICD works with a specialised unit of six Prosecutors, a specialised Investigative Unit within the Police, and a Government Analytical Unit with trained police officers. In my view, the ICD is not just a Division of the High Court but a competent court that is ready to try persons accused of war crimes and crimes against humanity. It is necessary to make more assertive efforts to entrench the ICD in Uganda's criminal justice system.

5.2. PROCEDURAL AND EVIDENTIAL CHALLENGES

The ICD does not have its own rules of procedure and evidence that enables it to effectively handle crimes against humanity, war crimes, or any other crimes that falls within its mandate. The Judicature Act Cap empowers the enactment of rules of procedure and evidence where there is a legislative vacuum. In such a situation, the relevant division crafts the necessary rules and forwards them to the Rules Committee for discussion and finalisation. The Rules Committee comprises, *inter alia,* the Chief Justice, the Principal Judge, the DPP, a representative of the Uganda Law Society and other crucial stakeholders. Currently, the momentum for the consideration of the Rules by the Rules Committee is on course. In May 2015, the Judges of the ICD met to validate the Draft Rules and bring them in line with existing laws of procedure and evidence whilst juxtaposing them with the rules relating to best practices of international procedures and evidence. The Judges were careful not to overstep the powers provided within the existing laws. A last validation was held at the end of 2014.[31] A cursory consideration of the Rules shows that the best practices as applied by the ICC and other international tribunals and courts have been adopted. This is premised upon the fact that the ICC Act 2010 has the Rome Statute as its Annexure. It seems as if Uganda would have liked to copy the Rome Statute

30 See Legal Notice Supplement No. 5 of 31 May 2011.

31 A prior review by the ICD Judges and other stakeholders took place in a Validation of the Rules of Procedure and Evidence Meeting at Spike Hotel, Munyonyo on 22–23 May 2015.

as much as possible, oblivious of its freedom to utilise any means to uphold the legal tenets enunciated in the Rome Statute.[32] One of the features of the Draft Rules is the proposal to set up a Pre-Trial Chamber. Already the Principal Judge has designated the relevant judge to help in this regard. There are also elaborate provisions of witness protection measures. The latter are necessary as the witness protection bill is being prepared for debate before Parliament. However, since 2016 is a year of elections its debate might tarry. Concerning the Pre-Trial Chamber, this is a completely new establishment whose approval, in the final analysis, will depend upon the Rules Committee. The Rules have endeavoured to include some provisions of reparation and reference has been made to legal provisions under our existing laws. This is also a bold step because currently Uganda does not have a comprehensive law on reparation. It is pertinent to note that the Rules will be applicable not only to war crimes but to all the crimes falling within the ICD's extended mandate such as human trafficking, terrorism and other trans-boundary crimes.

5.2.1. Response to Procedural Challenges

In the meantime in order to fill the vacuum, the High Court has invoked the principle of complementarity and guided the ICD on the applicable law. The Legal Notice provides some guidance on the matter. It states that:

> (i) The Division shall in the first instance apply the rules of procedure applicable to criminal trials in Uganda;
> (ii) Where no express provision is made under any written law, the Court shall adopt such other procedure as it considers to be justifiable and appropriate in all the circumstances, taking into account the provisions of section 141 of the Trial on Indictment Act and section 39 of the Judicature Act, and having regard to the rights and views of the parties;
> (iii) Subject to any law for the time being in force, the Division may from time to time adopt Practice Directions for the better management of cases and for the orderly and timely disposal of cases.[33]

The ICD is, therefore, permitted to utilise not only domestic laws, but international decisions and laws from other countries and courts, including the International Criminal Tribunal for the former Yugoslavia (ICTY), the International Criminal Tribunal for Rwanda (ICTR), and the Special Court for Sierra Leone (SCSL). In practice, the emphasis is on best practices. It is envisaged that there will not be wholesale application of those tribunals' or international court rules. The expectation is that of modifying the international procedural rules to suit Uganda's context. An opportunity to apply the best international practices arose

32 States have used different wording as well as different mechanisms – see Terracino 2007.
33 Practice Direction setting up the ICD.

during the trial of Thomas Kwoyelo when it was faced with a problem of how the Defence could move the court to present their motion on lack of jurisdiction, their request for disclosure and amnesty issues. The issue of jurisdiction is pivotal to any trial and legal jurists have now and again underscored the importance of a court's jurisdiction. A notable international lawyer from Bangladesh Mizanur Rahman opined that '[j]urisdiction is the critical legal issue underpinning the prosecution of war criminals in a state's courts.'[34]

Considering the importance of jurisdictional challenges, the lack of rules of procedure to enable the defendants to effectively bring such a challenge is a weakness of the ICD. Although the Defence in the *Kwoyelo case* raised such a motion prematurely, that is, prior to taking the plea, the Presiding Judge considered the legal notice provision *supra*. He resorted to the use of international legal standards and practices which would best determine the matter and directed the Defence Team to raise motions orally for consideration by the Court. As the Defence was not well prepared to deal with those motions during plea taking, the Court granted the Defence time within which to file formal written motions. However, by this time the Defence Counsel had read into the record a motion on amnesty as well as his challenge to the ICD's jurisdiction to try grave breaches. The record of proceedings regarding this motion was eventually expunged. Later, during the constitutional reference hearing, the Defence abandoned the request to interpret the jurisdictional question.

5.3. LACK OF FORMAL WITNESS PROTECTION MECHANISMS

Uganda has no law on witness and victims protection at the moment but efforts are being made to finalise the Witness Protection Bill. In the absence of a witness protection law, each judge becomes creative as they handle sensitive capital offences such as rape, defilement and murder cases. There are, however, some basic protections enshrined in the Evidence Act. Sections 150 and 151 of the Evidence Act provides some protections as shown below.

> Indecent and scandalous questions.
>
> The court may forbid any question or inquiries which it regards as indecent or scandalous, although the questions or inquiries may have some bearing on the questions before the court, unless they relate to facts in issue, or to matters necessary to be known in order to determine whether or not the facts in issue existed (Section 150).

34 Rahman and Billah, Prosecuting War Crimes in Domestic Level: The Case of Bangladesh, available at: www.banglajol.info/index/WUJL/article/download/18522/12972.

> Questions intended to insult or annoy.
> The court shall forbid any question which appears to it to be intended to insult or annoy, or which, though proper in itself, appears to the court needlessly offensive in form (Section 151).

The protection is limited to questions to be put to a witness but does not extend to physical protection. It is notable that these provisions cover only the control of courtroom appearance and questions put to witnesses but do not extend to other requisite courtroom witness protection mechanisms such as the non-disclosure of a witness's identity, and voice and facial distortion. Our criminal justice system does not have the gadgets to effect such measures.

The ICC Act 2010 contains two main provisions. The first protection pertains to a witness, who is also a victim. The second category concerns the enforcement of orders for victim reparation made by the ICC. Although these provisions exist, they must be developed and implemented so that witness protection mechanisms may effectively protect victims and witnesses who will appear in trials before the ICC whether in Uganda or at The Hague.

5.3.1. *Response to Lack of Witness Protection*

Protecting victims and witnesses should remain high on any court's agenda. Victim and witness cooperation is essential to ensure fair and successful prosecutions. Providing witness protection is therefore both expedient for law enforcement as well as a fundamental legal obligation. Yet, often, in post-conflict situations, individuals do not want to cooperate out of fear. The protection of witnesses from intimidation or harm is imperative to the integrity and success of a judicial process. Justice Navanethem Pillay has stated that:

> We know that most witnesses involved in investigations and Prosecutions have good reasons to fear retaliation. They often live in volatile and insecure environments where their human rights could be violated. Absent appropriate safety nets for the protection of witnesses, their physical and psychological integrity, privacy, dignity, their reputation and even lives may be at risk. The fear is more real than imaginary.[35]

It is therefore not debated that witnesses must be protected from intimidation, threats and harm. Victims need justice as well as Accused need their rights at trial. From a human rights and judicial perspective, it is important that the rights of the accused should not be undermined by the rights of the victim.[36] There is

---

35 As cited in Redress, *Ending Threats and Reprisals Against Victims of Torture and Related International Crimes: A Call To Action*, p. 7 (paper presented at OHCHR Expert meeting on Witness Protection for Successful Investigations and Prosecution of Gross Human Rights Violations and International Crimes, held on 29 September 2009 in Geneva).

36 See Croquet 2010, p. 4.

extensive jurisprudence on the 'balance' that must be struck between witnesses and victims' rights to be protected from threats and reprisals and the rights of the accused, particularly the right for each accused to know the case against him/her. The general view has been that in 'balancing' the rights, it should be understood that there is no implied hierarchy of rights with respect to victims and the accused, or that the rights of either party can be violated, dismissed or subsumed by the rights of the other. I posit that the balancing act is the basis of a fair trial and should not end at the stage of prosecution.

Regional human rights courts such as the European Court of Human Rights are at the forefront of balancing the rights of the victims against those of the accused persons. In general, witnesses who are completely anonymous would deprive the accused of the necessary information to challenge the witness's reliability thereby eroding the accused persons' rights to confront prosecution witnesses through effective cross-examination.

The European Court of Human Rights has generally indicated that the use of testimony from an anonymous witness does not necessarily violate an accused person's right to examine witnesses, but may render the trial to be wholly unfair as held in the *Doorson* case.[37]

Concerning the ICD and witness protection, several discussions in the form of conferences have been constantly carried out. In 2011, the UN Human Rights Office organised a Conference at which the ICD Judges interacted with prosecutors, defence lawyers and national NGOs and international NGOs.[38]

Additionally, over the past three years, the Justice Law and Order Sector (JLOS) had been working with consultants to oversee a needs assessment in respect of the risk posed to witnesses. In practice, the ICD has not yet had to deal with motions on witness protection as the first trial did not progress far enough for this to happen due to the Defence's request to have some matters placed as a constitutional reference before the Constitutional Court as already reflected in this paper. On the contrary, in the preparation of its trials, the ICD Prosecutorial Unit has grappled with this issue. The Director of Public Prosecutions is duty bound to disclose certain materials for purposes of a fair trial[39] but must take into account the need to protect witnesses given the lack of a witness protection law.

---

37 *Doorson v. The Netherlands*, 54/1994/501/583. Mr Doorson applied to the European Court of Human Rights on 27 June 1992 claiming that he was a victim of a violation of Arts. 6(1) and 3(d) of the European Human Rights Convention because he was convicted on evidence adduced from anonymous witnesses.

38 Judicial Colloquium on Witness and Victim Protection in Uganda held on 1–3 August 2011 in Gulu, Uganda.

39 *Soon Yeon Kong Kim and Another v. Attorney General*, Constitutional Reference No. 6 of 2007 from the Chief Magistrate's Court at Buganda Road arising from Criminal Case No. 4288 of 2005.

The solution would be to adopt the best practices applied at the ICC, the SCSL and the ad hoc Tribunals in accordance with the Practice Direction establishing the ICD.[40] Uganda can take a cue from international courts. As pointed out above under the ICD Rules, this aspect is being addressed. Protective measures may include physical protective measures for witnesses during testimony and the ensuing logistical procedures to physically ensure their protection. The non-disclosure of witness identity prior to trial is the most commonly used measure by the Prosecution.[41] However, anonymity is extremely important to maintain the protection of victims and witnesses during a trial. Other protective measures pertaining to psychologically vulnerable witnesses, particularly children, should also be considered. Vulnerable witnesses might be allowed to provide testimony in a closed session or via video link from the waiting room.[42] There is a pending motion before me in a kidnap for ransom case involving foreigners who are not willing to travel to Uganda owing to old age and the ordeal they suffered. The motion has just been filed and awaits a hearing date.

5.4. VICTIM PARTICIPATION IN THE PROCEEDINGS IN THEIR OWN STANDING AND LACK OF VICTIM REPARATIONS

Uganda's criminal justice system does not provide for independent appearance of victims. Rather, the DPP appears on their behalf. Similarly, the ICC Act 2010 does not specifically provide for the participation of victims in criminal proceedings nor does it make provision for victim reparations in Uganda. There is also no mention of the establishment of a Victims' Trust Fund, similar to what is authored in the Rome Statute.

There are several questions which come to mind when considering the issue of reparation. Some of them are: how can the victims of the LRA generally be given reparation considering that not all of them will be brought before the Court? Should victims' reparation be considered during or at the end of trial? What sort of reparations are the victims entitled to? Should they be individual or collective? There is also the most crucial question, why give reparation to the victims? Perhaps, this is a good stage, to make some interjections on reparations generally.

40 *Yeon Kong Kim and Another v. Attorney General*, Constitutional Reference No. 6 of 2007.

41 This is a lesson learnt from the ICTR's experience in cases like that of Rudasingwa where the ICTR Investigators visited his shop at numerous occasions in marked UN vehicles thus making him an easy target. He was later killed.

42 See also Rule 75 of the SCSL Rules of Procedure & Evidence; in Uganda, the Family Law Division has already started implementing this mechanism.

5.4.1. *Response to Lack of Victims' Participation*

Whether or not victims will appear independently in proceedings before the ICD is a policy issue to be decided by the administrators at the High Court. The ICD can incorporate and adopt ICC measures to create a specialised unit for victims and witnesses. The Victim and Witness Unit will cater for and support victims' needs such as physical or psychosocial protection or material support. Similar provisions have been included in the Draft Rules of the ICD. However, these are temporary measures. When the Witness and Victims' Protection Bill is finally passed, there will be regulations to cater for all these matters.

The ICD Rules of Procedure also include provisions on reparation, particularly court ordered to make the necessary orders on reparation. It is necessary for Parliament to enact an overarching primary law encompassing all aspects of reparation before the ICD Rules could meaningfully effect and emphasise its provisions on reparation. Currently, the DPP acts on behalf of the victims to initiate claims for compensation/reparation as envisaged under paragraph 58 of the Sentencing Guidelines. A State Attorney may apply for ancillary, compensatory/confiscatory orders with regard to the needs of the victims.

Although the ICD is a criminal court, Articles 50 and 126(2)(c) of the Constitution of the Republic of Uganda 1995 provide for remedies and compensation. This pertains where the rights of a person are violated. A wronged party may seek redress from the competent courts of law and he/she must get a remedy. Given the importance of remedy, the law and mechanisms of reparation must be given serious consideration by the Uganda Law Reform Commission and Parliament.

5.5. REPARATIONS FOR VICTIMS: TYPES OF REPARATION

Reparations are measures adopted by states that are intended to repair past harms, in particular the systematic violation of human rights associated with armed conflict or repression. The right to such redress is enshrined in international human rights instruments. There are two broad categories of reparations: one type involves reparations from one state, usually a defeated state to another state. The second type is the situation where a state pays reparations to non-state parties and individual victims of mass atrocities. Reparations are intended to redress the damage caused to the injured party.

5.5.1. *Reparation under International Law*

Under international law, reparations must, as far as possible, wipe out all the consequences of the illegal act and re-establish the situation, which would, in all probability, have existed if that act had not been committed.[43] According to the Juba Agreement on Accountability and Reconciliation, this involves wiping out all the consequences of the act. Reparations may take the form of restitution, compensation, rehabilitation as well as satisfaction and guarantees of non-repetition.[44] Reparations programmes can be put in place by governments for a large group of victims and may include individual compensation, possible opportunities for education and training, access to health and psychological rehabilitation and measures of collective reparations.[45]

5.5.2. *Other Forms of Reparations*

These constitute measures of satisfaction that may include a search for the disappeared, administrative or judicial sanctions against perpetrators, disclosure of the truth, memorials, official/public apologies or other symbolic measures like commemorations. The purpose of reparations is to provide acknowledgement of violations, a re-assertion of the violations of the survivors and means to redress the impact of crimes. Reparations impact on both the individual victim and the wider societies and communities affected. By focusing on restorative and retributive actions, reparations for mass atrocities play a big role in rebuilding war-torn societies through advancing truth and acknowledging the gravity of the crimes committed. Reparations should provide benefits directly to the victims of certain types of crimes and violations. International law obliges the government to provide reparations to victims of violations if the obligation to provide effective remedy is to be fulfilled. Article 2(3) of the International Covenant on Civil and Political Rights obliges government to ensure that:

a. Any person whose rights or freedoms recognized are violated shall have an effective remedy, notwithstanding that the violation has been committed by persons acting in official capacity;
b. Any person claiming such a remedy shall have his right thereto determined by competent judicial, administrative or legislative authorities, or by any other competent authority provided for by the legal system of the State, and to develop the possibilities of judicial remedy;
c. The competent authorities shall enforce such remedies when granted.

---

43 Article 1 of the draft Articles on State Responsibility adopted by the International Law Commission in 2001: 'Every internationally wrongful act of a state entails the international responsibility of the state' (UN Doc. A/CN.4/L.602/Rev.1, 26 July 2001).

44 Clause 1 of the Juba Agreement on Accountability and Reconciliation and its Annexure, 29 June 2007.

45 Clause 9(2), Juba Agreement cited above.

5.5.3. *The Convention against Torture and Other Cruel, Inhuman or Degrading Treatment or Punishment*

Article 14 of this Convention obliges the government to ensure that any victim of an act of torture obtains redress and has an enforceable right to fair and adequate compensation including the means for full rehabilitation where possible and in the event of the death of the victim as a result of torture, his dependants shall be entitled to compensation.

5.5.4. *Article 24 of the International Convention for the Protection of All Persons from Enforced Disappearance*

This states that each victim has the right to know the truth regarding the circumstances of the enforced disappearance, the progress and results of the investigation and the fate of the disappeared person. Each state party shall take appropriate measures in this regard.

Similar provisions can be found in Article 91 of the Additional Protocol to the Geneva Convention of 12 August 1949 relating to the Protection of Victims of International Armed Conflict (Protocol 1) of 8 June 1977; Articles 68 and 75 of the Rome Statute of the International Criminal Court; Article 7 of the African Charter on Human and Peoples Rights; Article 22 of the African Charter on the Rights and Welfare of the Child; and the 1985 UN Declaration on Basic Principles of Justice for Victims of Crime and Abuse of Power.[46]

The Rome Statute requires the institution of principles relating to reparations to or in respect of victims including restitution, compensation, and rehabilitation. The Assembly of States Parties is required to establish a Trust Fund for the benefit of victims of crimes within the ICC's jurisdiction. Uganda has also incorporated reparations for the survivor in a number of its enacted laws.[47] They include but are not limited to Section 126 of the Trial on Indictment Act (TIA) Cap 23 and Sections 123–124, 126, 188–189 and 239–247 of the TIA.

5.5.5. *The Juba Peace and Reparation Initiative*

The Agreement on Accountability and Reconciliation committed parties to acknowledging and addressing the suffering of victims including the most vulnerable groups. In addition to the retributive and traditional justice and

---

46 Article 91 of the Additional Protocol to the Geneva Convention of 12 August 1949 relating to the Protection of Victims of International Crimes [Protocol 1] of 8 June 1977; Articles 68 and 75 of the Rome Statute of the International Criminal Court; Article 7 of the African Charter on Human and Peoples Rights; Article 22 of the African Charter on the Rights and Welfare of the Child; and the 1985 UN Declaration on Basic Principles of Justice for Victims of Crime and Abuse of Power.

47 Articles 50, 21, 24, 44(a) and 53(2) of the Constitution of the Republic of Uganda 1995.

truth seeking mechanisms, the Agreement also provides for the provision of reparations to victims. It takes a broad approach to the concept of reparations, providing that they can include a range of measures such as 'rehabilitation; restitution; compensation; guarantees of non-recurrence and other symbolic measures such as apologies, memorials and commemorations'. It states that reparations should be 'collective as well as individual'. Clearly, such a holistic approach to reparations is important in ensuring the necessary infrastructure is in place for the IDPs to return to their villages.

Clause 9(1) of the Agreement on Accountability makes provision for reparations and states that reparations may include rehabilitation, restitution, compensation, guarantees of non-recurrence and other symbolic measures such as apologies, memorials and commemorations. The Agreement stipulates that 'priority shall be given to members of vulnerable groups' such as women and children. For both groups, it provides little detail on how this should be achieved. The Agreement does not even explicitly refer to child soldiers, although it does provide that the parties will 'ensure that children are not subjected to criminal justice proceedings, but may participate, as appropriate, in reconciliation processes.' There have already been some reparations by the Government of Uganda for lost or damaged property. This measure falls under the auspices of the Northern Uganda Reconstruction Program (I and II) and focuses on providing financial compensation. Priority is to be given to vulnerable groups. Collective and individual reparations are envisaged to be made via mechanisms to be adopted by the parties upon further consultation.

Clause 9(3) provides that reparations paid to a victim arising out of penalties and sanctions in accountability proceedings maybe paid out of resources identified for that purpose. The problem is that Uganda is yet to earmark such resources.

Another reason why LRA victims should receive reparation is that a clearly established right to remedy and reparation for serious violations of international human rights law and international humanitarian law exists.

5.5.6. *The United Nations General Assembly and Reparations*

In 2005, the United Nations General Assembly adopted the 'Basic Principles and Guidelines on the Right to a Remedy and Reparation for Victims of Gross Violations of International Human Rights Law and Serious Violations of international humanitarian law' ('The Basic Principles'). These enunciate the International law regarding the right to remedy and reparation based upon existing legal obligations under national and international laws.

5.5.7. *The Right to Remedy under Uganda's Basic Legal Instruments*

The right to remedy is also found in Article 50 of the Constitution of the Republic of Uganda. Section 64 of the ICC Act 2010 mentions enforcement of the

ICC's orders for victims' reparations. The Amnesty Act of 2000 does not address any aspects of compensation or reparations for the victims of such crimes. Due to lack of a comprehensive reparations programme in the country, survivors of the war in Northern Uganda have not yet received reparations. The existing law on reparations in the Penal Code Act has limitations. It provides for only compensation. Civil remedies may be granted by Courts arising from civil suits but cannot be used as a basis to grant reparations for the victims of the massive human rights violations committed during the war. As I have already pointed out, the Government of Uganda has made efforts in some parts of the country as for instance, through the development of the Peace Recovery and Development Plan (PRDP), to address needs of the Northern region and 'LRA war affected areas'. The Government was also extensively involved in resettlement exercises during which it issued the affected communities with resettlement packages. There have also been ad hoc directives by the executive in the form of monetary compensation for victims of the *Mukura* massacre in the Teso sub-region. The issue remains however, whether these reparations gave due regard to the needs of specialised victims of war crimes like women, children and persons with disabilities.

5.6. THE DRAFT TRANSITIONAL JUSTICE POLICY AND REPARATION

Some guidelines on reparations are necessary. During the first review of the ICD proposed Rules in September 2012, it became evident from the contribution of the JLOS representatives that there is a Draft Policy on reparations. It envisages that the Government of Uganda is considering the establishment of a reparation programme. What is planned shows the availability of two options. One is reparation attached to a Court Order. The other is reparation availed through the non-informal mechanism whereby a victim will be expected to make a formal application to a body to be set up. The latter reparative mechanism will cover those victims whose matters are not before court or are not participating in the trial as victims or witnesses.

The Uganda Draft Transitional Justice Policy is an effort by the Government of Uganda to implement a holistic Draft Transitional Justice policy, designed to address issues of accountability, reparation and reconciliation in post-conflict Uganda. The Draft Transitional Justice Policy marks a historic step by the Government of Uganda in creating a framework designed to implement the provisions of the Agreement on Accountability and Reconciliation.[48] The Government of Uganda committed itself to establishing and implementing

48 Item No. 3 of the Juba Peace Agreement which provides that victims have a right to: effective and meaningful participation in accountability and reconciliation proceedings; access

a reparations programme for victims affected by conflict. Compensating individuals may ultimately prove to be administratively impractical and counter-productive, potentially causing resentment both within and between communities. Victims have pointed fingers at the ex-LRA combatants who received a 'resettlement package' upon being granted amnesty. The package included a monetary payment of 200,000 Ugandan shillings (about 80 US dollars).

This has led to the perception by some victims that the ex-LRA fighters were rewarded for their role in the conflict since the victims did not receive any comparable individual reparation. The Draft Policy makes a general statement that the victims will be identified for the purposes of implementing a reparations programme. It falls short of explicitly providing that individual victims will be favoured over collective reparation. Overall, the Policy has catered for the reparations needs of affected communities in a more meaningful and comprehensive manner.

It is worthy to note that different victims suffered different forms of sexual violence during the war. Arguably, reparations are the most victim-centred measures among all available transitional justice mechanisms. It is also the most significant means of making a difference in the lives of the victims. However, the omission by the Policy to state the basis on which a determination can be made for those eligible to participate in the reparations programme poses a major challenge. A system must be devised to determine what form of reparation should be given to each victim.

There is another setback, which is that the recipient communities also exhibit high expectations. This is coupled with a missing link between recovery, healing or retrieval and justice. A JLOS survey done in the greater north of Uganda revealed an interesting pattern.[49] The victims wanted to know the truth about the past harms; they are interested in truth recovery and wished to know the identity of the perpetrators. Others want a historical clarification to understand the underlying causes of the conflict, while others emphasise the need for reconciliation and healing, particularly at family, community and inter-regional levels. They want a compilation of the serious violations that they encountered to be noted and recorded for posterity's sake.[50] The war-affected communities in Northern Uganda underscored individual and collective measures to address the social and economic effects of the conflict which the individuals and communities suffered. These communities want physical and mental health services, education, housing, restoration of their livelihoods, empowerment of the youth, public

to information about their experiences; truth telling and fact finding; and right to dignity, privacy and security.

49 *The Dust has not yet Settled: Victims' Views on the Right to Remedy & Reparation*: A Report from the Greater North of Uganda sponsored by United Nations Human Rights Office and the Uganda Human Rights Commission 2011.

50 Ibid, pp. 59–60.

land and inheritance, and the public acknowledgement of the harm which they had suffered.[51] It is imperative that efforts be made to strike a balance between individual and collective reparations for the different types of harm suffered by individuals and their communities. A specially tailored reparations programme that takes care of all the different types of human rights abuses suffered by the victims will be most suitable. Concerning the issue of what remedy should be availed to the communities that experienced the war, the JLOS Report indicates that the victims want to be involved in the design of the mandate of any official body to be established to unearth the truth and clarify historical events.[52]

6. CHALLENGE OF LACK OF CAPACITY

The ICD has the right calibre of judges but lacks corresponding support staff that possess the requisite competence of managing international cases. There is no standardised training requirement for judiciary support staff. The ICD has few trained court interpreters. ICD Registry has pin-pointed archive management as one of the necessary training areas as well as training in areas of witness protection. Added to these training limitations is the hindrance of frequent personnel transfers. The few competent support staff members are usually transferred from the ICD without due regard to the experience acquired which is crucial to the ICD. However, most staff working with the ICD, including judges, are civil servants who cannot resist being transferred because it is a prerogative of the Principal Judge (PJ) and the Human Resources Unit. Since the ICD's inception, four Registrars have been transferred from the Division and four judges have been reshuffled. The same predicament extends to both the ICD Prosecutorial Unit and the ICD Investigative Unit. Regarding the training of staff, although a number of trainings have been organised for judges, prosecutors and investigators, the need for continuous training cannot be overemphasised. The staff turnover has exacerbated the problem of lack of capacity and some trained staff members leave the ICD for greener pastures.

Another challenge is that the Ugandan legal community lacks knowledge of international criminal law, although some training for both prosecutors and defence lawyers has been conducted. Most Ugandan judges have been trained in public international law, but not specifically in the field of international criminal law. The ICD has been equipped to handle the trial of perpetrators of international crimes and thus, the four Judges in the ICD are exceptions. They either have practical or academic knowledge of international criminal law. However, Judges have been assigned only one legal researcher who is paid by the judiciary. Initially there were seven pro bono legal researchers but there were no

51 *Justice and Law Order Sector Report*, p. xvi.
52 *Ibid*, pp. xv–xvi.

funds to cover their salaries and they left. The administrators in the Ministry of Public Service argue that there is no position for legal assistants and researchers in the judiciary's structure.

6.1. LACK OF LEGAL EFFECTIVE LEGAL AID

There is a dire need for advocates willing and able to provide legal aid to the indigent accused persons in international crimes cases. The existing system is made up of several ad hoc arrangements made by local NGOs such as the Uganda Law Society's Legal Aid Project; the Law Development Centre Legal Clinic; Women Lawyers Association (FIDA); the Christian Lawyers Fraternity, the Public Defenders' Association and Justice Law Centers, most of whom have not benefited from the limited training availed to some defence counsels. For the *Kwoyelo* trial, the ICD Registry had assigned a team of three well-trained lawyers to Kwoyelo on state brief but Kwoyelo opted to engage private lawyers whose legal fees were paid by Joseph Kony.

6.2. LACK OF ADEQUATE EQUIPMENT

The ICD lacks proper facilitation in terms of equipment such as Court recording equipment and expertise in operating such equipment.

6.3. RESPONSE TO LACK OF CAPACITY, TRAINING, AND THE SHORTAGE OF PERSONNEL AND LACK OF LEGAL AID

In order to enhance their capacity to handle such high profile trials, the ICD Prosecutorial Unit has been working well with a dedicated War Crimes Investigation Unit of the Uganda Police Force. This follows the best practice in international courts and tribunals by carrying out prosecutorial-based investigations.

Regarding the incessant staff transfers, the ICD has dialogued with the PJ and continues to raise the matter at any possible opportunity. The logistical needs are being addressed by the JLOS Sector and the Judiciary.[53] The Office of

53 The Justice and Law Order Sector (JLOS), which usually galvanises funds for the judiciary and other institutions, has constantly made funds available to engage a legal researcher when a judge handles a criminal session and intends to extend this feature to areas of the judiciary. The necessity of such a legal researcher has now taken root in the institutional set-up of the judiciary and the position is being considered in the ongoing review of public posts within the Public Service Commission.

the Prosecutor of the International Criminal Court is in constant touch with the DPP Unit of the ICD through which the Office of the Prosecutor at The Hague shares some relevant information and materials with the DPP/ICD Unit which is useful and a true demonstration of positive complementarity. However, the initiative has been taken by the ICD-Prosecutorial Unit and not the ICC which falls short of genuine positive complementarity.

The training needs have been sponsored by JLOS and carried out by the Judicial Studies Institute (JSI). The more substantive training for judges and prosecutors has been done by international NGOs which are friendly to the ICD.[54] The JSI recently showed interest in a proposal to commence training the judges of the Court of Appeal and the Supreme Court in international criminal law and procedure. The ICD is still negotiating with an international NGO to fund legal researchers. They will come in handy considering the latest Ruling of the Supreme Court which held that the Kwoyelo Trial should resume.[55] The Judiciary has already embarked on the process of procuring court equipment for all the Divisions of the High Court.

As far as the issue of legal aid is concerned, the ICD's strategy is to encourage the provision of training for the advocates on the List of Counsel willing to take state briefs. The problem is also being addressed administratively to enhance the remuneration of state briefs in order to attract the best calibre of lawyers.

7. CHALLENGES OF OFFICE SPACE

In terms of physical infrastructure, the ICD and the DPP-ICD Unit share a rented compound with the Anti-Corruption Division of the High Court. The ICD needs a permanent building of its own. The ICD needs extra space to provide adequate space for offices, archives, a library and a teleconferencing room to give it a semblance of other courts in the world that adjudicate over international crimes.

7.1. RESPONSE TO THE LACK OF SPACE

There are future plans to relocate the ICD and other divisions. A step forward has been taken by securing land in a good location and construction arrangements are underway.

54 Recently, on 14–18 November 2015, the ICD judges and some Court of Appeal and Supreme Court judges were trained in Kampala by the Peace and Justice Initiative in diverse aspects of international criminal law, international criminal procedure and evidence and other related laws.

55 The trial of Kwoyelo is projected to resume in April 2016 after the elections have taken place.

8. CONCLUSION

The challenges that the ICD has faced and still faces have enabled us to work hard and resolve them using best practice principles as appropriate and within the available funds. The Kwoyelo trial had been halted, and only resumed under the Supreme Court's recent order. Consequently, the idea of making the ICD fully functional is gaining momentum. It is crucial that efforts geared towards improving the ICD's set up and its functionality should continue. This will facilitate the effective investigation, prosecution, defence and adjudication of the serious international crimes within the domestic jurisdiction. The ICD is also mandated to handle other crimes such as human trafficking, terrorism, drug trafficking, money laundering and other trans-boundary cases. Ideally, priority should be accorded to the adjudication of core crimes: genocide, crimes against humanity and war crimes, which were originally envisaged to be the main business of the ICD.[56]

BIBLIOGRAPHY

BOOKS AND JOURNAL ARTICLES

Bacio Terracino 2007
Bacio Terracino, J., 'National Implementation of ICC Crimes: Impact on National Jurisdictions and the ICC', 5 Journal of International Criminal Justice, 2007, pp. 421–440.

Croquet 2010
Croquet, N., 'Implied External Limitations on the Right to Cross-Examine Prosecution Witnesses: The Tension Between a Means Test and a Balancing Test in the Appraisal of Anonymity Requests', 11 Melbourne Journal of International Law, 2010.

Marshall 2010
Marshall, K.A., 'Prevention and Complementarity in the International Criminal Court: A Positive Approach', 17 Human Rights Brief, 2010.

Nouwen 2013
Nouwen, S.M.H., 'Complementarity in the Line of Fire: The Catalysing Effect of the International Criminal Court in Uganda and Sudan', Cambridge University Press, 2013.

Rahman and Billah 2010
Rahman, M. and Billah, S.M.M, 'Prosecuting "War Crimes" in Domestic Level: The case of Bangladesh', 1 Northern University Journal of Law, 2010.

56 It is worthy to note that the handling of trials depends on the investigations done by the ICD/DPP & ICD-Investigative Units. Those two Units have the prosecutorial discretion of which cases to commit to the ICD.

JURISPRUDENCE

Constitutional Court of Uganda 2011
Constitutional Court of Uganda, Uganda v. Thomas Kwoyelo, Constitutional Application No. 050 of 2011 [Arising out of Constitutional Reference No. 036/11], 10 November 2011.
Constitutional Court of Uganda 2011
Constitutional Court of Uganda, Thomas Kwoyelo v. Uganda, Constitutional Petition No. 036 of 2011 [Arising out of HCT -00-ICD-Case No. 02/10], 22 September 2011.
Constitutional Court of Uganda 2008
Constitutional Court of Uganda, Soon Yeon Kong Kim and Another v. Attorney General, Constitutional Reference No. 6 of 2007, 6 March 2008.
ECtHR 1996
ECtHR, Doorson v. The Netherlands, Application no. 20524/92, 26 March 1996.
ECtHR 1979
ECtHR, Sunday Times v. UK (Series A No. 30), (1979–80) 2 EHRR 245, 26 April 1979.
High Court of Uganda 2012
High Court of Uganda, Thomas Kwoyelo v. The Attorney General, (Miscellaneous Cause) No. 162 of 2011, 25 January 2012.
Supreme Court of Uganda 2015
Supreme Court of Uganda, Uganda v. Thomas Kwoyelo, Constitutional Appeal No. 01 of 2012, 8 April 2015.
Supreme Court of Uganda 2003
Supreme Court of Uganda, Arvind Patel v. Uganda, Criminal Application No. 1 of 2003, 16 June 2003.

TREATIES, LEGISLATION AND AGREEMENTS

African (Banjul) Charter on Human and Peoples' Rights, OAU Doc. CAB/LEG/67/3 rev. 5, 27 June 1981.
African Charter on the Rights and Welfare of the Child, OAU Doc. CAB/LEG/24.9/49, 11 July 1990.
Protocol Additional to the Geneva Conventions of 12 August 1949, and relating to the Protection of Victims of International Armed Conflicts (Protocol I), 8 June 1977.
Rome Statute of the International Criminal Court, 2187 UNTS 90/37, 17 July 1998.
Special Court for Sierra Leone, Rules of Procedure and Evidence, 16 January 2002.
Uganda, Agreement on Accountability and Reconciliation Between the Government of the Republic of Uganda and the Lord's Resistance Army/Movement (Juba Agreement), 29 June 2007.
Uganda, Amnesty Act, Cap 294, 2000.
Uganda, Constitution of the Republic of Uganda, 1995.
Uganda, High Court (International Crimes Division) Practice Directions 2011, Legal Notices Supplement No. 5, 31 May 2011.
Uganda, Judicature Act, Cap 13, 1996.
Uganda, Judicature (Court of Appeal Rules) Directions, 2000.

Uganda, Judicature (Judicial Review) Rules, 2009.
Uganda, Penal Code Act, Cap 120, 1950.
Uganda, Uganda Peoples' Defence Forces Act, Cap 307, 1992.
UN Declaration on Basic Principles of Justice for Victims of Crime and Abuse of Power, UN Doc. A/RES/40/34, 29 November 1985.

OTHERS

Agger, K., 'The End of Amnesty in Uganda: Implications of the LRA Defections', Enough Project, August 2012.
ICTY, 'Address of Serge Brammertz, Prosecutor of the International Criminal Tribunal for the Former Yugoslavia to the Security Council', 3 December 2009.
International Law Commission, Draft Articles on State Responsibility, UN Doc. A/CN.4/L.602/Rev.1, 26 July 2001.
Kaheru, C., 'Does the Bail Question Confirm Museveni's Mastery of the Political Law of Diversion?', PoliticalArticles.Net, September 2011.
Open Society Justice Initiative, 'Putting Complementarity into Practice: Domestic Justice for International Crimes in DRC, Uganda and Kenya', 2011.
Redress, 'Ending Threats and Reprisals against Victims of Torture and Related International Crimes: A Call to Action', December 2009.
Uganda Human Rights Commission and United Nations Human Rights Office of the High Commissioner, "The Dust has not yet settled': Victims' views on the Right to Remedy & Reparation – A Report from the Greater North of Uganda', 2011.
UN Secretary-General, Report of the Secretary-General Pursuant to Resolutions 1653 and 1663, UN Doc. S/2006/478, 29 June 2006.

LOOKING BACK, LOOKING FORWARD

The Implications of the Termination of the Kenyatta Case Before the ICC

George Kegoro

1. INTRODUCTION

In March 2015, the International Criminal Court formally terminated the case against Kenyan president, Uhuru Kenyatta, the Prosecutor having indicated that the evidence available was insufficient to prove beyond reasonable doubt that Kenyatta was guilty of the crimes against humanity charges that he was facing before the Court. The charges against Kenyatta arose in relation to the violence that followed the announcement of the results of the presidential elections held in Kenya in 2007 in which both the incumbent, Mwai Kibaki of the Party of National Unity (PNU), and his main challenger, Raila Odinga of the Orange Democratic Party (ODM), claimed victory. Large-scale violence followed the disputed results and the ICC eventually commenced investigations into the crimes committed during the violence.

The Prosecutor presented two separate cases, with three accused persons in each. The first case was against William Ruto, senior member of ODM at the time of the violence, and who had since been appointed a cabinet minister in a power-sharing government which came into place following a mediation process necessitated by the violence. Those charged alongside Ruto were Henry Kosgey, the chair of the ODM, who had also become a cabinet minister in the power-sharing government. The third accused person in the first case was Joshua Sang, a vernacular radio journalist based in Eldoret, the home area of both Ruto and Kosgey, and a major epicentre of the violence.

In the second case, other than Kenyatta, those charged were Francis Muthaura, the head of Kenya's civil service, and Mohammed Hussein Ali, who at the time of the violence was the Commissioner of Police.

In the end, the Court failed to confirm the charges against Kosgey in the first case but confirmed those against Ruto and Sang, both of whom have since been on trial. The Court also discharged Ali during the confirmation hearing, and only confirmed the charges against Kenyatta and Muthaura in the second case.

Eventually, however, in March 2013, the Prosecutor also withdrew the charges against Muthaura,[1] after a key witness had recanted his statement that linked Muthaura to the planning of the violence, a development which left Kenyatta as the sole accused person in the second case. Therefore, although the case against Ruto was ongoing, the termination of charges against Kenyatta signified the complete collapse of the second of the two cases that the Prosecutor brought in response to Kenya's post-election violence of 2007–2008.

The termination of the Kenyatta case is an important development of the Kenyan cases before the ICC. In the context of the termination of the Kenyatta case, this paper reviews decision-making in Kenya, which culminated in the referral of the country's situation to the ICC. The paper examines perceptions in Kenya on why the post-election violence was referred to the ICC, and whether, in view of the experiences faced before the ICC, the country's expectations of justice have been met.

A natural question that follows the termination of the Kenyatta case is whether there is a possibility that the case can be reinstated in the future. This paper discusses the possibility of bringing back the same case against Kenyatta, or a different case based on the same circumstances.

The paper is divided into the introduction, which is followed by background information, and a discussion of the work of the Waki Commission, whose recommendations led to the referral of the Kenyan situation to the ICC. The next section discusses efforts in Kenya to address the post-election violence and forestall the intervention of the ICC, followed by an analysis of the effects of the collapse of the Kenyan case before the ICC. Lastly there will be a discussion on the chances of a new case against Kenyatta and a number of concluding remarks.

1.1. BACKGROUND

The incumbent president of the Party of National Unity Mwai Kibaki, and his challenger, Raila Odinga of the Orange Democratic Party, both claimed victory in Kenya's presidential elections in 2007. Violence broke out in many parts of the country, which was characterised by acts of arson, leading to internal displacement of large sections of the population. Eventually, an African Union (AU)-led mediation process brokered a political settlement that led to the formation of a coalition government, with Kibaki retaining his position as president while Odinga was appointed the prime minister, a position specifically

1 See statement by ICC Prosecutor on the Notice to Withdraw charges against Mr Muthaura available at: www.icc-cpi.int/en_menus/icc/press%20and%20media/press%20releases/Pages/OTP-statement-11-03-2013.aspx.

created to accommodate a power-sharing agreement that constituted part of the mediation agreement.[2]

The mandate of the mediation process also established a commission of inquiry to investigate the causes of the violence, and propose how accountability for the violence could be achieved.

Finding that the post-election violence amounted to systematic attacks on Kenyans based on their ethnicity and their political leanings,[3] the report of the Commission[4] recommended that a special tribunal, to be known as the Special Tribunal for Kenya, be established 'as a court that will sit within the territorial boundaries of the Republic of Kenya and seek accountability against persons bearing the greatest responsibility for crimes, particularly crimes against humanity, relating to the 2007 General Elections in Kenya. The Special Tribunal shall achieve this through the investigation, prosecution and adjudication of such crimes.'[5]

The special tribunal would apply Kenyan law as well as the International Crimes Bill once it was enacted into law, and would have Kenyan and international judges, as well as Kenyan and international staff. The Commission recommended that '[i]n order to fully give effect to the establishment of the Special Tribunal, an agreement for its establishment shall be signed by representatives of the parties to the Agreement on National Accord and Reconciliation within 60 days of the presentation of the Report of the Commission of Inquiry into the Post-Election Violence to the Panel of Eminent African Personalities, or the Panel's representative' and that 'a statute (to be known as "the Statute for the Special Tribunal") shall be enacted into law and come into force within a further 45 days after the signing of the agreement.'[6]

The date of commencement of the functioning of the special tribunal would be determined by the President, in consultation with the Prime Minister, the Chief Justice, the Minister of Justice and Constitutional Affairs and the Attorney General, within thirty days after the giving of presidential assent to the bill enacting the statute.

If an agreement for the establishment of the special tribunal was not signed, the statute for the special tribunal failed to be enacted, with the result that it would fail to commence functioning as contemplated, or its purposes were subverted once it had commenced operating. A list containing the names and

2 For copies of all the agreements reached during the mediation process in Kenya, see The Office of the AU Panel of Eminent African Personalities, *Back from the Brink: The 2008 Mediation Process and Reforms in Kenya*, Geneva, Africa Union Commission, p. 245.

3 Republic of Kenya, *Report of the Commission of Inquiry into the Post Election Violence*, Nairobi: Government Printer, 17 October 2008, p. viii.

4 Officially known as the Commission of Inquiry into the Post Election Violence.

5 Republic of Kenya, *Report of the Commission of Inquiry into the Post Election Violence*, Nairobi: Government Printer, 17 October 2008, p. 472.

6 *Ibid.*

relevant information of those suspected to bear the greatest responsibility for crimes falling within the jurisdiction of the proposed special tribunal 'shall be forwarded to the Special Prosecutor of the International Criminal Court. The Special Prosecutor shall be requested to analyse the seriousness of the information received with a view to proceeding with an investigation and prosecuting such suspected persons.'[7]

The Waki Commission suggested that the bill establishing the special tribunal ensure that the special tribunal be insulated against objections on constitutionality and, to that end, it should be anchored in the Constitution of Kenya. The bill should provide that the special tribunal consist of four organs: the chambers (including an Appeals Chamber) and the prosecutor, which shall be independent of each other, the Registry, and the Defence Office.

The tribunal would have six independent judges, three in the Trial Chamber, and three in the Appeals Chamber. The presiding judge of each chamber was to be a Kenyan national while the other two judges in each chamber were to be non-Kenyan and drawn from member states of the Commonwealth.

The Commission recommended that the bill provide for the appointment procedure of the judges for each chamber and the prosecutor of the special tribunal with the President, in consultation with the Prime Minister, appointing the chair of the Trial Chamber, both acting on the advice of the Chief Justice, from among persons qualified to be appointed judges of the High Court of Kenya.

The AU mediation mechanism[8] was to identify the other two members who would be appointed by the President, in consultation with the Prime Minister, from among persons qualified to occupy the position of a judge of a superior court of record in any part of the Commonwealth. The same procedure was to be applied for the appointment of the chair and members of the Appeals Chamber.

The prosecutor of the tribunal was to be appointed by the President in consultation with the Prime Minister from among persons qualified to occupy the position of judge in a superior court of record in any part of the Commonwealth, from a list decided by the AU mediation mechanism.

The Commission further required that the bill establishing the special tribunal should provide for the tribunal's jurisdiction, which would include the jurisdiction to adjudicate criminal cases brought against persons bearing the greatest responsibility for serious crimes, particularly crimes against humanity related to the 2007 post-election violence; the right of appeal from the decisions of the Trial Chamber to the Appeals Chamber of the special tribunal; and the ouster of the jurisdiction of ordinary courts in relation to the proceedings of the special tribunal. The bill was to provide the special tribunal with sufficient authority and independence to conduct investigations and, in particular, give

7 *Ibid*, p. 473.

8 Otherwise known as the Panel of Eminent African Personalities.

the special tribunal the authority to recruit and control its own staff. This would include the necessary staff, working under the prosecutor, to conduct prosecutions, the head of investigations, and not less than three other members of the investigation team, who would be non-Kenyan so as to provide an independent approach to the tribunal's investigation function. The investigations team would have to report to and work under the general direction of the Prosecutor.

The Commission also recommended that the 'Special Tribunal should take custody of all investigative material and witness statements and testimony collected and recorded by this Commission.'[9] The Commission recommended that the International Crimes Bill 2008 be fast-tracked for enactment by Parliament to facilitate investigation and prosecution of crimes against humanity.

The Waki Commission further suggested that all persons holding public office and public servants charged with criminal offences related to post-election violence be suspended from duty until the matter was fully adjudicated upon, and that upon conviction of any person charged with post-election violence offences of any nature, such persons be barred from holding public office or contesting an electoral position.

1.2. IMPLEMENTING THE RECOMMENDATIONS OF THE WAKI COMMISSION

The sixty-day countdown which the Waki Commission provided for the signing of a political agreement to establish a special tribunal started on 17 October 2008, the date on which the Commission released its report. In an apparent display of determination to implement the recommendations, President Kibaki and Prime Minister Odinga signed a coalition agreement on 17 December 2008, the 60th day since the release of the Waki Report, committing to implement the Waki Commission's recommendations.[10]

Legislative measures to anchor the proposed special tribunal had to be presented within 45 days. In February 2009, the Minister of Justice introduced a bill in the Kenyan Parliament to amend the Constitution, which would allow for the establishment of a special tribunal. While the bill required the support of a special two-thirds majority, or 145 votes, in order to pass, it only obtained the support of 101 members of parliament of the 195 who participated in the vote.

---

9 Republic of Kenya, *Report of the Commission of Inquiry into the Post Election Violence*, Nairobi: Government Printer, 17 October 2008, p. 475.

10 The Office of the AU Panel of Eminent African Personalities, *Back from the Brink: The 2008 Mediation Process and Reforms in Kenya*, Geneva, Africa Union Commission, p. 245.

Following the defeat of the bill, the mediation mechanism granted the Kenyan government an extension of the deadline for the establishment of legislation on a special tribunal. However, having failed to meet the new deadline of May 2009, the government sought and was granted one more extension, which it also failed to meet.

In July 2009, the Kenyan cabinet rejected two draft bills on the special tribunal presented by the Minister of Justice, due to concern over three clauses. The first proposed to remove the president's immunity from prosecution for the post-election violence cases. The second proposed to remove the presidential power to grant mercy to persons convicted of involvement in the post-election violence. The third proposal exempted proceedings before the proposed special tribunal from the Attorney General's power to exercise *nolle prosequi*.

On 9 July 2009, Kofi Annan, Chair of the Panel of Eminent African Personalities established by the AU to assist in finding a peaceful solution to Kenya's post-election crisis, submitted the sealed envelope containing a list of persons allegedly implicated, and supporting materials previously entrusted to the Panel by the Waki Commission, to the ICC Prosecutor.

On 5 November, having failed to convince them to make one more attempt at establishing the special tribunal, Annan invited Kibaki and Odinga to voluntarily refer the Kenyan situation to the ICC, but the two declined.

Subsequently, a member of the Kenyan Parliament presented a private bill, similar in content to the one that had been tabled by the Minister of Justice in February, and whose intention was to establish a special tribunal, but debate on the bill failed to take place due to a lack of quorum. Only 18 MPs were present when the bill was presented. Repeat attempts were made on several occasions to bring the bill up for debate, but these were always defeated by MPs who stayed away in order to ensure that the quorum needed for deliberations to take place was not achieved.

1.3. THE ICC MOVES INTO KENYA

As the coalition government had failed to establish the special tribunal for Kenya that would have addressed the crimes committed during the violence, the ICC assumed jurisdiction for those crimes in March 2010, when the Court's Prosecutor applied for the ICC Pre-Trial Chamber's authorisation to commence investigations into the Kenyan situation.[11]

In January 2012, the Pre-Trial Chamber confirmed crimes against humanity charges including murder, torture, and forcible transfer of population against

11 See Decision Pursuant to Article 15 of the Rome Statute on the Authorization of an Investigation into the Situation in the Republic of Kenya, Pre-Trial Chamber II, 31 March 2010, ICC-01/09-19.

Ruto and Sang in the first case, and crimes against humanity charges of murder, rape, torture, and forcible transfer of population against Kenyatta and Muthaura in the second case.

2. UNDERSTANDING THE CHOICE OF THE ICC AS KENYA'S EVENTUAL JUSTICE MECHANISM

As seen above, the Kenyan Parliament rejected legislative measures on three occasions that would have established the special tribunal as a national justice mechanism that would respond to the post-election violence. Presumably, Parliament knew that by rejecting these proposals it was creating a situation where a referral of the country's situation to the ICC would become possible.

A significant amount of political backlash has characterised the Kenyan cases before the ICC. While international platforms like the AU and the United Nations have been arenas for the backlash, Kenya's domestic institutions have also played a significant role in expressing hostility towards the trials before the ICC. The Kenyan Parliament has played a leading role in this regard, and has emerged as the foremost forum for condemning and vilifying attempts at accountability through the ICC. In view of the Parliament's apparently contradictory roles, it is important to understand the Parliament's reasons for rejecting proposals for a special tribunal when presented with the opportunity to approve them. The record of the parliamentary debate on the Special Tribunal Bill is informative and can provide answers to some of these questions and is discussed at some length below.

The only substantive debate on a bill for the establishment of a special tribunal took place in late January and early February 2009, when the bill was presented for debate on the first of the three occasions discussed above. By the time the bill came up for substantive debate, the deadline for its enactment as required by the Waki Report had elapsed a few days before. An objection was raised by Gitobu Imanyara, a backbencher that would later present the alternative private bill discussed above, that the government bill was time-barred in view of the timelines provided by the Waki Commission.[12] However, the Speaker ruled that parliamentary autonomy meant that it could debate any legislative measures at any time and was not bound by the timelines imposed by an external entity like the Waki Commission. The Speaker referred to the constitutional provision that vests legislative power in the National Assembly, and added that 'it does not say … the President, the National Assembly, the Hague, Waki or Kofi Annan or anybody else for that matter.'[13] The important point, however, is that the

12 Kenya National Assembly, Official Record of Proceedings, 29 January 2009, p. 27.
13 *Ibid*, p. 35.

Kenyan government showed a clear commitment to complying with the Waki Commission's recommendations.

The Minister of Justice, Martha Karua, then moved the bill, explaining that it was intended that there be a constitutional amendment bill which, if approved, would pave the way for a bill detailing the procedures for the establishment of the special tribunal, which would be enacted as ordinary, as opposed to constitutional, legislation. The constitutional bill would require a special two-thirds majority to pass. She reminded the MPs that the bill was the result of the mediation process and remarked that 'it is time to take responsibility knowing that we have been brought here by the over 30 million Kenyans to look after their welfare' before adding that 'there are people who lost their loved ones, people who were maimed … We are opening a door so that those people can ventilate their grievances in a court of law, and where they can have their matters investigated.'[14]

An early indication of the trouble that the bill would face in the house was provided when a junior minister, Danson Mungatana, expected to support the government in Parliament because of the doctrine of collective responsibility, spoke in opposition of the bill, describing the proposed special tribunal as 'a huge monolith that is going to set up a parallel legal system in this country.' In his view, the fact that the bill proposed the establishment of a public prosecutor, a public defender, a court with a trial and appellate chamber, and a registrar, was 'a very big parallel structure to the legal system of Kenya that already exists.'[15] He noted that the country was going through famine and suggested that the public resources that would be used for setting up the tribunal would be put to better use by feeding citizens threatened with starvation.

He was concerned that the proposed tribunal would have two separate trial chambers, one for the trial of ordinary crimes, and the other for the trial of crimes under international law, and wondered whether it was 'really right to have two special courts, one for the big people who contemplated, funded and made plans for these things to happen, and another for the ordinary person.'[16] He summed up the proposed court as 'discriminatory, expensive and unnecessary' and suggested that MPs should stay away from the house in order to deny the bill the quorum necessary for enactment.

A recurrent concern during the debate was about the ability of the proposed tribunal to take action against top officials if these should be found culpable.

14 *Ibid*, p. 37.

15 *Ibid*, p. 39.

16 In a departure from the recommendations of the Waki Commission, the bill proposed a two-tier tribunal that would be made up of a Trial Chamber which 'shall exercise jurisdiction over persons bearing the greatest responsibility for crimes falling within the jurisdiction of the Tribunal', and special magistrates who would have jurisdiction 'with regard to persons other than persons bearing the greatest responsibility'. See clause 9 of the Special Tribunal for Kenya Bill available at: www.kenyalaw.org/Downloads/Bills/2009/The_Special_Tribunal_for_Kenya_Statute_2009.pdf.

This concern was articulated by a member of parliament, Cyrus Jirongo, who said that 'the perpetrators of post-election violence who are in government are busy building [a] war chest … to make sure they defeat any tribunal that will be set up in this country.'[17] Jirongo captured the main concerns about a special tribunal when he asked rhetorically:

> Suppose the investigations point, God forbid, at His Excellency the President, do you want to tell me that this country has the capacity to try him? Suppose the investigations point to the Prime Minister, do you want to convince the Republic of Kenya that we have the capacity to try him?

The record of debate in the Assembly shows that there was applause when Jirongo added:

> If we are genuine and we want those people to be punished, we should let them go [to The Hague]. That way they will not be able to mobilise their supporters. They will not be able to pay them with the money they are looting the country today. Justice shall come to prevail … This tribunal is being set up for small people. This country has a history of punishing small people when the big ones committed the crimes. We are putting up a tribunal for the young man who blocked the road. We are not putting up a tribunal for the person who paid him to block the road.[18]

The MPs who took this line of reasoning kept referring to previous experiences in Kenya's history, where the government had raised expectations for accountability by setting up elaborate commissions of inquiry whose recommendations were, however, shelved. It was clear from their remarks that some MPs had no clear understanding that the proposed special tribunal was to be a court, rather than a commission of inquiry. Indeed, when the Minister of Justice replied at the end of the debate, she felt compelled to clarify the purpose of the proposed special tribunal. She said she was 'saddened to notice that quite a number of [MPs] think that the proposed tribunal is a commission of inquiry' and clarified that 'what is thought to be brought about is an actual special court', and further emphasised that 'it is a criminal court and a court of law and not a tribunal.'[19]

The fact that the Waki Commission had created a secret envelope containing the names of leading suspects for the violence appears to have played a significant role in the eventual decisions made by the Kenyan Parliament. Traditionally, when a Kenyan commission of inquiry was required to investigate wrongdoing, it would, as part of its report, also identify and name

17 Kenya National Assembly, Official Record of Proceedings, 29 January 2009, p. 47.

18 *Ibid.*

19 Kenya National Assembly, Official Record of Proceedings, 5 February 2009, p. 43.

the wrongdoers.[20] The fact that the Waki Report had a separate and secret list of suspects was interpreted mostly negatively during the debate. For example, Mungatana warned against setting up the tribunal, asserting that what the public wanted was for people who had funded the violence to resign from office rather than to insulate themselves from accountability by setting up the tribunal. The idea that the special tribunal would enable insulation seems to have been a misunderstanding generated by the secret nature of the envelope. According to many MPs, persons suspected of being responsible for the post-election violence should have been publicly identified, and should then have immediately resigned. In a clear reference to the secret envelope, Jirongo also complained that 'we are clear in our documents that those involved will not be touched, and that their identity will be kept secret, so that they can continue looting and building further war chests to pay youth to kill Kenyans whenever you try to bring them to justice.'[21]

Another consequence of the secret envelope is that it allowed MPs the freedom to imagine that their political opponents could possibly form part of the list, and to oppose a local tribunal as a way of maximising political trouble for their opponents. Thus, MP Ababu Namwamba, observed:

> [A]n impression has been created that if the tribunal law does not pass, some of our political rivals could be fixed for eternity. Therefore, there are those who will come to this Floor to debate this law with the determination that this law does not pass with the determination that the tribunal will not be set up because the political rivals will be headed to The Hague.[22]

Other objections to the special tribunal were based on concerns about the inadequacy of witness protection mechanisms. Even though the text of the bill was clear on the matter, there was also concern that the bill was vague on whether the prosecutor would be subject to the control of the Attorney General.[23]

There was criticism that the government had not put sufficient effort into maximising support for the bill from among its ranks. It was pointed out that when the government had previously wanted to enact constitutional amendments to secure other agreements reached during the mediation process,

20 The Waki Commission seemed aware of this expectation when, in its report, it devoted an early portion to a discussion titled 'Alleged Perpetrators: To name or not to Name?' in which it justified its decision not to name suspects implicated following its investigation. The discussion opens with the sentence: 'We realize that Kenyans and the international community have been hoping the Commission's report will identify the individuals behind the 2007 post election violence.' See Republic of Kenya, *Report of the Commission of Inquiry into the Post Election Violence*, Nairobi: Government Printer, 17 October 2008, p. 15.

21 Kenya National Assembly, Official Record of Proceedings, 29 January 2009, p. 47.

22 Kenya National Assembly, Official Record of Proceedings, 5 February 2009, p. 34.

23 See objection by a member, Lewis Nguyai, Kenya National Assembly, Official Record of Proceedings, 4 February 2009, p. 40.

there had been extraordinary mobilisation, including the personal attendance in Parliament by the President and Prime Minister to support the efforts needed to achieve the special majority of votes to pass the legislation. By contrast, however, no special effort had been made to mobilise support for the bill on the special tribunal. Indeed, in her reply to the debate, the Minister of Justice acknowledged the truth in this criticism and regretted the lukewarm support that the President and Prime Minister had shown for the bill.[24] MP Rachel Shebesh, remarked that: 'If the government was sincere about this, this house would be full'.[25] Namwamba added:

> This is not the first Bill that this house has been seized of, and that seeks to make a fundamental adjustment to our Constitution. But unlike previous occasions when the house has been full to the brim; when we have had the pleasure of the President and the Prime Minister attending debate of this nature, we do not see similar political will.[26]

Some support for the bill emanated from the government ministers and female parliamentarians who saw the entrenchment of the bill in the Constitution as an assurance of protection from interference by men. In their view, women were protected by the Constitution, not by men, and since the bill amended the Constitution, it would be good for women. The female MPs said they had decided to entrust the business of the house to the Constitution and not to individuals.

Other reasons for supporting the bill lay in the fact that a trial before the ICC would be highly selective and would not involve the bulk of those who committed crimes in Kenya, who would thus go unpunished.[27] The constitutional amendment was explained as necessary to end the culture of impunity once and for all. It was necessary to bring cases of crimes committed during the 2007 elections to an early end so as to support electoral reforms that would ensure clean elections in 2013.[28] It was also argued that since the Waki envelope would only contain those most responsible for the violence, those who had been involved at a transactional level would go unpunished if the bill establishing the tribunal was not approved.[29] It was also pointed out that taking the Kenyan cases to the ICC would embarrass the country since Kenya was not a failed state.[30] Supporting the bill was presented as a chance to reclaim

---

24 Kenya National Assembly, Official Record of Proceedings, 5 February 2009.

25 Kenya National Assembly, Official Record of Proceedings, 4 February 2009, p. 47.

26 *Ibid*, p. 32.

27 *Ibid*, p. 34.

28 Kenya National Assembly, Official Record of Proceedings, 5 February 2009, p. 44.

29 See arguments by Moses Wetangula, Kenya National Assembly, Official Record of Proceedings, 4 February 2009, p. 35.

30 Kenya National Assembly, Official Record of Proceedings, 4 February 2009, p. 36.

the country's image, which had been dented by the post-election violence.[31] It was also pointed out that there was no reason to assume that the ICC would automatically assume jurisdiction over Kenya if there was a failure to enact the bill, and so such a failure might deny the country the only chance to hold those responsible for the post-election violence accountable.[32] In apparent response to concerns raised about witness protection, the Minister of Justice explained that the tribunal would have its own witness protection programme.[33]

Responding to the criticism about the involvement of foreign lawyers and judges in the special tribunal, the government said this would not be a big deal since 'they will be our employees and we shall control them', a response which was met with the retort: 'The control is the problem.'[34] At the end of the debate, a vote was prevented by the lack of quorum, and the Speaker deferred voting to the following week.

On the resumption of deliberations the following week, the Vice President, speaking in the Assembly as leader of the government, and having sensed that the bill would not pass if put to the vote that day, asked for a deferral of the vote, explaining that 'there is need for the government to be given more time in order to consult and carry everyone on board.'[35] He explained that the need to consult was due to the fact that 'people have different interpretations of The Hague, International Criminal Court (ICC), the Rome Statute and the need to have a local tribunal.'[36] He disclosed that a letter written by Kenyan civil society urging the government to enact the bill had lent weight to the decision for more consultations.

The Speaker, however, rejected the request for time to allow for more consultation, arguing that the matters for discussion in the house were exclusively the decision of the government controlled House Business Committee, which the Vice President chaired. Therefore, the proper procedure would have been to get the committee to defer further discussion, rather than to request the Speaker to do so. A vote was nevertheless prevented by the fact that there was still insufficient quorum. This necessitated another adjournment and the debate was to resume after a week.

The following week, a vote took place with Kibaki and Odinga present in the house for the first time since the debate began. In his capacity as the head of the civil service, Muthaura had sent a circular letter to all the ministers and assistant ministers, urging them to be in Parliament on that day in order to support the bill. The matter was then put to a vote without further debate. Neither the President nor the Prime Minister was given the opportunity to speak before the

31 *Ibid*, p. 43.
32 Kenya National Assembly, Official Record of Proceedings, 5 February 2009, p. 34.
33 *Ibid*, p. 44.
34 Kenya National Assembly, Official Record of Proceedings, 4 February 2009, p. 37.
35 Kenya National Assembly, Official Record of Proceedings, 10 February 2009, p. 30.
36 *Ibid*.

debate was called. The bill needed the support of 145 MPs but was only able to obtain support from 101, with 93 rejections and one abstention.[37]

2.1. A COMMENT ON THE PARLIAMENTARY PROCESS ON THE BILL

A combination of factors can be seen as having contributed to the defeat of the bill for the establishment of the special tribunal. The record of the debate shows that there was concern that a justice process on Kenyan soil would only bring accountability against low-end perpetrators and would not be able to deal with politically influential people who were the planners of the violence. By voting against a local tribunal, a section of the Kenyan Parliament was going out of its way to invite the ICC, as the only institution it regarded as capable of doing so, to bring accountability without regard to the position held by the perpetrators of the violence.

The fact that the persons who would be held accountable remained unknown at the time of the debate was very important in the debate. First, since there were rumours as to the contents of the envelope, a section of the legislators decided to support or oppose the bill based on the persons rumoured to have been named in the envelope.

It remained clear during the debate that there was no 'official' position on the bill. As a result, ministers found the freedom to oppose the bill without regard to the doctrine of collective responsibility. While at some stage the government asked for more time for consultations, the Speaker's answer made it clear that the government controlled the parliamentary calendar and therefore the speed at which the debate on the bill could move. Criticism about the lukewarm support that the President and the Prime Minister had shown for the bill finally led to the two turning up in person during the voting. Although an official circular letter had gone out on the day of the vote, calling on all ministers to be present in the house and support the bill, nothing was done about ensuring that they actually voted with the government. As a result, while the President and Prime Minister supported the bill, some of their ministers voted against it. As a result, the special majority needed to enact it into law was not achieved.

The parliamentary debate also showed that a section of MPs had concerns about the involvement of foreigners in the affairs of the country, as was implied in the setting up of the Tribunal whose establishment would involve the AU and a segment of whose judges and other key role players would also be foreigners. While the government sought to assuage these concerns by pointing out that these foreigners would be the employees of the Kenyan government, and therefore subject to its control, this concern seems to have also been a factor in rejecting the bill.

---

37 Kenya National Assembly, Official Record of Proceedings, 12 February 2009, p. 34.

Finally, the immediacy of the effects of the bill's approval must have been a factor in rejecting the bill. While the Waki Commission provided what could be viewed as short timelines within which decisions to establish a tribunal had to be made, the government had done well, and had substantially met the first of the two timelines, that requiring a political agreement. If the second timeline requiring Parliament to pass legislation on a special tribunal had been met, it would have immediately imposed the obligation to begin the process of setting up the tribunal. It is possible that processing all these decisions so quickly was too much for Kenya's political process, which therefore rejected the bill as a way of avoiding any further commitments to implement the Waki Report.

In the aftermath of the debate, a sense of regret was evident over the failure to pass the bill on the special tribunal. During a debate on an adjournment motion for the house, a minister observed: 'God is watching this country because we have the IDPs and these are the people who would have been victims under the Tribunal that we refused to set up.'[38] During the same debate, an MP disagreed with the general sentiment that the house had done a good job, having been recalled from recess specifically to enact legislation to give effect to the mediation process, including setting up the special tribunal. The MP observed that Parliament should desist from the self-congratulation that had gone on in the debate because it had failed to enact the bill.[39]

During the official opening of the next session of Parliament in April, Kibaki observed the failure of the previous session to enact the special tribunal and promised that the 'government would expand consultations with a view to re-formulating the establishment of a local tribunal to try the perpetrators of the post election violence.'[40]

The termination of the Kenyatta case provides an opportunity to review what happened within and around the case and the extent to which this contributed to the termination of the case. An important accompanying experience around the case is the amount of political backlash that was generated both by Kenyatta and the Kenyan state in an effort to influence the outcome.

Backlash began in December 2010, on the day the Prosecutor made public the names of those against whom he wanted to bring charges before the ICC. On that day, President Kibaki declared that contrary to the recommendations of the Waki Commission, persons accused of crimes during the post-election violence would be required to vacate office until they had cleared their names, a recommendation that was also made by the President–Prime Minister coalition. The public officials among the six persons against whom the Prosecutor intended to bring charges would remain in office until charges against them

38 See the remarks of Mutula Kilonzo, Kenya National Assembly, Official Record of Proceedings, 24 February 2009, p. 46.

39 Kenya National Assembly, Official Record of Proceedings, 24 February 2009, p. 37.

40 Kenya National Assembly, Official Record of Proceedings, 21 April 2009, p. 7.

were confirmed. Kibaki's early declaration pre-empted any other on the matter. Kenyatta and Muthaura served in office for another year, and played a key role in the decisions of the Kenyan state towards its relationship with the ICC, while being the accused persons before the Court.

During a highly charged debate held the same week, the Kenyan Parliament passed a motion, in a near-unanimous decision, calling upon the government to withdraw the country's membership from the Rome Statute.

In late January 2011, Kenyatta and Ruto organised a large rally in Eldoret, which President Kibaki attended. The fact that President Kibaki chose to attend a rally convened by the two leading ICC suspects, especially so soon after the Prosecutor had named them, was viewed as repudiating the Prosecutor's announcement, and an endorsement of the political agenda that Kenyatta and Ruto were pursuing. The rally became the first public indication that Kenyatta and Ruto had decided to unite their previously opposing platforms against the common threat of prosecution by the ICC. At various stages of the ICC proceedings, Kenyatta and Ruto organised large anti-ICC rallies around the country that strongly condemned the Court.

Kenya also embarked on a diplomatic campaign against the ICC. The Kenyan government obtained the support of the AU at the Heads of State Summit for the deferral of the Kenyan cases by the UN Security Council on the grounds of peace and security under Article 16 of the Rome Statute. In 2009, when the ICC issued arrest warrants for President Omar Al-Bashir of Sudan, the AU resolved that none of its member states should cooperate with the ICC in this matter. The AU would eventually incorporate even more sweeping provisions in its resolutions calling for its member states not to cooperate with the ICC, and including the Kenyan situation alongside that of Sudan.

In August 2010, President Al-Bashir visited Kenya during the promulgation of the new Constitution. There was much consternation both in the country and internationally since Kenya, as a State Party to the Rome Statute, was under the obligation to arrest and hand him over to the ICC, but had instead invited and feted Al-Bashir.

A cabinet reshuffle in March 2012 resulted in the replacement of the Minister of Justice and Constitutional Affairs, Mutula Kilonzo, who had emerged as a strong supporter of the ICC. His place was taken by a backbencher, Eugene Wamalwa, a member of the emerging political caucus uniting Kenyatta and Ruto. At the time, the new caucus claimed to be preparing the ground for a political coalition in which Kenyatta and Ruto would run for president on a shared ticket, something that would come to pass. Kilonzo had insisted that Ruto and Kenyatta could not run for president while facing charges before the ICC.

It was always understood that Kenyatta, who faced charges before the ICC long before he became president, was charged in a private capacity rather than as the President of Kenya. In the campaign that brought him to office, Kenyatta confirmed this understanding when he referred to the case as 'a personal challenge' which he would address privately while also leading the country as president.[41] However, this changed once he got to office.

An early indication of his changed position regarding the case occurred during his inauguration ceremony, where his guest, Uganda's President, Yoweri Museveni, delivered a strong attack against the ICC, saluting 'Kenyan voters on one other issue – the rejection of the blackmail by the ICC and those who seek to abuse this institution for their own agenda'.[42] Museveni added that while he had supported the setting up of the ICC, 'the usual opinionated and arrogant actors using their careless analysis have distorted the purpose of that institution', and 'are now using it to install leaders of their choice in Africa and eliminate the ones they do not like.'[43]

Kenyatta's own speech indicated a tightening of the Kenyan position on the ICC. While, previously, Kenyatta had maintained that Kenya would cooperate with the ICC if he became president, he later introduced the conditions under which Kenya would cooperate, for the first time, during his inauguration declaring:

> I assure you again that under my leadership, Kenya will strive to uphold our international obligations, so long as these are founded on the well-established principles of mutual respect and reciprocity.[44]

Kenyatta introduced a new discourse asserting that:

> Central to our continued contribution to the international community, will be the understanding that the world is made up of many countries, cultures, political experiences and world-views. We must remember that no one country or group of countries should have control or monopoly on international institutions or the interpretation of international treaties. While each state has a right to its own view, it must respect the fact that it holds just one view amongst many in the community of nations.[45]

Kenyatta also established a pan-African platform, which would prove important in the political fight against his case before the ICC, promising 'nations of Africa and the Africa Union' that 'you will continue to have [Kenya as] a partner and an ally' and adding: 'If we stand together in solidarity I am confident that we will find the strength to thrive and innovate solutions that work for us. Of course, we

41 See the record of the presidential debate held on 11 February 2013, available at: https://www.youtube.com/watch?v=i89bSa88dOE.

42 See Ndonga, 'Museveni praises Kenya for rejecting ICC "blackmail"', available at: www.capitalfm.co.ke/news/2013/04/museveni-praises-kenya-for-rejecting-icc-blackmail/.

43 *Ibid.*

44 Inauguration speech delivered on 9 April 2013, available at: www.capitalfm.co.ke/eblog/2013/04/09/president-kenyattas-inauguration-speech/.

45 *Ibid.*

join you in continuing to insist on relating with all nations as equals, not juniors. As partners, not subordinates'.[46]

As he settled down in office, the ICC cases took over and began dominating Kenya's official diplomacy. Deputy President William Ruto soon went on a hasty, but ill-explained, trip to West Africa, which was assumed to be a mission to solicit diplomatic support for Kenya against the ICC charges.

Two months later, the head of Kenya's Permanent Mission to the United Nations, Ambassador Macharia Kamau, wrote the first of a series of stridently worded letters to the Security Council, seeking an unconditional termination of the Kenyan cases, a demand which the Security Council could not legally meet. Kamau stated that the Kenyan cases were based on 'claims that might have been false or manufactured', that the charges could have been 'procured through inducement and or corruption' and that 'the manner in which the cases are being conducted is neither impartial nor independent'. He characterised the Kenyan elections as a referendum on the ICC question, and argued that 'the very suspects who are being prosecuted ... received the overwhelming support of the citizens of Kenya in the just concluded 4 March 2013 elections', and concluded that 'the votes garnered by Mr Uhuru Kenyatta and Mr William Ruto, suggest that the Kenyan populace is ready for them to be their political masters'.

In October, an extraordinary session of the AU endorsed Kenya's application to the UN Security Council for a deferral of the cases for one year. The AU also resolved, once again, that no serving African head of state should stand trial before the ICC, and urged President Kenyatta not to attend his trial at The Hague. The AU accused the ICC of targeting Africa. This was based on the fact that all the cases before the ICC were African. Kenyatta called the Court 'a painfully farcical pantomime' and 'a toy of declining imperial powers.'[47] The AU chairperson, Robert Mugabe of Zimbabwe called on African states to stage a mass pull out from membership of the ICC.

The Security Council ultimately declined Kenya's request for a deferral for the second time, and amid threats of a mass pull out from the ICC by African states, the power relations in respect of the ICC shifted.

The AU Summit raised real fears that unless Kenya was appeased in some way, there could be a mass walkout by the 34 ICC African member states. As a result, the international community seemed anxious to demonstrate that, contrary to the AU's accusation, the decision not to defer the Kenyan cases was not out of disrespect for the continent, but rather because there was no empirical reason for granting such a deferral.

The 2013 Meeting of the Assembly of States Parties to the ICC, which was held, by coincidence, soon after the Security Council's rejection of Kenya's

---

46 *Ibid.*

47 Speech delivered at the African Heads of State meeting on 12 October 2013, available at: www.capitalfm.co.ke/eblog/2013/10/12/uhuru-icc-is-a-toy-of-declining-imperial-powers/.

request for deferral, provided a forum for appeasing Kenya and the AU as evidenced by the late inclusion of an item in the ASP agenda for a general debate on the AU/ICC relations in the context of the AU position that no serving head of state should be put on trial. With the expected start of the Kenyan trials came the additional pressure of figuring out how to manage a situation where the President and his deputy would be away on trial.

While the Court had made it clear that it would not allow a situation where both would be at The Hague at the same time since they had a country to run,[48] the Assembly declined to support this position. It passed new rules of procedure and evidence, allowing for a person facing trial and 'extraordinary public duties at the highest national level' to apply to be excused from continuous presence at their trial. This was a compromise position, since Kenya had wanted the automatic excusal of its two leaders from being physically present at trial.[49]

Over the twenty months during which period the case was before the Court, Kenyatta himself, and through senior members of his government, unrestrainedly condemned the ICC and Western countries, who were seen as the Court's backers.

When the case was terminated, it became clear that Kenyatta had used the Kenyan state as a shield against his personal trial before the ICC, deploying the country's diplomatic and financial resources for this purpose. Moreover, the personal pressure he was under increased his government's intolerance, contributing to the shutting of the civic space. The high profile campaigns against the ICC created an atmosphere where it became difficult for witnesses to remain strong in their resolve to testify against Kenyatta.

2.2. EFFECTS OF THE KENYATTA CHARGES BEING DROPPED

The findings of the Waki Commission shaped the approach the ICC took in compiling the Kenyan cases. The Waki Commission found that the post-election violence was spontaneous in some geographic areas, and a result of planning and organisation in others, and had often involved politicians and business leaders. According to the Commission, some areas witnessed a combination

48 Speaking at a public rally on the eve of Ruto's departure for The Hague, Kenyatta cautioned the ICC that he and his deputy could withdraw their cooperation with the Court unless their trials are rescheduled and set at different times. See 'President Uhuru Kenyatta rejects parallel Hague trial with William Ruto', *Standard Media*, 9 September 2013, available at: www.standardmedia.co.ke/article/2000093115/president-uhuru-kenyatta-rejects-parallel-hague-trial-with-william-ruto. Thereafter, the ICC announced that the trials would run on different dates. See 'ICC: Uhuru, Ruto trial to run on different days', *Daily Monitor,* 10 September 2013, available at: http://mobile.monitor.co.ug/News/ICC++Uhuru++Ruto+trial+to+run+on+different+days/-/691252/1985872/-/format/xhtml/-/2k8mx5z/-/.

49 See Rule 134*quater* of the Rules of Procedure and Evidence.

of the two forms of violence, which started as a spontaneous violent reaction to the perceived rigging of elections, and later evolved into well-organised and coordinated attacks on members of ethnic groups associated with the incumbent president or the PNU. In these areas, there was an expectation that violence was inevitable regardless of the election results.

The Commission concluded that the post-election violence was more than a mere juxtaposition of citizen-to-citizen opportunistic assaults and that these were systematic attacks on Kenyans based on their ethnicity and their political leanings. The Commission established that attackers had organised along ethnic lines, assembled considerable logistical means, and travelled long distances to burn houses and maim, kill and sexually assault their occupants because they were of particular ethnic groups and political persuasion.

The Commission also found that the reasons behind the deadly 'revenge' attacks, with victims being identified not for what they did, but for their ethnic association to other perpetrators, was also guilty by association. The Commission observed that the free-for-all was made possible by the lawlessness stemming from an apparent collapse of state institutions and security forces.

These findings can be summarised into two strands of violence. The first was spontaneous, while also showing signs of organisation in some areas, and was perpetrated by supporters of the opposition ODM. It was based on both frustration over an electoral outcome they had not expected, and the fact that their victims had supported Kibaki in those elections.

The second strand of violence was the revenge attacks carried out in response to the first round of violence. The Commission was keen to note the involvement of 'guiding forces behind' this form of violence and also the fact that state failure was allowed for all these forms of violence to occur.

The case against Ruto, Kosgey, and Sang was grounded on the first strand of violence, while that against Kenyatta, Muthaura and Ali was grounded on the second strand of violence.

The collapse of the Kenyatta case, the sole person on trial for the second strand of violence, signifies an end to the search for accountability in relation to the second strand of violence, and meant that nobody was put on trial for the Naivasha and Nakuru violence.

As found by the Commission, the post-election violence was ethnically expressed. One of the effects of charging people from all sides involved in the violence was that it maintained a balance in ethnic terms when searching for justice for the post-election violence. The dropping of charges in relation to one side of the violence upset the balance, and can be viewed as constituting a revisionist view of the post-election violence, as if to suggest that only one form of the violence amounted to criminality while the other did not. The dropping of charges against Kenyatta is also seen as having the potential to affect local politics in the country.

It is the pursuit of accountability against both forms of violence that gave rise to the two separate cases, pitting former political opponents in a common legal battle with the Prosecutor of the Court. This battle was to have significant effects on Kenya's domestic politics. Although the suspects in the two cases were bitter political rivals in the 2007 elections, a rivalry that directly contributed to the violence, the common risk of prosecution led to a unification of their political platforms for purposes of managing the threat of prosecution. The platform was deployed in a highly successful mobilisation of sympathy from the Kenyan masses through a portrayal of the prosecution by the Court as a form of persecution against them by their political rivals.

With the case against Kenyatta now over, there have been fears that the coalition will come under pressure since it now lacks a common objective to remain together. The possibility of new forms of violence, based on the old schisms that have been papered over, cannot be ruled out.

3. FUTURE PROSPECTS OF THE KENYATTA CASE

In the wake of the termination of the case against Kenyatta, the question that has arisen is how to handle the expectations of the victims of the violence that occurred in Naivasha and Nakuru, which was the basis of the charges against Kenyatta, and, specifically, whether there is a chance that the case could be reinstated in some form in the future. The circumstances surrounding, and terms applicable to, the termination of the charges are both relevant factors in answering this question.

After exhausting a large number of pre-trial procedures, the trial of the Kenyatta case was eventually assigned a provisional commencement date of 5 February 2014. However, in late December 2013, the Prosecutor requested a three month deferral, in order to 'undertake additional investigative steps' in relation to the case. The Prosecutor also requested a status conference.[50] The Chamber vacated the assigned trial date and ordered a status conference to be convened in order to address procedural matters.[51]

Thereafter, the Prosecutor filed a second request for an adjournment of the commencement date, which had been rescheduled for 7 October 2014. This was based on differences in opinion between the Prosecutor on the one hand, and the defence and the Kenyan state on the other, regarding the quality of cooperation offered to the former in preparations for the trial. On 31 March 2014, to

---

50 *The Prosecutor v. Uhuru Muigai Kenyatta*, Notification of the removal of a witness from the Prosecution's witness list and application for an adjournment of the provisional trial date, ICC-01/09-02/11-875, 19 December 2013.

51 *The Prosecutor v. Uhuru Muigai Kenyatta*, Order vacating trial date of 5 February 2014, convening a status conference, and addressing other procedural matters, ICC-01/09-02/11-886, 23 January 2014.

resolve the problem, the Chamber directed the Prosecutor to submit a revised cooperation request to the Kenyan government and adjourned the provisional trial date.[52] Both the Prosecutor and the Kenyan government filed two updated cooperation requests each. The first was in May, the second in June, and the third in September.

In September, the Prosecutor filed a notice indicating that she would not be ready for the trial in October, as there was 'insufficient evidence to prove Mr Kenyatta's alleged criminal responsibility beyond reasonable doubt' and requested that the case be adjourned until the Kenyan state fully executed the Prosecutor's revised cooperation request.[53] This request was, however, opposed by the defence, which applied for a termination of the case against Kenyatta. The Chamber turned the provisional commencement date into a status conference that it required Kenyatta to attend.

During the status conference of 8 October, the Prosecutor requested an indefinite adjournment of the trial date until the Kenyan government complied with the Prosecutor's revised cooperation requests, arguing that while under ordinary circumstances the charges would be withdrawn when there was insufficient evidence, the situation that applied to the Kenyatta case was unique because the Kenyan government had failed to comply with cooperation requests, thus thwarting the investigation. The Prosecutor argued that under the Kenyan Constitution, the head of state was responsible for compliance with international obligations.

The October status conference was followed, the following month, by an application, submitted by the common legal representative for victims, for the disclosure of the pre-trial brief prepared by the prosecution. As this procedure is relevant to the discussion of the terms on which the Kenyatta case was terminated, it is discussed below.

3.1. THE PRE-TRIAL BRIEF IN THE KENYATTA CASE

In November 2014, the common legal representative for victims applied for the publication of a redacted version of the pre-trial brief that the Prosecutor would have relied on if the case had gone to trial. The victims' lawyer had argued that victims had 'the right to know the truth about the crimes committed against them and the identities of those most responsible'. The lawyer sought a reclassification of the brief that had originally been filed confidentially, which would allow its contents to be made public.

---

52 *The Prosecutor v. Uhuru Muigai Kenyatta*, Decision on the Prosecution's applications for a finding of non-compliance pursuant to Article 87(7) and for an adjournment of the provisional trial date, ICC-01/09-02/11-908, 31 March 2014, para. 98.

53 *The Prosecutor v. Uhuru Muigai Kenyatta*, Prosecution notice regarding the provisional trial date, ICC-01/09-02/11-944, 5 September 2014, paras. 1–2.

Kenyatta's defence had opposed the application for a disclosure of the brief, arguing that a disclosure of the material in question was 'an out-dated articulation of the Prosecution case, which now includes wholly unsupported allegations' and, further, that the disclosure 'would result in further unjustified damage to the reputation of Mr Kenyatta'. For her part, the Prosecutor had no objection to a release of the material in question.

In December, the Trial Chamber granted the application and ordered the Prosecutor to release a redacted version of the pre-trial brief on which her case against Kenyatta would have been based if she had not withdrawn the charges against him. In granting the application, the Chamber found, firstly, that there was no legal basis for continuing to keep the information secret, and, second, that since the evidence that the Prosecutor had gathered was insufficient to sustain a case against Kenyatta, the publication of the information was not likely to be prejudicial to his reputation. The Court, therefore, ordered the release of the information with the exception of the details that could endanger witnesses and victims.

When, in October, Kenyatta had appeared for what became the last status conference in the case against him, the Prosecutor provided an outline of her case against him, asserting that despite the investigative difficulties that she had suffered, 'there remains a considerable body of evidence that implicates Mr Kenyatta'.

The outline, said to have been derived from the evidence of nine available witnesses, made specific allegations against Kenyatta. In Kenya, the release of the pre-trial brief was regarded as an opportunity to make more details public and to specify more clearly what the Prosecutor's case against Kenyatta would have been.

While the case against him was in court, Kenyatta had insisted on his innocence, and Kenya had deployed a well-organised strategy characterising his trial as a witch-hunt and the preparations by the prosecution as shoddy. Although Kenyatta and the Kenyan state gave themselves the liberty of making extra-judicial statements about the case, most of which vilified the very idea of the trial, the Prosecutor had no matching ability to provide her version, and any outreach efforts on the Kenyan cases were greatly dwarfed by Kenya's massive campaign against the trials. Because it was assumed that the chance to provide a balanced view of the Kenyatta case would finally present itself during the trial, the fact that the case never went to trial removed the opportunity for the Prosecutor to meaningfully provide her version of the story.

Two reactions to the disclosure of the pre-trial brief are relevant. The first was a resolution in January by the governing Jubilee Coalition,[54] attended by both Kenyatta and Ruto, to repeal the International Crimes Act, the law that

54 The governing coalition in Kenya which brings together Uhuru Kenyatta's party, The National Alliance, and William Ruto's party, the United Republican Party.

domesticates the Rome Statute in Kenya. This resolution was made during a high profile retreat of the Coalition, which was attended by its MPs.

While there had been previous threats to repeal the International Crimes Act, and also to withdraw Kenya's membership from the ICC, none of them had materialised. Why, then, did the Jubilee government find it necessary to issue this new threat to withdraw from the ICC when previous ones had not been followed up?

The withdrawal of the Kenyatta case had provided Kenya with liberties it could not exercise as long as the case was still in court. Any hostile legislative action by Kenya, while the case was in court, would have undermined the country's claims that it was cooperating with the Court, an issue that remained central in the Kenyatta case, and played a role in its eventual termination. With the case ended, Kenya did not have to placate the Court or the international community. The Kenyan government, therefore, took early steps to assert its independence, based on a belief that hostile domestic action against the ICC would go towards correcting the international relations that the Kenyatta trial had distorted.[55]

Repealing the International Crimes Act was an act of backlash against international arrangements that dared to imperil Kenya's top leadership through a criminal trial. The resolution by Jubilee was a statement that the country's leadership would never again be put through what Kenyatta had faced before the ICC.[56]

The continuation of the trial against Ruto was a source of internal pressure in Jubilee, and was seen as partly explaining the resolution. The Jubilee Coalition was covering itself against the possibility of accusations down the line that, unlike the efforts made to defend Kenyatta when he was on trial, insufficient effort had been made to support Ruto's defence. This issue would be particularly important if Ruto's case ended in a conviction.[57]

The resolution to repeal the Act was also motivated by the uncertainties inherent in the fact that the terms for the termination of the Kenyatta case do not preclude its future revival if additional evidence should be found. A repeal of the Act would be viewed as sending the message that Kenya had broken relations with the ICC and would not engage with it in the future should the Court find this necessary.[58]

Also, pressure from people around Kenyatta was seen as a factor in the resolution. A prevalent view within Jubilee has been that while Kenyatta may be safe from the possibility of a future trial, the people around him could

---

55 See Kegoro, 'Why Jubilee is eager to repeal the International Crimes Act', *Sunday Nation*, 1 February 2015, available at: www.nation.co.ke/oped/Opinion/International-Crimes-Act-Uhuru-Kenyatta-ICC-Case/-/440808/2608874/-/y7rxi3z/-/index.html.

56 *Ibid.*

57 *Ibid.*

58 *Ibid.*

be vulnerable, without his protection, in the event that the ICC revisited the prosecution of the Naivasha and Nakuru violence on which the Kenyatta case was founded. They feel that the Court can still go against them while sparing Kenyatta, and in fact, some of the people mentioned in the Prosecutor's pre-trial brief had publicly appealed to the president for protection.[59] Repealing the Act would be viewed as the kind of protection these people craved.

The second notable reaction was an unprecedented statement by Kenyatta's lawyer, Stephen Kay, while responding to the pre-trial brief, which went out of its way to draw in opposition leader, Raila Odinga, by declaring that biased investigations by the National Commission on Human Rights were responsible for his exoneration from a trial by the ICC.

This reaction was seen as a reflection of how much Kenyatta's defence was stung by the content of the brief. The question though, was why the defence had drawn Odinga in, when this did not concern their case. One view was that this was an attempt by the defence to discredit the Prosecutor's brief as baseless by claiming that other people, besides Kenyatta, were involved in the post-election violence. Secondly, drawing in Odinga would raise the political cost of re-opening investigations into the Naivasha/Nakuru violence. Kenyatta's defence was, in effect, to demand that the re-opening of those investigations be matched with other investigations, particularly against Odinga.[60]

The relevance of this discussion for the question of the future prospects of a trial against Kenyatta is clear. The Jubilee Coalition's resolution is a communication of fervent hostility to the ICC, of a level that leaves no room for a constructive engagement on the possibility of future accountability based on what the Prosecutor tried to do to Kenyatta. As long as Kenyatta remains president of Kenya, the chances of a resumption of the case against him at the ICC, or of a fresh case based on the same circumstances, are remote.

4. CONCLUSION

One of the reasons why the Kenyan Parliament rejected the establishment of a special tribunal, as recommended by the Waki Commission, was the considerable doubt as to its ability to rise above the political pressure that the trial of cases arising from the post-election violence would have generated. The choice of the ICC was based on an expectation that, unlike national mechanisms that would be open to political pressure, the ICC would conduct an impartial trial of the cases and would bring about the requisite justice.

An examination of the record of the Kenyan cases before the ICC shows that the Court has been the subject of significant pressure calculated to undermine its

---

59 *Ibid.*

60 *Ibid.*

trial of the cases. It is even arguable that the pressure has had the intended effect. An example that proves this point is the hurriedly convened session during the 12th Meeting of the Assembly of States Parties at The Hague, as a response to the displeasure that the AU had expressed over the conduct of the Kenyan cases, during its Extraordinary Summit in October 2013.

Two lessons emerge in relation to the trial of the Kenyan cases. First, the assumptions that went into creating the ICC did not foresee, and therefore failed to make provisions for, the kind of political pressure that the Kenyan cases have generated. Part of the problem is that while the ASP is the top political organ of the ICC, and was, as stated by the Rome Statute, the organ in which the important decisions on the management of the Court would be taken, the practice has been quite different. Important discussions about the ICC take place elsewhere and create a binding effect on the ASP and the organs of the Court. For example, in relation to the Kenyan case, the AU emerged as an important forum where decisions are processed, often to the detriment of the Court. At the same time, decisions that are supposed to be friendly to the ASP, such as those made by the Security Council, take place outside the ASP yet often become the source of displeasure elsewhere, particularly for the AU.

A trend in these relationships is that states are able to act duplicitously towards the Court, depending on the forum involved. Thus, while Kenya's positions in the forums of the ASP are reasoned, the same cannot be said about the country's behaviour at the AU, or the UN, where Kenya has taken the habit of condemning the ICC in unrestrained terms.

The lesson to be learned from the Kenyan cases is that there is, at the moment, no political mechanism that is capable of playing as versatile a role in defending the ICC, as would be necessitated by the attacks that are mounted against the Court in a highly dynamic environment.

A related issue is the effect of political activities against the ICC within Kenya. As has been seen, Kenya's political institutions, and the country's political leaders, have been at the forefront of attacking the Court from within Kenya. These attacks have had a chilling effect on domestic support for the Court, and raised the political cost of supporting the ICC within the country, with the effect that witnesses and their families, as well as intermediaries of the Court, may have been greatly intimidated. In most domestic jurisdictions, there are mechanisms for sanctioning unjustified criticism meant to undermine ongoing judicial proceedings. These mechanisms include contempt of court proceedings. A regrettable situation is that the ICC looked the other way and never tried to address the extra-judicial conduct of Kenyatta and the Kenyan state, which was calculated to undermine the trials. While in many national jurisdictions, the equivalent conduct would probably attract sanctions for contempt of court, it is not clear why the ICC did not try to become more assertive in controlling what Kenya and Kenyatta did outside of Court, when this had an effect on the trials.

There are many questions in relation to the Kenyan cases: did the ICC become aware of the damaging effect that the conduct of Kenyan actors has had towards the cases, and was it in its province to do anything about it? If the answer is affirmative, what organs of the ICC should or could have taken action and at whose behest? Is the internal conduct of the Kenyan state towards the cases an issue the ASP should discuss, and does it undermine Kenya's claims that it is cooperating with the ICC?

The last set of issues relates to the future of the Kenyatta case in view of its termination. While, in theory, the case can be reinstated in the future if new evidence is found, the hostility emanating from Kenya, where Kenyatta, the potential accused, is president, together with the AU's position that no head of state can be tried while in office, makes it highly unlikely that such a trial could materialise on a practical basis. The Kenyan cases are a lesson that, notwithstanding the Rome Statute, a de facto immunity based on political hostility has been created within Africa in favour, at least, of serving heads of state, if not a larger number of high officials.

Since the ICC, which was expected to have a greater measure of autonomy than the special tribunal, faired so badly in the trial against Kenyatta, it must be concluded that, had it been established, a special tribunal might not have performed any better than the ICC.

Unlike cases from other countries, the Kenyan cases before the ICC are the only ones whose trial did not enjoy the support of the state from which the cases originated. In all the other cases, the cooperation of the state has largely been forthcoming and may have been taken for granted. The Kenyan cases provided the first opportunity where the ICC had to conduct trials while facing the hostility of the government of the state from which the cases originated, and have provided lessons on the levels of cooperation that may be expected from the concerned state. The differing views between the Kenyan government and the Prosecutor as to the adequacy of the cooperation that the country was offering, reflects the fact that the Kenyan government offered only the most perfunctory cooperation with the Court, enough to avoid being found guilty of non-cooperation, but otherwise useless for the purposes of giving meaningful support to the Prosecutor.

The experience in the Kenyatta case provides proof that as currently structured, the ICC is too weak to make high state officials accountable. Acknowledging this reality limits the choices that the Prosecutor has in relation to the future of the case against Kenyatta. Even if additional evidence was to emerge as would enable the Prosecutor to consider reinstating the trial, it is likely that political pressure would eventually derail such a trial. Under these circumstances, the only option available to the Prosecutor is a waiting game, one in which she would have to try to gather evidence for a possible reinstatement of the Kenyatta case that would be deliberately delayed until he leaves office.

BIBLIOGRAPHY

BOOKS AND JOURNAL ARTICLES

Office of the AU Panel of Eminent African Personalities 2014
Office of the AU Panel of Eminent African Personalities, 'Back from the Brink: The 2008 Mediation Process and Reforms in Kenya', April 2014.

JURISPRUDENCE

ICC 2014
ICC, Prosecutor v. Uhuru Muigai Kenyatta, ICC-01/09-02/11-875, 3 December 2014.
ICC 2014
ICC, Prosecutor v. Uhuru Muigai Kenyatta, ICC-01/09-02/11-944, 5 September 2014.
ICC 2014
ICC, Prosecutor v. Uhuru Muigai Kenyatta, ICC-01/09-02/11-908, 31 March 2014.
ICC 2014
ICC, Prosecutor v. Uhuru Muigai Kenyatta, ICC-01/09-02/11-886, 23 January 2014.
ICC 2010
ICC, Decision Pursuant to Article 15 of the Rome Statute on the Authorization of an Investigation into the Situation in the Republic of Kenya, ICC-01/09-19, 31 March 2010.

TREATIES, LEGISLATION AND AGREEMENTS

International Criminal Court, Rules of Procedure and Evidence, ICC-ASP/1/3 (Part II-A), 9 September 2002.
Kenya, The Special Tribunal for Kenya Bill, 2009.

OTHERS

Capital FM, 'President Kenyatta's inauguration speech', 9 April 2013.
Capital FM, 'Uhuru: ICC is a toy of declining imperial powers', 12 October 2013.
ICC, 'Statement by ICC Prosecutor on the Notice to Withdraw Charges against Mr Muthaura', Press Release, 11 March 2013.
Kegoro, G., 'Why Jubilee is eager to repeal the International Crimes Act', Sunday Nation, 1 February 2015.
Kenya National Assembly, Official Record of Proceedings, 21 April 2009.
Kenya National Assembly, Official Record of Proceedings, 24 February 2009.
Kenya National Assembly, Official Record of Proceedings, 12 February 2009.
Kenya National Assembly, Official Record of Proceedings, 10 February 2009.

Kenya National Assembly, Official Record of Proceedings, 5 February 2009.
Kenya National Assembly, Official Record of Proceedings, 4 February 2009.
Kenya National Assembly, Official Record of Proceedings, 29 January 2009.
Kenya, Report of the Commission of Inquiry into the Post Election Violence, 17 October 2008.
KTN News Kenya, 'Kenya Presidential Debate 2013 [Full Video]', YouTube, 12 February 2013.
Leftie, P. and Gaitho, M., 'ICC: Uhuru, Ruto trial to run on different days', Daily Monitor, 10 September 2013.
Ndonga, S., 'Museveni praises Kenya for rejecting ICC "blackmail"', Capital News, 9 April 2013.
Njagih, M., 'President Uhuru Kenyatta rejects parallel Hague trial with William Ruto', Standard Digital, 9 September 2013.

TRANSFORMING LEGAL CONCEPTS AND GENDER PERCEPTIONS

Brigid INDER

1. INTRODUCTION

There are numerous reasons for impunity for sexual and gender-based crimes. Obstacles at the domestic level include discriminatory corroboration requirements and constructions of 'consent', and inadequate and incomplete legal prohibitions on these crimes, amongst other issues. In the international courts and tribunals, some of the impediments to successful prosecutions for these crimes have been due to assumptions about who is a victim of sexual violence, lack of prioritisation in investigation plans and in the past the inclusion of sexual violence charges in plea bargain agreements. Beyond these considerations, there is an underlying element that contributes to the unique and epidemic levels of impunity for sexual violence, and that is the partial integration, rather than the full integration, of women and concepts of gender within the structure of justice.

The law, in its legal concepts and practice, typically lags behind the human experience, and nowhere is this more poignant than in relation to sexual violence and gender-based crimes. There has been landmark jurisprudence which has recognised the gender dimensions of sexual violence, as well as the gender dimensions of other forms of criminality. Such jurisprudential highlights include: the recognition of rape as an underlying act of genocide;[1] sexual violence as a form of torture;[2] the recognition of forced marriage as a distinct crime from the crime of sexual slavery;[3] and non-invasive acts such as forced nudity as a form of sexual violence.[4] Each of these judgments has shed light on a specific aspect of sexual and gender-based violence as international crimes, and collectively, this jurisprudence provides a pathway of legal reasoning available for others to draw and expand upon.

1 *The Prosecutor v. Jean-Paul Akayesu*, ICTR-96-4-T, 2 September 1998.
2 *The Prosecutor v. Duško Tadić*, IT-94-1-T, 7 May 1997.
3 *The Prosecutor v. Brima, Kamara & Kanu*, SCSL-04-16-T, 20 June 2007, Dissenting Opinion of Justice Doherty.
4 *The Prosecutor v. Jean-Paul Akayesu*, ICTR-96-4-T, 2 September 1998.

Yet, despite the overwhelming numbers, millions, of mostly women and girls throughout history, and continuing today, who have been victimised through acts of sexual and gender-based crimes, only 16% of those accused of war crimes, crimes against humanity and genocide have been convicted of sexual violence through international legal mechanisms.[5]

Notwithstanding the important benchmarks, overall there has been limited and inconsistent jurisprudential progress in interpreting the law and engendering the legal concepts through a lens for crimes not obviously, but often inherently, gendered.

Systemic 'blind spots' resulting in both direct and indirect gender-based discrimination persist amongst investigators, prosecutors and judges and are reflected in the selective incorporation of 'gender' within the development of legal theories and the incomplete integration of these issues within legal concepts and liability regimes. In practice, these 'blind spots' lead to an insufficient assessment of the evidence, too few prosecutions for sexual violence and unintended invisibility of gender issues in the adjudication and interpretation of the law, including in relation to gender-based crimes.

This historic and ongoing marginalisation in the law has created a gender debt, and unless and until we transform both legal norms and gender perceptions, the justice process will continue to fail current and future generations of victims/survivors.

This article will explore two cases before the International Criminal Court which demonstrate the normative power of some of these legal blind spots and exemplify occasions on which the law, in its application and adjudication, has lagged behind the human experience of crimes considered amongst the most grave.

1.1. *THE PROSECUTOR V. THOMAS LUBANGA DYILO*[6]

The case of *The Prosecutor v. Thomas Lubanga Dyilo* (Lubanga) provides one of the sharpest examples at the ICC of the need to engender the law.[7] Mr Lubanga, former President of the *Union des Patriotes Congolais* (UPC) and Commander-in-Chief of the *Forces Patriotiques pour la Liberation du Congo* (FPLC), was

5 Brigid Inder, Executive Director, Women's Initiatives for Gender Justice, Special Advisor on Gender to the ICC Prosecutor, speech at the 'Launch of the Policy on Sexual and Gender-based Crimes by the ICC Office of the Prosecutor', 7 December 2014 (United Nations, New York), available at: www.iccwomen.org/documents/Global-Summit-Speech.pdf. Research on file with the Women's Initiatives for Gender Justice.

6 This section is based on an interview with Brigid Inder, Executive Director, Women's Initiatives for Gender Justice, referenced in Durbach and Chappell 2014, pp. 543–562.

7 *The Prosecutor v. Thomas Lubanga Dyilo*, ICC-01/04-01/06-2842, 14 March 2012. See also Women's Initiatives for Gender Justice, 'First Conviction by the ICC', 14 March 2012, available at: www.iccwomen.org/documents/Press-Statement-on-Lubanga-conviction.pdf.

charged with the war crimes of conscripting and enlisting children under the age of 15, and using them to participate actively in hostilities in the Ituri province of the Democratic Republic of the Congo (DRC), between 1 September 2002 and 13 August 2003.[8] Mr Lubanga was ultimately convicted for these crimes as a co-perpetrator under Article 25(3)(a) of the Rome Statute.[9]

Although Mr Lubanga was not indicted explicitly for gender-based crimes, testimony about these acts comprised a significant part of the trial. At least 21 out of 25 prosecution witnesses testified about the presence of girl soldiers within the UPC and at least 15 witnesses testified about crimes of sexual violence including the rape of girl soldiers by UPC commanders and other combatants within their ranks.[10] The testimonies of former child soldiers and other former members of the UPC militia, described some of the gender dimensions within the crimes for which Mr Lubanga was convicted – acts of sexual violence, the roles to which girls within the UPC were assigned, and the treatment of female soldiers.

Interviews conducted in 2006 and 2007 by the Women's Initiatives for Gender Justice (or Women's Initiatives) with former UPC child soldiers highlighted the horror of being conscripted, and enlisted, by this militia.[11] Reportedly, girls were regularly raped, many from the moment of abduction, with some of the most intense periods of sexual violence occurring during the initial abduction phase and once they were relocated to the militia training camps.[12]

According to the interviewees, the life of a child soldier within the UPC was marked by violence, hardship and suffering on a daily basis. The Women's Initiatives' documentation indicates that at the training camps, the children were deprived of sleep, forced to consume drugs, and shown how to fight. Newly enlisted and conscripted children were often made to walk at the front of the troops in battle to provoke gunfire, thus enabling UPC armed fighters to see where the opposing militia combatants were located. The children, girls and boys, young men and women, were made to fight and forced to kill.[13]

Sexual violence, in armed conflict, is often used as an effective mechanism for demonstrating control and ownership including over child soldiers, and for severing attachment with their families and childhood associations prior

---

8 *The Prosecutor v. Thomas Lubanga Dyilo*, ICC-01/04-01/06-803-tEN, 29 January 2007. See also, Women's Initiatives for Gender Justice, *Gender Report Cards on the International Criminal Court 2008, 2009, 2010, 2011 and 2012.*

9 *The Prosecutor v. Thomas Lubanga Dyilo*, ICC-01/04-01/06-2842, 14 March 2012.

10 Women's Initiatives for Gender Justice, *Gender Report Card on the International Criminal Court 2012*, p. 160.

11 Documentation on file with the Women's Initiatives for Gender Justice. Inder 2013.

12 Brigid Inder, Executive Director, Women's Initiatives for Gender Justice, 'The ICC, Child Soldiers and Gender Justice', *The Parliament Magazine*, 21 November 2011, Issue 338; Inder 2013.

13 Brigid Inder, Executive Director, Women's Initiatives for Gender Justice, 'The ICC, Child Soldiers and Gender Justice', *The Parliament Magazine*, 21 November 2011, Issue 338.

to abduction. Based on documentation material produced by the Women's Initiatives for Gender Justice, rape and sexual enslavement of girls within the UPC appear to have been integral components of induction into the militia group, occurring to such an extent that perhaps rape could be considered an indicator of enlistment and conscription for girl soldiers. Being raped, witnessing rape and being forced to rape were regular occurrences within the militia group, especially for new conscriptees.[14]

In addition, girls and young women within the UPC were sometimes assigned as bodyguards to commanders and often simultaneously designated as their sexual property. As bodyguards they were required to procure other girls and young female civilians for the sexual pleasure of their commander. Amongst the many roles children are required to play within militias, including within the UPC, it appears that only girls and other female 'soldiers' are involuntarily assigned to militia leaders for the purpose of sex.

It is clear from the testimony in the Lubanga case, emblematic of experiences of other children instrumentalised as combatants by militias and armed forces worldwide, that the crimes of enlistment, conscription and use are gendered.

According to the testimony of Radhika Coomaraswamy, UN Secretary General's Special Representative (SRSG) on Children in Armed Conflict who was called by the Prosecution as an expert witness in the Lubanga trial, girls and young women within militias are required to perform multiple combat and non-combat roles.[15] Based on the work of her Office, SRSG Coomaraswamy testified that girl soldiers are often forced to provide domestic services within militia camps, they may also be required to patrol check-points or act as porters or scouts.[16] Girl soldiers are also forced into sexual slavery,[17] or given as 'bush wives' to commanders.

The UPC's enlistment, conscription and use of children and the gendered expressions of these crimes are not unique to this militia group or to the children of Ituri, north-eastern DRC.[18]

The commonality of the commission of these crimes and the harmed suffered, challenge the traditional legal concept of what it means to be victimised through the crimes of enlistment, conscription and use. The Lubanga case, therefore, was a significant opportunity for a review of the legal concepts of these crimes in light of the inherent gender dimensions exposed by the evidence in relation to the charges and the universality of this experience.

---

14 *Ibid.*

15 Transcript of the International Criminal Court, ICC-01/04-01/06-T-223-ENG, 7 January 2010, p. 30, lines 11–19.

16 *Ibid*, p. 14, lines 10–14.

17 *Ibid*, p. 14, lines 10–14, p. 30, lines 11–19.

18 *Annual report of the Special Representative of the Secretary-General for Children and Armed conflict*, A/HRC/28/54, 29 December 2014, available at: www.un.org/ga/search/view_doc.asp?symbol=A/HRC/28/54%20&Lang=E&Area=UNDOC.

Disappointingly, the Lubanga Trial Chamber did not appear to apply the full extent of the victimisation, harm and criminality apparent in the evidence to their consideration of the legal concepts of enlistment, conscription and use. The Chamber's apparent focus on culpability alone and its preoccupation with the absence of explicit charges for crimes of sexual violence, appear to have distracted the majority of the bench from fully applying the evidence to the crimes. It also appears to have led to a number of assumptions including: that without explicit sexual violence charges, there were no gender dimensions to be considered in relation to the charges; and that sexual violence could only be considered in the context of culpability and not in the context of the legal concepts of enlistment, conscription and use.

In the judgment, the Trial Chamber declined to substantively discuss the evidence of sexual violence in relation to the charges and made no legal finding on whether sexual violence could or should be properly included within the scope of the crime of use.[19] In addition, the majority did not address sexual violence or any other gender dimensions of this crime, or the crimes of enlistment and conscription.

Judge Elisabeth Odio Benito, offered a dissenting opinion specifically on the approach of the Chamber to the legal concept of 'use' and the issue of sexual violence, where she argued that:

> Although the Majority of the Chamber recognises that sexual violence has been referred to in this case, it seems to confuse the factual allegations of this case with the legal concept of the crime, which are independent. By failing to deliberately include within the legal concept of 'use to participate actively in the hostilities' the sexual violence and other ill-treatment suffered by girls and boys, the Majority of the Chamber is making this critical aspect of the crime invisible. Invisibility of sexual violence in the legal concept leads to discrimination against the victims of enlistment, conscription and use who systematically suffer from this crime as an intrinsic part of the involvement with the armed group.[20]

Attention to legal concepts in the context of a trial does not detract or add to the finding of guilt or innocence against an accused. Such considerations are not confined by the facts of a case and exist outside of the evaluation of the performance of the prosecution. Consideration of legal concepts is an investment in the development of the law, intended to add greater clarity and accuracy to its application.

The case against Thomas Lubanga was a missed opportunity for the law to catch up with the reality of the experiences of child soldiers and to contribute

---

19 *The Prosecutor v. Thomas Lubanga Dyilo*, ICC-01/04–01/06–2842, 14 March 2012, para. 630; Women's Initiatives for Gender Justice, *Gender Report Card on the International Criminal Court 2012*, p. 162.

20 *The Prosecutor v. Thomas Lubanga Dyilo*, ICC-01/04–01/06–2842, 14 March 2012, Dissenting Opinion of Judge Odio Benito, para. 16.

to international jurisprudence on these issues. As exemplified by the Lubanga judgment, the evolution of the law governing these crimes has not kept pace with the forms of conflict and the expansion and nuance of the gendered forms of criminality inherent in the crimes of enlistment, conscription and use of children in armed conflict.

2. INCLUSIVE JUSTICE

In many respects, there is a heightened judicial obligation in cases before the ICC, for judges to fully consider the legal concepts and in so doing ensure that the theory of the crime adequately captures the reality it exists to adjudicate.

Article 21(3) of the Rome Statute, perhaps one of the Statute's most important provisions, states that the application and interpretation of law must be consistent with internationally recognised human rights and be without adverse distinction founded on grounds such as gender.[21] This article creates a positive obligation for prosecutors and judges to ensure that in applying and interpreting the law, factors historically utilised to discriminate against groups and identities of people, such as gender, age, race, colour, sexual orientation and social origin, are dismantled in favour of inclusive justice. Avoiding 'adverse distinctions' in the application of the law cannot be achieved without being alert to the legal concepts, for this is where inherent bias or unintended discriminations are often embedded.

2.1. *THE PROSECUTOR V. GERMAIN KATANGA*[22]

The second case which demonstrates the need to transform both legal norms and gender perceptions relates to Germain Katanga (Katanga), who was convicted as an accessory under Article 25(3)(d) for the war crimes of attack upon a civilian population, destruction of property, pillaging and murder as both a war crime and crime against humanity, but he was acquitted under Article 25(3)(d) of the

---

21 Rome Statute of the International Criminal Court, 17 July 1998, Article 21(3) provides: 'The application and interpretation of law pursuant to this article must be consistent with internationally recognized human rights, and be without any adverse distinction founded on grounds such as gender as defined in article 7, paragraph 3, age, race, colour, language, religion or belief, political or other opinion, national, ethnic or social origin, wealth, birth or other status.' See also *The Prosecutor v. Thomas Lubanga Dyilo*, ICC-01/04-01/06-2904, 7 August 2012, para. 191; Office of the Prosecutor of the International Criminal Court, *Policy Paper on Sexual and Gender-Based Crimes*, June 2014, para. 27 and footnotes 23, 25.

22 This section is based on a speech given by Brigid Inder, Executive Director, Women's Initiatives for Gender Justice at the expert panel on 'Prosecuting Sexual Violence in Conflict', 11 June 2014, Global Summit to End Sexual Violence in Conflict (London), available at: www.iccwomen.org/documents/Global-Summit-Speech.pdf.

sexual violence charges of rape and sexual slavery.[23] Katanga was also acquitted under Article 25(3)(a) of the crimes of enlistment, conscription and use.

The Katanga judgment, the first at the ICC to analyse sexual violence, is emblematic of so many of the ways in which sexual violence is treated differently and where a higher standard is required to satisfy the threshold of beyond reasonable doubt.

Katanga was convicted as an accessory for his role as the commander of the Walendu-Bindi *collectivité*, a Ngiti militia group, which together with the Lendu militia group, *Front des Nationalistes et Intégrationnistes* (FNI), attacked Bogoro village in eastern DRC in February 2003. This was a village populated mostly by those of Hema ethnicity. At that time, the *Union des Patriotes Congolais*, a Hema militia group, was involved in an armed conflict with the Walendu-Bindi *collectivité*, later known as the FRPI,[24] and the FNI fuelled, as asserted by the Prosecution, by ethnic rivalry.[25]

In its judgment, the majority of the Trial Chamber found the three witnesses who testified in relation to the charges of sexual violence credible and stated that it believed rape and sexual slavery had been committed by Katanga's militia during and after the attack on Bogoro.[26] However, the Chamber found Katanga not guilty of contributing to the acts of sexual violence as it did not believe these crimes formed part of the common purpose of the attack, unlike the crimes of directing an attack against a civilian population, pillaging, murder and destruction of property, for which he was convicted.[27]

It reached these findings based on evidence that in the weeks leading up to the attack Katanga had been responsible for the transportation, stockpiling and distribution of arms and a large amount of ammunition to his militia.[28] The Trial Chamber found that these actions contributed to all of the crimes associated with the attack under Article 25(3)(d), except for the acts of sexual violence.

According to the majority, transporting, stockpiling and distributing weapons and ammunition demonstrated planning, intent and preparation for the attack and proved Katanga's contribution to the common purpose.[29] But more than that, it appears that the majority also explicitly connected the amassing and distribution of weapons with the ability of the combatants to commit the crimes of murder, destruction of property, pillaging and an attack on the civilian population.[30] In other words, it appears that the Judges made an

---

23 *The Prosecutor v. Germain Katanga*, ICC-01/04-01/07-3436, 7 March 2014, pp. 709–710. Katanga was also acquitted of the war crime of using child soldiers under Article 25(3)(a).

24 *Ibid*, paras. 679–680.

25 *Ibid*, paras. 433, 1463, 1688–1691.

26 *Ibid*, paras. 988–999, 1002–1019.

27 *Ibid*, paras. 1657–1664.

28 *Ibid*, paras. 1671, 1679–1681.

29 *Ibid*, paras. 1672–1673.

30 *Ibid*, paras. 1676–1681.

explicit connection between the type of contribution to the plan and the types of crimes committed.

Based on this reasoning, what would be the equivalent contribution to commit the crime of rape? What would judges be satisfied with, in a comparable way, to demonstrate the intent to rape, in order for this crime to be considered part of the common purpose?

Why couldn't the same preparation and contribution the Judges found beyond reasonable doubt facilitated the ability of the militia to commit all the crimes for which Katanga was convicted, why could this not also satisfy the Chamber in relation to the ability of the militia to rape and sexually enslave women of the village?

Alternatively, if amassing weapons connected Katanga to the commission of murder quite literally because it provided them with the ability to kill, would the gathering of a large number of combatants in the context of an armed conflict readying themselves to attack a civilian population not be an equivalent demonstration of the ability to commit acts of rape and other forms of sexual violence?

Katanga was found guilty of murder and for an attack against a civilian population under *dolus directus* in the first degree, meaning that these were acts he intended to engage in.[31] In its judgment, the Chamber did not find Katanga guilty of intending to commit rape and sexual slavery, but it also does not appear to have even considered *dolus directus* in the second degree, meaning whether Katanga knew that in the ordinary course of the attack, crimes of sexual violence would occur. By contrast, under this theory of intent, the majority did find him guilty of pillaging and destruction of property, believing he knew that in the ordinary course of events that these crimes would be committed.[32]

The majority decision describes the intensity of the fire power deployed in the attack, which according to the judges 'compelled it [the population] to flee, leaving it vulnerable to shooting and forcing it to abandon its property'.[33] However, the Chamber did not seem to consider that the attempts by the female members of the population to flee the gunfire might also have made them vulnerable to rape, capture and enslavement.

3. INDICATORS OF THE COMMON PURPOSE

In considering whether the crimes charged were part of the common purpose, the Judges identified four indicators:

31 *Ibid*, paras. 1658, 1690–1691.
32 *Ibid*, paras. 1662, 1690–1691.
33 *Ibid*, para. 1678.

- whether the crimes were numerous and committed repetitively;
- whether the crimes were necessary to fulfilling the common purpose;
- whether the perpetrators of rape and sexual slavery – in this case, the Ngiti combatants of Walendu-Bindi – had committed these crimes prior to the attack on Bogoro; and
- whether the rape and sexual slavery were ethnically motivated, in light of the Prosecution's theory that ethnic hatred was a key dimension of the common plan.[34]

3.1. WHETHER THE CRIMES WERE NUMEROUS AND COMMITTED REPETITIVELY

The Judges in this case were convinced that the crimes for which Katanga was convicted were within the common plan, in part because of the volume of these crimes within the attack. According to the judgment, more than sixty people were killed in the attack, destruction of property occurred on a grand scale, and pillaging was widespread.[35] Because of the scale of these crimes, the Chamber was able to conclude that these crimes must have been intended, and therefore part of the common plan.

On the charges of rape and sexual slavery, the judges stated that they were satisfied these crimes had been committed by Katanga's combatants during and after the attack on Bogoro, but they did not find these crimes to be part of the common purpose, in part because of the apparently low number of times these crimes were committed, based on the evidence presented by the Prosecution.[36]

Firstly, the issue of numbers is very complex, for what we count and how we count reflects what we value. There were three sexual violence witnesses in this case. Each of them testified to being raped multiple times. If numerousity was an essential indicator then what was counted was critical – was it the number of women raped or the number of times they were raped? Did the Chamber consider the evidence and determine that three women had been raped or that according to the testimonies, at least 17 acts of rape were committed during the attack on Bogoro? All of these witnesses were also enslaved at a camp in Ngiti following the attack. The terms of their enslavement varied from one month to one and a half years, during which time they were, in the words of one of the witnesses, 'at the disposal' of combatants and raped repeatedly. This evidence, which the judges stated they believed, did not satisfy the indicator of numerousity and repetition.

---

34 *Ibid*, para. 1663. See also Women's Initiatives for Gender Justice, *Gender Report Card on the International Criminal Court 2014*, pp. 179–180; Women's Initiatives for Gender Justice presentations at panel discussion on 'First Reflections on the ICC Katanga Judgment', 12 March 2014, T.M.C. Asser Institute (The Hague).

35 *The Prosecutor v. Germain Katanga*, ICC-01/04–01/07–3436, 7 March 2014, paras. 841, 950.

36 *Ibid*, para. 1663.

3.2. WHETHER THE CRIMES WERE NECESSARY TO FULFILLING THE COMMON PURPOSE

The Trial Chamber appeared to require that in order to find that rape and sexual slavery formed part of the common purpose, it had to be established that but for the commission of these crimes, the common purpose could not have been achieved.[37] However, the Trial Chamber does not provide explicit support for its finding that a crime must be necessary to achieving the common purpose in order for it to form part of the common purpose. Furthermore, this finding departs from established jurisprudence of the ad hoc tribunals which have found to the contrary.[38] For example, murder may be committed as part of a common purpose to forcibly transfer or deport the civilian population of a village, although murder is not necessary to achieving that common purpose. The same is true for rape.

It is well established that rape and sexual slavery are among the means regularly used during conflict to destroy communities. These crimes were found to have been highly effective as tools of ethnic cleansing in Bosnia and Rwanda, used to destroy the social fabric of communities and ensure that inhabitants would not return once the fighting ceased.

In concluding that it did not have evidence to find that the attack of Bogoro village necessarily occurred through the commission of rape and sexual violence, and therefore these crimes were not part of the common purpose, the Chamber appears to have ignored the well-established lineage of jurisprudence establishing that sexual and gender based crimes are commonly used to achieve such aims.[39]

3.3. WHETHER THE PERPETRATORS OF RAPE AND SEXUAL SLAVERY – IN THIS CASE, THE NGITI COMBATANTS OF WALENDU-BINDI – HAD COMMITTED THESE CRIMES PRIOR TO THE ATTACK ON BOGORO

In its judgment, the Chamber does not provide explicit support for its conclusion that the Ngiti combatants had not committed rape and sexual slavery prior to the Bogoro attack, and the relevance of this requirement also appears to be questionable. Necessitating the commission of these crimes in prior attacks

---

37 *Ibid*, para. 1663.

38 See e.g. *The Prosecutor v. Nikola Šainović, Nebojša Pavković, Vladimir Lazarević, Sreten Lukić*, IT-05-87-A, 23 January 2014; *The Prosecutor v. Milan Martić*, IT-95-11-A, 8 October 2008.

39 See e.g. *The Prosecutor v. Jean-Paul Akayesu*, ICTR-96-4-T, 2 September 1998; *The Prosecutor v. Duško Tadić*, IT-94-1-T, 7 May 1997; *The Prosecutor v. Anto Furundžija*, IT-95-17/1-T, 10 December 1998; *The Prosecutor v. Zejnil Delalić*, IT-96-21-T, 16 November 1998; *The Prosecutor v. Dragoljub Kunarac et al.*, IT-96-23-T, IT-96-23/1-T, 22 February 2001; *The Prosecutor v. Radislav Krstić*, IT-98-33-T, 2 August 2001.

committed by a militia group may have the effect of creating a threshold that is very difficult to meet. Whilst the prior commission of such crimes makes it easier to rationalise that the subsequent commission is possible and believable, *requiring* these acts to have been previously committed by the militia, is inherently flawed. For example, would this mean that any time acts are committed for the first time by a militia group, they cannot be found to form part of the common purpose and therefore will not result in convictions? At present, such reasoning appears to only apply to crimes of sexual violence.

In its confirmation of charges decision, Pre-Trial Chamber I, by majority, concluded that there was evidence that not only in subsequent attacks, but also 'in previous … attacks against the civilian population, the militias led and used by the suspects to perpetrate the attacks, [including the FNI and FRPI], repeatedly committed rape and sexual slavery against women and girls in Ituri.'[40] This was one of the factors, along with other reports and witness statements, it found supported its conclusion that although there was insufficient evidence to establish substantial grounds to believe that the common plan specifically instructed the soldiers to rape or sexually enslave women, there was sufficient evidence to establish substantial grounds to believe that in the ordinary course of events, the implementation of the common plan would inevitably result in the rape or sexual enslavement of civilian women in Bogoro.[41]

It is not reasonable to require the prior commission of rape to determine whether this crime also occurred in the incident at hand, as required by the Katanga Trial Chamber. However, if there is evidence of the prior commission of rape or other forms of sexual violence, it is reasonable to consider this material and such evidence should not be ignored, as reflected in the approach taken by the Pre-Trial Chamber I in the same case.

3.4. WHETHER THE RAPE AND SEXUAL SLAVERY WERE ETHNICALLY MOTIVATED, IN LIGHT OF THE PROSECUTION'S THEORY THAT ETHNIC HATRED WAS A KEY DIMENSION OF THE COMMON PLAN

In one of the most memorable statements of the judgment, the majority stated 'that women who were raped, abducted and turned to slavery had their life "spared" and escaped a certain death because they pretended to belong to an ethnicity other than Hema'.[42]

40 *The Prosecutor v. Germain Katanga*, ICC-01/04-01/07-717, 30 September 2008, para. 568.

41 *Ibid*, paras. 434, 442.

42 *The Prosecutor v. Germain Katanga*, ICC-01/04-01/07-3436, 7 March 2014, para. 1663. See also Women's Initiatives for Gender Justice, *Gender Report Card on the International Criminal Court 2014*, pp. 179–180.

This is a deeply troubling statement and reinforces a traditional hierarchy of crimes, which the Rome Statute explicitly dismantles. The Chamber's assessment of the evidence is also intriguing.

A review of the publicly available transcripts of the testimonies of the three sexual violence witnesses indicates that each of these witnesses was asked about her ethnicity by the Ngiti combatants and all testified that when they tried to claim they were not Hema, the combatants disbelieved them and they were told that they were lying.[43]

Witness 353 testified that her assailants questioned her about her ethnicity; that she denied being Hema, and responded that she was of Nande ethnicity. At that moment, one person recognised her and stated that she was Hema, to which she replied that she was not Hema but that she was living with a Hema. Two combatants then argued about whose 'wife' she would become and decided that she would become both of their 'wives'.[44]

Witness 132 testified that when she was found by her assailants, they told her to take off her clothes. They then accused her of being Hema, which she denied. The combatants continued to inquire about her ethnicity and insist that she was Hema. They raped her, told her she had become their 'wife', and took her to a camp where she was interrogated, imprisoned in a hole and raped again repeatedly. She recounted that one day, when the 'chief' of the camp asked her about her ethnicity, she claimed she was Nande, and he replied 'no, you are Hema'. According to the transcript, '[a]fter that, he decided that she would not be released'.[45]

Witness 249 also testified that she was asked about her ethnicity but only after she was repeatedly raped. She claimed not to be Hema but was told 'that she was Hema because they smelled her odour'. She was also told that if she would not inform her captors of the location of the Hema, she would have to choose between her life and becoming their 'wife'. She testified that she 'told them to make that choice'. Witness 249 also testified that she 'told [the combatants] that it would be better for them to kill me rather than treat me like that, like an animal'.[46]

Based on their testimonies, it is clear that all of these witnesses were asked about their ethnic identity, before and after being raped and when they arrived at the militia camp following their abduction. Each denial was met with disbelief. It

43 Transcripts of the International Criminal Court, ICC-01/04-01/07-T-213-Red-ENG, 4 November 2010, p. 2-26; ICC-01/04-01/07-T-139-Red-FRA, 11 May 2010, pp. 11-12, 61, 64; ICC-01/04-01/07-T-135-Red-FRA, 4 May 2010, pp. 58-59.

44 Transcript of the International Criminal Court, ICC-01/04-01/07-T-213-Red-ENG, 4 November 2010, pp. 24-26, 48. See also Women's Initiatives for Gender Justice, *Gender Report Card on the International Criminal Court 2014*, p. 179.

45 Transcript of the International Criminal Court, ICC-01/04-01/07-T-139-Red-FRA, 11 May 2010, pp. 9-13, 19-20, 22-23, 25, 28-30, 37, 40, 45, 48, 59, 61, 64. See also Women's Initiatives for Gender Justice, *Gender Report Card on the International Criminal Court 2014*, p. 179.

46 Transcript of the International Criminal Court, ICC-01/04-01/07-T-135-Red-FRA, 4 May 2010, pp. 40-43, 58-59. See also Women's Initiatives for Gender Justice, *Gender Report Card on the International Criminal Court 2014*, p. 179.

would appear that perhaps the judges focused on the assertions of the witnesses disclaiming Hema ethnicity to conclude that the crimes committed against them were unrelated to their ethnic identity. The fact that all of the witnesses were asked about their ethnicity suggests that this factor was of great relevance to the perpetrators, regardless of the actual ethnic identities of the witnesses, or whether their denials of Hema ethnicity were believed. At best, determining that the acts of rape and sexual slavery were unrelated to the issue of ethnicity does not appear to be a reasonable assessment of the evidence.

The Katanga judgment, emblematic of so many cases before the international tribunals, appears to demonstrate: a subconscious but clear bias requiring sexual violence to be a more explicit component of a common plan, than is expected of any other category of crimes; that the contribution considered necessary to commit rape and sexual slavery is different from the contribution necessary to commit other crimes which occur simultaneously; and that the scale and volume of sexual violence may be rendered invisible by an incomplete assessment of the evidence.

4. LOOKING AHEAD

Moving beyond the initial ICC jurisprudence, there are a number of forthcoming trials and judgments which provide important opportunities for a deeper consideration of these issues. In learning from its mistakes in the Lubanga case, the Prosecution included, and Pre-Trial Chamber II confirmed,[47] ground-breaking charges of rape and sexual slavery committed against child soldiers within its case against Bosco Ntaganda. This is the first time in international criminal and humanitarian law that a commander has been charged with crimes committed against children in his own militia group and under his command. The Prosecution's case against LRA commander Dominic Ongwen contains the largest number and widest range of charges for sexual and gender-based crimes brought by the Office of the Prosecutor (OTP) to date.[48] The case against Laurent Gbagbo and Charles Blé Goudé in relation to the post-election violence occurring between November 2010 – May 2011 in Côte d'Ivoire, includes charges of rape and persecution carried out through acts including rape.[49] This brings to trial the first former Head of State charged with crimes of sexual violence.[50] The judgment in the main case against Jean-Pierre Bemba, a former Vice-President of the DRC and the first

47 *The Prosecutor v. Bosco Ntaganda*, ICC-01/04-02/06-309, 9 June 2014.

48 *The Prosecutor v. Dominic Ongwen*, ICC-02/04-01/15-305-Red2, 24 September 2015.

49 *The Prosecutor v. Laurent Gbagbo and Charles Blé Goudé*, ICC-02/11-01/15-1, 11 March 2015. See also *Prosecutor v. Laurent Gbagbo*, ICC-02/11-01/11-656-Red, 12 June 2014; *The Prosecutor v. Charles Blé Goudé*, ICC-02/11-02/11-186, 11 December 2014.

50 *Prosecutor v. Laurent Gbagbo*, ICC-02/11-01/11-656-Red, 12 June 2014.

accused charged with command responsibility under Article 28(a) of the Rome Statute, is due to be issued in 2016. This case contains charges of rape as a war crime and crime against humanity and includes testimony from a male witness regarding the rape committed against him and female members of his family, allegedly by troops under Bemba's command.[51]

Learning from its case-based results during the first ten years of its work, in June 2014 Prosecutor Bensouda launched the OTP's Policy on Sexual and Gender-based Crimes.[52]

This is the first such policy developed by an international tribunal or court to address these issues. Eighteen months in production and involving a number of internal consultations with staff of the OTP and a review process with external stakeholders, the Policy outlines a comprehensive approach to integrating gender issues and concepts within each area of the OTP's operations – preliminary examination, investigations and analysis, and prosecutions. It addresses both legal practices and policy imperatives, and combines overarching principles for the OTP as a whole, as well as substantive operational strategies. Along with its historic status, the policy also includes an important innovation incorporating gender-analysis as a critical tool applicable to each step of the OTP's work and at every stage of proceedings. Until this policy, gender analysis had not been systematically used as a tool within the practice of international criminal law. Responding with a sense of urgency in relation to strengthening its work on sexual and gender-based crimes, implementation of some of the concepts and strategies contained within the Policy began while it was still in production. These efforts are visible in several of the cases identified above.

Importantly, the policy-based approach to sexual and gender-based crimes adopted by the OTP emphasises institutional responsibility, organisational methodologies and collective competence. These components are deemed necessary to achieve meaningful and sustainable progress towards fully integrating women and girls, and concepts of gender, within the structure of justice.

There are sound reasons for hopeful expectation regarding the gender-justice outcomes the OTP is becoming capable of producing. However, as demonstrated in the Lubanga and Katanga judgments, real progress on these issues is simply not possible without greater judicial attention to legal concepts, and the willingness to transform static legal reasoning with respect to individual criminal responsibility in sexual and gender-based crimes.

---

51 *Transcript of the International Criminal Court*, ICC-01/05–01/08-T-51-Red-ENG, 21 January 2011, p. 36, line 4 to p. 40, line 11.

52 Office of the Prosecutor of the International Criminal Court, *Policy Paper on Sexual and Gender-Based Crimes*, June 2014.

BIBLIOGRAPHY

BOOKS AND JOURNAL ARTICLES

Durbach and Chappell 2014
Durbach, A. and Chappell, C., 'Leaving Behind the Age of Impunity: Victims of Gender Violence and the Promise of Reparations', 16(4) International Feminist Journal of Politics, 2014, pp. 543–562.
Inder 2013
Inder, B., 'Partners for Gender Justice', in De Brouwer, A.M. et al., 'Sexual Violence as an International Crime: Interdisciplinary Approaches', Series on Transitional Justice Vol. 12, Intersentia, 2013, pp. 315–338.

JURISPRUDENCE

ICC 2015
ICC, Prosecutor v. Dominic Ongwen, ICC-02/04-01/15-305-Red2, 24 September 2015.
ICC 2015
ICC, Prosecutor v. Laurent Gbagbo and Charles Blé Goudé, ICC-02/11-01/15-1, 11 March 2015.
ICC 2014
ICC, Prosecutor v. Charles Blé Goudé, ICC-02/11-02/11-186, 11 December 2014.
ICC 2014
ICC, Prosecutor v. Laurent Gbagbo, ICC-02/11-01/11-656-Red, 12 June 2014.
ICC 2014
ICC, Prosecutor v. Bosco Ntaganda, ICC-01/04-02/06-309, 9 June 2014.
ICC 2014
ICC, Prosecutor v. Germain Katanga, ICC-01/04-01/07-3436, 7 March 2014.
ICC 2012
ICC, Prosecutor v. Thomas Lubanga Dyilo, ICC-01/04-01/06-2904, 7 August 2012.
ICC 2012
ICC, Prosecutor v. Thomas Lubanga Dyilo, ICC-01/04-01/06-2842, 14 March 2012.
ICC 2011
ICC, Transcript, ICC-01/05-01/08-T-51-Red-ENG, 21 January 2011.
ICC 2010
ICC, Transcript, ICC-01/04-01/07-T-213-Red-ENG, 4 November 2010.
ICC 2010
ICC, Transcript, ICC-01/04-01/07-T-139-Red-FRA, 11 May 2010.
ICC 2010
ICC, Transcript, ICC-01/04-01/07-T-135-Red-FRA, 4 May 2010.
ICC 2010
ICC, Transcript, ICC-01/04-01/06-T-223-ENG, 7 January 2010.
ICC 2008
ICC, Prosecutor v. Germain Katanga, ICC-01/04-01/07-717, 30 September 2008.

ICC 2007
ICC, Prosecutor v. Thomas Lubanga Dyilo, ICC-01/04-01/06-803-tEN, 29 January 2007.
ICTR 1998
ICTR, Prosecutor v. Jean-Paul Akayesu, ICTR-96-4-T, 2 September 1998.
ICTY 2014
ICTY, Prosecutor v. Nikola Šainović, Nebojša Pavković, Vladimir Lazarević, Sreten Lukić, IT-05-87-A, 23 January 2014.
ICTY 2008
ICTY, Prosecutor v. Milan Martić, IT-95-11-A, 8 October 2008.
ICTY 2001
ICTY, Prosecutor v. Radislav Krstić, IT-98-33-T, 2 August 2001.
ICTY 2001
ICTY, Prosecutor v. Dragoljub Kunarac et al., IT-96-23-T & IT-96-23/1-T, 22 February 2001.
ICTY 1998
ICTY, Prosecutor v. Anto Furundžija, IT-95-17/1-T, 10 December 1998.
ICTY 1998
ICTY, Prosecutor v. Zejnil Delalić, IT-96-21-T, 16 November 1998.
ICTY 1997
ICTY, Prosecutor v. Duško Tadić, IT-94-1-T, 7 May 1997.
SCSL 2007
Special Court for Sierra Leone, Prosecutor v. Brima, Kamara & Kanu, SCSL-04-16-T, 20 June 2007.

TREATIES, LEGISLATION AND AGREEMENTS

Rome Statute of the International Criminal Court, 2187 UNTS 90/37, 17 July 1998.

OTHERS

ICC, Office of the Prosecutor, 'Policy Paper on Sexual and Gender-Based Crimes', June 2014.
Inder, B., 'Launch of the Policy on Sexual and Gender-based Crimes by the ICC Office of the Prosecutor', Speech at the United Nations, 7 December 2014.
Inder, B., 'Prosecuting Sexual Violence in Conflict', Speech at the Global Summit to End Sexual Violence in Conflict, 11 June 2014.
Inder, B., 'The ICC, Child Soldiers and Gender Justice', The Parliament Magazine, Issue 338, 21 November 2011.
United Nations Special Representative of the Secretary-General for Children and Armed Conflict, Annual report, A/HRC/28/54, 29 December 2014.
Women's Initiatives for Gender Justice, 'First Conviction by the ICC', 14 March 2012.

Women's Initiatives for Gender Justice, 'Gender Report Cards on the International Criminal Court', 2008, 2009, 2010, 2011, 2012, and 2014.
Women's Initiatives for Gender Justice, presentations at panel discussion on 'First Reflections on the ICC Katanga Judgment', T.M.C. Asser Institute, 12 March 2014.

EXPLORING EFFORTS TO RESOLVE THE TENSION BETWEEN THE AU AND THE ICC OVER THE BASHIR SAGA*

Max du Plessis

1. INTRODUCTION

In international criminal justice circles, as between international law academics, and over discussions between government officials within and outside Africa, one theme dominated June of 2015: South Africa's decision to host President Omar Al-Bashir of Sudan who had been invited to attend the African Union (AU) Summit in South Africa.

The ingredients for drama were all there. First, Al-Bashir is a suspected international criminal wanted for an unholy trinity of crimes – genocide, war crimes and crimes against humanity. Second, South Africa is a leading African democracy which is a member of the International Criminal Court. Third, Al-Bashir's rumoured presence at the summit turned into a reality as images of him standing alongside President Zuma and other African leaders were beamed around the world. Fourth, ANC spin doctors and government spokespersons proclaimed that South Africa was obliged to honour the AU's call to respect Al-Bashir's immunity as a head of state. Fifth, and perhaps quite significantly, urgent court action was mobilised by civil society to ensure his arrest.[1] Sixth, contradictory accounts were given by government lawyers to the Court about his continued presence in South Africa, and controversially, while the Court was ordering that he not leave South Africa, he was in fact leaving under protection of a blue light brigade allegedly courtesy of the South African government.[2]

* This chapter is an updated and expanded version of a paper first commissioned by the Institute for Security Studies.

1 See the decision of the Full Court in *Southern Africa Litigation Centre v. Minister of Justice and Constitutional Development and Others* (27740/2015) [2015] ZAGPPHC 402 (24 June 2015) (hereinafter 'the SALC decision'). Given the importance of the matter, it was heard and decided by the Judge President (Mlambo JP), the Deputy Judge President (Ledwaba J), and Fabricius J (hence a decision of the Full Court).

2 See "We told Bashir to just relax": new details of S. Africa's effort to shield wanted Sudanese leader', *Mail & Guardian* (Africa), 21 June 2015, available at: http://mgafrica.com/

As one hears the back and forth between legal luminaries, academics, judges and politicians, the debate is reduced to one about competing obligations. The argument goes that regarding AU member states that are also states parties to the Rome Statute, there would appear to be a conflict between the binding obligations imposed by the Rome Statute and the binding obligations imposed by the Decisions of the AU. Given that there are obligations that pull in two different directions, the argument (by those attempting to justify South Africa's behaviour) is that South Africa can't be blamed for how it dealt with Al-Bashir's visit – since it was caught in a norm conflict.

The suggestion is that South Africa was a rabbit caught in the headlights (one beam shone from the ICC demanding arrest; the other light lasering in from the AU demanding respect for Al-Bashir's immunity). This is not the place to focus on the criticisms raised against South Africa, including that it deliberately put itself in this position or recklessly stumbled into the imbroglio, that it decided to invite Al-Bashir, it decided not to arrest him, it decided to ignore the ICC Pre-Trial Chamber's decision demanding that it arrest him, it ignored its own domestic court order, and it appeared to facilitate Al-Bashir's departure from South Africa.[3]

For now it is enough to appreciate the risk that South Africa's example will have repercussions for the international criminal justice project (at least on the continent). Other African states may well contend, as South Africa has done, that they too are confronted with a norm conflict. In so doing, they too might seek to counter any suggestion that the ICC's demand that they arrest Al-Bashir is the norm that takes supremacy over the AU's demand that Al-Bashir's immunity is to be respected.

Thus, the central legal and political theme that the drama accentuates is whether South Africa was caught in a double-bind of competing obligations. Was it, on the one hand, obliged to arrest and surrender Al-Bashir to the ICC, yet on the other hand, obliged to respect the AU's claims that Al-Bashir had immunity from such processes as a head of state?

---

article/2015-06-21-we-told-bashir-to-just-relax-new-details-of-s-africas-effort-to-shade-wanted-sudanese-leader (accessed on 12 October 2015).

3 See further De Wet 2015, p. 1049. As the Full Court put it in the SALC decision (at paras. 36 and 37):

> Perhaps the questions that can be asked about the apparent non compliance with this court's explicit order of Sunday 14 June are:
> 36.1 how was it possible that President Bashir would, with his whole entourage, travel from Sandton to Waterkloof Airbase, without any of the Respondents' knowledge?
> 36.2 how was it possible that the Sudanese plane would take off from the airbase without the Respondents knowing whether the President was on board or not?
> 36.3 how would that plane be able to land in Sudan by late afternoon if it had not departed at about noon that same day?
> 37. The answers suggest themselves.

For purposes of this chapter let us assume that South Africa set up Al-Bashir's visit and allowed itself to be the (African) test case for a fight for the soul of international (criminal) law.[4] Let us assume that there is truly a double bind. The question then is how would the stasis be broken? What should South Africa (and other states responsibly committed to international law) *now* be doing or thinking about to resolve the political dispute? Before coming to a discussion of deadlock-breaking options, it is important to sketch why there is a perceived deadlock in the first place.

2. THE PROCLAIMED DOUBLE BIND

South Africa became a state party to the Rome Statute of the International Criminal Court on 27 November 2000. In compliance with its duties under the Rome Statute, South Africa's legislature incorporated the obligations under the Rome Statute into domestic law through the Implementation of the Rome Statute of the International Criminal Court Act, 2002.[5] Through such accession and incorporation, South Africa became bound by the obligations under the Rome Statute, both internationally and on the domestic level.[6] Central to the Al-Bashir dispute is the duty upon South Africa as a state party to cooperate 'fully with the Court in its investigation and prosecution of crimes within the jurisdiction of the Court'.[7] Particularising this obligation further, Article 89 of the Rome Statute obliges state parties to comply with requests for arrest and surrender issued by the Court.[8]

On 4 March 2009 and 12 July 2010, the ICC issued two arrest warrants against Al-Bashir related to seven counts of war crimes and crimes against humanity and three counts of genocide.[9] The ICC accordingly requested state parties to the Rome Statute to arrest Al-Bashir in the event that he came into their jurisdiction.[10] The ICC's request was made under the Rome Statute and

4 See generally and presciently, Tladi 2009.

5 See further du Plessis 2007. The ICC Act 27 of 2002 is available at: www.gov.za/sites/www.gov.za/files/a27–02.pdf (last accessed 1 October 2015).

6 See *Southern Africa Litigation Centre v. Minister of Justice and Constitutional Development* (27740/2015) [2015] ZAGPPHC 402 (24 June 2015) para. 11, available at: www.southernafricalitigationcentre.org/cases/ongoing-cases/south-africasudan-seeking-implementation-of-icc-arrest-warrant-for-president-bashir/ (last accessed 2 October 2015).

7 Article 86 of the Rome Statute.

8 Section 89(1) reads in full as follows: 'The Court may transmit a request for the arrest and surrender of a person, together with the material supporting the request outlined in art 91, to any State on the territory of which that person may be found and shall request the cooperation of that State in the arrest and surrender of such a person. States Parties shall, in accordance with the provisions of this Part and the procedure under their national law, comply with requests for arrest and surrender.'

9 SALC decision, para. 2.

10 *Ibid*, para. 12.

with reliance on United Nations Security Council (UNSC) Resolution 1593 (2005),[11] in which the UNSC referred the situation in Darfur (Sudan) to the ICC for investigation and prosecution in accordance with the Chapter VII of the UN Charter.

It is this obligation to comply with a request for arrest or surrender that was put to the test for South Africa when Al-Bashir attended the AU summit in Johannesburg between 14 and 15 June 2015.[12]

The government's argument is that the request by the ICC to arrest Al-Bashir ran against a competing claim by the AU *not* to arrest and surrender Al-Bashir. Further, and, importantly, the government contended that the AU's claim to immunity 'trumped' South Africa's obligations to arrest and surrender Al-Bashir to the ICC.[13] To appreciate the AU's claim, one must recall that the relationship between African states and the ICC is both complex and contested. The participation of African states in negotiations at Rome in 1998 was crucial to both the ICC's inception and its relative independence. Since then 34 African countries have signed up to the ICC, making it the largest signatory bloc.[14]

However, the ICC has been criticised for its focus on Africa in its first decade of operation, with all of the situations under formal investigation and currently being prosecuted by the Court coming from Africa. In truth this focus is a reflection of other realities: including the sad preponderance of conflicts in

---

11 In UNSC Res 1593 (31 March 2005) the UNSC determined that:
Acting under Chapter VII of the Charter of the United Nations,

> 1. *Decides* to refer the situation in Darfur since 1 July 2002 to the Prosecutor of the International Criminal Court;
> 2. *Decides* that the Government of Sudan and all other parties to the conflict in Darfur, shall cooperate fully with and provide any necessary assistance to the Court and the Prosecutor pursuant to this resolution and, while recognizing that States not party to the Rome Statute have no obligation under the Statute, urges all States and concerned regional and other international organizations to cooperate fully. The UNSC Resolution was adopted with 11 in favour (including Tanzania and Benin) to none (while Algeria along with Brazil, China and the United States abstained).

See further Condorelli and Ciampi 2005, pp. 591–592.

12 The background to this visit is set out by the ICC itself in ICC-02, Decision following the Prosecutor's request for an order further clarifying that the Republic of South Africa is under the obligation to immediately arrest and surrender Omar Al-Bashir, /0501/09, PTC II, 13 June 2015 ('Full Bench decision').

13 As the SALC decision records at para. 6:

> On that Sunday morning Adv I. Ellis who appeared for all the Respondents, laid out the basis of Respondents' defence to Fabricius J who was on duty at that stage. The defence propounded was to the effect that the Cabinet had taken a decision to grant President Bashir immunity from arrest, and that this decision 'trumped' the government's duty to arrest the President on South African soil in terms of two warrants of arrest issued by the ICC, and its concomitant obligation in terms of the Implementation Act.

14 Notably since the first arrest warrant for Al-Bashir, four additional African countries have ratified the Rome Statute. These are: Seychelles, Tunisia, Cape Verde and Côte d'Ivoire.

Africa, the hostile political conditions that prevent the Court from pursuing more deserving cases from other parts of the world (viz. Gaza – although earlier in 2015, the Court indicated that it was considering opening an investigation into the situation), and the fact that as the biggest bloc the chances of states referring themselves to the Court being from Africa are far more likely. However, those who oppose the Court generally, or the situations under consideration in particular, have not wasted the opportunity to allege an anti-African bias on the part of the Court.

The ICC's opponents on the continent have marshalled their forces against the Court through the AU.[15] The backlash from the AU against the Court has reached its peak in respect of the Court's decision to seek an arrest warrant for Al-Bashir, and has taken a number of forms. For present purposes of relevance are the Decisions of the AU Assembly of Heads of State and Governments that African states will not cooperate in the arrest and surrender of Al-Bashir.[16]

Over time, even though Al-Bashir is the subject of an arrest warrant by the ICC, there have been reports of several states parties failing to enforce the warrant after inviting Al-Bashir to visit their territory. Before June 2015, there had been seven cases of African states refusing to comply with the duty to arrest and surrender Al-Bashir – Kenya, Djibouti, Chad (twice), Malawi, Nigeria and the Democratic Republic of Congo. Dire Tladi suggests that the AU position placed African states parties to the Rome Statute in the 'unenviable position of having to choose between their obligations as member states of the AU on the one hand, and their obligations as states party to the Rome Statute, on the other.'[17]

Arguably there are tools by which states parties like South Africa could and should navigate such a proclaimed norm clash.[18] That is particularly so where those states have under their domestic law – like South Africa – sought to express a preference for accountability over immunity and impunity for international crimes. And indeed South Africa had previously used such tools to good effect, expressing its preference for the ICC's norm (see further below), if only by refusing to allow itself to face a conflict head on. Whatever its previous position, something changed in June 2015.[19]

---

15 Established in 2001 to replace the Organisation of African Unity. See Constitutive Act of the AU (2001), available at: www.au.int/en/sites/default/files/Constitutive_Act_en_0.htm (last accessed 1 October 2015).

16 See generally Maunganidze and du Plessis 2015.

17 Tladi 2009.

18 See further du Plessis and Gevers 2011, available at: https://www.issafrica.org/uploads/Paper225.pdf (accessed 10 October 2015).

19 Although it should not be forgotten that Al-Bashir had previously threatened to arrive in South Africa and South Africa had then insisted that it would arrest Bashir if he stepped foot on its territory.

3. A WANTED WAR CRIMINAL COMES TO (AND LEAVES) TOWN

On 28 May 2015, the Registrar of the ICC, acting on the basis of media reports of Al-Bashir's potential travel to South Africa to attend the AU summit scheduled from 7 to 15 June 2015, notified the Embassy of South Africa and reminded South Africa of its obligations.[20]

On Saturday 13 June 2015, just before 23.00 hrs, following an urgent request from the ICC Prosecutor making reference to the fact that Al-Bashir had already arrived in South Africa to attend the summit, Pre-Trial Chamber II of the ICC made an order that South Africa immediately arrest and surrender Al-Bashir. The order clarified that South Africa had a duty to do so and that Al-Bashir's alleged immunity as a sitting head of state did not avail him (or South Africa in avoiding its obligations under the Rome Statute).[21] By now civil society in South Africa had mobilised to bring an urgent application before the Gauteng Division of the High Court, seeking an order, amongst others, that the South African authorities arrest and surrender Al-Bashir. On Sunday 14 June 2015 the Gauteng Division of the High Court ordered the government to take all reasonable steps to prepare to arrest Al-Bashir and detain him, pending a formal request for his surrender from the ICC.[22] As a stop-gap, the Court also ordered the government to take all necessary steps to prevent his departure and to that end directed the government to effect service of the order on the officials in charge of every point of entry into and exit from the Republic. The government was directed to provide proof of service, identifying the name of each person on whom the order was served.[23] As is now well known, it turned out that in the face of these orders the South African government facilitated Al-Bashir's departure from the country. On 15 June 2015 he was winging his way back to Khartoum while the court hearings (and the AU Summit) were underway.[24]

---

20 See Pre-Trial Chamber II, Order requesting submissions from the Republic of South Africa for the purposes of proceedings under Article 87(7) of the Rome Statute – 4 September 2015.

21 Full Bench decision para. 2.

22 *Ibid.*

23 SALC decision, para. 6.

24 SALC decision paras. 3, 6, 7 and 8. It is worth recalling what the Full Court found (paras. 7 and 8):

> Due to the importance of the matter, especially having regard to South Africa's constitutional and international legal obligations in respect of international crimes that are at issue, the Judge President of this Division took a decision that the application would continue before a Full Court on Monday, i.e. before three Judges, being Mlambo JP, Ledwaba DJP and Fabricius J. The Answering Affidavit was only filed at about 11:25 instead of 9:00 on Monday 15 June 2015, without any explanation being tendered as to why it was late. The lack of an explanation for the lateness is particularly significant as the Answering Affidavit only consisted of 24 typed pages, a supporting affidavit of four pages, and printed annexures of 87 pages. In our experience, all of this could easily have been produced within a few hours.

Of course, sight should not be lost of the fact that South Africa had already decided to host the AU Summit in January 2015, and so by then knew that Al-Bashir would be invited.

And recall too that up until this point South Africa had neatly side-stepped the conflict of obligations by always requesting the Sudanese President not to honour invitations to South African events – as confirmed in the judgment of the South African court, these examples include the two inaugurations of President Zuma in 2009 and again in 2014, the 2010 World Cup and the funeral of former South African President Nelson Mandela.[25] Previously, South Africa had elected to show fidelity to its ICC obligations. To illustrate, reports emerged that during May 2009 South Africa had invited Al-Bashir – by then wanted by the ICC – to President Zuma's inauguration. If he were to arrive, the country faced an embarrassing situation that threatened to undermine the jubilation of inauguration day.[26] On the eve of the inauguration the Government clarified that although the Sudanese government was invited, President Al-Bashir was not and that it was prudent for him not to attend given the Damoclean sword of the ICC arrest warrant. Al-Bashir chose not to visit South Africa at that time. Two months later, South Africa joined ranks with others at an AU meeting in Sirte, Libya, to support a 3 July 2009 AU resolution (apparently driven by Muammar Gaddafi) calling on its members to defy the international arrest warrant issued by the ICC for Al-Bashir. Confusingly, just shy of a month before that, South Africa's Justice Minister at a different AU meeting on 8 and 9 June in Addis

In view of the late filing of the Answering Affidavit and the need for the court and the applicant to peruse it, as well as the necessity to file a reply, if any, the proceedings were adjourned until just before 13:00. When adjourning the proceedings at 11:30 and upon resumption thereof the court specifically requested Adv Mokhari SC to provide an indication whether President Bashir was still in the country. This was rendered necessary in the light of media reports, which we took judicial notice of, that suggested that President Bashir was either in the process of flying out or had already left this country. Adv Mokhari SC, specifically disavowing reliance on media reports, stated that his instructions were that President Bashir was still in the country. During the entire hearing Adv Mokhari SC repeatedly re-assured us that President Bashir was still in the country, which fact was necessary for the court's jurisdiction. As it transpired later that day and after we handed down our order, all these assurances were not correct as President Bashir had, most probably left the country before argument commenced just before 13:00. We return to this aspect later.

The court concluded hearing argument just after 14:30 and handed down the order referred to in para. 2 above at about 15:00. It is only then that the court was informed by Adv Mokhari SC that President Bashir had left the country. This, in our view, is a clear violation of the order handed down by Fabricius J on Sunday afternoon. On being apprised of this state of affairs the court issued an order that the Minister in the Office of the Presidency and the Minister of State Security should file an affidavit within seven days explaining the circumstances under which President Bashir managed to fly out of this country despite the explicit court order prohibiting this...

25 See SALC decision at para. 12.

26 See du Plessis and Fritz, 'New Diplomatic Fiasco Looms', *Business Day*, 2 May 2009.

Ababa had joined with other African states to affirm a deep commitment to the Court.

The Sirte resolution of the AU – stressing that member states would not cooperate in the arrest and surrender of African heads of state – was quickly condemned as a betrayal of Africa's commitment to end impunity for human rights atrocities, and an international treaty violation. Only Botswana publicly distanced itself from the AU move, and in a letter dated 8 July 2009 to the ICC assured the Court that 'as a State Party to the Rome Statute of the ICC, Botswana will fully abide with its treaty obligations and will support the International Criminal Court in its endeavours to implement the provisions of the Rome Statute'.[27]

South Africa eventually clarified its position after directed criticism from civil society. The government issued a response, which suggested (despite its actions to the contrary in supporting the AU resolution) that it was committed to its legal obligations in relation to the possible arrest of President Al-Bashir. On 31 July 2009 Dr Ayanda Ntsaluba (then of Foreign Affairs) explained as follows at a Press Conference (which is worth quoting in full):

> South Africa is a (sic) State Party of the Rome Statute of the International Criminal Court and is therefore obliged to cooperate with the Court in its investigation and prosecution of crimes within the jurisdiction of the Court (Article 86), and hence also in the execution of arrest warrants. It is worth noting that Article 87(7) of the Statute provides that, when a State Party fails to comply with a request to cooperate, the Court may make a finding to that effect and refer the matter to the Assembly of States Parties, or in the case of a United Nations Security Council (UNSC) referral to the UNSC.
>
> Article 27 of the Rome Statute provides that the official capacity as Head of State or Government of an accused provides no exemption from criminal responsibility. Furthermore, Section 4(1) of the South African Implementation of the Rome Statute of the International Criminal Court Act also ousts the applicability of other domestic laws in respect of an accused, with the result that the immunity from prosecution that President El Bashir (sic) would normally have enjoyed in terms of the Diplomatic Immunities and Privileges Act, 2001 (Act No. 37 of 2001), is not be [sic] applicable.

Remarkably, at that press conference it was disclosed that an international arrest warrant for Al-Bashir 'has been received' (from the ICC) and 'endorsed by a [South African] magistrate'. Dr Ntsaluba explained that '[t]his means that if President El Bashir (sic) arrives on South African territory, he will be liable for arrest'.

---

27 Letter dated 8 July 2009 from the Minister of Foreign Affairs and International Cooperation of the Republic of Botswana to Justice Sang-Hyun Song, President of the International Criminal Court.

So much for 2009. In six years, Dr Ntsaluba's claims appear to have suffered a reversal. For present purposes it is enough to highlight that the government's argument is today squarely hinged on the immunity Al-Bashir is said to have, coupled with the duty to respect the decisions of the AU which demanded that African states not comply with the ICC's arrest warrant. Before the High Court in June 2015 the South African government argued that Al-Bashir enjoyed immunity from arrest in South Africa.[28] A central premise of its case remains this: after agreeing in January 2015 to host the AU summit, the government entered into a host state agreement with the AU Commission in order to facilitate the organisation of the summit. This agreement was eventually concluded around 4 June 2015.[29] Under Article VIII of the host state agreement, privileges and immunities were provided for the duration of the meeting to the members of the AU Commission and staff members and – so contended the government – the delegates and other representatives of inter-governmental organisations attending the meetings. The immunities in question included immunity from arrest and detention.[30]

By ministerial notice in the government gazette the host state agreement was effected on 5 June 2015.[31] Such a diplomatic step occurred under the provisions of the Diplomatic Immunities and Privileges Act 37 of 2001, by which South Africa gives domestic effect to the Vienna Convention on Diplomatic Relations 1961.

Like Dr Ntsaluba's claims made on behalf of the government in 2009 (recalling his statement that 'the Rome Statute of the International Criminal Court Act also ousts the applicability of other domestic laws in respect of an accused, with the result that the immunity from prosecution that President Al-Bashir [sic] would normally have enjoyed in terms of the Diplomatic Immunities and Privileges Act, 2001, is not [sic] applicable'), a full bench of the Gauteng Division of the High Court similarly concluded that Al-Bashir was not entitled to immunity in South Africa. That, said the Court, was because Article 27(2) of the ICC Statute provided that heads of state do not enjoy immunity under its terms; and South Africa's ICC Act was to the same effect. The consequence – according to the Court – is that Al-Bashir's immunity as head of state is excluded or waived in respect of crimes and obligations under the Rome Statute.[32] In this regard the Court drew support for its decision from the decision of the ICC Pre-Trial Chamber II which had – contemporaneous with Al-Bashir's visit to South Africa – made it abundantly clear that the immunities

28 Answering Affidavit of Respondent (Full Bench decision, para. 3), available at: www.southernafricalitigationcentre.org/cases/ongoing-cases/south-africasudan-seeking-implementation-of-icc-arrest-warrant-for-president-bashir/ (last accessed at 30 July 2015).

29 See the Full Bench decision, paras. 13–14.

30 *Ibid*, paras. 15–16.

31 Government Gazette No. 38860, available at: www.gov.za/sites/www.gov.za/files/38860_gon470.pdf (last accessed 2 October 2015); Full Bench decision, para. 17.

32 Full Bench decision, para. 28.8.

that Al-Bashir invoked under international law had been implicitly waived by the UNSC, so that South Africa's duty to arrest him was clear.[33]

By contrast with these clear rules stripping immunity and imposing obligations to surrender Al-Bashir to the ICC, the Court was of the view that the AU decisions (including its latest of 12 October 2013 according to which no serving head of state shall be required to appear before any international court or tribunal during his or her term of office) was merely of persuasive status in the domestic legal order.[34]

The Court's decision notwithstanding, the South African government has attempted to appeal to the Supreme Court of Appeal.[35] In its application for leave to appeal, the South African government recounts firmly the countervailing duty (it says) was imposed upon it by the AU decision and heralds the immunity that it says attaches to Al-Bashir by virtue of his status as President of Sudan.[36] It is accordingly clear that the dispute is far from over.

That the dispute – and South Africa's conduct – is being considered by the South African courts is in itself an important development. That is because it is clear that the government will be required to justify its course of action against the strictures not only of its international law commitments, but also as against its domestic obligations under the ICC Act. If on appeal the South African courts break the apparent deadlock (at least for South Africa) by concluding that South Africa's obligations to arrest and surrender Al-Bashir are not offset by any purported immunity claims, that will be binding on the South African government as a matter of domestic law. But it will also resonate heavily and persuasively as a contributing factor in the development of customary international law on this point.

Whatever the courts may say about the outcome, for present purposes it is clear that the government in line with the AU has posited an apparent contestation between two norms: the ICC's norm of arrest and surrender, and the AU's norm of immunity from that arrest and surrender. It is also clear that South Africa's position is shared by other members of the AU – and is reflected in the decisions of the AU itself. And while the South African courts will determine the legal questions under the strictures of the applicable South African legal regime (as read with international law), the regional and international politics cannot be resolved by the courts. As the Full Court put it:[37]

---

33 *Ibid*, para. 28.9.
34 *Ibid*, para. 28.13.3.
35 Supreme Court of Appeal application – on file with author. The original application for leave before the High Court was refused by the Court – hence the petition now by the government to the Supreme Court of Appeal.
36 Leave to appeal application – on file with author.
37 SALC decision, para. 34.

> We are further impelled to state that as a court of law we are obviously the wrong forum for the ventilation of regional and international policy considerations, which as we say above, were not ventilated before us. We however find it prudent to invite the ICC to take cognisance of the issues that arise in this matter. As we demonstrate in this judgement, South Africa is not the only Rome Statute signatory that has failed to carry out its duties in terms of that Statute when it could have done so, based on a conflict between its regional affiliation on the one hand and its broader international obligations on the other.

4. RESOLVING THE ICC/AU IMPASSE?

Assuming that both sides have true belief in their arguments (and without deciding which normative claim trumps the other as a matter of law), let us attempt to move forward. That is, for purposes of this paper, let us accept that there is a real question of competing obligations between the AU and the ICC. And let us assume what Dire Tladi suggests is an 'unenviable position' for African ICC states parties, with a *prima facie* conflict between two obligations under international law. The first is their obligation as signatories to the ICC under, amongst others, Article 87 of the Rome Statute to cooperate in the arrest and surrender of Al-Bashir; the second being the obligation under Article 23 of the Constitutive Act of the AU to comply with decisions of the AU Assembly not to cooperate with the ICC. And let us assume further that in this case there is a real absence of established hierarchy of norms under international law, with the recent proliferation of international legal rules and rule-making institutions (like the AU) enhancing the likelihood of such conflicts.

We might then start by noting that the question of resolving norm clashes in international law is a controversial one. While there is widespread agreement regarding the identification of legal obligations – guided in large measure by Article 38 of the International Court of Justice (ICJ) Statute – the question of resolving norm conflicts is less settled. As Milanovic notes:

> Crucially, international law lacks the key method for resolving genuine norm conflict that is used in domestic law: a centralized system with a developed hierarchy, and at that a hierarchy based on the sources of norms. Thus, in domestic systems a constitutional norm will prevail over a statutory one, while legislation will ordinarily prevail over executive orders or decrees. Not so in international law, where all sources of law are considered equal.[38]

Against that backdrop, is there a means by which to move beyond the stalemate? Certainly there is a need to think about such deadlock-breaking options since the confused situation created by the political posturing of the AU has left states –

[38] Milanovic 2009.

or at least those states that have not already abandoned their fidelity to the Rome Statute in favour of the AU's position on immunity – in Tladi's 'unenviable position'. What is more, the ICC's work on the Sudan case and its efforts to do justice to the Security Council's referral of the situation, are heavily dependent on the support of states parties. The current imbroglio means that the ICC cannot realistically rely on African states parties to arrest and surrender Al-Bashir. And in light of the AU's continued concerns about the ICC's action against the incumbent Sudanese leader, and the impasse that has resulted, there is a growing fear within the international criminal justice community in Africa and elsewhere about the Court's ability to achieve its mandate under the Security Council referral.

The first option is for better drafting at the Security Council. Perhaps the first thing to appreciate is that the Al-Bashir saga has a particular genesis: a UNSC Resolution (Resolution 1593) referring the situation in Sudan (a state that is not party to the ICC) to the ICC for investigation and prosecution. That decision was the first time that the UNSC invoked this power, under Article 13(b) of the Rome Statute of the ICC, to refer a particular situation to the ICC Prosecutor for investigation and possible prosecutions of genocide, crimes against humanity and war crimes.[39]

If the saga teaches anything, it is that in the context of UN Security Council referrals to the ICC, decisions taken in pursuance of such referrals take on a higher order of legal significance and must be properly crafted. The reason for this is that the Rome Statute requires such referral decisions to be taken under Chapter VII of the UN Charter. In terms of Article 103 of the UN Charter, obligations under Chapter VII take precedence over 'any other obligation'.[40] This argument is most often raised in the context of immunity but more recently has been used to address the AU decisions.[41] As we have seen debated before the Gauteng Division of the High Court (and in the academic literature), for the purposes of resolving the current conflict, if the obligation to arrest Al-Bashir stems from UN Security Council Resolution 1593 it will, by operation of Article 103 of the UN Charter, override the obligation on African states parties like South Africa to comply with the AU decisions.

Two schools of thought have emerged regarding the effect of Resolution 1593, and by extension Article 13(b) referrals generally, on subsequent cooperation proceedings (such as that played out before the Gauteng Division of the High Court) in pursuance thereof. The first posits that a referral by the UN Security

39 'The Court may exercise its jurisdiction with respect to a crime referred to in article 5 in accordance with the provisions of this Statute if: ... (b) A situation in which one or more of such crimes appears to have been committed is referred to the Prosecutor by the Security Council acting under Chapter VII of the Charter of the United Nations'.

40 Questions of Interpretation and Application of the 1971 Montreal Convention arising from the Aerial Incident at Lockerbie (*Libyan Arab Jamahiriya v. United States of America*), Provisional Measures, Order of 14 April 1992, ICJ Reports 1992, para. 42.

41 See Amnesty International, *Bringing power to justice: absence of immunity for heads of states before the International Criminal Court*, 2010.

Council under Chapter VII of a situation or case to the ICC automatically means that such proceedings trigger cooperation obligations generally for member states of the UN such that states are bound to cooperate in such circumstances per force of Article 103.

One can certainly see why proponents of the ICC would want to capitalise on the UN Security Council's Chapter VII authority to ensure that the strongest possible cooperation obligation is placed on the broadest number of states.[42] That has been the approach of the ICC, and was reflected in the latest decision of Pre-Trial Chamber II in relation to South Africa's obligations to arrest Al-Bashir.[43]

The second approach considers that the effect of such a referral on the subsequent proceedings can only be determined with reference to the *specific resolution* in question. The claim by proponents of the second approach is to say that in considering the effect of Resolution 1593 it is not the Rome Statute that is determinative, but rather the UN Charter. It is the UN Charter that is *the* instrument that would create an overriding obligation under Article 103 – albeit in relation to an Article 13(b) referral by the UN Security Council under the Rome Statute. UN Security Council resolutions must be interpreted with reference to their terms, with the language they are couched in and the discussions leading to their adoption and the provisions cited all being indicators of the UN Security Council's intent.[44]

The argument then goes that the question whether Resolution 1593 (or any future Security Council Resolution) imbues decisions taken by the ICC in furtherance thereof (such as a decision by the ICC to issue an arrest warrant for a sitting head of state) with a higher normative value than they would otherwise enjoy under the Rome Statute cannot be addressed with regard to Article 13(b) referrals generally, but rather must be determined with reference to the specific UN Security Council Resolution, and its terms.

There is furthermore (and relatedly) a debate between international lawyers about the meaning and impact of Security Council Resolution 1593 on the immunity of Al-Bashir – and the extent to which the resolution's requirement of 'full cooperation' by Sudan with the ICC means that Al-Bashir's immunity has been lifted.[45]

It is not necessary to resolve this dispute about the real meaning or effect of Security Council Resolution 1593 and its impact on Al-Bashir's immunity. It is enough to recognise that the dispute in relation to Al-Bashir might have been

---

42 Article 103 would bind all UN member states, not merely states parties.

43 See *The Prosecutor v. Omar Hassan Ahmad Al-Bashir*, Decision following the Prosecutor's request for an order further clarifying that the Republic of South Africa is under the obligation to immediately arrest and surrender Omar Al-Bashir, Pre-Trial Chamber II, ICC-02/05-01/02-242, 13 June 2015.

44 See ICJ, *Case Concerning East Timor (Portugal v. Australia)* [1995] ICJ Rep 90, para. 32.

45 See generally De Wet 2015, submitted to JICJ for publication on 2 August 2015, and on file with author.

avoided if the UN Security Council had chosen its wording more pointedly. In this regard, Sluiter sets out three possible models of cooperation available to the UN Security Council insofar as international judicial mechanisms are concerned:

> First, the Council could simply refer a situation without any reference to cooperation; this would mean that the 'normal' regime of the Statute applies and that only obligations for states parties can be established. In case the Council opts for the imposition of obligations for states non-parties there would be the choice, as to the substance of the duties, to apply the ICC Statute mutatis mutandis, or to develop a separate, possibly more demanding regime.[46]

The point is an obvious one. If the Security Council is going to refer situations to the ICC involving a non-party and implicating a head of state, then to avoid the type of legal wrangling that the AU and South Africa's legal advisers are now engaged in, and to close down the space for any point-taking about whether immunities have been lifted for international criminals, the Council ought to express itself clearly and unmistakably about the consequences of its referral for existing rules of international law. Notably, states themselves have affirmed the need for more precise drafting in future referrals to identify obligations regarding cooperation.[47]

The Security Council does have the power to subvert or deviate from the rules of international law. The Al-Bashir saga teaches that if it wishes to do so, it should do so clearly and firmly, particularly if its intention is to remove an otherwise accepted protection such as immunities.[48] Even if it has not ordinarily been its practice to do so, and even if good arguments exist as to why SC Resolution 1593 should be read as lifting Al-Bashir's immunity,[49] it behoves the Council – and those states that would wish to ensure clarity of purpose and outcome in this regard – to adopt and push for express resolutions confirming that indeed the Security Council's intention is to remove the customary international law immunities of officials who are subject to the referral of a situation to the ICC.

The second option is to refer the dispute to the International Court of Justice, the Assembly of States Parties to the Rome Statute or African Court for resolution. Another means of breaking the impasse between the ICC and the

46 Sluiter 2008.

47 See Statement of Australia, 2012 Open Debate on Peace and Justice UNSC 6849th meeting resumption cited in Verduzco 2015, p. 62 n 189.

48 Immunity is not (as a general rule) waived implicitly but explicitly. See International Law Commission, *Third Report on the Immunity of State Officials from Foreign Criminal Jurisdiction*, by the Special Rapporteur, Mr Roman Kolodkin, 24 May 2011, A/CN.4/646, paras. 39–42.

49 For an example of such arguments, see De Wet 2015; Akande 2012.

AU might be by seeking finality and clarity from an external international third party.

One might say: but surely the ICC's own judicial findings in this regard ought to be regarded as dispositive, particularly for states parties? It unfortunately seems clear – at least by its conduct – that the South African government is disinclined to accept the views of the ICC on the question of which competing obligation should prevail as between the ICC's claim for arrest and surrender and the AU's claim for the inviolability of the immunity of heads of state.[50] After all, the South African government acted in direct violation of the ICC's Pre-Trial Chamber II decision issued just before Al-Bashir arrived in South Africa. That also appears to be the position shared by the AU and other African member states, with the possible exception of Botswana.[51]

In such circumstances, and to avoid further undermining of the ICC as a treaty body (by states parties flagrantly disobeying its orders), one option is for South Africa (and the AU) to seek a resolution of the dispute by following through on a long standing AU decision made in January 2012, where the AU Assembly asked the AU Commission to seek an advisory opinion from the International Court of Justice (ICJ) on immunities of state officials under international law. That decision, issued at the summit of the Assembly of the AU held in Addis Ababa, Ethiopia, African Heads of States and Heads of Government, requested:

> the [AU] Commission to consider seeking an advisory opinion from the International Court of Justice regarding the immunities of state officials under international law.[52]

While the AU decision does not make this clear, presumably what the AU wants is an opinion that would clarify the immunity (or otherwise) of state officials from prosecution by the ICC and from enforcement action taken by states acting at the request of the ICC.

Under Article 96 of the UN Charter and Article 65 of the Statute of the ICJ, only organs of the United Nations or UN specialised agencies may be authorised by the UN General Assembly to request advisory opinions. So the AU Commission cannot itself seek an advisory opinion from the ICJ. For a request

---

50 See Fabricius, 'South Africa arms itself for battle with the ICC', *ISS Today*, 8 October 2015 available at: https://www.issafrica.org/iss-today/south-africa-arms-itself-for-battle-with-the-icc (accessed on 9 October 2015).

51 See 'Botswana would have arrested Al-Bashir', *News Day*, 17 June 2015, available at: https://www.newsday.co.zw/2015/06/17/botswana-would-have-arrested-al-bashir/ (accessed on 2 October 2015).

52 See Gevers, 'Updated: Africa's ICC gripes heading to the ICJ?', *War and Law*, 2 February 2012, available at: http://warandlaw.blogspot.co.za/2012/02/africa-icc-gripes-heading-to-icj.html (accessed on 2 October 2015).

to be made, it would most likely have to come from the General Assembly where African states might be able to muster greater support (certainly than in the Security Council) for an ICJ advisory opinion.

A significant issue that would arise in seeking an advisory opinion would be what question or questions should be put to the ICJ. Christopher Gevers notes as follows here that:

> If an advisory opinion is sought it could address a broad range of legal issues such as (i) immunity before international courts under international law (although this was addressed obiter in the Arrest Warrant case, it might be further clarified), (ii) immunity under the Rome Statute, both generally and in respect of cooperation obligations on states in particular, and (iii) the effect (if any) of Security Council resolutions referring matters to the Court on (i) and (ii).

A further option might be that the matter is referred to the ICC Assembly of States Parties under Article 119(2) of the Rome Statute under which any dispute relating to the interpretation or application of the ICC Statute, other than those concerning the judicial functions of the ICC, may be referred to the Assembly of States Parties.[53] The Assembly may either seek to settle the dispute itself or make recommendations as to how it may be settled, including referral to the ICJ. One issue that arises in this context is whether the dispute should be regarded as concerning a judicial function of the ICC, in which case the Assembly would not have competence to deal with it. In any case, the Assembly cannot itself refer a matter to the ICJ. All that this provision means is that the Assembly may recommend that disputing parties refer a dispute under the Rome Statute to the ICJ.

In this regard, it is worth recalling that African Ministers of Justice have in the past recommended that the issue of the relationship between Articles 27 and 98 of the Rome Statute be referred to the Assembly of States Parties of the ICC in terms of Article 119 of the Rome Statute.[54]

A number of questions then arise if this avenue is to be pursued. For example, does this issue of state cooperation in the arrest of Al-Bashir relate to 'judicial functions' of the Court or would it qualify as a dispute (i) not pertaining to judicial functions, (ii) arising between two or more state parties and (iii) concerning the interpretation or application of the Statute?

---

53 Article 119, which relates to 'general disagreements', states that 'disputes that do not pertain to judicial functions – that arise between two or more state parties – and relate to the interpretation or application of the Statute', shall be referred to the ASP which can: (i) seek to settle the dispute itself or; (ii) make recommendations on further means of dispute settlement, notably including referral to the International Court of Justice in conformity with the Statute of that Court.

54 See 'Ministerial Meeting of African States Parties to the Rome Statute of the ICC'; 8–9 June 2009, Addis Ababa, MinICC/Legal.

These questions (aside from others) will need to be confronted: and at the very least their existence means that a concerted effort will need to be adopted by African states if the AU's concerns regarding the ICC reach the ICJ.

A further option in this regard is to seek an advisory opinion from the African Court on Human and Peoples Rights. Notably a request is currently pending before the African Court, requesting the Court to provide a determination of the following question:[55]

> Whether the Treaty obligation of an African state party to the Rome Statute of the ICC to cooperate with the Court is superior to the obligation of that state to comply with the AU resolution calling for non-cooperation of its members with the ICC?
>
> If the answer to question (a) above is in the affirmative, whether all Africa State parties to the ICC have overriding legal obligation above all other legal or diplomatic obligations arising from resolutions or decisions of the AU to arrest and surrender President Omar Al-Bashir any time he enters into the territory of any of the African State parties to ICC?

The request has been lodged under Article 4 of the Protocol to the African Charter on Human and Peoples' Rights and Rule 68 of the Rules of the African Court on Human and Peoples' Rights. It was made shortly after President Al-Bashir visited Nigeria and was then forced to leave hurriedly due to an urgent court process against him.[56] The request is made by a coalition of civil society organisations in Nigeria led by the Nigerian Coalition for the International Criminal Court. While the case is pending, it is a further example of an effort to seek judicial – third party – resolution of the dispute.

Whichever external avenue is chosen, one of the points that may well take centre stage is whether ICC members, after being obligated to comply with the ICC arrest warrant, may permissibly seek to create (or vote for) a countervailing resolution in the AU which says that they don't have to comply with the ICC arrest warrant. In this regard the International Law Commission's Draft articles on the Responsibility of International Organisations 2011[57]

---

55 See African Court on Human and People's Rights, Advisory Opinion 001 of 2014, available at: http://arcproject.co.uk/wp-content/uploads/2012/12/001–2014-Advisory-Request-Case-Summary.pdf (accessed on 2 October 2015).

56 www.ncicc.org.ng/index.php/downloads (accessed on 2 October 2015).

57 Adopted by the International Law Commission at its sixty-third session in 2011, and submitted to the General Assembly as a part of the Commission's report covering the work of that session (A/66/10).

appear to loom large – in particular Articles 58[58] and 61,[59] both of which in different ways are aimed at prohibiting a state from breaching an obligation it already owes under international law by seeking to undermine that obligation through an international organisation (like the AU). As an example of a breach of Article 58, the ILC's commentary is instructive:

> Aid or assistance by a State could constitute a breach of an obligation that the State has acquired under a primary norm. For example, a nuclear-weapon State Party to the Treaty on the Non-Proliferation of Nuclear Weapons would have to refrain from assisting a non-nuclear-weapon State in the acquisition of nuclear weapons, and the same would seem to apply to assistance given to an international organization of which some non-nuclear-weapon States are members.

Article 61 in turn prohibits a State member of an international organisation from taking advantage of the fact that the organisation has competence in relation to the subject-matter of one of the state's international obligations, to circumvent that obligation by causing the organisation to commit an act that, if committed by the state, would have constituted a breach of the obligation.

Arising for consideration, then, is whether ICC member states through their work in supporting AU decisions that oblige non-cooperation in relation to Al-Bashir's arrest have circumvented their ICC obligations (under Article 61), or are responsible for the AU's breach of the obligation in passing such a resolution (under Article 58).

Accordingly, it may well be that recourse to the ICJ or the African Court is a means by which the impasse might be resolved. At the very least this option has the attraction of being a positive step towards a legal solution to a problem with immense political significance.

---

58 'Article 58 Aid or assistance by a State in the commission of an internationally wrongful act by an international organization.
1. A State which aids or assists an international organization in the commission of an internationally wrongful act by the latter is internationally responsible for doing so if:
(a) the State does so with knowledge of the circumstances of the internationally wrongful act; and
(b) the act would be internationally wrongful if committed by that State.
2. An act by a State member of an international organization done in accordance with the rules of the organization does not as such engage the international responsibility of that State under the terms of this article.'

59 'Article 61 Circumvention of international obligations of a State member of an international organization
1. A State member of an international organization incurs international responsibility if, by taking advantage of the fact that the organization has competence in relation to the subject-matter of one of the State's international obligations, it circumvents that obligation by causing the organization to commit an act that, if committed by the State, would have constituted a breach of the obligation.
2. Paragraph 1 applies whether or not the act in question is internationally wrongful for the international organization.'

The third option is to defer to findings by the ICC and accountability mechanisms under the Rome Statute. Article 87(7) of the Rome Statute states:

> Where a State Party fails to comply with a request to cooperate by the Court contrary to the provisions of this Statute, thereby preventing the Court from exercising its functions and powers under this Statute, the Court may make a finding to that effect and refer the matter to the Assembly of States Parties or, where the Security Council referred the matter to the Court, to the Security Council.

In this regard Pre-Trial Chamber II of the ICC decided to initiate official non-cooperation proceedings against South Africa under Article 87(7) on 4 September 2015.[60] In terms of that decision, South Africa was invited to submit by 5 October 2015 any observations on the report, in particular with regard to its alleged failure to comply with the cooperation requests issued by the Court regarding Al-Bashir's arrest. On the basis of this information the Chamber will decide what steps to be adopted, which will presumably include referring South Africa to the UN Security Council for further action to be taken.

Missing the deadline, South Africa's Department of International Relations and Cooperation said in a statement on 5 October 2015 that 'SA has now approached the court for more time to respond to this request. This was done in view of the complex and conflicting legal principles involved, both in international and in South African domestic law, and the fact that the South African domestic courts are still seized with the matter.'[61]

South Africa indicated in its report that 'the government remained committed to international criminal justice and to co-operating.'[62]

It also indicated that it would approach the Secretariat of the Assembly of States Parties (ASP) to the Rome Statute. This would be to ensure that talks take place during the ASP meeting in The Hague from 18 to 26 November 2015, on the rules and procedures that must be developed to provide clarity on the Article 97 consultation process and on the interpretation of Article 98, dealing with issues around the immunities of serving heads of state which are not parties to the Rome Statute, such as Sudan.[63] An approach through the ASP (and considerations for the ASP's expanded role in regard to the political and legal questions raised by the Al-Bashir debate) is an option considered further below under Option 5.

---

60 See *The Prosecutor v. Omar Hassan Ahmad Al-Bashir*, Order requesting submissions from the Republic of South Africa for the purposes of proceedings under Article 87(7) of the Rome Statute, Pre-Trial Chmaber II, ICC 02/05–01/09, 4 September 2015.

61 See 'SA government asks ICC for more time to explain why it did not arrest Bashir', *Business Day*, 5 October 2015, available at: www.bdlive.co.za/national/2015/10/05/sa-government-asks-icc-for-more-time-to-explain-why-it-did-not-arrest-bashir (accessed on 9 October 2105).

62 *Ibid.*

63 See further, Fabricius, 'South Africa arms itself for battle with the ICC', *ISS Today*, 9 October 2015, available at: https://www.issafrica.org/iss-today/south-africa-arms-itself-for-battle-with-the-icc (accessed on 9 October 2015).

For now let it be said that indications are that Pretoria is choosing the political ASP rather than the judicial Pre-Trial Chamber as its battleground precisely because it favours its chances before a political body over a judicial one that could rule very explicitly, that the obligations of all states regardless of status as an ICC state party, to prevent and punish the crime of genocide without exception, trump the obligation to respect immunity of heads of state and government.[64]

As a state party to the ICC, South Africa cannot escape the fact that the ICC will make a ruling under Article 87(7), and may therein attempt to provide (clearer) guidance on the interplay between the norm conflict and the reasons for one norm trumping the other. Of course, as Allan Ngari rightfully points out, 'a responsible government that says that it "remains committed to international criminal justice and to cooperate with the Court in the pursuit thereof as was envisaged in the Rome Statute" [as the government avowed in its statement] should then take the responsibility to seek this clarification by the judicial arm that has the mandate to clarify the matter.'[65] And if South Africa engages – as a state party – within that judicial process and in terms of the Rome Statute, then the Court's decision (whatever its outcome) ought to be respected.

Given that the decision made will be under Article 87(7), any finding that South Africa has failed to comply with a request by the Court will then have to be referred to the Security Council.[66] If nothing else, such a referral will serve to heighten the political stakes, given long-standing criticism by African and other states about the need for Security Council reform, criticism that has been exacerbated by and exemplified in the conduct of the Council as regards the ICC and its Sudan referral. It is thus appropriate that we next consider the prospect of Security Council reform as the fourth option.

The fourth option is to push for UN Security Council Reform. Today, from the perspective of many African leaders, the ICC's involvement in Sudan has come to reflect their central concern about the UN – the skewed nature of power distribution within the UN Security Council and global politics. Because of the Council's legitimacy deficit, many African and other developing countries see its work as 'a cynical exercise of authority by great powers',[67] in particular, the five permanent members. The Council's engagement with the ICC since the Rome Statute became operative will have exacerbated rather than softened those impressions.[68] And the result for the world's first permanent

64 *Ibid.*

65 *Ibid.*

66 Unless South Africa were to appeal such a decision to the Appeals Chamber of the ICC. If it were to do so, then it would apparently have to bring itself under Article 82(1)(d) of the Rome Statute, whereby either party may appeal a decision that 'involves an issue that would significantly affect the fair and expeditious conduct of the proceedings or the outcome of the trial, and which, in the opinion of the Pre-Trial or Trial Chamber, an immediate resolution by the Appeal Chamber may materially advance the proceedings.'

67 Schabas 2010.

68 *Ibid.*

international penal court? The result is that the uneven political landscape of the post-World War II collective security regime has become a central problem of the Court.

Arising from the ICC's Article 87(7) proceedings that have been initiated against South Africa, the ICC can, and on the available facts to date should, issue a notice of South Africa's non-compliance and send a complaint to the Security Council. Whether the Security Council will take any action in respect of South Africa is difficult to predict.

Certainly the Council has done itself and the cause of international criminal justice no favours in this regard as far as the Al-Bashir situation is concerned. As Tladi highlights:

> subsequent to the adoption of Resolution 1593, and in the light of the controversy about whether Resolution 1593 affects the immunities of Al-Bashir, the Council could have adopted a subsequent resolution confirming that indeed its intention was to waive the customary international law immunities of Sudanese officials.
>
> Moreover, twice a year, after the Prosecutor's briefing on ICC's activities in the situation in Sudan, members of the Security Council hold a debate on the report of the Prosecutor. The only member of the Security Council that has consistently referred to the question of immunities has been Russia. Russia's position has consistently been that Security Council Resolution 1593 had no effect on the immunities enjoyed under international law by the Sudanese. Moreover, the ICC transmitted its decisions on the non- cooperation of Malawi, Chad and the DRC to the Security Council. The Council has never acted on them, suggesting that, in its view, there is no non-compliance with its referral in Resolution 1593.[69]

If the Security Council were suddenly to shake itself from its previous slumber on its intentions with Resolution 1593, and were to issue some form of sanction against South Africa, that would be confirmation to African states of a Council that is a politically skewed body that cannot be trusted to do meaningful work on a principled basis (the clamour will go like this: why single out South Africa, when nothing of such significance was done in respect of Malawi, Chad and the DRC?).

Either way, whether the prospect of Security Council action is minimal or it selectively acts against South Africa, both inaction and selectivity would serve to bolster claims for the Council's reform and/or embolden proponents who see an expanded role for the Assembly of States Parties as a more democratic political counterpoint to the Security Council.

From an African perspective, frustration over the role that the Security Council plays, both in principle and practice, will almost certainly lead to a continental push for accelerated reform of the Council and its work, certainly in relation to ICC referrals. In this regard African states may themselves seek to engage with or work alongside other states or groupings of states that are working on Security

69 See Tladi 2015. See further Dicker 2015.

Council reform. Notably, some UN member states have formed a group called the Accountability, Coherence and Transparency Group (ACT), launched on 2 May 2013. ACT is aimed at enhancing the effectiveness of the Security Council through the improvement of its working methods.[70] Most recently, and closer to home, an initiative has gained traction in South Africa (hosted at the Institute for Security Studies in Pretoria), called Elect the Council. Elect the Council is a global civil society initiative to advocate for countries to be elected on a proportional basis to the UN Security Council and to do away with the system of permanent members and veto rights over a 15-year transitional period.[71]

Working with groupings like Elect the Council and ACT, African states may attempt to bring their concerns to the fore. For example, it may be contended by African states that if the Council is going to refer non-parties to the ICC for possible prosecution, then it is incumbent on the Council to pay for the referral (rather than members of the ASP).[72] African states might also insist that if the Council is going to refer situations involving non-parties, then it must (as indicated earlier) properly and clearly express itself on the removal of any immunities if that is the Council's intention. And finally, African states might insist that if a situation is referred to the ICC through a Security Council referral that explicitly removes immunities for international crimes, then all the members of the UN Security Council that decided on the referral (including non-members of the Rome Statute) should be similarly and expressly obliged to cooperate with the ICC in ensuring the arrest and surrender of high-standing individuals identified by the Court for possible prosecution. It seems anomalous that the Security Council (including members like the US, Russia and China that are not members of the Rome Statute) can proclaim that it is in the interests of peace and justice that a situation in a non-party state (like Sudan) requires referral to the ICC, impose obligations of cooperation with the ICC upon all UN member states (including states that are not party to the Rome Statute) which obligations override the immunities otherwise enjoyed by heads of state under international law, yet those members of the Council remain exempt from themselves cooperating in the arrest and surrender of such individuals. In short: if the Council is going to impose such potentially controversial obligations upon states, then all members of the Council should be held to the same standard they are so willing to impose on other states.

---

70 See further, Global Policy Forum, 'Reforming the Working Methods of the UN Security Council – The ACT Initiative', available at: https://www.globalpolicy.org/component/content/article/200-reform/52474-reforming-the-working-methods-of-the-un-security-council-the-act-initiative.html (accessed 10 October 2015). See also the ISS-led initiative to reform the UNSC. See Elect the Council, available at: www.electthecouncil.org (accessed 12 October 2015).

71 For further information, see Elect the Council, available at: www.electthecouncil.org (accessed on 19 January 2016).

72 To date, the only two successful Security Council referrals to the ICC (in respect of Sudan and Libya, both non-parties to the Court) contained provisions that imposed the entire financial burden of investigation and prosecution on the Court and its states parties. See UNSC Resolution 1593, operative para. 7; UNSC Resolution 1970, operative paras. 8 – and see further Dicker 2015.

While any attempted reform of the Security Council is an uphill struggle, as Richard Dicker highlights, a key challenge is 'to build a sense of momentum'.[73] The Al-Bashir saga demonstrates, if nothing else, the danger of stasis. It simultaneously confirms the need for the Security Council to take seriously claims for greater coherence and less selectivity in Council decisions on referrals and improving the substantive content of Security Council referral resolutions.

The fifth option is for the ASP to have an expanded role. Despite the issue of South Africa's non-cooperation now headed for deliberation by the ICC Pre-Trial Chamber, a judgment by the judicial arm – even though binding on states parties to the Rome Statute – does not mean that the AU will be satisfied. And South Africa's indications that it was simultaneously seeking to approach the ASP on these issues in December last year while responding to the ICC's Article 87(7) enquiry is an indication that the government is at the very least seeking a parallel answer from the political body that is the ASP.[74] It, moreover, did so at the same time as its ruling party was adopting strong-arm tactics by threatening to withdraw from the Rome Statute and invite Al-Bashir to a scheduled South Africa/China summit.[75] Whether or not African states are right to perceive the ASP as a more amenable body to answer questions about immunity of heads of state, and despite the regrettable tactics of South Africa's ruling party, the fact is that the ASP is an opportunity and a space for such debates.[76]

In that regard, the debates are not merely an occasion for hot-air venting. Article 112(6) of the Rome Statute allows for special sessions to be convened 'by

73 See Dicker 2015.

74 South Africa and Kenya were successful in adding to the 14th ASP's agenda items their specific concerns with the application and interpretation of Articles 97 and 98 of the Rome Statute. See 'Enabling constructive debate about Africa's international justice concerns', Institute for Security Studies, 26 November 2015, available at: https://www.issafrica.org/iss-spotlight/enabling-constructive-debate-about-africas-international-justice-concerns (accessed on 28 January 2016). However, no particular resolution was adopted by the Assembly in regard to the proposal, with the Assembly deciding to continue discussions in the ASP Bureau next year. See 'Fourteenth Session of the Assembly of States Parties – ICC', PILPG, 18 November 2015, available at: http://publicinternationallawandpolicygroup.org/practice-areas-2/war-crimes-prosecution/fourteenth-session-of-the-assembly-of-states-parties-icc-2/ (accessed on 28 January 2016).

75 See 'South Africa should leave ICC, ruling party says; will invite Bashir for China-Africa summit', *Mail & Guardian* (Africa), 11 October 2015, available at: http://mgafrica.com/article/2015-10-11-south-africa-should-leave-icc-ruling-party-says-willinvite-bashir-for-china-africa-summit (accessed on 12 October 2015). In the end Al-Bashir did not attend the summit, and to this day South Africa remains a member of the ICC.

76 Although there is a strong reminder from civil society groups that any such debates should not in any way impinge on the independence of the ICC. In this regard, in response to South Africa's efforts to raise the Article 98 debate before the ICC, Human Rights Watch wrote that it was 'deeply concerned that South Africa's proposal risks interference with ongoing judicial processes, and its concerns should instead be expressed through the pending litigation.' See Memorandum to African States Parties of the International Criminal Court for the Assembly of States Parties 14th Session, Human Rights Watch, 17 November 2015, available at: https://www.hrw.org/news/2015/11/17/memorandum-african-states-parties-international-criminal-court-assembly-states (accessed on 28 January 2016).

the Bureau on its own initiative or at the request of one third of the states parties'. Notably, 34 of the ICC's 123 states parties are African, where the African Bloc accordingly has a significant advantage. In any event, Kenya has already submitted proposals for the amendment of the Rome Statute, including a proposal that Article 27 be amended to preclude the ICC from prosecuting sitting heads of state or government.[77] It remains to be seen how the Assembly deals with such proposals, and whether it convenes a special session. For now the point is simply this: these types of proposals are likely to remain channelled through the ASP, and the South African and Kenyan governments sought to place further proposals on the ASP's agenda. What is important in this context is the following caution by O'Donohue:

> the Assembly faces serious challenges arising from efforts by some African states, including States Parties, to promote non-cooperation in some cases and seek amendments that threaten the effectiveness of the ICC. The Assembly should be the key forum for all States Parties to engage on these issues and consider the concerns raised, but discussions and any solutions explored must respect the independence of the prosecutor and the judiciary, the importance of the work of the ICC, and the integrity of the Statute.[78]

The Al-Bashir saga and African states' concerns over the Security Council might also be the catalyst for an expanded role for the ASP as more democratically viable alternative to the Council. African states have already proposed an amendment to Article 16 of the Rome Statute (which allows the Security Council to defer cases that are before the ICC for prosecution – for example in the interests of a peace settlement) that would give the UN General Assembly the power of deferral of cases before the ICC in the event of inaction by the Security Council, and continue to push for its adoption.[79] The primary legal obstacle faced by proponents of the current draft is the question of authority, as Article 16 relies on the Security Council's Chapter VII mandate as the guardian of international peace and security. The amendment attempts (optimistically) to overcome this problem by relying on the controversial Uniting for Peace Resolution, adopted by the UN General Assembly in 1950. In the context of amending Article 16,

---

77 See United Nations: Kenya, proposal for amendments, C.N. 1026.2013.TREATIES-XVIII.10, Depositary Notification, 14 March 2014. See further O'Donohue 2015, p. 123.

78 See O'Donohue 2015, p. 138.

79 The amendment proposal was again endorsed by the AU Assembly at its 16th Ordinary Session in January 2011. See Africa Union, Decision on the Implementation of the Decisions on the International Criminal Court, Assembly/AU/Dec.334 (XVI), 30–31 January 2011. For full discussion, see Akande, du Plessis and Jalloh, *An African expert study on the AU concerns about Article 16 of the Rome Statute of the ICC*, ISS Paper, October 2010, available at: www.elac.ox.ac.uk/downloads/AkandeDuPlessisJallohICCPositionPaper.pdf (accessed on 2 October 2015). See further the Extraordinary Session of the Assembly of Heads of State and Government of the AU, held at the AU Headquarters in Addis Ababa, Ethiopia, on 12 October 2013 in which Decision Ext/Assembly/Dec.1, October 2013, was adopted on Africa's relationship with the International Criminal Court.

it purports to grant the General Assembly authority to supplant the Security Council when the latter refuses to be moved by calls to defer investigations before the ICC. In the final analysis, this is probably the amendment's death knell; as even sympathetic countries are unlikely to support employing the controversial Uniting for Peace Resolution in this legally questionable manner.

In the current climate,[80] the amendment could conceivably be altered to require that the ASP, rather than the General Assembly, decide to defer the matter. In this regard it is notable that African states parties (and most recently again South Africa in response to the ICC's Article 87(7) process) have indicated their preference for using the ASP to settle disputes regarding Articles 27 and 98 of the Rome statute. For those states that see the Security Council as legitimate, the idea of relinquishing the Council's exclusive role regarding ICC referrals and deferrals of situations (including interpretations of immunities and states' compliance with Security Council referrals) to the ASP is unconscionable no doubt.

However, for those states that not only view the Council as unrepresentative, but also hostile to African requests regarding the ICC and the Security Council's work with the ICC, expanding the role of the ASP in this manner – as a more democratic body – is corrective.

These are difficult questions that also have a bearing on governance. In light of the Al-Bashir saga and the acute tensions that have arisen in regard thereto, their answers can no longer be stalled.

5. CONCLUSION

For African states parties to the ICC like South Africa,[81] an obvious way to avoid the apparent conflict of norms is by refusing to invite Al-Bashir or be party to

80 See e.g. Meeting of the open ended Committee of African Ministers on International Criminal Court (ICC), New York, USA, African Union, September 2015, available at: http://au.int/en/newsevents/13173/meeting-open-ended-committee-african-ministers-international-criminal-court-icc-new#sthash.Lgg1K8SY.dpuf (accessed on 2 October 2015) The African Union notes that the Committee of African Ministers of Foreign Affairs on the International Criminal Court has met in New York to address their concerns over Africa's relationship with the ICC which has been tested with the high profile cases against Kenya's Deputy President William Ruto and Sudanese leader Omar Al-Bashir. The committee is made up of members from Burundi, Chad, Côte d'Ivoire, Eritrea, Ethiopia, Kenya, Libya, Sudan, South Sudan and Senegal who are petitioning the UN Security Council to defer proceedings against Al-Bashir and Ruto. The group under the chairmanship of Ethiopia's Foreign Affairs Minister Tedros Adhanom Ghebreyesus has resolved to develop a comprehensive strategy for the speedy implementation and funding for the African Court of Justice on Human and Peoples' Rights in conformity with the decision of the Assembly on the ICC and Africa. The committee emphasised that 'African State Parties to the Rome Statute of the ICC should periodically assess and evaluate their continued membership as parties to the Rome Statute of the ICC'.

81 Supposing South Africa remains a state party and does not withdraw in line with Article 127 of the Rome Statute. Note that Article 127 requires a one-year notice of withdrawal from the Statute, and a state's withdrawal does not affect its obligations to the Court, including

hosting events that might attract his presence. However, the manner in which South Africa conducted itself – and allowed itself to be a haven for Al-Bashir – suggests either a calculated decision by Pretoria to set up a deliberate conflict between the ICC and the AU,[82] or a hapless move by a government that should have foreseen the weather coming its way. Certainly it would have required no great foresight by the government to realise the dilemma that would arise when Al-Bashir arrived for the AU Summit in Sandton and human rights groups predictably tried to have him arrested as a fugitive from justice.

Knowing what was coming, Pretoria could and arguably, should, simply never have offered to host the Summit – recalling that it had decided to do so in January 2015 after Chad told the AU it was unable to do so, and by then must have recognised that Al-Bashir's attendance at an AU Summit would be the consequence.

If African states wish to avoid the imbroglio attendant upon South Africa's conduct, then it may be preferable for them to act with greater foresight by avoiding any apparent clash of obligations through a simple choice of not allowing Al-Bashir anywhere near their territories.

That said, storm clouds have been gathering on the international criminal justice front years before Al-Bashir's visit to South Africa. His arrival in Sandton heralded forked lightning between the ICC and the AU – with both institutions demanding fealty to their obligations.

The tension, while palpable, is in need of resolution. If international criminal justice is to move forward there is a need for some form of lightning conductor. The difficulty is exacerbated by the fact that international criminal justice is often portrayed or perceived as a binary field: the ICC's obligations are unyielding in one direction, while the AU's demands are polar opposite and absolute; the ICC's pursuit of justice is (ig)noble, while the AU's protection of immunity for African heads of states is (dis)honourable.

We do ourselves a disservice if we allow ourselves to be stuck in such a binary world. Put differently, we need to move beyond the absolutist terms and positions adopted by opposing parties in the Al-Bashir debate.

Furthermore, all too often a simplistic and cynical view is peddled (particularly by Western states) about Africa's commitment to international norms. While critics have stressed that there is much within the Al-Bashir saga to raise serious doubts about South Africa's fealty to the obligations imposed by international law and its own domestic law, sight should nevertheless not be lost of the fact that

cooperation with existing cases and investigations, as well as future cases arising out of the same situation. As to the ability of South Africa to withdraw, see Viljoen, 'Five reasons why South Africa should not withdraw from the International Criminal Court', 23 June 2015, available at: www.up.ac.za/en/news/post_2100609-five-reasons-why-south-africa-should-not-withdraw-from-the-international-criminal-court-statute. He argues that any such withdrawal would be inconsistent with the Constitution.

82 See De Wet 2015.

proposals are being made by African states, including South Africa, for a resolution of the issue, possibly by a referral to the ICJ, and through recourse to the ASP.

As Mark Kersten points out:[83]

> Among observers and scholars, there is a propensity to judge the ICC, and international law more broadly, in all-or-nothing, black and white terms. Either international law must be enforced to its fullest or it is an ineffectual fantasy of liberal idealists. But the visit of Bashir in combination with South Africa's insistence that it is not in violation of international law or its obligations to the ICC may actually reinforce, rather than weaken, international criminal law. Here it is useful to recall the 1986 ruling of the International Court of Justice in The Republic of Nicaragua v. The United States of America:
>
> If a State acts in a way prima facie incompatible with a recognised rule, but defends its conduct by appealing to exceptions or justifications contained within the rule itself, then whether or not the State's conduct is in fact justifiable on that basis, the significance of that attitude is to confirm rather than to weaken the rule.

It seems to me that Kersten is correct. While many advocates of the ICC may be dismayed, and even horrified by (South) Africa's conduct and the decisions taken regarding Al-Bashir, sight should not be lost of the fact that most African states are engaged in the process of interpreting and negotiating the ICC's rules – rather than discarding them altogether. As Kersten says, 'That could very well end up strengthening international criminal law.'

One means by which this could be achieved, and international criminal law – and the institutions served by it (like the ICC, the ASP, and the Security Council) – could be enhanced and improved, is by reflecting seriously on the Al-Bashir debate and moving beyond the polarising binary that is exemplified in the stand-off between the ICC and the AU. A combination of clear-sighted thinking and open-minded debating of the options available to the international community to break the perceived deadlock may well achieve that. It is in that spirit that this chapter has offered the suggestion of five such exploratory steps.

BIBLIOGRAPHY

BOOKS AND JOURNAL ARTICLES

Akande 2012

Akande, D., 'The Effect of Security Council Resolutions and Domestic Proceedings on State Obligations to Cooperate with the ICC', 10 Journal of International Criminal Justice, 2012, pp. 299–324.

83 Kersten, 'Silver Linings: Bashir's Visit to South Africa and its Implications for the ICC', available at: http://justiceinconflict.org/2015/06/15/silver-linings-bashirs-visit-to-south-africa%E2%80%A8-and-its-implications-for-the-icc/ (accessed on 2 October 2015).

Condorelli and Ciampi 2005
Condorelli, L. and Ciampi, A., 'Comments on the Security Council Referral of the Situation in Darfur to the ICC', 3 Journal of International Criminal Justice, 2005.
De Plessis 2007
Du Plessis, M., 'South Africa's Implementation of the ICC Statute. An African Example', 5 Journal of International Criminal Justice, 2007.
De Wet 2015
De Wet, E., 'The implications of the visit of Al-Bashir to South Africa for international and domestic law', 13(5) JICJ, 2015.
Dicker 2015
Dicker, R., 'The ICC and Double Standards of International Justice', in Stahn, C. (ed.), 'The Law and Practice of the International Criminal Court', Oxford University Press, 2015.
Du Plessis and Gevers 2011
Du Plessis, M. and Gevers, C., 'Balancing Competing Obligations: the Rome Statute and AU Obligations', ISS Paper No. 225, 2011.
Maunganidze 2015
Maunganidze, O. and Du Plessis, A., 'The ICC and the AU', in Stahn, C., 'The Law and Practice of the International Criminal Court', Oxford University Press, 2015.
Milanovic 2009
Milanovic, M., 'Norm conflict in international law: whither human rights?', 20 Duke JCIL, 2009.
O'Donohue 2015
O'Donohue, J., 'The ICC and the ASP', in Stahn, C. (ed.), 'The Law and Practice of the International Criminal Court', Oxford University Press, 2015.
Schabas 2010
Schabas, W., 'The International Criminal Court: A Commentary on the Rome Statute', Oxford University Press, 2010.
Sluiter 2008
Sluiter, G., 'Obtaining cooperation from Sudan – where is the law?', 6(5) Journal of International Criminal Justice, 2008, pp. 871–884.
Tladi 2015
Tladi, D., 'The Duty on South Africa to Arrest and Surrender Al-Bashir under South African and International Law: Attempting to Make a Collage from an Incoherent Framework', Journal of International Criminal Justice, 2015.
Tladi 2009
Tladi, D., 'The African Union and the International Criminal Court: The battle for the soul of international law', 34 SAYIL, 2009.
Verduzco 2015
Verduzco, D.R., 'The Relationship between the ICC and the Security Council', in Stahn, C. (ed.), 'The Law and Practice of the International Criminal Court', Oxford University Press, 2015.

JURISPRUDENCE

ACHPR 2014
ACHPR, Request for an Advisory Opinion 001 of 2014, 2014.
ICC 2015
ICC, Prosecutor v. Omar Hassan Ahmad Al-Bashir, ICC-02/05-01/09-247, 4 September 2015.
ICC 2015
ICC, Prosecutor v. Omar Hassan Ahmad Al-Bashir, ICC-02/05-01/09-242, 13 June 2015.
ICJ 1995
ICJ, Case Concerning East Timor (Portugal v. Australia), Judgment, 30 June 1995.
ICJ 1992
ICJ, Questions of Interpretation and Application of the 1971 Montreal Convention arising from the Aerial Incident at Lockerbie (Libyan Arab Jamahiriya v. United States of America), Provisional Measures, 14 April 1992.
North Gauteng High Court 2015
NGHC, Southern Africa Litigation Centre v. The Minister of Justice and Constitutional Development and Others, Case no. 27740/2015, ZAGPPHC 402, 24 June 2015.

TREATIES, LEGISLATION AND AGREEMENTS

AU, Decision on Africa's Relationship with the International Criminal Court (ICC), Ext/Assembly/AU/Dec.1, October 2013.
AU, Decision on the Implementation of the Decisions on the International Criminal Court, Assembly/AU/Dec.334 (XVI), 30–31 January 2011.
Charter of the United Nations, 26 June 1945.
Constitutive Act of the African Union, 11 July 2000.
Rome Statute of the International Criminal Court, 2187 UNTS 90/37, 17 July 1998.
South Africa, Diplomatic Immunities and Privileges Act No. 37, 2001.
South Africa, Implementation of the Rome Statute of the International Criminal Court Act 27 of 2002, July 2002.
UN Security Council, Resolution 1593 (2005), UN Doc. S/RES/1593, 31 March 2005.
UN Security Council, Resolution 1970 (2011), UN Doc. S/RES/1970, 26 February 2011.

OTHERS

AU, 'Meeting of the open ended Committee of African Ministers on International Criminal Court (ICC), New York, USA', Media Advisory, 26 September 2015.
Akande, D., Du Plessis, M. and Jalloh, C.C., 'An African expert study on the African Union concerns about article 16 of the Rome Statute of the ICC', ISS Position Paper, 2010.

Amnesty International, 'Bringing Power to Justice: Absence of Immunity for Heads of States before the International Criminal Court', IOR 53/017/2010, 2010.
Du Plessis, M. and Fritz, N., 'New Diplomatic Fiasco Looms', Business Day, 2 May 2009.
Fabricius, P., 'South Africa arms itself for battle with the ICC', ISS Today, 8 October 2015.
Gevers, C., 'Africa's ICC gripes heading to the ICJ?', War and Law Blog, 2 February 2015.
Global Policy Forum, 'Reforming the Working Methods of the UN Security Council – The ACT Initiative', August 2013.
Hartley, W., 'SA government asks ICC for more time to explain why it did not arrest Bashir', Business Day Live, 5 October 2015.
Human Rights Watch, 'Memorandum to African States Parties of the International Criminal Court for the Assembly of States Parties 14th Session', 17 November 2015.
Institute for Securities Studies, 'Enabling constructive debate about Africa's international justice concerns', 26 November 2015.
International Law Commission, 'Third Report on the Immunity of State Officials from Foreign Criminal Jurisdiction – By Roman Anatolevich Kolodkin, Special Rapporteur', UN Doc. A/CN.4/646, 24 May 2011.
Kersten, M., 'Silver Linings: Bashir's Visit to South Africa and its Implications for the ICC', Justice in Conflict, 15 June 2015.
Letter dated 8 July 2009 from the Minister of Foreign Affairs and International Cooperation of the Republic of Botswana to Justice Sany-Hyun Song, President of the International Criminal Court.
Mail and Guardian Africa, 'South Africa should leave ICC, ruling party says; will invite Bashir for China-Africa summit', 11 October 2015.
Mail and Guardian Africa, "We told Bashir to just relax": new details of S. Africa's effort to shield wanted Sudanese leader', 21 June 2015.
Mushava, E., 'Botswana would have arrested Al-Bashir', NewsDay, 17 June 2015.
Public International Law and Policy Group, 'Fourteenth Session of the Assembly of States Parties – ICC', 18 November 2015.
Report of the Ministerial Meeting of African States Parties to the Rome Statute of the ICC 8 – 9 June 2009 Addis Ababa, MinICC/Legal (on file with the author).
Southern Africa Litigation Centre v. The Minister of Justice and Constitutional Development and Others (North Gauteng High Court, Case no. 27740/2015), Respondent's Answering Affidavit, 15 June 2015.
UN, Depository Notification C.N.1026.2013.TREATIES-XVIII.10 (Proposal of amendments by Kenya to the Rome Statute), 14 March 2014.
UN, 'Report of the International Law Commission', UN Doc. A/66/10, 2011.
Viljoen, F., 'Five reasons why South Africa should not withdraw from the International Criminal Court Statute', University of Pretoria News, 23 June 2015.

WHEN WE DON'T SPEAK THE SAME LANGUAGE

The Challenges of Multilingual Justice at the ICC

Lorraine SMITH VAN-LIN

If you talk to a man in a language he understands, that goes to his head.
If you talk to him in his language, that goes to his heart
– Nelson Mandela

1. INTRODUCTION

Delivering effective, fair and expeditious justice in a multilingual and multicultural context is never an easy task, but for the International Criminal Court (ICC or the Court) the challenge is even greater. The ICC is the only permanent international criminal justice institution in the world and with 123 member states parties to date[1] and the potential for others to be referred by the United Nations (UN) Security Council;[2] its jurisdictional reach spans virtually every country and language. All of the Court's cases are currently from Africa, the most linguistically diverse continent in the world with more than 2,000 different languages.[3] Ensuring that defendants, victims and affected communities are able to fully understand, participate in and follow proceedings has significant time and resource implications, both of which the ICC can ill afford.

The trial of *Abdallah Banda Abakaer Nourain (Abdallah Banda)* concerning war crimes committed against the African Union (AU) Peacekeeping Mission at the Haskanita Military Group Site in Darfur, Sudan is a case in point.[4] Abdallah

1 See ICC Website, 'The States Parties to the Rome Statute', available at: http://bit.ly/18zHW78.
2 Article 13(b) Rome Statute.
3 See Language Magazine, 'Africa's Linguistic Diversity', available at: http://languagemagazine.com/?page_id=123616.
4 See *The Prosecutor v. Abdallah Banda Abakaer Nourain*, ICC-02/05-03/09, ICC Case Information Sheet, available at: www.icc-cpi.int/iccdocs/PIDS/publications/BandaEng.pdf.

Banda speaks and understands only one language – Zaghawa, a little known unwritten language with a limited vocabulary of 5,000 words.[5] Taking steps to transliterate evidentiary material for the benefit of the accused has delayed the trial for several years at significant cost. The Banda challenges are likely to feature in several other cases in the coming years and states parties to the Rome Statute establishing the ICC are already complaining about the mushrooming budget.[6] Outside the courtroom, this Hague-based court is also hard-pressed to communicate and connect with affected communities in a language which they understand, a challenge which it dares not ignore.

Delivering justice in a linguistically and culturally diverse context is not peculiar to the ICC. Its predecessor ad hoc tribunals, the International Criminal Tribunal for the former Yugoslavia (ICTY) and the International Criminal Tribunal for Rwanda (ICTR) also grappled with language-related challenges where the language spoken by the majority of witnesses and accused differed from the Tribunal's working languages, English and French.

This article will explore the ICC's efforts to deliver justice in the context of linguistic diversity. The issues will be considered under three broad themes: *the challenges of multilingualism* – an examination of some of the pervasive difficulties in ensuring the right to language at the court; *language and rights*, specifically the steps taken by the ICC to enforce language rights for both defendants and victims; and finally, *language and complementarity* – how the ICC's approach to lesser known languages can provide valuable lessons for local courts.

2. LANGUAGE AND THE ICC

Language is defined as a means of conveying or communicating ideas; specifically, human speech, or the expression of ideas by written characters.'[7] It plays an essential role in the evolution and understanding of human existence, development and dignity.[8] Indeed it has been said that 'language bridges the gap between isolation and community, allowing humans to delineate the rights and duties they hold in respect of one another; and thus to live in society.'[9]

---

5 *The Prosecutor v. Adallah Banda Abakaer Nourain and Saleh Mohammed Jerbo Jamus*, Prosecutions Response to the Trial Chamber's Request for Written Submissions on issues to be addressed during the Status Conference on 19 April 2011, ICC-02/05-03/09-131, 14 April 2011, para. 7.

6 See Evenson, 'Budget cuts challenge the ICC', Genocide Watch, 7 August 2015, available at: http://genocidewatch.net/2015/08/13/budget-cuts-challenges-the-icc/.

7 Black's Law Dictionary, available at: http://thelawdictionary.org/language/.

8 Hlophe, 'Receiving justice in your own language the need for effective court interpreting in our multilingual society', April 2004, available at: www.sabar.co.za/law-journals/2004/april/2004-april-vol017-no1-pp42-47.pdf.

9 *Ibid.*

Nowhere is its power to unify or divide, to clarify or confuse, build up or tear down, more apposite than in the courtroom. The fact-finding nature of court proceedings necessarily relies on the oral and written expressions by the parties and participants, and the judges' ability to understand not only the spoken or written words, but the cultural nuances that are inherent to every communication exchange. Thus the existence of deeply entrenched socio-cultural values or issues that divide peoples within a nation become a part of the trial process through language, even where efforts are made to exclude them.

The ICC has five official languages namely English, French, Arabic, Spanish, Chinese and Russian.[10] English and French are the two working languages.[11] Officials of the Court including judges, the Registrar and Deputy Registrar, Prosecutor and Deputy Prosecutor, as well as defence counsel and legal representatives of victims, must have an excellent knowledge of and be fluent in at least one of its working languages.[12] In addition to the official languages, the ICC uses what are referred to as 'situational languages' that is, the local languages utilised by suspects, victims or witnesses who do not speak or understand any of the working languages of the Court.[13]

The Language Services Section (LSS) of the ICC Registry has full responsibility for language-related activities and services at the Court including translation, revision and editing of Court documents; consecutive and simultaneous interpretation for trial hearings, press conferences, and other events, among others.[14] Translation is outsourced when there is no in-house provision for the languages requested or when competing priorities mean that the translation cannot be done in house.[15] The Office of the Prosecutor (OTP)

10 Article 50(1) Rome Statute.

11 Article 50(2) Rome Statute.

12 See Articles 36(3)(c) and 42(3) of the Rome Statute; Rule 22 of the ICC Rules of Procedure and Evidence.

13 See Tomic and Montoliu, 'Translation before the International Criminal Court', ResearchGate, available at: www.researchgate.net/publication/236258793_Translation_at_the_International_Criminal_Court.

14 See *Proposed Programme Budget for 2016 of the International Criminal Court*, ICC-ASP/14/10, 2 September 2015, para. 474. The former Court Interpretation and Translation Section (STIC) was renamed the LSS under a restructuring exercise initiated by ICC Registrar Herman von Hebel. See *Report on the review of the organizational structure of the Registry Outcomes of Phase 4 of the ReVision Project Decisions on the structure of the Registry*, ICC-ASP/14/18, May 2015. The Section underwent a review said to be aimed at 'increasing efficiency, streamlining reporting lines to the Chief of Section and allocating responsibilities in a coherent and transparent manner.' The changes were designed to strengthen the capacity of LSS in the area of English and French translation, with the creation of additional Reviser positions, and facilitating more direct contact between revisers and translators in order to ensure stronger accountability for the quality and quantity of translations. The Registry Revision Project has been criticised as being aimed at disproportionately targeting Africans through so-called internal staff restructuring and abolition of key posts. See for example Africa Legal Aid E-reporter, 'ICC Alert – The Registrar's Questionable Revision Project', available at: www.imanager.nl/IManager/MailingWeb/13932/C1AHr4P1sczR.

15 *Ibid.*

has its own Language Services Unit (LSU) which is responsible for translation of OTP evidence and core office documentation.[16]

It is quite an irony that a global court of the ICC's stature and jurisdictional reach has chosen to carte blanche retain the 6 official UN languages rather than to adopt a flexible system more consistent with its working needs. This directly contrasts with the ICTY for example which has no official languages and utilises only two working languages (English and French) with the option for the language of the accused or the majority of the parties to become a working language where necessary.[17]

Retaining the six UN languages was a bad idea which only serves to reinforce deeply entrenched divisions between the so-called powerful states or former colonial masters and the ex-colonies within the UN system. Despite the fact that there are 23 cases arising from nine situations all originating from Africa currently before the Court, not even one (non-colonial) African language is listed among the Court's official languages.[18] Swahili for example, is the official language of Tanzania, widely spoken in Uganda and Kenya and is spoken by over 100 million persons in Africa.[19] It is listed as one of the official languages of the AU but is not officially recognised as a UN language and thus is not one of the ICC's official languages.[20]

While this may appear at first blush to be a matter of pure semantics, the non-inclusion of African languages in an official form in the ICC's legal texts reinforces the deeply entrenched perceptions of the ICC as a Western Court which is currently targeting Africa. Under its Statute and Rules of Procedure and Evidence (RPE) the ICC has a legal obligation to translate all judgments and decisions which are of fundamental importance into all of the official languages of the Court.[21] While there is the possibility under specified circumstances for a

---

16 *Ibid*, para. 164(g).

17 See Translation and Interpretation Section of the ICTY, available at: www.icty.org/sid/165.

18 The following situations are currently before the Court: Uganda, Democratic Republic of Congo, Kenya, Darfur Sudan, Côte d'Ivoire, Central African Republic I, Central African Republic II, Mali and Libya. In October 2015 the ICC opened a tenth situation in Georgia, the first time since the Court's inception that a situation was being opened outside of Africa.

19 See Africa Ranking, 'Top Ten Most Spoken Languages in Africa', available at: www.africaranking.com/most-spoken-languages-in-africa/4/.

20 See Article 11 Protocol on Amendments to the Constitutive Act of the African Union.

21 See Article 50(1): Rome Statute which provides *inter alia* that 'The judgments of the Court, as well as other decisions resolving fundamental issues before the Court, shall be published in the official languages.' Under Rule 40(1) of the ICC Rules of Procedure and Evidence decisions of fundamental importance include: all decisions of the Appeals decision; all admissibility and jurisdiction decisions; all Trial Chamber decisions on guilt or innocence, sentencing and reparations, and all decisions on Article 57(3)(d) (investigative steps in the absence of state cooperation). Rule 40(2) provides that confirmation of charges decisions and Article 70 decisions (administration of justice) are also to be published in all the official languages if the Presidency considers that they resolve fundamental issues. The Presidency may also decide to publish other decisions in all the official languages when they concern major issues regarding the implementation or interpretation of the Statute or major issues of general interest

language other than one of the official languages to become the working language of particular proceedings, there is no legal requirement for fundamental decisions to be published in non-official languages.[22] To date almost every single fundamental decision at the ICC concerns an African defendant, witness, victim or state party. There is no legal obligation to translate any of these decisions into languages that a significant number of Africans understand; yet ironically they must be translated into languages utilised by non-states parties some of whom have been noticeably intransigent towards the Court.[23]

3. MULTILINGUALISM AT THE ICC: CHALLENGES AND ACHIEVEMENTS

Delivering justice in the diverse multilingual context of the ICC has presented its own unique challenges, some of which have spawned creative solutions. One of the main challenges is the number of languages which must be supported. According to Alexander Tomic, Chief of the LSS, the Unit currently supports 45 languages including official, judicial cooperation and situational languages; and given the ICC's jurisdictional scope, there is in theory no limit to the number of languages which may be utilised at the Court.[24] In addition, the sheer volume of translations including key decisions such as arrest warrants and confirmation of charges coupled with strict judicial deadlines and divergent needs of the end-users, place a major burden on the resources of the LSS.[25]

The struggle with multilingualism in the context of international criminal trials can be traced as far back as the International Military Tribunal, also

(Rule 40(3)). Despite the legal requirement, the Court's approach to translation of decisions into all official languages is inconsistent, ad hoc and far from systematic. Given the Court's resource constraints, it is little wonder that in this case the practise does not follow the law. A quick glance at the ICC's website reveals that the Court has translated only a very limited selection of relevant decisions into the official languages. Three years after its issuance, the Lubanga judgment remained available in English and French only.

22 Article 50(3) Rome Statute. Thus for example in the case of Bosco Ntaganda, translation will also be provided into Kinyarwanda, the language spoken by the accused and a number of witnesses in the case. See ICC Q&A Opening of the Trial of the Ntaganda Case, 2 September 2015, available at: www.icc-cpi.int/iccdocs/PIDS/publications/Ntaganda_Q-A-ENG.pdf.

23 Article 50(1) of the Rome Statute requires translation into all official languages including Chinese and Russian. Neither Russia nor China is a state party to the Rome Statute establishing the ICC. Both are however members of the UN Security Council and used their powers to oppose the referral of Syria to the ICC. See UN Press, 'Referral of Syria to International Criminal Court Fails as Negative Votes Prevent Security Council from Adopting Draft Resolution', 22 May 2014, available at: www.un.org/press/en/2014/sc11407.doc.htm.

24 Tomic and Beltran Montoliu, 'Translation before the International Criminal Court', available at: www.researchgate.net/publication/236258793_Translation_at_the_International_Criminal_Court.

25 *Ibid.*

known as the Nuremberg Tribunal, credited with being the modern forefather of international criminal courts.[26] The Tribunal utilised four working languages – English, French, Russian and German (the language of the defendants). The Tribunal struggled with the obligation to conduct all court proceedings and produce all official documents in the working languages.[27] In addition, the freedom of every allied country representative (judges and prosecutors) to use their own language and the need to ensure that the public were kept informed took a toll on the Tribunal's linguistic capacity.[28] Struggles notwithstanding, the Nuremberg trials pioneered what has now evolved into the modern version of simultaneous translation, utilised in national and international criminal courts today.

The ICTY has also had its fair share of language-related challenges. Unlike the ICC, the ICTY's focus was on one single linguistic region which created slightly different language-related challenges.[29] As previously noted English and French are the Tribunal's two working languages; however, the accused before the Tribunal speak Bosnian Croatian Serbian (BCS), Albanian or Macedonian and consequently all court proceedings are held in at least three, and sometimes four, languages while the vast majority of its written documents are translated into anywhere from two to five languages.[30]

Like its predecessor ICTR, the ICC has had to grapple with local languages characterised by the absence of legal terminology and a paucity of written materials such as dictionaries, and glossaries. While English and French were the official languages of the ICTR, the majority of witnesses and several accused spoke Kinyarwanda thus the ICTR Registry had to codify Kinyarwanda terminology for important international criminal law concepts, for example 'indictment', a process which took some time and evolved over several years.[31] A similar approach was adopted by the ICC Registry with the LSS creating a legal dictionary of words and notions where these were non-existent in a

26 The Nuremberg Tribunal was set up for the purpose of bringing Nazi war criminals to justice. The Tribunal conducted a series of 13 trials in Nuremberg, Germany, between 1945 and 1949. The defendants, who included Nazi Party officials and high-ranking military officers along with German industrialists, lawyers and doctors, were indicted on such charges as crimes against peace and crimes against humanity. Nazi leader Adolf Hitler (1889–1945) committed suicide and was never brought to trial. Although the legal justifications for the trials and their procedural innovations were controversial at the time, the Nuremberg trials are now regarded as a milestone toward the establishment of a permanent international court, and an important precedent for dealing with later instances of genocide and other crimes against humanity. See Nuremberg trials, available at: www.history.com/topics/world-war-ii/nuremberg-trials.

27 Namakula 2014.

28 *Ibid.*

29 See Translating and Interpreting: Legacy of the ICTY, Hague, available at: www.kwintessential.co.uk/read-our-blog/translation-and-interpreting-legacy-of-the-icty-hague.html.

30 See Translation and Interpretation Section of the ICTY, available at: www.icty.org/sid/165.

31 Swigart 2015.

particular language. In the Uganda situation, one of the first to come before the Court, the Registry had to set up a panel of experts to create a legal dictionary in Acholi in order to be able to translate arrest warrants, as complex judicial terminology and notions contained in the ICC documents were unknown in Acholi.[32]

There was also a perpetual shortage of trained interpreters for specialised languages. The Registry's solution was to train local language speakers with no previous interpretation experience.[33] The individuals were then contracted by the Court as para-interpreters to facilitate hearings and other court-related contexts.[34] The Court has to date hired and trained simultaneous interpreters in Acholi (Uganda), Swahili Congolese variant (DRC), Lingala (DRC), Sango (Central African Republic), and Zaghawa (Sudan). Consecutive interpreters are available for other African languages as well, such as Alur (Uganda) and Lendu (DRC), and ultimately Fur (Sudan) and Sudanese Arabic.[35]

A more pervasive challenge is the need to ensure accurate interpretation and translations. This is particularly difficult in interpretation because of the need for speed, sensitivity and the ability not only to interpret legal terminology but also to convey nuances and emotions which are key to effective simultaneous translation, the most commonly practised form of interpretation at the Court.[36] These factors can result in the alteration of testimony through interpretation or an inaccurate rendering of the witness' testimony.

Inaccuracy in interpretation can be attributed to a number of factors, not all of which are the fault of the interpreters. These include 'the number of languages involved; the nuances of the local languages and dialects; the implementation of protective measures such as voice distortions; lack of diligence by persons in court using technical equipment (such as poor microphone use); and the need for parties to modify behaviour to facilitate interpretation (such as speaking in

32 Dubuisson et al. 2009, p. 569.

33 *Ibid.*

34 *Ibid.*

35 Swigart 2015, p. 34.

36 See Tomic and Montoliu, 'Translation before the International Criminal Court', available at: www.researchgate.net/publication/236258793_Translation_at_the_International_Criminal_Court; See also Regulation 61 of the Regulations of the Registry which provides for the various forms of interpretation at the ICC including: (a) simultaneous interpretation, where the interpreter renders the speaker's message immediately and continuously from a booth; (b) chuchotage or whispering, which is simultaneous interpretation by an interpreter whispering an interpretation of what is said to a maximum of two listeners; this was utilised in the case of Germain Katanga to provide interpretation into Lingala; (c) consecutive interpretation, where the interpreter interprets aloud, usually taking notes as the speaker speaks and then concisely interpreting several sentences at a time for an unlimited number of listeners; (d) Liaison interpretation, where the interpreter interprets aloud in and out of two or more languages, interpreting a few sentences at a time, for a very limited number of listeners; and (e) sight translation, for written documents that need to be translated orally.

slow, measured tones, waiting until the interpretation of one speaker is complete before another person continues).'[37]

Inaccurate interpretations can significantly impact the fairness of the proceedings both in terms of the accuracy of the official record and the judges' legal and factual assessment of the evidence, and also in relation to the delay occasioned by the need to check and correct the record. As former ICTY Judge Patricia Wald noted:

> The ICTY judges' job of assessing the demeanor of a witness is also more difficult than in a domestic court because the witness invariably speaks in a foreign language. Although simulcast translations by earphone are available, along with a written transcript on the TV screen, it is still very different from hearing the actual words and voice of a witness. Sometimes when a counsel speaks both Bosnian/Croatian/Serbian and English, he will jump up and object to a 'wrong' translation (sometimes he is right). But otherwise the judge is almost completely dependent on the translator for the content as well as the inflections of voice in which the witness's testimony is given.[38]

In the *Lubanga* case the trial proceedings were halted on at least one occasion due to substantial discrepancies between the French and English versions of the transcripts.[39] In his appeal against conviction and sentence, Mr Lubanga argued that there had been a mistranslation of the witness's 'particularly ambiguous statement' that General Kisembo's bodyguards had picked up 'children' to be 'in his court' (according to the French version of the transcript), rather than 'in his corps' (according to the English version of the transcript).[40]

It would be virtually impossible for the ICC to have judges, team members of the prosecution or defence, or other staff working at the Court who are able to speak or understand the local languages of all situations before the Court. This would of course be helpful in identifying linguistic and cultural nuances that only a native speaker could understand, and provide a check and balance for interpreters. At the Special Court for Sierra Leone – a hybrid court consisting of local and international staff – there were always local language-speakers who could constantly check the accuracy of interpretation. As Swigart noted, 'not only were Sierra Leonean legal assistants represented on the prosecution and defence teams, nationals played other roles among the large courtroom staff.

37 See International Bar Association, 'First Challenges: An examination of recent landmark developments at the International Criminal Court', June 2009.

38 Wald 2002, p. 237.

39 See *The Prosecutor v. Thomas Lubanga Dyilo*, Transcript of Hearing (Open Session), ICC-01/04–01/06-T-247-Red-ENG CT WT, 16 February 2010, pp. 28–29. See also, War Crimes Research Office, Expediting Proceedings before the International Criminal Court, p. 60, available at: https://www.wcl.american.edu/warcrimes/icc/documents/1106report.pdf.

40 See *The Prosecutor v. Thomas Lubanga Dyilo*, Judgment on the appeal of Mr Thomas Lubanga Dyilo against his conviction, ICC-01/04–01/06–3121-Red, para. 401.

Perhaps of particular importance was the presence of Sierra Leonean judges who could easily stop the proceedings in order to correct the official record if an interpretation was deemed inaccurate.'[41]

To alleviate this problem the ICC Registry has initiated a system of self-check and cross check wherein individual interpreters have a duty to take necessary steps to minimise inaccuracies and to self-revise, while revisers are tasked with cross checking for accuracy. A system is also in place whereby the parties can regularly request the Registry's translation services to conduct a review of the accuracy of the transcripts.[42] More importantly however, in light of the due process guarantees in the Statute, judges have an independent obligation to ensure the accuracy of the interpretation and that translations meet the necessary standards for a fair trial.[43] This is also consistent with the Chamber's duty to adjudicate the 'truth' which should not be based on translation and interpretation errors.[44] The Presiding Judge/Chamber should therefore *of its own motion* request a review of the accuracy of the transcripts/exhibits if it has grounds to believe that there may be errors.[45]

4. LANGUAGE SERVICES AT A COST

Resourcing the multilingual requirements of international criminal trials comes at a significant cost, one that states may not always be willing to pay. A former interpreter from the ICTR offered the following advice to the ICC concerning the resourcing of language services:

> Make the necessary investment in language services and it will save money in the end. Every time a trial is delayed because a necessary document has not been translated, it costs money ... People at the top need to understand that investment in language skills will shorten the proceedings and lower the costs of the Court. Creating a highly professional language staff with proper infrastructure makes sense, both practically and fiscally.[46]

In its 2016 Proposed Programme Budget, the ICC requested 153 million euros to fund its total activities for 2016, an increase of 22 million over the previous

41 Swigart 2015, p. 26.

42 A procedure for such requests is also established at the ICTY. See *Prosecutor v. Seselj*, Decision on the Accused's Motions Concerning the Quality of Interpretation (Submissions 352, 354 And 366), 15 July 2008, p. 6, available at: www.icty.org/x/cases/seselj/tdec/en/080715.pdf.

43 International Bar Association, 'First Challenges: An examination of recent landmark developments at the International Criminal Court', June 2009, p. 37.

44 *Ibid.*

45 *Ibid.*

46 Swigart 2015, p. 40.

year.[47] The increase was attributed to a steady growth in the overall workload of the court and an increase in judicial activities.[48] The LSS requested a significant increase in its budgetary allocation in order to meet the needs of the Unit.[49] The OTP also requested additional resources for the LSU due to changes in its investigative policy and more field-based presence.[50]

An increase in judicial activities places greater demands upon the resources of the LSS. Budgetary uncertainties will have an impact on the Unit's output as well as the ability to retain trained staff. In the *Banda* case, after painstakingly training two Zaghawa interpreters, the Registry was forced to not renew their contracts due to major cuts to the 2012 budget.[51] The result: further delay in a case which had been struggling from the beginning with managing a difficult language.

Investment in language services in the short term will pay dividends in the longer term. Where international courts such as the ICC are situated far from the countries under investigation and are required to facilitate the effective relay of information within court proceedings, they must be adequately resourced. Not only is this good business sense, it is the only way to ensure that proceedings are efficient and fair.

5. DEFENDANTS' RIGHT TO LANGUAGE, TRANSLATION AND INTERPRETATION

The need to define and give effect to language fair trial rights is by far the most difficult challenge of the ICC yet. Language rights are inextricably bound with the due process and fair trial guarantees afforded to persons charged with crimes before the Court and more seminally with the participatory rights to which other parties to the proceedings such as victims and witnesses are entitled. Resolving the tension between two congruent rights: the right to a fair trial, and the right to be tried expeditiously, has not been easy.

47 See Proposed Programme Budget for 2016 of the International Criminal Court, Executive Summary, August 2015, ICC-ASP/14/10/Add1.

48 *Ibid*, para. B1(a).

49 Proposed Programme Budget for 2016 of the International Criminal Court, September 2015, ICC-ASP/14/10, paras. 474 and 475.

50 *Ibid*, paras. 166–173. According to the OTP, since the implementation of the 2012–2015 Strategic Plan the budgetary allocation to the Services Section under which the LSU falls has seen a steady annual decline. Thus for the 2016 budget the Office has requested an increase consistent with the 'incremental complexity and volumes of missions, evidence and information determined by the new approach in investigative and prosecutorial activities'. The requested increase amounts to 12.8% (876.9 thousand euros) or 16.8% of the total OTP budget.

51 See *The Prosecutor v. Adallah Banda Abakaer Nourain and Saleh Mohammed Jerbo Jamus*, Fifth Joint Prosecution and Registry's Monthly Report on Translation and Interpretation Issues, ICC-02/05-03/09-299.

The ICTR and the ICTY expressly codify the right of accused persons to use his or her own language during proceedings at the Tribunal.[52] Counsel for the accused may also apply to a Judge for leave to use a language other than the two working ones or the language of the accused. If such leave is granted, the expenses of interpretation and translation shall be borne by the Tribunal to the extent, if any, determined by the President, taking into account the rights of the defence and the interests of justice. Witnesses and other persons appearing before the Tribunal have the right to use their own language if they do not have sufficient knowledge of either of the two working languages.[53]

The Rome Statute provides for both the right to translation and the right to interpretation at different stages of proceedings before the ICC, but the scope of the respective rights differ. 'Translation' has been described as 'the transfer of thoughts and ideas from one language (the source language) into another (the target language)', in either written or oral form.[54] Interpretation is said to refer to oral communication encompassing 'situations in which one person speaks in the source language, an interpreter processes this input and produces output in the target language, and another person listens to the interpreted target language version of the original speaker's message.'[55]

Specifically, accused persons are entitled to be informed promptly and in detail of the nature, cause and content of the charge, *in a language which s/he fully understands and speaks* and the right to have, free of any cost, the assistance of a competent interpreter and such translations *as are necessary to meet the requirements of fairness*, if any of the proceedings of or documents presented to the Court are not in a language which the accused *fully understands and speaks* (emphasis added).[56] The inclusion of the qualifying word 'fully' before 'understands and speaks', places the protection afforded to ICC defendants at a level above even the human rights instruments.[57]

52 Rule 3(B), Rules of Procedure of both the ICTR and ICTY.
53 *Ibid.*
54 Karton 2008.
55 *Ibid.*
56 Article 67(a) and (f), Rome Statute.
57 See Article 14(3)(a) and (f) ICCPR which affords the accused the right to be informed of the charges brought against him in a language he understands and to have the free assistance of an interpreter if he cannot understand or speak the language used in Court. See also Article 5(2) of the ECHR which provides that '[e]veryone who is arrested shall be informed promptly, in a language which he understands, of the reasons for his arrest and of any charge against him.' Article 6(3) of the ECHR specifies that '[e]veryone charged with a criminal offence has the following minimum rights: (a) to be informed promptly, in a language which he understands and in detail, of the nature and cause of the accusation against him; ... [and] (e) to have the free assistance of an interpreter if he cannot understand or speak the language used in court. The African Charter on Human and Peoples' Rights contains no specific provision in this regard; however, the African Commission on Human and Peoples' Rights has held that the right to a fair trial includes, *inter alia*, the requirement that persons arrested 'shall be informed at the time of arrest, in a language which they understand of the reason for their arrest and shall be informed promptly of any charges against them.'

But what does 'fully' mean? Namakula notes that 'the task of gauging linguistic and comprehension level in both cross-lingual (between different languages) and monolingual (within the same language) situations is problematic in many respects.'[58] The varying degrees of proficiency in any one language make it difficult to judge where on the scale of understanding a person should be situated.[59]

According to the Appeals Chamber (AC) in the case of *Germain Katanga*, the accused person fully understands and speaks a language when he is completely fluent in the language in ordinary, non-technical conversation.[60] Understanding based on legal or judicial training is not required. Doubt concerning the linguistic understanding of the accused must be resolved in his favour and his language request in such circumstances should be accommodated.[61]

The AC found that the right to interpretation as set out in Article 67 is an essential component of the right to a fair trial, thus the standard laid down therein is particularly high, higher even than similar provisions at the predecessor ad hoc tribunals – the ICTY and the ICTR – which exclude the word 'fully'.[62] Thus in order to give effect to this higher standard, an accused's request for interpretation into a language other than the Court's language *must be granted* as long as he or she is not abusing his or her rights under Article 67 of the Statute (emphasis added). Whether an accused is acting in bad faith, malingering or abusing the right to interpretation must be decided on a case-by-case basis.[63]

From an idealistic perspective the AC's decision certainly hits the right note. However, the case-by-case determination of whether or not to give effect to this right then introduces a number of scenarios that are not always easy to resolve. These include the need to guarantee the fair trial rights of the accused to receive documents in a language he fully understands, denial of which could impinge on his right to an expeditious hearing. For example, the confirmation of charges hearing in the *Abu Garda* case had to be postponed in order to allow the Prosecutor to provide the suspect with a list of evidence and the statements

58 Namakula 2012, p. 76.

59 *Ibid.*

60 *The Prosecutor v. Germain Katanga*, Judgment on the appeal of Mr Germain Katanga against the decision of Pre-Trial Chamber I entitled 'Decision on the Defence Request Concerning Languages', Appeals Chamber, ICC-01/04–01/07–522, 27 May 2008, para. 3 (hereafter 'Katanga Language Appeal Decision').

61 *Ibid.*

62 Article 21 (Rights of the accused) of the Updated Statute of the ICTY provides that: 'In the determination of any charge against the accused pursuant to the present Statute, the accused shall be entitled to the following minimum guarantees, in full equality: (a) to be informed promptly and in detail in a language which he understands of the nature and cause of the charge against him; ... (f) to have the free assistance of an interpreter if he cannot understand or speak the language used in the International Tribunal. Article 21 of the Statute of the ICTR mirrors this provision.

63 Katanga Language Appeal Decision, para. 60.

of witnesses in Arabic, the suspect's native language.[64] In the *Katanga* case, following the remittance to the Pre-Trial Chamber by the Appeal Chamber for the language issue to be determined, the Single Judge decided that a thorough factual determination of whether Germain Katanga's competence in French had reached the exact level of 'fully understands and speaks' as defined by the Appeals Chamber would effectively delay the pending confirmation of charges proceedings.[65] Thus the decision was made to proceed and to allow Germain Katanga to continue to have whispering interpretation in Lingala, the language he indicated that he fully understood, even though there were indications that he had a reasonable understanding of French.[66]

5.1. PARTIAL OR UNLIMITED TRANSLATION

The right to translation has been much more circumscribed. ICC Judges have ruled that the accused is not entitled to unlimited translation of every document- an approach which is consistent with the jurisprudence of the international tribunals and human rights bodies.[67] Thus where former President

---

64 *The Prosecutor v. Bahir Idriss Abu Garda*, Decision on the Prosecutor's Requests for Extension of Time-Limit, ICC-02/05-02/09-98, 11 September 2009. See also War Crimes Research Office, *Expediting Proceedings at the International Criminal Court*, June 2011, p. 59, available at: https://www.wcl.american.edu/warcrimes/icc/documents/1106report.pdf.

65 *The Prosecutor v. Germain Katanga and Mathieu Ngudjolo Chui*, Decision Implementing the Appeals Chamber Judgement concerning Languages, ICC-01/04-01/07-539, 2 June 2008.

66 *Ibid.*

67 *The Prosecutor v. Laurent Gbagbo*, Decision on Mr Gbagbo's request for translation and an extension of time for the filing of a response to the document in support of the appeal, ICC-02/11-01/11-489 (hereafter 'Gbagbo Translation Appeal') where the judges opined that '[t]here is no general requirement that filings of parties and participants submitted in English be translated into French, or vice versa, or that time limits begin to ran from the notification of decisions or orders in both working languages of the Court'. This is also confirmed with respect to the language which a suspect fully understands and speaks by the wording of regulation 40(6) of the Regulations of the Court, which provides that '[t]he Registrar shall ensure translation into the language of the [suspect], if he or she does not fully understand or speak any of the working languages, of all decisions or orders in his or her case. Counsel shall be responsible for informing that person of the other documents in his or her case.' For jurisprudence from the ECtHR see *Kamasinski v. Austria*, where the ECtHR found no breach of the Convention where 'all essential points of the indictment, of the witnesses' depositions, of the contents of the documents read out in court as well as of the judgment, including its reasoning' were translated. See generally *Kamasinski v. Austria*, 9783/82, 1989; *Husain v. Italy*, 18913/03, 2005; *Hermi v. Italy*, 18114/02, 2006; *Diallo v. Sweden* 13205/07, Admissibility Decision, 2010. For jurisprudence from the ICTY and ICTR see *Prosecutor v. Tolimir*, Decision on Interlocutory Appeal against Oral Decision of the Pre-Trial Judge of 11 December 2007, IT-05-88/2-AR73.1, 28 March 2008, para. 15; *Prosecutor v. Karadzic*, Decision on Interlocutory Appeal of the Trial Chamber's Decision on Prosecution Motion Seeking Determination that the Accused Understands English, IT-95-5/18-Ar73.3, 4 June 2009, paras. 2 and 18; and *Prosecutor v. Praljak*, Decision on Praljak's Request for Stay of Proceedings, IT-04-74-A, 27 June 2014, paras. 14-16. In all three decisions the Chamber reiterated that the obligation to provide translations in a language the accused understands

of Côte d'Ivoire, Laurent Gbagbo, requested that the AC delay its consideration of the appeal against confirmation of charges until he had received the French translation of several decisions and the Prosecution's appeal brief, the AC ruled that none of the documents were necessary to meet the requirements of fairness.[68] The judges also took into account the fact that the defence team had demonstrated its ability to respond to filings in English in the past and thus were in a position to properly advise Mr Gbagbo.[69]

Full translations inevitably require significant time and resources and depending on the language could greatly delay proceedings. Thus in the case of *Abdallah Banda*, the Prosecution proposed to disclose partial translations of witness statements and summaries to the defence given the practical challenges of translating in Zaghawa. The Prosecution argued that a pragmatic approach should be taken to the entire process in order to avoid extensive delays. The defence contended that challenges notwithstanding, the accused had an entitlement to full compliance with the terms of Article 67.

Pragmatism or fairness, which should prevail? Where the Prosecution proposes to do partial translations of witness statements or summaries at the trial stage of a case this tends to raise a red flag. Even with the most accurate translations there are serious risks that key information and nuances get 'lost in translation' particularly in languages such as Zaghawa, which is unwritten and has a limited vocabulary.

The Trial Chamber in the *Banda* case agreed with the defence that in the interest of fairness, signed witness statements and not summaries should be provided to the defence, even where these would need to be transcribed from previous audio-visual recordings.[70] The judges noted that:

> Although the defence accepted to receive disclosure in summary form at the confirmation stage, the rights of the accused enshrined in the Statute and the Rules require the disclosure of fully translated (signed) statements in a language the accused fully understand. The accused cannot be expected to accept a limitation of their statutory rights simply because they were previously willing to cooperate in order to assist the expedient conduct of the confirmation proceedings. Rule 76(3) of the Rules confers upon the accused the right to disclosure of the witness statements as opposed to summaries prepared by the prosecution. At this trial stage, the defence

---

extends only to 'relevant material' and that the determination of which translations are necessary should be decided on a case-by-case basis.

68 Gbagbo Translation Appeal, para. 12.

69 *Ibid*, para. 13.

70 *The Prosecutor v. Adallah Banda Abakaer Nourain and Saleh Mohammed Jerbo Jamus*, Order on translation of witness statements, Trial Chamber IV, ICC-02/05-03/09-199, 16 August 2011; *The Prosecutor v. Adallah Banda Abakaer Nourain and Saleh Mohammed Jerbo Jamus*, Reasons for the Order on translation of witness statements (ICC-02/05-03/09-199) and additional instructions on translation (ICC-02/05-03/09-214), Trial Chamber IV, 12 September 2011.

has not waived this right and therefore translations of the witness statements, as specified above, should be provided.

The AC reversed the decision but confined itself to the narrow issue of whether there was a legal obligation on the Prosecutor to provide signed narrative statements alongside audio or video recordings of the person's statement.[71] The AC decision did not resolve the issue of whether the provision of summaries at the trial phase would be unfair to the defence.[72]

The fact is that the requirement of full translation can significantly lengthen trial proceedings. It has taken almost four years for the Prosecution to translate and disclose the relevant witness statements to the defence in the *Banda* trial and more challenges are in sight. Issues such as these are likely to recur since the ICC will continue to investigate in situations in which lesser-known languages are utilised. But pragmatic solutions can lead to unfair trials.

In an effort to resolve the issue, ICC Judges presented three proposals for amending the relevant provisions in the RPE namely Rules 76(3), 101(3) and 144(2)(b) to the Study Group on Governance, a group established by the Assembly of States Parties (ASP) to review the levels of efficiency at the Court.[73] An amendment to Rule 76(3) was proposed which would allow the Court to authorise partial translations of prosecution witness statements, where such partial translations would not infringe the rights of the accused.[74] The proposed amendment to Rule 144(2)(b) concerned the partial translations of decisions of the Court and the proposed changes to Rule 101(3) would allow the Court to delay the commencement of time limits of certain decisions until their translations were notified.[75] According to the judges changes to Rule 76(3) were initiated because the provision of full translations of witness statements were becoming 'unwieldy' and creating extensive delays in Court proceedings. The proposed changes were expected to grant judges greater flexibility in decision-making which would 'balance considerations of fairness and expediency'.[76]

---

71 *The Prosecutor v. Abdallah Banda Abakaer Nourain and Saleh Mohammed Jerbo Jamus*, Judgment on the appeal of the Prosecutor against the decision of Trial Chamber IV of 12 September 2011 entitled 'Reasons for the Order on translation of witness statements (ICC-02/05-03/09-199) and additional instructions on translation', ICC-02/05-03/09-295, Appeals Chamber, 17 February 2012, paras. 1–2, 21 and 22.

72 *Ibid.*

73 See *Report of the Bureau on Study Group on Governance*, ICC-ASP/13/28, November 2014, Annex I, paras. 4–12.

74 *Ibid*, para. 4.

75 *Ibid*, para. 5. The proposed amendment to Rule 101(3) is actually one that works very much in the accused's favour. The judges explained that the proposed amendment was drafted in response to the ad hoc practice of extending time limits where translations of certain decisions were deemed necessary. The amendment would clarify that time would begin to run from the moment of notification of the translation. This would in principle give the accused considerably more time and force the LSS to ensure that documents are translated in a timely manner.

76 *Report of the Bureau on Study Group on Governance*, Annex I, para. 5.

Not surprisingly, the proposals generated fervent debate and opposing views. The detractors felt that the removal of the right to full translations would place additional pressure on the accused's counsel to make such translations since he is tasked with ensuring the full preparation of the defence case.[77] Thus rather than being an efficiency measure, the proposal would shift costs to the defence which would adversely affect the rights of the accused. Furthermore there were concerns about who was best suited to determine which of the 'relevant parts' of a statement should be translated to ensure fairness.[78] At the time of writing no decision had been taken by the Assembly on the proposed amendments.

Balancing the right to fairness and expeditiousness is difficult for every justice institution. The proposed judicial amendments are said to be aimed at codifying what already obtains in practice and facilitating consistency of approach among judges. However, the proposals touch on two very sensitive issues – fairness and efficiency – and it is likely to prove difficult to achieve consensus on these issues among states at the ASP level. In the absence of rule changes, the Court will have to continue with a case-by-case approach to dealing with language-related challenges. Nevertheless it is possible to learn key lessons from the *Banda* case namely: the importance of discussion and hopefully agreement between the Prosecution and defence concerning which statements do not require full translations at the trial stage; collaboration between the Registry and Prosecution concerning sharing of translation resources provided that this does not impinge on the rights of the defence; the need for early anticipation by the Prosecution of the likely translation needs during investigations and commencement of the process from that stage; and finally a creative and proactive approach by the Trial Chamber to ensuring fairness without compromising the expeditiousness of proceedings.

6. VICTIMS' LANGUAGE RIGHTS

One of the major innovations at the ICC is the right of victims to participate in proceedings before the Court. Victims at the ICC may be allowed to present their views and concerns at appropriate stages of proceedings where their personal interests have been affected and in a manner that is not prejudicial to or inconsistent with the rights of the accused and a fair trial.[79] There are no

---

77 *Ibid*, para. 11.

78 *Ibid*, para. 10.

79 Article 68(3) Rome Statute. Rule 85 of the ICC Rules of Procedure and Evidence defines victims as natural persons who have suffered harm as a result of the commission of any crime within the jurisdiction of the Court. Victims may include organisations or institutions that have sustained direct harm to any of their property which is dedicated to religion, education, art or science or charitable purposes, and to their historic monuments, hospitals and other places and objects for humanitarian purposes.

specific provisions in the Rome Statute or Rules of Procedure giving victims the right to use their own language or to interpretation and translation. However, it can be argued that the formal codification of victims' right to participate in Article 68 of the Statute implies a corresponding positive obligation on the part of the Court to take steps to give effect to those rights.

With the ICC's current focus in Africa, all of the victims before the Court and a significant number of witnesses are Africans many of whom speak only local languages and not the official languages of the Court. The Court makes allowances for victims who cannot speak any of the working languages to apply to participate in a language other than English or French. They are advised to contact the Court or Field Offices for assistance, although the Court warns that it may not have translators who can translate into all languages.[80] In practice most victims are assisted by intermediaries with their initial application to participate in proceedings before the ICC.

Victims are free to choose a legal representative to communicate with the Court on their behalf. That person is required to be fluent in one of the Court's working languages and can represent the victims' interests even where the victims do not speak any of the working languages.[81] Unrepresented victims may file documents in a language other than English or French if they do not have sufficient knowledge of a working language of the Court or any other language authorised by the Chamber or the Presidency.[82] There are however no clear provisions or guidelines on victims' rights to translation and interpretation at the ICC.

The European Union Directive on the minimum standards on the rights, support and protection of victims of crime is an instructive document which could provide useful insight for the ICC concerning the rights of victims to translation and interpretation.[83] The Directive forms an essential part of a horizontal package of measures, launched by the European Commission in May 2011, aimed at strengthening the rights of victims of crime so that any victim can rely on the same basic level of rights, whatever their nationality and wherever in the EU the crime takes place.[84]

---

80 See ICC Booklet, *Victims before the International Criminal Court, A guide for the participation of victims in the proceedings of the Court*, p. 21, available at: http://bit.ly/1iLl0YD.

81 Rule 22(1) and Rule 90 ICC Rules of Procedure and Evidence.

82 Regulation 39 Regulations of the Court.

83 See Directive 2012/29/EU of the European Parliament and of the Council of 25 October 2012 establishing minimum standards on the rights, support and protection of victims of crime, and replacing Council Framework Decision, 2001/220/JHA.

84 See *DG Justice Guidance Document related to the transposition and implementation of Directive 2012/29/EU of the European Parliament and of the Council of 25 October 2012 establishing minimum standards on the rights, support and protection of victims of crime, and replacing Council Framework Decision 2001/220/JHA*, December 2013, available at: http://ec.europa.eu/justice/criminal/files/victims/guidance_victims_rights_directive_en.pdf. (hereinafter 'DG Justice Guidance Document').

The Directive provides for victims to make a complaint in a language they understand.[85] To that end, they have the right to 'linguistic assistance' from the authorities free of charge, a notion that is sufficiently flexible to allow the victim to receive assistance from someone who speaks his/her language but who is not an official interpreter if this is deemed appropriate by the competent authorities.[86] Victims also have the right to request a translation of a written acknowledgement if they do not understand the language of the document. This translation must be provided free of charge in any language the victim understands (which does not necessarily mean the victim's mother tongue).[87]

The right to translation and interpretation is provided under Article 7 of the Directive. Only victims with a formal role in the proceedings have a right to interpretation. The assistance must be given free of charge and for a broad set of procedural actions from interaction with investigative and judicial authorities from first contact throughout investigation to trial. Victims also have the right to translation of information essential to the exercise of their rights.[88]

In practice, and with the assistance of intermediaries and legal representatives, victims of ICC crimes are able to communicate with the Court. Indeed, the Court has taken bold unprecedented steps to actualise the participatory rights of victims. However, the absence of clear guidelines on victims' rights to translation and interpretation is a challenge that could negatively impact other participatory rights. Formalising the right of victims and witnesses to linguistic assistance, interpretation and translation at all stages of proceedings is a further important step that should be taken by the Court.

7. LANGUAGES AND COMPLEMENTARITY

The ICC's approach to multilingualism in its proceedings could potentially benefit national courts in ICC situation countries, a type of positive complementarity. Complementarity refers to the shared approach to justice between the ICC and national courts whereby the latter retains the primary obligation to investigate and prosecute serious crimes and the ICC intervening only where the state is unwilling or unable to do so.[89] The phrase 'positive complementarity' was first coined by the ICC OTP in its 2009–2012 Prosecutorial Strategy to refer to a proactive policy of cooperation aimed at promoting national proceedings.[90]

---

85 See Directive 2012/29/EU, Article 5.
86 *Ibid.*
87 See DG Justice Guidance Document, Article 7 discussion.
88 *Ibid.*
89 See Preamble to the Rome Statute of the ICC.
90 ICC, *OTP Prosecutorial Strategy 2009–2012.*

National courts struggle with insufficient resources to guarantee access to interpretation and translation in multilingual contexts.[91] Even in countries in which multiple languages are spoken, judicial proceedings are often only conducted in one official language. Poor defendants and victims who communicate in local languages are often disproportionately placed at a disadvantage because of the lack of access to interpretation.[92]

Interpreters and translators trained by the ICC may be able to contribute to building a culture of and respect for interpretation in national courts. Unfortunately most national courts lack the resources of the ICC and would find it difficult to sustain this facility. Nevertheless, for ICC states parties attention and resources must be directed to ensuring effective translation and interpretation in order to ensure fairness of proceedings consistent with international standards.

Outreach is also one of the key ways for the Court to have a lasting impact on the affected communities. Communication in the local language is a very important tool for bridging the gap between the Court and the local population and ensuring that there is understanding about the ICC's role. The Court last produced an Outreach Report in 2010, detailing some of its activities to build relationships with local communities.[93] These included interactive weekly radio programmes presented in the local language, including Lingala, Swahili and Sango, predominantly spoken in the areas of operation. To date, outreach sessions have targeted a significant number of people in rural areas of several situation countries with no access to the Internet, phones or the printed press.[94]

As the Court evolves and learns from past errors such as being too focused in The Hague and dedicating insufficient resources to its field offices, important changes are being made to ensure greater field presence. Under the so-called Registry Revision Project, structural changes are being made to the Registry operations and specific attention is being paid to enhancing the Court's field presence.[95] The OTP has also implemented changes to its investigative approach with more field based focus and longer field missions which will require a more intensive recourse to language skills to enable the integrated teams to interview witnesses and victims, transcribe collected audio-video materials, and translate documents to be used as evidence.[96] Increased field presence will also hopefully lead to greater understanding of the ICC's role.

---

91 See for example in the Ugandan context, Namakula 2014.

92 *Ibid.*

93 See *ICC Outreach Report 2010,* p. 2–3, available at: www.icc-cpi.int/iccdocs/PIDS/publications/OUR2010Eng.pdf.

94 *Ibid.*

95 See *Report on the review of the organizational structure of the Registry Outcomes of Phase 4 of the ReVision Project Decisions on the structure of the Registry,* ICC-ASP/14/18, May 2015.

96 Proposed Programme Budget for 2016 of the International Criminal Court, ICC-ASP/14/10, September 2015, para. 170. See also *OTP Strategic Plan 2016–2018,* available at: www.icc-cpi.int/iccdocs/otp/070715-OTP_Strategic_Plan_2016–2018.pdf.

The ICC is understandably unable to engage directly in building capacity of local courts through training of court personnel. However through the training of interpreters and translators for ICC proceedings, recruitment and training of local staff for field operations, and sharing of best practices, the Court can contribute positively to ensuring that the right to interpretation and translation can also be realised in proceedings before national courts.

8. CONCLUSION

The diversity of languages in international criminal proceedings is a reflection of the global consensus towards closing the impunity gap for perpetrators of atrocity crimes. The ICC is the tangible realisation of this global consensus, mandated to investigate the most serious crimes of concern to the international community as a whole. Given the scope of its mandate and jurisdictional span, the ICC must deal with multiple defendants and victims and thus a multiplicity of languages. Defendants are entitled to accurate translation and interpretation if they do not understand and speak the language of the proceedings as part of their fundamental due process rights. Yet the Court finds itself struggling to balance the right to ensure fair proceedings and the right to be tried without delay. By virtue of the participatory rights enshrined in the Statute, victims also implicitly have the right to access language services at the Court and should be fully informed of this. All of this comes at a cost. Ensuring effective translation and interpretation services at the Court requires the allocation of considerable resources on an annual basis. While there is need for the ICC to be prudent money managers, inadequately resourced language services at the ICC could ultimately prove to be far more costly in the long term. That said, given the relative level of uncertainly concerning the number of and frequency with which the Court will need to utilise situational languages, outsourcing of translation needs will continue to remain one of the most pragmatic solutions to its language dilemma. Ultimately, in order for the ICC to meet its diverse multilingual needs, both pragmatism and fairness are required.

BIBLIOGRAPHY

BOOKS AND JOURNAL ARTICLES

Dubuisson et al. 2009

Dubuisson, M. et al., 'Contribution of the Registry to greater respect for the principles of fairness and expeditious proceedings before the ICC', in Stahn, C. and Sluiter, G. (eds.), 'The Emerging Practice of the International Criminal Court', Martinus Nijhoff, 2009.

Hlophe 2004
Hlophe, J.M., 'Receiving justice in your own language the need for effective court interpreting in our multilingual society', 17(1) Advocate, 2004.
Karton 2008
Karton, J., 'Lost in Translation: International Criminal Tribunals and the Legal Implications of Interpreted Testimony', 41 Vanderbilt Journal of Transnational Law, 2008.
Namakula 2014
Namakula, C., 'Language and the right to a fair hearing in International Criminal Trials', Springer, 2014.
Namakula 2014
Namakula, C., 'Language Fair Trial Rights in the Uganda Criminal Justice System', 20 East African Journal of Peace and Human Rights, 2014, pp. 122–151.
Namakula 2012
Namakula, C., 'Language in the Minimum Guarantees of Fair Trial', 19 International Journal of Speech, Language and the Law, 2012, pp. 74–93.
Swigart 2015
Swigart, L., 'African Languages in International Criminal Justice: the International Criminal Tribunal for Rwanda and Beyond', in Jalloh, C.C. and Marong, A.B.M. (eds.), 'Promoting Accountability Under International Law for Gross Human Rights Violations: Essays in Honour of Prosecutor Hassan Bubacar Jallow', Brill Nijhoff, 2015.
Tomic and Beltran Montoliu 2013
Tomic, A. and Beltran Montoliu, A., 'Translation before the International Criminal Court', 4 New Trends in Translation Studies (Legal Translation in Context), 2013.
Wald 2002
Wald, P., 'Dealing with Witnesses in War Crime Trials: Lessons from the Yugoslav Tribunal', 5 Yale Human Rights and Development Law Journal, 2002.

JURISPRUDENCE

ECtHR 2010
ECtHR, Diallo v. Sweden, Application no. 13205/07, 5 January 2010.
ECtHR 2006
ECtHR, Hermi v. Italy, Application no. 18114/02, 18 October 2006.
ECtHR 2005
ECtHR, Husain v. Italy, Application no. 18913/03, 24 February 2005.
ECtHR 1989
ECtHR, Kamasinski v. Austria, Application no. 9783/82, 19 December 1989.
ICC 2014
ICC, Prosecutor v. Thomas Lubanga Dyilo, ICC-01/04-01/06-3121-Red, 1 December 2014.
ICC 2013
ICC, Prosecutor v. Laurent Gbagbo, ICC-02/11-01/11-489, 22 August 2013.

ICC 2012
ICC, Prosecutor v. Adallah Banda Abakaer Nourain and Saleh Mohammed Jerbo Jamus, ICC-02/05-03/09-299, 20 February 2012.
ICC 2012
ICC, Prosecutor v. Adallah Banda Abakaer Nourain and Saleh Mohammed Jerbo Jamus, ICC-02/05-03/09-295, 17 February 2012.
ICC 2011
ICC, Prosecutor v. Adallah Banda Abakaer Nourain and Saleh Mohammed Jerbo Jamus, ICC-02/05-03/09-214, 12 September 2011.
ICC 2011
ICC, Prosecutor v. Adallah Banda Abakaer Nourain and Saleh Mohammed Jerbo Jamus, ICC-02/05-03/09-131, 14 April 2011.
ICC 2010
ICC, Prosecutor v. Thomas Lubanga Dyilo, ICC-01/04-01/06-T-247-Red-ENG CT WT, 16 February 2010.
ICC 2009
ICC, Prosecutor v. Bahir Idriss Abu Garda, ICC-02/05-02/09-98, 11 September 2009.
ICC 2008
ICC, Prosecutor v. Germain Katanga and Mathieu Ngudjolo Chui, ICC-01/04-01/07-539, 2 June 2008.
ICC 2008
ICC, Prosecutor v. Germain Katanga, ICC-01/04-01/07-522, 27 May 2008.
ICTY 2014
ICTY, Prosecutor v. Praljak, IT-04-74-A, 27 June 2014.
ICTY 2009
ICTY, Prosecutor v. Karadzic, IT-95-5/18-Ar73.3, 4 June 2009.
ICTY 2008
ICTY, Prosecutor v. Seselj, IT-03-67-T, 15 July 2008.
ICTY 2008
ICTY, Prosecutor v. Tolimir, IT-05-88/2-AR73.1, 28 March 2008.

TREATIES, LEGISLATION AND AGREEMENTS

Directive 2012/29/EU of the European Parliament and of the Council of 25 October 2012 establishing minimum standards on the rights, support and protection of victims of crime, and replacing Council Framework Decision 2001/220/JHA.
European Convention on Human Rights, 4 November 1950.
International Covenant on Civil and Political Rights, GA Res. 2200A (XXI), 16 December 1966.
International Criminal Court, Regulations of the Registry, ICC-BD/03-01-06-Rev.1, 6 March 2006.
International Criminal Court, Rules of Procedure and Evidence, ICC-ASP/1/3 (Part II-A), 9 September 2002.
International Criminal Tribunal for Rwanda, Rules of Procedure and Evidence, UN Doc. ITR/3/REV.1, 29 June 1995.

International Criminal Tribunal for the former Yugoslavia, Rules of Procedure and Evidence, UN Doc. IT/32, 11 February 1994.
Protocol on Amendments to the Constitutive Act of the African Union, 11 July 2003.
Rome Statute of the International Criminal Court, 2187 UNTS 90/37, 17 July 1998.

OTHERS

Africa Legal Aid, 'ICC Alert – The Registrar's Questionable Revision Project', 15 July 2015.
Africa Ranking, 'Top Ten Most Spoken Languages in Africa'.
Assembly of State Parties to the Rome Statute of the ICC, 'Report of the Bureau on Study Group on Governance', ICC-ASP/13/28, November 2014.
Black's Law Dictionary.
DG Justice, Guidance Document related to the transposition and implementation of Directive 2012/29/EU of the European Parliament and of the Council of 25 October 2012 establishing minimum standards on the rights, support and protection of victims of crime, and replacing Council Framework Decision 2001/220/JHA, December 2013.
Evenson, E., 'Budget cuts challenge the ICC', Genocide Watch, 7 August 2015.
History, 'Nuremberg Trials', 2010.
ICC, List of 'The States Parties to the Rome Statute'.
ICC, Office of the Prosecutor, Prosecutorial Strategy 2009–2012, 1 February 2010.
ICC, Office of the Prosecutor, Strategy Plan 2016–2018, 6 July 2015.
ICC, 'Outreach Report 2010', 2010.
ICC, 'Proposed Programme Budget for 2016 of the International Criminal Court: Executive Summary', ICC-ASP/14/10/Add1, 31 August 2015.
ICC, 'Proposed Programme Budget for 2016 of the International Criminal Court, ICC-ASP/14/10, 2 September 2015.
ICC, 'Prosecutor v. Abdallah Banda Abakaer Nourain Case Information Sheet', ICC-PIDS-CIS-SUD-04-006/15_Eng.
ICC, 'Q&A Opening of the Trial of the Ntaganda Case', ICC-PIDS-Q&A-DRC-04-02/06_Eng, 2 September 2015.
ICC, Report on the review of the organizational structure of the Registry Outcomes of Phase 4 of the ReVision Project Decisions on the structure of the Registry, ICC-ASP/14/18, 8 May 2015.
ICC, 'Victims before the International Criminal Court – A guide for the participation of victims in the proceedings of the Court' Booklet.
ICTY, 'Translation and Interpretation at the ICTY'.
International Bar Association, 'First Challenges: An examination of recent landmark developments at the International Criminal Court', ICC-01/04-01/07-2153-AnxC, June 2009.
Language Magazine, 'Africa's Linguistic Diversity', 24 April 2015.
Security Council Press Statement, 'Referral of Syria to International Criminal Court Fails as Negative Votes Prevent Security Council from Adopting Draft Resolution', SC/11407, 22 May 2014.

The Culture Vulture, 'Translation and Interpreting: Legacy of the ICTY, Hague', Kwintessential, 2 April 2013.
War Crimes Research Office, 'Expediting Proceedings before the International Criminal Court', June 2011.

THE ROLE OF THE AFRICAN UNION IN INTERNATIONAL CRIMINAL JUSTICE

Force for Good or Bad?

Godfrey M. Musila

1. INTRODUCTION

With the concretisation and expansion of international criminal justice, intergovernmental bodies other than the United Nations Security Council (UNSC) are increasingly becoming important role players. While African countries have been active at various times in the decisions to establish the International Criminal Tribunals for Yugoslavia (ICTY) and Rwanda (ICTR), the Special Court for Sierra Leone (SCSL) and more recently the proposed Special Court for Central African Republic, the African Union (AU), as a grouping of African states is assuming greater and broader roles in the functioning of the international criminal justice system. With the adoption of the Malabo Protocol on the African Court of Justice and Human Rights, the AU has waded into previously unexplored territory. In the same vein, the AU's role in the creation of the Extraordinary African Chambers for the trial of former Chadian dictator Hissène Habré for alleged torture and crimes against humanity committed in Chad is another example of the AU's expanding forays into the unfolding system of international criminal justice. The voices of various AU organs, in particular the Assembly, Pan-African Parliament and the Peace and Security Council in debates around universal jurisdiction and the International Criminal Court and its work in Africa add to the stack of new forms of engagement.

This contribution locates international criminal prosecutions – at the national and international levels – within a broader context of responses to conflict and associated atrocities. It discusses the evolving roles of the African Union and its various organs – political, deliberative and judicial. The contribution argues that regional and sub-regional bodies have a role to play in international criminal justice: directly in respect of prosecutions at the international and national levels; and indirectly in a number of other ways that has a bearing on international criminal justice. Noting that this involvement by regional and sub-regional bodies in international criminal justice is for the most part novel, it argues that this heralds a new and exciting era of engagement that should contribute to the fight against impunity and by extension to peace and security on the continent. However, the approach adopted (ad hoc, reactive and in some measure antagonistic) and certain measures taken by some of these bodies have the potential of undermining or rolling back gains made so far in the fight against impunity.

The contribution integrates the more traditional mandates of regional bodies – in maintenance of peace and security – into the debate, arguing that some of these functions have relevance for international criminal justice. The contribution argues that while the potential contribution of the regional and sub-regional bodies under discussion cannot be underrated, various factors dictate a reasoned and politically prudent approach that recognises the important – yet in some crucial respects limited ability of these bodies to respond effectively and speedily to international crimes. While suggesting that judicial mechanisms at this level fit within a broadly conceived notion of complementarity in international criminal justice and respond to the imperative of burden sharing with the permanent International Criminal Court in responding to atrocities and international crimes, it argues that it is critical to recognise the legal and practical limitations attendant to their variety of mandates.

2. GLOBAL CONTEXT AND OVERVIEW OF REGIONAL AND SUB-REGIONAL BODIES

In the post-Cold War era, regional and sub-regional bodies have emerged and grown as important players in many spheres of engagement. While the United Nations Security Council (UNSC) has ultimate responsibility in the maintenance of international peace and security under Chapter VII of the UN Charter, the roles of regional and sub-regional organisations in this area has expanded tremendously over the years. Although such a role was already foreseen in Chapter VIII of the UN Charter[1] – albeit subject to the UNSC's overarching mandate[2] – this power remained largely underutilised by regional

1 Article 52(1) of the UN Charter provides that: 'nothing in the present Charter precludes the existence of regional arrangements or agencies for dealing with such matters relating to the maintenance of international peace and security as are appropriate for regional action provided that such arrangements or agencies and their activities are consistent with the Purposes and Principles of the United Nations.'

2 The relevant part of Article 53(1) of the UN Charter provides that 'no enforcement action shall be taken under regional arrangements or by regional agencies without the authorization of the Security Council, with the exception of measures against any enemy state'. For its part, Article 54 of the UN Charter provides that 'the Security Council shall at all times be kept fully informed of activities undertaken or in contemplation under regional arrangements or by regional agencies for the maintenance of international peace and security.'

bodies, including the African Union, until they begun to formulate regional security strategies in the early 1990s.[3] As the UNSC waded into new territory notably by establishing international criminal tribunals to prosecute individuals for genocide, war crimes and crimes against humanity, the range of possible interventionist action under the UN Charter has expanded. By the same token, the potential arenas of action by regional and sub-regional bodies within the Charter framework have expanded accordingly.

At the African level, there has been an increase – perhaps proliferation – of regional and sub-regional mechanisms, respecting both security and human rights in recent years. This is due in part to perceived weaknesses within the global arrangements that have produced weak or inadequate responses to various situations, and in part as a result of the natural process of 're-generation' brought about by new impulses to reform independence-era institutions better attuned to latter-day challenges and to embody principles of democracy, human rights and the rule of law.

For various reasons, the Organisation of African Unity (OAU) – the predecessor of the AU – was a reluctant, sometimes unwilling actor respecting issues of peace, security, and human rights. Over the years, however, in particular with the transition in 2002 from the OAU to the AU, the regional body is increasingly becoming a willing and bolder actor in various conflicts on the continent.[4] At an organisational level, there is today a multiplicity of institutions and peace and security initiatives, all aimed at ensuring greater human security.[5]

The sub-regional bodies – Economic Community of West African States (ECOWAS), East African Community (EAC) and Southern African Development Community (SADC) have become important actors in these spheres. However, the sub-regional bodies or Regional Economic Communities (RECs) as they are commonly known – did not emerge to address common security needs in respective regions. Rather, they have evolved as economic blocs with a clear agenda of economic integration.[6] They subsequently took on peace and security issues and were integrated into the AU's peace and security

3 It is only in 1993 during the 29th OAU Assembly of Heads of State and Government in Cairo that the decision to establish the Mechanism for Conflict Prevention, Management and Resolution was taken. On the emerging relationship between the UNSC and African regional mechanisms, see Murithi, 'Between Paternalism and Hybrid Partnership: the Emerging UN and Africa Relationship in Peace Operations', FES Briefing Paper, May 2007.

4 The AU's mixed record is informed, at some level, by a residual reticence based on old notions of sovereignty and non-intervention. See generally Udombana 2002.

5 The African Union set itself the objective of establishing a comprehensive architecture of peace and security comprising the following structures: (1) Peace and Security Council, (2) Continental Early Warning System, (3) Panel of the Wise, (4) African Standby Force and (5) Special Fund.

6 See generally, the ECOWAS Treaty of 1975, the South African Development Community (SADC) Treaty and the Treaty of the East African Community (EAC).

architecture (APSTA).[7] Some also took on limited human rights mandates insofar as they were considered necessary corollaries of the key objective: pursuing economic development and integration.[8] The third aspect, which is shared with the trend at the AU level reflects that in practice, international criminal justice has not featured prominently, if at all, as an important area of concern in peace and security debates at this level and that conceptually justice appears to be incorrectly pitted – in somewhat absolute terms – against considerations of peace that preoccupy actors at both levels.

Alongside the AU's peace and security architecture, gains by the human rights movement have seen the establishment of regional and sub-regional human rights systems fitted with judicial or quasi-judicial oversight mechanisms vested with varying powers of adjudication including powers to entertain petitions from individuals alleging human rights violations.[9] The African Charter on Human and Peoples' Rights adopted in 1981 anchors the African human rights system[10] and is now complemented by several other regional human rights treaties (some of which create implementing bodies) and the emerging sub-regional frameworks of human rights protection and the fight against impunity.[11]

The remaining sections in this contribution interrogate the relevance of the AU to the fight against impunity and international criminal justice in particular. It considers the political, deliberative and judicial organs, and also discusses generic themes in respect of which the AU's role has emerged and is likely to take root. I argue that with the concretisation and expansion of international criminal justice, intergovernmental bodies such as the AU are increasingly becoming important role players. With the adoption of the Malabo Protocol on the African Court of Justice and Human Rights in June 2014,[12] the AU has controversially waded into previously unexplored territory. In the same vein, its role in the creation of the Extraordinary African Chambers to try former

7 See Article 3(l) AU Constitutive Act. For general readings on the place of sub-regional bodies within the AU's peace and security framework see Hammerstad 2003/4; Ajayi, 'The UN, the AU and ECOWAS – A Triangle for Peace and Security in West Africa?', FES Briefing Paper 11 November 2008; Makinda and Okumu 2007.

8 Viljoen 2007.

9 For an overview, see generally Akokpari and Zimbler 2008; Viljoen 2007; and Nmehielle 2001.

10 The African Charter on Human and Peoples' Rights, OAU Doc CAB/LEG/67/3 Rev 5 was adopted in June 1981 and entered into force in October 1986.

11 See two relevant protocols of the Great Lakes Pact signed by seven countries: Protocol on the Prevention and Suppression of Sexual Violence Against Women and Children (Sexual Violence Protocol) and Protocol on the Prevention and Punishment of the Crimes of Genocide, War Crimes and Crimes Against Humanity.

12 Protocol on Amendments to the Protocol on the Statute of the African Court of Justice and Human Rights Adopted at Malabo, Equatorial Guinea, 27 June 2014, available at: http://au.int/en/treaties/protocol-amendments-protocol-statute-african-court-justice-and-human-rights.

Chadian dictator Hissène Habré for alleged torture and crimes against humanity committed in Chad is another example of unprecedented action and evidences the AU's expanding forays into the unfolding system of international criminal justice. As discussed in greater detail elsewhere in this chapter, the voices of various AU organs, in particular the Assembly, Pan-African Parliament and the Peace and Security Council in debates around universal jurisdiction and the ICC and its work in Africa add to the stack of new forms of engagement.

This contribution locates international criminal prosecutions – at the national and international levels – within a broader context of responses to conflict and associated atrocities. I argue that the AU has a role to play in international criminal justice: directly in respect of prosecutions at the international and national levels; and indirectly in a number of other ways that has a bearing on international criminal justice. I integrate the more traditional mandates of regional bodies – in maintenance of peace and security – into the debate, arguing that some of these functions have relevance for international criminal justice. The contribution argues that while the potential contribution of the AU under discussion cannot be underrated, various factors dictate a reasoned and politically prudent approach that recognises the important – yet in some crucial respects limited – ability of the AU to respond effectively and speedily to international crimes. While suggesting that judicial mechanisms at this level fit within a broadly conceived notion of complementarity in international criminal justice and respond to the imperative of burden sharing with the International Criminal Court, it argues that it is critical to recognise the legal and practical limitations attendant to their variety of mandates.

3. THE ROLE OF THE AU'S POLITICAL AND DELIBERATIVE ORGANS

The transformation of the continental body from the defunct OAU to the AU was said to herald a new dawn on the continent, especially in the protection of human rights.[13] State security and sovereignty over 'human and material resources', rather than the realisation of human rights, informed calls for African Unity following independence in the late 1950s and 1960s.[14] With the establishment of the OAU in 1963, it was not surprising that human rights were not a prominent feature in the new continental arrangement.[15] Even with the adoption of the African Charter on Human and Peoples' Rights in 1981 as the continent's comprehensive human rights instrument, gross human rights violations remained a key feature in many of Africa's conflict zones. Against this backdrop,

13 Nmehielle 2003.
14 See Nkrumah at p. 163 cited in Ebobrah 2007.
15 See Naldi 1999, for a discussion of the objectives of the OAU.

most of the initial praise lavished on the AU was motivated not only by the fact that it 'represents the start of a new political, judicial and economic organisation of the continent', but also more particularly by the renewed commitment to among others, principles of human rights and the fight against impunity.[16]

Having defined the promotion of peace, security and stability and the promotion and protection of human and peoples' rights as core objectives of the Union, the Constitutive Act of the AU commits member states to a number of fundamental principles including 'respect for the sanctity of human life, condemnation and rejection of impunity'.[17] More broadly, the Act enshrines the principle of humanitarian intervention which is framed as a 'right of the Union to intervene in a Member State pursuant to a decision of the Assembly in respect of grave circumstances, namely: war crimes, genocide and crimes against humanity.'[18] Additionally, the Act provides as one of the objectives of the AU to 'promote and protect human and peoples' rights in accordance with the African Charter on Human and Peoples' Rights and other relevant human rights instruments'.[19]

These principles are meant to inform how the AU functions as an organisation. To give effect to these commitments at the continental level, the Act establishes various organs with diverse mandates, all of which contribute to the common objectives of the Union.[20] As discussed in the following sections, the Assembly of Heads of State and Government, Executive Council (of Ministers), the AU Commission (Secretariat), the Peace and Security Council, Court of Justice and the Pan-African Parliament[21] all have mandates in varying degrees of relevance to the fight against impunity.[22]

As the main regional intergovernmental body – especially one that commits itself to the fight against impunity – the idea that the AU necessarily has a role to play in international criminal justice is not difficult to fathom. When referring the Darfur situation to the Prosecutor of the ICC for investigation, the UNSC invited the Court and the African Union 'to discuss practical arrangements that would facilitate the work of the Prosecutor and of the Court, including the possibility of conducting proceedings in the region'.[23] For his part, the Prosecutor of the ICC, Luis Moreno-Ocampo stated when launching the investigation into crimes in Darfur that:

16 See Packer and Rukare 2002; Nmehielle 2003; Gutto 2002; Udombana 2002.
17 Art. 4(o) AU Constitutive Act.
18 Art. 4(h) AU Constitutive Act.
19 Art. 3(h) AU Constitutive Act.
20 Art. 3 AU Constitutive Act.
21 Arts. 5 and 17 AU Constitutive Act; Protocol to the Treaty Establishing the African Economic Community Relating to the Pan-African Parliament (PAP Protocol) signed in Abuja, Nigeria 1991.
22 See Art. 5 AU Constitutive Act.
23 UNSC Res 1593 (31 March 2005).

> [t]he investigation will require sustained cooperation from national and international authorities. It will form part of a collective effort, complementing African Union and other initiatives to end the violence in Darfur and to promote justice. Traditional African mechanisms can be an important tool to complement these efforts and achieve local reconciliation.[24]

In this statement, the Prosecutor alludes – in a broad and general fashion – to the ways in which the AU can be active in international criminal justice, and in particular the work of the ICC. Taking an expansive view of the possible role of relevant bodies at the AU and sub-regional level, the following sections consider the role of relevant organs in turn. However, the strategies available to these bodies will in large part correspond to the mandates of its various organs. As revealed by the discussions below, these strategies may range from benign diplomatic measures to more invasive sovereignty-breaching military/ humanitarian intervention at the other end of the scale.

As elaborated in detail in the following sections, the contribution conceives an expansive role for political and deliberative organs in international criminal justice at the AU, and their role goes beyond creating and enabling criminal tribunals to punish perpetrators of international crimes. Typically, action by these bodies may be preventive or reactionary, general or specific. In the texts, it appears that the only specific role of intergovernmental organisations such as the AU that is envisaged in the Rome Statute framework is contained in Rule 98(4) of the ICC's Rules of Procedure and Evidence. Rule 98(4) provides that 'the Court may order that an award for reparations be made through the Trust Fund to an intergovernmental, international or national organisation approved by the Trust Fund'. This provision will be scrutinised at a later stage. Other direct roles for intergovernmental bodies such as the AU in the work of the ICC and international criminal justice broadly could only be derived by interpretation of specific provisions of the Rome Statute and its Rules, as well as treaties establishing those intergovernmental organisations. The Appeals Chamber's recent interpretation of Rule 103 of the Rules of Procedure and Evidence to grant leave to the African Union to file an *amicus curiae* brief making representations on the interpretation of Rule 68 of RPE, which has generated controversy in the case of *Prosecutor v. William Samoei Ruto and Joshua Arap Sang*, is a good example.[25]

---

24 See Press Release, 'The Prosecutor of the ICC opens investigation in Darfur', 6 June 2005, ICC-OTP-0606-104-En, available at: https://www.icc-cpi.int/en_menus/icc/press%20and%20media/press%20releases/2005/Pages/the%20prosecutor%20of%20the%20icc%20opens%0investigation%20in%20darfur.aspx.

25 *The Prosecutor v. William Samoei Ruto and Joshua Arap Sang*, Decision on applications for leave to submit amicus curiae observations pursuant to Rule 103 of the Rules of Procedure and Evidence, Appeals Chamber, ICC-01/09-01/11-1987, 12 October 2015.

More broadly, the ever-increasing willingness of these intergovernmental bodies to engage in preventive diplomacy, peacemaking, peacekeeping[26] and post-conflict peacebuilding has an indirect yet vital bearing on international criminal justice. Peacebuilding, which is understood, in the narrowest sense, to refer to a long-term process that occurs after violent conflict has slowed down or ended and consists of 'a wide range of activities associated with capacity building, reconciliation, and societal transformation.'[27] In this sense, peacebuilding is the phase of the peace process that takes place after peacemaking and peacekeeping. Peacebuilding can also be understood in a broader sense, in reference to a variety of interventionist action and long term transformative efforts, which is not irrelevant for international justice.[28] For purposes of this contribution, the relevance of peacebuilding and related concepts to international criminal justice does not turn on definition. Rather, the brief outline above is meant as an illustration of the wide range of spheres in which regional and sub-regional bodies can intervene in conflict and post conflict societies and it is in this context that we locate international criminal justice. In the following sections, the most relevant interventions are discussed in reference to the main political organs of the AU.

4. THE AU ASSEMBLY OF HEADS OF STATE AND GOVERNMENT AND THE PEACE AND SECURITY COUNCIL

The Assembly of Heads of State and Government (the AU Assembly) which is composed of heads of states and governments or their duly accredited representatives is the governing body of the AU, vested with numerous powers including that to 'determine policies of the Union' and 'receive, consider and take decisions on reports and recommendations from the other organs of the Union'.[29] The Assembly's decisions on a range of issues and initiatives is Within the AU's Framework for a Common African Defence and Security Policy (CADSP)[30] – the Union's strategic plan on peace and security – the Assembly

26 See Haugerudbraaten 1998, who outlines the various dimensions of 'peacebuilding'. See also Paris 1997, p. 55.

27 See Boutros-Ghali 1992. See also Francis et al. 2005, p. 24.

28 According to some accounts, peacebuilding is 'an umbrella concept that encompasses not only long-term transformative efforts, but also peacemaking and peacekeeping. In this regard, peacebuilding entails a number of interventionist mechanisms, irrespective of time dimension and the actors: 'early warning and response efforts, prevention of violence, advocacy work, civilian and military peacekeeping, military intervention, humanitarian assistance, ceasefire agreements, and the establishment of peace zones.' See Malese 2003, available at: www.beyondintractability.org/essay/peacebuilding (accessed on 9 June 2009).

29 Arts. 6(1)–(2) and 9(1)(a) of Constitutive Act of the AU.

30 The Framework for a Common African Defence and Security Policy (CADSP) was formally adopted as the master plan for Africa's search for peace, security and stability on the

works closely with the Peace and Security Council (AU PSC), which serves as the standing decision-making mechanism for the prevention, management and resolution of conflicts.[31] The PSC is also the 'collective security and early-warning arrangement to facilitate timely and efficient response to conflict and crisis situations in Africa.'[32] In terms of Article 2(2) of the AU PSC Protocol, the PSC is to be supported by the AU Commission (secretariat), a Panel of the Wise,[33] a Continental Early Warning System,[34] an African Standby Force[35] and a Special Fund.[36] These institutions, together with arrangements at the Regional Economic Community (RECs) level, jointly constitute what is commonly referred to as the African Union's Peace and Security Architecture (APSA).[37]

The African Standby Force, which derives its legal mandate from the AU Constitutive Act, is worth a special mention.[38] The ASF's policy framework outlines several possible 'conflict and mission scenarios' the AU and the Standby Force are likely to confront. Mission Scenario Six is directly relevant for international criminal justice. The ASF policy foresees the Standby Force's role in 'intervening in genocide situations when the international community does not act promptly'.[39] Article 13 of the PSC Protocol outlines the functions and roles of the ASF, which are, among others 'intervention in a Member State in respect of grave circumstances or at the request of a Member State in order to restore peace and security, in accordance with Article 4 of the Constitutive Act'. Grave circumstances under Article 4 of the AU Constitutive Act relate to situations of 'genocide, war crimes and crimes against humanity'. These provisions make a good entry point into the discussion on the AU's role in international criminal justice.

Continent at the meeting of the AU Assembly of Heads of State and Government in Addis Ababa in July 2004, available at: www.peaceau.org/uploads/declaration-cadsp-en.pdf.

31 Art. 2(1) of Protocol Relating to the Establishment of the Peace and Security Council of the African Union (AU PSC Protocol).

32 *Ibid.*

33 On the Panel of the Wise see Abdellaoui 2009; Nathan, 'Mediation and the African Union's Panel of the Wise', LSE Discussion Paper No. 10, 2005.

34 See generally African Union, *Framework for the operationalization of the continental early warning system*, 2006.

35 Kent and Malan 2003; Alusala 2004; Cilliers and Malan, 'Progress with the African Standby Force', ISS Occasional Paper 98, May 2005.

36 Art. 2(2) AU PSC Protocol.

37 See generally, Powell, 'The African Union's emerging peace and security regime', ISS Monograph 119, May 2005.

38 Art. 4(d) of the Constitutive Act of the AU calls for the establishment of 'a common defence and security policy for the African Continent'.

39 Other mission scenarios are: providing AU/regional military advice to a political mission; performing AU/regional observer missions co-deployed with a UN mission; performing stand-alone AU/regional observer missions; acting as an AU/regional peacekeeping force for Contribution VI and preventive deployment missions and acting as an AU peacekeeping force for complex multidimensional missions with low-level spoilers (a feature of many current conflicts) deployed.

5. PREVENTIVE ACTION AND PREVENTIVE DIPLOMACY

Conflict prevention targets structural sources or root causes of conflict. It can incorporate a variety of elements including early economic, social and development engagement in the relevant country.[40] Depending on context, preventive action aims to prevent: disputes from arising between parties or; existing disputes from escalating into full-blown conflicts and to limit the spread of the latter when they occur.[41] At the UN level, and to an extent at the AU level, intervention has moved from 'preventive diplomacy' to 'preventive action' to accommodate the range of available forms of intervention for purposes of preventing conflict.[42] While diplomacy has been the main political tool for conflict prevention both at the UN and AU level and has been the mainstay of AU activity in Africa's hotspots over the years, other forms of preventive intervention have crystallised: preventive deployments of troops (mainly to contain emerging crisis);[43] preventive disarmament; fact-finding missions (Zimbabwe, Darfur); early warning (Mauritania, Madagascar);[44] inspections, monitoring[45] and peacekeeping. Although peacekeeping missions for the most part are deployed to enforce peace in post conflict situations or situations where conflict has waned (often after a negotiated agreement), peacekeeping was conceived at the AU as part of the expanded mandate of the continental early warning mechanism.

6. PEACEMAKING, PEACEKEEPING AND PEACE ENFORCEMENT

Between the AU and its predecessor the OAU, there have been a number of peacekeeping or observer missions, either on their own or in partnership with the UN. A number of AU deployments have served as precursor for UN-sanctioned missions. The OAU deployed its first military mission, an inter-African force, in Chad in 1981 in an attempt to resolve the conflict in that

40 UN Secretary General Report, *Agenda for Peace*, 1992; Francis et al. 2005, p. 23.

41 *Ibid.*

42 *Ibid.*

43 At the UN level, one example of this form of preventive action is the UN peacekeeping mission in Macedonia (UNPREDEP) in 1995–1999.

44 See AU's Continental Early Warning System (CEWS), as provided for by Article 12 of the Protocol Relating to the Establishment of the Peace and Security Council (PSC).

45 The OAU and AU have sent observer and monitoring missions to a number of countries: Rwanda (OAU Neutral Military Observer Group, ONMOG); Comoros (OAU Observer Mission in the Comoros, OMIC); Congo (OAU Observer Mission in the Democratic Republic of Congo); Comoros (AU Military Observer Mission in the Comoros, MIOC).

country.[46] The OAU was presented another opportunity to intervene in the armed conflict between the Rwandan Government and Rwanda Revolutionary Front rebels. The organisation was able to facilitate peace talks hosted in Arusha (between June 1992 and August 1993) and the deployment of a Neutral Military Observer Group to Rwanda (ONMOG) to secure a buffer zone between the warring parties.[47] The OAU mission ONMOG was replaced by the United Nations Observer Mission Uganda-Rwanda (UNOMUR) and later by the United National Assistance Mission in Rwanda (UNAMIR) created to intervene in the enforcement of the Arusha Peace Agreement in the months preceding the 1994 genocide. Although the two interventions by the OAU in Chad and Rwanda were beset by serious problems, the lack of interest in African conflicts generated by the tragic outcomes of the UN's interventions in Rwanda and later in Somalia emphasised the need for stronger African responses to African conflicts.[48]

Since 2002, the AU has deployed several missions: African Union Mission in Burundi (AMIB); African Union Mission in Sudan (AMIS); AU Mission for Support to the Elections in the Comoros (AMISEC); African Union Mission in Somalia (AMISOM); AU Electoral and Security Assistance Mission to the Comoros (MAES); AU Military Observer Mission in the Comoros (MIOC); and United Nations African Union Mission in Darfur (UNAMID Hybrid force). The Burundi mission in May 2003 consisting of soldiers from South Africa, Ethiopia, and Mozambique was the first to be deployed by the newly transformed AU. The peacekeeping force was mandated to oversee the implementation of agreements signed by various warring parties in Burundi.[49] Since this deployment, a practice is evolving where the AU is disposed to taking timely measures to enforce peace in various situations on the continent. Peacekeepers have since been deployed in Sudan (Darfur), Somalia and Central African Republic.

With respect to Sudan and Somalia, the African Union Mission in the Sudan (AMIS) was set up by the AU PSC following the Addis Ababa Agreement of May 28 2004 to implement the decisions made in response to the situation in Darfur after the signing of the N'djamena Humanitarian Ceasefire Agreement on April 8 2004 between the Government of Sudan and the two rebel movements: the Sudan Liberation Movement/Army and the Justice and Equality Movement.[50] AMIS eventually became the joint AU-UN force UNAMID when the AU handed over the mission to the United Nations on 1 January 2008.[51] On 19 January 2007, the

46 De Coning, 'The Role of the OAU in Conflict Management in Africa, Monograph No. 10, Conflict Management, Peacekeeping and Peacebuilding', April 1997.

47 For a detailed discussion of the OAU intervention in the Rwandan conflict see Khadiagala 2004.

48 See Khadiagala 2004, p. 75 commenting on the US Presidential Decision Directive 25 and the influence of events in Somalia on the UN's intervention in Rwanda.

49 Aboagye 2004.

50 Generally on AMIS, see Appiah-Mensah 2006; Mansaray 2009.

51 On UNAMID see Aboagye, 'The hybrid operation for Darfur: A critical review of the concept', ISS Paper 149, August 2007.

AU PSC established the African Union Mission in Somalia (AMISOM). AMISOM has peacekeeping troops from Uganda and Burundi. On 20 February 2007 the UNSC adopted Resolution 1744, authorising the deployment of AMISOM. The UN supports AMISOM by means of an assistance cell to the AU in Addis Ababa and by providing military planners.[52] In the Central African Republic, the AU took over mission deployed by the Economic Community of Central African States (ECCAS) deployed MICOPAX to secure Bangui, and to protect civilians from attacks by both Seleka and Anti-Balaka. The AU's peacekeeping mission, known by its French acronym *Mission internationale de soutien en Centrafrique* (MISCA)[53] transitioned into MINUSCA, the UN Mission in CAR in 2014.

Both the Sudan (Darfur) and Somalia missions demonstrate the limits of peacekeeping or peace enforcement missions as a measure to intervene in ongoing conflicts to prevent the commission of war crimes and crimes against humanity. The much vaunted 'protect through presence' has not yielded deterrence. Attacks against civilians have continued. The AU peacekeepers themselves sustained fatal attacks in both Darfur (Haskanita) and different parts of Somalia particularly Mogadishu. The tragic killing of ten AU peacekeepers became subject to ICC investigations and indictments in the cases of Abu Garda and Abdallah Banda Abakaer Nourain.[54] A number of commentators have identified weaknesses in AU deployments in both Darfur and Somalia, which if addressed could improve the interventionist value of such missions: limited mandates respecting use of force to protect civilians; lack of resources; inadequacy of the force itself in view of vast geographic areas of operation; uncooperative and hostile host states; and a range of operational difficulties.[55]

Despite these difficulties, the cases of both Darfur and DRC where judicial inquiries into international crimes are ongoing demonstrate the value of peacekeeping missions to the work of courts investigating and prosecuting international crimes – the ICC in both Sudan and DRC, as well as military courts in the latter. In the CAR, MINUSCA (and BINUCA before it) has been instrumental in the documentation of human rights violations while in the DRC, the UN Mission there (MONUC) has been involved in various aspects of

52 Murithi 2008.

53 The deployment of MISCA was authorised by the AU Peace and Security Council on 19 July 2013 and subsequently on 5 December 2013 by the UNSC Res. 2127. See in this regard AU PSC '1er Rapport Intérimaire de la Commission de l'Union Africaine sur la situation en République Centrafricaine et les activités de la Mission Internationale de Soutien à la Centrafrique sous conduite Africaine', available at: www.peaceau.org/fr/article/1er-rapport-interimaire-de-la-commission-de-l-union-africaine-sur-la-situation-en-republique-centrafricaine-et-les-activites-de-la-mission-internationale-de-soutien-a-la-centrafrique-sous-conduite-africaine.

54 On the two cases, *The Prosecutor v. Bahar Idriss Abu Garda* and *The Prosecutor v. Abdallah Banda Abakaer Nourain*, see https://www.icc-cpi.int/en_menus/icc/situations%20and%20cases/situations/situation%20icc%200205/Pages/situation%20icc-0205.aspx.

55 Aboagye 2005; International Crisis Group, *Darfur: Failure to protect: Africa Report No. 89*, March 2005.

the ICC and national courts' work: arresting indicted individuals; documenting commission of crimes and other issues in their area of operation that are of evidentiary value for ICC and prosecutions by military courts; and, crucially, providing security for ICC activities on the ground such as investigations and outreach.[56] In Darfur, where the peacekeeping forces on the ground (AMIS then UNAMID) are very weak, and where the host country has been uncooperative, the ICC (office of the Prosecutor) does not seem to have derived any benefit from the presence of such missions on the ground. After initial permission granted to the ICC Prosecutor by the government was no longer forthcoming, unable to guarantee security for teams on the ground, the Prosecutor has contented himself with gathering information and evidence from refugee camps in Chad rather than in Darfur itself.

While the areas of mutual benefit between the ICC and the peacekeepers in Darfur do not seem to have been explored fully, if at all, the situation demonstrates that the potential role of such missions to protecting civilians and to contribute in various ways to the work of international criminal tribunals and international criminal justice generally depends on various interrelated factors: mandates granted to them; logistical and other capabilities; political will; and pressures wielded by various actors. Revealingly, Khartoum's opposition to a strong force on the ground – in particular initial opposition to the transition of the peace mission from the AU's AMIS to UNAMID – betrayed the government's fear that such a force would strengthen effective protection and the ICC's work in particular. Pointing to the lack of progress by the ICC in Darfur, Aptel rightly concluded that 'international criminal justice does not operate in a political vacuum'.[57]

7. HUMANITARIAN INTERVENTION AND INTERNATIONAL CRIMINAL JUSTICE

The doctrine of humanitarian intervention, although controversial and fraught with uncertainties, can be understood at a basic level to mean the use of force by a state unilaterally, a group of states or an international organisation (multilateral) against a sovereign state for the purpose of protecting human rights in a variety of contexts: internal war, insurgency, repression or state failure in circumstances where the relevant state is unwilling or unable to act to protect civilians from

---

56 For a more detailed discussion of the role of MONUC in promoting justice in the DRC, see Musila, 'Between rhetoric and action: The politics, processes and practice of the ICC's work in the DRC', ISS, 2009, pp. 29–32, available at: http://papers.ssrn.com/sol3/papers.cfm?abstract_id=2379993.

57 On the difficulties encountered by the ICC in its early days in Darfur, see generally Aptel 2006, pp. 20–31.

gross human rights violations.[58] Humanitarian intervention therefore differs from peacekeeping and peace enforcement missions in one important respect: while peacekeeping is a less invasive interventionist mechanism contingent upon consent from the host country, humanitarian intervention is an invasive military intrusion undertaken without the consent of the government.

The controversy surrounding humanitarian intervention and its lack of universal appeal among states and commentators alike arises from: its supposed incompatibility with the foundational notions of sovereignty and non-intervention;[59] selectivity in its invocation;[60] lack of agreement on basic criteria as well as reluctance to embrace such a right even among states with a history of intervention;[61] and the fear among many states, particularly African states, that such a notion provides pretexts for war and aggressive action.[62] Even the attempt to temper the language used and to establish a formal legal framework with clear criteria for interventionist action through the Responsibility to Protect (R2P) initiative[63] has not yielded collective support. Although the R2P norm recast the debate from one that ranges human rights against sovereignty to one in which the responsibility of a sovereign nation to protect its citizens is preeminent, many still wrongly consider R2P to be a euphemism for humanitarian intervention.[64] These doubts persist despite endorsement of R2P by key actors including the AU,[65] the UN General Assembly (UNGA)[66] UN and the UNSC.[67]

---

58 See Murphy 1996, pp. 11–12.

59 See UN Press Release SG/SM/7136, 20 September 1999. Kofi Annan explains that humanitarian intervention presents a 'core challenge to the Security Council and the United Nations as a whole in the next century'. See also Parekh 1997, arguing that humanitarian intervention is logically unstable, because it contradicts the foundational notions of international law.

60 Mayall 2000.

61 See United Kingdom Foreign Office, Policy Document No. 148, reprinted in 1986 British Yearbook of International Law, p. 619. See also Goodman 2006, p. 109, citing reservations by the USA, China and the Netherlands.

62 Generally Goodman 2006; Brownlie 1973, pp. 147–148, noting that humanitarian intervention 'is a general license to vigilantes and opportunists to resort to hegemonial intervention.'

63 On Responsibility to Protect, see International Commission on Intervention and State Sovereignty, *Responsibility to Protect Report*, 2001 and generally, Kindiki, 'Intervention to Protect Civilians in Darfur: Legal Dilemmas and Policy Imperatives', ISS Monograph 131, 1 May 2007.

64 On reservations by AU and G77 states, see Ping, 'Keynote address at the Roundtable high-level meeting of experts on the responsibility to protect in Africa', Addis Ababa, 23 October 2008.

65 See 7th Extraordinary Summit of the Heads of States and Government of the African Union, Ext./EX.CL/2(VII), March 2005 and the 'Ezulwini Consensus' relating to UN reforms. See also African Commission on Human and Peoples' Rights, Resolution on Strengthening the Responsibility to Protect in Africa, 42nd Ordinary Session in Congo Brazzaville, 15–28 November 2007.

66 United Nations Summit Declaration – Outcome Document 2005, paras. 138 and 139.

67 UNSC Res. 1674 (2006) on the Protection of Civilians in Armed Conflict.

Despite the fact that 'international law is currently incapable of providing a clear legal position in respect of the lawfulness of humanitarian interventions',[68] there seems to be near-universal agreement – at least in rhetoric – that the existence of certain circumstances warrants intervention (whether framed as a right or duty): gross human rights violations, genocide, war crimes and crimes against humanity. At the continental level, there is formal collective embrace of the idea of humanitarian intervention, a clear break from OAU's absolutist position on sovereignty and non-intervention. The Constitutive Act of the AU – in fact the only international treaty to expressly provide for humanitarian intervention – enacts for 'the right of the Union to intervene in a Member State ... in respect of grave circumstances, namely war crimes, genocide and crimes against humanity', if it is determined to be necessary by the Assembly of Heads of State and Government.'[69] In the same vein, the AU PSC is to be guided by among other principles, humanitarian intervention in the circumstances mentioned above.[70] While there is lack of precision on the scope of the new principle of humanitarian intervention, it is clear that it is aimed at ensuring that the AU may take interventionist action in situations where grievous harm is threatened or occurs.[71]

A brief survey of postcolonial African history discloses several cases where humanitarian intervention has been invoked. With the exception of Tanzania's foray into Uganda in 1978–79, all these cases have been by Western powers.[72] In more contemporary times, some have cited humanitarian intervention as the 'appropriate' response to the ongoing conflict in Darfur, yet the UN and AU seem to eschew the idea[73] even after the UNSC had invoked it in its important Resolution 1706.[74] It could be argued that apart from demonstrating the limits of the AU's ability to respond to complex conflicts,[75] Darfur also provided an excellent illustration of the limits of humanitarian intervention. The debate around the effectiveness of AMIS and UNAMID peacekeeping forces raised the question as to whether the response by the AU and UN had been adequate

68 Harhoff 2001, p. 107.

69 Art. 4(h) of the Constitutive Act as amended by the Protocol on Amendments to the Constitutive Act of the African Union adopted by the 1st and 2nd Extraordinary Sessions of the AU Assembly on 3 February 2003 and 11 July 2003 respectively.

70 Art. 4(j) Protocol relating to the Establishment of the Peace and Security Council.

71 For a discussion of humanitarian intervention under the AU Constitutive Act, see Kioko 2003; Kuwali 2009; and International Refugee Rights Initiative, 'Some reflections on the legal and political mechanisms bolstering the responsibility to protect: The African Union and the Great Lakes, Eastern, Southern and Horn of Africa sub-regional arrangements', 21 October 2008.

72 See Francis et al. 2005, p. 84, citing interventions by Belgium in Congo (1960); US and Belgium in Congo (1964); South Africa in Angola (1975); Tanzania in Uganda (1978–79); and France in Central Africa (1979).

73 Straus 2005, p. 124.

74 On R2P and Sudan, see Udombana 2005.

75 Grono 2006, p. 624; Mansaray 2009; and International Crisis Group, *Darfur: The Failure to Protect*, Africa Report No. 89, 8 March 2005, which describes AU and UN efforts in Darfur and identifying constraints.

and appropriate.[76] Some discussion occurred around the issue of intervention in Darfur and the application of the Responsibility to Protect (R2P).[77] The debate related not only to the legality of possible action and attendant questions about thresholds for intervention and legitimacy, but also to the willingness of relevant actors to commit financial, political and human resources to effect the mission. Even after the UNSC had referred the Darfur situation to the ICC prosecutor for investigation in 2005,[78] debate continued to rage over whether the atrocities committed amounted to genocide, which would presumably serve to inform humanitarian intervention.[79]

The genocide debate was problematic at two levels. First, it reflected inaccurately that only situations of genocide warrant humanitarian intervention. The contention over whether genocide was happening in Darfur became some kind of crutch for those who were less than positively inclined to take action. Secondly, the debate prevented actors from confronting the real issues by misdirecting (or withholding) efforts that would have gone into fashioning appropriate responses to the humanitarian tragedy. In his commentary, Strauss captured this aptly:

> Darfur has shown that the energy spent fighting over whether to call the events there 'genocide' was misplaced, overshadowing difficult but more important questions about how to craft an effective response to mass violence against civilians in Sudan.[80]

The referral by the UNSC to the ICC itself poses problems of a legal and practical character on broad questions of attribution and responsibility. For our purposes, it disclosed some of the difficult challenges that confront the AU and regional actors such as Inter-Governmental Authority on Development (IGAD) with respect to humanitarian intervention. While some commentators criticised the AU for failing to take more forceful action beyond the deployment of AMIS, legal responsibility rests with the UNSC. The AU's unequivocal formal commitment to intervene in 'grave circumstances' involving genocide, war crimes and crimes against humanity notwithstanding, this critique of the AU ignores the fact that there is a broader international legal framework within which the continental body's role in humanitarian intervention and international peace and security more generally must be considered.

---

[76] See for instance Grono 2006, p. 6–7.

[77] See for instance UNSC Res. 1706 of 2006 regarding the transitioning of UNMIS mandate. While the resolution does not authorise humanitarian intervention, contributions by various representatives of the sitting UNSC members at the time (5519th UNSC Meeting) touched the issue of R2P within the context of Sudanese and UN obligations.

[78] UNSC Res. 1593 (2005), available at: www.un.org/en/ga/search/view_doc.asp?symbol=S/RES/1593(2005).

[79] See generally Prunier 2005. See also relevant parts of the Report of the International Commission of Inquiry on Darfur to the United Nations Secretary General, Pursuant to UNSC Res. 1564 of 18 September 2004, Geneva, 25 January 2005.

[80] Straus 2005, p. 124.

On the broad issue of international peace and security, the UNSC is the primary authorising body for the use of international force, either by itself or by other actors except in the case of self-defence.[81] However, the UN Charter recognises that regional and sub-regional bodies may play a role in international peace and security: it provides that such bodies may undertake enforcement action, but only after authorisation from the UNSC.[82] Article 54 of the UN Charter then establishes a monitoring mechanism, requiring that when regional bodies undertake action, they must keep the Council informed at all times. While the possibility may still exist for regional bodies to take interventionist military action without authorisation, prior action by the UN Council with respect to the same situation removes this possibility.[83] However, in exercise of its Contribution VII powers, it is routine – as in the case of Darfur – for the UNSC to reserve its right to take further action (after initial deliberation or action) to the exclusion of all other actors.[84] With the expansion by the UNSC of the scope of its Contribution VII powers in recent years, the areas where regional bodies can engage on their own appears to have narrowed considerably. It can be argued that while the UNSC referral of the situation in Darfur was justified, it had the effect – especially with the exclusivity claimed by the UNSC – of severely limiting action by the regional and sub-regional bodies.

UNSC inaction – or limited action – after the referral of the Darfur situation to the ICC may be interpreted in various ways.[85] For our purposes, it seems to reflect the misguided, although rather widespread view that the ICC – or any other judicial process for that matter – could be a panacea to the host of difficult questions arising out of the Darfur conflict. The Council's approach – discernible more in its silence than action – not only overstates the role of judicial or quasi-judicial processes in dealing with complex crimes and conflict more broadly, but also underplays the role other responses can and should play in these situations.[86]

81 Art. 24 (1) UN Charter. See also Art. 51 UN Charter.

82 Art. 53(1) UN Charter.

83 The AU itself has acknowledged this limitation, but suggested that regional bodies should be able to intervene without prior UNSC authorisation in 'emergency' situations. See the African Union Executive Council, Common African position on the reform of the United Nations ('Ezulwini Consensus'), 7th Extraordinary session, 7–8 March 2005, recommendation B(i).

84 See Res. 1593, para. 9, in which the UNSC decided 'to remain seized of the matter'. This is a formulation attached to all UNSC resolutions.

85 See Grono, 'The Role of the International Criminal Court in African Peace Processes: Mutually Reinforcing or Mutually Exclusive?', Institute for Public Policy Research Paper, 28 November 2006, p. 629 provides a complex mix of reasons for the lack of bold action in Darfur: national interests (US, China); indecision within the UN; ideology (China, Russia); regional (Arab League); and inability and fear of marginalisation (AU).

86 From a 'justice perspective', it is noteworthy that that UNSC foresaw the creation of truth commission alongside the ICC. It emphasised 'the need to promote healing and reconciliation and encourages in this respect the creation of institutions, involving all sectors of Sudanese society, such as truth and/or reconciliation commissions, in order to complement judicial processes and thereby reinforce the efforts to restore long lasting peace, with African Union and international support as necessary'. See Res. 1593, para. 5.

In making an argument for the important role of humanitarian intervention and other forms of responses in conflict situations, Smith[87] argues rather presciently that legal responses have their limits and that although the ICC is but one facet of international justice, its existence may diminish the possibilities for humanitarian intervention to prevent atrocities. When one considers how the situation in Darfur has unfolded, Smith's observation – although not made in specific reference to Darfur – turns out to be rather prescient.

Since the referral of the situation in Darfur to the ICC, the UNSC seems unwilling to consider or to undertake any other meaningful action, including humanitarian intervention. For their part, the AU's effort – pursuit of alternative justice mechanisms – is constrained in various ways and does not seem to go beyond the legal.[88] The more constructive and appropriate approach in such cases as proposed by Smith, is the parallel development and strengthening of existing political frameworks for intervention to balance the pursuit of international justice.[89] It is argued here that this view captures the multifaceted approach that a broad conceptualisation of international criminal justice should take. The best approach is for 'legal aspects' of international criminal justice to tap into and complement non-legal mechanisms, and vice versa.

The argument here – as is the case in the entire contribution – is not that non-judicial/legal approaches such as humanitarian intervention, peacekeeping, peace negotiation and other forms of interventions should supersede the work of criminal tribunals, whether international, regional or national. The suggestion rather is that an appropriate approach is one that locates the work of such tribunals within their proper context, recognising their strengths and limits. In arguing for the work of tribunals in conflict situations, Grono cites the case of Sudan and Uganda arguing that often, the ICC [will be] 'one of the few credible threats faced by leaders of warring parties'.[90] However, he also recognises that 'fear of prosecution can lead to entrenchment of culpable leaders', and suggests that in the short term, 'the leverage gained by the threat of prosecution has to be weighed against the likely entrenchment of threatened government leaders'.[91] In this regard, it is suggested here that these sorts of calculations must inform those seeking to fashion responses to complex conflict situations, which entail balancing a range of competing goals: those of international and state actors and various interests and objectives of various actors at the national level.

On the strength of these arguments, it is my view that the AU's main failure as regards the ICC in Darfur may not be providing political cover and support for President Al-Bashir, but in failing to seize opportunities presented by the

87 Smith 2002.

88 See *Report of the African Union High Level Panel on Darfur* (AUPD), launched on 8 October 2009.

89 Smith 2002.

90 Grono, 'The Role of the International Criminal Court in African Peace Processes: mutually reinforcing or mutually exclusive?', Institute for Public Policy Research Paper, 2006.

91 *Ibid.*

ICC process to extract desired forms of conduct from Khartoum (for instance, movement on the local justice, cooperation with the ICC, political reform and peace process fronts).[92] Inevitably, many of these situations will boil down to an analysis of imperatives of peace and justice, which often are pitted against each other. Grono argues that interventionist measures in conflict situations should lean towards justice and suggests, usefully, that approaches favouring impunity (such as amnesty) should always be a last resort. This view is consistent with recent developments in international law and national practice in terms of which issues of accountability have gained prominence in post conflict transitional processes.[93]

8. THE AU AND AD HOC COURTS: THE EXTRAORDINARY AFRICAN CHAMBERS IN SENEGAL

The AU's role in the creation of the Extraordinary African Chambers in Senegal to try former Chadian President Hissène Habré for crimes against humanity and torture demonstrate the AU's willingness to play a role in more direct ways in international criminal justice. The case saw the unprecedented involvement of the AU in ordering prosecution of an individual for alleged international crimes in a member state, Senegal exercising universal jurisdiction.[94]

Hissène Habré was first arrested in Senegal in February 2000 on charges of torture stemming from his 1982–1990 rule in Chad. Senegal had initially declined to prosecute him in 2001 after a court ruling dismissing charges brought against him.[95] An extradition request from Belgium in 2005 had been rejected. Confronted with the need to definitively settle the matter – either to try him or extradite him to Belgium or to a third country for trial – Senegal sought 'guidance and direction' from the AU Assembly on the question, in every way a weighty one because of the status of the alleged perpetrator. Keen to assert its voice on the matter, the AU Assembly decided in January 2006 to establish a Committee of Eminent African Jurists' to advise it on how to respond to the Senegalese request.[96] On receiving the report of the Committee, the Assembly

92 See section ahead on the AU and the ICC.

93 Grono, 'The Role of the International Criminal Court in African Peace Processes: mutually reinforcing or mutually exclusive?', Institute for Public Policy Research Paper, 2006, p. 5. See also Seils and Wierda 2005, pp. 1–3, available at: www.ictj.org/images/content/1/1/119.pdf.

94 Williams 2013.

95 Decision of the Indicting Chamber of the Appellate Court of Dakar (République du Sénégal, Cour d'Appel de Dakar, Chambre d'Accusation), Arrêt No. 135 of 4 July 2000.

96 AU HSG Decision on the Hissène Habré Case and the African Union, Doc. Assembly/AU/8 (VI)) Add.9, in Decisions, Declarations and Recommendation of the Sixth Ordinary Session, Khartoum, 23–24 January 2006.

noted that while in its present state the AU had no legal organ competent to try Hissène Habré, the AU 'has jurisdiction' over the matter in terms of provisions in the Constitutive Act relating to the AU's commitment to principles of human rights and the fight against impunity.[97] On this reasoning, the Assembly decided that Habré must be tried on the continent.[98] Pointing to among others, Senegal's obligations as signatory under the UN Convention Against Torture, the Assembly accepted the recommendations of the jurists that a Senegalese court should try Habré. Accordingly, Senegal accepted the Assembly's request to stage Habré's trial on 'the AU's behalf'.[99]

To effect the request, Senegal had to amend its Constitution and adopt a law on universal jurisdiction to provide for the exercise of extraterritorial jurisdiction by its courts – that is, to try torture and crimes against humanity and genocide committed abroad. Senegal also amended its constitution to cushion such action against any claims of unconstitutionality.[100] While the AU's action in ordering Habré's prosecution was rightly celebrated, as it should, by many as one that breathes life in the continental body's commitment to the fight against impunity,[101] there were further twists and turns in the saga over the ensuing years – including a case brought against Senegal by Belgium at the International Court of Justice for the former's inaction[102] – before the Chambers were eventually established, with the AU's participation following the signing of an agreement between the AU and the government (President) of Senegal on 28 December 2012.[103] Habré's trial eventually commenced on 20 July 2015.

97 Arts. 3(h), 4(h) and 4(o) of the AU Constitutive Act.

98 See AU HSG Décision sur le Procès d'Hissène Habré et l'Union Africaine, Assembly/AU/Dec.127 (VII), in Decisions and Declarations of the Seventh Ordinary Session of the Assembly, Banjul (VII).

99 African Union, *Report of Committee of Eminent Jurists.*

100 See AU Assembly Decision on the Trial of Mr Hissène Habré and the African Union, Assembly/AU/Dec.157 (VIII), in Decisions and Declarations of the Eighth Ordinary Session, Addis Ababa, 23–30 January 2007, reporting on Senegal's progress in this regard.

101 See Human Rights Watch, Press Release, 'Ex-Chad Dictator Indicted in Senegal: Hissène Habre, "The African Pinochet", To Face Trial', 3 February 2000. See also weekly statement by President Mbeki noting that the decision to try Hissène in Senegal 'unequivocally demonstrates the determination of the African continent to ensure that our peoples should never again fall victim to tyranny and the denial or violation of their human rights.' ANC Today, Vol. 6, No. 26, 7–13 July 2006, available at: www.anc.org.za/docs/anctoday/2006/at26.htm; Briefing by the Deputy Minister of Foreign Affairs, Ms Sue van der Merwe to the Heads of Mission accredited to South Africa on the Outcomes of the 7th African Union Summit, CSIR International Convention Centre, 14 July 2006, available at: www.dfa.gov.za/docs/speeches/2006/merw0714.htm.

102 ICJ, *Case Concerning Questions Relating to the Obligation to Prosecute or Extradite (Belgium v. Senegal), Request for the Indication of Provisional Measures*, Decision, 28 May 2009.

103 On the Agreement between the African Union, Senegal and the Annexed Statute of the Extraordinary African Chambers, see www.chambresafricaines.org/pdf/Accord%20UA-Senegal%20Chambres%20africaines%20extra%20Aout%202012.pdf.

9. SHAPING THE DEBATE ON IMPORTANT QUESTIONS IN INTERNATIONAL CRIMINAL JUSTICE

In the recent past, particularly as the impact of the work of the ICC has begun to be felt with its mounting caseload, the AU has become increasingly active, even aggressive, in shaping debates in international criminal justice. Nowhere is this more evident than in debates around universal jurisdiction – prompted in part by the Habré case as well as the issuing of arrest warrants against top Rwandan officials in France and Spain – and the work of the ICC in Africa, in particular the indictment of Sudan's President Omar Al-Bashir. The indictment by the ICC of Uhuru Kenyatta and William Samoei Ruto, who would become Kenyan President and Deputy President respectively, reignited debate on immunities of heads of state at the AU and raised new questions on Rule 68 of the ICC's Rules of Procedure and Evidence. These are discussed in turn.

10. UNIVERSAL JURISDICTION DEBATE

Faced with indictments issued by French and Spanish judges against 45 senior military and government officials for their alleged roles in the fatal downing of President Habyarimana's plane in 1994 and other crimes allegedly committed against ethnic Hutus,[104] Rwanda responded in various ways. One response was to launch a public campaign to discredit these actions as an abuse of judicial process for political ends. In so doing, Kigali sought to distinguish these 'political' uses of universal jurisdiction from its 'good' uses, of which Rwanda has been a major 'beneficiary' since the 1994 genocide.[105] To generate political support at the continental level for its position against the arrest warrants considered by Kigali a de-legitimisation campaign against the Rwanda Patriotic Front (RPF) regime, Rwanda had approached the AU's political organs. The PAP was the first to respond by adopting the Johannesburg Declaration on Universal Jurisdiction on 15 May 2008.[106]

---

104 French indictments on 22 November 2006 by Judge Jean-Louis Bruguière, against ten high-ranking Rwandan officials and; Spanish indictments by Judge Fernando Merrelles against forty top military and civilian officials came in February 2008. See Pan-African Parliament, 'Motion for a resolution of Parliament on the concerns by the Republic of Rwanda on the Indictments issued by top civil and military leadership of the Republic of Rwanda', Ninth Ordinary Session of the Pan-African Parliament, 8 May 2009, available at: http://jkanya.free.fr/rwandamotion.pdf (accessed on 15 November 2015). See Contribution Three, Part III.4 in this volume.

105 A number of courts in Belgium, Canada, Switzerland, the Netherlands and Germany have prosecuted numerous cases linked to the 1994 Rwanda genocide.

106 Johannesburg Declaration on Universal Jurisdiction, 15 May 2008. 'Motion for a resolution of Parliament on the concerns by the Republic of Rwanda on the Indictments issued by top

While acknowledging that universal jurisdiction is a 'universally entrenched principle of international law' that could be claimed by a state in cases of torture, war crimes, crimes against humanity and genocide when these crimes are committed outside its boundaries, the PAP made two significant resolutions that kicked off the debate within the AU. First, it condemned the Spanish and French indictments as 'an affront to the sovereignty' of Rwanda and urged that the AU Assembly add its voice in denouncing the action.[107] Second, PAP urged the AU Commission to undertake a study into universal jurisdiction and to take measures to safeguard member states against abuse and misinterpretation of universal jurisdiction.[108]

As the PAP was debating the Rwanda motion, a meeting of AU justice ministers was addressing the same issue in Addis Ababa. The Johannesburg and Addis Ababa meetings resulted in an AU Commission study on universal jurisdiction on the basis of which the now ubiquitous Sharm el-Sheikh Declaration on Universal Jurisdiction was based.[109] Acknowledging both processes, the AU Assembly resolved at Sharm el-Sheikh as follows:[110]

> The abuse of the principle of universal jurisdiction is a development that could endanger international law, order and security … The political nature and abuse of the principle of universal jurisdiction by judges from some non-African States against African leaders, particularly Rwanda, is a clear violation of the sovereignty and territorial integrity of these states … The abuse and misuse of indictments against African leaders have a destabilizing effect that will negatively impact on the political, social and economic development of states and their ability to conduct international relations … Those warrants shall not be executed in African Union Member States … There is need for establishment of an international regulatory body with competence to review and/or handle complaints or appeals arising out of abuse of the principle of universal jurisdiction by individual States.

In an attempt to address concerns over pending and future indictments, the Assembly requested the Chairperson of the AU Commission to arrange a meeting between the AU and EU to discuss the legal and political issues around the exercise of universal jurisdiction and to find 'a lasting solution to the Rwandan indictments'.[111] This has been the most significant resolution in

civil and military leadership of the Republic of Rwanda', moved by Higiro Prosper (Rwanda), seconded by Lassane Sawadogo (Burkina Faso) and Gitobu Imanyara (Kenya).

107 Johannesburg Declaration on Universal Jurisdiction, Resolution 2.

108 *Ibid.*

109 See AU Assembly Decision on the report of the Commission on the abuse of the principle of universal jurisdiction, Doc. Assembly/AU/14 (XI), 1 July 2008 (hereinafter 'Sharm el-Sheikh Declaration'). Available at: http://au.int/en/sites/default/files/decisions/9558-assembly_en_30_june_1_july_2008_auc_eleventh_ordinary_session_decisions_declarations_tribute_resolution.pdf (accessed on 12 November 2015).

110 Sharm el-Sheikh Declaration, Resolution 5.

111 *Ibid*, Resolution 7.

terms of clarifying relevant issues around universal jurisdiction, in particular EU and African practice. An AU-EU Committee of Experts appointed by both sides following Sharm el-Sheikh eventually produced a report aimed at clarifying 'the respective understanding on the African and EU side on the principle of universal jurisdiction'.[112]

The arrest of Rose Kabuye, Chief of Protocol in the Rwandan Presidency in Frankfurt Germany on the strength of an arrest warrant issued by judge Bruguière in France prompted the AU Assembly's response at the close of its 12th Summit in February 2009. The Assembly reiterated its condemnation of the abuse of universal jurisdiction and regretted Rose Kabuye's arrest despite its previous call for a moratorium on pending warrants until discussions were concluded between the EU and the AU on this issue.[113] The Executive Council and the Assembly's 13th Summit meeting in Sirte on 3 July 2009 renewed this call.[114] The AU subsequently adopted a model law on universal jurisdiction, which states were encouraged to adopt.[115] The Extraordinary African Chambers provide an opportunity for practical application of universal jurisdiction with the AU playing a pivotal role in the creation of the internationalised court.

11. BLOWING HOT AND COLD? THE AU AND THE INTERNATIONAL CRIMINAL COURT

Following the indictment of President Al-Bashir in 2008 for war crimes and crimes against humanity, the debate around the work of the Court took a controversial turn. The AU has featured prominently in the debates, which revolved around immunities of heads of states, peace and justice and the role of the UNSC in international criminal justice. The AU forcefully inserted itself into the ICC debate in Sudan, and subsequently in Kenya, where it stood on weaker moral legs and had a weaker case for pushing an argument on immunities, but it became a site for the Kenyan leadership to take swipes at the ICC in the lead up to the trials of Uhuru Kenyatta and William Ruto. The AU Assembly and the

---

112 Report of the African Union-European Union (AU-EU) Technical Ad-hoc Expert Group set up by the Eleventh AU-EU Ministerial Troika (16 April 2009), para. 2, available at: www.africa-eu-partnership.org/sites/default/files/documents/rapport_expert_ua_ue_competence_universelle_en_0.pdf.

113 AU Assembly Decision on the Implementation of the Assembly Decision on the Abuse of the Principle of Universal Jurisdiction. Assembly/AU/3(XII), January 2009.

114 Executive Council, Decision on the Abuse of the Principle of Universal Jurisdiction – Doc. EX.CL/522(XV) available at: http://au.int/en/sites/default/files/decisions/9633-council_en_24_30_june_2009_executive_council_fifteenth_ordinary_session.pdf.

115 African Union (Draft) Model National Law on Universal Jurisdiction over International Crimes (2012) (AU Model Law), adopted by the Meeting of Government Experts and Ministers of Justice/Attorneys General on Legal Matters, 7–15 May 2012, Addis Ababa, Ethiopia.

PSC have been at their most vocal in respect to the situation in Darfur, by far the most controversial and clearly the epicentre of what some have called 'the struggle for the ICC in Africa'.[116]

The controversy hinged in part on the fact that one of the targets of ICC arrest warrants was a serving head of state. In four short years, the AU moved from a stance supportive of the ICC, to a less than enthusiastic and obstructionist posture. Its most famous, and most criticised decision came out of its Sirte Summit in 2009. At the conclusion of its Summit in Sirte on July 1 2009, the AU Assembly decided that 'AU Member States shall not cooperate pursuant to the provisions of Article 98 of the Rome Statute of the ICC relating to immunities, for the arrest and surrender of President Omar Al-Bashir of the Sudan.'[117] The merits of this decision notwithstanding, the AU position with respect to the case against President Al-Bashir – while specific to that case – augurs badly for the future of the ICC, a project for which many struggled for so long to see realised.[118] Yet it was not always like this.

The *double entendre* notwithstanding, the ICC could rightly be regarded as an 'African Court', and a number of commentators have described the important role played by the AU and African states in the negotiations that led to creation of the Court.[119] Since the Court commenced investigations in Uganda, the AU had been supportive of its work, reiterating severally the need to fight impunity on the continent. The AU Assembly and PSC demanded, on a number of occasions, compliance by parties in the Darfur conflict with UNSC Resolutions as well as their own resolutions.[120] In his periodic reports to the UNSC, the ICC prosecutor continues to emphasise the important role the AU can play.[121] However, since the indictment of President Al-Bashir of Sudan in 2008 and arrest warrants issued against him on 4 March 2009 and 12 July 2010,[122] the AU has come under attack as its relationship with the ICC has soured.

---

116 See Odinkalu, 'Saving international justice in Africa', Oxford Transitional Justice Research Working Paper Series, available at: http://africanarguments.org/2009/08/saving-international-justice-in-africa/. Odinkalu argues that international justice was in the midst of a crisis.

117 AU Assembly Decision on the meeting of African States Parties to the Statute of the Rome Statute of the International Criminal Court, Doc. Assembly/AU/13(XIII), Sirte, Libya, 3 July 2009, para. 10.

118 This contribution does not address the merits of Article 98 (and Article 27) of the Rome Statute, which raise complex legal and policy issues. For some initial thoughts on immunities of heads of state before the ICC, see African Union, 'Concept Note For The Meeting of African States Parties to the Rome Statute of the International Criminal Court', 8–9 June 2009, Addis Ababa, Ethiopia; Akande 2009; Gaeta 2009.

119 See Jalloh 2009; Jallow and Bensouda 2008; Mochochoko 2005; and Maqungo 2000.

120 See for instance para. 4(b)(iv) Communiqué of the 46th meeting of the AU Peace and Security Council, 10 March 2006.

121 See various reports of OTP to UNSC, available at: https://www.icc-cpi.int/en_menus/icc/situations%20and%20cases/situations/situation%20icc%200205/reports%20to%20the%20unsc/Pages/reports%20to%20the%20security%20counsel%20of%20the%20united%20nations%20organisation.aspx.

122 See Situation in Sudan, *The Prosecutor v. Omar Hassan Ahmad Al-Bashir*, Warrant of Arrest for Omar Hassan Ahmad Al-Bashir Decision, ICC-02/05-01/09-1, 4 March 2009, available

The Sirte decision sits at the apex of other decisions that depict the progressive hardening AU position on the ICC. On 21 July 2008, the AU PSC passed a resolution expressing concern over perceived 'double standard' in the conduct of international justice and condemning the indictment of President Al-Bashir noting that it could seriously undermine the pursuit of peace and reconciliation.[123] The PSC also requested the Chairperson of the Commission to take steps to establish an independent High-Level Panel made up of distinguished Africans of high integrity, to examine the situation in depth and submit recommendations to Council on how best the issues of accountability and combating impunity, on the one hand, and reconciliation and healing, on the other, could be effectively and comprehensively addressed.[124] The AU High Level Panel was subsequently constituted. It rendered its report, making comprehensive proposals on the triple questions of justice, peace and reconciliation in Darfur and Sudan.[125]

On 3 January 2009, the AU Assembly reiterated its condemnation of its earlier decision on the abuse of universal jurisdiction. In the same decision, the Assembly made its first indication that it was collectively dissatisfied with the conduct of ICC process, in particular in the situation relating to Darfur, Sudan, and would be prepared to request members to opt out of the Rome Statute. The Assembly requested the AU Commission:

> in consultation with the African Commission on Human and Peoples' Rights, and the African Court on Human and Peoples' Rights, to examine the implications of the Court being empowered to try international crimes such as genocide, crimes against humanity and war crimes, and report thereon to the Assembly in 2010.[126]

Internal deliberations on this issue continue.[127] In another decision, the Assembly reiterated the condemnation of the indictment against President Al-Bashir's indictment and called for a meeting of African states parties to the ICC to take a unified stand.[128] At the meeting held on 9 June 2009, withdrawal

---

at: https://www.icc-cpi.int/iccdocs/doc/doc639078.pdf; Situation in Darfur, *The Prosecutor v. Omar Hassan Ahmad Al-Bashir,* Second Warrant of Arrest, ICC-02/05-01/09-95, available at: https://www.icc-cpi.int/iccdocs/doc/doc907140.pdf.

123 AU PSC Communique on Al-Bashir 21 July 2008, 142nd Meeting.

124 *Ibid.*

125 AUPD Report, available at: www.africa-union.org and at: www.scribd.com/doc/21963057/AUPD-Final-Report-on-Darfur.

126 Decision on the Implementation of the Assembly Decision on the Abuse of the Principle of Universal Jurisdiction, Assembly/AU/3(XII), January 2009, para. 9.

127 Coalition for an Effective African Court on Human and Peoples' Rights et al., *Implications of the African Court on Human and Peoples' Rights being empowered to try international crimes such as genocide, war crimes and crimes against humanity* (2009).

128 AU Assembly Decision on the application by the International Criminal Court Prosecutor for the indictment of the President of the Republic of Sudan, 12th Ordinary Summit, February 2009.

from the ICC did not attract universal appeal, although the need for strong and capable domestic criminal justice systems was emphasised in a series of important recommendations.[129]

In rationalising its overall stand on the Darfur issue and the ICC, the AU maintained that the approach (by the UNSC) privileged justice and that inadequate attention was paid to reconciliation. The PSC has stated that the ICC process, in particular its indictment of a sitting head of state is not conducive for pursuit of peace and that justice should be pursed in a manner not to jeopardise peace.[130] The AU PSC is on record requesting the UNSC to defer the process initiated by the ICC in accordance with the provisions of Article 16 of the Rome Statute of the ICC, taking into account the need to ensure that peace efforts are not jeopardised, as well as the fact that prosecution of Omar Al-Bashir may not be in the interest of the victims and justice.[131] The AU PSC reiterated this decision in a communiqué after the 175th meeting held on 5 March 2009 condemning issuance of the arrest warrant by the ICC.[132] In a press statement issued on 14 July 2009, two weeks after the Sirte declaration on non-cooperation with the ICC, the AU stated that its decision requesting African countries not to cooperate in the Al-Bashir matter 'bears testimony to the glaring reality that the situation in Darfur is too serious and complex an issue to be resolved without recourse to an harmonised approach to justice and peace, neither of which should be pursued at the expense of the other.'[133] In its well-considered report, the AU High Level Panel on Darfur offers an excellent blue print for a multifaceted approach that pays due regard to the imperatives of justice, peace and reconciliation.

12. PAN-AFRICAN PARLIAMENT (PAP)

Above, I made reference to the role that the PAP played in the debate on universal jurisdiction. Here, I briefly review the mandate of the PAP to establish whether it can support additional roles. As one of the nine bodies provided for in the Treaty Establishing the African Economic Community, the idea of a PAP predates the AU.[134] However, the PAP was only established in March 2004 as one of the eight main organs of the AU.[135] The purpose of the PAP is 'to ensure the full participation of African peoples in the development and economic integration

129 See African Union, Report of the Meeting of African States Parties to the Rome Statute of the ICC, 8–9 June 2009, Addis Ababa, Ethiopia, MinICC/Legal/3.

130 AU PSC Communique on Al-Bashir, 21 July 2008, 142nd Meeting, Resolution 3 and 9.

131 PSC Communique on Al-Bashir, 21 July 2008, 142nd Meeting, Resolution 11(i).

132 AU PSC Communique, 5 March 2009 Addis Ababa, 175th Meeting.

133 AU Commission Press Release, 'Decision on the meeting of African States Parties to the Rome Statute of the International Criminal Court', Addis Ababa, 14 July 2009.

134 Protocol to the Treaty Establishing the African Economic Community Relating to the Pan-African Parliament (PAP Protocol) signed in Abuja, Nigeria 1991.

135 Arts. 5 and 17 of the Constitutive Act of the African Union.

of the continent.'[136] Although the PAP is not a true legislative body, as it lacks a legislative mandate, it is vested with a number of 'powers'.[137] In its relevant parts, the PAP Protocol provides that the PAP has power to:

> examine, discuss or express an opinion on any matter, either on its own initiative or at the request of the Assembly or other policy organs and to make any recommendations it may deem fit relating to, inter alia, matters pertaining to respect of human rights ... and the rule of law; make recommendations aimed at contributing to the attainment of the objectives of the AU ...; and promote the programmes and objectives of the AU, in the constituencies of the member states.[138]

It is clear that without true legislative power, the PAP must strive to achieve its objectives and perform its functions with only advisory and consultative capabilities.[139] In the absence of any legislative mandate, and with its power limited to an advisory role in respect of the Assembly of Heads of States and Government, PAP is in the process of finding its niche within the AU's institutional framework, until its Protocol is amended to extend this power to it.[140] As a starting point, it is notable that the PAP is already emerging as an influential player within the AU framework in three important respects: (1) fact finding; (2) recommending action to the AHSG; and (3) shaping relevant debates. Its growing influence on matters that affect international criminal justice issues on the continent – in particular the debates on universal jurisdiction and the work of the ICC – belies its lack of real powers.

While the Pan-African Parliament's role in international criminal justice is not specified in its protocol, fact-finding has emerged as one of its main responses in respect of situations of gross human rights violations and international crimes. Apart from the broad powers outlined above, the PAP Protocol reserves a residual – seemingly all-encompassing – power for the continental parliament. It enacts that PAP may 'perform such other functions as it deems appropriate to achieve the objectives set out in article 3 of the Protocol.'[141] These objectives include 'promotion of the principles of human rights and democracy in Africa' and 'promote peace, security and stability.' The PAP seems to have interpreted this residual power to include a sanction for fact-finding missions in various circumstances.

In one of its first actions following its creation, the PAP agreed during its Second Ordinary Session held from 16 September to 1 October 2004 to send a

---

136 Art. 17(1) of the Constitutive Act of the AU.

137 Art. 11(1)–(9) PAP Protocol.

138 See relevant provisions of Art. 11 of the PAP Protocol.

139 For a discussion of reforms necessary to the PAP, see Musila, 'United States of Africa: Positioning the Pan-African Parliament and Court in the political union debate', ISS Paper 142, June 2007.

140 Art. 2(3) of the PAP Protocol provides that this is to happen at the end of the PAP's first five-year term, sometime in 2009.

141 Art. 11(9) PAP Protocol.

fact-finding mission to Darfur.[142] It invoked the objectives of PAP, which seek to promote peace, security and stability as well as promote the principles of human rights and democracy in Africa, by encouraging good governance, transparency and accountability in member states.[143] The fact-finding mission rendered its report on 23 February 2005.[144]

Although PAP did not explore its possible role in international criminal justice in the Darfur Report in any depth, some of its recommendations made in the report are instructive. PAP commended the AU's intervention in Darfur through the deployment of the AU Mission to Sudan (AMIS). It suggested that the move to send peacekeepers without waiting to determine whether the situation in Darfur amounted to genocide, war crimes or crimes against humanity was proactive.[145] The PAP Mission to Darfur recommended that PAP's standing committees develop and maintain a policy of constructive engagement with all sectors in Darfur. It also proposed that the PAP should establish a trust fund for humanitarian assistance to populations in conflict situations.[146]

The rest of PAP's recommendations focused on how the AU could engage in Darfur. Specifically, it urged the AU, through the Assembly, to take immediate steps to influence the Sudanese government to find ways and means of quantifying and qualifying the losses caused by the war. It also made a case for the launching of a 'Trust Fund' with the support of the African Union and the international community to finance a comprehensive resettlement programme for refugees and displaced persons. PAP also recommended that the mandate of the African Union Mission be improved to include a strong component on the protection of the population in Darfur.

Perhaps energised by its perceived success in the Darfur Fact-Finding Mission, the PAP under Rule 5(1)(a) of its Rules of Procedure passed a resolution for a peace mission to Côte d'Ivoire commencing in May 2005.[147] Similarly, at the same session another resolution was passed for a Peace Mission to the Democratic Republic of Congo (DRC).[148] On 14 May 2007, during its 7th Ordinary Session, the PAP (building from its Darfur precedent) voted to send a fact-finding mission to Zimbabwe to investigate allegations of the abuse of human rights and the rule of law relating to the arrest and detention, assault and

142 PAP-RE/002/04, Report of the Pan-African Parliament fact-finding mission to Darfur, the Sudan AU/PAP/CIRCR.CTTEE, PAP resolution available at the website of the PAP: www.pan-african-parliament.org.

143 See Protocol to the Treaty Establishing the African Economic Community Relating to the Pan-African Parliament (PAP Protocol) signed in Abuja, Nigeria, 1991, Article 3.

144 Report of the Pan-African Parliament fact-finding mission on Darfur Sudan presented by Abdul Katuntu, 23 February 2005.

145 A group of soldiers sent under the auspices of the African Union to help maintain peace and stability in Darfur.

146 Report of the Pan-African Parliament fact-finding mission on Darfur Sudan presented by Abdul Katuntu, AU/PAP/RPT/CIRCR.CTTEE, 23 February 2005.

147 PAP-Res. 006/05, 3rd Session General Resolution.

148 PAP-Res. 007/05, 3rd Session General Resolution.

murder of political activists and members of the media. Suzanne Vos, a South African Member of Parliament, had tabled the motion in Parliament calling for a fact-finding mission to Zimbabwe 'to investigate matters relating to human rights, good governance, transparency and the rule of law pertinent to the mandate of the Pan-African Parliament and report to the next plenary session of PAP.' Vos noted that PAP could not sit on the side-lines nor could it be silent on the range of issues affecting Zimbabwe and the security of its citizens. She noted: 'We must ask ourselves in all honesty whether we can place on the agenda of this Parliament debate on the Great Lakes Region, the situation in Darfur, the Côte d'Ivoire, Chad, Somalia and the Saharawi Arab Democratic Republic and omit Zimbabwe'. Based on information available, these two missions do not appear to have materialised, and there has been no follow up action on the PAP's report and recommendations arising from its mission to Darfur.

13. THE ROLE OF JUDICIAL AND ADJUDICATIVE BODIES

There are more than ten international judicial and quasi-judicial tribunals operating in Africa, excluding the International Criminal Tribunal for Rwanda (ICTR). The regional and sub-regional tribunals are: the African Commission on Human and Peoples' Rights (ACHPR); the African Court of Human and Peoples' Rights (ACtHPR); the proposed African Court of Justice and Human rights (ACJ & HR); the East African Community Court of Justice (EACJ); the Tribunal of the Southern African Development Community (SADC Tribunal, defunct); the ECOWAS Court of Justice; the Common Market for Eastern and Southern Africa (COMESA) Court of Justice; and the Union Economique et Monétaire Ouest-Africaine.

This contribution discusses only the African Commission on Human and Peoples' Rights and the proposed African Court of Justice and Human Rights, which includes an international criminal section.

14. AFRICAN COMMISSION ON HUMAN AND PEOPLES' RIGHTS (ACHPR)

The African Commission on Human and Peoples' Rights is the African regional treaty oversight body established under the African Charter on Human and Peoples' Rights[149] with the mandate to promote and protect human rights

[149] African Charter on Human and Peoples' Rights, adopted 27 June 1981, OAU Doc. CAB/LEG/67/3 rev. 5, 21 ILM 58 (198a2), entered into force 21 October 1986.

in Africa.[150] The Commission is not an organ of the AU (it is not listed in the Constitutive Act) but is a key African continental organ, with responsibility for monitoring compliance with the African Charter on Human and Peoples' Rights (the African Charter). Its protective mandate entails, in the main, receiving and determining inter-state and individual petitions alleging human rights violations.[151] While its mandate is one of oversight in relation to purely human rights issues arising under the African Charter and other relevant instruments, the African Commission has been fairly active on issues related to international criminal justice and the ICC in particular.

One of the working methods of the African Commission, and a key mechanism of promoting human rights, is the adoption of resolutions. Resolutions are either thematic, country-specific or relate to a particular procedural or administrative issue. Since 1987, when the Commission became operational, it has adopted – often with NGO input and lobbying – more than 145 resolutions on diverse human rights issues.[152]

Following the adoption of the Rome Statute in 1998, the African Commission has adopted at least three resolutions on ratification of the Rome Statute and has repeatedly made this call to AU states.[153] Perhaps the most relevant resolution on international criminal justice is its resolution on ending impunity, which among others: called on African states to ratify and implement the Rome Statute at the national level; ensure that the perpetrators of crimes under international human rights law and international humanitarian law should not benefit from impunity and; urged withdrawal from Article 98 Bilateral Immunity Agreements and restraint from acts that would weaken the effectiveness of the ICC in line with international obligations accepted by African states.[154] Another important thematic resolution is on the right to a remedy and reparation for women and girls victims of sexual violence, which refers to the Rome Statute and other international instruments.[155]

---

150 On the African Commission on Human Rights and its role in the promotion and protection of human rights, see generally Ankumah 1996; Viljoen 2007.

151 Articles 54 and 55 of the African Charter on Human and Peoples' Rights. On its application see Odinkalu 1998, p. 359.

152 The majority of the resolutions of the African Commission may be accessed at: www.achpr.org/resolutions/ (accessed on 3 December 2015).

153 ACHPR, Resolution on the Ratification of the Treaty on the International Criminal Court, Banjul, 31 October 1998; and ACHPR Resolution on the Ratification of the Statute on the International Criminal Court by AU Member States, Pretoria, 2–6 May 2002.

154 ACHPR Resolution on ending impunity in Africa and on the domestication and implementation of the Rome Statute of the International Criminal Court, 8th Ordinary Session held in Banjul, 21 November–5 December 2005, available at: www.iccnow.org/documents/ACHPR-ResolutionEndingImpunity5Dec2005eng.pdf.

155 Resolution on the Right to a Remedy and Reparation for Women and Girls Victims of Sexual Violence of the African Commission on Human and Peoples' Rights (the African Commission or ACHPR), meeting at its 42nd Ordinary Session held in Brazzaville, Republic of Congo, 15–28 November 2007, available at: www.achpr.org/sessions/42nd/resolutions/111/.

The Commission has also adopted several country-specific resolutions of relevance to the work of the ICC in particular. On the situation in Northern Uganda, it called for support for the ICC Prosecutor's work in that country and urged other specific action on the part of the parties to the conflict.[156] The Commission has passed similar resolutions in relation to the situation in the Democratic Republic of the Congo.[157] On Darfur[158] the African Commission has adopted a number of resolutions urging action on the part of the government of the Sudan and other parties to the conflict in terms of their obligations under various instruments including the Constitutive Act of the AU. More recently, the Commission adopted two resolutions on the situation in Central African Republic calling on warring parties (anti-Balaka and ex-Seleka rebels) to stop targeting civilians, and called on the transitional government, the AU and UN to undertake specified measures.[159]

Fact-finding missions have evolved as another important working method of the African Commission, with particular relevance for international criminal justice, particularly as a source of information on crimes. In this regard, the focus of the Commission has been largely on situations of mass atrocities – which essentially constitute international crimes over which the ICC has jurisdiction. Article 58(1) of the African Charter provides that when the Commission learns of 'special cases which reveal the existence of a series of serious or massive violations of human and peoples' rights', it shall draw the attention of the Assembly of Heads of State and Government to these special cases. In turn, the AU Assembly may request the Commission 'to undertake an in-depth study of these cases and make a factual report, accompanied by its findings and recommendations'.[160] One relevant mission undertaken in terms of this procedure can be cited here. In July 2004, the African Commission conducted a fact-finding mission in Darfur supported logistically by the AU Commission in Addis Ababa and prepared a report on the human rights

156 Resolution on the Human Rights Situation in Uganda by the African Commission on Human and Peoples' Rights, meeting at its 38th Ordinary Session held in Banjul, The Gambia, 21 November–5 December 2005, available at: www.achpr.org/sessions/38th/resolutions/94/.

157 ACHPR Resolution on the Human Rights Situation in the Democratic Republic of Congo, Banjul, 38th Ordinary Session, 21 November–5 December 2005; Resolution on the Situation of Women in the Democratic Republic of Congo, adopted during its 40th Ordinary Session held in Banjul, The Gambia, on 29 November 2006.

158 See Resolution ACHPR/Res.68 (XXXV) 04 adopted on 4 June 2004 by the African Commission on Human and Peoples' Rights during the 35th Session on the situation in the Darfur Region of The Sudan, and Resolution ACHPR /Res.74 (XXXVII) 05 adopted on 11 May 2005 on the Human Rights Situation in Darfur, Sudan.

159 Resolution on the Human Rights Situation in the Central African Republic by the African Commission on Human and Peoples' Rights meeting at its 14th Extraordinary Session held in Nairobi, Kenya, 20–24 July 2013 and Resolution on the Human Rights Situation in the Central African Republic, the African Commission on Human and Peoples' Rights meeting at its 15th Extraordinary Session held in Banjul, The Gambia, from 7–14 March 2014, available at: www.achpr.org/sessions/15th-eo/resolutions/266/.

160 Art. 58(2) African Charter HPR.

situation in that country, and Darfur in particular.[161] The mission produced a report that has been cited in various AU Assembly and PSC resolutions and decisions on the situation in Darfur. In addition, the Commission adopted in May 2005, a resolution on the human rights situation in Darfur. It called on the government of Sudan to:

> cooperate fully with the Prosecutor of the ICC … in order to investigate and bring to justice all persons suspected of perpetrating crimes of concern to the international community; on the UNSC to continue monitoring the implementation of its resolutions on the Darfur, in particular the cooperation by the government of Sudan with the Prosecutor of the ICC; and urged Sudan to submit to the African Commission its overdue comments on the recommendations made in the Report of the African Commission's Fact-Finding Mission undertaken in July 2004 to Darfur.[162]

A broader review of the work of the African Commission as well as the discussion above of its emerging role in international criminal justice shows that it has pedigree in the promotion and protection of human rights on the continent. Although the compliance rate with its decisions remains woefully low,[163] the Commission's decisions carry increasing traction among African states. The AU could make use of the African Commission's developed and tested mechanisms on fact-finding, country-specific rapporteurs and special (thematic) rapporteurs to conduct inquiries into alleged violations of human rights which can inform decisions of its political organs. While these efforts are useful in post conflict situations, the Commission's decisions and reports on specific countries could inform pre-emptive action by feeding into the AU's various mechanisms, including the early warning arrangements.

15. AFRICAN COURT ON HUMAN AND PEOPLES' RIGHTS (ACtHPR)

The African Court of Human and Peoples' Rights, which was established to complement the protective mandate of the African Commission on Human Rights has jurisdiction over the African Charter and 'any other relevant human

161 Report of the African Commission on Human and Peoples' Rights' Fact-finding Mission to the Republic of Sudan in the Darfur Region, 8–18 July 2004, available at: www.achpr.org/files/sessions/41st/mission-reports/sudan/misrep_factfind_sudan_2004_eng.pdf.

162 Resolution on the Human Rights Situation In Darfur, Sudan of the African Commission on Human and Peoples' Rights meeting at its 37th Ordinary Session, 27 April–11 May 2005 in Banjul, The Gambia, para. 5, available at: www.achpr.org/sessions/37th/resolutions/74/.

163 Viljoen and Louw 2007.

rights instrument ratified by States [parties].'[164] These instruments include the African Charter on the Rights and Welfare of the Child and the Protocol to the African Charter on the Rights of Women in Africa and the Convention Governing the Specific Aspects of Refugee Problems in Africa. The extent to which the Court's jurisdiction over 'any other relevant human rights instrument' can be stretched, however, to include sub-regional protocols addressing impunity for human rights violations (such as for example the Protocol for the Prevention and Punishment of the Crime of Genocide, War Crimes, Crimes against Humanity and all Forms of Discrimination, signed by all eleven states of the International Conference on the Great Lakes (ICGLR) is an open question.[165] The interim rules of procedure of the Court, which were adopted at its ninth session in June 2008, do not shed any light on this issue. Similarly, the Court's Protocol is not explicit as to whether the jurisdiction of the Court itself could extend to the consideration of international crimes. However, if one takes the view that since the Court is nothing but a human rights court – it lacks a specific criminal mandate – then this question is easy to resolve.

The African Court became operational in 2006 and received its first case in 2008. It has so far received over 54 cases (applications), of which half are still pending, with the rest decided, struck out or transferred to the African Commission.[166] When the idea of complementarity is viewed not in the technical sense as framing the relationship between the ICC and states but in the broad sense in which it connotes a supplementary relationship in which various commissions and courts contribute to the fight against impunity when they adjudicate complaints relating to human rights or try cases, then the contribution of the African Court to international criminal justice is obvious. In any case, to the extent that human rights cases brought to the court highlight potential hotspots where international crimes are likely to be committed, or when such courts contribute to inculcating the culture of respect for human rights and rule of law in target states, they contribute to prevention of human rights violations and commission of international crimes.

Other than this general contribution, the African Court has adjudicated at least one case brought on behalf of former Chadian President *Hissène Habré* who is facing trial in Senegal for alleged international crimes of torture and crimes against humanity committed during his rule in Chad. In the case of *Michelot Yogombaye v. Senegal*[167] the applicant sought to stop the criminal

164 Art. 7 Protocol to the African Charter on Human and Peoples' Rights on the Establishment of an African Court on Human and Peoples' Rights.

165 Eleven states in the region (including Sudan) have signed the Pact on Security, Stability and Development in the Great Lakes Region Pact that came into force in early 2008.

166 For the status of the work of the African Court, see www.african-court.org/en/index.php/2012-03-04-06-06-00/cases-status1 (accessed on 3 December 2015).

167 *Michelot Yogombaye v. Senegal*, African Court on Human and Peoples Rights Application No. 001/2008.

case commenced in Senegal against *Hissène Habré* arguing that Senegal had pollicised the process and that the trial constituted *ex post facto* justice and as such offended against principles of legality and was consequently in violation of Mr Habre's rights under the African Charter. This case, which raised interesting questions, was unfortunately dismissed for want of jurisdiction as Senegal has not filed the required declaration under Article 34(6) of the Protocol Establishing the Court, which would allow individuals and NGOs to bring cases to the Court. Currently, individuals and NGOs can only do so indirectly through the African Commission before which they have standing. This does not guarantee that the Commission will bring the case before the Court under Article 5(1)(a) of the Protocol as this is discretionary.

16. AFRICAN CRIMINAL COURT

On 27 June 2014, the African Union Assembly of Heads of States adopted the Malabo Protocol, which expands the mandate of the African Court of Justice and Human Rights to include a section with jurisdiction over international crimes of genocide, war crimes, crimes against humanity, aggression, the crime of unconstitutional change of government, piracy and several transnational crimes.[168] The Malabo Protocol amended the Protocol on the Statute of the African Court of Justice and Human Rights (Protocol on the Merged Court) adopted by the Assembly at its 6th Ordinary Session in Sharm el-Sheikh, Egypt in July 2008 and which had not come into force.[169] The Protocol on the Merged Court had the objective of merging the existing African Court on Human and Peoples Rights with the yet-to-be-created African Court of Justice foreseen in the Constitutive Act of the AU of 2002. It is at the height of the controversy on universal jurisdiction and the indictment of President Al-Bashir discussed above, barely six months after the adoption of the Protocol on the Merged Court that the Assembly requested the AU Commission (Secretariat), in consultation with the African Commission on Human and Peoples' Rights, and the African Court on Human and Peoples' Rights, 'to examine the implications of the Court being empowered to try international crimes such as genocide, crimes against humanity and war crimes'.[170] It took over five years for a text to emerge from the legislative process, and eventually adopted in June 2014.

---

168 Protocol on Amendments to the Protocol on the Statute of the African Court of Justice and Human Rights, adopted at Malabo, Equatorial Guinea, 27 June 2014, available at: http://au.int/en/treaties/protocol-amendments-protocol-statute-african-court-justice-and-human-rights.

169 For an early critique of the Protocol on the Merged Court and the proposal for an African Criminal Court, see Musila 2013.

170 See Decision on the Implementation of the Assembly Decision on the Abuse of the Principle of Universal Jurisdiction, Assembly/AU/3(XII), January 2009, para. 9.

Once established, the African Court of Justice and Human Rights will be the main judicial organ of the AU.[171] Other than adjudicating inter-state disputes, providing advisory opinions to AU organs, it will prosecute international crimes detailed in Article 28A *et seq.* of the Malabo Protocol and complement the protective functions of the African Commission on Human and Peoples' Rights and the African Committee of Experts by adjudicating human rights cases. The Court shall thus have three sections: a General Affairs Section, Human and Peoples' Rights Section and; the International Criminal Law Section. According to Article 10 of the Malabo Protocol, the Court will have 15 judges distributed as follows: the General Affairs Section and Human Rights Sections have three judges each, while the International Criminal Law Section has nine judges divided (one judge in the Pre-Trial Chamber, three judges in the Trial Chamber and five judges in the Appeals Chamber).

Its subject matter jurisdiction is quite broad. It includes not only the core international crimes over which the ICC has jurisdiction but extends to new international crimes created by the Malabo Protocol: the crime of unconstitutional change of government, piracy, terrorism, corruption, money laundering, human trafficking, trafficking in drugs, dumping of hazardous wastes and illicit exploitation of natural resources.[172]

With respect to human rights violations arising under various treaties – the African Charter on Human and Peoples' Rights, the Women Rights Protocol, the African Charter on the Rights and Welfare of the Child and other instruments – the parties that have automatic access to the Court are the African Commission on Human and Peoples Rights, the African Committee of Experts on the Rights and Welfare of the Child and African intergovernmental organisations.[173] Individuals and African non-governmental organisations (NGOs) may only bring cases against states that have accepted this jurisdiction when ratifying the Court Protocol.[174] There is no bar to such declaration being made at a later date by a state party. Before the Court was merged, only Burkina Faso had lodged a declaration accepting standing for individuals and NGOs before the African Court of Human Rights. Subsequently, six other countries have made the declaration. With respect to the admissibility of cases relating to human rights protection, the Court Protocol, like the African Charter on Human and Peoples Rights[175] requires, as a general rule, that individuals and NGOs bringing cases to the Court must first exhaust domestic remedies.

The Malabo Protocol has already attracted criticism, particularly from civil society, not least for its Article 46Abis, which appears to grant heads of

171 Art. 4 of Statute on the African Court of Justice and Human Rights.
172 See Arts. 28A–28M of the Malabo Protocol.
173 Art. 29(a, b & c) of the Statute of the Merged Court and Arts. 15 and 16 of the Malabo Protocol.
174 Art. 29(d) of the Statute of the Merged Court.
175 Arts. 55 and 56 of the African Charter on Human and Peoples' Rights regarding admissibility to the African Commission on Human and Peoples' Rights.

state and other public officials immunity from investigation and prosecution by the African Court. Other provisions of interest include Article 46H on complementarity, which establishes a complementarity relationship between the Court and states but also between the Court and sub-regional courts created by regional economic communities such as ECOWAS, SADC and the East African Community, but not with the ICC.

17. CONCLUSION: LOOKING TO THE FUTURE

Having reviewed various instruments and discussed the AU's contribution to international justice based on various treaties, I now turn in this concluding section, to ways in which the AU can play a role in advancing the work of the ICC, the permanent international criminal court.

To begin with, the AU and its organs can be a source of information by conducting studies, missions etc. As noted, this aspect was pioneered in the case of Darfur, where the African Commission and PAP undertook missions. The Report of the Pan-African Parliament Mission to Darfur partly informed the ICC Prosecutor's decision to launch an investigation in Darfur.[176] As noted already, the African Human Rights Commission also conducted a mission to Darfur and prepared a report.[177] More can be done in this regard. In particular, mechanisms should be put in place to coordinate such missions between AU organs and institutions with a view to avoiding duplication and cutting costs. The African Commission, which has established fact-finding mechanism and Special Rapporteurs and has experience in fact finding, should be encouraged to take a lead in such missions.

Second, while contact was made between the ICC and AMIS, it appears that both did not properly explore mutually beneficial strategies in Darfur, in part because of restrictions on ICC investigating teams, which were unable to visit Sudan, and limits in AMIS's capacities on the ground in Darfur. Several proposals on how the ICC can engage in mutually beneficial ways with the African Commission were made here. When the ICC opens investigations in a particular situation, there will often be AU or joint AU/UN peacekeepers on the ground that can provide coordinated security for investigators, victims and other people involved. AU peacekeepers could assist in apprehending suspects, as has happened in the case of the DRC. In this context, the role that MONUSCA has played in providing capacity building and technical assistance to mechanisms

176 According to the ICC, multiple sources of information were used for the OTP analysis (in deciding to investigate Darfur), including reports from the Government of Sudan, the African Union, the United Nations, and other organisations, local and international media, academic experts and others.

177 *Report of the African Commission on Human and Peoples' Rights' Fact-finding Mission to the Republic of Sudan in the Darfur Region*, 8–18 July 2004.

charged with prosecuting international crimes in the DRC provides interesting lessons as well. Taking into consideration admitted restrictions on the ICC engagement in this sector, established missions, including those in which AU is involved can provide support to domestic justice institutions that complement the work of the ICC in prosecuting international crimes.

Third, the AU can, and should do more to create a conducive environment for ICC operations in situation countries. This can be done in a number of ways, including through the pursuit of peace. In Darfur for instance, there is an extent to which the success of ICC work cannot be de-linked from that of the AU. The case of northern Uganda, and DRC and Darfur itself demonstrates clearly that some form of stability and peace is necessary for the ICC to carry out investigations and prosecutions, let alone succeed in its overall mission. The AU's role in shaping discourse on particular issues in international criminal justice has been discussed. The AU can do more to encourage a discourse that is favourable to the fight against impunity and the work of the ICC, which includes withholding support from anti-ICC actors. If universal subscription is essential for the legitimacy of the ICC, then urging ratification, implementation and assisting member states to building capacity to prosecute crimes themselves will greatly enhance the work of the ICC and advance the fight against impunity. On building the capacity of domestic justice institutions, the recommendations of the meeting of African States Parties to the ICC of 9 June 2009 elaborate on how this can be done.[178]

Fourth, the ICC's strategic plan recognises that the Court's success depends on effective cooperation and clarity of functions with its strategic partners, including the AU.[179] In the case of the Darfur for instance, the outreach plan identified one focus of outreach activity as clarifying the difference between the ICC's functions and those of other international players such as the AU.[180] The strategic plan recognised that while cooperation is important, success may depend on clear distinction of functions between the ICC and its partners, including the AU and the UN.

Of all aspects of the Court's work, its approach on outreach has suffered the most trenchant criticisms. This critique has focused on the fact that the Court has for the most part maintained a low profile, with the result that its work is little understood in important sectors of society, and that the ICC's outreach programme has tended to be belated, coming as it does long after the Prosecutor had commenced investigations in various situations. Because of its limited reach, outreach has not been effective in reaching victims and their

---

178 See *Report of Ministerial meetings of African States Parties to the ICC*, 9 June 2009.

179 See ASP, *Strategic Plan for Outreach of the International Criminal Court*, ICC-ASP/5/12, 29 September 2006, available at: www.icc-cpi.int/library/asp/ICC-ASP-5-12_English.pdf (accessed 5 June 2008).

180 ASP, Strategic Plan for Outreach of the International Criminal Court, ICC-ASP/5/12, 29 September 2006, p. 25.

communities. While experiences differ from one situation to another, and taking into consideration the increasing sophistication of measures adopted by those opposed to the Court, the result has been that outreach has generated less than adequate levels of legitimacy for the Court among victims, their communities and wider public. Further, the judicial character of the Court is lost to many, with the result that it has drawn fire directed at UNSC, UN and individual states, with a negative impact on the legitimacy of the Court. As illustrated by the case of Sudan and Kenya cited above, this is one area where the AU can be lumped together with the ICC's opponents. In view of its own formal commitments to the fight against impunity to support the work of the ICC, it is suggested that the AU can, and should do more as it repeatedly affirms. The starting point is cultivating a constructive relationship with the Court.

The AU is important, not only because some of the criticism of the ICC has come from Africa's political regional body, but also because the ICC's outreach strategy and the Court's Rules identify important roles of the continental body. In 2009, the AU itself, through its members that are party to the ICC, identified ways in which it can play an important role in advancing the goals of the ICC: generating political support, constructive engagement, and raising awareness about the work of the Court. Other activities include: building and maintaining cooperation and support, for the activities of the Court; engaging and making public aware of the judicial activities of the Court, which is integral to delivering public and transparent justice; increasing the broader impact of the Court, contributing to lasting respect for and enforcement of international justice; increasing the awareness of ICC activities; and building networks in the course of ICC activities, which will help to foster national measures and international cooperation and contribute to the prevention of crimes.[181]

Fifth, as noted already, Rule 98(4) ICC RPE allows for the possibility of reparations awards to be made to or in respect of victims through the Victims' Trust Fund to among others, intergovernmental organisations. Little else exists in the Rules to clarify how such organisations may be of use in this regard. The AU enjoys goodwill among the majority of its members, which is crucial in mobilising support for the Court more broadly but also in respect of specific programmes in which the AU and its members could play a role. Further, the network of organisations associated with the AU: sub-regional bodies and civil society organisations could be useful for broad-based victims programmes. While the role of such organisations is needless where reparations awards are made by the Court or Trust Fund to an individual victim, or a small number of victims, mass reparations programmes would require a wide network of actors, including intergovernmental organisations, civil society and victim rights groups.

---

181 AU, *Report of the Ministerial Meeting of African States Parties to the ICC*, held in Addis Ababa, Ethiopia, 9 June 2009.

It is critical that the AU and ICC establish a formal structure and framework for cooperation, akin to negotiated agreement between the ICC and the United Nations.[182] Discussions on an agreement have been drawn out but in the meantime, the annual seminar between the two entities is encouraged. Moreover, *amicus curiae* facility under Rule 103 of the RPE which the African Union has described as 'a new form of dialogue' between the AU and the ICC provide an apolitical, non-adversarial and constructive process through which the AU can channel its views on the interpretation of the Rome Statute.[183]

BIBLIOGRAPHY

BOOKS AND JOURNAL ARTICLES

Akande 2009
Akande, D., 'The Legal Nature of Security Council Referrals to the ICC and its Impact on Al-Bashir's Immunities', 7 Journal of International Criminal Justice, 2009, pp. 333–352.

Akokpari and Zimbler 2008
Akokpari, J. and Zimbler, D.S. (eds.), 'Africa's Human Rights Architecture', Jacana Media, 2008.

Alusala 2004
Alusala, N., 'African Standby Force: East Africa moves on', 13(2) African Security Review, 2004.

Ankumah 1996
Ankumah, E.A., 'The African Commission on Human and Peoples' Rights: Practice and Procedures', Martinus Nijhoff Publishers, 1996.

Appiah-Mensah 2006
Appiah-Mensah, S., 'The African mission in Sudan: Darfur dilemmas', 15(1) African Security Review, 2006, pp. 2–19.

Appiah-Mensah 2005
Appiah-Mensah, S., 'AU's critical assignment in Darfur: challenges and constraints', 14(2) African Security Review, 2005, pp. 7–21.

Aptel 2006
Aptel, C., 'Empowered or Hampered: the International Criminal Court in Darfur', 15(1) African Security Review, 2006, pp. 20–31.

182 *Negotiated Relationship Agreement between the International Criminal Court and the United Nations*, available at: https://www.icc-cpi.int/NR/rdonlyres/916FC6A2-7846-4177-A5EA-5AA9B6D1E96C/0/ICCASP3Res1_English.pdf.

183 See Appeals Chamber, Situation in the Republic of Kenya, *Prosecutor v. William Samoei Ruto and Joshua Arap Sang*, the African Union's Amicus Curiae Observations on the Rule 68 Amendments at the Twelfth Session of the Assembly of States Parties, ICC-01/09-01/11, 19 October 2015, available at: https://www.icc-cpi.int/iccdocs/doc/doc2090973.pdf.

Brownlie 1973
Brownlie, I., 'Thoughts on kind-hearted gunmen', in Lillich, R.B. (ed.), 'Humanitarian intervention and the United Nations', University of Virginia Press, 1973.
Francis et al. 2005
Francis, D.J. et al., 'Dangers of Co-deployment', Ashgate, 2005.
Gaeta 2009
Gaeta, P., 'Does President Al-Bashir enjoy immunity from arrest?', 7 Journal of International Criminal Justice, 2009, pp. 315–332.
Goodman 2006
Goodman, R., 'Humanitarian Intervention and Pretexts for War', 100(1) American Journal of International Law, 2006, pp. 107–141.
Grono 2006
Grono, N., 'Briefing: The International Community's Failure to Protect', 105(421) African Affairs, 2006, pp. 621–631.
Gutto 2002
Gutto, S., 'The reform and the renewal of the African Regional and Peoples' Rights', 2 African HRLJ, 2002.
Hammerstad 2003/4
Hammerstad, A., 'SADC and the African Union's Evolving Security Architecture', South African Yearbook of International Affairs, 2003/4.
Harhoff 2001
Harhoff, F., 'Unauthorised Humanitarian Interventions – Armed Violence in the Name of Humanity?', 70 Nordic Journal of International Law, 2001, pp. 65–119.
Haugerudbraaten 1998
Haugerudbraaten, H., 'Peacebuilding: Six dimensions and two concepts', 7(6) African Security Review, 1998.
Jalloh 2009
Jalloh, C.C., 'Regionalising international criminal law?', 9 International Criminal Law Review, 2009, pp. 445–499.
Jallow and Bensouda 2008
Jallow H. and Bensouda, F., 'International criminal law in an African Context', in Du Plessis, M. (ed.), 'African Guide to International Criminal Justice', Institute for Security Studies, 2008, pp. 15–54.
Kent and Malan 2003
Kent, V. and Malan, M., 'African Standby Force: progress and prospects', 12(3) African Security Review, 2003, pp. 71–81.
Khadiagala 2004
Khadiagala, G.M., 'Intervention in Internal Conflict: The Case of Rwanda', in Lahneman, W. (ed.), 'Military Intervention: Cases for the Twenty-First Century', Rowman and Littlefield Publishers, 2004, pp. 67–88.
Kioko 2003
Kioko, B., 'The right of intervention under the African Union's Constitutive Act: From non-interference to non-intervention', 852 International Review of the Red Cross, 2003, pp. 807–825.

Kuwali 2009
Kuwali, D., 'The End of Humanitarian Intervention: an Evaluation of the African Union's Right of Intervention', African Journal in Conflict Resolution, 2009.

Makinda and Okumu 2007
Makinda, S. and Okumu, W., 'The African Union: Challenges of Globalization, Security, and Governance', Routledge, 2007.

Mansaray 2009
Mansaray, A.V., 'Amis in Darfur: Africa's litmus test in peacekeeping and political mediation', 18(1) African Security Review, 2009, pp. 35–49.

Maqungo 2000
Maqungo, S., 'The Establishment of the International Criminal Court: SADC's Participation in the Negotiations', 9 African Security Review, 2000.

Mayall 2000
Mayall, J., 'The Concept of Humanitarian Intervention Revisited', in Schnabel, A. and Thakur, R. (eds.), 'Kosovo and the challenge of humanitarian intervention: selective indignation, collective action and international citizenship', UNU Press, 2000.

Mochochoko 2005
Mochochoko, P., 'Africa and the International Criminal Court', in Ankumah, E.A. and Kwakwa, E. (eds.), 'African Perspectives on International Criminal Justice', Africa Legal Aid, 2005.

Murithi 2008
Murithi, T., 'The African Union's evolving role in peace operations: the African Union Mission in Burundi, the African Union Mission in Sudan and the African Union Mission in Somalia', 17(1) African Security Review, 2008, pp. 70–82.

Murphy 1996
Murphy, S.D., 'Humanitarian Intervention: The United Nations in an Evolving World Order', Pen Press, 1996.

Musila 2013
Musila, G.M., 'The African Union and the Evolution of International Criminal Justice: Challenges Opportunities and Controversies', SSRN, 2013.

Naldi 1999
Naldi, G.J., 'The Organization of African Unity: An analysis of its Role', Bloomsbury Academic, 1999.

Nmehielle 2001
Nmehielle, V.O., 'The African Human Rights System: Its Laws, Practice and Institutions', Martinus Nijhoff, 2001.

Nmehielle 2003
Nmehielle, V.O., 'The African Union and African Renaissance: A new era for human rights protection in Africa', 7 Singapore J Intl & Comparative Law, 2003.

Odinkalu 1998
Odinkalu, C.A., 'The individual complaints procedures of the African Commission on Human and People's Rights: a preliminary assessment', Transnational Law and Contemporary Problems, 1998.

Packer and Rukare 2002
Packer, C.A.A. and Rukare, D., 'The new African Union and its Constitutive Act', 96 American JIL, 2002.

Parekh 1997
Parekh, B., 'Rethinking humanitarian intervention', 18(1) International Political Science Review, 1997.
Paris 1997
Paris, R., 'Peacebuilding and the limits of liberal internationalism', 22(2) International Security, 1997.
Prunier 2005
Prunier, G., 'Darfur: The ambiguous genocide', Cornell University Press, 2005.
Smith 2002
Smith, T.W., 'Moral Hazard and Humanitarian Law: The International Criminal Court and the Limits of Legality', 39(2) International Politics, 2002, pp. 175–192.
Straus 2005
Straus, S., 'Darfur and the Genocide Debate', 84(1) Foreign Affairs, 2005, pp. 123–133.
Udombana 2005
Udombana, N.J., 'When Neutrality Is a Sin: The Darfur Crisis and the Crisis of Humanitarian Intervention in Sudan', 27(4) Human Rights Quarterly, 2005, pp. 1149–1199.
Udombana 2002
Udombana, N.J., 'Can the leopard change its spots: The African Union Treaty and Human Rights', 17 American University Int'l Law Review, 2002.
Viljoen 2007
Viljoen, F., 'International human right law in Africa', Oxford University Press, 2007.
Viljoen and Louw 2007
Viljoen, F. and Louw, L., 'State compliance with the recommendations of the African Commission on Human and Peoples' Rights, 1994–2004', 101(1) American Society of International Law, 2007.
Williams 2013
Williams, S., 'The Extraordinary African Chambers in the Senegalese Courts: An African Solution to an African Problem?', 11(5) Journal of International Criminal Justice, 2013, pp. 1139–1160.

JURISPRUDENCE

AfCHPR 2009
AfCHPR, Michelot Yogombaye v. Senegal, Application No. 001/2008, 10 December 2009.
Appellate Court of Dakar 2000
Appellate Court of Dakar, Souleymane Guengueng and Others Against Hissène Habré, Arrêt No. 135, 4 July 2000.
ICC 2015
ICC, Prosecutor v. William Samoei Ruto and Joshua Arap Sang, ICC-01/09-01/11, 19 October 2015.
ICC 2015
ICC, Prosecutor v. William Samoei Ruto and Joshua Arap Sang, ICC-01/09-01/11-1987, 12 October 2015.

ICC 2010
ICC, Prosecutor v. Omar Hassan Ahmad Al-Bashir, ICC-02/05-01/09-95, 12 July 2010.
ICC 2009
ICC, Prosecutor v. Omar Hassan Ahmad Al-Bashir, ICC-02/05-01/09-1, 4 March 2009.
ICJ 2009
ICJ, Case concerning questions relating to the obligation to prosecute or extradite (Belgium v. Senegal), 28 May 2009.

TREATIES, LEGISLATION AND AGREEMENTS

African (Banjul) Charter on Human and Peoples' Rights, OAU Doc CAB/LEG/67/3 Rev 5, 27 June 1981.
Agreement between the Government of the Republic of Senegal and the African Union on the Establishment of Extraordinary African Chambers within the Senegalese Judicial System, Doc No. LC11888, 22 August 2012.
AU PSC, Communiqué of the 142nd Meeting of the Peace and Security Council, Doc. PSC/MIN/Comm(CXLII), 21 July 2008.
AU PSC, Communiqué of the 175th Meeting of the Peace and Security Council, Doc. PSC/PR/Comm(CLXXV) Rev.1, 5 March 2009.
AU PSC, Communiqué of the 46th Meeting of the Peace and Security Council, Doc. PSC/MIN/Comm(XLVI), 10 March 2006.
AU, Decision on the Abuse of the Principle of Universal Jurisdiction - Doc. EX.CL/522(XV), June 2009.
AU, Decision on the Hissène Habré Case and the African Union, Doc. Assembly/AU/8 (VI) Add.9, January 2006.
AU, Decision on the Implementation of the Assembly Decision on the Abuse of the Principle of Universal Jurisdiction, DOC. Assembly/AU/3(XII) Jan 2009.
AU, Decision on the meeting of African States Parties to the Statute of the Rome Statute of the International Criminal Court (ICC), Doc. Assembly/AU/13(XIII), 3 July 2009.
AU, Decision on the Trial of Mr Hissène Habré and the African Union, Doc. Assembly/AU/Dec.157 (VIII), January 2007.
AU, Décision sur le Procès d'Hissène Habré et l'Union Africaine - Doc. Assembly/AU/3 (VII), Doc. Assembly/AU/Dec.127 (VII), July 2006.
AU, The Common African position on the proposed reform of the United Nations ('The Ezulwini Consensus'), Doc. Ext/EX.CL/2 (VII), March 2005.
Charter of the United Nations, 26 June 1945.
Constitutive Act of the African Union, 11 July 2000.
Johannesburg Declaration of the Pan-African Parliament (on Universal Jurisdiction), 15 May 2008.
Negotiated Relationship Agreement between the International Criminal Court and the United Nations, ICC-ASP/3/Res.1, 7 September 2004.
Pact on Security, Stability and Development in the Great Lakes Region, December 2006.
Pan-African Parliament, Resolution on the Dispatch of A Pan-African Parliament Peace Mission to the Democratic Republic of Congo during the First Fortnight of May 2005, PAP-Res. 007/05, 11 April 2005.

Pan-African Parliament, Resolution on the Dispatch of the Pan-African Parliament Peace Mission to Côte d'Ivoire at the Beginning of May 2005, PAP-Res. 006/05, 11 April 2005.
Protocol on Amendments to the Protocol on the Statute of the African Court of Justice and Human Rights (Malabo Protocol), 27 June 2014.
Protocol on the Prevention and Punishment of the Crimes of Genocide, War Crimes and Crimes against Humanity, 29 November 2006.
Protocol on the Prevention and Suppression of Sexual Violence against Women and Children (Sexual Violence Protocol), 30 November 2006.
Protocol Relating to the Establishment of the Peace and Security Council of the African Union, 9 July 2002.
Protocol to the African Charter on Human and Peoples' Rights on the Establishment of an African Court on Human and Peoples' Rights, 10 June 1998.
Protocol to the Treaty Establishing the African Economic Community Relating to the Pan-African Parliament (PAP Protocol), 1991.
Rome Statute of the International Criminal Court, 2187 UNTS 90/37, 17 July 1998.
Statute of the Extraordinary African Chambers within the courts of Senegal created to prosecute international crimes committed in Chad between 7 June 1982 and 1 December 1990.
Statute on the African Court of Justice and Human Rights, 1 July 2008.
Treaty for the Establishment of the East African Community (EAC), 30 November 1999.
Treaty of the Economic Community Of West African States (ECOWAS), 28 May 1975.
Treaty of the South African Development Community (SADC), 17 August 1992.
UN Security Council, Resolution 1593 (2005), UN Doc. S/RES/1593, 31 March 2005.
UN Security Council, Resolution 1674 (2006), UN Doc. S/RES/1674, 28 April 2006.
UN Security Council, Resolution 1706 (2006), UN Doc. S/RES/1706, 31 August 2006.
UN Security Council, Resolution 2127 (2013), UN Doc. S/RES/2127, 5 December 2013.

OTHERS

Aboagye, F., 'The African Union in Burundi: Lessons from the first African Union Peacekeeeping Operation', ISS Africa, 2004.
Aboagye, F., 'The Hybrid operation for Darfur: A Critical Review of the Concept', ISS Paper 149, August 2007.
ACHPR, Report of the African Commission on Human and Peoples' Rights' Fact-finding Mission to the Republic of Sudan in the Darfur Region, EX.CL/364 (XI) Annex III, 20 September 2004.
ACHPR, Resolution on Darfur, ACHPR/Res 68-(XXXV) 04, 4 June 2004.
ACHPR, Resolution on Ending Impunity in Africa and on the Domestication and Implementation of the Rome Statute of the International Criminal Court, 5 December 2005.
ACHPR, Resolution on Strengthening the Responsibility to Protect in Africa, 28 November 2007.
ACHPR, Resolution on the Human Rights Situation in Darfur, Sudan, ACHPR/Res.74 (XXXVII) 05, 11 May 2005.

ACHPR, Resolution on the Human Rights Situation in the Central African Republic, 24 July 2013.
ACHPR, Resolution on the Human Rights Situation in the Central African Republic, 14 March 2014.
ACHPR, Resolution on the Human Rights Situation in the Democratic Republic of Congo, 5 December 2005.
ACHPR, Resolution on the Human Rights Situation in Uganda, 5 December 2005.
ACHPR, Resolution on the Ratification of the Statute on the International Criminal Court by AU Member States, 16 May 2002.
ACHPR, Resolution on the Ratification of the Treaty on the International Criminal Court, 31 October 1998.
ACHPR, Resolution on the Right to a Remedy and Reparation for Women and Girls Victims of Sexual Violence, 28 November 2007.
ACHPR, Resolution on the Situation of Women in the Democratic Republic of Congo, 29 November 2006.
AfCHPR, Cases – List of Applications Received By the Court.
Ajayi, T., 'The UN, the AU and ECOWAS – A Triangle for Peace and Security in West Africa?', FES Briefing Paper 11, November 2008.
ASP, 'Strategic Plan for Outreach of the International Criminal Court', ICC-ASP/5/12, 29 September 2006.
AU and European Union, 'AU-EU Technical Ad hoc Expert Group on the Principle of Universal Jurisdiction Report', 2009.
AU Commission, 'Decision on the meeting of African States Parties to the Rome Statute of the International Criminal Court', Press Release, 14 July 2009.
AU Peace and Security Council, '1er Rapport Intérimaire de la Commission de l'Union Africaine sur la situation en République Centrafricaine et les activités de la Mission Internationale de Soutien à la Centrafrique sous conduite Africaine', 2014.
AU, 'Concept Note For The Meeting of African States Parties to the Rome Statute of the International Criminal Court', 8–9 June 2009.
AU, '1er Rapport Intérimaire de la Commission de l'Union Africaine sur la situation en République Centrafricaine et les activités de la Mission Internationale de Soutien à la Centrafrique sous conduite Africaine'.
AU, 'Framework for the Operationalization of the Continental Early Warning System', PSD/EW/EXP/FRAMEWORK (I), December 2006.
AU, 'Report of the African Commission on Human and Peoples' Rights (ACHPR)' Fact-finding Mission to the Republic of Sudan in the Darfur Region, EX.CL/364 (XI) Annex III, 20 September 2004.
AU, Report of Committee of Eminent Jurists on the Case of Hissene Habre, 2 July 2006.
AU, Report of the African Union: High Level Panel on Darfur I, PSC/AHG/2(CCVII), 29 October 2009.
AUPD, 'The Quest for Peace, Justice and Reconciliation', Report of the African Union High Level Panel on Darfur, 8 October 2009, Annex I UN Doc. S/2009/599.
Cilliers, J. and Malan, M., 'Progress with the African Standby Force', ISS Occasional Paper 98, May 2005.
Coalition for an Effective African Court on Human and Peoples' Rights et al., 'Implications of the African Court on Human and Peoples' Rights being empowered

to try international crimes such as genocide, war crimes and crimes against humanity', 2009 (on file with author).

De Coning, C., 'The Role of the OAU in Conflict Management in Africa', in Conflict Management, Peacekeeping and Peacebuilding, ISS Monograph No. 10, April 1997.

Ebobrah, S., 'A rights-protection goldmine or a waiting volcanic eruption: Competence of, and access to, the human rights jurisdiction of the ECOWAS Community Court of Justice', 7 African Human Rights Law Journal, 2007.

El Abdellaoui, J., 'The Panel of the Wise: A comprehensive introduction to a critical pillar of the African Peace and Security Architecture', ISS Paper 193, August 2009.

Grono, N., 'The Role of the International Criminal Court in African Peace Processes: Mutually Reinforcing or Mutually Exclusive?', Institute for Public Policy Research Paper, 28 November 2006.

Human Rights Watch, 'Ex-Chad Dictator Indicted in Senegal: Hissène Habre, "The African Pinochet", To Face Trial', Press Release, 3 February 2000.

ICC, 'The Prosecutor of the ICC opens investigation in Darfur', Press Release, ICC-OTP-0606–104-En, 6 June 2005.

ICC, Situation in Darfur, Sudan, ICC-02/05.

International Commission on Intervention and State Sovereignty, 'The Responsibility to Protect' Report, December 2001.

International Crisis Group, 'Darfur: The Failure to Protect', Africa Report No. 89, 8 March 2005.

International Refugee Rights Initiative, 'Some reflections on the legal and political mechanisms bolstering the responsibility to protect: The African Union and the Great Lakes, Eastern, Southern and Horn of Africa sub-regional arrangements', 21 October 2008.

Kindiki, K., 'Intervention to Protect Civilians in Darfur: Legal Dilemmas and Policy Imperatives', ISS Monograph 131, 1 May 2007.

Maiese, M., 'Peacebuilding', in Burgess, G. and Burgess, H. (eds.), Beyond Intractability, Conflict Information Consortium (University of Colorado, Boulder), September 2003.

Murithi, T., 'Between Paternalism and Hybrid Partnership: the Emerging UN and Africa Relationship in Peace Operations', FES Briefing Paper, May 2007.

Musila, G.M., 'Between Rhetoric and Action: The Politics, Processes and Practice of the ICC's Work in the DRC', ISS Monograph 164, July 2009.

Musila, G.M., 'United States of Africa: Positioning the Pan-African Parliament and Court in the political union debate', ISS Paper 142, June 2007.

Nathan, L., 'Mediation and the African Union's Panel of the Wise', LSE Discussion Paper No. 10, June 2005.

Odinkalu, C.A., 'Saving International Justice in Africa', Oxford Transitional Justice Research Working Paper Series, 4 August 2009.

PAP, Report of the Pan-African Parliament fact-finding mission on Darfur, the Sudan, Doc. AU/PAP/RPT/CIRCR.CTTEE, 23 February 2005.

Ping, J., 'Keynote address at the Roundtable high-level meeting of experts on the responsibility to protect in Africa', High-Level Meeting of Experts on the Responsibility to Protect in Africa, 23 October 2008.

Powell, K., 'The African Union's Emerging Peace and Security Regime', ISS Monograph 119, May 2005.

Seils, P. and Wierda, M., 'The International Criminal Court and Conflict Mediation, International Center for Transitional Justice', June 2005.

South Africa Department of International Relations and Cooperation's, 'Briefing by the Deputy Minister of Foreign Affairs, Ms Sue van der Merwe to the Heads of Mission accredited to South Africa on the Outcomes of the 7th African Union Summit, CSIR International Convention Centre', 14 July 2006.

UN General Assembly, 2005 World Summit Outcome, UN Doc. A/RES/60/1, 24 October 2005.

UN Secretary General, 'An Agenda for Peace', UN Doc. A/47/277, 17 June 1992.

UN, 'Report of the International Commission of Inquiry on Darfur to the United Nations Secretary General: Pursuant to Security Council Resolution 1564 of 18 September 2004', 25 January 2005.

UN, 'Secretary-General Presents His Annual Report To General Assembly', Press Release SG/SM/7136, 20 September 1999.

United Kingdom, United Kingdom Foreign Office Policy Document No. 148, reprinted in 1986 British YB of Int'l Law.

A SEED FOR WORLD PEACE GROWING IN AFRICA

The Kampala Amendments on the Crime of Aggression and the Monsoon of Malabo

Jutta F. Bertram-Nothnagel

1. INTRODUCTION

In 1758, Emmerich de Vattel wrote of 'the great guilt of the sovereign' who undertakes 'an unjust war':

> He is chargeable with all the evils, all the horrors of the war: all the effusion of blood, the desolation of families, the rapine, the acts of violence, the ravages, the conflagrations, are his works and his crime. He is guilty of a crime against the enemy, whom he attacks, oppresses, and massacres without cause; he is guilty of a crime against his people, whom he forces into acts of injustice, and exposes to danger, without reason or necessity, – against those of his subjects who are ruined or distressed by the war, – who lose their lives, their property, or their health, in consequence of it: finally he is guilty of a crime against mankind in general, whose peace he disturbs, and to whom he sets a pernicious example...[1]

In 1998, the Rome Statute of the International Criminal Court[2] echoed Vattel's condemnation by listing the crime of aggression[3, 4] as one of the four core

1 De Vattel 1758, Chapter XI (Of the Sovereign who Wages an Unjust War), para. 184. I am grateful to Don Ferencz who first alerted me to these observations by Vattel.

2 Rome Statute of the International Criminal Court, adopted 17 July 1998, UN Doc. A/CONF.183/9, 2187 UNTS 90, entered into force 1 July 2002.

3 While De Vattel, *supra* n. 1, did not use the term 'crime of aggression' and while the justifications he pondered for war-making may not have been exactly the same as those for the use of force under the Charter of the United Nations, his vivid description of the range of individual criminal responsibility at issue bears recalling whenever the armed force of a state is unleashed against another state without adequate legal basis.

4 Already in 1918, the Entente considered a proposal to prosecute the just-abdicated Kaiser Wilhelm II for starting an aggressive war, but the proposal focused exclusively on a crime that had already taken place (see Sellars 2014, pp. 195–211). Similarly, the mandates of the Nuremberg and Tokyo Tribunals to prosecute crimes against peace were looking to the past

crimes under the Court's jurisdiction.[5] Yet the exercise of jurisdiction remained suspended in the absence of agreement about the definition and about the jurisdictional conditions for the crime.[6] Looking back over the decade that followed, the world is left to wonder how it might look different today if the crime had been fully included in the Rome Statute from the beginning and despair about the crime's brutality had been etched already then with a stronger acid into international criminal law.

2. KAMPALA

2.1. ADOPTION OF THE AMENDMENTS ON THE CRIME OF AGGRESSION

Finally in 2010, the long-missing international accord on the definition and the jurisdictional conditions was achieved in Kampala, Uganda, when the Review Conference of the Rome Statute of the International Criminal Court adopted its historical resolution on the crime of aggression.[7] A new seed for world peace was planted in Africa.[8] Deciding by consensus and aiming at the full integration of provisions on the crime of aggression into the legal framework of the International Criminal Court, the Review Conference adopted amendments to the Rome Statute,[9] amendments to the Elements of Crimes,[10] and a series of

and restricted to crimes that had already taken place. In contrast, under the much wider legislative scope of the Rome Statute, international criminal jurisdiction was for the first time expressly established for crimes of aggression that might be committed in the future and anywhere around the globe.

5 Article 5(1) Rome Statute. In addition, the preamble of the Rome Statute reaffirms explicitly the obligation of states to refrain from the threat or use of force inconsistent with the Purposes of the United Nations (see preamb. para. 7.).

6 Article 5(2) Rome Statute.

7 Resolution RC/Res.6, 11 June 2010, in Review Conference Official Records, RC/11, part II, 17. The Review Conference adopted also an amendment resolution expanding with new Article 8(2)(e)(xiii),(xix) and (xv) on the war crime of employing prohibited weapons Resolution RC/Res.5, 10 June 2010, in Review Conference Official Records, RC/11, part II, 13. See Clark 2010, p. 689.

8 Bertram-Nothnagel 2010, pp. 9–27, also posted 19 December 2014, pp. 1–27, at: www.africalegalaid.com/news/the-provisions-on-the-crime-of-aggression-kampala-conference.

9 'Amendments to the Rome Statute of the International Criminal Court on the crime of aggression', Resolution RC/Res.6, Annex I. The new version of the Rome Statute containing the Kampala Amendments on both the crime of aggression and on certain war crimes is available at: http://treaties.un.org. For the amendments on the crime of aggression, see also the Depository Notification circulated by the UN Secretary General, C.N.651.2010.TREATIES-8, 29 November 2010. For the amendments on certain war crimes, see Depository Notification C.N.651.2010.TREATIES-6, 29 November 2010. In the context of this paper, the term 'Kampala Amendments' refers to those concerning the crime of aggression.

10 'Amendments to the Elements of Crimes', Resolution RC/Res.6, Annex II.

Understandings.[11] The amendments to the Rome Statute spell out the definition of the crime of aggression in a new Article 8*bis* and specify the conditions for the ICC's exercise of jurisdiction in new Articles 15*bis* (for referrals by a state party and *ex proprio motu* of the Prosecutor) and 15*ter* (for referrals by the Security Council). Aggression is a leadership crime not only under Article 8*bis*: a new paragraph 3*bis* for Article 25 also restricts the application of the general principles on criminal *participation* to persons in a leadership position.[12] Significantly too, the *ne bis in idem* rule in Article 20(3) is extended to the crime of aggression. Article 9 clarifies that the Elements of the Crimes, as amended, assist the Court also for this crime.

Still, the resolution did not immediately enable the ICC to proceed: in accordance with Article 15*bis*(2) and Article 15*ter*(2), the Court may only exercise jurisdiction with regard to crimes of aggression committed one year after the ratification or acceptance of the Kampala provisions by thirty states parties. Moreover, under paragraph 3 of both Article 15*bis* and Article 15*ter*, the Court's exercise of jurisdiction is still 'subject to a decision to be taken after 1 January 2017 by the same majority of States Parties as is required for the adoption of an amendment to the Statute.'

These two stipulations, whichever is later, are not only relevant for the Court's authority to start exercising jurisdiction, they matter also for temporal jurisdiction, i.e. how far the Court can reach into the past to prosecute crimes of aggression.[13] While Article 15*bis*(2) and Article 15*ter*(2) are clear about the thirty ratifications (plus one year) as the time point for temporal jurisdiction, Understandings 1 and 3[14] refer to both stipulations and state that the Court shall also not exercise jurisdiction over crimes committed before the activating decision. These temporal jurisdiction requirements apply to all three trigger mechanisms, Security Council referrals, state party referrals and *proprio motu*. At the same time, it should be noted that the two stipulations influence and hold up only the *exercise of jurisdiction*, including the temporal reach of jurisdiction, but not *entry into force*. They also appear only in the provisions on the jurisdictional conditions and not in the definition of the crime.

Throughout the long negotiations for the Kampala Amendments, advocacy by African states towards a full inclusion of the crime of aggression under the Rome Statute had been widespread and pronounced, most certainly

11 'Understandings regarding the amendments to the Rome Statute of the International Criminal Court on the crime of aggression', Resolution RC/Res.6, Annex III.

12 'In respect of the crime of aggression, the provisions of this article shall apply only to persons in a position effectively to exercise control over or to direct the political or military action of a State.'

13 Compare jurisdiction *ratione temporis* for the other three core crimes in Article 11 of the Rome Statute.

14 See 'Understandings regarding the amendments to the Rome Statute of the International Criminal Court on the crime of aggression', Resolution RC/Res.6, *supra* n. 7, Annex III.

by those party to the Statute.[15] To cite just one example from the pre-Kampala negotiations: Cutting through the long-ongoing debate whether the provisions should enter into force under Article 121(3), (4) or (5)[16] of the Rome Statute, Nigeria submitted a proposal[17] that combined features of

15 See also McNamee, 'The ICC and Africa – Between Aspiration and Reality: Making International Justice Work Better for Africa – Reflections on a High-Level Roundtable', 2 Brenthurst Discussion Paper (2014), 1, at 8: 'African States have been largely supportive of inclusion of the crime of aggression.'

16 Article 121(3) determines the process for the adoption of an amendment. Arguments for entry into force by adoption relied on the wording in Article 5(2): 'The Court shall exercise jurisdiction… once a provision is adopted…' They also relied on Articles 12(1) and 5(1) of the Rome Statute to point out that states parties had already accepted the Court's jurisdiction over the crime of aggression. – Under Article 121(4) an amendment enters into force for all states parties together, one year after instruments of ratification or acceptance have been deposited by seven-eighths of them. A state party that has not accepted the amendment may withdraw from the Statute in accordance with Article 121(6). – The first sentence of Article 121(5) provides that any amendment to Articles 5, 6, 7 and 8 enters into force only 'for those States Parties which have accepted the amendment, one year after the deposit of their instruments of ratification or acceptance.' The sentence does not include wording on entry into force *as such*, i.e. the moment when an amendment becomes part of the Statute and supports proceedings based on Security Council referrals. (Compare Article 126 on the moment of entry into force *as such* for the Statute.) In the course of the discussions, states referred to either one of two possibilities: The Security Council could start referring situations from the moment of the adoption of the amendment or after the first ratification becomes effective. (These discussions took place long before the two postponing stipulations for the exercise of jurisdiction were added with regard to the crime of aggression.) – The second sentence of Article 121(5) sets out conditions for the *exercise of jurisdiction* (not for *entry into force*): 'In respect of a State Party which has not accepted the amendment, the Court shall not exercise its jurisdiction regarding a crime covered by the amendment when committed by that States Party's nationals or on its territory.' (The sentence does not refer to non-parties to the Statute, only to states parties that do not ratify or accept an amendment.) There was general consensus throughout the negotiations that this second sentence was *irrelevant for Security Council referrals*. Possible reinterpretations or modifications debated with regard to the second sentence were likewise considered irrelevant for Security Council referrals. See explicitly on the irrelevance of state consent in the case of Security Council referrals: 'Non-paper by the Chairman on outstanding issues regarding the conditions for the exercise of jurisdiction', footnote 6 and text above footnote 7, in Report of the Working Group on the Review Conference, in Official Records of the Assembly of States Parties to the Rome Statute of the International Criminal Court [Official ICC-ASP Records], Eighth Session (resumption), New York, 22–25 March 2010, ICC-ASP/8/20/Add.1, Annex II [2010 WGRC Report], Appendix I. For the irrelevance of state acceptance of the provisions on the crime of aggression in the case of Security Council referrals, see also Report of the Special Working Group on the Crime of Aggression, ICC-ASP/7/SWGCA/2, 20 February 2009 [2009 SWGCA Report], paras. 28–29, in Official ICC-ASP Records, Seventh Session (first and second resumptions), New York, 19–23 January and 9–13 February 2009, ICC-ASP/7/20/Add.1, Chapter II, Annex II.

17 'Non-Paper Submitted by Nigeria on the Draft Resolution of 19 November 2008'. The proposal was submitted in the Special Working Group on the Crime of Aggression during the seventh session of the Assembly of States Parties to the Rome Statute, 14–22 November 2008. During the second resumption of the seventh session of the Assembly, 9–13 February 2009, the original Non-Paper was followed by the 'Revised Non-paper Resubmitted by Nigeria of 9 February 2009'. (Both Non-Papers are on file with the author.) See also 2009 SWGCA Report, *ibid*, paras. 7–8.

paragraphs 4 and 5.[18] While the specific idea did not find sufficient support, the intent to build a bridge was welcomed and inspired further efforts towards creative answers. After all, creativity was badly needed in light of the unique 'half-in/half-out' position of the crime of aggression under the Statute.[19] The determination by African states parties to achieve the adoption of amendments on the crime of aggression was also strongly expressed in Kampala.[20] During the General Debate, Kenya, on behalf of the African states parties, spoke of the 'promise' in Rome with respect to the crime of aggression and added: 'We believe that the time is opportune for the ICC to assume its mandate' over this crime.[21] The statement listed the two issues still be resolved – both jurisdictional – namely, the question of a filter mechanism and the question of the need for consent by the aggressor state to the Court's jurisdiction. The statement reiterated well-known African positions aimed at the widest possible reach of the Court: primarily, there should be no court-external filter, particularly not a requirement for a determination by the United Nations Security Council of a state act of aggression. The objections against the Security Council filter, voiced not only by African states parties but also by many other states, were practically never based on concern about politicised overuses of Security Council

18 Under the Nigerian proposal, the amendments would initially enter into force in line with Article 121(5), namely for each state party individually, ratification by ratification. But once ratifications or acceptances by seven-eighths of the states parties would be achieved (the number relevant under Article 121(4)), the amendments would enter into force for all.

19 Shortly before adoption of the Rome Statute, Article 121(5) referred only to amendments to Article 5 (and not yet to amendments to Articles 6, 7 and 8). Article 5 consisted of one paragraph setting out the list of core crimes. Inclusion of the crime of aggression in this list had not yet been agreed upon. According to the delegate of the state proposing the second sentence of Article 121(5), *supra* n. 16, that sentence was put forward exactly with the crime of aggression in mind, i.e. for a future addition of the crime *after* adoption of the Statute. (See Scheffer, 'Unwilling Hands – U.S. Sabotages International Court at its Own Peril', *The Seattle Post-Intelligencer*, 1 February 2004.) When the crime of aggression *was* included in the list of core crimes after all, i.e. *before* the adoption of the Statute, Article 121(5) became, arguably, no longer applicable to that crime. Especially the second sentence of Article 121(5) became an ill fit: In accordance with Article 12(1) of the Rome Statute, states parties agree to the Court's jurisdiction over the crime of aggression already with the ratification of the Statute. On the other hand, the addition to the list of core crimes was accompanied by the suspension of the exercise of jurisdiction in a new paragraph 2 for Article 5. And in yet another late development at the Rome Conference, the Drafting Committee extended Article 121(5) to Articles 6, 7 and 8, thus restricting it no longer to amendments of the list of crimes in Article 5.

20 See e.g. 'Statement by Deputy-Minister A.C. Nel, MP, Deputy Minister of Justice and Constitutional Development, Republic of South Africa', General Debate at the Review Conference of the Rome Statute of the International Criminal Court, 31 May 2010. The speeches at the General Debate can be found at the Review Conference website: www.icc-cpi.int/en_menus/asp/reviewconference/Pages/review%20conference.aspx.

21 'Statement by Hon. Amos Wako, Attorney General of the Republic of Kenya, on Behalf of the African States Parties to the International Criminal Court', General Debate at the Review Conference of the Rome Statute of the International Criminal Court', 31 May 2010. Available *ibid.*

determinations but on concern about paralysis in the Council due to the veto power of its permanent members and thus on concern about politicised *failures* to make a determination, failures that would block the Court.[22] In Kampala, the statement on behalf of the African states parties continued: 'We have been told that to avoid political prosecutions, it is important that the alleged Aggressor State should have consented to the Court's exercise of jurisdiction … The truth is that all the crimes in the Statute are capable of being politicised. It is for this reason that the Statute has put in place internal mechanisms, including the Pre-Trial Chamber, to ensure the judicial appropriateness of any investigation.' Significantly, the resolve to find a solution and the openness towards compromise were at the same time clearly conveyed: 'we are of the firm belief that the differences between the delegations are not insurmountable and that there is sufficient will at this Review Conference to overcome them. We are of the firm view that during this Review Conference, our efforts should be aimed at bridging the differences'.[23] The statement highlighted the outcome of the 'roll call' during the resumed eighth session of the Assembly of States Parties on four different combinations of jurisdictional conditions[24] concerning state party referrals and *ex proprio motu*:[25] then too, the African states parties had individually indicated their support for 'combination 4', namely for jurisdictional conditions that would neither require a Security Council determination nor acceptance by the aggressor state.[26] Yet again, the statement in Kampala repeated the willingness for compromise: '[T]he overwhelming majority of States Parties expressed their support for combination 3 and 4. We

---

22 Telling in this respect had been also the pre-Kampala discussions on the *substantive* rather than jurisdictional effect of determinations of an act of aggression by organs outside the Court. (Such determinations might exist irrespective of any filter requirement.) Already in the Special Working Group on the Crime of Aggression, states had achieved preliminary agreement that prior determinations of an act of aggression by organs outside the Court would be without prejudice to the Court's own findings. The considerations were not propelled by worries about politicised determinations and politicised prosecutions but by the possibility of new evidence and by the due process rights of the accused as a matter of principle.

23 In contrast, the statement of the African Union – reflective also of the opinions of non-parties to the Rome Statute – expressed reluctance about the adoption of crime of aggression provisions. See 'Statement by Mr Ben Kioko, Legal Counsel of the African Union Commission on Behalf of the AU Commission', General Debate at the Review Conference of the Rome Statute of the International Criminal Court, 1 June 2010, available *supra* n. 20. The arguments were quite similar to those of some of the permanent members of the United Nations Security Council.

24 'Illustrative chart on conditions for the exercise of jurisdiction', in 'Non-paper by the Chairman on outstanding issues regarding the conditions for the exercise of jurisdiction', 2010 WGRC Report, *supra* n. 16, Appendix I, Attachment.

25 'Illustrative chart', *ibid*, chapeau: 'The focus is on State referrals and *proprio motu* proceedings, since Security Council referrals do not require the consent of the State(s) concerned.' See in this regard also *supra* n. 16.

26 Combination 4 did require the Victim State's acceptance of the Court's jurisdiction over the crime of aggression, 'Illustrative chart', *supra* n. 24.

are convinced that the adherents of these two combinations can work towards a consensus position.' Like combination 4, combination 3 excluded the need for a Security Council determination but required acceptance by the aggressor state.[27]

2.2. THE JURISDICTIONAL CONDITIONS

One of the preferences of the African states parties was clearly met: a determination by the Security Council of an act of aggression is not required for any of the three trigger mechanisms. Instead, for both state party referrals and the Prosecutor's *proprio motu*, the Kampala Amendments use a court-internal instead of an external filter mechanism: In the absence of a determination by the Security Council, the full Pre-Trial Division, rather than a Pre-Trial Chamber must authorise the Prosecutor to proceed with the investigation.[28] Apart from differences with regard to temporal jurisdiction,[29] Security Council referrals work for the crime of aggression exactly as for the other three core crimes.[30] Security Council referrals are effective irrespective of any ratification or acceptance requirements existing under the other two trigger mechanisms. In their universal applicability to situations around the globe, Security Council referrals under the Rome Statute are comparable to the Council's authority to establish ad hoc tribunals. As with regard to the setting up of ad hoc tribunals, the Council, in referring a situation to the ICC, is 'acting under Chapter VII of the Charter of the United Nations'.[31]

---

27 The combinations for the roll call encompassed more variability than indicated above: With regard to the question of a filter mechanism, combinations 3 and 4 were favored both by those states parties who preferred no external filter at all and those who would be open to any filter other than the Security Council. With respect to the latter option, the chart boxes referred to the external filters of the United Nations General Assembly and the International Court of Justice. A footnote to combination 3 mentioned that the Pre-Trial Chamber of the ICC could serve as an internal filter. – Combination 1 required both acceptance by the aggressor state and a Security Council filter. Combination 2 entailed the latter but not the former requirement. – Significantly too, the two types of jurisdictional requirements were tied to two different stages of the proceedings. The question of acceptance by the aggressor state was relevant for the initiation of an investigation, the question of a requirement for a Security Council determination mattered at the next procedural stage when the Prosecutor decides to proceed with an investigation. *Ibid.*

28 Article 15*bis*(6)–(8) of the Rome Statute.

29 See *supra* n. 13, 14 with main text.

30 Article *15ter* (Security Council referrals) – in contrast to Article 15*bis* (state party referrals and *proprio motu*) – does not provide for exemptions when relevant states are non-parties to the Statute or when the state committing an act of aggression has made a declaration that it does not accept jurisdiction over the crime. In addition, Understanding 2 provides expressly that the Court shall exercise jurisdiction on the basis of Security Council referrals irrespective of whether the state concerned has accepted the Court's jurisdiction with regard to aggression. See also *supra* n. 16.

31 Articles 15*ter*(1) and 13(b) Rome Statute.

For referrals by a state party and *proprio motu*, the Kampala Amendments on the crime of aggression clearly fall more under combination 3 than 4. Two parameters apply. First, the Court will not be able to exercise jurisdiction over a crime of aggression committed by the nationals or on the territory of a state that is not a party to the Rome Statute.[32] Second, when the act of aggression was committed by a *state party*, the Court may exercise its jurisdiction over the respective individual crime, unless *that* state has previously declared that it does not accept the Court's jurisdiction over the crime of aggression.[33, 34] Ultimately, with regard to these two trigger mechanisms, it remains very much up to the

32 Article 15*bis*(5) Rome Statute.

33 Article 15*bis*(4) Rome Statute.

34 Whether and how far the *exercise of jurisdiction* over the crime of aggression requires the ratification or acceptance of the Amendments has been a point of contention with regard to state party referrals and *proprio motu*, see Barriga 2012, pp. 3, 52 n. 260. For this question, it is essential to differentiate between (1) entry into force *as such*, *supra* n. 16; (2) entry into force *for a state* (relevant in particular for the State's treaty obligations, – and possibly but not necessarily for the ICC's exercise of jurisdiction); and (3) *exercise of jurisdiction* by the ICC over the *individual* crime. Those who argue that the Court's exercise over the crime of aggression requires the ratification or acceptance of the Kampala Amendments by either the state of the accused or the state where the crime was committed, i.e. that ratification or acceptance by the victim state would be sufficient, draw on the pattern in Article 12 and/or on the so-called 'positive understanding' of the second sentence of Article 121(5). With regard to Article 12, it should be noted that its ratification or acceptance requirements refer to the Statute and not to amendments. Yet, insofar as the Amendments represent the completion of the Statute and since Article 12 must mean the full Statute, it could be argued that ratification or acceptance of the 'completion' must be added by at least one of these two states referred to in Article 12, in order to allow exercise of jurisdiction after state party referral or *proprio motu*. At the same time, states parties have already accepted the ICC's jurisdiction over the crime of aggression under Article 12(1), providing food for argument that mere adoption of the Amendments suffices for exercise of jurisdiction, in accordance with Article 5(2), *supra* n. 16. – Those who argue that the Amendments must have been ratified or accepted by *both* the state party of the accused and the state party of the territory of the crime, i.e. the aggressor state must have ratified or accepted the amendments, rely on the ordinary meaning of the second sentence of Article 121(5) under a so-called 'negative understanding'. Yet the latter argument does not fit well with operative paragraph 1 of Resolution RC/Res.6, *supra* n. 7. That paragraph notes that any state party may lodge an opt-out declaration *prior* to ratification or acceptance. Why would such an opt-out be needed when the Court's exercise of jurisdiction were anyway blocked? The triple-stitching (requiring what amounts to an opt-in by the state party of the accused *and* an opt-in by the state party where the crime was committed *and* the absence of an opt-out by the aggressor state) does also not fit well with the history of the negotiations. With regard to the second sentence of Article 121(5), states discussed mainly whether it should be applied equally to non-ratifying states parties and non-party states, whether an opt-out or opt-in system should be used, and whether the consent by the aggressor state or by the victim state would be sufficient. This observer does not recall that states ever argued for an arrangement that would both require opt-in and permit opt-out by the same state. (See 2009 SWGCA Report, *supra* n. 16, paras. 31–37, and 'Non-Paper on other substantive issues on aggression to be addressed by the Review Conference', 2009 SWGCA Report, *supra* n. 16, Annex II; also 2010 WGRC Report, *supra* n. 16, paras. 4–8, and 'Non-Paper by the Chairman on outstanding issues regarding the conditions for the exercise of jurisdiction', 2010 WGRC Report, *supra* n. 17, Appendix I.).

individual state party whether it wishes its leaders to be deterred and its people and the world to be protected.[35]

African states parties, moving in Kampala towards compromise on a consent-based regime, advocated that the right to opt out should be more limited and accompanied by a mandatory sunset clause.[36] After all, the dependency of the Court's exercise of jurisdiction on the consent of the aggressor state is plainly counterproductive for the prevention of the crime of aggression.

Looking at the three trigger mechanisms together, the limitations to the exercise of jurisdiction are serious – yet not quite as restrictive as may be assumed.

First, the unavailability of one trigger mechanism may often be compensated by the availability of another trigger mechanism.

Second, with regard to state party referrals and the Prosecutor's *proprio motu*, states may be ill advised to make an opt-out declaration or to refrain from ratifying the Statute. Leaders who have the power to steer their country into an act of aggression probably have as well the wherewithal to obtain an opt-out declaration. The question is if they really should. After Rome and Kampala, crimes of aggression are less and less likely to remain without legal, political or economic consequence. Escape from prosecution has become less and less assured – the train has left the station. Establishment of a Nuremberg-type ad hoc court may, as a matter of course, become the juridical alternative when the ICC is unavailable. Yet due process as granted in a post-war ad hoc court may not measure up to the due process offered in the ICC. Notably, both Article 15*bis*(9) and Article 15*ter*(4) of the Rome Statute make it explicit that a determination by an organ outside the Court of a state act of aggression shall be without prejudice to the Court's own findings under the Rome Statute.[37] Such a protection of the rights of the accused can be easily forgotten in a court set up directly after a war, at a time when the commission of an act of aggression may have become a foregone conclusion

35 Since the conditions for the exercise of jurisdiction with regard to state party referrals and *proprio motu* differ from the wording of the second sentence of Article 121(5) in two respects, it is important to keep in mind that Article 5(2) had given states the authority, with regard to the crime of aggression, to agree on new conditions for the exercise of jurisdiction, conditions that could be different from those already existing in the Statute. The second sentence of Article 121(5) does not speak about entry into force but about the exercise of jurisdiction. Article 5(2) can be argued to top that sentence. Otherwise, what had been accomplished in Rome with Article 5(1)(d) and (2) would be nullified. (See also Permanent Mission of the Principality of Liechtenstein to the United Nations et al., *Handbook – Ratification and Implementation of the Kampala Amendments to the Rome Statute of the ICC – Crime of Aggression – War Crimes,* (Liechtenstein Institute on Self-Determination, 2013) 9, available at: www.crimeofaggression.info.)

36 See Barriga 2012, *Travaux, supra* n. 34, p. 53.

37 See also *supra* n. 22. With regard to a prior determination by the Security Council, the rule against prejudice does not preclude one procedural effect: When the Security Council has made a determination that an act of aggression was committed by the state concerned, the Prosecutor does not need to obtain an authorisation by the Pre-Trial Division.

immune to the mere thought of new evidence. Yet the prior determination by another organ may have used a different definition or a different evidentiary standard. The evidence may have been incomplete. The accused must be heard.

Third, while the veto power of the permanent members of the Council may work as a barrier against Security Council referrals and 'protect' in particular the leaders of a permanent member or the leaders of its allies against this trigger mechanism (not necessarily against the other two trigger mechanisms), such a barrier is not assured in the long term. Different governments of a permanent member can arrive at different positions about a prior use of force and about the soundness of a referral. Even where a state is able to block all three trigger mechanisms, the leader cannot dismiss the possibility of prosecution for a crime of aggression outright. Digging out from underneath the rubble of war, a future government may turn against the former leader and even seek prosecution by the ICC, especially where the exercise of domestic jurisdiction could be criticised for bias and retroactivity under national law. At least with regard to Security Council referrals, the *temporal* jurisdiction of the ICC would not be dependent on the acceptance of the Kampala Amendments by the particular state *before* its act of aggression.[38] Admittedly, the scenario of a permanent member of the Security Council changing its mind about its own or an ally's use of force is not a very likely one, but it is also not absurd. The small measure of deterrence that might flow from it could even be helpful to leaders who try to resist being drawn into uses of force.

2.3. THE DEFINITION AND A 'BREATHING ROOM'

Again, as in Rome, the glass in Kampala was half full and half empty, especially in light of the still required activating decision[39], but it is a glass less breakable. The adoption *per se* of the Amendments sent a sharp and powerful signal, a *cri de cœur* more piercing than in 1998: The prohibition of the use of force inconsistent with the Purposes of the Charter of the United Nations, a command

---

38 On temporal jurisdiction, see *supra* main text with n. 13, 14. Ratification or acceptance of the Amendments by the individual state, and entry into force for that state, is not mentioned as a relevant time point for *temporal* jurisdiction, i.e. how far back into the past the Court may reach. Article 11(2) of the Rome Statute, significant for state party referrals and the Prosecutor's *proprio motu*, refers only to entry into force of the *Statute* for the individual state as another relevant time point for temporal jurisdiction. For the developments on temporal jurisdiction, see especially Kreß 2012, pp. 83–89: for earlier wording that had still indicated an analogue application of Article 11(2), see 87. Ultimately, and still somewhat ambiguously, the reference to Article 11(2) was considered 'no longer enough' and the thirty ratifications and activating decision became 'instead' 'the decisive temporal points', see 89. In the case of state referrals and *proprio motu*, entry into force of the *Statute* (for the state concerned) under Article 11(2) continues to matter with regard to the crime of aggression, in case the temporal point under Article 11(2) comes later. (The application of Article 12(3) constitutes a point of argument that will not be addressed here.)

39 Articles 15*bis*(3) and 15*ter*(3) Rome Statute, *supra* p. 3.

for humanity carved already deep into the tablets of international law, must not be belittled, must not be disregarded and must not be forgotten. Decisions to use force are not a matter of discretionary political strategy; they are first and foremost ruled by a peremptory norm.[40] In the absence of an exceptional justification recognised under international law, human beings must not be turned into 'cannon fodder' and 'collateral damage', they must not be forced, ordered or manipulated into killing other human beings, and the hearts of families must not be cut to pieces. The fiat of the state does not suffice to sanctify aggression's assault on human dignity and human rights.

The Kampala adoption of the *definition* reaffirmed more loudly and clearly than ever that individual conduct to bring about an act of aggression is one of 'the most serious crimes of concern to the international community as a whole'.[41]

Significantly, the definition of the crime of aggression had been already agreed upon in the Special Working Group on the Crime of Aggression[42] and none of the states parties sought to reopen discussion at the Review Conference. Significantly too, the requirements of thirty ratifications and of an activating decision are only included in the provisions on the exercise of jurisdiction and not in the provision on the definition.

The definition of the crime of aggression under the Kampala Amendments is set out in two paragraphs of Article 8*bis* of the Rome Statute, with the first one spelling out the elements of the individual crime, and the second one further defining one of these elements, the state act of aggression:

> 1. For the purpose of this Statute, 'crime of aggression' means the planning, preparation, initiation or execution, by a person in a position effectively to exercise control over or to direct the political or military action of a State, of an act of aggression which, by its character, gravity and scale, constitutes a manifest violation of the Charter of the United Nations.
> 2. For the purpose of paragraph 1, 'act of aggression' means the use of armed force by a State against the sovereignty, territorial integrity or political independence of another State, or in any other manner inconsistent with the Charter of the United Nations. Any of the following acts, regardless of a declaration of war, shall, in accordance with United Nations General Assembly resolution 3314 (XXIX) of 14 December 1974, qualify as an act of aggression:
>   (a) The invasion or attack by the armed forces of a State
>   ...
>   (g) ...[43]

40 Orakhelashvili 2006, pp. 50–51.

41 Preamble, Rome Statute, preamb. para. 9.

42 'Proposals for a provision on aggression elaborated by the Special Working Group on the Crime of Aggression, in 2009 SWGCA Report, *supra* n. 16, Annex I, also in Official ICC-ASP Records, Seventh Session (first and second resumptions), *supra* n. 18, Appendix I.

43 The generic definition of the state act of aggression in the first sentence of the second paragraph is followed by a list of specific acts (a)–(g) that would qualify as an act of aggression.

Yet, as pointed out, before the Court can act at all, before any of the trigger mechanisms can kick in effectively, it remains first up to the Assembly of States Parties to adopt, 'as early as possible',[44] the still required decision to activate the Court's authority to exercise jurisdiction. The delay, backed in addition by the requirement for thirty ratifications,[45] was intended to provide 'breathing room',[46] a euphemism if ever there was one. 'Breathing room' for whom? For the people around the world who fear and suffer the crime of aggression? 'Breathing room' for what? For more mind-doping to fuel the addiction to 'solutions' by force? In an age of nuclear weapons, how can the international community afford procrastination in raising one of the shields against aggression?

Or does this 'breathing room' deserve its positive ring after all? Will the time until January 2017 be used to advance the organisational preparation for a more integral authority of the Court? Will states parties update their national criminal codes and cooperation agreements with the Court? It would be more than ironic to drag out activation based on concerns that the crime of aggression 'overburdens' the Court. Strengthening deterrence against this crime means less breeding ground for the other crimes and thus a *lessening* of the burden for the Court. At bottom, the Court is overburdened by the unfairness of its *inability* to prosecute the crime of aggression, by the substantive selectivity in the types of crimes it may touch. How long may the Court prosecute the war crimes of the victim state but not the war-making of the aggressor state? How long are the handcuffs on the Court instead of on the perpetrator of the crime of aggression? How long is *humankind* overburdened by the commission of crimes of aggression?

It is true that the activating decision will introduce a new set of jurisdictional differences for the crime of aggression, some of them sensible, such as the requirement of authorisation by the Pre-Trial Division, some of them decidedly less so, such as the overdependence of two trigger mechanisms on consent by the aggressor state. It is also true that these differences could again produce unjust unevenness when the Court may be able to prosecute the three other crimes but not this one. In its origin, it is a problem similar to the one already existing with regard to the unevenness in the prosecution of the other three crimes. Both problems are ultimately traceable to the unwillingness of the international community to endow the ICC with inherent universal jurisdiction. But both are also an insufficient reason for preventing the Court from even starting to respond to at least some of the victims of these four core crimes.

---

44 Resolution RC/Res.6, 'The Crime of Aggression', 11 June 2010, preamb. para. 6.

45 At the time of writing, 24 ratifications have been already deposited. It is quite likely that thirty ratifications will be already reached in either 2015 or 2016.

46 Barriga 2012, *Travaux*, *supra* n. 34, at 47, 51, 53; Barriga and Grover 2011, p. 530.

3. MALABO

3.1. THE ADOPTION OF THE MALABO PROTOCOL

In the meantime, during the interim between the adoption of the Kampala Amendments and a future activating decision, African states have moved closer towards establishing regional criminal jurisdiction over fourteen crimes of international concern, *including the crime of aggression*: during its 23rd Ordinary Session in Malabo, Equatorial Guinea, the Assembly of the African Union adopted for this purpose the Protocol on Amendments to the Protocol on the Statute of the African Court of Justice and Human Rights (Malabo Protocol).[47] Neither the new Protocol nor the earlier Protocol[48] that it amends has yet entered into force.[49] Both together entail rather complicated legislative steps: The earlier Protocol, adopted in 2008 in Sharm el-Sheikh, Egypt, would merge the African Court of Justice[50] with the African Court on Human and Peoples Rights[51] in order to create an African Court of Justice and Human Rights. The Malabo Protocol[52] would add criminal jurisdiction to this merged Court and create an African Court of Justice and Human and Peoples Rights (ACJHPR).[53] The future Court would have three Sections, the General Affairs Section, the Human and Peoples Rights Section and the International Criminal Law Section. In the context of this paper, reference to the ACJHPR will generally mean the International Criminal Law Section of the African Court of Justice and Human and Peoples Rights.

---

47 Adopted 27 June 2014, available at: www.au.int/en/treaties.

48 Protocol on the Statute of the African Court of Justice and Human Rights, adopted 1 July 2008, available at: www.au.int/en/treaties.

49 At its 24th Ordinary Session, the Assembly of the African Union has underscored the need to ratify both Protocols, see 'Decision on the Progress Report of the Commission on the Implementation of Previous Decisions on the International Criminal Court Doc. Assembly/AU/18(XXIV), Assembly/AU/Dec.547(XXIV), para. 15.

50 See with regard to this Court, Constitutive Act of the African Union, adopted by the 36th Ordinary Session of the Assembly of Heads of State and Government, Lome, Togo, 11 July 2000 (7 November 2000), entry into force 26 May 2001, Articles 5 and 18; and Protocol of the Court of Justice of the African Union, adopted by the 2nd Ordinary Session of the Assembly, Maputo, 11 July 2003, entry into force 11 February 2009, both available at: www.au.int/en/treaties.

51 For this Court see Protocol to the African Charter on Human and Peoples' Rights on the Establishment of an African Court on Human and Peoples' Rights, adopted 9 June 1998, entered into force 25 January 2004 available at: www.au.int/en/treaties.

52 The Malabo Protocol, *supra* n. 47, consists of three parts, the paragraphs of the Protocol *per se*, followed by amendments to the earlier Protocol, and then, in an Annex, the Statute of the African Court of Justice and Human and Peoples Rights (ACJHPR Statute), containing the changes to the earlier Statute of the African Court of Justice and Human Rights (not yet in force).

53 Articles 1, 6[16] and 7[17] ACJHPR Statute.

Depending on the jurisdictional interplay with national and international, sub-regional and ad hoc jurisdictions, regional criminal courts can make eminent sense. Or they cannot. Sadly, the idea for an ACJHPR was born in the middle of acrimony about the ICC, acrimony underpinned most prominently by three complaints, namely that the ICC focuses disproportionately on African situations, pays too little attention to the objective of peace and is wrongly disrespectful of the immunity of governmental leaders.[54] Dismay about exercises of universal jurisdiction was another strong driving force.[55] The charged atmosphere appears to have left scant room for a detailed and comprehensive assessment of the drafting of the Malabo Protocol, and for a calm evaluation how the interplay of national, regional and international jurisdiction could best advance the judicial response to crimes of international concern.[56] Might a regional court be especially suitable for international crimes of strong regional concern? Might it serve not only as alternative but preferred jurisdiction when the exercise of national jurisdiction is unwise or unsatisfactory, as may occur with regard to transnational, inter-state or multi-state crime? Or vice versa, might the regional jurisdiction suffer from the same maladies or drawbacks that national or, for that matter, international jurisdiction could be faced with *in a particular situation*? In general, does the establishment of regional criminal jurisdiction seek to assist the jurisdiction of another level – notably where that level cannot or should not face the burden of coping with the situation – or does it seek to block other jurisdictions that would be more suitable and effective? Does the door remain wide open for the exercise of whichever jurisdiction might do best what most needs to be done,

---

54 See e.g. Jalloh 2013, available at: http://ssrn.com/abstract=2325520; McNamee, 'The ICC and Africa – Between Aspiration and Reality: Making International Justice Work Better for Africa – Reflections on a High-Level Roundtable', 2 *Brenthurst Discussion Paper* (2014), *supra* n. 15; Nkansah 2014, p. 8; Kimani, 'Princes versus the Liberals and the Fate of the Negotiated Peace', *Brenthurst Analysis: Newsletter Item*, available at: www.thebenthurstfoundation.org/a_sndmsg/news_view.asp?|=161748&PG=290; Richardson, 2013, p. 81, available at: http://papers.ssrn.com/sol3/papers.cfm?abstract_id=2285474; Tladi 2009, p. 57; Udombana 2014, p. 57.

55 Pan-African Lawyers Union et al., 'Implications of the African Court of Human and Peoples' Rights Being Empowered to Try International Crimes Such as Genocide, Crimes Against Humanity, and War Crimes – An Opinion' (2009) 1–24, at 6, 22 (on file with the writer). The critical opinion, submitted by eight non-governmental organisations of lawyers and other legal experts to the African Union Commission, offered an early warning about problems that the African Court's jurisdictional extension would face. Subsequently, the African Union Commission contracted the Pan-African Lawyers Union in January 2010 to produce an extensive study. For a more positive assessment of the project to extend the African Court's jurisdiction and for emphasis on the issue of universal jurisdiction and other concerns as genesis for the project, see Deya, 'Worth the Wait: Pushing for the African Court to Exercise Jurisdiction for International Crimes', available at: www.osisa.org/sites/default/files/is_the_african_court_worth_the_wait_-don_deya.pdf.

56 Du Plessis 2014, p. 2–3; Du Plessis 2012, pp. 5, 11, calling the process 'rushed'.

namely help the victims, help prevent future crimes, and help reweave and reconcile a human community torn apart?

Considering specifically the crime of aggression, would such an evaluation have to shift? The light and shadow of complementarity between national, regional and international jurisdictions are thrown into starker relief when looking at a leadership crime particularly affected by the issue of immunity, an individual crime linked by its very definition to an act of state. What exactly does the Malabo Protocol signal with regard to the Kampala seed for peace? Drawing from nature's gifts to the wide island bay of Malabo, will the deluges and thunderstorms of the monsoon sweep the kernel into the ocean and into oblivion? Will the heavy cloud cover of long wet seasons leave too little light for growth? Or quite the opposite, do the Malabo Protocol's provisions on the crime of aggression promise more intensive nurturing for what was planted earlier? After all, the inclusion of the crime in Article 28A(1)(14) and Article 28M of the Statute of the African Court of Justice and Human and Peoples Rights (ACJHPR Statute)[57] reflects again the recognition of states that this crime must be prosecuted. In the preamble of the Protocol, the member states of the African Union reiterate 'their respect for the sanctity of human life, condemnation and rejection of impunity and political assassination, acts of terrorism and subversive activities, unconstitutional changes of governments and acts of aggression'.[58] They further reiterate 'their commitment to fighting impunity in conformity with the provisions of Article 4(o) of the Constitutive Act of the African Union'.[59] Crucially too in light of the crime of aggression's broad-based attack on human dignity, freedom, life, health, self-determination and peace, the Malabo Protocol recognises the assault on human rights by the crimes under ACJHPR jurisdiction.[60] Might both the Kampala and the Malabo provisions serve as seeds for peace and inter-grow as mutually beneficial companion plants? Could the lush vegetation on Malabo's Bioko Island serve as harbinger of good things to come?

---

57 *Supra* n. 52.

58 Malabo Protocol *per se*, *supra* n. 52, preamb. para. 10.

59 *Ibid*, preamb. para. 11. Article 4 of the Constitutive Act of the African Union, *supra* n. 50, lists the principles of the African Union, with para. (o) citing 'respect for the sanctity of human life, condemnation and rejection of impunity and political assassination, acts of terrorism and subversive activities'.

60 See Malabo Protocol *per se supra* n. 52, preamb. para. 9 which 'reiterates... respect for democratic principles, human and peoples' rights, the rule of law and good governance', and preamb. para. 16, 'the present Protocol will complement national, regional and continental bodies and institutions in preventing serious and massive violations of human and peoples rights in keeping with Article 58 of the Charter and ensuring accountability for them wherever they occur'.

3.2. THE JURISDICTIONAL CONDITIONS

The crime of aggression is one of fourteen crimes that can be tried by the ACJHPR.[61] Significantly, the conditions for the exercise of jurisdiction are the same for all fourteen.

Under Article 46E*bis*(1) of the ACJHPR Statute, '[a] State which becomes a Party to this Protocol and Statute thereby accepts the jurisdiction of the Court with respect to the crimes referred to in Article 28A.'[62] Article 46E*bis*(2) of the ACJHPR Statute addresses the question whose acceptance is required to permit the *exercise* of jurisdiction. The provision reflects a more progressive outlook than Article 12 of the Rome Statute.[63] The ACJHPR may exercise its jurisdiction if at least one of four types of states is a party: (a) the state where the conduct in question occurred; (b) the state of the accused; (c) the state of the victim of the crime; and/or (d) the state whose vital interest is threatened by 'extraterritorial acts by non-nationals'. The ACJHPR has jurisdiction not only over individual persons but also over legal persons, with the exception of states.[64]

In accordance with Article 46F, the exercise of jurisdiction may be triggered when a situation is referred to the Prosecutor by a state party, or by the Assembly of Heads of State and Government of the African Union, or by the Peace and Security Council of the African Union, or when the Prosecutor initiates an investigation *proprio motu*.[65] In the latter case, Article 46G requires authorisation by the Pre-Trial Chamber, corresponding to Article 15 of the Rome Statute. This court-internal filter is the same for all crimes. No special hurdle applies for the crime of aggression, in contrast to the Kampala Amendments which require authorisation by the whole Pre-Trial Division, including for referral by a state party. Partly this can be explained by the different structure of the two courts. Under Article 6/16 of the ACJHPR Statute, the International Criminal Law Section of the African Court is directly divided into Chambers and thus does not use Divisions.[66]

Interestingly, the conditions under Article 46E*bis*(2) are not restricted to state party referrals and the Prosecutor's own initiatives. Thus, also for referrals

61 Article 28A(1) ACJHPR Statute.

62 According to Article 28A(2), '[t]he Assembly may extend upon the consensus of States Parties the jurisdiction of the Court to incorporate additional crimes to reflect developments in international law.' No Statute of limitations applies, Article 28A(3) ACJHPR.

63 This interpretation is a bit adventuresome since Article 46E*bis*(2) appears to be missing some wording. The meaning of Article 46E*bis*(2) becomes most apparent over the first half sentence of Article 46E*bis*(3).

64 Article 46C ACJHPR Statute.

65 Article 16 indicates that African individuals and African non-governmental organisations may submit cases with regard to a state that has made a declaration accepting this competence of the Court. But this option is not mentioned under Article 46F and might not apply for the International Criminal Law Section.

66 For the Divisions and Chambers of the ICC, see Articles 34(b) and 39 Rome Statute.

by the Assembly or the Peace and Security Council, one of the four states cited must be a party to the Malabo Protocol and Statute. But here too, the wording of Article 46E*bis* may be unintentionally incomplete.

Article 46H(1) of the ACJHPR Statute provides that the jurisdiction of the ACJHPR shall be complementary to that of the national courts.[67] As set out in Paragraphs 2–4 of Article 46H, the jurisdiction shifts to the ACJHPR when the national court is or has been unable or unwilling to investigate and prosecute the crime. The conditions of and definitions for inability and unwillingness parallel those in the related provisions in Article 17 of the Rome Statute, even though they are not quite identical. Importantly in the context here, national courts have primary jurisdiction for all crimes under the ACJHPR's jurisdiction, including the crime of aggression.

The Malabo Protocol does not contain a provision analogue to Article 15*bis*(9) and Article 15*ter*(4) of the Rome Statute explicitly mandating that the determination by an organ outside the Court of a state act of aggression shall be without prejudice to the findings of the Court.[68] On first sight such an omission may not seem troubling. After all, the rights of the accused are protected under Article 46A of the ACJHPR Statute. Moreover, the Principles and Guidelines on the Right to a Fair Trial and Legal Assistance proclaimed by the African Commission on Human and Peoples' Rights[69] will be a highly authoritative basis for due process as well. In addition, the Malabo Protocol provides better support for the defence than the Rome Statute, notably through a Defence Office as an independent, separate organ of the ACJHPR.[70] But the need for an express provision or understanding on 'non-prejudice' must not be underestimated. In the wake of a determination by another organ of an act of aggression, the due process requirements and higher evidentiary standard in criminal proceedings may be easily forgotten and one significant element of the individual crime may be treated as already judged.

In this context, it is especially relevant that the ACJHPR as a whole, as conceived under the Malabo Protocol, is divided into three Sections.[71] The risk is high that a determination by one of the other two Sections, specifically the General Affairs Section[72] might be given automatically great weight in the International Criminal Law Section. The door could then close rather quickly

---

67 According to Article 46H(1) ACJHPR Statute, the jurisdiction of the African Court shall also be complementary to that of the courts of regional economic communities where specifically provided for by the communities.

68 *Supra* n. 22, n. 37 with main text.

69 African Commission on Human and Peoples' Rights, Principles and Guidelines on the Right to a Fair Trial and Legal Assistance in Africa, DOC/OS(XXX)247.

70 Article 22C ACJHPR Statute. The Office is headed by a Principal Defender. See also Du Plessis 2014, pp. 3–4.

71 *Supra* p. 13.

72 On the extensive jurisdiction of the General Affairs Section see Du Plessis 2012, pp. 5–6.

against the evaluation of new evidence and challenges by the accused. Thus, it should be understood that not only determinations by other organs outside the Court but also by other Sections within the Court are without prejudice to the findings of the International Criminal Law Section. Protection against prejudice does not mean that a prior determination could not be taken into account at all. But the rights of the accused must remain fully applicable and the burden of proof must not be reversed. Vice versa, *if* determinations by the General Affairs Section of an act of aggression were treated as conclusive for the respective element of the definition of the individual crime, the accused must have been heard and all fair trial rights should have been respected within the proceedings of the General Affairs Section.[73]

With regard to determinations by organs *outside* the ACJHPR, the non-prejudicial effect would be particularly essential when the definition used by the other organ may have been different from the one under the Malabo Protocol. Organs using a different definition may include national and other courts. The leaders of a presumed aggressor state may be prosecuted by different courts. For example, a national court may have convicted one of the leaders, but decided not to undertake proceedings against another one of the leaders due to new political tension within the country. In proceedings by the ACJHPR against the second leader, the determination of the national court with regard to the state act of aggression should be non-prejudicial. The leader before the ACJHPR had not been heard before the national court in his or her own cause. And even if the definition may have been the same, new evidence may be available.

3.3. THE DEFINITION

The definition of the crime of aggression in Article 28M of the ACJHPR Statute reads:

> A. For the purpose of this Statute, 'Crime of Aggression' means the planning, preparation, initiation or execution, by a person in a position effectively to exercise control over or to direct the political of military action of a state or organization, whether connected to the state or not, of an act of aggression which, by its character, gravity and scale, constitutes a manifest violation of the Charter of the United Nations or the Constitutive Act of the African Union and with regard to the territorial integrity and human security of the population of a State Party.
>
> B. The following shall constitute acts of aggression, regardless of a declaration of war by a State, group of States, organizations of States, or non-State actor(s) or by any foreign entity:

[73] See also *infra*, main text above n. 171.

1. The use of armed forces against the sovereignty, territorial integrity and political independence of any state, or any other act inconsistent with the provision of the Constitutive Act of the African Union and the Charter of the United Nations
2. The invasion or attack by armed forces against the territory of a State...

   ...

   8...[74]

Different from the Kampala definition, the Malabo definition is not restricted to the Charter of the United Nations as its core legal reference point. Instead, the crime of aggression requires the planning, preparation, initiation or execution of 'an act of aggression which, by its character, gravity and scale, constitutes a manifest violation *of the Charter of the United Nations or the Constitutive Act of the African Union and with regard to the territorial integrity and human security of the population of a State Party*' (emphasis added). Under Article 4(f) of the Constitutive Act of the African Union[75] the Union shall function in accordance with the principle of 'the prohibition of the use of force and threat to use force among Member States'. Article 4(i) of the Constitutive Act sets out the principle of 'peaceful co-existence of Member States and their right to live in peace and security'. It is not clear whether the phrase starting 'and with regard to the territorial integrity and human security' appears to have been intended as a further element for an act of aggression under the Constitutive Act, or as a third form of an act of aggression. The phrase may recall wording in the definition of 'Aggression' in Article 1(c) of the African Union Non-Aggression and Common Defence Pact:[76]

> 'Aggression' means the use, intentionally and knowingly, of armed force or any other hostile act by a State, a group of States, an organization of States or non-State actor(s) or by any foreign or external entity, against the sovereignty, political independence, *territorial integrity and human security of the population of a State Party* to this Pact, which are incompatible with the Charter of the United Nations or the Constitutive Act of the African Union.[77]

---

74 The Malabo definition uses a two-partite structure similar to the one of the Kampala definition, but the definition of the act of aggression appears to forego a generic definition and to use solely a list of eight specific acts. The generic definition in the first sentence of the second paragraph of the Kampala definition becomes, with significant changes, the first subparagraph of the specific list.

75 *Supra* n. 50.

76 African Union Non-Aggression and Common Defence Pact, adopted 31 January 2005, Abuja, Nigeria, available at: www.au.int/en/treaties.

77 Emphasis added. This wide generic definition in the Pact is followed by a list of eleven specific acts of aggression. (Interestingly, even though the definition seems to relate more to an act of aggression rather than to an individual crime, it requires mental elements.).

A meaning for 'human security' can be found in Article 1(k) of the African Union Non-Aggression and Common Defence Pact.[78]

In another distinction from the Kampala definition, the Malabo definition covers also perpetrators who hold leadership positions in organisations other than a state and unconnected to a state. Acts of aggression seem to include uses of armed force by non-state entities against a state.[79]

On first glance, an expansion of the definition of the crime of aggression to uses of force by non-state actors may seem understandable considering the threat to the attacked state and the deaths and injuries that may be caused by states and non-state actors alike – but there are serious drawbacks. First, the expansion dilutes the essence of the crime of aggression, or at least one essential aspect of it, namely the misuse of the authority of the *state* to sanctify illegal uses of force. The state, directed by the criminal leader to betray its sovereign responsibilities towards peace and freedom, life and human dignity, turns into an outlaw state, a traitor to its people and the world. It is exactly the marshalling of state power that makes the commission of the crime of aggression so overwhelming and so difficult to prevent, resist, evade or prosecute. Second, calling the use of force by a non-state actor an 'act of aggression' carries a risk that might not have been intended, namely the risk of a too wide interpretation of the right to self-defence. In the face of an 'act of aggression', an immediate right to self-defence against the non-state actor's innocent host state may be assumed too readily. Approaches that should come first, such as offers of support for the innocent host state's enforcement measures against the non-state actor, may then be too easily neglected even where they would still be an option.[80] This note of caution

78 '"Human Security" means the security of the individual in terms of satisfaction of his/her basic needs. It also includes the creation of social, economic, political, environmental and cultural conditions necessary for the survival and dignity of the individual, the protection of and respect for human rights, good governance and the guarantee for each individual of opportunities and choices for his/her full development.'

79 While the reference to non-state actors in the chapeau of paragraph B is somewhat ambiguous and might relate to the irrelevance of a declaration of war, the first and second subparagraph in the list of acts of aggression do not require that the prohibited uses of force are by a state. Compare also Article 1(c) of the African Union Non-Aggression and Common Defence Pact, *supra* n. 76, which covers force by non-state actors more extensively. Both its generic definition and nearly all specific definitions of an act of aggression encompass acts by non-state actors.

80 The situation is obviously quite different when a host state is complicit. (But complicity should not be automatically assumed whenever a host state does not accept law enforcement assistance by the attacked state. The host state may reasonably fear that the assistance will make matters worse.) The situation is also different when a host state is powerless against a non-state actor and an attack by the non-state actor against another state is imminent and unpreventable without intrusion into the territory of the host state. The discussion on this topic cannot be reflected in the space available for this article. For a recent sample of the debate about self-defence and non-state actors, see Ruys, 'Guest Post: Self-Defence and Non-State Actors in the Cold War Era – A Response to Marty Lederman', *Opinio Juris, Blog Archive* 12 March 2015, available at: http://opiniojuris.org/2015/03/12/guest-post-self-defence-and-non-state-actors-in-the-cold-war-era-a-response-to-marty-lederman. See also

about the definition under the Malabo Protocol is not meant to imply that the right to self-defence *never* comprises uses of force intruding upon an innocent host state or that such intrusions themselves must always give rise to prosecution for crimes of aggression.

3.4. CRIMINAL PARTICIPATION AND IMMUNITY

To understand the substantive reach of the Malabo definition, it is noteworthy too that Article 28M of the ACJHPR Statute is *not* accompanied by a provision analogue to Article 25(3)*bis* in the Kampala Amendments.[81] Thus, while the crime of aggression under the ACJHPR Statute is defined as a leadership crime, Article 28N on 'Modes of Responsibility' would arguably permit the prosecution of *non-leaders* who aid or abet the crime.[82]

At the same time, with the definition clearly requiring a leadership role at least for the primary perpetrator(s), the treatment of immunity becomes inherently more relevant for the crime of aggression than for the other three core crimes under the Rome Statute or the other thirteen core crimes under the Malabo Protocol.[83] Article 46B(2) of the ACJHPR Statute states: 'Subject to the provision of Article 46A*bis* of this Statute, the official position of the accused person shall not relieve such person of criminal responsibility nor mitigate punishment.' Article 46A*bis* provides: 'No charges shall be commenced or continued before the Court against any serving AU Head of State or Government, or anybody acting or entitled to act in such capacity, or other senior state officials based on their functions, during their tenure of office.'

It is not possible in the space available here to do justice to the international law on the immunity of state officials from criminal jurisdiction.[84] Only a very short sketch is attempted, in order to signal the main issues under Article 46A*bis*. In principle, respect for the immunity of state officials is essential for international relations and is most pronounced as protection against the *national* criminal jurisdiction of another state. Exceptions to immunity from criminal jurisdiction depend on the seriousness of the crime, the type or level of jurisdiction – notably national or international –

Bethlehem 2012, and the various critiques of this Article under Notes and Comments, 107 ASIL 378–395 (2013) and 108 *ASIL* 563–579, plus D. Bethlehem's response to the critiques at 108 *ASIL* 579–585.

81 *Supra* n. 12.

82 See also at p. 24.

83 See Article 28A(1) ACJHPR Statute.

84 For a particularly valuable study of the subject, see 'Immunity of State officials from foreign criminal jurisdiction', Memorandum by the Secretariat, International Law Commission, Sixtieth Session, Geneva, 5 May–6 June and 7 July–8 August 2008, UN Doc. A/CN.4/596. The Annex of the Memorandum, 177–206, contains an extensive bibliography. See also Murphy 2014, p. 41.

the applicability of a treaty denying immunity, or the existence of a waiver of immunity. The loss of immunity is most firmly established for the prosecution of atrocity crimes in international courts and tribunals. The protection of state officials against criminal jurisdiction varies also with the type of immunity at issue, namely personal immunity (immunity *ratione personae*) or functional immunity (immunity *ratione materiae*).[85] Absent an exception, immunity *ratione personae* is usually recognised in national courts for Heads of State, also Heads of Government, and widely too for Ministers of Foreign Affairs, the so-called *troika*.[86] If and how far personal immunity covers other state officials is a matter of debate.[87] Personal immunity extends to both official and private activities. It is temporary, restricted to the time in office.[88]

In contrast, functional immunity or immunity *ratione materiae* is applicable to 'acts performed in an official capacity' – undertaken in the exercise of official functions rather than in private capacity.[89] This immunity lasts indefinitely. Functional immunity is widely considered to be inapplicable to atrocity crimes including in national jurisdictions,[90] even though opinions have not been consistent.[91]

In a recent statement to the International Law Commission, the High Commissioner on Human Rights underlined: 'what immunity means, is, clearly, impunity – a denial of justice that freezes into place the broken relationships and violated trust that crime has caused. To break the culture of impunity that feeds so many human rights violations, it is crucial that prosecutions be allowed to proceed.' He called for 'clear parameters' and 'two distinct sets of limits that could be set where international crimes are concerned: First, it should be clear

85 Sukhija, 'Head of State Immunities and Article 98 of the Rome Statute: Interpretations That Avoid Obstacles to Cooperation in the Execution of ICC Arrest Warrants, ICC Forum, 10 March 2014, 1–27, available at: http://iccforum.com/forum/permalink/93/4084.

86 From the draft articles and commentaries provisionally adopted by the International Law Commission on 'Immunity of State officials from foreign criminal jurisdiction' see: 'Article 3: Persons enjoying immunity *ratione personae* – Heads of State, Heads of Government and Ministers for Foreign Affairs enjoy immunity *ratione personae* from the exercise of foreign criminal jurisdiction.' In Report of the International Law Commission on the Work of its Sixty-Fifth Session, UN Doc. A/68/10 (2013), at 52, para. 48, commentary 58–66.

87 Murphy 2014, p. 41; *supra* n. 84, p. 45.

88 See draft Article 4 provisionally adopted by the International Law Commission, Report of the International Law Commission on the Work of its Sixty-Fifth Session, UN Doc. A/68/10 (2013), at 52, para. 48, commentary at 66–70.

89 See draft Articles 2(f) and 6 in 'Immunity of State official from foreign jurisdiction – Text of the draft Articles provisionally adopted by the Drafting Committee at the sixty-seventh session', International Law Commission, Sixty-sixth [sic] Session, Geneva, 4 May–5 June and 6 July–7 August 2015, UN Doc. A/CN.4/L.865, 29 July 2015.

90 Sukhia, 'Head of State Immunities and Article 98 of the Rome Statute: Interpretations That Avoid Obstacles to Cooperation in the Execution of ICC Arrest Warrants, ICC Forum, 10 March 2014, at 3; Du Plessis 2014, p. 3.

91 Hernández, Special Rapporteur, 'Fourth Report on the immunity of State officials from foreign criminal jurisdiction', International Law Commission, Sixty-seventh Session, 4 May–5 June and 6 July–7 August 2015, UN Doc. A/CN.4/686, 29 May 2015.

that any immunity is personal, and ceases when the person leaves office, since immunity results solely from the need to allow states to function effectively. Recognising functional immunity when international crimes have been committed would inadvertently signal that the commission of international crimes can be legitimate acts of states. This would defeat all the human rights obligations of states and, beyond, would undermine the very system of international law. Second, the categories of individuals deemed to benefit from this limited personal immunity must be as restricted as possible, along the lines of the provisions of Article 7(2)(a) of the 1969 Vienna Convention on the Law of Treaties and Article 21(2) of the 1961 Vienna Convention on Diplomatic Relations.'[92]

Article 46A*bis* of the ACJHPR Statute grants immunity *ratione personae.* For the recipients of the immunity, the provision does not use the formula for the *troika,* but lists 'serving AU Heads of State or Government', and continues rather ambiguously 'or anybody acting or entitled to act in such capacity, or other senior state officials based on their functions'.[93] Criminal charges are only ruled out during the tenure of office.[94] Unfortunately, for the purpose of ending impunity over the crimes under the Malabo Protocol, such tenure of office may not be as temporary as it sounds. Especially with regard to senior state officials, the tenure may last throughout a working life. Nor is the seemingly time-sensitive reference to 'serving' Heads of State or Government of much help against impunity when a ruler clings to his or her office without end in sight.[95]

Article 46A*bis* is roughly aligned with the customary law on immunity from the *national* jurisdiction of another state and diverges from the relevant provisions on immunity in the Rome Statute where Article 27 mandates the irrelevance of immunity, no matter if the person is still in office and no matter

---

92 Statement by Mr Zeid Ra'ad Al Hussein, United Nations High Commissioner for Human Rights, at the International Law Commission, 21 July 2015. With regard to the case maybe most frequently cited on behalf of immunity in national courts, Arrest Warrant of 11 April 2000 (*Democratic Republic of Congo v. Belgium*), 2002 ICJ Rep. 3, the High Commissioner recalled that the International Court of Justice had underlined that 'the immunity enjoyed by certain senior State officials does not mean that they enjoy impunity in respect to any crimes they might have committed, especially the gravest crimes.' He also cited from the judgment: 'while jurisdictional immunity is procedural in nature, criminal responsibility is a question of substantive law. Jurisdictional immunity may well bar prosecution for a certain period or for certain offenses; it cannot exonerate the person to whom it applies from all criminal responsibility.'

93 The words 'acting or entitled to act' sound as if they include acting without legitimate entitlement. It is not quite clear whether 'other senior state officials' are meant to be also only those from the African Union. 'Based on their functions' is reminiscent of functional immunity criteria and immunity *ratione materiae,* but the immunity is spelled out for a limited time period.

94 It is essential in this regard that the ACJHPR has no statute of limitations, *supra* n. 62.

95 For a discussion of Article 46A*bis* at a digital forum see Amani, 'Article 46A*bis*: Implications for Peace, Justice, and Reconciliation in Africa', *On the Spot*, 21 October 2014, available at: http://forums.ssrc.org/kujenga-amani/category/on-the-spot/.

if the conduct at issue could be claimed to be part of an official duty. Article 98 of the Rome Statute, concerning requests for surrender or assistance, recognises at the same time the obligations states may have with respect to the immunity of a person of another state. Under the latter provision, it will matter especially whether not only the requested state but the third or sending state is a party to the Rome Statute or otherwise duty-bound to cooperate with the ICC, for example based on a Security Council resolution.[96]

Article 46A*bis* can be seen as an indication that the regional jurisdiction may have been conceptualised as substitute for national rather than international jurisdiction, thus suggesting a quicker channel to international jurisdiction when neither national nor regional jurisdiction would be available. The question nevertheless arises whether the exercise of regional jurisdiction really engenders the same need for immunity as the exercise of national jurisdiction. Is the risk of the political misuse of criminal jurisdiction against state officials as high in regional as in foreign national jurisdictions? And would the tenure-linked regional immunity not add a new incentive to commit one of the other crimes under the ACJHPR Statute, namely the Crime of Unconstitutional Change of Government under Article 28A(1)(4) and Article 28E?

During the time when personal immunity applies for leaders who might be responsible for a crime of aggression, the ACJHPR could theoretically proceed in line with Article 28N and prosecute participants below the leadership level,[97] including soldiers. While one of the most atrocious aspects of the crime of aggression is the large-scale violation of the human dignity of soldiers – who are being turned into war tools of the state, lied to about the illegality of the use of force, and ordered and manipulated into killing others without justification under international law – this widespread pattern does not preclude situations where soldiers know that the use of force constitutes an act of aggression, are free in their decision to participate, and share in the intent to commit the crime. To understand fully the implications of Article 28N, notably with respect to aiding and abetting crimes of aggression, it would be necessary to know more about the required mental elements and the personal grounds for the exclusion of criminal responsibility under the ACJHPR Statute. The general principles in the ACJHPR Statute are largely silent in these regards and would benefit from an expansion.[98] Yet apart from the problem how then to determine the participatory guilt of

---

96 For a narrow reading of Article 98, see Sukhija, 'Head of State Immunities and Article 98 of the Rome Statute: Interpretations That Avoid Obstacles to Cooperation in the Execution of ICC Arrest Warrants', ICC Forum, 10 March 2014.

97 For a proposal to adjust the ICC Prosecutor's strategy of prosecuting those most responsible for a crime and to pursue instead lower-level participants, see e.g. Lafontaine and Tachou-Sipowo 2014, available at: http://ssrn.com/abstract-2550453. Under the Kampala Amendments, specifically Article 25(3)*bis*, such a change in strategy would not have much leeway for the crime of aggression.

98 For a major study on the mental elements of crimes see Badar 2013.

non-leaders, prosecutions of low-level secondary perpetrators would not so much compensate for the temporary immunity of the leadership but highlight and exacerbate inequality before the law: by definition, crimes of aggression cannot be brought under way without persons in a leadership position. It would seem here doubly unfair to 'immunise' those who led, but not those who have been led.

Altogether, Article 46A*bis* is in strange tension with principles 4(d), (h) and (j) of the Constitutive Act of the African Union[99] and related instruments and provisions.[100] The Union can, based on decisions by the Assembly and the Peace and Security Council,[101] intervene in a member state to stem atrocity crimes, it can join a member state in self-defence, thus it can fight against the presumed perpetrators of crimes of aggression, genocide, crimes against humanity and war crimes – but as long as they are in power, the ACJHPR cannot prosecute them. To find a better equilibrium between the immunity provisions under the Malabo Protocol and principles 4(d), (h) and (j) of the Constitutive Act, an option might be to modify Article 46A*bis* and deny immunity based on a decision by the Assembly or the Peace and Security Council. Exceptions to immunity could also be considered when the tenure in office derives from unconstitutional action.

The issues raised by Articles 28N and 46A*bis* of the ACJHPR Statute in relation to the jurisdiction of the ICC shall be returned to shortly below.

4. MALABO AND KAMPALA

4.1. THE MUTUAL IMPACT BETWEEN THE MALABO PROTOCOL AND THE ROME STATUTE: COMPLEMENTARITY?

At the time of this writing, not only the Malabo Protocol's date of entry into force but also its ultimate interrelationship with the Rome Statute remains open. Against the background of the three main complaints about the ICC, the voices from states in the African Union, including from states parties to the Rome Statute, vary with regard to the basic role of the Malabo Protocol. Some envision

---

99 *Supra* n. 50, 'Article 4 Principles – The Union shall function in accordance with the following principles: ... (d) establishment of a common defence policy for the African Continent; ... (h) the right of the Union to intervene in a Member State pursuant to a decision of the Assembly in respect of grave circumstances, namely: war crimes, genocide and crimes against humanity; ... (j) the right of Member States to request intervention from the Union in order to restore peace and security'.

100 Protocol Relating to the Establishment of the Peace and Security Council of the African Union, adopted by the 1st Ordinary Session of the Assembly of the African Union, Durban, 9 July 2002; African Union Non-Aggression and Common Defence Pact, *supra* n. 76.

101 Protocol Relating to the Establishment of the Peace and Security Council of the African Union, *ibid*, Articles 3(b)(e), 4(j)(k), 6(d),(f),(g) and 7(e),(f),(h).

the ACJHPR Statute as a full regional replacement for the Rome Statute and call for withdrawal from the latter. Others pursue complementarity of the ICC with both national *and* regional jurisdiction. Still others persist in their wholehearted support for the ICC, but may nevertheless draw on the existence of the Malabo Protocol to fortify the argument that the Assembly of States Parties to the Rome Statute must do more to overcome the complaints.[102]

Withdrawal from the Rome Statute, as preferred by the first group of voices,[103] does not necessarily achieve its objective of barring the ICC from Africa. Withdrawal does not prevent Security Council referrals to the ICC – except that the need for such referrals subsides when a regional jurisdiction can fill the impunity gap left by an inactive, unable or unwilling national jurisdiction. The effect of withdrawal on the *other two trigger mechanisms* depends on the crime and the situation: whereas prosecutions of the crime of aggression would here be effectively disabled when committed by the national or on the territory of a state that has withdrawn from the Rome Statute, the exercise of jurisdiction over the other three core crimes may still be possible – assuming that the state of the accused and the state where the crime was committed are not the same and one of these two is still a party to the Statute.

Those who argue for withdrawal will be aware that it means a reduction of influence in the Assembly of States Parties to the Rome Statute and in the development of international criminal law. Possibly, involvement in the development of regional criminal law is seen as compensating for this loss.

The second group of voices was exemplified in a statement by the delegate of Kenya on 29 April 2015, in the Working Group on Amendments of the

---

102 'Statement by Lesotho on Behalf of African States Parties to the Rome Statute at the Thirteenth Session of the Assembly of States Parties to the Rome Statute of the International Criminal Court', General Debate, 8 December 2014, available at: www.icc-cpi.int/iccdocs/asp_docs/ASP13/GenDeba/ICC-ASP13-GenDeba-Lesotho-AfricanStatesPrties-ENG.pdf. The statement refers to 'consistent, active backing for the ICC among African governments and civil society' while also highlighting African concerns and amendment proposals: 'African States Parties would like to express their strong conviction that the search for justice should be pursued in a way that does not impede or jeopardize efforts aimed at promoting lasting peace and reiterate AU's concern with the misuse of indictments against African leaders; and stress the need for international justice to be conducted in a transparent and fair manner, in order to avoid any perception of double standards, in conformity with the principles of international law. Therefore, African States Parties would like to strongly urge this Assembly to ensure that concerns raised by Africa are addressed. This includes proposals to amend the Articles 16 and 27 of the Rome Statute.' The Statement also explained that the African Union 'premised its call for non-cooperation with the ICC on the Security Council's ignoring its July 2008 request to defer the case against President Al-Bashir. Concern has mounted that the Security Council has disrespected the AU by failing to respond either positively or negatively to its deferral request.'

103 Ngirachu, 'Uhuru Kenyatta: Let's have an African-funded court', *Daily Nation,* 31 January 2015; Mataire, 'AU must pull out of ICC: President', *Chronicle*, 5 February 2015; Moyo and Mambo, 'Mugabe reluctant to ratify African court protocol', *Zimbabwe Independent*, 7 April 2015. But see also Kegoro, 'African Union might shelf plan for expanded continental court', *Daily Nation*, 14 March 2015.

Assembly of States Parties to the Rome Statute. Kenya has deposited several amendment proposals to the Rome Statute,[104] among them one which would amend the preamble to include a reference to the ICC's complementarity to regional jurisdiction.[105] The delegate pointed out that the establishment of African regional jurisdiction 'is not a way to oust the ICC. It is the opposite. The regional jurisdiction gets just the first bite. National jurisdiction may be difficult to exercise. Rather than spring-boarding [from national to international jurisdiction], the ICC would be what it was meant to be, the last resort.'[106]

Even if not expressly stated in the Rome Statute, complementarity to regional jurisdiction could materialise by itself, at least in some circumstances. To circumvent the need for amendment, it could be argued that complementarity to the national jurisdiction of a state includes complementarity to a jurisdiction established by several states. Notably too, where a regional court has tried a person for conduct that is also proscribed under the Rome Statute, the ICC would have to abide by the principle of *ne bis in idem* under Article 20 and abstain from trying that person for the same conduct, unless the exceptions under Article 20(3)(a) and (b) apply.[107] Where the relevant regional court has not undertaken any proceedings, the ICC would simply move forward with its usual evaluation of complementarity in relation to national jurisdiction and examine the criteria for admissibility under Article 17. Still, the principle of *ne bis in idem* might not prevent possible confusion and conflict when the proceedings in the regional court are still in the planning stage or still under way. Nor would the principle be of sufficient help when the regional court has investigated the case but decided not to prosecute. Such uncertainties could be partially overcome by

104 United Nations Depository Notification C.N.1026.2013.TREATIES-XVIII.10 of 14 March 2014 (Proposal of amendments by Kenya to the Statute). In a meeting of the Working Group of Amendments on 5 November 2014, the delegate of Kenya clarified, that the amendment proposals had been made on behalf of the African states parties.

105 *Ibid*, 'Proposed amendment 5': the preambular paragraph would read: 'Emphasizing that the International Criminal Court established under this Statute shall be complementary to national and regional criminal jurisdictions'. The amendment consists of two added words. The proposal explains that the amendment is intended 'to allow recognition of regional judicial mechanisms'.

106 The citation reflects the notes taken by the writer and might not absolutely mirror each word spoken. The essence of the statement was confirmed in a short conversation with the delegate at the end of the Working Group meeting. For a statement on complementarity between several jurisdictional levels, see also Ambassador Smail Chergui, African Union Commissioner for Peace and Security, 24th Summit of the African Union, Press Briefing, 31 January 2015, available at: livestream.com/account/2466140/events/3771885, at 17:28.

107 Article 20(3) of the Rome Statute: 'No person who has been tried by another court for conduct also proscribed under Article 6, 7, 8 or 8 *bis* shall be tried by the Court with respect to the same conduct unless the proceedings in the other court: (a) Were for the purpose of shielding the person concerned from criminal responsibility for crimes within the jurisdiction of the Court; or (b) Otherwise were not conducted independently or impartially in accordance with the norms of due process recognized by international law and were conducted in a manner which, in the circumstances, was inconsistent with an intent to bring the person concerned to justice.'

consultation and cooperation, but the proposed amendment could also help to forestall confusion. Supposing the amendment proposal would find sufficient support, states parties to the Rome Statute might want to add a corresponding amendment to Article 1. After all, this is the Article that expressly provides that the ICC shall be complementary to national criminal jurisdiction.[108] They might also prefer to make clear that the ICC's complementarity to regional jurisdiction should follow conditions analogue to those for complementarity to national jurisdiction.[109] States parties could indicate this intention by adopting an Understanding that Article 17 of the Rome Statute shall apply *mutatis mutandi*. Or, they could consider amending Article 17: a new fourth paragraph could explicitly clarify that the admissibility criteria under the existing three paragraphs apply *mutatis mutandi* in complementarity relationships with regional, sub-regional or other multi-state courts or tribunals. Whether and how the notifications under Article 18 and the challenges under Article 19 of the Rome Statute should be extended to multi-state organisations that have established courts for crimes of international concern is another question that might come up in the future. Yet as pondered further below, these basic conceptions alone, to allow for a multi-step ladder of complementarity, do not by themselves assure the best ways to harvest justice – certainly not for the crime of aggression and also not for the other crimes. Where to anchor the rungs of 'inactivity', 'inability' or 'unwillingness' of a primary jurisdiction, how steeply to lean the ladder, where to place hand and foot – these may be decisions highly dependent on the particular crime situation and requiring more skill and flexibility than may have been anticipated in the original quest for complementarity under the Rome Statute.

The third group of voices ties the geographical distortion in the reach of the ICC less to over-focus on Africa than to under-focus on other regions, an imbalance at least partially due to the handicaps within the jurisdictional conditions under the Statute.[110] Here, the sorrow and frustration arise on behalf of the peoples who are deprived of international judicial back-up. As is well known, Security Council resolutions, including referrals to the ICC, are at the mercy of national interests prevailing in the Council and at the mercy of the veto power of the permanent members. The two other trigger mechanisms, referral by a state party or initiation by the Prosecutor, cannot lead to proceedings before the ICC when a ratification or acceptance required for the exercise of

108 The amendment proposal, *supra* n. 105, focuses only on the preamble.

109 The meetings of the Working Group on Amendments attended by the writer left the impression that states were quite open to the substance of the proposed amendment but concerned that the change in the preamble might require maybe more complicated amendments in addition.

110 The argument that the International Criminal Court's focus is discriminatory and not sufficiently explained by the jurisdictional conditions under the Statute has been made for example by Richardson 2013, p. 81, *supra* n. 54, p. 108 f.

jurisdiction is missing.[111] Differences among the jurisdictional conditions for the crime of aggression, the other three core crimes, the new weapons crimes added in Kampala,[112] and crimes included under future amendments, will lead to various further distortions. It will not help to have illusions: the problem of the ICC's under-focus due to the jurisdictional restrictions under the Rome Statute diminishes with each ratification of the Rome Statute, but it is unlikely to disappear in the near future. Sadly too, even insofar as the jurisdictional restrictions can serve as an explanation for the unequal reach of the ICC, they do not fully neutralise the hurt: even when the prosecution of a particular crime is just, the lack of attention to the same type of crime elsewhere subtracts from the perception of fairness. Still worse, when past discrimination has amounted to unspeakable cruelty, as it has countless times for Africa, every new difference in treatment, malevolent or not, can resurrect the memory of the trauma and be perceived that much more sharply. Hopefully, the courage of states parties from Africa to brace themselves against the ICC's uneven and incomplete reach is accompanied by consolation – the knowledge that the ratification of the Rome Statute remains a wise decision, bringing affirmation *for* each state party and its people, building more rather than less protection against crimes of serious international concern.

Hopefully too, with respect to the crime of aggression, an indirect protective effect of the ratification of the Kampala Amendments may even provide consolation when a different form of unevenness arises, namely when the ICC cannot act despite an African victim state's ratification. Ratification amounts to a firmer shield against the crime than may be obvious from the jurisdictional conditions. Through the ratification of the Kampala Amendments, the exercise of national or regional, special hybrid tribunal or ad hoc court jurisdiction gains in ethical authority and becomes more compelling: The victim state had warned its own leaders and it had warned the leaders of all other states of its commitment against the crime. The effort to seek out a jurisdictional alternative to the unavailable ICC honours that commitment to justice and peace.

This depiction of three groups of African voices about the respective roles of the Rome Statute and the Malabo Protocol is only a rough and incomplete rendering of the full range of positions. The focus is here not on an evaluation of the various approaches with regard to the future of the Malabo Protocol or on the multi-faceted considerations that have already gone or might still go into the decision-making about it. Rather, looking at the Malabo Protocol as it currently exists and trying to keep the unpredictability of future development in mind, it is argued that support for the Kampala provisions on the crime of aggression continues to be not only justified but also urgent, even though they

111 The 'Statement on behalf of African States Parties', *supra* n. 102, urged: 'We therefore need to step up our collective efforts to promote the universality of the Rome Statute.'

112 *Supra* n. 7.

are a product of compromise and may fall short of an ideal once pursued. The crime of aggression provisions in the ACJHPR Statute do not dilute but highlight this urgency, – may the Protocol enter into force or not, be reconfigured or not, or serve for ad hoc extensions of the existing African Court.[113] Importantly, the Malabo Protocol signals the potential richness in the interplay of different jurisdictional levels and different courts. Limitations in the crime definitions or jurisdictional conditions applicable in a particular court may be offset by the availability of other courts. Positive features in one tribunal's exercise of jurisdiction may over time set a pattern for other tribunals, as reiterated in more detail further below. The chance for mutual assistance and enhancement between the ICC and the ACJHPC can truly exist in both directions.

4.2. THE URGENCY OF ACTIVATING THE ICC'S AUTHORITY OVER THE CRIME OF AGGRESSION

Altogether, prompt activation of the ICC's capacity to prosecute the crime of aggression has not become superfluous with the Malabo Protocol. It remains, just like the adoption of the Amendments in Kampala, a matter of life over death:

Even with the Malabo Protocol in place, African states will be more protected when the ICC can prosecute crimes of aggression. For example, while the ACJHPR can prosecute a crime of aggression by a non-African person against an African state – as long as the jurisdictional conditions are fulfilled[114] – back-up by the jurisdiction of the ICC adds to deterrence, just like the ACJHPR would add to the deterrence of the ICC. One court may be able to proceed when the other cannot. One court may gain the cooperation necessary in a particular situation when the other does not. One court may be more suitable than the other. Moreover, the fully activated voice of the Kampala Amendments in the Rome Statute is indispensable when any war, anywhere, affects all regions of the world and disrupts the global cooperation desperately needed to protect environmental, social and economic sustainability.

Activation of the ICC's jurisdiction over the crime of aggression is urgently needed to oppose, most adamantly, the use of human beings as expendable tools of the state, starting with the use of soldiers as killing tools for crimes of aggression. The crime, from its very conception, violates human dignity to the core. The earliest activation possible, 2 January 2017, would send the most poignant signal *around the world* against both the degradation and the

---

113 Pan-African Lawyers Union et al., *supra* n. 55, at 17, addresses the possibility of using the African Court for criminal jurisdiction on an ad hoc basis. The financial costs of a court may speak for ad hoc use as well. On funding, see e.g. McNamee, 'The ICC and Africa – Between Aspiration and Reality: Making International Justice Work Better for Africa – Reflections on a High-Level Roundtable', 2 Brenthurst Discussion Paper 2014, p. 13.

114 See Article 46E*bis* ACJHPR Statute and *supra* p. 16.

slaughter inflicted by the crime. It would be a signal with repercussions against other machinations that reduce human beings to tools and numbers. While the ACJHPR can eventually span its protective umbrella over a whole continent, crimes of aggression no matter where they occur have a devastating global effect on human consciousness.

An end to the ICC's paralysis with regard to the crime of aggression is instrumental in moving states and non-state actors alike away from violence as the far too dominant approach to the resolution of political, economic and social conflict. The Kampala Amendments, different from the Malabo Protocol, do not cover the use of force by non-state actors, but this makes them far from useless. Wars between states frequently ferment the use of force by non-state actors. Thus, the prevention of crimes of aggression has a preventive effect on other illegal uses of armed force. Moreover, in order to achieve a stronger taboo against non-state violence, it would suggest itself to begin by first building a stronger taboo against state violence.

Like each ratification of the Kampala Amendments, the ICC's activated jurisdiction will help to overcome blindness about the criminality of aggression. The adoption of the Kampala Amendments already reinforced the visibility of the crime, yet procrastination about the activating decision would run the risk of flattening out the Kampala effect and giving new room to those who abet the crime by putting on blinders. Prompt activation of the ICC's jurisdiction and increased visibility of the criminality of aggression promises to advance the prevention of aggression in at least three ways. With the activating decision, temporal jurisdiction[115] commences (assuming the thirty ratifications are attained before and assuming the ICC follows Understandings 1 and 3). Thus, with activation, the possibility of prosecution with regard to crimes occurring after that moment commences as well. From that day on, concern about prosecution by the ICC enters the evaluation when uses of armed force against another state are contemplated. Deterrence of the crime stemming directly from fear about the Prosecutor's reach under the Kampala Amendments may be less acute than the prosecutorial deterrence[116] for the other core crimes. But the restrictions in the jurisdictional conditions do not nullify prosecutorial deterrence and thus do not nullify the value of the activating decision. Nor is activation made valueless because the African Court, other regional, national, or various forms of hybrid tribunals and ad hoc courts may have precedence or 'substitute' for the ICC when the latter is not available. Apart from the impact gained when the ICC *can* proceed, greater visibility of the criminality

115 *Supra* main text with n. 13, 14; and n. 38.

116 Jo and Simmons, 'Can the International Criminal Court Deter Atrocities', 18 December 2014, available at: http://ssrn.com/abstract=2552820. The authors have found statistical evidence for prosecutorial deterrence, i.e. due to fear of prosecution and sentencing, as well as for social deterrence, i.e. due to fear of informal, non-legal consequences, measured with regard to the crime of intentionally killing civilians.

of aggression would facilitate political, economic and social activism against the crime, before and after its commission, and thus add a fresh measure of social deterrence. More importantly, once activation beams the criminality of aggression around the globe, it cuts through the resignation about war as uncontrollable 'human fate' and war as unavoidable outgrowth of human nature;[117] it cuts through the insinuation that peacefulness is weakness; it cuts through the nonchalance about 'politics by other means';[118] and it cuts through the demons of hatred and greed. In that moment, and stronger over time, another form of deterrence stands a chance to burn more sharply worldwide: conscience – the pain of the soul warning against the commission of the crime.

Activation helps to advance due process for the accused. As pointed out earlier, by spelling out the non-prejudicial effect of court-external determinations of a state act of aggression, the Kampala Amendments address one particular due process issue unique to the crime. Even though the prohibition against prejudice from the determinations by other organs could be deducted from general due process provisions, including those in the Rome Statute and in the Malabo Protocol, it could be easily forgotten, especially when the existence of the act of aggression is already treated as a foregone conclusion and the prior determination carries great authority. Thus the explicit affirmation of the rule against prejudice is crucial. With the activation of the Kampala Amendments, the option opens up to try suspects of the crime of aggression before the ICC rather than before a national or other court burdened by the perception of bias, a court that may, in addition, lack an explicit safeguard against the prejudicial effect from prior determinations. At the same time, the activation of the ICC's jurisdiction over the crime of aggression illuminates this safeguard and helps to set a pattern for other courts, leading to the inclusion of the rule in criminal court statutes as a matter of course and resulting in decisive due process gains, notably in the national court of the presumed victim state, the court of the presumed aggressor state ruled by a new government, or in an ad hoc court established after the use of armed force at issue.[119] A similar effect can be hoped for from the establishment of an independent Defence Office under the ACJHPR Statute. More criminal courts may follow the example. Both these advancements for due process are essential not only for the accused, but for the victims. Victims deserve full efforts to establish the truth; they do not deserve another betrayal, this time by a half-baked trial.

---

117 For a short introduction to the scientific literature on aggressive and cooperative tendencies in human nature, see e.g. Cortright 2008, pp. 243–246.

118 'War is a mere continuation of politics by other means'/'*Der Krieg ist eine bloße Fortsetzung der Politik mit anderen Mitteln*', in Von Clausewitz 1832, pp. 1, 24. The much-cited sentence has received various interpretations. Drawing from the context within the book, Clausewitz underlined the primacy of politics, with war as an instrumentality of politics, not a replacement.

119 On the jurisdiction of these courts, see below section 4.3.

Without the activation of the ICC's full authority over the crime of aggression the international security architecture would continue to miss an essential component. Nothing can underline more emphatically that the international community meant what it said in Article 2(4) of the Charter of the United Nations[120] than the ability of international criminal jurisdiction to break through the 'corporate veil' of the state and demand accountability from those who do not take the prohibition seriously.

But would the spectre of prosecution not make ending wars more difficult? Concerns about conflicts between peace and justice have long been raised with regard to the other three core crimes and cited among the reasons for African considerations to withdraw from the Rome Statute, for establishing an ACJHPR, and for the immunity provisions in the Malabo Protocol. With the worry about wars that might be prolonged due to fear of prosecution for the crime of aggression, the 'peace versus justice' paradigm straining the ICC's jurisdiction has found its renewed expression, this time to counter the very activation of the jurisdiction over that crime.

The juxtaposition of 'peace versus justice' has been called a 'false dichotomy'[121] and it frequently is. At the same time, conflicts between peace and justice, where they might truly arise, must not be dismissed lightly. Kay Rala Xanana Gusmão, the former President and Prime Minister of East Timor, has said: 'Many believe that justice is a necessary condition for reconciliation, that without justice there can be no reconciliation. In my view, it is precisely the opposite – without reconciliation there is no real justice. We cannot pursue justice merely based on revenge and hatred.'[122] These observations are a highly valuable counterpoint when justice is disfigured for retaliation or used too automatically as the singular lodestar. Peace and justice are interdependent in both directions. Yet without knowing the contingencies of a particular situation, it is unnecessary and maybe impossible to assign conclusively a hierarchical relationship between the two values, one way or the other. Rather, each value must carry the kernel of the other one within it. It is also helpful to keep in mind how their objectives overlap. True reconciliation and true justice must pursue the same: heal the victims, prevent future crimes and reweave the torn fabric of societies. Peace and justice are best pursued in the context of the actual situation. Here, only a basic position is set out: the difficulties to end war, due to a 'peace versus justice' conflict, are less likely to arise than may be feared,

---

120 'All Members shall refrain in their international relations from the threat or use of force against the territorial integrity or political independence of any state, or in any other manner inconsistent with the Purposes of the United Nations.' See also Article 2(3) of the Charter of the United Nations: 'All Members shall settle their international disputes by peaceful means in such a manner that international peace and security, and justice, are not endangered.'

121 See the citation in Jo and Simmons 2014, p. 5.

122 Interview with Kay Rala Xanana Gusmão, in Fried (ed.), *Beyond the 'Never Agains'*, Regeringskansliet, Statsrådsberedningen, Government of Sweden, 2005, pp. 116–122, at 116.

and where they might, they are surmountable. They are not a reason against activation.

First of all, the spectre of prosecution for a crime of aggression complicates the *beginning* of war before it could ever complicate the *ending* of war. There is no need to end a war that has never begun. The activating decision is not just a means to advance *justice*, it is a direct means to advance *peace*. Peace and justice are in many ways mutually supportive, in the case of the prevention and prosecution of crimes of aggression even more so. Preventing crimes against peace means, as a matter of logic, protecting peace.

Second, after a war has begun, occasions for peace and justice conflicts are limited. They are a non-issue when the aggressor state is losing at a quicker pace than the process of peace negotiations. They are a non-issue too when the aggressor state wins. (In the latter case, the world is confronted with a quite different problem.) Conflict between peace and justice could only arise, if at all, when the war drags on and successful peace negotiations could end it earlier rather than later. (Peace negotiations for a faster conclusion of the war tend to be in any event rather unpromising as long as both sides still believe they can win.)

Third, activation of the ICC's jurisdiction does not make prosecution inevitable. The Security Council does not *have to* refer the situation to the Court, especially not if it is concerned that this would impact negatively on peace negotiations. The victim state does not *have to* refer the situation, especially not when it fears this would make matters worse. This might not prevent other states parties to the Rome Statute from referring the situation – depending on the circumstances, it may be helpful to the victim state if another state party refers – but no state party *has to* make use of its right to refer a situation.

With regard to the Prosecutor acting *ex proprio motu*, as well as with regard to the Prosecutor's proceedings under the other two trigger mechanisms, the considerations are more complex. But first a note to recall the most prominent provision intended to give room for the possible deferral of Court proceedings: Under Article 16 of the Rome Statute[123] the Security Council, acting under its mandate to maintain peace and security, may suspend proceedings at the ICC.

Article 16 may not be sufficiently reassuring for everyone: the Assembly of the African Union has expressed its disappointment that a request to the Security Council by Kenya, supported by the African Union, to defer the proceedings against the President and Deputy President of the Republic of Kenya, has not yielded the expected result.[124] A request by the African Union to defer the

---

123 'No investigation or prosecution may be commenced or proceeded with under this Statute for a period of 12 months after the Security Council, in a resolution adopted under Chapter VII of the Charter of the United Nations, has requested the Court to that effect; that request may be renewed by the Council under the same conditions.'

124 Assembly of the African Union, Twenty-Second Ordinary Session, Addis Ababa, Ethiopia, 30–31 January 2014, 'Decision on the Progress Report of the Commission on

proceedings against the President of the Republic of the Sudan has similarly caused disappointment.[125] But part of the disappointment was tied to procedural inadequacies in the Security Council's response, or at least the perception of procedural inadequacies. Thus, based on a decision by African states parties, South Africa has proposed an amendment to Article 16 of the Rome Statute, giving a state formally the authority to request the Security Council to defer the matter before the Court. Where the United Nations Security Council fails to decide on the request within six months, the state may request the United Nations General Assembly to assume, consistent with GA Resolution 377(v), the responsibility of the Security Council under Article 16.[126] It is a matter of debate whether the ICC should be made dependent on a further political body. A set of procedural steps within the Security Council dedicated to requests for deferral could possibly address part of the objective of the amendment proposal. To protect the ICC's independence, court-internal mechanisms for temporary suspensions, where truly needed, would seem much preferable.

Back to the Prosecutor: assuming the aggressor state had not opted out from the Court's jurisdiction and the Prosecutor may act *ex proprio motu*, she or he is not *obligated* to initiate an investigation. Nor is the Prosecutor *obligated* to initiate an investigation based on the other two trigger mechanisms. The Prosecutor first needs to establish a 'reasonable basis' for the initiation of an investigation and has a measure of discretion in this preliminary examination. In accordance with Article 53(1), the Prosecutor must not only consider whether the information available provides a reasonable basis to believe that a crime within the jurisdiction of the Court has been or is being committed[127] and whether the case is admissible under Article 17 of the Rome Statute,[128] but also whether '[t]aking into account the gravity of the crime and the interests of victims, there are nonetheless substantial reasons to believe that an investigation would not serve the interests of justice.'[129] Significantly, the Office of the Prosecutor (OTP) has recently noted again that the preliminary examination has no time line prescribed under the Rome Statute.[130] Timing alone can already help to diffuse possible conflict with peace negotiations. In the same report, the OTP has explained, that it 'seeks to contribute to two overarching goals of the Statute: the ending of impunity by encouraging genuine national proceedings, and the prevention of crimes, thereby potentially obviating the need for the

the Implementation of the Decisions on the International Criminal Court Doc. Assembly/AU/13(XXII)', Assembly/AU/Dec.493(XXII), para. 6.

125 *Ibid*, para. 7.

126 United Nations Depository Notification C.N.851.2009.TREATIES-10 of 30 November 2009 (Proposal of amendment by South Africa to the Statute).

127 Article 53(1)(a) Rome Statute.

128 Article 53(1)(b) Rome Statute.

129 Article 53(1)(c) Rome Statute.

130 ICC, OTP, *Report on Preliminary Examination Activities 2014*, 2 December 2015, Section I.13.

Court's intervention.'[131] While acknowledging that peace and justice are interdependent and that the 'interests of justice' under Article 53(1)(c) refer to a concept of justice wider than criminal justice,[132] the OTP has stated in 2007 that the 'interests of justice' 'must be interpreted in accordance with the objects and purposes of the Statute. Hence, it should not be conceived so broadly as to embrace all issues related to peace and security.'[133] In other words, the OTP sees that the interests of peace are part of the interests of justice but seeks to keep them aligned with the objects and purposes of the Statute. Nevertheless, if the interests of justice do not embrace *all* issues related to peace and security, they may embrace *some* – the door is left narrowly ajar. The OTP 'recognizes a role for the Security Council to defer ICC action',[134] but notes at the same time 'the obligation of the Prosecutor to consider all relevant factors. The Office will consider issues of crime prevention and security under the interests of justice, and there may be some overlap … [with] the duty to protect victims and witnesses'.[135] The reference to this specific 'overlap' indicates that the Prosecutor could weigh the risk of prolonged war already in the evaluation of the 'interests of the victims' under Article 53(1)(c). In other words, the interests of the victims might not only speak for an investigation, they might speak against it. It would be, moreover, inconceivable that the creation of more and more victims by the same ongoing crime could be outright disregarded.[136] But this all assumes that the prolongation of a war is at all linked to the fear of prosecution. The OTP calls a decision not to proceed 'a course of last resort' and recalls that such a decision can be revisited under Article 53(4).

In 2013, the OTP reiterated that 'the interests of justice should not be perceived to embrace all issues related to peace and security. In particular, the interests of justice provision should not be considered a conflict management tool requiring the Prosecutor to assume the role of mediator in political negotiations: such an outcome would run contrary to the explicit judicial

131 *Ibid*, Section I.16.

132 ICC, OTP, *Policy Paper on the Interests of Justice*, September 2007, ICC-OTP-2007, Section 6 b. 'Peace Processes', p. 8.

133 *Ibid.*

134 *Ibid.*

135 *Ibid*, p. 9.

136 The issue whether the interests of victims could mean that the Court should *refrain* from exercising its jurisdiction was pondered in 2004: 'Informal inter-sessional meeting of the Special Working Group on the Crime of Aggression', held at the Liechtenstein Institute on Self-Determination, Woodrow Wilson School, at Princeton University, New Jersey, United States, from 21–23 June 2004, ICC-ASP/3/SWGCA/INF.1, paras. 25–27. The question was raised in the context of Articles 17 and 53(1)(c). The concern was not focused on situations where the victim state, after the end of a war, is merely beholden to a victorious aggressor state, but on situations where the victim state has to fear additional suffering. Could the issue be addressed through interpretation or did it require an explicit understanding or an amendment? The meeting concluded that amendments were not necessary and it was stated that the concern, as well as other concerns raised (see further below), could be addressed though interpretation of the Articles.

functions of the Office and the Court as a whole.'[137] The OTP observed that 'the UN Secretary General has called for mediators to adjust to the legal process, rather than for the legal process to accommodate political negotiations'[138] and cites his advice: 'Now that the ICC has been established, mediators should make the international legal position clear to parties. They should understand that if the jurisdiction of the ICC is established in a particular situation, then, as an independent judicial body, the Court will proceed to deal with it in accordance with the relevant provisions of the Rome Statute and the process of justice will take its course.'[139]

The Prosecutor's narrowly tailored approach to peace considerations does not preclude flexibility about timing in the ICC. Providing some room to bring peace negotiations to fruition and to *shorten* rather than lengthen the very crime to be prosecuted is a more compelling situation-specific need than serving generically as 'conflict management tool'. The risk that the negotiations will then be dragged out is curtailed: Each additional day of the war aggravates the seriousness of the crime of aggression and thus the seriousness of the Court's reaction.

Thus, fourth, the likelihood that an activated criminal jurisdiction makes the ending of a war *easier* instead of more difficult should not be underestimated: Mediators or peace negotiators may very well find that the prospect of ICC prosecution moves a state and its leaders towards rather than away from ending the war. No matter how long the aggressor state fights, the possibility that its leaders end up before the Court does not disappear. Quite the opposite, pressure towards the Court's exercise of jurisdiction may grow, with the crime having become more and more unbearable. This does not underestimate the weakness of the enforcement power of the Court, especially against the leaders of an aggressor state with might, but even then the likelihood of prosecution does not shrink to zero. The leaders of the aggressor state may prefer a faster ending of the war exactly to obtain more lenient treatment and to forestall a higher sentence.

In addition, the actual initiation of investigations and commencement of proceedings against the leader of an aggressor state can make the ending of a war easier instead of more difficult. Based on a warrant by the ICC, a concentrated endeavour to arrest the leader of an aggressor state could turn out to be feasible, at least in some circumstances. Immunity would not be a hindrance for proceedings by the Court. Again depending on the political constellation in the

137 ICC, OTP, *Policy Paper on Preliminary Examinations*, November 2013, Section IV.69, at 17. For a somewhat different view, commenting on internal armed conflict, see Arbour 2014, p. 55: 'considering that some of [those most responsible for the most serious crimes] might be able to hold the peace process hostage to their personal interest, there must be incentives for them to come forward. Without compromising the core integrity of justice, this could include lenient treatment in exchange for disclosing facts, expressing remorse, and making some form of restitution.'

138 ICC, OTP, *Policy Paper on Preliminary Examinations*, November 2013, n. 47.

139 Report of the Secretary General, *Enhancing Mediation and its Support Activities*, UN Doc. S/2009/189, 8 April 2009, para. 37.

aggressor state, the surrender of the leader may quickly quell the fighting spirit of the remaining government and its armies.

The contribution of an activated ICC jurisdiction to the *faster* ending of a war is also significant in the context of temporal personal immunity under the ACJHPR Statute. Even if such immunity is arguably necessary before *national* criminal courts, it is a relatively crude tool to protect peace efforts against the feared disruption from *regional* and *international* criminal courts. After all, these courts are set up exactly to prosecute those most responsible for international crimes. Yet immunity shields the guilty as much as the innocent, the dictator as much as the democratically elected leader, the war-maker as much as the peacemaker. Here too, the activated jurisdiction of the ICC over the crime of aggression, together with the ratifications of the Rome Statute and the Kampala Amendments, can assist African states suffering under a crime of aggression. If the immunity is anyway soon to pass and the ACJHPR intends to exercise its jurisdiction in the near future, the ICC may refrain from pressing ahead and offer instead technical cooperation. When the immunity presents a more enduring hindrance for the ACJHPR, or other considerations[140] advise against action by the ACJHPR, the ability of the ICC to step in[141] can be a relief for African states enduring a crime of aggression. Again, the Prosecutor would have an explicit measure of discretion when evaluating whether the interests of the victims of the crime of aggression and the interests of justice speak for or against immediate proceedings: the Prosecutor can either await the imminent conclusion of peace negotiations and postpone the proceedings till afterwards or work as speedily as possible towards a warrant for arrest, especially when this would not only serve justice but end the war more expeditiously. Kenya may have had these various reasons for discretion in mind when it proposed an amendment to the irrelevance of official capacity under Article 27 of the Rome Statute. A new paragraph 3 would read: 'Notwithstanding paragraph 1 and 2 above, serving Heads of State, their deputies and anybody acting or is entitled to act as such may be exempt from prosecution during their current term of office. Such an exemption may be renewed by the Court under the same conditions.'[142] Yet while the exemption is discretionary, its emphasis on immunity and wide applicability jar with the objectives of the Rome Statute to finally move beyond the hurdles against national prosecutions and to end the impunity of international crimes. After all, those most responsible for international crimes are typically high-level persons in the state. Those who commit crimes of aggression are leaders by definition. Procedural accommodations based explicitly on the status of the person or the status of his or her official duties are fundamentally at odds with

140 See further below.
141 On immunity and complementarity, see *infra* n. 154.
142 *Supra* n. 104, 'Proposed amendment 2'.

the Rome Statute.[143] Moreover, the proposed exemption could become a non-discretionary pattern and thus be counterproductive to both democracy and peace, as much as to justice.[144] The discretion already existing under the Rome Statute is the wiser tool.

4.3. (MORE) QUESTIONS OF COMPLEMENTARITY

The plea to make the ICC available for crimes of aggression is *not* based on the claim that the exercise of national or even regional jurisdiction over this crime is constrained in principle. It *is* based on the observation that different levels of jurisdiction may offer different advantages and disadvantages for peace and justice and that it will be wise to give room for flexibility, depending on the circumstances of the situation. International jurisdiction will often be the best or only option for prosecution, even after entry into force of the Malabo Protocol.

With regard to the interplay of different jurisdictional levels, much hinges on the interpretation of Article 17 under the Rome Statute and Understanding 5 of the Kampala Amendments. Much depends too on the degree of overlap between regional and international jurisdictional reach. As described above, all the ACJHPR trigger mechanisms require ratification or acceptance by just one of four different types of states. In contrast, one of the ICC trigger mechanisms requires no state ratification or acceptance (but voting by the Security Council under Chapter VII of the Charter of the United Nations), and the two other ICC trigger mechanisms are dependent – in the case of the crime of aggression – on the ratification or acceptance of the *Rome Statute* by both the state of the accused and the state where the crime was committed, plus, possibly, on the ratification or acceptance of the *Kampala Amendments* by either one of these states, and, moreover, on the absence of an opt-out by the aggressor state.[145] At the same time, temporary personal immunity can throw a wrench into the process of the ACJHPR. Discrepancies between the national, regional and international definitions of the crime of aggression may likewise permit prosecution by one court but not by another.

Under the Malabo Protocol, as under the Rome Statute, national courts have primary jurisdiction. Presumably, the ACJHPR would have primary jurisdiction before the ICC, in case a future relationship between the two courts closely

143 Rule 134*quater* of the ICC Rules of Procedure and Evidence, is a case in point, as it permits excusal from presence at trial due to extraordinary public duties. Why not extraordinary private duties, such as the care of a dying relative? A less accommodating Rule 134*ter* on excusals from presence at trial is applicable to all accused persons. Under both Rules an excusal can be given to accused persons only if they are subject to a summons to appear, not subject to a warrant for arrest. See Resolution ICC-ASP/12/Res.7, 27 November 2013.

144 The more the discretionary rule turns into a non-discretionary pattern, the more it makes sense for the leader to cling to power. See also *supra* main text after n. 96.

145 *Supra* sections 2.2 and 3.2.

parallels the relationship between a national court and either the ACJHPR or the ICC. Yet does a too automatic application of complementarity do justice to justice?

According to Understanding 5 of the Kampala Amendments, they 'shall not be interpreted as creating the right or obligation to exercise domestic jurisdiction with respect to an act of aggression committed by another State.' The impact of the Amendments on the complementarity principle under the Rome Statute is carefully circumscribed. The Understanding does not subtract from the domestic jurisdiction of a former aggressor state against its own leaders. It does also not preclude that the described right or obligation might already exist under national or international law. Interestingly too, the Understanding speaks of the state act and not the individual crime, maybe in an allusion to the opinion of the International Law Commission which took a narrow view: A state may only exercise jurisdiction over crimes of aggression 'arising' from the state's own acts of aggression.[146] Otherwise international jurisdiction is exclusive. The jurisdiction of the aggressor state is termed 'permissive' rather than obligatory. Determinations by national courts about the acts of other states (as necessary in the context of determining the individual crime) 'would be contrary to the fundamental principle of international law *par in parem imperium non habet*' and 'would have serious implications for international relations and international peace and security'.[147] The International Law Commission excluded national jurisdiction by states other than the aggressor state in one swoop, without a separate focus on the victim state. At least with regard to the latter state, the argument is difficult to accept and rather ironic. After all, it is the act of the aggressor state that has had 'serious implications for international relations and international peace and security'! It seems contradictory that the victim state would be permitted to fight back, but not permitted to make a judicial determination of the act of aggression and to prosecute those responsible for it. The Nuremberg Trial is a case in point. The victim state gained its jurisdictional authority the hard way and can only be expected to forego this authority where genuine alternatives exist, be it through proceedings in the national courts of the aggressor state, in the ICC, in a future ACJHPR, or otherwise. For example, the victim state may be well advised to set up a special hybrid tribunal with an international component. But where such alternatives are not available, would a victorious victim state have to let the leaders of the aggressor state go their way? Or execute them without trial?

Even with regard to the exercise of universal jurisdiction by national courts, the argument of the International Law Commission appears to give too little weight to the *erga omnes* character of the obligation to abstain

---

146 'Draft Code of Crimes against the Peace and Security of Mankind', Article 8 and Commentary para. 13–15, in Report of the International Law Commission. 48th Session (1996), para. 50, ILC Yearbook (1996), Vol.II part 2, pp. 17 and 20.

147 *Ibid.*

from the illegal use of force.[148] An act of aggression may have succeeded, the leadership remained in power, the victim state is occupied or subordinated, and international jurisdiction may be unavailable. While it might be rather unlikely that *any* criminal court proceedings would be feasible under such circumstances, other states should have, at least in principle, the right to step in, notably when both the people of the aggressor state and the victim state long to be freed and the effort to prosecute those in power would not aggravate the suffering of the peoples under their rule.[149] To overcome immunity before national courts and nevertheless guard against politicised prosecution, states could act together, in a meaningful number and across a wide political spectrum, by setting up an ad hoc court. Some features of such an ad hoc court are similar to those of a regional court. Vice versa, a regional court, such as the ACJHPR, can be drawn up in a preliminary fashion and employed like an ad hoc court.[150]

The suggestion for special tribunals and ad hoc courts indicates concern with the shortcomings of national jurisdiction, but it is not meant to subtract from the existence of such jurisdiction. Quite the opposite, the authority of special tribunals and ad hoc courts flows from it. So does the authority of regional and international courts. In general, with regard to national jurisdiction, it might be more circumspect for a state to anticipate not only its aggressor state jurisdiction but also its victim state and possible universal jurisdiction, and to prepare its

---

148 The ILC concern about a national criminal court's pronouncement on the act of another state may also assign *too much* weight to such a pronouncement. It is a finding on one of the elements of the individual crime, an intermediate step in the judgment on the crime. The national criminal court's finding of a state act of aggression is not generally binding under international law. Not even a finding *by the ICC* of an act of aggression is binding beyond the framework of the Rome Statute. During the negotiations on the crime of aggression, specifically in the discussions on the non-prejudicial effect of determinations by organs outside the ICC, it was clearly stated that, vice versa, the determination of the state act by the Court would not bind the Security Council. Neither would the International Court of Justice be bound. The definition of the crime, including of the state act, in the Kampala Amendments is for the purposes of the Rome Statute. Moreover, according to Article 25(4), '[n]o provision in this Statute relating to individual criminal responsibility shall affect the responsibility of States under international law.' Comparable considerations apply with regard to the findings by national, regional or other criminal courts. Neither the International Court of Justice nor the Security Council would be stopped from making an own determination with regard to the state act of aggression. On the autonomy of the Court and the Security Council in determining an act of aggression, see 'Informal Inter-sessional Meeting of the Special Working Group on the Crime of Aggression, held at the Liechtenstein Institute on Self-Determination, Woodrow Wilson School, Princeton University, United States, from 11 to 14 June 2007', ICC-ASP/6/SWGCA/INF.1, para. 54.

149 See in this context, AFLA 2007, Appendix 91, in particular principle 8, 'universal jurisdiction shall not be used as a pretext to pursue politically motivated prosecutions', and principle 16, 'prosecution and sentencing of gross human rights offenders shall be guided not only by the need for deterrence, but also by the need to reconcile, rehabilitate and reconstruct the society where the offence was committed.'

150 See also Pan-African Lawyers Union et al., 'Implications of the African Court of Human and Peoples' Rights Being Empowered to Try International Crimes Such as Genocide, Crimes Against Humanity, and War Crimes – An Opinion', 2009.

criminal code accordingly, with due process rules and extradition parameters firmly in place, than to leave the question up to the heat of the moment when it might have obtained custody over the (former) leaders of the aggressor state. Preparatory legislation could also anticipate some of the criteria, indicated below, that might speak for the use of another jurisdiction. Such criteria, going beyond a mechanical application of complementarity, could also ease the interplay between the ICC and a future ACJHPR and be part of a Relationship Agreement.

These arguments on behalf of wide jurisdictional ability to prosecute crimes of aggression do not mean that the application of the usual concept of complementarity would be the ideal. Using the higher rather than the lower jurisdictional level and pursuing what might be called a *reverse, flexible*, or *mutual* complementarity concept could at times be the much more sensible approach. In other words, the higher level might be given more readily priority, with the lower level only proceeding when the higher level does not, depending on a variety of circumstances. For example, pondering investigation and prosecution of the crime of aggression by national courts *versus* by the ACJHPR *versus* by ad hoc courts *versus* by the ICC, it could matter whether both the aggressor state and the victim state belong to the African Union, or whether only either one – or neither one – does. But these constellations are not determinative by themselves. To decide on the appropriate jurisdictional level, additional questions might include:

Does the jurisdiction have the power and independence to achieve proceedings against governmental leaders?

Does the jurisdiction have the capacity to achieve the necessary cooperation by states, the United Nations, and other relevant institutions, especially with respect to the collection of evidence? Are cooperation and relationship agreements in place?

Which court's exercise of jurisdiction carries a lesser risk of causing new political tension? Or, in case the war is ongoing despite the arrest of one or more of the leaders of the aggressor state, which jurisdiction might be most conducive to peace?

Would the court of a particular jurisdiction be susceptible to bias or the perception of bias? Would a fair trial be less likely? Are due process rules firmly in place?[151]

Does the jurisdiction address the rights of victims? Would the proceedings pursue the full recognition of the crime and offer or facilitate reparation?[152]

---

151 Forum shopping for the most lenient court is here not the point, protection of human dignity is – for the victims, for the accused. Without due process, the odds are simply too high against finding and comprehending the truth about the crime and about those most responsible. The recognition of guilt remains fake and the relief for victims elusive.

152 The victims of the crime of aggression do not only include individuals, institutions and peoples, but also states. The question arises whether this aspect of the crime requires

Which court's exercise of jurisdiction would most contribute to reconciliation? Which court's exercise of jurisdiction would most contribute to the prevention of future crimes of aggression?

Of course the very first question would be which courts – national, regional, international, ad hoc – are available at all, in light of jurisdictional restrictions, immunities or other legal hindrances. But here the focus is on the complementarity ladder, which way around it should be placed, when more than one jurisdictional level would actually be available. Could the higher-level jurisdiction be exercised even if it is complementary to the lower-level one?

The observations start here with the leeway available under the basic complementarity concept in the Rome Statute and the ACJHPR Statute. When a state with jurisdiction does *not* insist on exercising it, giving up its priority would seem quite feasible both under the ACJHPR and the Rome Statute. For instance, a former aggressor state ruled by a new government, or a victim state, may reasonably fear that a trial by its national court would be biased, or perceived as biased, *against* the accused. Or, fear of renewed political tension and conflict may speak for a trial at a higher jurisdictional level. Under the introductory wording of both Article 17(1) of the Rome Statute and Article 46H(1) of the ACJHPR Statute, a case is *inadmissible if it has been or is being investigated or prosecuted* by a state with jurisdiction *unless* that state is *unwilling* or *unable* to (genuinely)[153] investigate or prosecute. Thus the case is *admissible* when it is *not* or has *not* been investigated or prosecuted by that state: it is irrelevant whether the state is 'unwilling' or 'unable' and whether the reasons abstaining from the exercise of jurisdiction fit under the definitions of inability or unwillingness under the Rome Statute or the ACJHPR Statute. The OTP of the ICC has pointed out: 'An admissibility determination is not a judgment or reflection on the national justice system as a whole. If an otherwise functioning judiciary is not investigating or prosecuting the relevant case(s), the determining factor is the absence of relevant proceedings … The absence of national proceedings, i.e. domestic inactivity, is sufficient to make the case admissible. The question of unwillingness or inability does not arise and the Office does not need to consider the other factors set out in Article 17.'[154] Even though national courts have

adjustments in existing provisions on the rights of victims or not. Peace negotiations and peace treaties may be already addressing the issue of reparations. In all likelihood, the perpetrator would be the wrong addressee for the restitution of territory. (From a small unpublished 2004 paper by the writer.).

153 The provision in the ACJHPR Statute does not use the term 'genuinely'.

154 ICC, OTP, *Policy Paper on Preliminary Examinations*, November 2013, Section IV.(b), paras. 46, 47. In para. 48, the OTP cites not only legal restrictions as possible reasons for national court inactivity: 'Inactivity in relation to a particular case may result from numerous factors, including the absence of an adequate legal framework; the existence of laws that serve as a bar to domestic proceedings such as amnesties, immunities or statutes of limitations; the deliberate focus on proceedings on low-level or marginal perpetrators despite evidence on those more responsible, or other, more general issues related to the lack of political will

primary jurisdiction under the Rome Statute and under the Malabo Protocol, the complementarity principle does not *require* them to exercise this jurisdiction. Nor would either the ACJHPR or the ICC be *prevented* from proceeding when the national court foregoes to exercise its jurisdiction.[155] Similarly, assuming the ICC would be complementary to the ACJHPR, the former could proceed when the latter refrains from exercising its jurisdiction, even if the reasons for inactivity are not due to legal restrictions.[156] The definitions of unwillingness or inability under the Rome Statute and the ACJHPR Statute are beside the point.

In contrast, when a state *insists* on the exercise of its national jurisdiction, the application of the concept of a *reverse, flexible or mutual* complementarity, even if for good reason, is problematic. Absent legal basis, leverage or enforcement power, it is not easy to stop a state from exercising its jurisdiction or to free a person from the prison of a state bent on retribution. Similar difficulties may have to be anticipated where a regional court insists on its exercise of jurisdiction even though particular circumstances might strongly speak for international jurisdiction. Thus, it would be greatly relevant to see whether the complementarity provisions in the Rome Statute and in the ACJHPR Statute exceptionally accommodate priority of their jurisdiction, with an obligation for the national jurisdiction to abstain from its own proceedings.[157] If yes, a comparable complementarity reversal would come into play in case the same complementarity provisions were to be used *mutatis mutandi* for the relationship between the ACJHPR and the ICC.

In the course of the negotiations on the crime of aggression, some of the aspects of this quandary were considered in the context of discussions on complementarity, admissibility and *ne bis in idem*. Complementarity with regard to the crime of aggression was debated intermittently, starting with the first Pre-Rome Committee session[158] and also, shortly, in other sessions before and after the Rome Conference.[159] Those who were reluctant about complementary international jurisdiction called national courts unsuitable for the crime of aggression and expressed concern about insufficient respect for the rights of the accused. It was not always clear if the preference would have

---

or judicial capacity.' Immunity exemptions or the focus on low-level actors would mean inactivity by the national court. But so would any other ground.

155 The ICC-OTP or ACJHPR-OTP may try to encourage national action. Or they too may find national action inadvisable.

156 But it should be kept in mind that it will be relevant too whether the states involved in a situation of interest to either court are states parties to the Rome Statute and/or the ACJHPR Statute and which trigger mechanisms can be or have been used.

157 For a careful study of complementarity with regard to the crime of aggression, see Trahan 2012.

158 The writer relies here on her notes from the meetings.

159 Before Rome, arguments for primary or exclusive international jurisdiction were at times difficult to differentiate from arguments on behalf of inherent jurisdiction for the International Criminal Court. Inherent jurisdiction would have been independent of the ratification or acceptance of the Rome Statute by the states concerned.

been for primary or exclusive international jurisdiction. But other states, notably one of the European states, argued strongly for complementary international jurisdiction, i.e. primary national jurisdiction, typically linking their position to the state right of self-defence or pointing out that prosecution of the other three core crimes can face the same problems. That the crime was a crime *erga omnes* was underlined too. From early on – also starting with the first pre-Rome Preparatory Committee session – one of the counterpoints to the concerns about unfair national trials was that the ICC should not be a court of appeals for national judgments.[160] Over time, support increased for using the same complementarity principle for the crime of aggression as for the other core crimes. Delegates tended more and more to simply remain silent in response to reminders, by another one[161] of the European states, to reconsider the question of complementarity. In the first inter-sessional meeting in Princeton,[162] a non-governmental representative asked if the prospect of victor's justice might speak for special efforts to move jurisdiction to the ICC, specifically whether Article 17(2)(c) should and could cover this constellation. Under that provision, the Court, in order to determine unwillingness, must consider, 'having regard to the principles of due process recognized by international law', whether '[t]he proceedings were not or are not being conducted independently or impartially, and ... were or are being conducted in a manner which, in the circumstances, is inconsistent with an intent to bring the person concerned to justice.' While the wording itself could cover biased proceedings *against* the person concerned, the negotiations on 'unwillingness' had been clearly focused on the opposite danger, namely national proceedings that shield or favour the person concerned. The same thrust seems to pervade the Article as a whole when read together.[163] At the Princeton meeting, one response to the concern about unfair trials was again that the ICC was not intended as a court of appeals for national decisions. The non-governmental inquirer had in mind that the ICC should be able to act *instead* of the national court, but the answer indicated the hurdles in the absence of cooperation by the national jurisdiction. Interestingly, it was also argued that the problem could be addressed through interpretation. The main preliminary

---

160 After Rome, complementarity was listed as an issue with regard to the crime of aggression in 'Preliminary list of possible issues relating to the crime of aggression – Discussion paper proposed by the Coordinator', Preparatory Commission for the International Criminal Court, Working Group on the Crime of Aggression, PCNICC/2000/WGCA/RT.1, 29 March 2000.

161 According to notes of the writer, this delegation referred explicitly to the position of the International Law Commission, *supra* n. 149, for example during the fourth post-Rome Preparatory Commission session.

162 'Informal inter-sessional meeting of the Special Working Group on the Crime of Aggression, held at the Liechtenstein Institute on Self-Determination, Woodrow Wilson School, at Princeton University, New Jersey, United States, 21–23 June 2004, ICC-ASP/3/SWGCA/INF.1.

163 But compare recently McDermott, 'How Libya became the International Criminal Court's latest failure', *The Conversation*, 6 August 2015, available at: http://theconversation.com.

conclusion was that no amendment was required and Articles 17, 18 and 19 were applicable in their current wording.[164] At the same meeting, the reluctance of using the ICC as appeals court was also apparent in discussions about *ne bis in idem*. Under Article 20(3)(b) of the Rome Statute, the ICC may exceptionally try a person who has been already tried by another court for the same conduct, when the proceedings in the other court 'were not conducted independently or impartially in accordance with the norms of due process recognized by international law and were conducted in a manner ... inconsistent with an intent to bring the person concerned to justice.' Here it was asked whether the provision could also be applied when the other court, possibly the court of a victorious state, had been partial *against* the accused. In response, it was noted that the crime of aggression was in this regard not unique *vis-à-vis* the other three crimes and that 'it was preferable to leave the matter to judicial interpretation, on a case-by-case basis, which would take into account the respective elements of the crime.'[165]

In the third session of the Assembly of States Parties to the Rome Statute, a small island developing state took the argument against complementarity up again: national courts may not be in a position to exercise jurisdiction or may not have legislation with respect to the crime of aggression, the ICC should perhaps have primary or exclusive jurisdiction. But no one ran with the ball. Instead, in other sessions, states repeated that the principle of complementarity must be upheld.[166] Altogether, the position of states during the negotiations did not leave much room for a wide interpretation of the exceptions to both primary national jurisdiction and *ne bis in idem*.

The writer did not attend the discussions that went into the drafting of Article 46H ('Complementary Jurisdiction') and 46I ('*Non bis in idem*') of the ACJHPR Statute, but both provisions are nearly identical to Articles 17 and 20 of the Rome Statute. Thus the intentions under both instruments may largely parallel each other.

Again, if a future relationship between the ICC and the ACJHPR is structured along similar lines, similar considerations on complementarity and *ne bis in idem* could apply.

The rather complex issue which situations might speak for a *reverse, mutual* or more *flexible* complementarity could be one of the agenda items of the future review conference that is required for the Kampala Amendments seven years after the beginning of the ICC's exercise of jurisdiction over the crime of aggression.[167] The subject might be of interest not only to other regions but also for other crimes, especially crimes where the accused, the victims, and the

---

164 *Ibid*, paras. 25–27.

165 *Ibid*, paras. 32, 33.

166 To cite one instance, such a statement was made by an Asian state in the resumed fifth session of the Assembly of States Parties to the Rome Statute. (author's notes.)

167 Resolution RC/Res.6, 'The Crime of Aggression', 11 June 2010, op. 4.

territory concerned do not belong to the same state. This does not underestimate the significance of the state act element in the definition of the crime of aggression. But the insights achieved from the discussion can very well have general value, exactly because situations involving other crimes too stir up the question if and when it might be wiser that a complementary jurisdiction should be given priority.

At the same time, much can be done to diminish resistance against the priority of national and possibly regional jurisdiction over the crime of aggression. Protecting due process in *all* courts promises to be the most direct way to soften concerns about the 'misplacement' of prosecutions and about the very proposition of prosecution. Due process not only helps the accused and the victims of the crime but also supports the authority and acceptability of judicial proceedings. It counters perceptions of bias, pre-empts and calms political tension and contributes to reconciliation. To strengthen due process and give further credence to national and regional jurisdiction over the crime of aggression, states and regional jurisdictions could consider adding non-national or non-regional judges to their criminal courts. This could be arranged on an ad hoc basis. Judges with expertise in public international law will be needed for the evaluation of the element of the state act of aggression. The ACJHPR may reach out to its General Affairs Section, 'borrowing' judges for the International Criminal Law Section or sitting in full court.[168] The ICC, in turn, would do well by further strengthening its institutional support for the defence. Importantly, permitting acrimony between available courts would contradict the common commitment against crimes of aggression. Instead, cooperation assists with the larger goal. Peace is still best sown by peace.

Ultimately, the contribution that prosecution by national, regional or international courts can make to the prevention of crimes of aggression is based on something more profound than fear of punishment. It is based on achieving a greater understanding of the hurt caused by the crime and a greater understanding of the roots of the crime. While the main objective of a trial is to establish guilt or innocence, more than the accountability of the *person accused* is under examination. The proceedings speak also to a common accounting of all human beings: Every trial amounts to an inquiry into human nature. Especially with the prosecution of international crimes, the whole world is asked to dig deeper into questions of human identity, into choices between the submission and the resistance to evil. With each trial of such crimes, everyone's accountability, everyone's conscience and quest for a conscious life are at issue. Human-rights-based approaches to prosecution advance this wider objective more strongly than a shaming by unfair trial. In this regard particularly, the closeness of the International Criminal Law Section to the Human and Peoples

168 Other options exist for the interaction between the ACJHPR Sections, all with the proviso that the rules of due process apply for the accused. See *supra* main text above n. 73.

Rights Section will be of great value to the ACJHPR. The fruits of such closeness could become an inspiration for other courts.[169]

No one shall suffer the cruelty of the crime of aggression evermore. No one evermore shall incur the burden of the guilt.

The storms around the Malabo Protocol will pass, leaving fertile ground for peace.

'Rainy season ends –
Water lilies in the pond
suddenly open.'
– Sasabune

BIBLIOGRAPHY

BOOKS AND JOURNAL ARTICLES

AFLA 2007
Africa Legal Aid (AFLA), 'The Cairo–Arusha Principles on Universal Jurisdiction in Respect of Gross Human Rights Offences: An African Perspective', AFLA Quarterly, July–December 2007.

Arbour 2014
Arbour, L., 'Freedom, Peace and Justice', 27 The Berlin Journal, 2014.

Badar 2013
Badar, M.E., 'The Concept of Mens Rea in International Criminal Law – The Case for a Unified Approach', Hart Publishing, 2013.

Barriga 2012
Barriga, S., 'Negotiating the Amendments on the crime of aggression', in Barriga, S. and Kreß, C. (ed.), 'The Travaux Préparatoires of the Crime of Aggression', Cambridge University Press, 2012.

Barriga and Grover 2011
Barriga, S. and Grover, L., 'A Historic Breakthrough on the Crime of Aggression', 105 ASIL, 2011.

Bertram-Nothnagel 2010
Bertram-Nothnagel, J.F., 'A Seed for World Peace Planted in Africa: The Provisions on the Crime of Aggression Adopted at the Kampala Review Conference for the Rome Statute of the International Criminal Court', AFLA Quarterly, April–June 2010.

Bethlehem 2012
Bethlehem, D., 'Principles Relevant to the Scope of a State's Right of Self-Defense Against an Imminent or Actual Armed Attack by Non-State Actors', 106 ASIL, 2012.

169 See in this context Zappalà 2003.

Clark 2010
Clark, R.S., 'Amendments to the Rome Statute of the International Criminal Court Considered at the First Review Conference on the Court, Kampala, 31 May–11 June 2010', 2(2) Göttingen J Int'l, 2010.

Cortright 2008
Cortright, D., 'Peace – A History of Movements and Ideas', Cambridge University Press, 2008.

De Vattel 1758
De Vattel, E., 'Of the Sovereign who Wages an Unjust War', in 'The Law of Nations or the Principles of Natural Law', 1758.

Du Plessis 2014
Du Plessis, M., 'Shambolic, shameful and symbolic – Implications of the African Union's immunity for African leaders', 278 Institute for Security Studies Paper, 2014.

Du Plessis 2012
Du Plessis, M., 'Implications of the AU decision to give the African Court jurisdiction over international crimes', 235 Institute for Security Studies Paper, June 2012.

Fried 2005
Fried, E., (ed.), 'Beyond the "Never Agains"', Swedish Government, 2005.

Jalloh 2013
Jalloh, C.C., 'Africa and the International Criminal Court: Collision Course or Cooperation?', University of Pittsburgh School of Law Legal Studies Research Paper Series, No. 2013–31, 2013.

Jo and Simmons 2014
Jo, H. and Simmons, B.A., 'Can the International Criminal Court Deter Atrocities', SSRN, 2014.

Kreß 2012
Kreß. C. et al., 'Negotiating the Understandings on the Crime of Aggression', in Barriga, S. and Kreß, C. (ed.), 'The Travaux Préparatoires of the Crime of Aggression', Cambridge University Press, 2012.

Lafontaine and Tachou-Sipowo 2014
Lafontaine, F. and Tachou-Sipowo, A.-G., 'Le Débat Paix/Justice Après 10 Ans de Cour Pénale Internationale: Une Réévaluation à la Lumière de la Stratégie de Poursuite Limitée aux Plus Hauts Responsables', Dossiers de la Revue de droit pénal et de Criminologie, 2014.

Murphy 2014
Murphy, S.D., 'Immunity Ratione Personae of Foreign Government Officials and Other Topics: The Sixty-Fifth Session of the International Law Commission', 108 ASIL, 2014.

Nkansah 2014
Nkansah, L.A., 'International Criminal Court in the Trenches of Africa', 1 African Journal of International Criminal Justice, 2014.

Orakhelashvili 2006
Orakhelashvili, A., 'Peremptory Norms in International Law', Oxford University Press, 2006.

Richardson 2013
Richardson, H., 'African Grievances and the International Criminal Court: Issues of African Equity under International Criminal Law', Temple University Legal Studies Research Paper Series, No. 2013–24, 2013.
Sellars 2014
Sellars, K., 'Trying the Kaiser: The Origins of International Criminal Law', in Bergsmo, M., Cheah, W.L. and Yi, P. (eds.), 'Historical Origins of International Criminal Law: Volume I', FICHL Publication Series No. 20, 2014.
Tladi 2009
Tladi, D., 'The African Union and the International Criminal Court: The battle for the soul of international law', 34 SAYIL, 2009.
Trahan 2012
Trahan, J., 'Is Complementarity the Right Approach for the International Criminal Court's Crime of Aggression? – Considering the problem of 'Overzealous' National Court Prosecutions', 45 Cornell Int'l. L.J, 2012.
Udombana 2014
Udombana, N.J., '"Can These Dry Bones Live?" In Search of a Lasting Therapy for AU and ICC Toxic Relationship', 1 African Journal of International Criminal Justice, 2014.
Von Clausewitz 1832
Von Clausewitz, C., 'Vom Kriege', Dümmlers Verlag, 1832.
Zappalà 2003
Zappalà, S., 'Human Rights in International Criminal Proceedings', Oxford Monographs in International Law, Oxford University Press, 2003.

TREATIES, LEGISLATION AND AGREEMENTS

African Union Non-Aggression and Common Defence Pact, 31 January 2005.
AU, Decision on the Progress Report of the Commission on the Implementation of the Decisions on the International Criminal Court, Doc. Assembly/AU/13(XXII), 30–31 January 2014.
AU, Decision on the Progress Report of the Commission on the Implementation of Previous Decisions on the International Criminal Court (ICC), Doc. Assembly/AU/18(XXIV), 30–31 January 2015.
Charter of the United Nations, 26 June 1945.
Constitutive Act of the African Union, 11 July 2000.
Protocol on Amendments to the Protocol on the Statute of the African Court of Justice and Human Rights (Malabo Protocol), 27 June 2014.
Protocol of the Court of Justice of the African Union, 11 July 2003.
Protocol on the Statute of the African Court of Justice and Human Rights, 1 July 2008.
Protocol Relating to the Establishment of the Peace and Security Council of the African Union, 9 July 2002.
Protocol to the African Charter on Human and Peoples' Rights on the Establishment of an African Court on Human and Peoples' Rights, 9 June 1998.
Resolution RC/Res.5 'Amendments to article 8 of the Rome Statute', 10 June 2010.

Resolution RC/Res.6 'The Crime of Aggression', 11 June 2010.
Rome Statute of the International Criminal Court, 2187 UNTS 90/37, 17 July 1998.

OTHERS

African Commission on Human and Peoples' Rights, Principles and Guidelines on the Right to a Fair Trial and Legal Assistance in Africa, DOC/OS(XXX)247, 2001.
Assembly of States Parties to the Rome Statute of the ICC, 'Crime of Aggression – Non-paper by the Chairman on outstanding issues regarding the conditions for the exercise of jurisdiction', in Report of the Working Group on the Review Conference, ICC-ASP/8/20/Add.1, Annex II, Appendix I, March 2010.
Assembly of States Parties to the Rome Statute of the ICC, 'Informal inter-sessional meeting of the Special Working Group on the Crime of Aggression', held at the Liechtenstein Institute on Self-Determination, Woodrow Wilson School, at Princeton University, New Jersey, United States, from 21 to 23 June 2004', ICC-ASP/3/SWGCA/INF.1, 13 August 2004.
Assembly of States Parties to the Rome Statute of the ICC, 'Non-paper on other substantive issues on aggression to be addressed by the Review Conference', in Report of the Special Working Group on the Crime of Aggression, ICC-ASP/7/20/Add.1, Chapter II, Annex II, February 2009.
Assembly of States Parties to the Rome Statute of the ICC, 'Report of the Special Working Group on the Crime of Aggression', ICC-ASP/7/SWGCA/2, 20 February 2009.
Assembly of States Parties to the Rome Statute of the ICC, Report of the Working Group on the Review Conference, in Official Records of the ICC-ASP, ICC-ASP/8/20/Add.1, Annex II, 42, March 2010.
Assembly of States Parties to the Rome Statute of the ICC, Special Working Group on the Crime of Aggression, 'Non-Paper Submitted by Nigeria on the Draft Resolution of 19 November 2008', November 2008.
Assembly of States Parties to the Rome Statute of the ICC, Special Working Group on the Crime of Aggression, 'Revised Non-Paper Resubmitted by Nigeria', 9 February 2009.
Assembly of States Parties to the Rome Statute of the ICC, Statement by Lesotho on Behalf of African States Parties to the Rome Statute at the Thirteenth Session of the Assembly of States Parties to the Rome Statute of the International Court, General Debate, 8 December 2014.
Deya, D., 'Worth the Wait: Pushing for the African Court to Exercise Jurisdiction for International Crimes', Open Society Justice Initiative for Southern Africa, 2012.
ICC, Office of the Prosecutor, 'Policy Paper on Preliminary Examinations', ICC-OTP 2013, November 2013.
ICC, Office of the Prosecutor, 'Policy Paper on the Interests of Justice', ICC-OTP-2007, September 2007.
ICC, Office of the Prosecutor, 'Report on Preliminary Examination Activities 2014', 2 December 2015.
International Law Commission, 'Draft Code of Crimes against the Peace and Security of Mankind', 2(2) Yearbook of the International Law Commission, 1996.

International Law Commission, 'Immunity of State official from foreign jurisdiction – Text of the draft Articles provisionally adopted by the Drafting Committee at the sixty-[sixth] session', UN Doc. A/CN.4/L.865, 29 July 2015.
International Law Commission, 'Immunity of State officials from foreign criminal jurisdiction', Memorandum by the Secretariat, UN Doc. A/CN.4/596, 31 March 2008.
International Law Commission, Report of the International Law Commission on the Work of its Sixty-Fifth Session, UN Doc. A/68/10 (2013), 2013.
International Law Commission, Special Rapporteur's 'Fourth Report on the immunity of State officials from foreign criminal jurisdiction', UN Doc. A/CN.4/686, 29 May 2015.
Kegoro, G., 'African Union might shelf plan for expanded continental court', Daily Nation, 14 March 2015.
Kimani, M., 'Princes versus the Liberals and the Fate of the Negotiated Peace', Brenthurst Analysis: Newsletter Item.
Kujenga Amani Editors, 'Article 46Abis: Implications for Peace, Justice, and Reconciliation in Africa', On the Spot, 21 October 2014.
Mataire, L., 'AU must pull out of ICC: President', Chronicle, 5 February 2015.
McDermott, Y., 'How Libya became the International Criminal Court's latest failure', The Conversation, 6 August 2015.
McNamee, T., 'The ICC and Africa – Between Aspiration and Reality: Making International Justice Work Better for Africa – Reflections on a High-Level Roundtable', 2 Brenthurst Discussion Paper 2014.
Moyo, H. and Mambo, E., 'Mugabe reluctant to ratify African court protocol', Zimbabwe Independent, 7 April 2015.
Ngirachu, J., 'Uhuru Kenyatta: Let's have an African-funded court', Daily Nation, 31 January 2015.
Pan-African Lawyers Union et al., 'Implications of the African Court of Human and Peoples' Rights Being Empowered to Try International Crimes Such as Genocide, Crimes Against Humanity, and War Crimes – An Opinion', 2009.
Permanent Mission of the Principality of Liechtenstein to the United Nations et al., 'Handbook – Ratification and Implementation of the Kampala Amendments to the Rome Statute of the ICC – Crime of Aggression – War Crimes', Liechtenstein Institute on Self-Determination, 2013.
Preparatory Commission for the International Criminal Court, Working Group on the Crime of Aggression, 'Preliminary list of possible issues relating to the crime of aggression – Discussion paper proposed by the Coordinator', PCNICC/2000/WGCA/RT.1, 29 March 2000.
Press Briefing of Ambassador Smail Chergui, African Union Commissioner for Peace and Security, 24th Summit of the African Union, 31 January 2015.
Review Conference of the Rome Statute of the International Criminal Court, 'Statement by Deputy-Minister A.C. Nel, MP, Deputy Minister of Justice and Constitutional Development of the Republic of South Africa', General Debate, 31 May 2010.
Review Conference of the Rome Statute of the International Criminal Court, 'Statement by Hon. Amos Wako, Attorney General of the Republic of Kenya, on Behalf of the African States Parties to the International Criminal Court (ICC)', General Debate, 31 May 2010.

Review Conference of the Rome Statute of the International Criminal Court, 'Statement by Mr Ben Kioko, Legal Counsel of the African Union Commission on Behalf of the AU Commission', General Debate, 1 June 2010.

Ruys, T., 'Guest Post: Self-Defence and Non-State Actors in the Cold War Era – A Response to Marty Lederman', Opinio Juris, 12 March 2015.

Scheffer, D.H., 'Unwilling Hands – U.S. Sabotages International Court at its Own Peril', The Seattle Post-Intelligencer, 1 February 2004.

Sukhija, T., 'Head of State Immunities and Article 98 of the Rome Statute: Interpretations That Avoid Obstacles to Cooperation in the Execution of ICC Arrest Warrants', ICC Forum, 10 March 2014.

UN High Commissioner for Human Rights (Hussein, Z.R.), Statement at the International Law Commission, 21 July 2015.

UN, 'Report of the Secretary General on Enhancing Mediation and its Support Activities', UN Doc. S/2009/189, 8 April 2009.

UN, Depository Notification C.N.1026.2013.TREATIES-XVIII.10 (Proposal of amendments by Kenya to the Rome Statute), 14 March 2014.

UN, Depository Notification C.N.851.2009.TREATIES-10 (Proposal of amendment by South Africa to the Rome Statute), 30 November 2009.

UN, Depository Notification C.N.651.2010.TREATIES-6 (Amendments to the Rome Statute on certain war crimes), 29 November 2010.

UN, Depository Notification C.N.651.210.TREATIES-8 (Amendments to the Rome Statute on the crime of aggression), 29 November 2010.

THE RIGHTS OF VICTIMS OF SERIOUS VIOLATIONS OF INTERNATIONAL HUMAN RIGHTS LAW AND INTERNATIONAL HUM ANITARIAN LAW

A Human Rights Perspective

Cécile Aptel*

1. INTRODUCTION

International law is increasingly recognising the rights of victims of gross violations of international human rights law (IHRL) and serious violations of international humanitarian law (IHL). It is first and foremost incumbent upon states, as duty bearers within the human rights framework, to ensure that these rights are respected. A growing number of states are fulfilling, or at least trying to fulfil their responsibility in this regard. In certain contexts, when states are unwilling or unable to render justice to the victims of these violations, international criminal jurisdictions, in particular the International Criminal Court can step in and help contribute to filling the impunity gap. However, their ability to do so is often limited.

This short paper examines the emergence and consolidation of the rights of victims of gross violations of IHRL and serious violations of IHL under international law and the role of national and international courts in realising them.[1] First, it sets out the definition and sources of these rights. It then briefly surveys the obligations incumbent on states to uphold them, before exploring how the ICC also constitutes an avenue, albeit a limited one, through which the rights of victims of such violations can be given effect. It emphasises that

* The views expressed in this article are those of the author and do not necessarily represent the views of, and should not be attributed to, the United Nations.

1 This piece reiterates some of the arguments I developed in the article 'Prosecutorial Discretion at the ICC and Victims' Right to Remedy: Narrowing the Impunity Gap', 10 Journal of International Criminal Justice 2012, pp. 1357–1375.

states have the primary obligation to investigate and prosecute those responsible for international crimes, and that failure to do so does not relieve them of responsibility under international human rights law, even when other courts, such as the ICC, do step in and exercise their jurisdiction. It also argues that, due to its limited jurisdiction and resources, the ICC can fill the impunity gap left by states with regards to only a small number of cases. Therefore, many victims are left without a forum where they can seek and be granted a remedy.

2. DEFINITION OF VICTIMS OF GROSS VIOLATIONS OF IHRL AND SERIOUS VIOLATIONS OF IHL

The UN Basic Principles and Guidelines on the Right to a Remedy and Reparation for Victims of Gross Violations of International Human Rights Law and Serious Violations of International Humanitarian Law (the 'Basic Principles and Guidelines'), adopted by the UN General Assembly in 2005,[2] set out a general definition of victims of gross violations of IHRL and serious violations of IHL. Paragraph 8 provides that, for the purposes of the Basic Principles, 'victims are persons who individually or collectively suffered harm, including physical or mental injury, emotional suffering, economic loss or substantial impairment of their fundamental rights, through acts or omissions that constitute gross violations of international human rights law or serious violations of international humanitarian law'.[3]

3. NATURE AND SOURCES OF VICTIMS' RIGHTS

One of the fundamental rights of victims of gross violations of IHRL and serious violations of IHL enshrined in international law is the right to remedy. This right is broad in scope and fulfilment of this right often entails the fulfilment of other rights including the right to an investigation and the right to have an alleged violation heard before a court or tribunal. A number of sources of IHRL provide for the right to remedy, including international treaties, the jurisprudence of

2 General Assembly Resolution 60/147 (Basic Principles and Guidelines on the Right to a Remedy and Reparation for Victims of Gross Violations of International Human Rights Law and Serious Violations of International Humanitarian Law), 16 December 2005.

3 In the same vein, the Committee Against Torture, in its General Comment No. 3, indicated that: 'Victims are persons who individually or collectively suffered harm, including physical or mental injury, emotional suffering, economic loss or substantial impairment of their fundamental rights, through acts or omissions that constitute violations of the Convention'. Committee Against Torture, General Comment No. 3 on Implementation of Article 14 by States Parties, 19 November 2012, para. 3.

regional courts as well as broadly accepted sources of 'soft law' such as principles and guidelines.

One of the international treaties which enshrine this right is the Universal Declaration of Human Rights, which has acquired customary international law status. Article 8 provides that everyone has the right to an effective remedy by competent national tribunals for acts violating the fundamental rights granted by the constitution or by law. In addition, the International Convention for the Protection of All Persons from Enforced Disappearance,[4] the International Covenant on Civil and Political Rights,[5] the International Convention on the Elimination of All Forms of Racial Discrimination,[6] and the Convention against Torture and Other Cruel, Inhuman or Degrading Treatment or Punishment[7] all explicitly acknowledge the right of victims to an effective remedy.

The right to remedy is also grounded in regional human rights treaties and in the jurisprudence of regional courts. The African Charter on Human and People's Rights,[8] the American Convention on Human Rights[9] and the European Convention for the Protection of Human Rights and Fundamental

---

4 International Convention for the Protection of All Persons from Enforced Disappearance, Article 8(2): 'Each State Party shall guarantee the right of victims of enforced disappearance to an effective remedy during the term of limitation.'

5 International Covenant on Civil and Political Rights, Article 2(3):
'Each State Party to the present Covenant undertakes:
(a) To ensure that any person whose rights or freedoms as herein recognized are violated shall have an effective remedy, notwithstanding that the violation has been committed by persons acting in an official capacity;
(b) To ensure that any person claiming such a remedy shall have his right thereto determined by competent judicial, administrative or legislative authorities, or by any other competent authority provided for by the legal system of the State, and to develop the possibilities of judicial remedy;
(c) To ensure that the competent authorities shall enforce such remedies when granted.'

6 International Convention on the Elimination of All Forms of Racial Discrimination, Article 6: 'States Parties shall assure to everyone within their jurisdiction effective protection and remedies, through the competent national tribunals and other State institutions, against any acts of racial discrimination which violate his human rights and fundamental freedoms contrary to this Convention, as well as the right to seek from such tribunals just and adequate reparation or satisfaction for any damage suffered as a result of such discrimination.'

7 Convention against Torture and Other Cruel, Inhuman or Degrading Treatment or Punishment, Article 14: 'Each State Party shall ensure in its legal system that the victim of an act of torture obtains redress and has an enforceable right to fair and adequate compensation, including the means for as full rehabilitation as possible. In the event of the death of the victim as a result of an act of torture, his dependents shall be entitled to compensation.'

8 African Charter on Human and People's Rights (ACHPR), Article 7: 'Every individual shall have the right to have his cause heard.'

9 American Convention on Human Rights, Article 25: 'Everyone has the right to simple and prompt recourse, or any other effective recourse, to a competent court or tribunal for protection against acts that violate his fundamental rights recognized by the constitution or laws of the state concerned or by this Convention, even though such violation may have been committed by persons acting in the course of their official duties.'

Freedoms[10] all recognise a right to have an alleged violation heard before a competent authority, thus placing an obligation upon states to develop and enforce a framework to provide judicial remedies.[11]

The right has been more explicitly acknowledged by some regional courts, namely the Inter-American Court of Human Rights[12] and the European Court of Human Rights.[13] In 1996, the European Court of Human Rights ruled against Turkey in the case of *Aksoy v. Turkey*, in which the applicant alleged that he had been arrested, taken into police custody and tortured. According to the Court, 'the notion of an effective remedy entails, in addition to the payment of compensation where appropriate, a thorough and effective investigation capable of leading to the identification and punishment of those responsible and including effective access of the complainant to the investigatory procedure.'[14] In particular, the Court considered that Article 13 of the Convention against Torture and Other Cruel, Inhuman or Degrading Treatment or Punishment imposes, 'without prejudice to any other remedy available under the domestic system, an obligation on States to carry out a thorough and effective investigation of incidents of torture.'[15]

Three years later, the Inter-American Court ruled against Guatemala in the case of the *Street Children (Villagrán-Morales et al.) v. Guatemala*. The case concerned the alleged kidnapping, torture and death of four minors and the murder of a fifth one in the city of Guatemala by members of the security forces and the state's subsequent failure to provide adequate access to justice to the victims' families. The Inter-American Court held that Guatemala had violated, *inter alia*, Article 25 of the American Convention on Human Rights regarding the right to effective recourse, to the detriment of the five victims and their immediate next of kin.[16]

Furthermore, other key human rights bodies including the Human Rights Committee[17] and the African Commission on Human and Peoples' Rights[18]

---

10 Convention for the Protection of Human Rights and Fundamental Freedoms, Article 13: 'Everyone whose rights and freedoms as set forth in this Convention are violated shall have an effective remedy before a national authority notwithstanding that the violation has been committed by persons acting in an official capacity.'

11 For example, under Article 25 of the American Convention on Human Rights, States Parties undertake 'to develop the possibilities of judicial remedy' and 'to ensure that the competent authorities shall enforce such remedies when granted'.

12 See for example *Caracazo v. Venezuela*, Judgment (IACtHR, 29 August 2002), para. 115.

13 See for example *Silver v. the United Kingdom*, Judgment, (ECtHR, 25 March 1983), para. 113.

14 *Aksoy v. Turkey*, Judgement (ECtHR, 18 December 1996), para. 98.

15 *Ibid.*

16 *Villagrán-Morales v. Guatemala*, Judgment (IACtHR, 19 November 1999), para. 238.

17 Human Rights Committee, General Comment No. 31, Nature of the General Legal Obligation on States Parties to the Covenant, UN Doc. CCPR/C/21/Rev.1/Add.13 (2004), 80th session, adopted on 29 March 2004 (2187th meeting), para. 15.

18 See the African Commission's Principles and Guidelines on the Right to a Fair Trial and Legal Assistance in Africa, DOC/OS(XXX)247, 2001, Principle C(a); see also *The Social and*

have underlined the duty of states to provide an effective remedy to victims of gross violations of human rights.

Building on this normative framework, the Basic Principles and Guidelines expand on the right to remedy as it applies to victims by setting out three fundamental aspects, namely the right to: (1) equal and effective access to justice; (2) adequate, effective and prompt reparation for harm suffered; and (3) access to relevant information concerning violations and reparation mechanisms. These rights are also broadly identified by the so-called Joinet/Orentlicher Principles,[19] which were formulated to protect and promote human rights through combating impunity and which set out the duties of states to investigate violations of IHRL and IHL and bring the perpetrators to justice. The Joinet/Orentlicher Principles highlight three key rights of the victims of such violations: the right to justice, the right to know the truth about violations, and the right to reparation and guarantee of non-recurrence.

International conventions, the jurisprudence of regional human rights bodies and soft law are therefore unanimous in recognising the various rights of victims under IHRL. These can be divided into three broad categories of rights: 'access to justice', 'the right to reparation', and 'the right to truth'.

3.1. ACCESS TO JUSTICE

Principle 12 of the Basic Principles and Guidelines sets out the duty to ensure access to justice. States are required, amongst other things, to take measures to minimise any harm to victims and their representatives and ensure their safety from intimidation and retaliation before, during and after judicial, administrative or other proceedings, as well as to make available all appropriate legal, diplomatic and consular means to ensure that victims can exercise their rights to remedy.[20] Principle 12 also obliges states to ensure that '[o]bligations arising under international law to secure the right to access justice and fair and impartial proceedings [are] reflected in domestic laws.'

The interconnected nature of the relationship between the broad right to remedy and the right to access justice has been highlighted by the Convention against Torture and Other Cruel, Inhuman or Degrading Treatment or Punishment. In its General Comment No. 3, the Committee against Torture declared that states have both procedural and substantive obligations as regards the provision of redress, the former requiring states to 'enact legislation and

---

Economic Rights Action Center and the Center for Economic and Social Rights v. Nigeria, Communication (ACHPR 2001), para. 61.

19 Updated set of principles for the protection and promotion of human rights through action to combat impunity, Addendum to the Report of the independent expert to update the set of principles to combat impunity, Diane Orentlicher, 8 February 2005.

20 Basic Principles and Guidelines, *supra* n. 2, Principle 12(b) and (d).

establish complaints mechanisms, investigation bodies and institutions, ... capable of determining the right to and awarding redress for a victim of torture and ill-treatment'.[21] It also stipulated that compensation for victims is a key component of the right to a remedy.[22]

3.2. THE RIGHT TO REPARATION

Access to justice is also interrelated with the right of victims' to adequate, effective and prompt reparation for any harm they have suffered. Principle 15 of the Basic Principles and Guidelines, states that reparation is intended to promote justice by redressing gross violations of IHRL and serious violations of IHL.

According to the Basic Principles and Guidelines, states' obligations to ensure that this right is upheld are manifold. States should endeavour to establish national programmes for reparation in the event that the parties liable for the harm suffered are unable or unwilling to meet their obligations; enforce domestic judgments for reparation against the individuals or entities liable for the harm suffered; and provide effective mechanisms for the enforcement of reparation judgments under their domestic laws.[23]

Reparation itself is understood as encompassing restitution, compensation, rehabilitation, satisfaction and guarantees of non-repetition.[24] Further, the prosecution of offenders is integral to reparation. The Joinet/Orentlicher Principles also link guarantees of non-recurrence of violations with the reform of state institutions and provide that 'States must take all necessary measures, including legislative and administrative reforms, to ensure that public institutions are organised in a manner that ensures respect for the rule of law and protection of human rights.'[25] Article 24(5) of the International Convention for the Protection of All Persons from Enforced Disappearance, which came into force less than an year after the Basic Principles and Guidelines, broadly confirms the definition of reparation provided in the Basic Principles and Guidelines and specifies that it covers both material and moral damages.

The Committee against Torture's General Comment No. 3 also elaborates on the concept of rehabilitation, which is defined as 'the restoration of function or the acquisition of new skills required by the changed circumstances of a

---

21 See Committee Against Torture (CAT), General Comment No. 3 on Implementation of Article 14 by States Parties, 19 November 2012, para. 5.

22 CAT General Comment No. 3, paras. 5, 9 and 10: 'Victims are persons who individually or collectively suffered harm, including physical or mental injury, emotional suffering, economic loss or substantial impairment of their fundamental rights, through acts or omissions that constitute violations of the Convention'.

23 Basic Principles and Guidelines, Principles 16 and 17.

24 *Ibid*, Principle 18.

25 Joinet/Orentlicher Principles, Principle 36.

victim'.[26] According to the Committee, '[r]ehabilitation for victims should aim to restore, as far as possible, their independence, physical, mental, social and vocational ability; and full inclusion and participation in society.'[27]

3.3. THE RIGHT TO TRUTH: ACCESS TO RELEVANT INFORMATION CONCERNING VIOLATIONS AND REPARATION MECHANISMS

The right to truth is rooted in IHL as well as in IHRL. Articles 32 and 33 of the 1977 Additional Protocol I to the Geneva Conventions of 1949 (AP I) place an obligation on parties to armed conflicts to search for missing persons and recognise the right of families and of the opposing side to a conflict to know the fate of their relatives and fellow soldiers, respectively. Article 32 states that in the implementation of Section III of AP I, the activities of the various parties to the conflict and of international humanitarian organisations, 'shall be prompted mainly by the right of families to know the fate of their relatives.'[28] Article 33 provides that, *inter alia*, '[a]s soon as circumstances permit, ... each Party to the Conflict shall search for the persons who have been reported missing by an adverse Party. Such adverse Party shall transmit all relevant information concerning such persons in order to facilitate such searches.'[29]

The notion of the right to be given information has now led to the identification and recognition, under IHRL, of a broader 'right to truth' regarding violations suffered. Victims of gross violations of IHRL and serious violations of IHL are now deemed to be entitled to seek and obtain information on the causes and conditions relating to the violations they have suffered and to learn the truth.[30] Principle 2 of the Joinet/Orentlicher Principles states that '[e]very people has the inalienable right to know the truth about past events concerning the perpetration of heinous crimes and about the circumstances and reasons that led, through massive or systematic violations, to the perpetration of those crimes. Full and effective exercise of the right to truth provides a vital safeguard against the recurrence of violations.' Indicative of the recognition of the right to truth was the 2011 decision of the Human Rights Council to appoint a 'Special Rapporteur on the promotion of truth, justice, reparation and guarantees of non-recurrence', pursuant to resolution 18/7.[31] The duties

26 CAT General Comment No. 3, para. 11.

27 *Ibid.*

28 Protocol Additional to the Geneva Conventions of 12 August 1949, and Relating to the Protection of Victims of International Armed Conflicts of 1977, Article 32.

29 *Ibid*, Article 33(1).

30 Basic Principles and Guidelines, Principle 24.

31 Human Rights Council Resolution 18/7, Special Rapporteur on the promotion of truth, justice, reparation and guarantees of non-recurrence, 13 October 2011.

of the Special Rapporteur include identifying, exchanging and promoting good practices and lessons learned with a view to recommending ways and means to improve and strengthen the promotion of truth, justice, reparation and guarantees of non-recurrence as well as working to improve strategies and policies for addressing gross violations of IHRL and serious violation of IHL.[32]

According to the Joinet/Orentlicher Principles, the right to know implies that archives must be preserved and that access to archives should be facilitated.[33] Principle 24 of the Basic Principles and Guidelines also provides that states should develop means of informing the general public, as well as victims themselves, of the rights and remedies addressed by the Basic Principles and Guidelines and of any legal, medical, psychological, social, administrative or other services to which victims may have a right of access.

Regional human rights instruments such as the African Charter on Human and Peoples' Rights also provide that 'every individual shall have the right to receive information.'[34] The Inter-American Court of Human Rights, described as one of the regional mechanisms at the forefront of developing jurisprudence on the right to know the truth,[35] declared in the *Myrna Mack Chang* case that 'every person, including the next of kin of the victims of grave violations of human rights has the right to truth. Therefore, the next of kin of the victims and society as a whole must be informed of everything that has happened in connection with said violations. This right to the truth has been developed by International Human Rights Law; recognised and exercised in a concrete situation, it constitutes an important means of reparation.'[36] The underlying rationale is that providing this information can aid the healing process of victims, their families and communities. It helps bring closure and restore the dignity of the victims and their relatives. In addition, the right to truth encourages the development of more transparent and accountable governments, while enabling society to understand the underlying causes of conflicts or widespread human rights violations in order to ensure that these do not occur again.

Principle 4 of the Joinet/Orentlicher Principles states that, '[i]rrespective of any legal proceedings, victims and their families have the imprescriptible right to know the truth about the circumstances in which violations took place and, in the event of death or disappearance, the victims' fate.' This is also reflected in Article 24(2) of the International Convention for the Protection of All Persons from Enforced Disappearance, which states, 'each victim has the right to know

32 *Ibid*, paras. 1(c) and 1(e).

33 Joinet/Orentlicher Principles, Principles 14 and 15.

34 ACHPR, Article 9(1). See also Declaration of Principles on Freedom of Expression in Africa, African Commission on Human and Peoples' Rights, 32nd Session, 17–23 October 2002, Article I and IV.

35 Report of the Special Rapporteur on the promotion of truth, justice, reparation and guarantees of non-recurrence, Pablo de Greiff, 28 August 2013, para. 19.

36 *Myrna Mack Chang v. Guatemala*, Judgment (IACtHR, 25 November 2003), para. 274.

the truth regarding the circumstances of the enforced disappearance, the progress and results of the investigation and the fate of the disappeared person.' States parties are required under the Convention to take appropriate measures in order to ensure respect for this right.[37] Already in 1988, the Inter-American Court of Human Rights ruled in favour of a victim of torture and enforced disappearance emphasising that: 'Even in the hypothetical case that those individually responsible for crimes of this type cannot be legally punished under certain circumstances, the State is obligated to use the means at its disposal to inform the relatives of the fate of the victims and as may be the case, the location of their remains.'[38]

4. THE RESPONSIBILITY OF STATES TO REALISE VICTIMS' RIGHTS

The above review of the legal framework governing the rights of victims who have suffered gross violations of IHRL and serious violations of IHL reveals an increasing recognition of such rights at the international level. Victims are not mere spectators in justice – they have fundamental rights devised to remedy the effects of any harm and loss they have experienced, and above all to affirm their dignity despite the injury and humiliations they have endured.

A variety of mechanisms, including international and mixed or hybrid tribunals, have been created to provide some remedy for victims' sufferings. However, this does not in any way relieve states from their primary responsibility to ensure that these rights are respected. These rights have been developed under IHRL, which addresses the responsibility of states towards individuals under their jurisdiction. Furthermore, specific instruments such as the Basic Principles and Guidelines and the Joinet/Orentlicher Principles also reiterate that the onus is on states to uphold and enforce the rights provided for therein.

Principle 19 of the Joinet/Orentlicher Principles, which deals with the duties of states with regard to the administration of justice, provides that 'States shall undertake prompt, thorough, independent and impartial investigations of violations of human rights and international humanitarian law and take appropriate measures in respect of the perpetrators, particularly in the area of criminal justice, by ensuring that those responsible for serious crimes under international law are prosecuted'. In addition, the eighth preambular paragraph of the Basic Principles and Guidelines recalls that 'international law contains the obligation to prosecute perpetrators of certain international crimes in accordance with international obligations of States and the requirements of

37 International Convention for the Protection of All Persons from Enforced Disappearance, Article 24(2).

38 *Velásquez Rodríguez v. Honduras*, Judgment, (IACtHR, 29 July 1988), para. 181.

national law or as provided for in the applicable statutes of international judicial organs'.

According to the Joinet/Orentlicher Principles, states' failure to meet their obligations to investigate violations, take appropriate measures in respect of the perpetrators, particularly in the area of justice, and also provide victims with effective remedies, are some of the reasons for impunity.[39] With regard to prosecution in particular, international and regional human rights bodies such as the former UN Commission on Human Rights,[40] the Human Rights Committee,[41] the Inter-American Court and Commission on Human Rights,[42] the European Court of Human Rights[43] and the African Commission on Human and Peoples' Rights[44] have emphasised the importance of states' obligation to prosecute offenders in the fight against impunity surrounding gross violations of IHRL and serious violations of IHL.

Encouraging initiatives of some states in recent years prove that there is an increasing willingness to enforce the rights of such victims, albeit to varying degrees. After the long struggle by the victims of Hissène Habré, former President of Chad, the Assembly of Heads of State and Government of the African Union mandated Senegal to try Habré 'on behalf of Africa'.[45] In so doing, it invoked 'the right of the Union to intervene in a Member State … in respect of grave circumstances, namely: war crimes, genocide and crimes against humanity',[46] as well as the Union's principle of 'respect for democratic principles, human rights, the rule of law and good governance'.[47] The Extraordinary African Chambers, established within the Senegalese courts to prosecute atrocities that occurred in Chad between 1982 and 1990, were granted jurisdiction to adjudicate these crimes.[48] Senegalese law was in fact amended in order to permit the country's courts to prosecute cases of genocide,

39 Joinet/Orentlicher Principles, Principle 1.

40 See Resolutions E/CN.4/RES/2003/72, paras. 2, 10; E/CN.4/RES/2002/79, paras. 2, 11; E/CN.4/RES/2001/70, para. 2; E/CN.4/RES/2000/68, para. 4.

41 *Irene Bleier Lewenhoff and Rosa Valiño de Bleier v. Uruguay*, Communication No. 30/1978, UN Doc. CCPR/C/OP/1 at 109 (1985), para. 11.

42 *Velásquez Rodríguez v. Honduras*, Judgment, (IACtHR, 29 July 1988), paras. 166 and 175.

43 *X and Y v. the Netherlands*, Judgment (ECtHR, 26 March 1985), para. 27.

44 *The Social and Economic Rights Action Center and the Center for Economic and Social Rights v. Nigeria*, Comm. No. 155/96 (ACHPR October 2001).

45 Decision of the Assembly of the African Union, Assembly/AU/Dec.127 (VII), para. 5(ii).

46 Constitutive Act of the African Union, adopted in 2000 at the Lomé Summit (Togo), entered into force in 2001, Article 4(h).

47 *Ibid*, Article 4(m).

48 See the Agreement Between the Government of the Republic of Senegal and the African Union on the Establishment of Extraordinary African Chambers within the Senegalese Judicial System, and the Statute of the Extraordinary African Chambers within the Senegalese judicial system for the prosecution of international crimes committed on the territory of the Republic of Chad during the period from 7 June 1982 to 1 December 1990, both available at: http://legal.au.int/en/sites/default/files/Agreement%20AU-Senegal%20establishing%20AEC-english_0.pdf.

crimes against humanity, war crimes and torture, even when such crimes are committed outside of Senegal.[49]

Arguably, a general trend towards the enforcement of victims' rights has also been interpreted as a consequence of the increasing legitimacy of the norms of individual criminal accountability for human rights violations and an increase in related prosecutions.[50] Indeed, since the 1980s, a number of transitional justice mechanisms such as truth commissions, criminal prosecutions and reparations, have been increasingly employed to address past human rights violations.[51]

Although some states appear to be increasingly willing to enforce the rights of victims of gross violations of IHRL and serious violations of IHL and have taken commendable steps in this direction, many hurdles remain to the full realisation of victims' rights. Amnesty laws and immunities figure prominently among the main obstacles. Despite the clarification by the International Court of Justice in its 2002 judgment in the *Arrest Warrant* case, that the immunity recognised as being attached to certain senior state officials due to their function does not equate to impunity in respect of international crimes,[52] in a number of countries, heads of states and other prominent officials still benefit from immunity under customary as well as domestic law and use it to escape prosecution for violations of IHRL and/or IHL. In this context, a recent decision by certain African leaders to vote that, *inter alia*, sitting heads of state 'or other senior state officials' be granted immunity from prosecution[53] is worrying, as it may seriously undermine accountability efforts.

A recent report of the Special Rapporteur on extrajudicial, summary or arbitrary executions highlights the critical role of effective investigations in providing a remedy to victims: '[a]n effective remedy is dependant on an effective investigation. The General Assembly has also addressed the obligation of all states 'to conduct exhaustive and impartial investigations ... to identify and bring to justice those responsible ... and to adopt all necessary measures ... to put an end to impunity.'[54] Moreover, the European Court of Human

---

49 See *Case Concerning Questions Relating to the Obligation to Prosecute or Extradite (Belgium v. Senegal)*, Counter-Memorial of the Republic of Senegal, ICJ, 23 August 2011, para. 223.

50 See notably Sikkink 2011.

51 See, for example, the South African Truth and Reconciliation Commission, established in 1995 by the Promotion of National Unity and Reconciliation Act 34; the Sierra Leone Truth and Reconciliation Commission, established in 1999 by the Lomé Peace Agreement; the Colombian National Commission for Reparation and Reconciliation, established in 2005 by Law 975/2005 (Justice and Peace Law).

52 *Case Concerning the Arrest Warrant of 11 April 2000 (Democratic Republic of the Congo v. Belgium)*, Judgment, ICJ, 14 February 2002, para. 60.

53 Protocol on Amendments to the Protocol on the Statute of the African Court of Justice and Human Rights, Article 46(B), available at: www.au.int/en/sites/default/files/PROTOCOL%20ON%20AMENDMENTS%20TO%20THE%20PROTOCOL%20ON%20THE%20AFRICAN%20COURT%20-%20EN_0.pdf.

54 *Report of the Special Rapporteur on Extrajudicial, Summary or Arbitrary Executions*, Christof Heyns, 1 April 2014, para. 83.

Rights also underlined the importance of effective investigations and held that the notion of an effective remedy for violations enshrined in Article 13 of the European Convention on Human Rights 'entails, in addition to the payment of compensation where appropriate, a thorough and effective investigation capable of leading to the identification and punishment of those responsible'.[55]

The European Court has also long held that the right to life enshrined in Article 2 of the Convention 'requires by implication that there should be some form of effective official investigation when individuals have been killed as a result of the use of force'[56] and that the failure to carry out an effective investigation constitutes a separate violation of Article 2.[57] Consequently, when an alleged violation of an individual's right to life is met with a failure to investigate ultimately leading to impunity, the victim can be considered to have endured a 'second violation'. It should be emphasised that this second violation occurs whenever there is a failure to investigate, regardless of whether accusations in respect of the first violation are ultimately upheld. Some positive judicial developments suggest that this conception of the failure to investigate as an additional implied violation of a particular right may eventually apply to violations of other rights such as, for instance, the prohibition of torture.[58]

Significantly, even where states are willing to enforce victims' rights, they do not always have the capacity to do so. Indeed, upholding the rights of victims requires not only the existence of laws providing for domestic prosecution of international crimes, but also effective enforcement mechanisms and a functioning judicial system. However, this is obviously not always the case in a number of situations such as, for instance, in countries affected by an armed conflict, or transitioning from an authoritarian regime to democracy.

It is precisely in order to overcome the limits of states not willing or not able to ensure effective prosecution and redress to victims of international crimes that the ICC was established. As Kofi Annan, former Secretary-General of the

55 *Kaya v. Turkey*, Judgment (ECtHR, 19 February 1998), para. 107.

56 *Ibid*, para. 86. See also *McCann and Others v. The United Kingdom*, Application No. 18984/91, Judgment, 27 September 1995, para. 161; *Mahmut Kaya v. Turkey*, Application No. 22535/93, Judgment, 28 March 2000, para. 102.

57 *Ibid*, para. 92. See also *Report of the Special Rapporteur on Extrajudicial, Summary or Arbitrary Executions*, para. 79.

58 See *Assenov and Others v. Bulgaria*, Judgment (ECtHR, 28 October 1998), para. 102: 'The Court considers that, in these circumstances, where an individual raises an arguable claim that he has been seriously ill-treated by the police or other such agents of the State unlawfully and in breach of Article 3, that provision, read in conjunction with the State's general duty under Article 1 of the Convention to "secure to everyone within their jurisdiction the rights and freedoms defined in … [the] Convention", requires by implication that there should be an effective official investigation. This investigation, as with that under Article 2, should be capable of leading to the identification and punishment of those responsible … If this were not the case, the general legal prohibition of torture and inhuman and degrading treatment and punishment, despite its fundamental importance (see paragraph 93 above), would be ineffective in practice and it would be possible in some cases for agents of the State to abuse the rights of those within their control with virtual impunity'.

United Nations observed, '[i]n the prospect of an international criminal court lies the promise of universal justice ... Only then will the innocents of distant wars and conflicts know that they, too, may sleep under the cover of justice; that they, too, have right, and that those who violate those rights will be punished.' The Court is born out of the recognition that impunity for international crimes has too often prevailed. However, it is a court of last resort, which can only step in if and when domestic judicial systems fail to do so. Indeed, the principle of complementarity enshrined in the Rome Statute establishes that the ICC can only exercise its jurisdiction where the state is unwilling or unable to provide for investigation or prosecution at the domestic level.[59]

The ICC emphasises victims' rights by: (1) giving them access to justice and remedies, (2) enabling their active participation in justice, and (3) acting as a means through which they can access reparations. The ICC has also taken steps to realise other fundamental rights. The Trust Fund for Victims created by the Rome Statute, for instance, is mandated to implement Court-ordered reparations and to provide physical and psychosocial rehabilitation or material support to the victims of crimes within the jurisdiction of the ICC.[60]

Yet the ICC cannot fully fill the vacuum left by states with regard to their obligations towards victims and so cannot be considered a substitute for states in this respect. It only has the mandate and resources to prosecute a few cases and, furthermore, it does not have the resources to realise the rights of most of victims. Thus, although the ICC is a particularly useful mechanism when it comes to upholding victims' rights, in no way should its existence be viewed as an excuse for states to abnegate their responsibilities towards victims.

The call by victims for justice guarantees of non-repetition and reparation for their suffering needs to be answered. Despite all possible efforts, the ICC cannot answer this call alone. States must do all that is in their capacity to ensure the respect of the rights of victims of gross violations of IHRL and serious violations of IHL by providing the necessary means for effective prosecution and redress at the national level.

5. CONCLUSION

Despite the important normative developments pertaining to the rights of victims of gross violations of IHRL and serious violations of IHL, the tragic reality is that, today, far too many victims of international crimes still have no access to any form of remedy whatsoever. Rather than feeling that the suffering they have been through is being acknowledged and recognised, these victims too often fall within the so-called impunity gap, resulting from the combined

59 Rome Statute of the ICC, 17 July 1998, Article 17(1)(a).

60 *Ibid*, Article 79. See also the ICC Rules of Procedure and Evidence, Article 98.

effect of shortcomings in national criminal judicial accountability and of limited international criminal prosecutions.[61] Much more needs to be done at the international, regional and most importantly, national levels, to ensure that the rights of victims of gross violations of IHRL and serious violations of IHL are fully respected. States have the primary responsibility to implement these rights, and should do their part to uphold their duty to victims. Victims should not be subjected to so-called 'second violations' by being denied justice and seeing that the crimes committed against them have been met with impunity.

BIBLIOGRAPHY

BOOKS AND JOURNAL ARTICLES

Aptel 2012
Aptel, C., 'Prosecutorial Discretion at the ICC and Victims' Right to Remedy: Narrowing the Impunity Gap', 10 Journal of International Criminal Justice, 2012, pp. 1357–1375.

Sikkink 2011
Sikkink, K., 'The Justice Cascade: How Human Rights Prosecutions Are Changing World Politics', W.W. Norton & Company, 2011.

JURISPRUDENCE

ACHPR 2001
ACHPR, The Social and Economic Rights Action Center and the Center for Economic and Social Rights v. Nigeria, Comm. No. 155/96, October 2001.

ECtHR 2000
ECtHR, Mahmut Kaya v. Turkey, Application no. 22535/93, 28 March 2000.

ECtHR 1998
ECtHR, Assenov and Others v. Bulgaria, Application no. 24760/94, 28 October 1998.

ECtHR 1998
ECtHR, Kaya v. Turkey, Application no. 22535/93, 19 February 1998.

ECtHR 1996
ECtHR, Aksoy v. Turkey, Application no. 21987/93, 18 December 1996.

ECtHR 1995
ECtHR, McCann and Others v. the United Kingdom, Application no. 18984/91, 27 September 1995.

ECtHR 1985
ECtHR, X and Y v. the Netherlands, Application no. 8978/80, 26 March 1985.

---

61 De Guzman and Schabas 2011, pp. 8–11.

ECtHR 1983
ECtHR, Silver v. the United Kingdom, Application no. 5947/72; 6205/73; 7052/75; 7061/75; 7107/75; 7113/75; 7136/75, 25 March 1983.
IACtHR 2003
IACtHR, Myrna Mack Chang v. Guatemala, (Ser. C) No. 101, 25 November 2003.
IACtHR 2002
IACtHR, Caracazo v. Venezuela, (Ser. C) No. 95, 29 August 2002.
IACtHR 1999
IACtHR, Villagrán-Morales v. Guatemala, (Ser. C) No. 63, 19 November 1999.
IACtHR 1988
IACtHR, Velásquez Rodríguez v. Honduras, (Ser. C) No. 4, 29 July 1988.
ICJ 2011
ICJ, Case Concerning Questions Relating to the Obligation to Prosecute or Extradite (Belgium v. Senegal), Counter-Memorial of the Republic of Senegal, 23 August 2011.
ICJ 2002
ICJ, Case Concerning the Arrest Warrant of 11 April 2000 (Democratic Republic of the Congo v. Belgium), Judgment, 14 February 2002.
HRC 1985
HRC, Irene Bleier Lewenhoff and Rosa Valiño de Bleier v. Uruguay, Communication No. 30/1978, UN Doc. CCPR/C/OP/1 at 109 (1985).

TREATIES, LEGISLATION AND AGREEMENTS

African (Banjul) Charter on Human and People's Rights, OAU Doc. CAB/LEG/67/3 rev. 5, 27 June 1981.

Agreement between the Government of the Republic of Senegal and the African Union on the Establishment of Extraordinary African Chambers within the Senegalese Judicial System, Doc No. LC11888, 22 August 2012.

American Convention on Human Rights, 'Pact of San Jose, Costa Rica' (B-32), 22 November 1969.

Basic Principles and Guidelines on the Right to a Remedy and Reparation for Victims of Gross Violations of International Human Rights Law and Serious Violations of International Humanitarian Law, GA Res. 60/147, 16 December 2005.

Colombia, Justice and Peace Law 975/2005, 25 July 2005.

Constitutive Act of the African Union, 11 July 2000.

Convention against Torture and Other Cruel, Inhuman or Degrading Treatment or Punishment, UN Doc. A/RES/39/46, 10 December 1984.

Convention for the Protection of Human Rights and Fundamental Freedoms, 3 September 1953.

Decision of the Assembly of the African Union, Décision sur le Procès d'Hissène Habré et l'Union africaine (Decision On The Trial Of Hissene Habre and the African Union), Assembly/AU/Dec.127 (VII), July 2006.

International Convention for the Protection of All Persons from Enforced Disappearance, UN Doc. A/RES/61/177, 20 December 2006.

International Convention on the Elimination of All Forms of Racial Discrimination, UN Doc. A/RES/20/2106, 21 December 1965.

International Covenant on Civil and Political Rights, GA Res. 2200A (XXI), 16 December 1966.

International Criminal Court Rules of Procedure and Evidence, ICC-ASP/1/3 (Part II-A), 9 September 2002.

Protocol Additional to the Geneva Conventions of 12 August 1949, and relating to the Protection of Victims of International Armed Conflicts (Protocol I), 8 June 1977.

Protocol on Amendments to the Protocol on the Statute of the African Court of Justice and Human Rights, 27 June 2014.

Rome Statute of the International Criminal Court, 2187 UNTS 90/37, 17 July 1998.

Sierra Leone, Lomé Peace Agreement, 7 July 1999.

South Africa, Promotion of National Unity and Reconciliation Act 34 of 1995, 19 July 1995.

Statute of the Extraordinary African Chambers within the Senegalese judicial system for the prosecution of international crimes committed on the territory of the Republic of Chad during the period from 7 June 1982 to 1 December 1990.

OTHERS

African Commission on Human and Peoples' Rights, Declaration of Principles on Freedom of Expression in Africa, ACHPR/Res.62(XXXII)02, October 2002.

African Commission on Human and Peoples' Rights, Principles and Guidelines on the Right to a Fair Trial and Legal Assistance in Africa, DOC/OS(XXX)247, 2001.

Committee Against Torture, General Comment No. 3, 'Implementation of Article 14 by States Parties', UN Doc. CAT/C/GC/3, 19 November 2012.

De Greiff, P., Report of the Special Rapporteur on the promotion of truth, justice, reparation and guarantees of non-recurrence, UN Doc. A/HRC/24/42, 28 August 2013.

De Guzman, M.M. and Schabas, W.A., 'Initiation of Investigations and Selection of Cases', in 'General Rules and Principles of International Criminal Procedure and Recommendations of the International Expert Framework', Hague Institute for the Internationalisation of Law, October 2011.

Heyns, C., Report of the Special Rapporteur on extrajudicial, summary or arbitrary executions, UN Doc. A/HRC/26/36, 1 April 2014.

Orentlicher, D., Updated set of principles for the protection and promotion of human rights through action to combat impunity, Addendum to the Report of the independent expert to update the set of principles to combat impunity, UN Doc. E/CN.4/2005/102/Add.1, 8 February 2005.

UN Commission on Human Rights, 'Impunity', Commission on Human Rights Res. 2003/72, UN Doc. E/CN.4/RES/2003/72, 25 April 2003.

UN Commission on Human Rights, 'Impunity', Commission on Human Rights Res. 2002/79.

UN Doc. E/CN.4/RES/2002/79, 25 April 2002.

UN Commission on Human Rights, 'Impunity', Commission on Human Rights Res. 2001/70, UN Doc. E/CN.4/RES/2001/70, 25 April 2001.
UN Commission on Human Rights, 'Impunity', Commission on Human Rights Res. 2000/68, UN Doc. E/CN.4/RES/2000/68, 26 April 2000.
UN Human Rights Committee, General Comment 31, Nature of the General Legal Obligation on States Parties to the Covenant, UN Doc. CCPR/C/21/Rev.1/Add.13, 29 March 2004.
UN Human Rights Council, Resolution 18/7, Special Rapporteur on the promotion of truth, justice, reparation and guarantees of non-recurrence, UN Doc. A/HRC/RES/18/7, 13 October 2011.

BOKO HARAM'S INSURGENCY IN NIGERIA

Exploring the Justice, Peace and Reconciliation Pathways

Idayat HASSAN and Benson CHINEDU OLUGBUO

1. INTRODUCTION

The government of Nigeria is currently battling Boko Haram, a militant Islamic group accused of committing several human rights abuses against civilians.[1] Literally translated, Boko Haram means 'Western education or influence is sinful and forbidden.' However the group who prefers to call itself *'Jama'atu Ahlus-Sunnah Lidda'Awati Wal Jihad'*, which means 'People Committed to the Propagation of the Prophet's Teachings and Jihad' has recently changed its name to Islamic State's West Africa Province (Iswap).[2] The name change came about upon the group's pledge of allegiance to the dreaded Islamic State (IS) and establishes an international dimension to the insurgency.

The insurgency in the last six years has claimed a conservative estimate of over 13,000 victims, inclusive of people killed both by Boko Haram and the Nigerian security forces. This is based on the allegations of serious human rights violations and extra judicial killings levelled against the Nigerian security forces in their bid to curtail the insurgency.[3] Boko Haram's *modus operandi* includes bombing civilian and military targets; kidnappings; arsons; lootings; murders;

---

1 Hassan and Olugbuo, 'Winning the War, and Not Just the Battle: Masterplan for Ending the Boko Haram Insurgency in the North-East', Centre for Democracy and Development, August 2015; Badejogbin 2013; Human Rights Watch, 'Spiraling Violence: Boko Haram Attacks and Security Force Abuses in Nigeria', October 2012; Walker, 'What Is Boko Haram?', United States Institute for Peace Special Report 308, June 2012; Onuoha 2010.

2 'Boko Haram changes name to "Islamic State in West Africa", *News24 Nigeria*, 24 April 2015, available at: www.news24.com.ng/National/News/Boko-Haram-changes-name-to-Islamic-State-in-West-Africa-20150424.

3 See Amnesty Report, *Stars on Their Shoulders, Blood on Their Hands*, 3 June 2015. See also Human Rights Watch, *Spiraling Violence: Boko Haram Attacks and Security Force Abuses in Nigeria*, October 2012.

sex slavery; causing grievous bodily harm to civilians, taking territory, etc.[4] The conflict is exacting a huge toll on the civilian population. The number of property and lives lost, internally displaced persons and refugees have changed the face of North East Nigeria. This is leading many to call for accountability. Victims and survivors of crimes want justice. Several of them are demanding that the perpetrators be punished while others want peace and reconciliation. There is no easy way to define the relationship between justice and reconciliation. While some see the two as diametrically opposed to each other, others insist that they both have to work together to move a nation forward. The case of the Lord's Resistance Army (LRA) in Uganda is a good example where justice, peace and reconciliation became controversial. In the face of the consistent terror the people of Northern Uganda face from the LRA, they pressurised the government of President Yoweri Kaguta Museveni to enact an Amnesty Law granting the LRA members immunity from prosecution.

Spurred by the threat that the Niger Delta militants posed to the economic mainstay of the country's oil, the government of late President Umaru Musa Yar'Adua granted the Niger Delta militants amnesty through a money for weapon and rehabilitation programme to end the insurgency. With the escalation of the Boko Haram insurgency in Nigeria, the issue of amnesty has come to the front burner again. Several factors can be attributed to the rise of Boko Haram in Northern Nigeria. These include the *Almajiri* school system, which is a practice of sending young children to Koranic school without adequate provision for their sustenance; financial inducement attracting unemployed youths; and alleged extra-judicial killings of families and relatives by the Nigerian security forces. The ideology factor is also a probable basis of recruitment and recent source of forceful conscription and blackmail.

Despite these challenges, the call for the peace and reconciliation option remains high on the agenda. Since the inauguration of the new administration of President Muhammadu Buhari, the insurgency in the North East continues to fester with an estimated 1,000 people killed within the administration's sixty days in office. More than fourteen months have passed since the abduction of more than 200 girls from the Chibok Government Girls Secondary School, and the inability of the state to rescue these girls has raised the stakes of the conflict. The country is currently under preliminary examinations by the International Criminal Court as the prosecutor has declared the conflict in Nigeria as an internal armed conflict between the government of Nigeria and the Boko Haram terrorists.

---

4 Boko Haram in 2014 and first quarter of 2015 was in total occupation/complete control of 13 local governments (and other swathes of land) in Borno and two each in Yobe and Adamawa. See Hassan, 'Nigeria Forum: IDPs, Boko Haram and elections likely to be settled by the courts', available at: http://africanarguments.org/2015/01/30/nigeria-forum-idps-boko-haram-,and-elections-likely-to-be-settled-by-the-courts-by-idayat-hassan/.

The new All Progressive Congress (APC) government has promised to deliver a Marshall Plan on ending the insurgency, including a time limited partial amnesty and truth and reconciliation commission.[5] The Borno state governor, Kashim Shettima continues to insist that amnesty cannot be ruled out.[6] It becomes imperative to begin to broaden the discussions beyond military options as a solution to limiting the insurgency. There is a need to critically assess other options in ending the conflict. So, one can ask the following questions: is Boko Haram ready to lay down its arms and embrace dialogue with the federal government? And also is it important to evaluate such a possibility within the context of the international criminal justice system? This paper uses the Nigerian experience, namely the Niger Delta rebellion and the Boko Haram insurgency, as case studies to discuss the difficult choices to make when dealing with justice, peace and reconciliation.

2. JUSTICE, PEACE, RECONCILIATION AND THE 'INTERESTS OF JUSTICE' IN THE ROME STATUTE

There have been several definitions of justice. For example, Plato argues that 'justice is harmony' and 'doing one's job.'[7] There are other definitions of justice by moral and political philosophers like David Hume[8] and John Rawls.[9] However, for the purposes of this paper, we will adopt a definition that brings into focus our arguments. The United Nations defines 'justice' as:

> An ideal of accountability and fairness in the protection and vindication of rights and the prevention and punishment of wrongs. Justice implies regard for the rights of the accused, for the interests of victims and for the well-being of society at large. It is a concept rooted in all national cultures and traditions and, while its administration usually implies formal judicial mechanisms, traditional dispute resolution mechanisms are equally relevant.[10]

In the same vein, the Nuremberg Declaration on Peace and Justice defines 'justice' as accountability and fairness in the protection and vindication of rights, and the prevention and redress of wrongs, and insists on the necessity

---

5 'A New Party for A New Nigeria', *The APC Manifesto*, see also: www.buharimeter.ng.

6 Borno State is the most affected by the insurgency. It is said to be birthplace of the Boko Haram group.

7 Plato's Republic Book 4, 434c and 443b.

8 For the writings of David Hume, see: www.davidhume.org (accessed 17 August 2014).

9 See generally Rawls 2001; Rawls 1971.

10 Paragraph 7 of the *Report of the Secretary General on the Rule of Law and Transitional Justice in Conflict and Post-Conflict Societies*, UNSC S/2004/616.

for 'Peace', more specifically, sustainable peace.[11] Another concept that plays an important part in any justice and peace process is reconciliation, which can be defined as a transitional justice procedure where two warring parties are reconciled. In Africa, for example, it is embedded in the continent's cultural experience and has been documented in several countries like Uganda and Rwanda where mechanisms like *Mato oput* and *Gacaca* were used as instruments for justice and reconciliation.[12] It has been shown that citizens of these countries identify more closely to these ceremonies than to western justice mechanisms because they provide opportunity for truth, and reconciliation of warring parties to a considerable extent.[13] However, there have been arguments and counter arguments on whether to prosecute individuals who commit international crimes or to grant them amnesty, which reinforces the option of reconciliation.[14] For example, Diane Orentlicher supports the view that prosecution of international crimes promotes peace and justice by arguing that criminal prosecutions act as deterrence against impunity and future abuses and repression.[15] However, Charles Villa-Vicencio contends that there are instances, especially in transitional societies, when amnesties and alternative means of conflict resolution will have to be applied to ensure the survival of the state.[16] Charles Villa-Vicencio's position may easily align to the Boko Haram insurgency in the North East and the position of the people in support of partial amnesty. The argument has been that there is hardly any family in the three states under insurgency without a member belonging to the dreaded group, mainly the very young and impressionable minds abducted or hoodwinked into joining the group. They further argued that no interest of justice will be served by prosecution under international justice.

The 'interests of justice' provision in Article 53 of the Rome Statute of the ICC presents the dilemma between peace and justice and has been the subject of intense debates, discussions and analyses by academics and practitioners. Several authors and commentators are divided on the meaning of interests of justice and whether Article 53 of the Rome Statute accommodates alternative justice mechanisms. While this section's discussion cannot be conclusive on the issue, it reflects the general view of scholars on the matter. The ideas and views on interests of justice are actually divergent and vary from one author to the other regarding the relationship between the 'interest of justice' and alternative forms of justice. Most authors recognise that Article 53 of the Rome Statute extends

11 Nuremberg Declaration on Peace and Justice General Assembly of the United Nations A/62/885 of 19 June 2008.
12 Olugbuo and Wachira 2011, p. 624.
13 *Ibid.*
14 Mallinder 2007, pp. 208–209.
15 Orentlicher 1991, p. 2542.
16 Villa-Vicencio 2000, p. 208.

beyond criminal sanctions of the ICC.[17] However, the Prosecutor of the ICC prefers a restrictive interpretation of the 'interests of justice' on the assumption that the primary responsibility of the ICC is exclusively criminal prosecution.[18] This view is shared by non-governmental organisations like Human Rights Watch and Amnesty International and is endorsed by some scholars.[19] From the discussion above, it can be concluded that 'interests of justice' provisions accommodate amnesties and alternative justice mechanisms, and the analyses of Article 53 of the Rome Statute supports this claim. The Office of the Prosecutor (OTP) has the opportunity to defer investigations and prosecution of crimes when it is in the 'interests of justice', though this should be limited in scope and practice. Furthermore, it is reiterated that the alternative means of justice states embarked upon should meet minimum standards of justice and have the support and input of victims and their survivors. Applying the discussion above in the Nigerian context, one can argue that there is nothing wrong with Nigeria granting amnesty to her citizens in promoting justice and reconciliation.

2.1. JUSTICE, PEACE, RECONCILIATION AND TRANSITIONAL JUSTICE: THE NIGERIAN EXPERIENCE

There have been various attempts to address human rights abuses in Nigeria through transitional justice mechanisms. For example, in June 1999, the Nigerian government set up the Human Rights Violations Investigation Commission (Oputa Panel), which sat from June 1999 to May 2002, and then submitted its report to the government of Nigeria. The Oputa Panel Report holds military incursion into politics as one of the issues responsible for human rights violations in Nigeria. The report argues that '[m]ilitary rule has left, in its wake, a sad legacy of human rights violations, stunted national growth, a corporatist and static state, increased corruption, destroying its own internal cohesion in the process of governing, and posing the greatest threat to democracy and national integration.'[20] The open and transparent process adopted by the Oputa Panel allowed several Nigerians to openly present their views and seek

17 Ambos 2009, p. 85; Scharf 1999, p. 522; Arsanjani 1999, p. 67; Clark 2005, p. 407; Villa-Vicencio 2000, p. 214; Dukic 2007, p. 700; Hafner et al. 1999, p. 112; Blumenson 2006, p. 859; Goldstone and Fritz 2000, p. 656; Gallavin 2003, p. 184; Gavron 2002, p. 110; Stahn 2005, p. 698.

18 International Criminal Court, *Policy Paper on the Interests of Justice*, September 2007.

19 See Human Rights Watch, *Policy Paper: The Meaning of 'Interests of Justice' in Article 53 of the Rome Statute*; Amnesty International, 'Open letter to the Chief Prosecutor of the International Criminal Court: Comments on the Concept of the Interests of Justice', AI Index: IOR 40/023/2005, 17 June 2005; Mendes 2010, p. 33.

20 Paragraph 89 of the Oputa Panel Report.

redress.[21] However, the government of Nigeria refused to release the report, citing the judgment of the Supreme Court of Nigeria in *Fawehinmi v. Babangida* as the reason behind the decision.[22] As political fallout to the Oputa Panel Report and the Supreme Court decision, several Nigerian states set up truth and reconciliation commissions to address human rights abuses. These include the Rivers State Truth and Reconciliation Commission set up in November 2007; the Osun State Truth and Reconciliation Commission set up in February 2011; and the Ogun State Truth and Reconciliation Committee set up in September 2011.

We argue in this paper that transitional justice mechanisms in Nigeria have never been endowed with enough powers or resources, nor enjoyed the political will of the government in the implementation of its recommendations. For instance, the Oputa Panel recommended the investigations into 150 human rights violations; the reports of the Osun, Ogun and Rivers commissions were never fully implemented.

3. THE NIGER DELTA CONFLICT *VIS-À-VIS* THE NORTHERN NIGERIA CONFLICT

The conflicts in the Niger Delta and Northern Nigeria are not the only conflicts that have been recorded in Nigeria. For example, from 1967 to 1970, there was a civil war between the government of Nigeria and the country's south-eastern provinces that attempted secession as the sovereign Republic of Biafra. There have been several inter-ethnic, political and religious conflicts in Nigeria since independence. However, it is argued that the Niger Delta and Northern Nigeria conflicts actually reflect the deep-rooted contradictions of the Nigerian State. They touch on the fundamental issues that threaten the peaceful coexistence of people in Nigeria. These are issues of religion, resource control, self-determination; corruption and state failure, aptly represented by the Niger Delta militancy and the Boko Haram insurgency. It is conceded that Boko Haram has been denounced by mainstream Muslim organisations locally and internationally.[23] However, its attraction to radical Muslims in the region

---

21 See 'Synoptic Overview of HRVIC Report: Conclusions and Recommendations (Including Chairman's Foreword)', presented to President, Commander-in-Chief of the Armed Forces of the Federal Republic of Nigeria, Chief Olusegun Obasanjo. GCFR submitted by Human Rights Violations Investigation Commission May 2002.

22 *Fawehinmi v. Babangida* (2003) 12 WRN 1; (2003) NWLR (PT 808) 604. The Supreme Court in that case held that under the 1999 Constitution, the Federal Government of Nigeria had no power to set up a Tribunal of Inquiry as the power was now under the residual legislative list exercisable by states only, and not the federal government unlike the 1966 Constitution which made provision for such.

23 For instance, the Organisation of the Islamic Conference (OIC) labelled the group as criminal, See 'Islamic body OIC distances itself from Boko Haram calling it a criminal group', *Nigerian Watch*, 3 June 2014.

remains a recipe for disaster and reinforces the argument that its religious leanings cannot be denied. In fact, some similarities can be drawn between Boko Haram and the Lord's Resistance Army (LRA) that operated in northern Uganda for more than two decades. While the LRA uses the Ten Commandments in the Bible as a weapon of influence and power, Boko Haram uses the Koran as a rallying point for its activities in Nigeria. Another striking similarity between Boko Haram and the LRA is that they both aim to overthrow their governments, using religion and a brutal insurgency as weapons of warfare and as foundation for their political dreams and aspirations.

4. NIGERIA AND RESOURCE CONTROL IN THE NIGER DELTA

The complex mix between religion, ethnicity, politics and control of natural resources in Nigeria has led to the emergence of several ethnic based militia groups, including the Movement for the Actualization of the Sovereign State of Biafra (MASSOB); the Oodua People's Congress (OPC); the Movement for the Emancipation of the Niger Delta (MEND); and the Movement for the Survival of Ogoni People (MOSOP), amongst several others. The Niger Delta crisis is as old as the Nigerian nation. Early agitation for the emancipation of the Niger Delta was led by Isaac Adaka Boro who, with others, declared the Niger Delta Republic in 1967.[24] Though the insurrection lasted just twelve days, it ignited a quest for the emancipation of minority groups in the region. The quest for self-determination in the Niger Delta led to the formation of militant groups such as the Niger Delta People's Volunteer Force (NDPVF) led by Asari Dokubo, MEND led by Henry Okah, Government Ekpelumo, etc. These groups exerted maximum pressure on Nigeria's oil wells and threatened the mainstay of Nigeria's economy.

In June 2009, the government of late Umaru Musa Yar'Adua declared an amnesty which allowed militants to hand in weapons for cash and other benefits of rehabilitation.[25] Asari Dokubo, Henry Okah and several other militant surrounded their arms thereby benefitting from the amnesty.[26] This was pursuant to the provisions of section 175 of the 1999 Constitution of Nigeria as amended.

---

24 Osaghae 1995.

25 See 'Text of President Yar'Adua's Amnesty Proclamation', *Nigeria First*, 25 June 2009.

26 Okah was rearrested in October 2010, due to his alleged involvement in the 1 October 2010 bombing during the independence celebration. He was convicted and sentenced to twenty-four years imprisonment in 2013 by a South African Court, see 'Breaking news: S/Africa court convicts Henry Okah of 13 acts of 'terrorism', *The Vanguard Newspaper*, 21 January 2013.

During the Goodluck Jonathan Presidency, the Niger Delta insurgency reduced. It is however interesting to note that Boko Haram is the current existential threat to Nigeria. However, the political dynamics of the Niger Delta insurgency has refused to fade away. Following the loss of the Presidential elections by Dr Goodluck Jonathan and his concession to President Muhammad Buhari, there are fears in several quarters that the insurgency may resume. This is not unrelated to the fears that the Amnesty Program may be terminated by the new administration. The Niger Delta militancy has therefore adopted a political stand, mixing a campaign for self-determination and control of power. This trend can be witnessed in the discussion below regarding the political leanings of Boko Haram.

4.1. PEACE, JUSTICE, RECONCILIATION AND BOKO HARAM

The raging Boko Haram insurgency in Nigeria calls for a closer introspection within the context of international criminal justice. Amnesty International recently accused high ranking military officials in Nigeria of committing international crimes in the conflict between the military and Boko Haram forces.[27] Also, the Office of the High Commissioner for Human Rights argues that some of the crimes committed by Boko Haram amounts to crimes against humanity and has urged the Nigerian government to ensure that perpetrators of the violence are brought to justice.[28] The ICC has listed Nigeria as a country under preliminary examination and the OTP has received several communications since 2005 regarding the matter. These include the ethnic and religious conflicts that have occurred in central Nigeria since 2004, and the recent violent clashes in the wake of the 2011 general elections.[29] The Prosecutor of the ICC, Fatou Bensouda, has stated that Nigeria is not under investigation, but under preliminary analysis and that, as long as the government is prosecuting those responsible for international crimes, the jurisdiction of the ICC will not be activated.[30] This means that Nigeria has the primary responsibility to hold her citizens accountable. It is only when Nigeria is inactive, unwilling, and unable to act will the ICC become involved. A first step to fulfilling this obligation is the domestic implementation of the Crimes Against Humanity, War Crimes,

27 Amnesty International, 'Stars on their shoulders, blood on their hands: War Crimes committed by the Nigerian Military', June 2015. See also Mazen, 'Amnesty International Accuses Nigerian Military of Committing War Crimes, Claims Videos Show Abuses', *Huffington Post*, 4 August 2014.

28 Schlein, 'UN Human Rights Chief Condemns Boko Haram Attacks', *Voice of America*, 23 June 2012.

29 International Criminal Court, *The Office of the Prosecutor: Report on Preliminary Examination Activities*, 13 December 2011.

30 Onuora, 'Nigeria backs ICC's efforts to check impunity', *Guardian Newspapers*, 4 July 2012.

Genocide and Related Offences Bill, 2012. The Bill provides for the investigation and prosecution of those accused of committing international crimes in Nigeria as well as a Special Victims Trust Fund.

The current war on terror against the Boko Haram sect is not a new phenomenon. The troubling issue is that Boko Haram has assumed a wider dimension linking up with other terrorist organisations across the world including the recent allegiance to the Islamic State.[31] In addition, the intensity of the violence since the inception of the new APC government is worrisome. A body count done 49 days into this administration revealed that 675 people have been killed.[32] The sect is also launching attacks in neighbouring Niger, Chad and Cameroon. Furthermore, the United Nations' Security Council Al-Qaida Sanctions Committee had added Boko Haram to its Sanctions List.[33] The kidnapped Chibok girls are yet to be rescued 470 days since their abduction (at the time of writing), and have led to both a local and an international campaign for the release of the girls.[34]

Although President Buhari has given marching orders to the Nigerian military to end the Boko Haram insurgency by December 2015, many Nigerians are wary of the possibility of ending the Boko Haram conflict through military success.[35] This is mainly because of the increasing number of civilian causalities recorded in the conflict. Innocent citizens are killed in great numbers by Boko Haram insurgents and government forces waging a counter-insurgency military operation. Besides Boko Haram activities in Nigeria, the sources of conflicts in Nigeria are myriad. These include corruption, religious and ethnic issues, competition for scarce resources, and the inability to implement laws for national development. Several conflicts in Nigeria have a combination of religious, ethnic and political connotations. In fact, most religious conflicts in Nigeria usually assume inter-ethnic coloration, even when they begin as purely religious disagreements. In addition, the reverse is sometimes the case where socio-economic conflicts often degenerate into inter-religious conflicts. Hence, the boundary between ethnic and religious conflicts in Nigeria is very hazy and not well defined.[36] Nigeria has witnessed ethnic, economic, religious and political conflicts since independence and the current threat by Boko Haram and its affiliated groups is threatening the security of the Nigerian state. The limited success recorded by the amnesty granted to the Niger Delta militants may have

---

31 *Ibid*, p. 2.

32 Internal count done by the Centre for Democracy and Development (CDD).

33 United Nations Security Council SC/11410 of 22 May 2014.

34 The 'BringBackOurGirls' campaign has gained worldwide fame both in capitals of the world and social media. Although a few of the girls have escaped, a good number of them are still being held hostage by Boko Haram's members.

35 'Boko Haram insurgency will end by December, Buhari insists', *Vanguard Newspers*, 14 October 2015, available at: www.vanguardngr.com/2015/10/boko-haram-insurgency-ll-end-by-december-buhari-insists/.

36 Alabi 2007, p. 95.

prompted several highly placed Nigerians, including the Sultan of Sokoto to ask the Federal Government to grant amnesty to Boko Haram's members.[37] Although the Jonathan government set-up a Committee for advice on the possibility of granting amnesty to Boko Haram members, it seems that there is no interest in or appetite for such an approach and, possibly, no political gain for the endeavour in the current dispensation. Moreover, Boko Haram's leadership has rejected any form of amnesty from the government.

4.2. BOKO HARAM AND EMERGING TRENDS IN CONFLICT RESOLUTION

There are several emerging trends in the conflict between Boko Haram and the Nigerian government that warrant a serious review. Boko Haram is more and more becoming an ideology and less and less a movement of religious extremists. It seems that Boko Haram's core leadership has split into different camps with different motives and persuasions. Boko Haram has also become a franchise in Nigeria. This means that not all terrorist-related activities attributed to Boko Haram are actually committed by its members. In addition, the abuses committed against hapless innocent civilians caught in the cross-fire between Boko Haram and government forces has threatened a vital link to achieving effective security in information gathering. The use of teenage female suicide bombers is a worrying sign of the metamorphosis of Boko Haram into a dangerous terrorist group. Although the identities of the female bombers are not yet known, there are speculations that they may be part of the girls abducted during their incessant raids on communities.[38] Boko Haram's insistence that the girls must be exchanged with its members currently held in various detentions centres in Nigeria brings up a difficult dilemma. But this is not an insurmountable task; it just demands sacrifices and a good understanding of the dynamics of the conflict and the operationalisation of Boko Haram's leadership. For instance, some convicted and detained Boko Haram's members have been seen asking for clemency and leniency from the government. Are these genuine requests? Is it possible to exchange these prisoners for the girls abducted, and in the same vein possibly isolate the leadership of Boko Haram in the process? Is it possible to have an all-inclusive reconciliation negotiation between the Nigerian government and Boko Haram's elements? Can Nigeria afford a home grown *Mato oput* as practiced in Northern Uganda or *Gacaca* in Rwanda, which might heal the wounds inflicted by the Boko Haram conflict and by Nigeria's federal government's counter-insurgency activities?

---

37 'Sultan of Sokoto requests full amnesty for Boko Haram members', *Nigerian Watch*, 6 March 2013.

38 This includes the Chibok girls.

5. CONCLUSION

It is a difficult choice to make when asked to choose between peace, reconciliation and justice. They are all very important elements of a conflict resolution. However, there are possibilities that 'peace' and 'justice' can work together when they are used effectively. The granting of amnesty to Niger Delta militants achieved the goal of ensuring that the oil wells continued to flow in the Niger Delta. It however did not solve the Niger Delta question as the underlying issues remain yet to be addressed. Nevertheless, the emergence of Goodluck Jonathan as Nigeria's President appeared to have pacified the Niger Delta militancy. Whether the shift of power to the North with the victory of President Mohammadu Buhari in the 2015 general elections will play a role in ending the Boko Haram insurgency in the North is subject to speculation. As the peace, justice and reconciliation option continue to be favoured in several quarters, it is worthy of note that the affiliation of Boko Haram to other terrorist networks have raised the stakes; and the involvement of the ICC is also significant. This is because the ICC is not bound by any amnesty or reconciliation programme entered between the Nigerian government and Boko Haram. Although it can be argued that Article 53 of the Rome Statute allows the Prosecutor to recognise non-judicial mechanisms, the interpretation of the ICC Prosecutor is different and very restricted in application. Until there is a shift in that interpretation, the likes of Boko Haram can only enjoy transitional justice mechanisms that operate within the boundaries of Nigeria and may still be liable for prosecution if indicted by the ICC. In addition, the transnational nature of Boko Haram means that any of the West and Central African countries neighbouring Nigeria, where Boko Haram members operate, can actually prosecute them for international crimes.

BIBLIOGRAPHY

BOOKS AND JOURNAL ARTICLES

Alabi 2007

Alabi, D., 'Religious Conflicts in Northern Nigeria: A Critical Analysis', in Joab-Peterside, S. and Ukiwo, U. (eds.), 'The Travails and Challenges of Democracy in Nigeria, 1999–2003 and Beyond', Centre for Advanced Social Sciences, 2007.

Ambos 2009

Ambos, K., 'The Legal Framework of Transitional Justice', in Ambos, K., Large, J. and Wierda, M. (eds.), 'Building a Future on Peace and Justice: Studies on Transitional Justice, Peace and Development', Springer, 2009.

Arsanjani 1999

Arsanjani, M.H., 'International Criminal Court and National Amnesty Laws: The Future of the International Criminal Court', 93 American Journal of International Law, 1999.

Badejogbin 2013

Badejogbin, O., 'Boko Haram: An enquiry into the socio-political context of Nigeria's counter-terrorism response', Law, Democracy & Development, 2013, pp. 226–252.

Blumenson 2006

Blumenson, E., 'The Challenge of a Global Standard of Justice: Peace, Pluralism, and punishment at the International Criminal Court', 44 Columbia Journal of Transnational Law, 2006.

Clark 2005

Clark, T.H, 'The Prosecutor of the International Criminal Court, Amnesties and the Interests of Justice: Striking a Delicate Balance', 4 Washington University Global Studies Law Review, 2005.

Dukic 2007

Dukic, D., 'Transitional justice and International Criminal Court – in "the interests of justice?", 89(867) International Committee of the Red Cross, 2007.

Gallavin 2003

Gallavin, C., 'Article 53 of the Rome Statute of the International Criminal Court: In the interests of justice?', 14 Kings College Law Journal, 2003.

Gavron 2002

Gavron, J. 'Amnesties in Light of Developments in International Law and the Establishment of the International Criminal Court', 51 International and Comparative Law Quarterly, 2002.

Goldstone and Fritz 2000

Goldstone, R. and Fritz, N., "In the Interests of Justice" and Independent Referral: The ICC Prosecutor's Unprecedented Powers', 13 Leiden Journal of International Law, 2000.

Hafner, Boon, Rubesame, and Huston 1999

Hafner, G., Boon, K., Rubesame, A. and Huston, J., 'A Response to the American View as Presented by Ruth Wedgewood', 10 Journal of International Law, 1999.

Mallinder 2007

Mallinder, L., 'Can Amnesties and International Justice be Reconciled?', International Journal of Transitional Justice, 2007.

Mendes 2010

Mendes, E.P., 'Peace and Justice at the International Criminal Court: A Court of Last Resort', Edward Elgar Publishing, 2010.

Olugbuo and Wachira 2011

Olugbuo, B. and Wachira, M., 'Enhancing the Protection of the Rights of Victims' of International Crimes: A Model for East Africa', 11(2) African Human Rights Law Journal, 2011, pp. 608–638.

Onuoha 2010

Onuoha, F., 'The Islamist challenge: Nigeria's Boko Haram crisis explained', 19(2) African Security Review, 2010, pp. 54–67.

Orentlicher 1991
Orentlicher, D.F., 'Settling Accounts: The Duty to Prosecute Human Rights Violations of a Prior Regime', Yale Law Journal, 1991.
Osaghae 1995
Osaghae, E.E., 'The Ogoni Uprising: Oil Politics, Minority Agitation and the Future of the Nigerian State', 94(376) African Affairs, 1995, pp. 325–344.
Plato
Plato, 'The Republic', Book IV.
Rawls 2001
Rawls, J., 'Justice as Fairness: A Restatement', Harvard University Press, 2001.
Rawls 1971
Rawls, J., 'A Theory of Justice', Harvard University Press, 1971.
Scharf 1999
Scharf, M.P., 'The Amnesty Exception to the Jurisdiction of the International Criminal Court', 32 Cornell International Law Journal, 1999.
Stahn 2005
Stahn, C., 'Complementarity, Amnesties and Alternative Forms of Justice: Some Interpretative Guidelines for the International Criminal Court', 3 Journal of International Criminal Justice, 2005.
Villa-Vicencio 2000
Villa-Vicencio, C., 'Why perpetrators should not always be prosecuted: Where the International Criminal Court and Truth Commissions Meet', 49 Emory Law Journal, 2000.

JURISPRUDENCE

Supreme Court of Nigeria 2003
Supreme Court of Nigeria, Fawehinmi v. Babangida, SC. 360/2001, 31 January 2003.

OTHERS

All Progressive Congress (APC), The APC Manifesto – A New Party for A New Nigeria, Press Releases.
Amnesty International USA, 'Stars on Their Shoulders, Blood on Their Hands: War Crimes Committed by the Nigerian Military', 3 June 2015.
Amnesty International, 'Open letter to the Chief Prosecutor of the International Criminal Court: Comments on the Concept of the Interests of Justice', IOR 40/023/2005, 17 June 2005.
Hassan, I. and Olugbuo, B., 'Winning the War, and not Just the Battle: Masterplan for Ending The Boko Haram Insurgency in the North-East', Centre for Democracy and Development, August 2015.
Hassan, I., 'Nigeria Forum: IDPs, Boko Haram and elections likely to be settled by the courts', African Arguments, 30 January 2015.

Human Rights Violations Investigation Commission (Oputa Panel), 'Synoptic Overview of HRVIC Report: Conclusions and Recommendations (Including Chairman's Foreword)', May 2002.
Human Rights Watch, 'Spiraling Violence: Boko Haram Attacks and Security Force Abuses in Nigeria', 11 October 2012.
Human Rights Watch, 'The Meaning of "Interests of Justice" in article 53 of the Rome Statute', 1 June 2005.
ICC, Office of the Prosecutor, 'Policy Paper on the Interests of Justice', September 2007.
ICC, Office of the Prosecutor, 'Report on Preliminary Examination Activities', 13 December 2011.
Mazen, M., 'Amnesty International Accuses Nigerian Military of Committing War Crimes, Claims Videos Show Abuses', Huffington Post, 4 August 2014.
News 24 Nigeria, 'Boko Haram changes name to "Islamic State in West Africa", 24 April 2015.
Nigeria First, 'Text of President Yar'Adua's Amnesty Proclamation', 25 June 2009.
Nigerian Watch, 'Islamic body OIC distances itself from Boko Haram calling it a criminal group', 3 June 2014.
Nigerian Watch, 'Sultan of Sokoto requests full amnesty for Boko Haram members', 6 March 2013.
Onuora, M., 'Nigeria backs ICC's efforts to check impunity', The Guardian Nigeria, 4 July 2012.
Schlein, L., 'UN Human Rights Chief Condemns Boko Haram Attacks', Voice of America, 23 June 2012.
United Nations General Assembly, 'Nuremberg Declaration on Peace and Justice', UN Doc. A/62/885, 19 June 2008.
United Nations Security Council, 'Security Council Al-Qaida Sanctions Committee Adds Boko Haram to Its Sanctions List', SC/11410, 22 May 2014.
United Nations Security Council, 'The rule of law and transitional justice in conflict and post-conflict societies', Report of the Secretary General, UNSC S/2004/616, 23 August 2004.
Vanguard, 'Boko Haram insurgency'll end by December, Buhari insists', 14 October 2015.
Vanguard, 'Breaking news: S/Africa court convicts Henry Okah of 13 acts of "terrorism"', 21 January 2013.
Walker, A., 'What Is Boko Haram?', United States Institute for Peace Special Report 308, June 2012.

TEN YEARS OF INTERNATIONAL CRIMINAL COURT PRACTICE – TRIALS, ACHIEVEMENTS AND TRIBULATIONS

Is the ICC Today what Africa Expects or Wants?

Akbar KHAN*

1. INTRODUCTION

With the Prosecutor's announcement in January 2013 of the formal opening of another investigation on the African continent, into alleged crimes on the territory of Mali, the theme of this paper 'Ten Years of International Criminal Court Practice – Trials, Achievements and Tribulations. Is the ICC Today what Africa Expects or Wants?' is extremely timely.

Let me start first by framing the discussion by what I consider Africa expects or wants from the ICC and then take stock of ICC court practice over the past ten years. In order to do this it is pertinent to recall Africa's significant contribution in the run up to the adoption of the Rome Statute in 1998.

At the time of the adoption of the Rome Statute African nations and civil society had played a vital role in shaping the Rome Statute; Ministers of Justice and Attorneys-General of the Southern African Development Community (SADC) helped to facilitate a continent wide discussion on the creation of the Court through their development of a set of principles that subsequently formed the basis of negotiations at Rome. These principles articulated the vision of a court with an independent prosecutor unfettered by UN Security Council control with inherent jurisdiction over the core international crimes of war crimes, crimes against humanity and genocide. These broad principles were also reflected in the Dakar Declaration, which was noted by the Council of Ministers of the Organisation of African Unity in February 1998 (now AU). The Council

* This paper is adapted from a presentation delivered on behalf of the International Bar Association at a conference convened by Africa Legal Aid (AFLA) titled 'Africa and the ICC: 10 Years On' held in Tanzania from 28 February to 1 March 2013.

of Ministers subsequently called on all OAU members to support the creation of the ICC, which was later adopted by OAU Heads of State in June 1998. It is also worth noting that Article 4 of the African Union's Constitutive Act underscores that the Union functions on principles of respect for human rights, the rule of law and a rejection of impunity.

Against this background the important role that Africa played on the run up to the adoption of the Rome Statute cannot be overstated. The expectations of Africa and the other member states were set by the framework of the Rome Statute, which represented a landmark development in international criminal law. The goals and aspirations set out in the preamble of the Rome Statute state, *inter alia*:

> Affirming that the most serious crimes of concern to the international community as a whole must not go unpunished and that their effective prosecution must be ensured by taking measures at the national level and by enhancing international co-operation.
>
> Determined to put an end to impunity of perpetrators of these crimes and thus to contribute to the prevention of such crime.

And at Article 1 of the Statute:

> It shall be a permanent institution and shall have the power to exercise its jurisdiction over persons for the most serious crimes of international concern … and shall be complementary to national criminal jurisdictions.

Kofi Annan, former United Nations Secretary-General, summed up the aspirations of the international community in 1998 well when he welcomed the birth of the world's first permanent International Criminal Court, by referring to it as 'a gift of hope to future generations, and a giant leap forward in the march towards universal human rights and the rule of law'. He further observed that 'Until now, when powerful men committed crimes against humanity, they knew that as long as they remained powerful no earthly court could judge them.'

Ten years after the entry into force of the Rome Statute have these aspirations been realised?

2. SELECTIVITY OF CASES

The ICC has opened eight investigations on the African continent and has only concluded two trials. The Prosecutor has brought 16 cases involving 29 suspects. Two individuals (Lubanga and Katanga) have been convicted and another (Ngudjulo Chui) acquitted.

The exclusive focus on investigations on the African continent has led some commentators to refer to the ICC as the International Criminal Court for Africa. Although understandable at first glance this observation fails to rightly place the investigations in context. Of the eight investigations on the African continent, three country situations were self-referrals (Uganda, Democratic Republic of Congo, Central African Republic), two were UNSC referrals (Darfur – UNSCR 1593 [2005] and Libya – UNSCR 1970 [2011]), and three were proprio motu (Côte d'Ivoire with full support of government, Kenya and Mali).

The understandable criticism of a perceived over focus by the Prosecutor in conducting investigations on the African continent was in my view correctly addressed by Kofi Annan (Op-Ed *New York Times* 30 June 2009) when he stated: 'The African opponents of the international court argue that it is fixated on Africa because its … cases so far all concern alleged crimes against African victims. One must begin by asking why African leaders shouldn't celebrate this focus on Africa victims. Do these leaders really want to side with the alleged perpetrators of mass atrocities rather than victims? Is the Court's failure to date to answer the calls of victims outside of Africa really a reason to leave the calls of African victims unheeded?'

While it cannot be seriously argued that the investigations already opened in Africa are unwarranted, the Prosecutor must be mindful that atrocities are also being committed across the globe; an over focus on Africa not only damages the Court's credibility as an international institution but also its global mission to combat impunity. The Prosecutor needs to open investigations on continents other than Africa where sufficient evidence justifies such action and governments outside of Africa should be encouraged to make referrals to the Court. Such steps will not only help to fill the impunity gaps that exist but will hopefully act as a catalyst for promoting national investigations and prosecutions.

A further area of concern regarding investigations that potentially damages the Court's credibility is the apparent imbalance in the Prosecutor's selection of cases. In the investigations conducted in the DRC, Uganda and Central Africa Republic no charges were brought against government officials or the armed forces despite widely circulated allegations of serious abuse. The absence of any reasonable explanation for such omissions erodes the Court's legitimacy. The recent Kenyan investigations indicate a welcome break from past selective practice but greater transparency is required to fully explain decisions taken by the Prosecutor. An opportunity now arises in the Mali investigation for the Prosecutor's office to consolidate progress by ensuring that any decisions taken on prosecuting cases are fully explained in a transparent and open manner.

3. RELATIONSHIP WITH THE UNITED NATIONS SECURITY COUNCIL (UNSC)

The relationship between the UNSC and the ICC is an uneasy one. Referrals by the UNSC to the ICC risk being seen as a political tool unless carefully managed and widely supported. This means that it is essential when making referrals (pursuant to Article 13(b) of the Rome Statute) or in exercising its power (pursuant to Article 16 of the Rome Statute) to defer an investigation or prosecution that the Council fully respects the judicial mandate of the ICC and avoids taking any steps which may be construed as using the Court as a political tool to respond to an immediate crisis situation. The Council should also ensure that once a situation is referred to the ICC it is the Court that is empowered to drive the process. This requires the Council to provide any necessary follow-up support to the Court on issues of cooperation especially in respect of referrals made. But, in this regard, the UNSC has a poor record to date in promoting co-operation. In both referrals, the Council diluted the impact of its resolutions by primarily obliging only the states on whose territory where the crimes were allegedly committed to cooperate while only 'urging non-states parties' to the Rome Statute to cooperate. Such differential treatment undermines the effectiveness of a Chapter VII resolution aimed at maintaining and/or restoring peace and security. Furthermore, the Council has failed to take any specific follow-up action where it has been notified of instances of non-cooperation by the ICC in respect of executing arrest warrants in the Darfur case.

However, despite these challenges, referrals by the Council provide an opportunity for the ICC to become a truly global court by having universal reaching but there is uneasiness about the three P5 non-ICC Member States and other such states on the Council referring situations involving other non-ICC states to the Court. Such uneasiness might be mitigated by the Council developing a consistent practice based on objective and credible evidence before deciding whether to refer a situation to the Court. This might include, for example, reference to a resolution from the Human Rights Council as in the case of Libya (the HRC passed a resolution on 25 February 2011 condemning the gross and systematic violation of human rights in Libya before UNSCR 1970 was passed by unanimous vote on 26 February) or the results of an Independent Expert Inquiry as in the case of Darfur.

Another aspect of this uneasy relationship is reflected in the ability of the Council pursuant to Article 16 of the Rome Statute to defer an investigation or prosecution in order to maintain or restore peace and security under Chapter VII of the UN Charter. Although there have been attempts to use this power, notably in the instance of peace negotiations with the leader of the Lord's Resistance Army and again by the Government of Kenya in late

2010 claiming that the potential ICC cases could be addressed through local mechanisms, neither attempt has been successful. This is an area where the political nature of the UNSC cuts across the judicial work of the ICC and therefore needs to be handled with extreme care to ensure that the judicial independence of the ICC is not undermined and the functions of the two institutions are not blurred.

4. EFFICIENT AND EFFECTIVE FUNCTIONING OF THE COURT

As a judicial institution the fairness of trials is at the heart of justice. Linked to this is the notion that justice delayed is justice denied. It has taken nearly 6 years since the surrender of Congolese militia leader Thomas Lubanga in 2006 for the Court to conclude its first full judicial cycle. With a staff of approximately 700 individuals and after ten years of operation at a cost of nearly USD 1 billion, it is clear that the status quo cannot continue. Thankfully the conclusion of the trials of accused Ngudjolo Chiu and Germain Katanga have progressed more quickly suggesting improvement in trial efficiency. However, even after discounting for the fact that the Court is a new operation and that institution building is difficult, to use Judge Song's own words of 4 June 2012: 'it is … important that we recognise that shortcomings and obstacles remain.' It is therefore welcome news that the Court is undertaking a 'lessons learnt' exercise to review criminal procedures. The amendment made at ASP 11 to the Court's Rules of Procedure and Evidence which introduces a new Rule 132*bis* designating a single trial judge in place of the full bench of three judges to adjudicate certain trial preparation matters in order to expedite proceedings and to promote cost efficiency is therefore an important step in the right direction.

Other intended steps to review personnel conditions and the operation of the legal aid system are also warranted in the interests of prudent management given that they are both major cost drivers. While it is in everyone's interest to ensure that the Court's oversight and budgetary processes are aligned in accordance with the 'One Court principle' to provide optimal transparency and accountability it is also incumbent on all member states to ensure that the Court is adequately resourced so that it is fit for purpose. Overburdening the court without adequate resources will only lead to further delays in investigations which in turn will impact the court's ability to dispense justice and act as a real deterrence. In this context it is regrettable that the UNSC placed the cost of progressing its two referrals on the Court rather than allowing the UN General Assembly to determine whether to fund the costs of referral (Article 17 of the UN Charter and Article 115 of the Rome Statute).

5. COOPERATION, COMPLEMENTARITY AND UNIVERSALITY

Issues of cooperation especially in relation to the execution of arrest warrants have dogged the ICC over the last ten years and will continue to do so unless member states step up and fulfil their legal obligations. Without cooperation the Court will fail and impunity will flourish. Without executed arrest warrants there can be no trials and no justice for the victims. A Court without trials is not a credible institution. Delays in executing arrest warrants corrode victims' confidence in the Court's mission and destroy any deterrent effect. Although the Assembly of States Parties has adopted procedures for addressing non-co-operation the procedures have yet to be implemented. Similarly, the UNSC has failed to take any measures after the notification of instances of non-co-operation. The result is that 12 suspects remain at large increasing delays in progressing justice for the victims. Another disappointing aspect after ten years of operations indicating a lack of support for the Court is the low number of witness relocation and sentence enforcement agreements in place. With 123 states parties to the Rome Statute and only a dozen or so agreements in place the international community can surely do better.

In many ways the importance of the Rome Statute regime lies in building on the principle that primary responsibility for investigating and prosecuting Rome Statute crimes lies with all states through their national legal systems and the International Criminal Court will only step in where the state with jurisdiction is genuinely unable or unwilling to carry out investigation or prosecution. The full implementation of this principle is the only feasible avenue to closing the impunity gap as it is well recognised that the ICC will be unable to prosecute too many individuals. Discussions in Kampala resulting in a stand-alone resolution have helped to provide a much needed focus in this area but in the end it is only political will matched by sufficient development assistance that will make any significant difference to building capacity at the national level to enable domestic investigations and prosecutions.

The continuing failure of well over half of the membership to put in any place any implementing legislation in spite of the wide availability of free technical assistance is a stark reminder that building domestic capacity is not just about the provision of development assistance but also requires political will.

Universality of the Rome Statute remains the ultimate goal but this will remain illusory in the absence of more ratifications. With 122 ratifications to date, the Rome Statute commands well over half of UN states. But the conspicuous absence of three P5 states and under representation in other significant regions of the world, for example from the Middle East, continues to undermine the Court's global fight against impunity and its mission to promote the international rule of law and respect for human rights. More work needs to be done by all stakeholders to increase ratifications in the coming years to achieve a truly global Court.

6. CONCLUSION

The ICC over the past ten years has largely been faithful to its mandate regarding the intentions of the states at Rome, whether African or otherwise. Although progress on trials has been slow, there have nonetheless been some notable successes. The conviction of Thomas Lubanga, a notorious Congolese warlord has highlighted the plight of child soldiers; the unanimous referral by the UNSC of the Libya situation together with cases opened by the Court against heads of state demonstrate that no one is above the law which has significantly helped to alter the paradigm from one of absolute impunity to accountability while promoting the international rule of law.

As a court of last resort, success should not be measured according to the number of convictions achieved but rather by the fairness of the trials conducted and even by the number of acquittals. The fact that six suspects in the Kenya cases and three suspects in the Darfur cases voluntarily appeared at pre-trial proceedings is growing evidence of the confidence in the fairness of proceedings at the ICC. Furthermore, for the first time in the field of international criminal justice victims have been given a voice and the prospect of receiving reparations. Retributive and restorative justices are finally being reconciled in the fight against impunity.

The ICC remains the only hope left to victims ravaged by atrocity crimes where there is little or no prospect of domestic investigations or prosecutions being undertaken. This is especially pertinent given that the ICC operates in areas of 'ongoing armed conflict or post conflict' where institutions and the rule of law are usually weak or fragile. As the ad hoc tribunals close and the international communities' appetite for creating such limited institutions fade the ICC offers the only truly independent and permanent international judicial mechanism to bring to justice the perpetrators of atrocity crimes and therefore provides justice for victims.

It is clear that the ICC has been through a challenging first decade; several indictees including President Bashir of Sudan remain at large, there is a perception that Africa is being unfairly targeted, and there are concerns over the relationship between the UNSC and the Court, including on how to enforce state cooperation to mention a few areas. Arguably, these are all growing pains that should be anticipated, but the challenge now is to learn the lessons of past institutional practice and from the other ad hoc tribunals as they phase out and to use these lessons to strengthen the institution's efficiency and effectiveness for the future. The ICC serves as an important part of the global architecture for sustainable peace and security.

As the ICC moves into its second decade it must continue to build its credibility as a judicial body through its focus on holding fair trials and delivering justice in an efficient manner. But the ICC must also reach for universality through reconnecting with its core constituencies, especially with civil society and Bar Associations that have nurtured and sustained the idea of a permanent international criminal court to realisation. The Court's relevance and legitimacy depends on the confidence of all of its stakeholders and especially its court users such as the legal profession and the victims it serves. Much of the negative perceptions arising from various stakeholders in response to certain decisions made by the Office of the Prosecutor may have been better handled and managed by the Court through greater dialogue, transparency and openness where possible with its stakeholders.

In conclusion, its seems appropriate to close by recalling the prescient remarks of Ambassador Intelmann, immediate past President of the Assembly of States Parties, when she rightly observed: 'We have come far, but as we strive to end impunity for the most serious crimes of concern to the international community, we still have a long road ahead'.

UNIVERSAL JURISDICTION, AFRICAN PERCEPTIONS OF THE INTERNATIONAL CRIMINAL COURT AND THE NEW AU PROTOCOL ON AMENDMENTS TO THE PROTOCOL ON THE STATUTE OF THE AFRICAN COURT OF JUSTICE AND HUMAN RIGHTS*

Manuel J. VENTURA and Amelia J. BLEEKER

1. INTRODUCTION

On 27 June 2014, the African Union (AU) adopted the Protocol on Amendments to the Protocol on the Statute of the African Court of Justice and Human Rights (Protocol) at the 23rd Annual Session of the Assembly of Heads of State and Government of the AU held in Malabo, Equatorial Guinea.[1] The Protocol will come into effect at such time as it receives 15 ratifications.[2] The Protocol, among other things, expands the *ratione materiae* jurisdiction of the African Court of Justice and Human Rights (African Court), which is itself a merger of the African Court of Human and Peoples' Rights and the African Court of Justice, so as to encompass international and transnational crimes. This move

---

* This chapter is an expanded version of a speech first delivered by Manuel Ventura at the Africa Legal Aid symposium on Universalizing the Rome Statute of the International Criminal Court held in Johannesburg, South Africa on 18–19 May 2015. The views expressed herein are those of the authors and do not necessarily reflect the views of the Special Tribunal for Lebanon.

1 For this reason, this protocol is occasionally referred to in the literature as the 'Malabo Protocol'.

2 See Art. 11 of the Protocol. As of 1 April 2016, nine Member States of the AU – Benin, Chad, Congo, Ghana, Guinea-Bissau, Kenya, Mauritania, Sierra-Leone, and São Tomé and Principe – have signed (but not ratified) the Protocol. See http://www.au.int/en/sites/default/files/treaties/7804-sl-protocol_on_amendments_to_the_protocol_on_the_statute_of_the_african_court_of_justice_and_human_rights_19.pdf (accessed 1 April 2016).

to create a regional African court for international crimes was triggered, in part, by negative perceptions in Africa concerning the International Criminal Court and its alleged selective exercise of jurisdiction over crimes on the African continent.[3]

After first examining the disconnect between rhetoric and reality that exists regarding African perceptions of the ICC, this chapter will discuss the potential role that universal jurisdiction can play at the African Court with its expanded international criminal jurisdiction based on the principle of complementarity. Specifically, the chapter will consider exercises of universal jurisdiction that have occurred outside of Africa over international crimes committed by African nationals on African soil and the limited examples to date of African states exercising universal jurisdiction over such crimes. The chapter will then discuss the rich possibilities that exist for African states to exercise universal jurisdiction over atrocities committed in Africa, the key obstacles facing African authorities in this endeavour and ways in which these obstacles can be overcome. The chapter concludes that, while the Protocol has created a regional African court with jurisdiction over both international and transnational crimes, the primary responsibility still rests with African states to investigate and prosecute atrocities committed in Africa. The domestic exercise of universal jurisdiction is one way in which Africa as a continent can counter the alleged abuse of the principle of universal jurisdiction by European states over African crimes and take ownership over justice processes that affect them.

2. NEGATIVE AFRICAN PERCEPTIONS OF THE ICC: THE DISCONNECT BETWEEN RHETORIC AND REALITY

It is no secret that today Africa and the ICC are not on good terms. Indeed, there is deep suspicion of the ICC on the continent, with the predominant rhetorical line (usually emanating from African leaders and politicians) being that the ICC unfairly targets Africans. This sentiment was perhaps most vividly encapsulated by the comments of then incumbent Chairperson of the AU and Prime Minister of Ethiopia Hailemariam Desalegn in May 2013, when he accused the ICC of 'degenerat[ing] into some kind of race hunting'.[4] Such feelings have manifested themselves in, among other things, the creation of the African Court with jurisdiction over many of the same crimes as the ICC. But things were not

3 See Du Plessis, Maluwa and O'Reilly, 'Africa and the International Criminal Court', July 2013, Chatham House, pp. 8–11, available at: www.chathamhouse.org/sites/files/chathamhouse/public/Research/International%20Law/0713pp_iccafrica.pdf (accessed 24 January 2016).

4 Desalegn, cited in BBC, 'African Union accuses ICC of "hunting" Africans', 27 May 2013, available at: www.bbc.com/news/world-africa-22681894 (accessed 24 January 2016).

always this way. As is well known, in the beginning, Africa was one of the biggest supporters of the ICC and is still the largest regional block of states parties to the Rome Statute.

Objectively viewed, there can be little doubt that this change in attitude to the ICC was directly associated with the ICC's proceedings against Sudanese President Omar Al-Bashir[5] and later exacerbated when Uhuru Kenyatta and William Ruto were elected President and Deputy President of Kenya respectively.[6] It was only then that attitudes, by the AU in particular, took a sharp turn away from the ICC[7] and accusations that the ICC has a 'bias against Africa' and was 'targeting Africans' began to take hold.[8]

Putting to one side the usual responses to such comments,[9] it should be remembered that the ICC was actively involved in the investigation and prosecution of cases on the African continent before the proceedings against President Al-Bashir in 2009 (and later President Kenyatta and Deputy President Ruto). In fact, in 2009, the ICC had in its custody a number of suspects, including Thomas Lubanga Dyilo, Germain Katanga, Mathieu Ngudjolo Chui and Jean-Pierre Bemba. Further, it had issued numerous arrest warrants against other suspects for crimes committed on the African continent. It is irrefutable that all of these persons are Africans who were being called to answer for serious

5 The ICC issued a warrant of arrest for President Al-Bashir in March 2009 for war crimes and crimes against humanity and later for genocide in July 2010. *See* ICC, *Prosecutor v. Al-Bashir*, Warrant of Arrest for Omar Hassan Ahmad Al-Bashir, ICC-02/05-01/09-1, Pre-Trial Chamber I, 4 March 2009; ICC, *Prosecutor v. Al-Bashir*, Second Warrant of Arrest for Omar Hassan Ahmad Al-Bashir, ICC-02/05-01/09-95, Pre-Trial Chamber I, 12 July 2010.

6 Kenyatta and Ruto were first summoned to appear by the ICC with respect to crimes against humanity in March 2011. See ICC, *Prosecutor v. Ruto et al.*, Decision on the Prosecutor's Application for Summons to Appear for William Samoei Ruto, Henry Kiprono Kosgey and Joshua Arap Sang, ICC-01/09-01/11-01, Pre-Trial Chamber II, 8 March 2001; ICC, *Prosecutor v. Muthaura et al.*, Decision on the Prosecutor's Application for Summonses to Appear for Francis Kirimi Muthaura, Uhuru Muigai Kenyatta and Mohammed Hussein Ali, ICC-01/09-02/11-01, Pre-Trial Chamber II, 8 March 2001. Subsequently, both men were elected President and Deputy President of Kenya respectively and took up their offices in April 2013.

7 See Murithi 2014, pp. 182–184.

8 See Batohi 2014, p. 50.

9 While it is true that all nine of the ICC's current active investigations are on the African continent, these have either: (1) been referred to the ICC by the UN Security Council; or (2) have been referred to the ICC by the relevant African state itself. The two exceptions where the ICC Prosecutor has exercised her *proprio motu* power to initiate an investigation have been with respect to Kenya and Côte d'Ivoire and even then, with respect to the latter, Côte d'Ivoire itself submitted an ad hoc declaration accepting the ICC's jurisdiction before a *proprio motu* investigation was initiated. In any event, the notion that the ICC targets Africans ignores the fact that another nine preliminary examinations are currently active by the ICC Prosecutor and only two of those (Guinea and Nigeria) involve an African state. Further, in October 2015, the ICC Prosecutor requested authorisation to begin an investigation into the situation in Georgia, which, if approved by the Pre-Trial Chamber, will mark the commencement of the first ICC investigation outside of the African continent. See ICC, Situation in Georgia, Request for Authorisation of an Investigation Persuant to Article 15, ICC-10/15-4, Office of the Prosecution, 13 October 2015.

allegations before the ICC. And yet, with respect to these persons, one did not hear accusations by the AU or African states that the ICC was 'unfairly targeting Africans'. As mentioned above, the present groundswell of anti-ICC sentiment only really began with the proceedings against President Al-Bashir and then in the Kenya cases when two of the accused became the President and the Deputy President of Kenya. And yet, both groups of persons are undoubtedly African. If the objections to the ICC revolve around its supposed focus on Africa alone, then one would have expected the AU and African states to, at some point, also object to other cases involving Africans before the ICC. That has not been the case.

Viewed in this light, it is submitted that the sentiment expressed by African states concern not that the ICC is targeting Africans *per se*, but rather that it is targeting *politically powerful* Africans. This is what differentiates the two set of cases described above. One group involves persons in positions of power within their relevant states (namely, Sudan and Kenya) and the other concerns individuals who have fallen from political grace, or are leaders of non-state armed groups – persons who lack political power. Indeed, one need only consider the recent case of Dominic Ongwen – one of those indicted for crimes committed by the Lord's Resistance Army in Uganda[10] – and how quickly and with very little protest he was handed over to the ICC in January 2015 for prosecution after he surrendered himself in the Central African Republic, despite the present anti-ICC stance among African states.

For these reasons, it would appear that the rhetoric emanating from Africa against the ICC, which was part of the impetus for the creation of the African Court, is disconnected from the facts. While it may be politically advantageous to give the impression that Africa is being unfairly targeted by the ICC, the way in which African states have acted as a whole with respect to ICC cases involving Africans gives another impression: that one standard appears to apply to Africans without political power and another to Africans who possess political power. The former, it seems, can and should be investigated and prosecuted by the ICC, the latter cannot – as per Article 46A*bis* of the Protocol which grants immunity for incumbent heads of state and senior state officials.[11]

10 See ICC, *Situation in Uganda*, Decision on the Prosecutor's Application for Warrants of Arrest under Article 58, ICC-02/04-01/05-1-US-Exp, Pre-Trial Chamber II, 8 July 2005.

11 Art. 46A*bis* of the Protocol reads, in full: 'No charges shall be commenced or continued before the [African] Court against any serving AU Head of State or Government, or anybody acting or entitled to act in such capacity, or other senior state officials based on their functions, during their tenure of office.' On this matter, see Tladi 2015; Babington-Ashaye 2015, pp. 406–425.

3. THE JURISDICTION OF THE AFRICAN COURT UNDER THE PROTOCOL

At first glance, linking universal jurisdiction and the African Court may appear odd given that the Protocol does not actually grant the African Court this form of jurisdiction. As is well known, universal jurisdiction provides states with the competence to investigate, prosecute and judge alleged perpetrators of certain serious crimes under international law – including genocide, crimes against humanity, war crimes, and torture – irrespective of where the crime took place and the nationality of the perpetrator or the victim. The concept is based on the idea that certain acts affect the common interests of the entire international community and, as a result, any state may investigate and prosecute such acts as a trustee for the international community.[12]

However, instead of endowing the African Court with universal jurisdiction, the Protocol grants the African Court commonly recognised jurisdiction bases: active personality jurisdiction (when the accused is a national of a state party to the Protocol) and territorial jurisdiction (when the accused committed crime(s) on the territory of a state party to the Protocol).[13] In addition, the Protocol also endows the African Court with less popular jurisdictional bases: passive personality jurisdiction (where the victim is a national of a state party to the Protocol) and protective jurisdiction (where a vital interest of a state party to the Protocol is threatened by extraterritorial conduct of non-nationals).[14] The latter two jurisdiction bases are a first: no international or regional court in history has been endowed with them. Until the African Court, such jurisdictional bases had only been previously exercised by some states for specific crimes within their domestic legal systems.

Nevertheless, despite its express absence in the Protocol, universal jurisdiction has a potential role to play at the African Court. This is due to the Court's expanded international criminal jurisdiction being based on the principle of complementarity.[15] Complementarity, which was also a founding

---

12 See Jeßberger 2009, pp. 555–557.

13 Art. 46E *bis* (a)–(b) of the Protocol.

14 Art. 46E *bis* (c)–(d) of the Protocol.

15 Art. 46H(2) of the Protocol. Art. 46(H) states, in full:
(1) The jurisdiction of the Court shall be complementary to that of the National Courts, and to the Courts of the Regional Economic Communities where specifically provided for by the Communities.
(2) The Court shall determine that a case is inadmissible where:
(a) The case is being investigated or prosecuted by a State which has jurisdiction over it, unless the State is unwilling or unable to carry out the investigation or prosecution;
(b) The case has been investigated by a State which has jurisdiction over it and the State has decided not to prosecute the person concerned, unless the decision resulted from the unwillingness or inability of the State to prosecute;
(c) The person concerned has already been tried for conduct which is the subject of the complaint;
(d) The case is not of sufficient gravity to justify further action by the Court.

feature of the ICC, dictates that cases are admissible before the relevant court only if a state with jurisdiction over an international crime is unwilling or unable to investigate or prosecute such crimes themselves.[16] Article 46H of the Protocol replicates the notion of complementarity as found in Article 17(1) of the Rome Statute. Thus, the Protocol refers to 'a State which has jurisdiction' over the relevant case.[17] In other words, a case is only admissible before the African Court if a state with jurisdiction is unwilling or unable to investigate or prosecute or, alternatively, if an investigation has taken place by a state with jurisdiction and a decision not to prosecute results from an unwillingness or inability to prosecute.[18]

The complementarity provision of the Protocol plainly refers to 'a State' with jurisdiction.[19] It does not refer, for example, to a 'Member State' (which is defined in the Protocol as a Member State of the African Union) with jurisdiction.[20] Since the criminal jurisdiction of a state can take the form of any of the various recognised jurisdictional bases, including universal jurisdiction, where a state – any state – has vested its courts with universal jurisdiction over the crimes found in the Protocol and her domestic authorities have exercised this jurisdiction, the African Court could be prevented from hearing such a case based on the principle of complementarity. It would simply be a situation where a state with jurisdiction (in this case, universal jurisdiction) is willing and able to investigate and prosecute the relevant international crimes – in the spirit of Article 46H of the Protocol. Such an interpretation of Article 46H is aligned with interpretations of the relevant provisions of the Rome Statute (namely, Article 17 and Article 19).[21]

---

(3) In order to determine that a State is unwilling to investigate or prosecute in a particular case, the Court shall consider, having regard to the principles of due process recognized by international law, whether one or more of the following exist, as applicable:
(a) The proceedings were or are being undertaken or the national decision was made for the purpose of shielding the person concerned from criminal responsibility for crimes within the jurisdiction of the Court;
(b) There has been an unjustified delay in the proceedings which in the circumstances is inconsistent with an intent to bring the person concerned to justice;
(c) The proceedings were not or are not being conducted independently or impartially, and they were or are being conducted in a manner which, in the circumstances, is inconsistent with an intent to bring the person concerned to justice.

(4) In order to determine that a State is unable to investigate or prosecute in a particular case, the Court shall consider whether, due to a total or substantial collapse or unavailability of its national judicial system, the State is unable to obtain the accused or the necessary evidence and testimony or otherwise unable to carry out its proceedings.

16 Art. 17(1) of the Rome Statute.
17 Art. 46H(2) of the Protocol.
18 *Ibid.*
19 Art. 46H(2)–(3) of the Protocol.
20 Art. 1 of the Protocol.
21 Schabas 2010, pp. 340–341 (emphasis added): '[t]he real question, then, is whether any proceedings have taken place *anywhere*'; Hall, Nsereko and Ventura 2016, margin no. 26,

4. THE EXERCISE OF UNIVERSAL JURISDICTION OVER INTERNATIONAL CRIMES COMMITTED IN AFRICA

The question, then, is how likely is it that universal jurisdiction will be exercised over international crimes committed by African nationals on African soil? Recent history shows we cannot discount this possibility altogether. For example, one of the more well-known exercises of universal jurisdiction over events in Africa in recent times was Belgium's proceedings against Mr Abdulaye Yerodia Ndombasi – the then incumbent Minister for Foreign Affairs of the Democratic Republic of the Congo. That case resulted in the (in)famous holding of the International Court of Justice (ICJ) in the *Case Concerning the Arrest Warrant of 11 April 2000* that incumbent Ministers of Foreign Affairs (and later incumbent Heads of State)[22] enjoyed complete (personal) immunity from criminal proceedings before domestic courts – even when the crimes alleged were international crimes.[23]

Other exercises of universal jurisdiction over crimes committed in Africa have arisen in the context of the Rwandan genocide in 1994. This includes Canada's successful prosecution of Désiré Munyaneza[24] and Belgium's prosecution of the *Butare Four*[25] and *Two Brothers* cases.[26] Other cases include France's conviction of Ould Dah *in absentia* for torture committed in Mauritius in 1990–1991,[27] and France's current investigation of the *Brazaville Beach* case in the Republic of the Congo.[28] Similarly, in September and December 2015, German courts convicted three persons across two cases for international crimes, including Onesphore Rwabukombe, a former Rwandan mayor, for

p. 869 (original emphasis): '[i]t would thus appear that *any* State – so long as it has jurisdiction over the relevant case – can file challenges under article 19 para. 2(b)'.

22 See ICJ, *Case Concerning Certain Questions of Mutual Assistance in Criminal Matters (Djibouti v. France)*, Judgment of 4 June 2008, ICJ Reports 2008, pp. 236–237, para. 170.

23 ICJ, *Case Concerning the Arrest Warrant of 11 April 2000 (Democratic Republic of the Congo v. Belgium)*, Judgment of 14 February 2002, ICJ Reports 2002, pp. 24–26, paras. 58–61.

24 Canada, Superior Court of Quebec – Criminal Division, *The Queen v. Munyaneza*, 2009 QCCS 2201, 22 May 2009. Munyaneza's appeal was subsequently rejected: Canada, Court of Appeal of Quebec, *Munyaneza v. The Queen*, 2014 QCCA 906, 7 May 2014.

25 Belgium, Cour d'assises de Bruxelles, *Higaniro et al.*, 8 June 2001. Their appeal in cassation was subsequently rejected. *See* Reydams 2003.

26 Belgium, Cour d'assises de Bruxelles, *Nzabonimana and Ndashyikirwa*, 29 June 2005.

27 France, Cour d'assises du Gard, 1 July 2005. Ould Dah's appeal to the European Court of Human Rights (ECtHR) was subsequently rejected: ECtHR – Fifth Section, *Ould Dah v. France*, Admissibility, Case No. 13113/03, 17 March 2009.

28 On 9 October 2014, the Chambre de l'instruction de la Cour d'Appel de Paris confirmed the indictment of Norbert Dabira for crimes against humanity. The case is ongoing. For further information about the status of this case, see: https://www.fidh.org/International-Federation-for-Human-Rights/Africa/congo/the-disappeared-of-the-beach-case/ (accessed 24 January 2016).

events that took place during the Rwandan genocide in 1994[29] and Ignace Murwanashyaka and Straton Musoni – leaders of a Rwandan rebel group – for war crimes and crimes against humanity committed in the Democratic Republic of the Congo.[30] There have been numerous other such proceedings, mostly in Europe, concerning crimes on the African continent pursuant to universal jurisdiction.[31]

If these cases had fallen within the jurisdiction of the African Court with its expanded international criminal mandate – and therefore been subject to the principle of complementarity – the language of the Protocol would require the African Court to hold that such cases were inadmissible before it. This is because a (European) state with jurisdiction – universal jurisdiction – was actively investigating and prosecuting the case. Given the political atmosphere and rhetoric that led to the Protocol's drafting and adoption, this result would be an odd one. The Protocol came into being partly as a result of African views that the ICC is biased against Africa or a 'tool' of Western states. It would be truly ironic if the AU's response – an African Court with international criminal jurisdiction – would be unable to adjudicate upon crimes that have occurred on the African continent on the basis that these same Western states are investigating and prosecuting them on the basis of universal jurisdiction.

5. AFRICAN EXERCISE OF UNIVERSAL JURISDICTION

While African states have condemned European states for their 'abuse of the principle of universal jurisdiction',[32] there are rich possibilities for African states to counter this alleged abuse by utilising their own domestic universal jurisdiction over atrocities committed in Africa. Indeed, the

---

29 Germany, Higher Regional Court of Frankfurt (Oberlandesgericht Frankfurt an Main), Case No. 4-3 StE 4/10-4-1/15, 29 December 2015. At his original trial, Rwabukombe was found guilty as an accessory: Germany, Higher Regional Court of Frankfurt (Oberlandesgericht Frankfurt an Main), Case No. 5-3 StE 4/10-4-3/10, 18 February 2014. However, on appeal, the Federal Court of Justice of Germany (Bundesgerichtshof) held that the trial court had erred with respect to the *mens rea* of genocide and in their holding that the evidence was only sufficient for criminal liability to attach as an accessory rather than a principal, sending the case back to a different chamber of the Higher Regional Court of Frankfurt as a result: Germany, Federal Court of Justice of Germany (Bundesgerichtshof), Case No. 3 StR 575/14, 21 May 2015.

30 Germany, Higher Regional Court of Stuttgart (Oberlandesgericht Stuttgart), Case No. 5-3 StE 6/10, 28 September 2015.

31 For an overview of such cases, see International Federation for Human Rights, 'Universal Jurisdiction Annual Review 2015: Make Way for Justice', available at: https://www.fidh.org/IMG/pdf/trial-ecchr-fidh_uj_annual_review_2014.pdf (accessed 24 January 2016).

32 AU, Decision on Africa's Relationship with the International Criminal Court, Doc No. Ext/Assembly/AU/Dec. 1 (Oct. 2013), 12 October 2013, para. 3.

principle of complementarity permits African states to demand that both the African Court and the ICC defer to their competence and right to investigate international crimes. While a 2012 Amnesty International study found that 37 out of 54 African states possessed universal jurisdiction over one or more of the international crimes that currently fall within the African Court's competence,[33] the exercise of African universal jurisdiction over crimes committed by Africans is scant. In 2009, an AU-EU expert group concluded that no African state had effectively exercised universal jurisdiction over international crimes.[34] The reality, until recently at least, was that '[c]ourts and prosecutors located in Africa do not prosecute and punish crimes under international law on the basis of universal jurisdiction – although their statutory law often explicitly allows for it.'[35]

However, recent developments suggest that change may be on the horizon. On 30 October 2014, the Constitutional Court of South Africa issued its landmark judgment in *National Commissioner of the South African Police Service v. Southern Africa Human Rights Litigation Centre and Another*, or, as it is more commonly known, the *Zimbabwe Torture Docket* Case.[36] At issue before the Constitutional Court was the National Prosecuting Authority's (NPA) refusal to exercise universal jurisdiction, as provided for in domestic legislation,[37] in order to initiate an investigation into allegations of torture as a crime against humanity committed against Zimbabwean political opponents in Zimbabwe by the Zimbabwean state. The Court held that South Africa not only had the power but also a domestic and international *duty* to investigate such crimes and ordered the commencement of an investigation. The decision was based on three considerations: (1) that South Africa had a domestic duty to investigate all crime – regardless of its classification as an international crime or domestic crime; (2) that South Africa had endowed her courts with universal jurisdiction over international crimes; and (3) that the presence of the accused

---

33 This includes African countries like, among others, Algeria, Burkina Faso, Burundi, Cameroon, Ethiopia, Ghana, Niger, Rwanda, Senegal and Uganda. See Amnesty International, 'Universal Jurisdiction: A Preliminary Survey of Legislation Around The World – 2012 Update', 9 October 2012, p. 16 *et seq.*, available at: https://www.amnesty.org/download/Documents/24000/ior530192012en.pdf (accessed 24 January 2016).

34 See Council of the EU, *AU-EU Expert Report on the Principle of Universal Jurisdiction*, Doc No. 8672/1/09 Rev. 1, 16 April 2009, para. 19. At the time of the report, Senegalese authorities had issued an indictment against former Chadian leader Hissène Habré on the basis of universal jurisdiction. However, proceedings had not then been pursued. See below for further discussion of the Habré case.

35 Jeßberger 2014, p. 164.

36 South Africa, Constitutional Court, *National Commissioner of the South African Police Service v. Southern Africa Human Rights Litigation Centre and Another* [2014] ZACC 30, 30 October 2014 ('*Zimbabwe Torture Docket* Case'). For an analysis of this decision, see Ventura 2015.

37 Specifically, section 4(3)(c) of the ICC Act. For a review of this legislation as a whole, see Du Plessis 2007.

was not a requirement for the commencement of investigations.[38] The Court also provided useful guidelines by limiting the duty to investigate upon the principles of subsidiarity and practicability. First, the principle of subsidiarity, according to the Constitutional Court, requires the existence of 'a substantial and true connection between the subject matter and the source of the jurisdiction' and before an investigation and prosecution of international crimes can proceed, the state with jurisdiction must unwilling or unable to do so itself.[39] Second, before the state assumes universal jurisdiction over a crime, it must consider whether an investigation is reasonable and practicable in light of the specific circumstances of the relevant case.[40] While the Court adopted these principles so as to guide South African authorities, they can equally be applied to other states in their exercise of universal jurisdiction.

Furthermore, in the wake of the successful challenge in the lower courts to the NPA's decision not to investigate in the *Zimbabwe Torture Docket* Case, in May 2012, the NPA announced that it would investigate, pursuant to South Africa's universal jurisdiction, crimes against humanity allegedly committed by former Madagascan President Marc Ravalomanana, who had fled Madagascar and was exiled in South Africa.[41] In November 2012, Ravalomanana's passport was confiscated and he was subjected to travel restrictions by order of the High Court.[42] Then, in October 2014, Ravalomanana apparently slipped out of South Africa, despite these restrictions, and is now in Madagascar.[43]

The saga surrounding the prosecution of former Chadian leader Hissène Habré in Senegal on charges of crimes against humanity, war crimes and torture is a further rare example of the exercise of universal jurisdiction in Africa by Africans.[44] Habré's ongoing trial before the Extraordinary African Chambers (EAC) – an ad hoc court set up within the Senegalese justice system to try those responsible for serious crimes committed under Habré's rule from 1982 to 1990 – is the culmination of a 15-year ordeal beginning with his indictment in Senegal in 2000. When Senegalese courts held that they did not have the jurisdiction to try Habré,[45] the victims turned to Belgium, which found that her courts possessed jurisdiction to hear the case on the basis of a domestic law that

---

38 South Africa, Constitutional Court, *Zimbabwe Torture Docket* Case, paras. 47–60.

39 *Ibid*, para. 61.

40 *Ibid*, para. 63.

41 See 'NPA Investigating Ravalomanana for crimes against humanity', *Times Live*, 5 August 2012, available at: www.timeslive.co.za/local/2012/08/05/npa-investigating-ravalomanana-for-crimes-against-humanity (accessed on 24 January 2016).

42 See South Africa, North Gauteng High Court, *Rakoto and Others v. Head: Directorate for Priority Crimes Investigation and Others* [2012] ZAGPPHC 281, 19 November 2012.

43 See 'Ex-president's mysterious exit', *Mail and Guardian*, 24 October 2014, available at: http://mg.co.za/article/2014-10-23-ex-presidents-mysterious-exit (accessed 24 January 2016).

44 On this case, see generally Brody 2015.

45 Senegal, Cour d'appel de Dakar, *Guengueng and Others v. Habré*, Arrêt No. 135, 4 July 2000; Senegal, Cour de cassation, *Guengueng and Others v. Habré*, Arrêt No. 14, 20 March 2001.

endowed Belgian courts with universal jurisdiction over the crimes with which Habré stood accused.[46] In September 2005, a Belgian judge indicted Habré and requested his extradition. After the request was refused, Belgium filed suit at the ICJ, which in the end ordered Senegal to either prosecute Habré without delay or extradite him to a country that would.[47] Finally, in February 2013, Senegal set up the EAC with the support of the AU.[48] On 13 February 2015, the EAC ruled that there was sufficient evidence to indict Habré to stand trial for crimes against humanity, war crimes, and torture.[49] However, it was only with immense external pressure and the involvement of a European state, regional and international mechanisms, and civil society over a period of 15 years, that the proceedings against Habré in a Senegalese court finally opened on 20 July 2015.

While the proceedings against Habré in Senegal and the *Zimbabwe Torture Docket* Case, in particular, offer hope as well as practical guidance for the exercise of universal jurisdiction in Africa, the general progress of international criminal justice on the continent took a backwards step in June 2015 when the South African government failed to facilitate the arrest and surrender of Sudanese President Omar Al-Bashir, who the ICC has charged with genocide, war crimes and crimes against humanity, during his visit to South Africa for an AU summit.[50] Although this matter appears to involve a failure on the part of South Africa to honour its obligations under the Rome Statute and does not specifically relate to the exercise of universal jurisdiction, it is emblematic of the current lack of political will prevailing in a number of African states when it comes to politically sensitive allegations of international crimes committed in other African states. Such a lack of political will does not bode well for future investigations and trials on the basis of universal jurisdiction in South Africa and Africa generally. Indeed, as the Constitutional Court of South Africa rightly held, '[p]olitical inter-state tensions are, in most instances, virtually unavoidable as far as the application of universality … is concerned.'[51] For this reason, it was held that the decision to investigate and prosecute international crimes in South Africa should not be influenced by political considerations.[52] However, without a show of support (or, at the very least, non-interference) by states where international crimes took place to those states that are actively investigating or prosecuting such crimes pursuant to universal jurisdiction, such criminal proceedings will likely face immense difficulties.

---

46 Belgium, Cour de cassation, Case No. P. 02.1139.F/1, 12 February 2003.

47 ICJ, *Questions Concerning the Obligation to Prosecute or Extradite (Belgium v. Senegal)*, Judgment of 20 July 2012, ICJ Reports 2012, p. 422.

48 For further discussion on the EAC, see Cimiotta 2015.

49 See EAC, Chambre d'instruction, Ordonnance de non-lieu partiel, de mise en accusation et de renvoi devant la Chambre africaine extraordinaire d'assises, Case No. 01/13, 13 February 2015.

50 On this matter, see Ventura 2015; Tladi 2015; De Wet 2015.

51 South Africa, Constitutional Court, *Zimbabwe Torture Docket* Case, para. 74.

52 *Ibid.*

6. SURMOUNTING OBSTACLES TO THE AFRICAN EXERCISE OF UNIVERSAL JURISDICTION OVER INTERNATIONAL CRIMES COMMITTED IN AFRICA

Although international criminal justice tends to take one step forward for every two back on the African continent, the *Zimbabwe Torture Docket* Case and the establishment of the EAC have opened the door for other African states to assume universal jurisdiction over atrocities committed in Africa. As mentioned above, numerous states in Africa have universal jurisdiction in their books over one or more international crimes.[53] Nonetheless, as demonstrated by the recent developments in Senegal and South Africa, increasing the exercise of universal jurisdiction by African states over crimes committed on their continent will not be without challenges. The key obstacles facing domestic African courts in exercising universal jurisdiction are a lack of political will to investigate and prosecute such crimes, a lack of cooperation between states when it comes to extraditing suspects and acquiring evidence, inadequate domestic legislation concerning international crimes, a lack of technical expertise in international criminal law, securing adequate levels of funding, and in some cases, unfortunately, a lack of judicial independence and a weak judiciary.

As the cases discussed above show, one of the biggest impediments to the exercise of universal jurisdiction in Africa is a lack of political will by African states to institute criminal proceedings with respect to international crimes. Whilst technical hurdles can be overcome more easily, convincing states of the need for international criminal justice will be a long-term and multifaceted process. A number of African states already struggle to guarantee the independence and impartiality of their courts and to deal with their own domestic criminal problems without taking on the additional burden of prosecuting international crimes carried out in other African states. Nevertheless, in 2012, the AU adopted a Model Law on Universal Jurisdiction (AU Model Law), which recognises that 'certain crimes are of most serious concern to member states of the African Union and the international community as a whole and they must not go unpunished'.[54] The AU Model Law provides for universal jurisdiction over not only genocide, crimes against humanity, war crimes and piracy, but also trafficking in narcotics and terrorism. It further endorses the view that there is no requirement under the principle of universal jurisdiction for a suspect to be within the relevant state at the time when an investigation is commenced.[55] Unfortunately, the Model Law is less aspirational

53 See *supra* n. 33.

54 Preamble, AU Model National Law on Universal Jurisdiction Over International Crimes, Doc. No. EX.CL/731(XXI)c, July 2012 ('AU Model Law').

55 Article 4(1) AU Model Law.

with regard to its inclusion of immunity for state officials.[56] Nonetheless, this endorsement of the principle of universal jurisdiction by the AU and her member states sets an important precedent that ought to make it more difficult for African states to turn a blind eye to atrocities simply on the basis that they occurred on the territory of another African state.

If enough political will can be garnered, the successful exercise of universal jurisdiction also requires access to victims and witnesses, and, ideally, the crime scene. It goes without saying that gathering sufficient evidence for a successful prosecution is difficult, if not impossible, where investigators and prosecutors do not have such access. Given that the exercise of universal jurisdiction is only necessary where a state fails to investigate or prosecute an international crime itself, cooperation is likely to be an issue. A state exercising universal jurisdiction will often need to exert significant political will and possibly even enlist the assistance of the international community to pressure the state in question to comply with its requests.

Interstate cooperation for the extradition of suspects is also essential to the exercise of universal jurisdiction. The process of extradition is impeded when states do not have effective (or any) mutual legal assistance treaties or arrangements in place. Indeed, there currently exists no comprehensive multilateral extradition treaty for all African states. Whilst such provisions do exist in specific treaties – such as the Organisation of African Unity (OAU) Convention on the Prevention and Combating of Terrorism[57] and the AU Convention on Preventing and Combating Corruption[58] – they only apply to those suspected of the specific offences covered by those treaties, namely, terrorism and corruption-related offences. At the sub-regional level in Africa, the Southern Africa Development Community has adopted two Protocols on Extradition and Mutual Legal Assistance aimed at enhancing cooperation in transnational criminal matters.[59] Similarly, the Economic Community of West African States (ECOWAS) has also adopted a Convention on Extradition.[60] However, these treaties are ill-suited to extradition for international crimes, as they do not reflect specific exceptions that generally apply to such crimes. For example, international human rights law recognises that states can prosecute

56 Article 16(1) AU Model Law. Note however that this provision does not specify when exactly the immunity is to be accorded. See D. Akande, 'The African Union, the ICC and Universal Jurisdiction: Some Recent Developments', *EJIL: Talk!* Blog, 29 August 2012, available at: www.ejiltalk.org/the-african-union-the-icc-and-universal-jurisdiction-some-recent-developments/ (accessed 24 January 2016).

57 The OAU Convention on the Prevention and Combating of Terrorism (1999) entered into force on 6 December 2002.

58 The AU Convention on Preventing and Combating Corruption (2003) entered into force on 5 August 2006.

59 The Protocol on Mutual Legal Assistance in Criminal Matters (2002) entered into force on 1 March 2007. The Protocol on Extradition (2002) entered into force on 1 September 2006.

60 The ECOWAS Convention on Extradition (1994) entered into force on 8 December 2005.

international crimes retroactively under domestic law – so long as they constituted an offence under international law at the time of their commission.[61] Similarly, it is a well-accepted proposition that statutes of limitation do not apply where international crimes are concerned.[62] Some African states have even legislated to prohibit the extradition of their citizens where they are to be prosecuted for international crimes. For example, the Sudanese Criminal Procedure Act 1991 prohibits anyone in Sudan from assisting in the extradition of any Sudanese person for the prosecution of war crimes, crimes against humanity and genocide.[63] However, one should not lose sight of the fact that this is a particularly extreme example that was in response to moves by the ICC to indict senior Sudanese officials for crimes that took place in the Darfur region of that country.

The domestic legislation of African states is also lacking in other areas with inevitable impacts on the exercise of universal jurisdiction. Without national legislation, domestic authorities have no framework to guide investigations and prosecutions on the basis of universal jurisdiction. National legislation is also necessary to give concrete content to universal jurisdiction principles. While 37 African states have enacted legislation endowing their courts and authorities with universal jurisdiction over one or more of the crimes of genocide, war crimes, crimes against humanity, and torture, many of these states have failed to properly define one or more of these crimes under national law. Alternatively, many existing definitions of international crimes under domestic law do not align with the accepted definitions under international law.[64] Where persons are prosecuted under such laws, legitimate *nullum crimen sine lege* concerns can be raised. At present, South Africa's ICC Act is one of the few examples of domestic legislation in Africa that adequately criminalises and defines international crimes at the domestic level.[65]

As far as building technical expertise is concerned, there is a multitude of NGOs that are willing and able to assist states to build their capacity to investigate, prosecute, and manage international crimes trials. There is no doubt that successful investigation and prosecution of international crimes requires a high degree of organisation and expertise. Experiences in Europe have shown that the setting up of specialised units within the police and prosecution

---

61 See Article 15(2) of the International Covenant on Civil and Political Rights (1966).

62 See Kok 2007, pp. 380–382. The author similarly concludes that it is now also a general principle of international law as well a general principle of law common to the major legal systems of the world.

63 Amendment to the Criminal Procedure Act adopted in the Sudanese National Assembly on 20 May 2009 and signed into law on 9 July 2009.

64 See Amnesty International, 'Universal Jurisdiction: A Preliminary Survey of Legislation Around the World – 2012 Update', 9 October 2012, p. 22 *et seq.*, available at: https://www.amnesty.org/download/Documents/24000/ior530192012en.pdf (accessed 24 January 2016).

65 For other African states with domestic legislation implementing the Rome Statute, see Kemp 2014, pp. 61–77.

authorities of a state to handle serious international crimes is central to the successful exercise of universal jurisdiction.[66] Moreover, national prosecutors are unlikely to be familiar with the legal framework within which international crimes sit, as well as strategies for managing the immense volume of evidence, witness testimony, expert witness statements, and relevant documents that international criminal cases inevitably entail. In this respect, NGOs, along with other international organisations and states with experience in such matters, can assist African national authorities to set up specialised units, provide training and other assistance to law enforcement officials, prosecutors, defence counsel, investigators and judges, and assist in developing capacity to ensure the protection of victims and witnesses. This will help to avoid cases being pursued but failing later in the judicial process due to weaknesses in the evidence and threats to witnesses and victims.

African states will also have to find ways to secure funding for international criminal prosecutions on the basis of universal jurisdiction. States conducting international criminal trials of their own nationals over crimes committed on their own territory struggle to fund such proceedings. However, the problem is exacerbated for states seeking to exercise universal jurisdiction. Proper funding needs to be secured or made available without jeopardising the effectiveness and impartiality of the judicial process. In particular, any international funding must avoid the perception of political manipulation by interested international actors.

7. CONCLUSION: A FUTURE FOR UNIVERSAL JURISDICTION IN AFRICA?

The Protocol has created a regional African court with jurisdiction over both international and transnational crimes. But this court, like the ICC, is a court of last resort. Under the principle of complementarity, the primary responsibility still rests with African states to investigate and prosecute atrocities committed in Africa. However, for a multitude of reasons, African states often fail to investigate and prosecute crimes committed within their borders. In such situations, other African states should consider exercising their universal jurisdiction over these

66 See Human Rights Watch, *The Long Arm of Justice: Lessons from Specialized War Crimes Units in France, Germany, and the Netherlands*, September 2014, available at: https://www.hrw.org/sites/default/files/reports/IJ0914_ForUpload.pdf (accessed 24 January 2016). Some African countries have already set up specialised units for the investigation and prosecution of international crimes. For example, in 2003, South Africa created a specialised unit within the NPA for, *inter alia*, the prosecution of international crimes: the Priority Crimes Litigation Unit. Since 2008, Uganda's High Court has had a specialised division – the International Crimes Division – dedicated to the prosecution of international crimes. See Human Rights Watch, *Justice for Serious Crimes before National Courts: Uganda's International Crimes Division*, January 2012, available at: https://www.hrw.org/sites/default/files/reports/uganda0112ForUpload_0.pdf (accessed 24 January 2016).

crimes as a trustee for Africa as whole, not to mention the entire international community. This would help minimise the problems that affect trials taking place far away from the site of the crime(s) and give Africans the chance to take ownership over justice processes that affect them. While universal jurisdiction is unlikely to bring the bulk of perpetrators of international crimes committed in Africa to justice, it can form part of the multi-layered system of international criminal justice that is developing on the continent. At the end of the day, it is in Africa's best interest for Africans themselves to address international crimes committed on their continent.

BIBLIOGRAPHY

BOOKS AND JOURNAL ARTICLES

Babington-Ashaye 2015

Babington-Ashaye, A., 'International Crimes, Immunities and the Protocol on Amendments to the Protocol of the Merged African Court: Some Observations', in Jalloh, C.C., and Elias, O. (eds.), 'Shielding Humanity: Essays in International Law in Honour of Judge Abdul G. Koroma', Brill Nijhoff, 2015.

Batohi 2014

Batohi, S., 'Africa and the International Criminal Court: A Prosecutor's perspective', in Werle, G., Fernandez. L. and Vormbaum, M. (eds.), 'Africa and the International Criminal Court', T.M.C. Asser Press/Springer, 2014.

Brody 2015

Brody, R., 'Bringing a Dictator to Justice: The Case of Hissène Habré', 13(2) Journal of International Criminal Justice, 2015, pp. 209–217.

Cimiotta 2015

Cimiotta, E., 'The First Steps of the Extraordinary African Chambers: A New Mixed Criminal Tribunal?', 13(1) Journal of International Criminal Justice, 2015, pp. 177–197.

De Wet 2015

De Wet, E., 'The Implications of President Al-Bashir's Visit to South Africa for International and Domestic Law', 13(5) Journal of International Criminal Justice, 2015, pp. 1049–1071.

Du Plessis 2007

Du Plessis, M., 'South Africa's Implementation of the ICC Statute: An African Example', 5(2) Journal of International Criminal Justice, 2007, pp. 460–479.

Hall, Nsereko and Ventura 2016

Hall, C.K., Nsereko, D.D.N. and Ventura, M.J., 'Article 19: Challenges to the Jurisdiction of the Court or the Admissibility of a Case', in Triffterer, O. and Ambos, K. (eds.), 'The Rome Statute of the International Criminal Court: A Commentary', 3rd ed., C.H. Beck/Hart Publishing/Nomos, 2016.

Jeßberger 2014
Jeßberger, F., '"On behalf of Africa": Toward the Regionalization of Universal Jurisdiction', in Werle, G., Fernandez, L. and Vormbaum, M. (eds.), 'Africa and the International Criminal Court', T.M.C. Asser Press/Springer, 2014.

Jeßberger 2009
Jessberger, F., 'Universal Jurisdiction', in Cassese, A. (ed.), 'The Oxford Companion to International Criminal Justice', Oxford University Press, 2009.

Kemp 2014
Kemp, G., 'The Implementation of the Rome Statute in Africa', in Werle, G., Fernandez. L. and Vormbaum, M. (eds.), 'Africa and the International Criminal Court', T.M.C. Asser Press/Springer, 2014.

Kok 2007
Kok, R.A., 'Statutory Limitations in International Criminal Law', T.M.C. Asser Press, 2007.

Murithi 2014
Murithi, T., 'Between Political Justice and Judicial Politics: Charting a Way Forward for the African Union and the International Criminal Court', in Werle, G., Fernandez, L. and Vormbaum, M. (eds.), 'Africa and the International Criminal Court', T.M.C. Asser Press/Springer, 2014.

Reydams 2003
Reydams, L., 'Belgium's First Application of Universal Jurisdiction: The *Butare Four* Case', 1(2) Journal of International Criminal Justice, 2003, pp. 428–436.

Schabas 2010
Schabas, W.A., 'Article 17: Issues of Admissibility / Questions relatives à la recevabilité', in 'The International Criminal Court: A Commentary on the Rome Statute', Oxford University Press, 2010.

Tladi 2015
Tladi, D., 'The Duty on South Africa to Arrest and Surrender President Al-Bashir under South African and International Law: A Perspective from International Law', 13(5) Journal of International Criminal Justice, 2015, pp. 1027–1047.

Tladi 2015
Tladi, D., 'The Immunity Provision in the AU Amendment Protocol: Separating the (Doctrinal) Wheat from the (Normative) Chaff', 13(1) Journal of International Criminal Justice, 2015, pp. 3–17.

Ventura 2015
Ventura, M.J., 'Escape from Johannesburg? Sudanese President Omar Al-Bashir Visits South Africa and the Implicit Removal of Head of State Immunity by the UN Security Council in light of Al-Jedda', 13(5) Journal of International Criminal Justice, 2015, pp. 995–1025.

Ventura 2015
Ventura, M.J., 'The Duty to Investigate Zimbabwe Crimes Against Humanity (Torture) Allegations: The Constitutional Court of South Africa Speaks on Universal Jurisdiction and the ICC Act', 13(4) Journal of International Criminal Justice, 2015, pp. 861–889.

JURISPRUDENCE

Constitutional Court of South Africa 2014
SACC, National Commissioner of the South African Police Service v. Southern Africa Human Rights Litigation Centre and Another, CCT 02/14, ZACC 30, 30 October 2014.

Cour d'appel de Dakar 2000
Cour d'appel de Dakar, Guengueng and Others v. Habré, Arrêt No. 135, 4 July 2000.

Cour d'assises de Bruxelles 2005
Cour d'assises de Bruxelles, Nzabonimana and Ndashyikirwa, 29 June 2005.

Cour d'assises de Bruxelles 2001
Cour d'assises de Bruxelles, Higaniro et al., 8 June 2001.

Cour d'assises du Gard (France) 2005
Cour d'assises du Gard (France), 1 July 2005.

Cour de cassation de Belgique 2003
Cour de cassation de Belgique, Case No. P. 02.1139.F/1, 12 February 2003.

Cour de cassation du Sénégal 2001
Cour de cassation du Sénégal, Guengueng and Others v. Habré, Arrêt No. 14, 20 March 2001.

Court of Appeal of Quebec 2014
Court of Appeal of Quebec, Munyaneza v. The Queen, 2014 QCCA 906, 7 May 2014.

ECtHR 2009
ECtHR, Ould Dah v. France, Application no. 13113/03, 17 March 2009.

Extraordinary African Chambers 2015
Extraordinary African Chambers, Ordonnance de non-lieu partiel, de mise en accusation et de renvoi devant la Chambre africaine extraordinaire d'assises, Case No. 01/13, 13 February 2015.

Federal Court of Justice of Germany 2015
Federal Court of Justice of Germany (Bundesgerichtshof), Case No. 3 StR 575/14, 21 May 2015.

Higher Regional Court of Frankfurt 2015
Higher Regional Court of Frankfurt (Oberlandesgericht Frankfurt an Main), Case No. 4-3 StE 4/10-4-1/15, 29 December 2015.

Higher Regional Court of Frankfurt 2014
Higher Regional Court of Frankfurt (Oberlandesgericht Frankfurt am Main), Case No. 5-3 StE 4/10-4-3/10, 18 February 2014.

Higher Regional Court of Stuttgart 2015
Higher Regional Court of Stuttgart (Oberlandesgericht Stuttgart), Case No. 5-3 StE 6/10, 28 September 2015.

ICC 2010
ICC, Prosecutor v. Al-Bashir, ICC-02/05-01/09-95, 12 July 2010.

ICC 2009
ICC, Prosecutor v. Al-Bashir, ICC-02/05-01/09-1, 4 March 2009.

ICC 2005
ICC, Situation in Uganda, Decision on the Prosecutor's Application for Warrants of Arrest under Article 58, ICC-02/04-01/05-1-US-Exp, 8 July 2005.

ICC 2001
ICC, Prosecutor v. Muthaura et al., ICC-01/09-02/11-01, 8 March 2001.
ICC 2001
ICC, Prosecutor v. Ruto et al., ICC-01/09-01/11-01, 8 March 2001.
ICJ 2012
ICJ, Questions Concerning the Obligation to Prosecute or Extradite (Belgium v. Senegal), Judgment, 20 July 2012.
ICJ 2008
ICJ, Case Concerning Certain Questions of Mutual Assistance in Criminal Matters (Djibouti v. France), Judgment, 4 June 2008.
ICJ 2002
ICJ, Case Concerning the Arrest Warrant of 11 April 2000 (Democratic Republic of the Congo v. Belgium), Judgment, 14 February 2002.
North Gauteng High Court 2012
NGHC, Rakoto and Others v. Head: Directorate for Priority Crimes Investigation and Others, ZAGPPHC 281, 19 November 2012.
Superior Court of Quebec 2009
Superior Court of Quebec, The Queen v. Munyaneza, 2009 QCCS 2201, 22 May 2009.

TREATIES, LEGISLATION AND AGREEMENTS

African Union Convention on Preventing and Combating Corruption, 1 July 2003.
African Union Model National Law on Universal Jurisdiction Over International Crimes, EX.CL/731(XXI)c, July 2012.
AU, Decision on Africa's Relationship with the International Criminal Court (ICC), Ext/Assembly/AU/Dec.1(Oct. 2013), 12 October 2013.
ECOWAS, Convention A/P1/8/94 on Extradition, 6 August 1994.
International Covenant on Civil and Political Rights, GA Res. 2200A (XXI), 16 December 1966.
OAU Convention on the Prevention and Combating of Terrorism, 14 July 1999.
Protocol on Amendments to the Protocol on the Statute of the African Court of Justice and Human Rights (Malabo Protocol), 27 June 2014.
Rome Statute of the International Criminal Court, 2187 UNTS 90/37, 17 July 1998.
SADC, Protocol on Extradition, 3 October 2002.
SADC, Protocol on Mutual Legal Assistance in Criminal Matters, 3 October 2002.
Sudan, Criminal Procedure Act 1991 (as amended on 20 May 2009).

OTHERS

Akande, D., 'The African Union, the ICC and Universal Jurisdiction: Some Recent Developments', EJIL: Talk! Blog, 29 August 2012.
Amnesty International, 'Universal Jurisdiction: A Preliminary Survey Of Legislation Around The World – 2012 Update', 9 October 2012.
AU, List of OAU/AU Treaties, Conventions, Protocols & Charters.

BBC, 'African Union accuses ICC of 'hunting' Africans', 27 May 2013.
Council of the EU, 'AU-EU Expert Report on the Principle of Universal Jurisdiction', Doc No. 8672/1/09 Rev. 1, 16 April 2009.
Human Rights Watch, 'Justice for Serious Crimes before National Courts: Uganda's International Crimes Division', January 2012.
Human Rights Watch, 'The Long Arm of Justice: Lessons from Specialized War Crimes Units in France, Germany, and the Netherlands', September 2014.
International Federation for Human Rights (FIDH), 'The Disappeared of the Beach Case'.
International Federation for Human Rights (FIDH), 'Universal Jurisdiction Annual Review 2015: Make Way for Justice', 2015.
Journalists for Justice, 'Benin, Guinea Bissau, Kenya and Mauritania sign the International Crimes Protocol', 25 March 2015.
Mail and Guardian, 'Ex-president's mysterious exit', 24 October 2014.
Plessis, M., Maluwa, T. and O'Reilly, A., 'Africa and the International Criminal Court', Chatham House, July 2013.
Times Live, 'NPA Investigating Ravalomanana for crimes against humanity', 5 August 2012.

PUNISHMENT AS PREVENTION?
The International Criminal Court and the Prevention of International Crimes

Kjell Follingstad Anderson

1. INTRODUCTION

The International Criminal Court, like all international criminal courts and tribunals, was created with a view to the prevention of international crimes. Yet, as a judicial mechanism, the court is designed with the core and sole purpose of punishing international crimes through the process of investigation, trial, and, in cases of guilt, detention. The court operates under the assumption that the punishment of crimes will itself lead to prevention. Indeed, this belief, which is near-orthodoxy among international lawyers and jurists, is enshrined in the preamble of the Rome Statute, which states that the signatories are 'determined to put an end to impunity for the perpetrators of these crimes and thus to contribute to the prevention of such crimes'.

In order for the court to effectively address this laudable goal it is important to critically assess the potential impact of the court in preventing international crimes. This chapter will attempt to do so from a criminological, socio-legal perspective. It will draw from the author's extensive research on the causes of genocide and crimes against humanity, particularly in terms of the moral context and its effect on perpetrator motivation.[1] This chapter is intended to be forward-looking and prescriptive, rather than focusing entirely on the past record of the court.

The analysis of the prevention of international crimes involves several aspects. Firstly, we must consider the nature of international crimes and the international criminal justice system. What makes international crimes distinct from domestic crimes? How is the international criminal justice system distinct

---

1 This research was largely conducted for my PhD thesis on the criminology of genocide. It involved interviews with 138 perpetrators and victims of international crimes in Rwanda, Burundi, Uganda, Bosnia, India, Bangladesh, and Cambodia. It is currently being converted into a book manuscript to be published under the title *Killing Without Consequence*.

from domestic criminal justice systems? Secondly, this chapter will draw from criminological theory to theorise the prevention of international crimes. Could the ICC stop international crimes while they are still occurring or prevent the future commission of crimes through timely prosecutions? Does the ICC directly or indirectly deter perpetrators? Does it trigger other forms of accountability and policy responses through its complementarity regime and/or its moral condemnation of named perpetrators? Could it undermine the conditions that contribute to criminal behaviour, such as an enabling moral context and armed conflict?

Each of these questions will be considered in reference to theoretical insights, as well as the record of the ICC in the decade since its inception. In the absence of detailed empirical studies this chapter will advance new theoretical frameworks for the analysis of the prevention of international crimes. It will also adduce that, firstly, the ICC has a mixed record with regards to its impact on the commission of mass atrocities, and secondly, that the prevention of international crimes requires a far more thoughtful and systematic approach than is currently the case.

2. INTERNATIONAL CRIMES AND INTERNATIONAL CRIMINAL JUSTICE

Crime prevention strategies at the domestic level have only limited applicability. This is because international crimes differ significantly from domestic crimes in terms of their causes, context, and complexity; moreover, international criminal justice is also far more politicised and decentralised than domestic systems.

International crimes are generally *political crimes*; they are committed pursuant to policy objectives. These policies may be directly communicated through orders and policy statements or they may be implicitly understood as a logical extension of policy objectives (I am speaking here of something less like a *dolus eventualis,* the foreseeable consequences of an act, and more like what the historian Ian Kershaw referred to as 'working towards the Fuhrer', i.e. acting in anticipation and interpretation of policy demands).[2] The sanctioning of criminal acts may come from *de jure* or *de facto* authorities. This does not mean that individuals never act in isolation to commit international crimes, rather that crimes against humanity and genocide cannot be committed without, at least, acquiescence from those exercising effective control in the area where the crime takes place.

We can also draw a distinction here between war crimes, on the one hand, and crimes against humanity and genocide on the other. War crimes (such as the murder of a single prisoner of war) may occur as a result of indiscipline, whereas

2 Kershaw 1999.

genocide and crimes against humanity require a higher level of concerted action, thus they are *crimes of conformity*.[3]

The political nature of international crimes does not mean that collective intent and motive (the group objective and rationale for seeking that objective) are synonymous with individual intent and motive. Individual intent and motive is still multivariate. It is possible, in fact quite normal, to act in furtherance of international crimes for highly personalised reasons. As my own research has shown, individuals may commit acts of genocide for motivations as mundane as a desire to steal their neighbour's tin roof.[4] Although these individuals may not possess genocidal intent (as classically conceived), they are still knowingly acting in furtherance of the crime of genocide. This reality predicates a move from intent-based approaches to international crimes, to knowledge-based approaches.

As crimes of conformity, genocide and crimes against humanity are generally *state crimes*. In other words, they are committed by the state, with the encouragement of the state, or with the acquiescence of the state. Genocide and crimes against humanity require a level of systematic design – they cannot be the simple aggregate of hundreds or thousands of wrongful acts. What binds these perpetrators together is the expressed or implied intent of state authorities. Propaganda is one of the central vectors of this enabling moral context. Of course, genocide and crimes against humanity may also be committed by state-like authorities, exercising effective control over a given area.

They are also *mass crimes* with a massive number of perpetrators and a massive number of victims. Punishment and prevention efforts must address this mass nature of genocide and crimes against humanity by focusing not only on individual perpetrators but also on institutional structures and cultures of violence. This would also dictate that prevention efforts focusing only on individual criminal liability will fail to adequately address causal factors.

The importance of groups in the commission of international crimes is also evinced in the prosecution of international crimes through the prosecution of groups (i.e. the joint criminal enterprise mode of liability and co-perpetration, in the case of the ICC), as well as the joinder of similar cases.[5] For example, at the International Criminal Tribunal for Rwanda (ICTR) there have been two 'military trials', a 'media trial', and an 'MRND trial' (*Mouvement républicain national pour la démocratie et le development),* while in the post-Nuremberg Control Council Number Ten trials there were Krupp, I.G. Farben, High Command, *Einsatzgrüppen*, and RuSHA (*Rasse- und Siedlungshauptamt- Schutzstaffel*) cases, and at the 'Khmer Rouge Tribunal' in Cambodia there is a 'government' case. The Nuremberg judgment went so far as to declare entire organisations as

---

3 Humphreys and Weinstein 2006, p. 433.

4 Anderson, *The Dehumanisation Dynamic: A Criminology of Genocide*, PhD thesis, Galway, Ireland: National University of Ireland, 2011.

5 Balint 2008, p. 318.

'criminal' such as the Nazi party leadership, Gestapo, and *Schutzstaffel* (SS). The mass nature of the perpetration of crimes against humanity and genocide has also informed the Elements of Crimes of the ICC, which declares that genocide must occur within a 'pattern of similar attacks' and that crimes against humanity must be pursuant to a 'state or organizational policy.'

The nature of genocide and crimes against humanity (and often war crimes) as mass crimes, political crimes, crimes of conformity, and state crimes means that, where they occur, they are also positively normative. In other words, in societies where the crime of genocide is committed, genocide is not only accepted but actually encouraged. These *criminogenic* (crime-producing) states create an enabling moral context whereby previous (universal) moral rules, such as the prohibition on murder, are lifted or reframed in specific instances. In such societies entire groups effectively become criminalised and violence against these groups is no longer criminal. Rather, violence becomes an imperative in the name of individual and collective self-defence.

Indeed the individual and collective become merged among both perpetrator and victim populations as victims become abstracted and, ceasing to be individuals, every potential victim is a symbolically attractive target through the mere fact of their common membership in the targeted group. This objectification of the victims is accompanied by a self-objectification on the part of perpetrators who come to view themselves as the object of greater external forces. Such self-objectification ties individual perpetrators to the group and also aids perpetrators in reframing their behaviour so that perpetration is either imperative or understandable.[6]

Although individual acts of ordinary murder and rape may occur within permissive subcultures, they lack the powerful influence of legitimate authorities, who are often physically or symbolically present at the scene of international crimes. Any preventive strategies for international crimes must address these collective, normative dimensions. Moreover, they must address the lack of guardianship for victims of international crimes – where authorities normally responsible for the prevention and punishment of crime are themselves acting as perpetrators.

This brings us to the nature of the international criminal justice system. In spite of the proliferation of international criminal courts and tribunals in recent years – the ICTR, the International Criminal Tribunal for the former Yugoslavia (ICTY), the Special Court for Sierra Leone, the East Timor Special Panel for Serious Crimes, the ICC, etc. – it is questionable whether international criminal justice institutions, when viewed as a whole, constitute a system. The word 'system' implies a level of coherence, integration, and universality which may not entirely characterise international criminal justice efforts to date. This is not to dismiss

---

6 For further discussion of these concepts please see my forthcoming book *Killing Without Consequence*.

the tremendous strides made, rather we must recognise the lack of coherence (in terms of sentencing, for example), integration (in terms of coordination between the courts), and universality (in terms of universal coverage).

Focusing on this issue of universality, although the ICC now has 123 member states, there are still many states which are not members; in fact, personal jurisdiction does not yet cover a majority of the world's population. Moreover, limited prosecutorial resources force the court to only focus on the gravest situations and a very limited subset of cases within these situation countries. For example, in the Central African Republic, a situation of grave and systematic *ongoing* human rights abuses, only one arrest warrant has been issued to date. The investiture of deferral and referral powers in the UN Security Council also creates a system where the court has effective blind spots. The lack of ICC action in response to the grave human rights violations in Syria is indicative of several of these problems – Syria is not a party to the Rome Statue, so the court lacks jurisdiction, and the countries comprising the UN Security Council, particularly Russia, refuse to refer the situation in Syria due to their own national interests.

Of course the ICC was never intended to be a universal trier of international crimes. Rather the system of complementarity was devised so as to ensure that most international crimes should be tried at the national level. Complementarity should also function as a bridge between national and international trials for international crimes; where states are willing and able to prosecute international crimes domestically, the court does not need to expend its resources to prosecute at the international level. Moreover, one could argue that the *indigenisation* of such trials brings them closer to relevant populations, strengthening their impact. Complementarity may also be effective in encouraging the domestication of international criminal law – a prospect which will be examined below in greater detail.

Complementarity should function as the linchpin of the international criminal justice system, ensuring universal coverage for the Rome Statute crimes, and, the prosecution of lower-level perpetrators in situation countries. Yet domestic prosecutions for international crimes remain relatively rare, with recent examples (and mixed success) in countries such as Canada, The Netherlands, Bosnia, Norway, Colombia, Finland, Rwanda, the Democratic Republic of Congo, and Uganda. This scarcity of domestic prosecutions, combined with an ever-increasing number of situations and preliminary investigations before the ICC, have created a situation of ongoing and massive capacity and impunity gaps. It is far too soon to say that complementarity has failed, but it is clear that much greater emphasis needs to be placed on encouraging and supporting the prosecution of international crimes at the domestic level.

The international criminal justice system is effectively a system of pluralistic judicial and enforcement power. There are many different authorities responsible for the investigation and prosecution of international crimes. These include international courts, national governments (encompassing the legislative, judicial, and executive branches of government), the UN, regional organisations, and even non-government organisations (though they lack formal powers, their investigations often complement official efforts). Moreover, state parties and non-state parties alike are called upon to cooperate with the functioning of the ICC in myriad ways such as facilitating access to indictees, witnesses, evidence, and the resettlement of acquitted accused. Although the court has received a great deal of cooperation from diverse stakeholders, situations of non-cooperation (such as the failure to execute the arrest warrant for President Bashir of Sudan) remain its Achilles heel.

Domestic criminal justice systems also experience impunity and political influence, yet domestic systems do not face the sheer level of complexity that the ICC does in its day-to-day functioning. It possesses no police force, no real coercive power (or at least none that is not reliant on the compliance of states), and limited control over post-trial issues such as witness protection. At the policy and complementarity level the ICC is, by necessity, a political actor. In this sense, it *is* politicised. The execution of the court's mandate is partly a function of political negotiations, considerations, and processes. As much as proponents of the court would love for it to operate at a purely functional level it exists within a political reality that dictates otherwise. Ultimately this makes the court far less powerful than domestic systems in terms of its ability to execute its mandate. Preventive strategies must also take account of these limitations.

3. THE PREVENTION OF INTERNATIONAL CRIMES

3.1. INTRODUCTION

The prevention of international crimes has received relatively little attention. Much of what has been written thus far about prevention constitutes mere platitudes about the importance of prevention, without the enactment of real policy frameworks for prevention. While it is beyond the scope of this chapter to reach empirical findings on the preventive impact of the ICC, it is hoped that the theoretical framework contained in the following pages can form a basis for further critical discussion and research.

Preventive tools for international crimes fall into several categories. Firstly, we can distinguish between *direct prevention* (preventive efforts which have the potential to directly impact perpetrators) and *indirect prevention* (preventive strategies which may have distal effects, i.e. they impact other actors, who then have the capability of impacting perpetrators). Most focus has been on the potential (but unproven) directly preventive effects of the court, especially the notion of deterrence. Yet, given the limitations in scope and resources inherent in the structure of the ICC, it may be the indirect effects which are the most important. These indirect effects give the court the potential to leverage its impact through third parties.

In terms of direct effects there are two primary possibilities (which I will discuss in greater detail below): firstly *deterrence*, the notion that by holding perpetrators accountable for violations of international criminal law this will prevent these perpetrators, and the public as a whole, from perpetrating international crimes. The second possibility is that international criminal law can address *underlying causes of criminal behaviour*, such as the development of criminal norms, impunity (the lack of external controls), and armed conflict.

In order to prevent international crimes, we must first have a clear understanding of perpetration. The perpetration of international crimes is highly socially situated.[7] Very few perpetrators are pathological; rather most perpetrators kill out of a reluctance to breach social obligations, and/or a fear of confronting the state. These perpetrators live within a moral context which permits or encourages criminal behaviour. Perpetrators use a variety of rationalisations in order to recharacterise their behaviour as being consistent with old (universal) moral rules such as the prohibition on unjust killing. For example, the victim is recast as being the perpetrator (a threat), the perpetrator claims that they had no power to stop the killing, or the perpetrator claims to be acting out of obedience. Effectively perpetrators self-objectify, making themselves the object of external powers, just as they objectify the victims. Perpetrators react to the changed moral context in states committing mass atrocities through cognitive adaptation, in order to avoid the cognitive dissonance which may result from actions inconsistent with beliefs and self-image. It is likely that many of these features of the perpetration of international crimes are also present in domestic criminality yet it is the exercise of state power which makes international crimes especially unique, and which makes it especially difficult for individuals to resist social pressures, particularly in the face of collective mobilisation on a massive scale.

Of course, not all perpetrators are reluctant – there are also the true believers, the ideologues, who will violently target others out of a belief in the fundamental righteousness of their cause, as well as sadists, who will commit violence in order to satisfy a need for control. However, through what I have labelled the *sadistic* shift, many perpetrators that cannot be clinically diagnosed as sadists will come to behave sadistically in situations of omnipotent power over the victims and a complete lack of accountability.[8] So what do these findings mean for preventive strategies? Can international crimes be deterred?

---

7 Anderson 2011, p. 133.

8 *Ibid*, p. 123.

3.2. DETERRENCE AND THE INTERNATIONAL CRIMINAL COURT

The promise of deterrence theory is that criminal sanctions do more than just punish serious deviant acts – they also dissuade potential future offenders by increasing the risk and decreasing the rewards of criminal behaviour. This notion is frequently voiced by actors in international criminal justice, particularly in sentencing hearings. When asked whether the ICC could deter international crimes, Ocampo responded:

> The legal advisor of NATO (North Atlantic Treaty Organisation), the most important military organisation, told me that they told their staff to imagine: in 15 years you are retired as a two-star general, on the beach with your family. Suddenly you're surrounded by policemen who handcuff you and you go to the ICC and the evidence is documentation from NATO. You have to be aware that if you commit crimes, you could be prosecuted. So that's it. Armies all over the world are adjusting to this.[9]

Likewise, in the Kambanda judgement at the ICTR, the court argued that 'it is clear that the penalties imposed on accused persons found guilty by the Tribunal must be directed, on the one hand, at retribution, and, over and above that, on the other hand at deterrence.'[10] The Lubanga Sentencing Judgement at the ICC also makes mention of the importance of deterrence in the Rome Statute but fails to further discuss how sentencing will affect deterrence.

Classical criminologist Césare Beccaria argued that in order for deterrence to be effective there must be a certainty of swift and appropriate punishment.[11] Severe punishment will not offer a strong deterrent effect if the criminal believes that impunity is a significant possibility. Unfortunately, in the international criminal law context impunity still appears to be likely. This is especially true when one considers the lack of true supranational authority in the international system (with the possible exception of the UN Security Council). Furthermore, as state crimes, perpetrators of genocide and crimes against humanity are acting at the behest of the state, thus they are protected by state power. The inconsistency of punishment would appear to undermine the effectiveness of deterrence.

This notion of general deterrence (to deter all potential criminals in society) can be contrasted with *specific deterrence*, which seeks to deter specific individual criminals. A central element of specific deterrence is incapacitation – making it impossible for criminals to commit crimes by imprisoning them. It is held that

9 Smith, 'Interview: Luis Moreno-Ocampo, ICC Prosecutor', *The Africa Report*, 21 September 2009, p. 42. Quoted in Tiemessen 2014.

10 ICTR, *Prosecutor v. Jean Kambanda*, ICTR-97-23-S, Trial Chamber Judgement, 4 September 1998, para. 28.

11 Lanier and Henry 2004, p. 76.

by isolating certain individuals, crime becomes less likely and society as a whole is safer.[12] In the case of the ICC there is some possibility that the mere issue of arrest warrants has the deterrent effect of restricting the movement of leaders likely to commit international crimes, although the Bashir case calls this into question. Specific deterrence may also include such measures as restrictions and conditions on convicted perpetrators after their release.

General deterrence is predicated on three notions: that perpetrators are rational actors, that the rewards available to perpetrators are measureable in order to design punishments that counteract this gain, and finally that perpetrators understand and are aware of potential risks. Criminogenic societies are often closed systems so within these societies there is an internal rationalising effect to criminal acts, even if these acts may be considered to be irrational in an 'ordinary' context. Perpetrators of international crimes are also likely less entrepreneurial than perpetrators of ordinary crimes – many are serving a particular role within a larger, legitimised (state-directed) joint criminal enterprise. Deterrence in the context of international crimes is also problematic because the perpetrators are usually sheltered within a state which is itself committing international crimes. Furthermore, general deterrence theory does not account for individual differences in personality and motivation.

Criminological research shows that sanctions do have the power to deter criminal conduct, but only under certain circumstances. Sanctions are effective where individuals are closely bonded to the broader social community, where they perceive the system as fair and legitimate, and where they feel shame at having committed a wrongful act.[13] Thus, the effectiveness of deterrence is differential and dependent on the individual and on their relationship to broader society. Lawrence Sherman argues that, when the converse is true, that sanctions may actually contribute to criminal behaviour, i.e. that deterrence will backfire.[14] According to this 'defiance theory' defiance occurs where the offender considers the sanction unfair, they are weakly bonded to the community, they consider the offence to have arisen from stigmatisation rather than unlawful behaviour, and they do not feel or acknowledge any shame from the criminal act.[15] Unfortunately many of these criteria are met in the application of international criminal law, perhaps indicating that the ICC might have a weak deterrent effect.

The first element, the perceived unfairness of the sanction could be either objective (i.e. the judicial system is itself unfair), or subjective (police and court officials have behaved disrespectfully towards the accused).[16] Both of

12 *Ibid*, p. 86.

13 Sherman 1993, p. 448.

14 *Ibid*, p. 448.

15 *Ibid*, p. 460. Other relevant individual differences include such factors as emotional/pharmacological arousal and self-control. See Piquero et al., 2011.

16 Sherman 1993, p. 461.

these criteria are relevant at the ICC. The selectivity of the court – as dictated by its mandate, limited resources, and prosecutorial strategy – can contribute to notions of selective justice, thus fundamental unfairness. In terms of the ICC we can distinguish between unfairness on the *policy* level (i.e. case and situation section at the pre-trial and preliminary investigation stages), *structural* level (unfair elements embedded in the very structure of the court, i.e. the Rome Statute, such as non-state parties exercising a degree of control over the court in the UN Security Council under Articles 13(b) and 16), and, finally, *procedural* unfairness. Each of these elements of potential unfairness decreases the legitimacy of the court as an institution, which, by implication, lessens its deterrent force.

There are ways to address this impression of unfairness. Firstly, procedural unfairness, which will always be an issue at any court, must be combated by ensuring that the rights of the accused are fully respected. This means that the ICC's success cannot be measured by states parties solely on the basis of convictions.

In contrast, overcoming structural unfairness is a near impossibility. As a treaty-based court the ICC will always be reliant on the consent of states in order to exercise its jurisdiction and these states may refuse the exercise of jurisdiction on the basis of other interests. The court's inability to address situations like Syria is a frequent critique of its work. Universal ratification, as well as the strengthening of prosecutions at the national level, both through the complementarity regime as well as prosecutions by non-state parties, is the best way to reduce this element of structural unfairness. It is also wise to bear in mind the limitations inherent in the nature of the court.

Finally, policy unfairness, in terms of the selection of cases and situations, is also bound to be an ongoing issue. In particular, the 'sufficient gravity' requirement for admissibility under Article 17 of the statute, and the Article 53 provision allowing the prosecutor not to proceed with an investigation if to do so would not serve the 'interests of justice', introduce an element of variability into case selection at the court.[17] These provisions are necessary to ensure the court only prosecutes the most serious cases, leaving less serious cases to national authorities, also that it has flexibility to consider non-juridical factors. The Office of the Prosecutor should do its utmost to achieve a consistent and transparent policy with regard to case selection. This means, if necessary, not being afraid to prosecute government officials in cases of self-referrals. Greater clarity may also come from decisions of the Pre-Trial Chamber once the court hears more cases.

Sherman also argues that defiance may be manifested as collective retaliation.[18] If systems are deemed to be unfair on the collective level, such as

---

17 For further information see the *Policy Paper on the Interests of Justice* of the Office of the Prosecutor (2007).

18 Sherman 1993, p. 467.

where there is systemic discrimination or oppression, then defiance can occur on the collective level; in other words, individuals will come to see a system as unworthy of compliance on the basis of their membership in an identifiable group facing perceived discrimination. In times of increased conflict and polarisation, there is a tendency towards a narrowing of awareness where one vector of identity becomes all important. This collective retaliation can occur against another collectivity, whether or not that collectivity is the source of the unfairness in question. If the ICC is active in a particular conflict zone, and its intervention is seen as unfair or one-sided, this may actually contribute to perceived unfairness and to the desire to perpetrate crimes as an act of equalisation or even self-defence.

The other elements which can generate defiance (weak bonding and lack of shame) are also all inherent in the kinds of cases before the ICC. As previously argued, genocide and crimes against humanity (and sometimes war crimes) are crimes of conformity committed pursuant to the political goals of criminogenic states. Within these states, perpetrators will face conflicting internal and external messages as to rightful behaviour. If perpetrators are not clearly aware that behaviour is wrongful how can they be deterred? However, as mass crimes, most perpetrators of genocide and crimes against humanity are not pathological, rather they are unlikely offenders. This increases the prospect that deterrence could have a strong preventive effect.[19]

The case of Kenya is informative. In Kenya the ICC indicted several Kenyans in relation to the 2007–2008 election violence. One would expect that such charges would isolate the indictees, doing serious damage to their political reputation in the process; yet the 2013 Kenyan presidential election was won by one of the indictees, Uhuru Kenyatta, and his running mate, William Ruto, also an indictee. During their campaign Kenyatta and Ruto successfully leveraged the political impact of the ICC charges by crafting a narrative of Kenyan persecution at the hand of great powers. This narrative also evoked Kenya's history of brutal colonial rule, as the Kenyan government successfully garnered political support from many other African states, as well as the African Union.

The Kenyan case illustrates the vulnerability of the ICC to attacks on its legitimacy. However, although the narrative of Kenyatta appears to have resonated with many Kenyan voters, one could also argue that this drew international scrutiny to the 2013 elections, thus helping to prevent mass violence during that campaign. Kenya's vibrant democratic life has also ensured that Kenyatta's narrative is not the only narrative. This is crucial in ensuring that the perceived unfairness of the court among some Kenyans is not universal, and cannot be used to legitimise further criminal behaviour.

One of the key policy implications of deterrence theory for the ICC is that perceptions matter: the ICC must be seen to be fair, and the possibility of

19 *Ibid.*

prosecution for international crimes must also be clearly communicated to potential perpetrators. This is a task for all organs of the court, particularly the Office of the Prosecutor and the Outreach Office. Both the current prosecutor (Fatou Bensouda) and the former prosecutor (Luis Moreno Ocampo) issued statements warning of the possibility of ICC prosecutions in ongoing conflicts (in the Central African Republic, Syria, and Ivory Coast respectively). These 'preventive statements in order to deter the escalation of violence' are called for in the OTP's *Policy Paper on Preliminary Examinations*.[20]

Outreach activities communicate the work of the court to affected populations and also may have a 'magnifier effect' deterring future crimes by communicating that accountability is a real risk if you perpetrate international crimes. The court is not doing enough in this area – the Lubanga decision was not even broadcast in the Ituri region of Democratic Republic of Congo.[21] Outreach efforts must be prioritised within the work of the court in order for it to realise its full effectiveness as a tool of prevention.

We must also ask whether perceptions of apprehension risk are societal or formed on the basis of apprehension risk for specific crimes (in the case of the ICC the Rome Statute crimes). It would be reasonable to expect that fears of apprehension and accountability are linked to a general sense of, firstly, the wrongfulness and illegality of the specific acts in question, secondly, the general sense of law and order present in the country, and thirdly, the enforcement of specific offences. One could foresee situations where states have relatively well-functioning justice systems, yet there is a high prospect of impunity for international crimes. These acts may not be internally defined as criminal and may not be enforced by state organs; thus impunity is not only a perception but reality. Where there is a general state of lawlessness for all crimes perceptions of impunity will also be strong.

Moreover, in order for perpetrators to fear the risk of apprehension, they must be aware of the illegality of their acts and the existence and relevance of the ICC more generally. I remain sceptical that most perpetrators in mass atrocities have a high degree of awareness of the court, with the exception of countries where the courts work is highly visible and politically relevant, e.g. Kenya. Moreover, they are often protected within perpetrating regimes that have no intention of cooperating with the court (e.g. Sudan). Deterrence research shows that deterrence is the most effective when formal punishment is accompanied by informal sanctions.[22] In cases where the ICC is acting in isolation, without cooperation, and without a broader context of coming to terms with atrocities

---

20 Office of the Prosecutor, *Policy Paper on Preliminary Examinations*, November 2013, p. 24.

21 Kersten, 'Lubanga and the Trouble with ICC Deterrence', 20 March 2012, available at: www.justiceinconfict.org.

22 Nagin 1998, p. 18.

(i.e. peacebuilding and other transitional justice mechanisms), the court is bound to have little impact.

The ICC is the first permanent international criminal court, so it is reasonable to expect that the deterrence of international crimes is an ongoing possibility for the first time. Prior to the establishment of the court, prosecutions of international crimes had been highly sporadic and context specific. Other efforts at accountability for international crimes, such as the ICTY, do not have universal territorial or temporal applicability. Moreover, their jurisdiction is now entirely retrospective (even though the ICTY began operation while the conflict in the Former Yugoslavia was still ongoing).

Perceptual deterrence theories tell us that the effectiveness of sanctions depends on their certainty and severity.[23] In order to achieve this level of certainty impunity gaps must be closed. The key to this endeavour are the complementarity and cooperation regimes. Both issues have received increasing attention in recent years, with dedicated sessions at the Assembly of States Parties meetings, as well as the Belgian, Dutch, Argentine, and Slovenian initiative for mutual legal assistance and extradition. While the non-cooperation of ICC state parties with arrest warrants is damaging for the court (for example when South Africa failed to arrest Sudanese President Omar Al-Bashir and surrender him to the ICC), the relative scarcity of domestic prosecutions for international crimes has greater impact in perpetuating impunity. Ideally, domestic prosecutions should work in concert with prosecutions at the ICC to create a comprehensive international criminal justice system.

There is mixed evidence supporting the effectiveness of the general deterrence of international crimes, although the establishment of the ICTY did appear to have significant effects on political developments in Serbia (both Karadzić and Mladić were removed from the Dayton peace negotiations). This isolation of genocidal leaders may have a preventive effect in and of itself. According to intercept evidence, the ICTY greatly concerned Bosnian Serb leaders when the idea of creating the tribunal was first discussed in August of 2002; this possibility may have also contributed to a momentary lull in the fighting.[24]

Furthermore, Juan Mendez argues that when he sent a note to the UN Security Council in November of 2004 (while he was still the UN Special Advisor on the Prevention of Genocide), indicating that ICC jurisdiction could be extended to cover instigation and incitement of all of the crimes in the Rome Statute, this had the effect of calming the hate media firestorm then taking place in Côte d'Ivoire.[25] The Sudan researcher for Human Rights Watch also claimed that the referral of Sudan to the ICC was a 'real deterrent in that the people in

---

23 *Ibid*, p. 7.

24 Robertson 1999, p. 69.

25 Mendez, 'Transitional Justice and Prevention', in 'Genocide Prevention: Where are we now?', Politorbis No. 47, February 2009, p. 94.

Khartoum were worried ... that they might have to go to The Hague.'[26] However, during the Moscow Conference of October 1943, Roosevelt, Churchill, and Stalin had issued a joint statement warning that German war criminals would be 'brought back to the scene of their crimes to be judged on the spot by the peoples whom they have outraged', yet the genocide continued unabated.[27]

This illustrates one of the central problems with deterrence – the certainty of many genocidal elites that their hold on power is secure, thus that they will never have to face international justice or transitional justice mechanisms within their own state. In November of 1945 Nuremberg Prosecutor Robert Jackson wisely observed that '[w]ars are started only on the theory and in the confidence that they can be won. Personal punishment, to be suffered only in the event that the war is lost, will probably not be a sufficient deterrent to prevent a war where the war makers feel the chances of defeat are negligible.'[28] Similarly, one Rwandan génocidaire argued 'we didn't think we would be prosecuted because we thought we would win the war.'[29] Nonetheless, we are moving towards a global state of affairs where perpetrators of international crimes increasingly face international judgement and suffer negative sanctions for their acts. Even if it is not immediately apparent that leaders will be punished for genocide, it should be apparent that the incentives for genocide are few and the risks are great.

In the context of international crimes, the propensity of perpetrators to commit genocide may come from a general orientation towards violence as well as ideological justification, rather than recidivism (past criminal acts). For instance a Rwandan perpetrator told me 'we killed him [the victim] because we thought that there wouldn't be any consequences. The leaders were doing the same thing ... If one person who killed was prosecuted everyone else would have stopped killing.'[30] Moreover, the criminal prosecution of individuals for genocide may also have other preventive effects such as norm-setting and removing the means of genocidal mobilisation.

In criminology, deterrence theory (the notion that the prosecution of crimes can dissuade potential offenders) is often contrasted with labelling theory – which posits that sanctions themselves are stigmatising, thus they contribute to further crime. This perspective seems to have little relevance for the analysis of the prevention of international crimes; international crimes, such as genocide, are of such perceived gravity that they receive virtually universal opprobrium. Even regimes that commit genocide and crimes against humanity seek to conceal or recharacterise these crimes. Although notions of victors' justice or of prosecutorial bias do posit that the selectivity of the punishment of international crimes is a product of political considerations or prejudice, these are *tu quoque*

---

26 Mennecke 2007, p. 324.

27 *Ibid*, p. 321.

28 *Ibid*, p. 325.

29 Rwandan Perpetrator Interview R62, farmer, Mont Kigali TIG Camp, 15 October 2009.

30 Rwandan Perpetrator Interview R37, farmer, Rwaza TIG Camp, 30 August 2009.

arguments rather than fundamental disagreements over the wrongfulness of alleged criminal acts.

3.3. BEYOND DETERRENCE: PROSECUTION AS PREVENTION

The prosecution of crimes by the ICC may have other preventive effects. These include: undermining the conditions which contribute to international crimes, incapacitating perpetrators, interdicting inchoate forms of criminality, thus preventing further crimes, isolating offenders, and contributing indirectly to prevention by encouraging prosecution and other responsive policies from other actors.

Beginning with the conditions that contribute to international crimes – international crimes are resultant partly from a norm shift, in which the commission of international crimes becomes acceptable or positively normative within the state, or at least within the group. One could ask whether the further development of an international criminal justice system, of which the ICC is a central piece, could contribute to the entrenchment of norms against crimes against international crimes. Already crimes against humanity and genocide are considered 'manifestly unlawful' under the grounds for excluding criminal responsibility provision of the Rome Statute (Article 31). In a sense then, the ICC assumes that the criminal acts encompassed by genocide and crimes against humanity are *mala in se*, against intuitive understandings of wrongful behaviour. Perhaps these norms can be strengthened further by entrenching international crimes in domestic law, through the domestication of the Rome Statute, as well as through the prosecution and appropriate punishment of these crimes. There is also a substantial public education component to this task; something that the ICC is not really designed to do beyond minimal activities like hosting groups of visitors in The Hague and offering public information sessions in situation countries.

Impunity is another criminogenic condition for international crimes. Most perpetrators are risk-averse, and with increased prosecutions the risk of punishment should increase parallel to a reluctance to offend.[31] Once again this requires the court and its partners to regularly and forcefully communicate the consequences of criminal behaviour.

The commission of international crimes almost always occurs in tandem with an armed conflict. In fact, multiple forms of violence such as war crimes (in the context of an armed conflict), crimes against humanity (widespread or systematic attacks targeting civilians such as opponents of the regime), and genocide (the intent to destroy a racial, national, ethnic, or religious group in

[31] Anderson 2011, p. 149.

whole or in part) often occur concomitantly. Armed conflict provides a useful cover for other atrocities as the confusion which predominates in armed conflict, and the removal of external observers, increase the prospects for the concealment of atrocities among other lawful uses of force. Moreover, in armed conflict polarisation often intensifies; in some sense genocide and crimes against humanity constitute the most extreme alternatives along a continuum of forms of violence. In armed conflict people also become socialised to accept the use of violence as a matter of policy, and adapt to committing acts of violence themselves. It may also be easier to demonise and dehumanise opponents of the regime once they have taken up arms.

The 'peace versus justice' debate is one of the central controversies in the application of international criminal law. The 'justice' side of this debate uses fundamentally deontological reasoning to argue that pursuit of justice (human rights) is a social good in and of itself. Thus, the pursuit of justice cannot be held to be subordinate to any other concern, such as the achievement of sustainable peace. In contrast, the 'peace' side of the debate contends that considerations of conflict resolution should be prioritised and that sometimes justice will need to be sacrificed, or put aside, in order to achieve the greater social good of peace.[32] Neither side believes that either peace or justice is unimportant, rather the controversy is really a question of priority and strategy.

This debate has many practical implications, not the least of which are decisions about when to pursue prosecutions for international crimes. The proponents of the 'peace' side of the peace-justice debate argue that, in some cases, the court may have a detrimental effect on human rights if the threat of prosecutions prevents lasting peace, leading to further violence and gross human rights violations.

Thus far the evidence for the ICC's impact on conflict resolution is unclear. Uganda provides an interesting case study. The Government of Uganda's referral of the 'situation concerning the Lord's Resistance Army' (LRA) in December of 2003 was clearly politically motivated; the regime sought to further isolate the LRA and Joseph Kony. When the ICC unsealed its arrest warrants for five top LRA officials in 2005, it was clear that the court was content to focus solely on the LRA. In a sense the LRA, nearly universally condemned, represented an easy target for the ICC as it sought to establish its legitimacy.[33] At the time there was some concern that the presence of the ICC arrest warrants would limit the incentive for the LRA and its leaders to negotiate peace, as well as for LRA combatants to take up the amnesty offered under Uganda's Amnesty Law of 2000.

---

32 Consult, for example, Akhavan 2009; or Nouwen and Werner 2011.

33 Kersten, 'Peace, justice and politics in Northern Uganda', European Council on Foreign Relations, 2013, available at: www.ecfr.eu/ijp/case/uganda.

The ICC charges against LRA leaders appear to have encouraged LRA negotiations with the government. ICC Prosecutor Luis Moreno Ocampo argued at the time: 'The negotiations currently taking place are partially a result of pressure from the ICC arrest warrants', and also that: 'We believe the best way to stop the conflict and restore security to the region is to arrest the top leaders.'[34] The ICC charges may have also influenced Sudan in ceasing its support for the LRA and signing a cooperation agreement with the ICC for the LRA investigation in 2005. However, those negotiations have been complicated by the stipulation that the ICC would not respect government amnesties for top LRA leaders. Withdrawal of the arrest warrants has been a precondition of the LRA for a final agreement. No such agreement was reached but the LRA did cease its attacks in Northern Uganda; unfortunately, the conflict has been exported to the Democratic Republic of Congo. A 2008 Act to set up a Special War Crimes Chamber stipulates that the gravity of the crime will be taken into account but also the need for reconciliation. The act does not apply to ICC indictees.

So what can we make of all this? As Mark Kersten argues the government of Uganda, which has since become a vocal critic of the ICC, may not have been very serious in its intention to negotiate peace with the LRA. However, the ICC has proven to be a useful tool in stigmatising the LRA and legitimising military solutions.[35] The self-referral mechanisms allowed the Ugandan government to expose the LRA's atrocities without exposing itself to the political (and judicial risk) of international prosecutions.

The use of self-referrals to trigger jurisdiction may also affect the ICC's impact on conflict resolution. In the three cases of self-referrals, Uganda, Democratic Republic of Congo, and Central African Republic, only individuals from one party to the conflict, namely rebel forces, have been indicted. This is problematic as it undermines the court's perceived fairness and reinforces perceptions that the court is one-sided and a tool for the powerful. Of course, there are very practical reasons for not indicting agents from the referring state but this strategy has a distorting effect on the work of the court.

It is often held that accountability processes encourage conflict resolution by stigmatising and socially isolating perpetrators, which leads to the *de facto* lustration of officials implicated in mass atrocities increasing the prospects for peace. Yet the issue of arrest warrants by the ICC also blocks the exit strategies of perpetrators, effectively disincentivising peace. We can distinguish here between the potential short-term risks of ICC involvement in conflict zones and the long term benefits in terms of norm-setting, incapacitation (specific deterrence), and general deterrence.

Juan Mendez argues that amnesties in the case of mass atrocities contribute to impunity and that amnesties for genocide, war crimes, and crimes against

---

34 ICC, 'Statement by Prosecutor Luis Moreno-Ocampo', ICC-OTP-20060706–146.

35 Kersten 2013, non-paginated.

humanity are illegal (although amnesties for domestic crimes such as treason are permissible).[36] As a principle this is logical: amnesties may be contemplated, or even encouraged, for political offences but not for international crimes, which are a matter of concern to the international community as a whole. Building the foundation of peace negotiations on the recognition of impunity for atrocities is counter-productive in the long-term.

Under the Rome Statute the Prosecutor has the power to decide that prosecution may not be in the interests of justice at a particular time; this allows sequencing to take place whereby criminal prosecutions are put on hold in the short term until negotiated settlements can be reached. Of course the ICC is an independent institution, which will not respect domestic amnesties. In a sense, then, the ICC is not really an element in transitional justice strategies, as it has no level of integration with such strategies. While respecting the founding principles of the court, more can be done to ensure that prosecutorial policy at the ICC works in harmony with broader transitional justice and peacebuilding initiatives. The court is not designed with this purpose in mind, so such a cultural shift would require the court to take on board additional expertise.

The active prosecution of early phases of mass atrocities, such as incitement, conspiracies, and biological forms of genocide, may increase the preventive power of international criminal law and disempower the mobilisation of mass atrocities.[37] Widespread or systematic crimes cannot occur without incitement and conspiracy. Incitement to genocide has the effect of mobilising genocidal forces – for instance, one Rwandan perpetrator recalls 'there were some in our group who were promoters – it was they who told us to find and kill the cockroaches.'[38] Leaders use incitement to coalesce disparate individuals into a mass with the shared purpose of destroying the victim group – the formation of such collective intent does not occur spontaneously. This purposeful destruction is only possible with the prior dehumanisation of the victim group through a discourse of hate speech and incitement to genocide. The incapacitation of leaders inciting violence may also stop such incitement, and violence, from occurring.

Moreover, incitement/propaganda can provide perpetrators with 'vocabularies of motive' – authorities claim that the destruction (killing) of the victims would not only be legitimate but imperative for the protection of the perpetrators' families, nation, and highest ideals.[39] Incitement also narrows the discursive space, reducing the perceived range of options available to the perpetrator. Further, it

---

36 Mendez, 'Transitional Justice and Prevention', in 'Genocide Prevention: Where are we now?' Politorbis, No. 47, February 2009, p. 94.

37 These biological forms of genocide are set out in Article 6 of the Rome Statute and include preventing births and the forcible transfer of children from one group to another.

38 Anderson 2011, p. 222. Interview R39 (Rwandan Perpetrator), farmer, Nyarusenge TIG Camp, 31 August 2009.

39 *Ibid*, p. 9.

fills 'gaps' in the scope of formal criminal conspiracies by providing guidance for collective action.

In order to counteract the effect of inchoate incitement, it must first be identified. This can be difficult because of the use of coded language. Moreover, incitement often works in an indirect manner as accusations are made of atrocities committed by the victim group as a means of providing authorisation for the perpetrator group to commit these same atrocities.[40]

Beyond direct and public incitement to commit genocide, combating the most egregious forms of hate speech is also essential to the prevention of international crimes. Case law indicates that certain forms of hate speech may be criminalised as the crime against humanity of persecution.[41] As reasoned in the Media Trial at the ICTR, hate media can condition the population and create 'a climate of harm.'[42] Hate speech may also be strongly indicative of the presence of a persecutory campaign targeting a group.

Conspiracy, like incitement, is instrumental for the commission of international crimes. Genocide and crimes against humanity are not individual offences and their implementation requires many elements. Often leadership (in the form of a small clique of leaders) provides the necessary impetus for these elements to be put into place. This was the case with the Holocaust (undoubtedly led by Hitler and his inner circle), the Rwandan genocide (with its ruling clique, the *Akazu*), and other mass atrocities. This does not mean that international crimes never enjoy mass support or participation, rather that the criminal conspiracy and planning of a group of individuals is necessary to push the masses in the correct direction. Furthermore, many individuals may be aware of the existence of an implicit conspiracy (for example the collective goal of exterminating the Tutsis). The Rome Statute has a narrower view of conspiracy than the ad hoc tribunals – the term conspiracy is never used in the provisions on criminal liability (Article 25), rather conspiracy is a form of complicity or attempted co-perpetration.

The prosecution of inchoate forms of international crimes, such as incitement and attempt, may greatly increase the preventive power of international criminal law. If incitement is stopped at an early stage by the prosecution of inciting individuals in vulnerable societies, perhaps these states can be pulled

40 Gutman 1993.

41 ICTR, *Prosecutor v. Georges Ruggiu*, ICTR-97-31-I, Judgement, 1 June 2000, para. 22. The Canadian Supreme Court reached a similar conclusion in *Mugesera*: 'hate speech, particularly when it advocates egregious acts of violence, may constitute persecution.' See *Prosecutor v. Mugesera*, Case No. 30025, judgement, 28 June 2005, para. 67 as well as: *Prosecutor v. Kupreskic et al.*, IT-95-16, 'Lasva Valley', Judgement, 14 January 2000, para. 621; and *Prosecutor v.Bikindi*, ICTR-01-72-T, Judgement, para. 393.

42 ICTR, *Prosecutor v. Nahimana*, ICTR-99-52, Judgement, para. 1073. Instigation (a form of liability listed in Article 6 of the ICTR Statute) differs from incitement to commit genocide in that it *does* require a direct causal link between the communication and the principal physical perpetration.

back from the brink. The 'marketplace of ideas' thesis, often espoused by the Americans (that all ideas should be heard because the best ideas will triumph), is unconvincing because in genocidal societies *there is no marketplace of ideas*.[43] As a state-directed crime the diversity of discourse is substantially reduced or non-existent – access to the mass media is disproportionately, or exclusively, held by those inciting genocide.

Attempt was included in the Rome Statute with the caveat that responsibility for attempted crimes is precluded in cases where the individual in question voluntarily and completely abandons their criminal purpose.[44] The defence of voluntary abandonment exists in many domestic judicial systems, including the United States. It is often only available as a defence if the abandonment of the criminal purpose is *completely* voluntary.[45]

Presumably voluntary abandonment was included to strengthen the preventive function of the law – it provides a measure of positive inducement to potential perpetrators to abandon their criminal efforts before the actual commission of other international crimes. Voluntary abandonment operates in concert with deterrence; perpetrators have no risk of punishment if they abandon their attempt at international crimes, yet they face criminal sanction if they do not.

However, as with deterrent effects, it is uncertain whether voluntary abandonment will actually motivate perpetrators to forgo their criminality. It is reliant on the assumption that potential attempters are sufficiently apprised of the defence (highly unlikely) and that they would not abandon their attempted crime otherwise.[46] One could also hypothesise that even if voluntary abandonment reduces completed attempts, it may provide incentives to initiate attempts. Moreover, individuals who attempt international crimes are likely dangerous persons (there may be a correlation between attempted crimes and further criminal behaviour), who intend to violate the substantive rules of society. This is why the punishment of attempted crimes is so important.

Historically, inchoate forms of international crimes have only been prosecuted after the actual occurrence of genocide and crimes against humanity. Needless to say, this nullifies the preventive effects of the law. It also reduces inchoate offences to mere forms of complicity, only criminalised because mass atrocities have already occurred.

There are some practical reasons for this prosecutorial conservatism. Firstly, gathering evidence of intended genocide is difficult in the absence of genocide itself. How can you prove the existence of a (explicit) conspiracy to commit genocide without locating direct evidence? Implicit conspiracies essentially cannot

43 Benesch 2008, p. 496.
44 Rome Statute of the International Criminal Court, 17 July 1998.
45 Crew 1988, p. 445.
46 *Ibid*, p. 450.

be proven without the occurrence of genocide itself. Secondly, indicting and arresting individuals before genocide has occurred would be difficult, requiring the full cooperation of the state in which they reside. This is often not possible, as that state is generally itself complicit or directing this preparation for genocide. Finally, indicting for 'potential' crimes may appear to be overly speculative and interventionist. The International Criminal Court is in the process of building its legitimacy and the prosecutor might be wary of expending political capital on a seemingly quixotic quest to stop mass crimes before they occur.

These problems notwithstanding, there are ways of gathering evidence on the existence of inchoate offences (for example through the context of incitement, or through conspirators that have abandoned their criminal purpose). It also must be reiterated that inchoate crimes are themselves crimes whether or not the underlying offence subsequently occurs. Genocide is a process and unsuccessful incitement or genocidal planning may have a pernicious effect – dehumanising victim groups and increasing the threat of future genocides. Furthermore, it might have the general deterrent effect of showing that crimes will be prosecuted. Perhaps, also the incarceration of criminal leaders may have the specific deterrent effect of ensuring that these individuals are no longer able to endeavour to bring about genocide. Although international crimes involve mass participation, it is leaders who undoubtedly cultivate and organise collective action. The prosecution of these leaders is essential to the prevention of international crimes, yet if only leaders are prosecuted by the ICC, absent broader domestic transitional justice activities, the ICC risks contributing to tokenistic responses to international crimes.

In the Lubanga case the Court debated this deterrent and preventive effect of prosecuting leaders. The Pre-Trial Chamber argued that leaders 'are the ones who can most effectively prevent or stoop the commission' of crimes and that 'only by concentrating on this type of individual can the deterrent effects of the Court be maximised.'[47] The Appeals Chamber regarded this reasoning as 'questionable', arguing rather that: 'It seems more logical to assume that the deterrent effect of the Court is highest if no category of perpetrators is *per se* excluded from potentially being brought before the Court.'[48] The Appeals Chamber continued:

> The imposition of rigid standards primarily based on top seniority may result in neither retribution nor prevention being achieved. Also, the capacity of individuals to prevent crimes in the field should not be implicitly or inadvertently assimilated to the preventive role of the Court more generally. Whether prevention is interpreted as a long-term objective, i.e., the overall result of the Court's

47 ICC, *Prosecutor v. Lubanga*, ICC-01/04-01/06-8, Decision on the Prosecutor's Application for a Warrant of Arrest, 10 February 2006, paras. 54–55.

48 ICC, *Situation in the Democratic Republic of the Congo*, ICC-01/04, Judgment on the Prosecutor's Appeal Against the Decision of Pre-Trail Chamber I Entitled 'Decision on the Prosecutor's Application for Warrants of Arrest, Article 58', 13 July 2006, para. 73.

> activities generally, or as a factor in a specific situation, the preventive role of the Court may depend on many factors, much broader than the capacity of an individual to prevent crimes. The predictable exclusion of many perpetrators on the grounds proposed by the Pre-Trial Chamber could severely harm the preventive, or deterrent, role of the Court which is a cornerstone of the creation of the International Criminal Court, by announcing that any perpetrators other than those at the very top are automatically excluded from the exercise of the jurisdiction of the Court.[49]

Leaders, of course, have a legal duty to intervene to prevent the commission of crimes under the law of command responsibility. It does seem, however, that the prosecution of leaders has more utility as a *post facto* mechanism for attributing wrongs than it does as a preventive measure. If the law is serious about prevention, inchoate forms of international crimes must be prosecuted, domestically and internationally *before* atrocities occur.

3.4. THE INDIRECT, PREVENTIVE EFFECTS OF PROSECUTION

The final aspect of the ICC's potential impact on the prevention of international crimes that we must consider is the indirect effects – namely that the ICC, through its work, could trigger preventive policy responses from other actors. These responses range from the judicial (the prosecution of international crimes in domestic jurisdictions through the complementarity regime) to political responses (mobilising political and military responses to mass atrocities through the moral opprobrium visited on the perpetrators).

The preliminary investigation authorised by the Prosecutor of the situation in Columbia seems to have had a positive effect in encouraging domestic prosecutions for international crimes. Likewise a war crimes chamber has been created in Uganda. There were efforts to set up a special court in Kenya to investigate the 2008 electoral violence but this has not borne fruit. Perhaps some of these courts would be created otherwise but there can be little doubt that the desire to avoid the scrutiny of the ICC has contributed to these policies. The maximum penalties under Colombia's Justice and Peace Law are only eight years imprisonment, while they are sixty years under other Columbian statues and thirty years under the Rome Statute.[50]

Unfortunately, the court seems to have had less of a political impact. Although the determination of *prima facie* evidence of crimes against humanity and war crimes may have contributed to the political isolation of Sudan – Omar Al-Bashir continues to visit African countries free from fear

49 *Ibid*, paras. 73–74.

50 Unger and Wierda 2009, p. 280.

of arrest. Moreover, the determination that mass atrocities are occurring in Sudan by the ICC and others has not created any further impetus for diplomatic, economic, or military measures against the regime in Khartoum. Indeed, there is a danger that action on the part of the ICC, even in the form of unexecuted arrest warrants after a Security Council referral, could be seen as 'dealing with the problem.' Thus, in certain cases, the ICC may actually inadvertently serve the purpose of precluding more meaningful policy responses. Unfortunately, even in the face of ICC charges, the Bashir government has continued to commit mass atrocities in the Nuba Mountains region and elsewhere in Sudan. One might question whether there is value added in the stigmatisation offered by ICC arrest warrants, on top of widespread condemnation from human rights organisations. The simple fact is that the ICC cannot overcome a lack of political will to catalyse action in the face of ongoing mass atrocities.

3.5. COURTS AND THEIR LIMITATIONS (OTHER PREVENTIVE STRATEGIES)

Even if it can be proved that the ICC has had a demonstrable effect in the prevention of international crimes over these past ten years, the Court has not acted in isolation. One must consider, more generally, the limits inherent in the use of legal and judicial tools for the resolution of social problems such as mass atrocities. Courts without strong enforcement mechanisms will have limited impact. Arrest warrants without arrests are not a deterrent. Moreover, once atrocities are imminent or underway, judicial orders are simply insufficient to halt them. Such judicial mechanisms can only work in tandem with other, more robust, forms of international engagement. International justice is simply not quick enough or universal enough to directly interdict international crimes. Ocampo argued as much himself, saying that the Court's mandate 'cannot realistically be viewed as a duty to protect all the victims in Darfur regardless of their lack of connection to the investigation.'[51] Alongside intervention, upstream prevention strategies, which seek to build the rule of law and respect for human rights, are crucial in the prevention of international crimes. Communities which are empowered and respected within a robust legal framework are less likely to become targets of international crimes. Conflict prevention is another essential aspect of the prevention of international crimes. The Policy Paper on Preliminary Examinations seems to envisage a broader role for the Office of the Prosecutor

---

51 ICC, Prosecutor's Response to Cassese's Observation on Issues Concerning the Protection of Victims and the Preservation of Evidence in the Proceedings on Darfur Pending before the ICC, 11 September 2006, ICC-02/05, 30.

and the ICC which includes an 'early warning function' going beyond the receipt of communications, and undertaking of preliminary examinations and investigations to encompass the proactive collection of open-source information on possible crimes within the jurisdiction of the Court.[52] Through such an approach the ICC is taking on a much broader role and mandate in terms of the interdiction of international crimes. Yet, is the Office of the Prosecutor, with its significant resource constraints, really well-equipped to perform such a role?

4. CONCLUSION: THE ICC AND THE PREVENTION OF INTERNATIONAL CRIMES

In order to take meaningful action to prevent international crimes, we must go beyond what Alex Hinton called 'the transitional justice imaginary' to enact thoughtful policy responses.[53] Hinton was referring to the set of normative assumptions which uncritically govern our ways of thinking about transitional justice. We must go beyond these normative assumptions to critically examine and strategise how the ICC might play a role in the prevention of international crimes. As this chapter has set out some of the key considerations include:

(1) deterrence requires legitimacy and perceived fairness;
(2) outreach must be a core function of the ICC in order to ensure its effectiveness; and
(3) inchoate crimes must be prosecuted by the ICC.

Addressing these points will require concerted effort by all international justice stakeholders.

Courts like the ICC do not have an instant and wide-ranging deterrent or preventive function. Rather, they exist within a broader political context comprised of numerous factors. The ICC must be situated within the broader framework of transitional justice and diplomatic policy responses in order to be effective. As an island in a sea of impunity, the ICC will continue to have only limited impact on the prevention of international crimes.

52 Office of The Prosecutor, *Policy Paper on Preliminary Examinations*, November 2013, p. 24.
53 Hinton 2013, p. 87.

BIBLIOGRAPHY

BOOKS AND JOURNAL ARTICLES

Akhavan 2009
Akhavan, P., 'Are International Criminal Tribunals a Disincentive to Peace? Reconciling Judicial Romanticism with Political Realism', 31(3) Human Rights Quarterly, 2009.

Anderson 2016
Anderson, K.F., 'The Criminology of Genocide: Killing without Consequence', Routledge, 2016 (forthcoming).

Balint 2008
Balint, J., 'Dealing with International Crimes: Towards a Conceptual Mode of Accountability and Justice', in Smeulers, A. and Haveman, R. (eds.), 'Supranational Criminology: Towards a Criminology of International Crimes', Intersentia, 2008.

Benesch 2008
Benesch, S., 'Vile Crime or Inalienable Right: Defining Incitement to Genocide', 48(3) Virginia Journal of International Law, 2008.

Crew 1988
Crew, M.A., 'Should Voluntary Abandonment be a Defense to Attempted Crimes?', 26(2) American Criminal Law Review, 1988.

Gutman 1993
Gutman, R., 'A Witness to Genocide: Dispatches on the Ethnic Cleansing of Bosnia', Macmillan, 1993.

Hinton 2013
Hinton, A.L., 'Transitional Justice Time: Uncle San, Aunty Yan, and outreach at the Khmer Rouge Tribunal', in Mayersen, D. and Pohlman, A., 'Transitional Justice in Asia: Legacies and Prevention', Routledge, 2013.

Humphreys and Weinstein 2006
Humphreys, M. and Weinstein, J.M., 'Handling and Manhandling Civilians in Civil War', 100(3) American Political Science Review, 2006.

Kershaw 1999
Kershaw, I., 'Working Towards the Führer: Reflections on the Nature of the Hitler Dictatorship', in Leitz, C. (ed.), 'The Third Reich', Blackwill, 1999.

Lanier and Henry 2004
Lanier, M. and Henry, S., 'Essential Criminology', Westview Press, 2004.

Mennecke 2007
Mennecke, M., 'Punishing Génocidaires: A Deterrent Effect or Not?', Human Rights Review, 2007.

Nagin 1998
Nagin, D.S., 'Criminal Deterrence Research at the Outset of the Twentieth Century', 23 Crime and Justice, 1998.

Nouwen and Werner 2011
Nouwen, S. and Werner, W., 'Doing Justice to the Political: The International Criminal Court in Uganda and Sudan', 4(21) European Journal of International Law, 2011.

Piquero, Paternoster, Pogarsky and Loughran 2011
Piquero, A.R., Paternoster, R., Pogarsky, G. and Loughran, T., 'Elaborating the Individual Difference Component in Deterrence Theory', 7 Annual Review of Law and Social Science, 2011.
Robertson 1999
Robertson, G., 'Crimes Against Humanity', Penguin, 1999.
Sherman 1993
Sherman, L.W., 'Defiance, Deterrence, and Irrelevance: A Theory of the Criminal Sanction', 30 Journal of Research in Crime and Delinquency, 1993.
Tiemessen 2014
Tiemessen, A., 'The International Criminal Court and the politics of prosecutions', 18 The International Journal of Human Rights, 2014.
Unger and Wierda 2009
Unger, T. and Wierda, M., 'Pursuing Justice in Ongoing Conflict: A Discussion of Current Practice', in Ambos, K., Large, J. and Wierda, M. (eds.), 'Building a Future on Peace and Justice', Springer, 2009.

JURISPRUDENCE

ICTR 2008
ICTR, Prosecutor v. Bikindi, ICTR-01–72-T, 2 December 2008.
ICC 2006
ICC, Prosecutor's Response to Cassese's Observation on Issues Concerning the Protection of Victims and the Preservation of Evidence in the Proceedings on Darfur, ICC-02/05, 11 September 2006.
ICC 2006
ICC, Judgment on the Prosecutor's Appeal Against the Decision of Pre-Trial Chamber I Entitled 'Decision on the Prosecutor's Application for Warrants of Arrest, Article 58', ICC-01/04, 13 July 2006.
ICC 2006
ICC, Prosecutor v. Lubanga, ICC-01/04–01/06–8, 10 February 2006.
ICTR 2003
ICTR, Prosecutor v. Nahimana et al., ICTR-99–52, 3 December 2003.
ICTR 2000
ICTR, Prosecutor v. Georges Ruggiu, ICTR-97–31-I, 1 June 2000.
ICTR 1998
Prosecutor v. Jean Kambanda, ICTR-97–23-S, 4 September 1998.
ICTY 2000
ICTY, Prosecutor v. Kupreskic et al., IT-95–16, 14 January 2000.
Supreme Court of Canada 2005
SCC, Mugesera v. Canada, Case no. 30025, 28 June 2005.

TREATIES, LEGISLATION AND AGREEMENTS

Rome Statute of the International Criminal Court, 2187 UNTS 90/37, 17 July 1998.

Statute of the International Criminal Tribunal for Rwanda, SC Res. 955, UN Doc. S/RES/955, 8 November 1994.

OTHERS

Anderson, K.F., 'The Dehumanisation Dynamic: A Criminology of Genocide', PhD Thesis, National University of Ireland, October 2011.

ICC, Office of the Prosecutor, 'Policy Paper on Preliminary Examinations', ICC-OTP 2013, November 2013.

ICC, Office of the Prosecutor, 'Policy Paper on the Interests of Justice', ICC-OTP-2007, September 2007.

ICC, 'Statement by Prosecutor Luis Moreno-Ocampo', ICC-OTP-20060706-146.

Kersten, M., 'Lubanga and the Trouble with ICC Deterrence', Justice in Conflict, 20 March 2012.

Kersten, M., 'Peace, justice and politics in Northern Uganda', European Council on Foreign Relations, 2013.

Mendez, J., 'Transitional Justice and Prevention', in 'Genocide Prevention: Where are we now?', Politorbis No. 47, February 2009.

Smith, P., 'Interview: Luis Moreno-Ocampo, ICC Prosecutor', The Africa Report, 21 September 2009.

COMPLEMENTARITY AND AFRICA

Tackling International Crimes at the Domestic Level

Angela Mudukuti

[T]he number of cases that reach the Court should not be a measure of its efficiency. On the contrary, the absence of trials before this Court, as a consequence of regular functioning of national institutions, would be a major success
– Luis Moreno Ocampo
Former Prosecutor of the International Criminal Court[1]

1. INTRODUCTION

Ending impunity and ensuring accountability for the most serious crimes is a priority for the international community. This united concern for crimes against humanity, war crimes, and genocide resulted in the creation of a permanent international court in 2002. The first twelve years of the International Criminal Court's existence have been characterised both by successes and evident shortcomings. However, as the first permanent international accountability mechanism, the ICC cannot wage the war against international crimes alone, and so it falls to domestic systems to assist by signing, ratifying, domesticating ICC legislation, and litigating core crimes in a domestic context.

Whilst universal jurisdiction has been a popular and useful method to try international crimes over the past twenty years, (particularly in Switzerland, Denmark, Belgium, Germany, and the United Kingdom) the domestication of ICC legislation is proving to be a far more efficient and pragmatic augmentation to customary international law notions of universal jurisdiction in an African context. Advancing the African international criminal justice project means that there must be a true understanding of international criminal law as a matter of national importance.

1 Luis Moreno Ocampo at the ceremony for the solemn undertaking of the Chief Prosecutor of the International Criminal Court, 16 June 2003.

Ensuring that there is justice beyond the bounds of The Hague involves the realisation and actualisation of the principle of complementarity. This principle, as enshrined in the Rome Statute of the International Criminal Court, allows the ICC to be a court of last resort, giving the domestic systems primary jurisdiction. Complementarity is one of the founding principles of the Rome Statute, and the vision of the drafters at the Rome Conference was a comprehensive system of international justice, where states take it upon themselves to investigate and prosecute international crimes. As a court of last resort, the ICC acts when a state is unwilling or unable to carry out its responsibilities.[2] For maximum complementarity to work, states are required to sign, ratify, and domesticate the Rome Statute, effectively giving them the legislative framework to address crimes that shock the conscience of humanity.

The ongoing perpetration of crimes against humanity and war crimes coupled with the accusation that the ICC is targeting Africa (which has resulted in serious backlash from certain African countries including threats of withdrawal from the ICC and acts of non-cooperation) has made the application of justice on a domestic level vital, now more than ever. Justice and accountability are the main objectives and they must be pursued from a domestic and international perspective.

In Africa, to date only South Africa, Kenya, Uganda, Burkina Faso and Senegal have amended their laws to allow the prosecution of core international crimes. In South Africa, the Implementation of the Rome Statute of the International Criminal Court Act 27 of 2002 (ICC Act) has paved the way for ground-breaking and precedent setting jurisprudence in the form of *Southern Africa Litigation Centre and Another v. The National Director of Public Prosecutions and Others*[3] colloquially known as the Zimbabwe Torture Case. This paper will address the legislative framework developed by South Africa in this regard, the first case brought in terms of the ICC Act and its impact on the international criminal justice project in South Africa.

Similar initiatives on the African continent will also be discussed briefly to show that litigation at the domestic level can provide substantive and practical content that can shape jurisprudence on the continent and help foster a culture of accountability. Civil society is the driving force behind accountability efforts for international crimes in a domestic context and so this paper will also briefly address the pivotal part played by these actors.

2 Article 17 of the Rome Statute.

3 The case was heard in the North Gauteng High Court under that name and changed in the Supreme Court of Appeal to *National Director of Public Prosecutions and Another v. Southern Africa Litigation Centre and Another*. In the Constitutional Court the case became *National Commissioner of the South Africa Police Service v. Southern Africa Litigation Centre and Another*.

2. INTERNATIONAL LAW AND ITS PLACE IN THE SOUTH AFRICAN LEGISLATIVE FRAMEWORK

South Africa's initial acknowledgment of international law and its place in the legal system came *vis-à-vis* the South African Constitution, Act 108 of 1996. Section 233 of the Constitution states that 'when interpreting any legislation, every court must prefer any reasonable interpretation of the legislation that is consistent with international law over any alternative interpretation that is inconsistent with international law.' Customary international law is also recognised in the Constitution in section 232 which states that: 'Customary international law is law in the Republic unless it is inconsistent with the Constitution or an Act of Parliament.' The South African Constitution also includes provisions on the role of international law with regard to the interpretation of the Bill of Rights and statutory interpretation in general. The requirement in section 39(1)(b) that courts 'must consider international law when interpreting the Bill of Rights' is one of the most important provisions that have influenced the use of international law in a domestic context. South Africa's dualist legal system and common law heritage have allowed for the reception and domestication of international criminal law. The domestication of the Rome Statute is the prime example.

3. THE ICC ACT

Until South Africa domesticated the Rome Statute, the core international crimes – war crimes, genocide and crimes against humanity – were not criminalised in South African law.[4] The ICC Act was adopted in 2002 and it criminalised these core crimes. Although the ICC Act has expansive territorial jurisdiction, its temporal jurisdiction is limited, as no crimes committed prior to its enactment can be brought before the relevant authorities, ensuring that there is no retrospective application.

The ICC Act is structured to provide extra-territorial jurisdiction by allowing the National Prosecuting Authority (NPA) to handle cases brought against any person accused of having committed a crime in the Republic and beyond the borders of the Republic if all the requirements are met. It also allows jurisdiction over people who are South African, and foreign nationals who are present in the country after the commission of the crime, regardless of the nationality of the victims.

To give effect to this far reaching legislation a Priority Crimes Litigation Unit (PCLU), staffed by five advocates and one administrator, was established

---

4 Du Plessis et al., 'Africa Efforts to Close the Impunity Gap', ISS Series, November 2012, available at: www.issafrica.org/uploads/Paper241.pdf.

within the NPA through a Presidential Proclamation issued on 23 March 2003. A Special Director of Public Prosecutions leads the PCLU and is mandated to 'manage and direct' the prosecution of crimes mentioned in the ICC Act and other serious offences. The South African Police Service (SAPS) are required to assist the PCLU. The establishment of professional units, tasked and mandated to handle priority crimes is a reflection of South Africa's commitment to the investigation and prosecution of international crimes. The existence of a useful legislative framework and the bodies mandated to investigate core crimes was identified by the Southern Africa Litigation Centre (SALC) as an opportunity to seek justice for victims of torture (committed as a crime against humanity) in neighbouring Zimbabwe.

3.1. *SOUTHERN AFRICA LITIGATION CENTRE AND ANOTHER V. THE NATIONAL DIRECTOR OF PUBLIC PROSECUTIONS AND OTHERS*[5]

The most meaningful invocation of South Africa's ICC Act to date is in the case of *Southern Africa Litigation Centre and Another v. The National Director of Public Prosecutions and Others*. This case was the first judicial pronouncement on South Africa's ICC Act. The events that gave rise to this case took place in Zimbabwe, in March 2007 when state police raided the headquarters of the opposition party, the Movement for Democratic Change (MDC), and subsequently tortured and detained a number of suspected and actual MDC members. Acts of torture included waterboarding, electrocution and severe beatings. SALC, in conjunction with the South Africa-based Zimbabwe Exiles Forum (ZEF), complied a detailed dossier containing evidence of widespread and systematic torture implicating high ranking Zimbabwean officials. The dossier was submitted by SALC to the PCLU requesting that the authorities investigate these crimes pursuant to the ICC Act. The evidence in SALC's dossier demonstrated that the raid on the MDC headquarters and the subsequent acts of torture were not isolated and formed part of a larger campaign of state-sanctioned torture sufficient to fall under the definition of crimes against humanity.

However, more than a year after the submission of the docket, the NPA and the SAPS notified SALC that they would not be initiating an investigation into the allegations of torture as requested by SALC. SALC was of the view that the authorities had not dealt with the dossier in accordance with South Africa's obligations in terms of the ICC Act and so had acted unlawfully. SALC accordingly approached the North Gauteng High Court seeking judicial review of the decision not to investigate.

5 Also known as the 'Zimbabwe Torture Case'.

3.1.1. *The High Court Proceedings*

The High Court was tasked with determining a number of issues including the legal standing of the applicants; the nature and extent of the obligation on the South African authorities to investigate and prosecute international crimes; the threshold for investigations; matters of jurisdiction; and the relevance of political considerations.

The authorities submitted that SALC had no legal standing and that they lacked sufficient interest to bring this matter to court. In response, SALC submitted, that in accordance with South African law, an organisation can bring a matter before the court provided the matter is of public interest and being brought on behalf of people who cannot act in their own name. The Court agreed with SALC indicating that denying legal standing would 'lead to the untenable situation that it would deny victims of international crimes standing in South African proceedings.'[6]

The nature and extent of the obligation on the South African authorities to investigate and prosecute international crimes was central to this case and the Court made it abundantly clear that there is an obligation on South Africa to investigate and prosecute crimes against humanity. The Court also shed light on the requisite threshold for the initiation of an investigation in terms of the ICC Act, and determined that there must be a 'reasonable basis' upon which to open an investigation. This is the same standard used at the ICC when the Prosecutor is deciding whether or not to initiate an investigation.

This determination by the High Court was significant because the ICC Act itself is silent on this aspect of investigations. SALC used relevant jurisprudence from cases before the ICC itself, to demonstrate that the authorities had conflated different thresholds by using the sufficiency of evidence for prosecution standards, not that for investigation standards. The authorities should have asked themselves whether there is enough evidence to open an investigation, not whether there is enough evidence in the docket to prosecute.

The most important aspect of this case was the discourse on matters of jurisdiction. Understanding whether a South African court has jurisdiction over crimes against humanity perpetrated in Zimbabwe by Zimbabweans who visit South Africa hinges on the correct interpretation of section 4(3)(c) of the ICC Act which states: 'Any person who commits [an ICC] crime outside the territory of the Republic, is deemed to have committed that crime within the territory of the Republic if that person, after the commission of the crime, is present in the territory of the Republic'.

The authorities argued that section 4(3)(c) created what they referred to as conditional universal jurisdiction, meaning that South Africa could

6 *Southern Africa Litigation Centre and Another v. National Director of Public Prosecutions and Others*, 2012 (10) BCLR, para. 13.

not exercise any form of jurisdiction over the crimes in the docket until the suspects were physically present in the country. SALC countered this argument by invoking section 4(1) of the ICC Act which states that '[d]espite anything to the contrary in any other law in the Republic, any person who commits an [international] crime, is guilty of an offence'. SALC argued that when section 4(1) and 4(3)(c) are read together, the legislation confers jurisdiction on South African authorities to investigate alleged offences because section 4(1) relates to prescriptive jurisdiction (the power to make laws) and section 4(3) pertains solely to enforcement jurisdiction (the power to enforce laws and rules). SALC explained that presence is required when exercising enforcement jurisdiction (to avoid trials in absentia) but not for prescriptive jurisdiction – and so presence was not required for investigations. The Court agreed with this argument, and rejected the authorities' view that investigations can only occur when the suspect is present in the country, as flawed.

The relevance of taking political considerations into account when deciding whether to investigate was also discussed as the authorities argued that foreign policy concerns dictated that they should not initiate investigations into Zimbabweans. They submitted that investigations would sour relations between South Africa and Zimbabwe and affect South Africa's position as the SADC mediator between the two political camps in Zimbabwe. The Court held that political considerations have no place when deciding whether or not to investigate crimes under the ICC Act.

In summation, Judge Hans Fabricius of the North Gauteng High Court held that the decision not to investigate was unlawful and inconsistent with the Constitution and therefore invalid. The NPA and the SAPS were found not to have acted in accordance with their obligations under the ICC Act, as well as the National Prosecuting Authority Act 32 of 1998 and the South African Police Service Act 68 of 1995. The Judge ordered that they do the 'necessary expeditious and comprehensive investigation of the crimes alleged in the torture docket.'[7]

The High Court judgment was particularly significant and unique in its tone and emphatic language, but, more importantly, it provided practical and substantive content to the obligations to investigate and prosecute international crimes. It was the first judgment to underscore South Africa's international criminal law obligations and confirmed that South Africa would not be a safe haven for perpetrators of egregious crimes. This judgment also confirmed that civil society organisations do have the required legal standing to challenge government's failure to adhere to legal obligations and demonstrated the vital role that civil society can play when authorities are unwilling or when they have misunderstood their responsibilities.

The decision was taken on appeal to the Supreme Court of Appeal (SCA) by the NPA and SAPS and was heard in November 2013.

---

7 *Ibid*, para. 33.5.

4. THE SUPREME COURT OF APPEAL PROCEEDINGS

A full bench of the SCA heard the case and the following three issues were tackled: whether the South African authorities are competent to investigate allegations of international crimes when the suspect is not present in South Africa; whether investigations and prosecutions are subject to the same jurisdictional requirements under the ICC Act; and if there is indeed competence to investigate, if there is a duty to investigate in every situation. Submissions from all parties remained largely unchanged and judgment on the matter was issued on 29 November 2013.

The SCA judgment was less riveting in comparison to the High Court judgment, however, the SCA held that SAPS is both empowered and required to investigate the crimes against humanity detailed in the dossier. The judgment effectively set aside the High Court ruling and distanced itself from some of the statements made by Judge Fabricius in his High Court judgment. The SCA opted for a more careful approach and made it clear that, although it was sufficiently empowered to order that an investigation take place it was not within the Court's mandate to tell the authorities how to go about their work. The SCA also made it clear that this ruling is intrinsically linked to the facts of the case and the evidence in the dossier, and so removed the concern that its judgment would open the floodgates and make South Africa responsible for core crimes committed everywhere. Despite two judgments in favour of investigation, the matter did not end there as the SAPS took the SCA judgment on appeal to the Constitutional Court.

5. CONSTITUTIONAL COURT PROCEEDINGS

By this time the NPA had fallen out of the matter leaving the SAPS to tackle the SCA judgment. The appeal was heard in May 2014, and judgment was handed down on 30 October 2014. The argument in this Court was limited to whether SAPS has the power to investigate international crimes committed outside South Africa if the suspect is not present within South Africa's territory. The question of presence became the focus of the case as it was commonly accepted by both parties that prosecution could not commence without the physical presence of the suspect in the country. The Constitutional Court was tasked with determining whether the link between investigations and prosecutions was so close that the same presence restrictions apply to investigations.

The Court had to decide whether the SAPS has the power, then whether there is a duty to investigate in this case, and whether the SCA was correct in ordering an investigation.

The SAPS argued that the SCA had usurped the power of the SAPS by ordering an investigation and submitted that the correct decision would be to remit the decision back to the SAPS to allow the relevant bodies to make decisions that fall within their area of expertise. They argued that it would be against the separation of powers[8] doctrine for the Court to order an investigation. The SAPS also submitted that the presence of the suspected perpetrators in this case was highly unlikely. They contended that the SCA had employed an 'extreme variant of absolutism as regards universal jurisdiction'[9] by expecting the SAPS to investigate the docket. The SAPS remained adamant that they simply did not have the power to investigate crimes committed outside the country unless the suspects were present in South Africa, and that even if they did have the power, they should not be expected to do so in this case as there is no duty to investigate.

SALC's submissions focused on the state's duty to investigate and prosecute crimes against humanity under the Rome Statute and the ICC Act, reiterating that the SAPS have the power to investigate crimes against humanity committed in Zimbabwe by Zimbabweans who visit South Africa. SALC also argued that international law does not prohibit 'investigations in absentia' and provided the Court with a number of examples of the different approach countries take to investigations. SALC submitted that this indicated that there was no international law rule requiring physical presence before an investigation can be initiated. SALC added that the SAPS's complaint that the SCA substituted its decision not to investigate instead of referring the matter back to the SAPS for consideration was without merit.

The Court had to establish whether SAPS has the power to investigate crimes committed outside South Africa whilst the suspect is not present in South Africa, and if so, if there is a duty to investigate in this case. The Court essentially had to rule on whether a court of law is competent to order investigation or whether that is a decision best left in the hands of the SAPS.

At this level of adjudication the case attracted four *amici curiae* including distinguished experts like Professor John Dugard whose submissions highlighted that there is nothing in international law that prohibits investigations without physical presence in the territory of the investigating country. Other submissions came from the Peace and Justice Initiative, a Netherlands based network of international law professionals, the South African non-governmental organisation, the Centre for Applied Legal Studies (CALS), and the Tides Centre, an American non-governmental organisation.

---

8 The division of the state power into three branches, namely the executive, the legislature and the judiciary.

9 SAPS Constitutional Court Heads of Argument, p. 4 at para. 6, available at: www.southern-africalitigationcentre.org/1/wp-content/uploads/2012/11/SAPS-CC-HEADS.pdf.

On 30 October 2014, in a unanimous judgment, South Africa's highest court ruled that the SAPS has a legal duty to investigate allegations of crimes against humanity committed in Zimbabwe by Zimbabweans, against Zimbabweans.

Central to the judgment are the following issues: (a) in terms of international and domestic law, the presence of the suspect is not required for investigations but is required for prosecution; and (b) universal jurisdiction is applicable, but must be subject to the principles of subsidiarity and practicability.

In this judgement the Court drew a clear distinction between investigation and prosecution of international crimes on the basis of universal jurisdiction. Whereas the dominant position in international law suggests that the presence of the accused in a state is a prerequisite to prosecution,[10] there is no such presence requirement as a prerequisite to investigation. In terms of domestic law, the Court ruled that the Constitution requires the 'presence of an accused during his or her trial',[11] and is silent on whether presence is required for investigations. In the Court's view, the exercise of universal jurisdiction, for purposes of the investigation of an international crime committed outside South Africa's territory, can take place in the absence of a suspected perpetrator without violating the Constitution or international law.[12]

The Court then noted several reasons for following this approach, including that requiring presence for an investigation would render futile South Africa's attempts to combat extraterritorial crimes against humanity, because it would not make practical sense to initiate charges or prosecution against a suspected perpetrator, who is only temporarily within the state, without having conducted a certain degree of prior investigation.[13] The Court indicated that to understand the issue of presence, the following three jurisdictional distinctions[14] should be made: (1) prescriptive jurisdiction, which empowers states to prohibit conduct through domestic legislation; (2) adjudicative jurisdiction, which allows states to enforce prohibitions on conduct through investigations and prosecutions for example; and (3) enforcement jurisdiction, which refers to the state's capacity 'to determine the outcome of matters pursued through the exercise of adjudicative jurisdiction by, for example, enforcing decisions on proscribed conduct'.[15]

The judgment then links the different types of jurisdiction to universality, which is an integral component of this case. The Court reasoned that domestic criminal jurisdiction based on universality applies to prescriptive jurisdiction, but can also apply to adjudicative jurisdiction as long as the latter is subject to

10 *National Commissioner of the South African Police Service v. Southern Africa Human Rights Litigation Centre and Another* [2014] ZACC 30, para. 47.

11 *Ibid*, para. 43.

12 *Ibid*, para. 47.

13 *Ibid*, para. 48.

14 *Ibid*, para. 25.

15 *Ibid*, para. 25.

the constraints of territoriality.[16] The Court concluded that investigations – which constitute an exercise of adjudicative jurisdiction – are allowed under the principles regulating universal jurisdiction, as long as they are confined to the territory of the investigating state.

The application of universal jurisdiction in this case is particularly noteworthy given the existing universal jurisdiction landscape.

Universal jurisdiction was very popular during the 1990s in Europe. However, European states have been circumspect about universal jurisdiction of late, limiting its use by amending their laws. In the past, nations like Belgium were trailblazers with regard to the application of universal jurisdiction as Belgium had the most far reaching and purest form of universal jurisdiction that required no nexus whatsoever between the acts, the accused, and the state of Belgium.[17]

In 2001 and 2003 respectively, Belgium boldly initiated cases against Ariel Sharon, in a bid to prosecute him for the massacre of innocent civilians in Lebanon in 1982, and against former president George H.W. Bush for the bombing in Baghdad during the first Gulf War.[18] Unfortunately, the initiation of these cases resulted in the United States of America and NATO threatening to withdraw the NATO base from Brussels if Belgium did not amend the scope of its universal jurisdiction laws.[19] The legislation was amended and significantly limited in 2003. Currently, a nexus to Belgium is required before complaints can be filed under Belgian universal jurisdiction laws.

The steady decline in the use of universal jurisdiction globally is particularly what makes the Constitutional Court judgement in the Zimbabwe Torture case significant. The judgment effectively breathes new life into the application of universal jurisdiction, and shows the way in which universal jurisdiction principles might be embraced whilst safeguarding against the potential risks of an absolutist approach. The Court did this by articulating two very important and sobering limitations to the application of universal jurisdiction: the principles of subsidiarity[20] and practicability.[21]

---

16 *Ibid*, para. 29.

17 In 1993 the Belgian Loi du 16 juin was enacted. It codifies the use and application of universal jurisdiction (for international crimes) in Belgian courts over war crimes, crimes against humanity, and genocide regardless of where they were perpetrated. Loi relative à la repression des violations graves de droit international humanitaire [Act on the repression of serious violations of the international humanitarian law] of 16 June 1993 Moniteur Belge [M.B.] 5 Aug 1993 Art. 7 ('Belgian jurisdictions are competent to hear offenses provided for under this act, regardless of the location where they have been committed').

18 Ratner 2003, p. 890.

19 *Ibid*, pp. 890–91.

20 *National Commissioner of the South African Police Service v. Southern Africa Human Rights Litigation Centre and Another* [2014] ZACC 30, para. 61.

21 *Ibid*, para. 63.

Subsidiarity means that South Africa may investigate international crimes committed abroad only if the state with traditional jurisdiction is 'unwilling or unable'[22] to prosecute, and only if the investigation is confined to the territory of the investigating state. The Court made it clear that if Zimbabwe were able and willing to investigate and prosecute the alleged instances of torture, South Africa would not have any jurisdiction.[23] The principle of practicability requires that before assuming universal jurisdiction over an extraterritorial international crime, South African authorities must consider whether embarking on an investigation is 'reasonable and practicable in light of the particular circumstances of the case.'[24] In making this assessment, the following must be considered: whether the investigation is likely to lead to a prosecution; and accordingly, whether the alleged perpetrators are likely to be present in the investigating state on their own, or through an extradition request. Simply put, the Court stated that the ultimate enquiry (having considered all the relevant facts) is whether it is reasonable to investigate crimes against humanity committed in another country.

These limits and well-articulated considerations are not only legally sound, but provide a road map for the application of universal jurisdiction. With the limits of subsidiarity, practicability, and reasonableness, the principle of universal jurisdiction can be viewed with less scepticism. The Constitutional Court judgment could also be a very useful model for other jurisdictions grappling with the concept of universal jurisdiction and could also show legislatures and judiciaries that universal jurisdiction need not be feared, but should rather be embraced.

Accountability for serious crimes should be a priority for the international community, and if principles like universal jurisdiction can assist in the eradication of impunity, they should be utilised.

6. CONCLUDING REMARKS ON THE ZIMBABWE TORTURE CASE

Litigating international crimes at a domestic level is not without its challenges. The Zimbabwe Torture Case was initiated in 2008 and after six years of litigation a final order was given and investigations are underway. It is unfortunate and untenable for victims to have to wait six years for justice. However, important ground has been covered and international criminal justice will mark the Zimbabwe Torture Case as the point where public interest litigation was used to try to secure accountability for crimes regardless of where they were committed.

22 *Ibid*, para. 62.
23 *Ibid*, para. 62.
24 *Ibid*, para. 64.

This case also highlights the fact that South Africa has a brave and daring judiciary that will seek to uphold the rule of law and consistent and correct application of the law. This case was politically sensitive and had extraterritorial implications, yet this did not deter the judiciary from upholding the law.

7. THE BASHIR CASE (*SALC V. THE MINISTER OF JUSTICE AND OTHERS*)

In 2015, the 25th African Union Summit was held in Johannesburg, South Africa, and Sudanese President Omar Al-Bashir was invited to attend. President Bashir has been indicted by the ICC on seven counts of crimes against humanity and war crimes and three counts of genocide. The first indictment came in 2009,[25] followed swiftly by a 2010[26] indictment.

Bashir's alleged crimes stem from the brutal suppression of an insurgency mounted by rebel groups in 2003, in Darfur. The rebel groups, including the Justice and Equality Movement (JEM), and the Sudanese Liberation Army (SLA), felt marginalised and discriminated by Bashir's government, and in a bid to address this, they challenged the government.[27]

The conflict rages on today with United Nations figures indicating that roughly 300,000[28] people have died, and an additional 4.7 million have been directly affected by the conflict. These crimes continue to be perpetrated with impunity. The ICC has also identified other suspected perpetrators including members of Bashir's government as well as leaders form the rebel groups.[29]

As a signatory to the Rome Statute, South Africa committed itself to cooperating with the Court, which included compliance with regard to the enforcement of arrest warrants. South Africa has also made commitments at the domestic level by domesticating the Rome Statute, where it articulates its intention to ensure that South Africa adheres to its international obligations, including the arrest and surrender of suspected perpetrators sought by the ICC.[30]

---

25 Issued 4 March 2009. *The Prosecutor v. President Omar Al-Bashir*, available at: www.icc-cpi.int/en_menus/icc/situations%20and%20cases/situations/situation%20icc%200205/related%20cases/icc02050109/pages/icc02050109.aspx.

26 Issued 12 July 2010. *The Prosecutor v. President Omar Al-Bashir*, available at: www.icc-cpi.int/en_menus/icc/situations%20and%20cases/situations/situation%20icc%200205/related%20cases/icc02050109/pages/icc02050109.aspx.

27 'Q and A Sudan's Darfur Conflict', *BBC*, available at: http://news.bbc.co.uk/2/hi/africa/3496731.st (accessed 1 June 2015).

28 UNICEF, 'Darfur Overview', available at: www.unicef.org/infobycountry/sudan_darfur overview.html (accessed 12 July 2015).

29 ICC, 'Sudan Darfur Situation', available at: www.icc-cpi.int/en_menus/icc/situations%20and%20cases/situations/situation%20icc%200205/Pages/situation%20icc-0205.aspx (accessed 12 July 2015).

30 Preamble, ICC Act.

Following the news of his arrival and the fact that he had not been arrested, SALC took the matter to the North Gauteng High Court on a Saturday evening seeking the implementation of the ICC arrest warrant. The matter was heard the following morning on an urgent basis.

The government of South Africa opposed the court application and requested that the matter be postponed. The matter was postponed until later that afternoon but having learnt lessons from previous experience in Nigeria, as discussed below; SALC requested that the Court issue an interim order mandating the government of South Africa to ensure that every port of entry and exit is made aware that President Bashir should not be allowed to leave the country.

When the matter resumed in Court the following day, the judges ruled that President Bashir should be arrested and detained for subsequent transfer to The Hague. It was at that point that the state informed the Court that they believed that President Bashir had left the country. The Court then requested that the state produce an explanatory affidavit detailing how it is that President Bashir was allowed to leave in direct contravention of the Court's order.[31]

This case caused a rule of law crisis in South Africa as the government that is meant to uphold the Constitution and the rule of law acted in contravention of constitutionally enshrined values. By allowing President Bashir to leave, the South Africa government not only failed to uphold the rule of law but it failed the victims of egregious crimes in Darfur. South Africa has a duty, as a member of the community of nations committed to ending impunity and defending human rights, to make sure that suspected perpetrators like President Bashir have their day in court.

However, there were some positive outcomes from this situation as the South African judiciary stood firmly in support of the nation's Constitution and in support of justice.

8. OTHER INITIATIVES

Other organisations have also been engaged in similar initiatives. In 2011, prior to the Zimbabwe Torture Case High Court judgment, the Media Review Network and the Palestinian Solidarity Alliance, two Johannesburg based civil society organisations, submitted a dossier to the PCLU, alleging that international crimes had been committed in the Gaza area by the Israeli authorities including the former Israeli Foreign Minister Tzipi Livni. The NPA were asked to investigate and if appropriate prosecute those involved in the perpetration of war

---

31 All the legal papers and judgment are available at: www.southernafricalitigationcentre.org/cases/ongoing-cases/south-africasudan-seeking-implementation-of-icc-arrest-warrant-for-president-bashir/.

crimes and crimes against humanity during Israel's Operation Cast Lead.[32] The PCLU indicated that there was insufficient evidence to proceed. Although this did not lead to prosecutions it is once again an example of civil society pushing for accountability.[33]

In August 2012, after the High Court Judgment in the Zimbabwe Torture Case, the NPA announced that it had opened an investigation into Madagascar's former head of state Marc Ravalomanana following pressure from a group known as the Association of the Martyrs of Antananarivo Merrina Square. The group claimed that Ravalomanana had committed crimes against humanity in Madagascar when he reportedly ordered the shooting of protesters at the presidential palace in the capital Antananarivo on 7 February 2009.[34] According to reports 71 people were killed and over 698 injured.[35] This was the first time that the NPA took a decision to investigate crimes under the ICC Act. Ravalomanana was in exile in South Africa at the time the decision to investigate was made. He allegedly escaped South Africa and returned to Madagascar in 2014.[36]

Also in 2012 the South Africa based Ogaden Community approached the NPA seeking the arrest of the late Prime Minister of Ethiopia Meles Zenawi for his alleged role in crimes against humanity and genocide perpetrated against the Ogaden people in the Ogaden region. However, the NPA refused to pursue the matter.[37]

Securing accountability at a domestic level is also being attempted in other parts of the African continent. In Kenya, four civil society organisations[38] have begun public interest litigation with regard to the crimes committed during the 2007/2008 post-election violence (PEV) in Kenya. In particular they are working with victims of sexual and gender-based violence and have brought a case before the Constitutional and Human Rights Division of the High Court, against the Attorney General, the Director of Public Prosecutions, the Inspector General of the National Police Service, the Independent Police Oversight Authority, the Ministry of Medical Service and the Ministry of Public Health and Sanitation.

---

32 A three-week armed conflict in the Gaza Strip between Israel and Palestinian militants that began on 27 December 2008 and ended on 18 January 2009 in a unilateral ceasefire.

33 Du Plessis et al., 'Africa Efforts to Close the Impunity Gap', 2012, ISS Series, p. 16, available at: www.issafrica.org/uploads/Paper241.pdf.

34 Gevers, 'South Africa Investigating 'Crimes Against Humanity' in Madagascar', 7 August 2012, available at: http://warandlaw.blogspot.com/2012/08/south-africa-investigating-elleged.html.

35 'NPA called on to probe crimes outside SA', 2 April 2012, *Sunday Independent*, available at: www.iol.co.za/sundayindependent/npa-called-on-to-probe-crimes-outside-sa-1.1268181#.U6qLOfmSyAU.

36 'Ex-Presidents mysterious exit', 24 October 2014, *Mail and Guardian*, available at: http://mg.co.za/article/2014-10-23-ex-presidents-mysterious-exit.

37 Du Plessis et al., 'Africa Efforts to Close the Impunity Gap', 2012, ISS Series, available at: www.issafrica.org/uploads/Paper241.pdf.

38 The Coalition on Violence against Women (COVAW), the Kenyan Section of the International Commission of Jurists (ICJ-Kenya), Physicians for Human Rights and the Independent Medico-Legal Unit (IMLU).

The Kenyan authorities have been taken to court to answer for their failure to adequately train and prepare police to protect the civilian population from acts of sexual violence. Allegedly, after the PEV the police declined or neglected to investigate and sufficiently document allegations of sexual and gender based violence. This failure, the organisations argue, constitutes an obstruction of justice. The Kenyan government has also been accused of depriving the population of emergency medical services, and failing to provide compensation for pain and suffering. The civil society organisations are hoping to get the government to make a public apology to the victims; provide appropriate compensation, including psycho-social, medical, and legal assistance to the victims; investigate sexual violence and prosecute those who are responsible; and establish a special team within the Department of Public Prosecutions to ensure that such investigations and prosecutions are credible.[39] The litigation was filed on 20 February 2013 and so is still in its early stages but will hopefully be one of many domestic efforts in Kenya to secure accountability for the crimes committed during the PEV.

Further west from Kenya, in the Democratic Republic of Congo (DRC), is another example of litigating international crimes in a domestic system. The mobile courts used in the DRC are a novel and efficient way of administering justice in that particular context. Due to the unprecedented level of sexual and gender based violence in remote areas of the DRC, the American Bar Association's Rule of Law Initiative (ABA ROLI) helped establish mobile courts that are designed to hold criminal trials in the remote rural areas. The courts are staffed by Congolese individuals and aim to administer justice, train lawyers and judges on matters of international and domestic criminal law and sensitise communities to the ills of sexual and gender based violence whilst sending a message that will hopefully deter future perpetrators. The courts effectively apply international and domestic law and make it accessible and palatable for local communities. This model is also a good example of cooperation between different sectors as the DRC government, the non-governmental organisations and the United Nations all work together to see that the mobile courts are efficient and effective. Between October 2009 and October 2012 the mobile courts in South Kivu had heard 382 cases, had 204 convictions for rape and 82 convictions for other offences and 67 acquittals.[40]

Securing accountability for international crimes in a domestic context can apply to crimes committed in one's territory or crimes committed outside of one's territory. Like the Zimbabwe Torture Case, the Nigerian Coalition of the ICC (NCICC) has also been engaged in litigation for crimes committed outside Nigerian territory. The NCICC has been litigating in Nigeria's domestic courts in an attempt to arrest Sudanese president Omar Al-Bashir who has been charged

---

39 For more information visit: http://covaw.or.ke/.

40 'Justice in the DRC Mobile Gender Courts Combat Rape and Impunity in Eastern Congo', 2013, Open Society Foundations, available at: www.opensocietyfoundations.org/sites/default/files/justice-drc-20130114.pdf.

with crimes against humanity and genocide by the ICC. The NCICC has been engaged in efforts to ensure that he does not set foot in Nigeria without risking arrest and subsequent transfer to The Hague. Their efforts are particularly interesting as, unlike the South African example highlighted above, there is no domestic legislation to incorporate the Rome Statute in Nigeria, which has resulted in the NCICC trying to use treaty obligations (in the form of Nigeria signing the Rome Statute) and to use domestic law to secure an arrest warrant.[41]

On 14 July 2013 Bashir arrived unannounced in Nigeria, and the NCICC promptly filed their court documents on 15 July 2013 requesting that the courts issue a domestic arrest warrant for Bashir in the case of *NCICC & Others v. Federal Republic of Nigeria*. However, during the court proceedings the news that Bashir had unexpectedly left Nigeria reached the court and the proceedings were abandoned. However, the NCICC were quick to act and this time hoped to secure a standing provisional arrest warrant that would be executed at any time should Bashir return to Nigeria. This case was filed as *NCICC & Others v. Federal Republic of Nigeria No. 2*.[42]

If the NCICC succeeds with its litigation it will show that judicial orders encouraging the implementation of treaty obligations can be used to secure accountability regardless of whether the Rome Statute has been incorporated on a domestic level or not. This could be a niche form of litigation and a viable option for signatories to the Rome Statute that are yet to domesticate it.

The Kenyan section of the International Commission of Jurists has also been involved in efforts to arrest Bashir.[43] In 2011 the organisation filed an application before the High Court seeking an arrest warrant for Bashir should he be found in Kenya. The Kenyan High Court issued a provisional arrest warrant, but ICJ Kenya did not stop there. After the arrest warrant was issued they managed to ensure that should the Kenyan Attorney General and the Minister of Internal Security hear of Bashir's travelling to Kenya, they are under a legal obligation to prepare to arrest him and surrender him to the ICC.

9. THE ROLE OF CIVIL SOCIETY

All of these initiatives are due to civil society efforts to ensure that justice and accountability remain as priorities. Civil society can and should play a role in promoting international criminal justice at the domestic level. The existence of a constitutionally guaranteed space that allows civil society actors to litigate in the interest of the public is fundamental to bringing issues of international criminal justice to the courts. The existence of this space allows civil society organisations

---

41 For more information visit: www.ncicc.org.ng/index.php/component/content/article/37-news/latest-news/71-press-statement-release-date-15th-july-2013.

42 At the time of writing the outcome of this case was unknown.

43 For more information visit: www.icj-kenya.org/index.php/component/content/article/7-news/491-icj-kenya.

to represent the interests of the victims, engage with experts and bring strategic and well-conceived issues before the courts. The ICC should not be the only mechanism tasked with accountability for egregious crimes and civil society are well positioned to push for national accountability. Where governments fail to act, civil society must navigate this space and aim for accountability.

With regard to matters like universal jurisdiction that can raise political concerns, civil society as neutral, non-aligned bodies should advance the view that political considerations should not be given precedence over accountability for human rights violations. Public interest litigation is a very good way to raise awareness and ventilate complex issues like universal jurisdiction.

Litigation must be accompanied with strong advocacy that is tailor made to spread an accurate and compelling message and civil society are well placed to do so. Civil society are also at the forefront of ensuring that once a precedent is set, implementation and application follow.

10. CONCLUSION

Securing accountability for international crimes involves a collaborative effort from various sectors of society and it should not be a task left to the ICC alone. Civil society have been the driving force from various angles including pushing for domestication of international legislation, gathering evidence for prosecution, instituting strategic litigation and being a voice for the victims. In all the case studies highlighted above, civil society have provided the impetus and urged the relevant authorities to ensure accountability. As non-partisan entities, civil society has the space to manoeuvre and do the job that parliamentarians and government officials are hesitant to do.

There are great challenges in pursuing accountability for core crimes including gathering sufficient evidence in a manner that will meet the professional investigative standards, securing the support of the authorities, financial constraints, and the fact that litigation is time consuming. However, litigation at a domestic level is a good way to raise awareness and generate discussion around issues of international justice. The idea of making international law a matter of national importance makes the issues digestible on a policy making level and fortifies the resolve to combat impunity. The ICC's strenuous mandate can be alleviated by more domestic litigation for international crimes, which would echo former Prosecutor Luis Moreno Ocampo's words, 'the number of cases that reach the Court should not be a measure of its efficiency. On the contrary, the absence of trials before this Court, as a consequence of regular functioning of national institutions, would be a major success'.[44]

---

44 Luis Moreno Ocampo at the ceremony for the solemn undertaking of the Chief Prosecutor of the International Criminal Court, 16 June 2003.

BIBLIOGRAPHY

BOOKS AND JOURNAL ARTICLES

Ratner 2003
Ratner, S.R., 'Belgium's War Crimes Statute: A Postmortem', American J of Int'l Law, 2003.

JURISPRUDENCE

Constitutional Court of South Africa 2014
SACC, National Commissioner of The South African Police Service v. Southern African Human Rights Litigation Centre and Another, CCT 02/14, ZACC 30, 30 October 2014.
ICC 2010
ICC, Prosecutor v. Omar Hassan Ahmad Al-Bashir, ICC-02/05–01/09, 12 July 2010.
ICC 2009
ICC, Prosecutor v. Omar Hassan Ahmad Al-Bashir, ICC-02/05–01/09, 4 March 2009.
North Gauteng High Court 2012
NGHC, Southern African Litigation Centre and Another v. National Director of Public Prosecutions and Others, 77150/09, ZAGPPHC 61, 8 May 2012.
Supreme Court of Appeal of South Africa 2013
SCA, National Director of Public Prosecutions and Another v. Southern Africa Litigation Centre and Another. 485/2012, 27 November 2013.

TREATIES, LEGISLATION AND AGREEMENTS

Belgium, Loi du 16 juin 1993 relative à la repression des violations graves de droit international humanitaire (Act on the repression of serious violations of international humanitarian law of 16 June 1993), 16 June 1993.
Rome Statute of the International Criminal Court, 2187 UNTS 90/37, 17 July 1998.

OTHERS

BBC, 'Q and A Sudan's Darfur Conflict', 2010.
Du Plessis, M. et al., 'Africa Efforts to Close the Impunity Gap', ISS Paper No. 241, November 2012.
Fabricius, P., 'NPA called on to probe crimes outside SA', The Sunday Independent, 2 April 2012.
Gevers, C., 'South Africa Investigating "Crimes Against Humanity" in Madagascar', War and Law Blog, 7 August 2012.
ICC, Situation in Darfur, Sudan, ICC-02/05.

International Commission of Jurists (Kenyan Section), 'ICJ asks government of Kenya to arrest Sudan President Bashir on his intended visit'.
Louw-Vaudran, L., 'Ex-Presidents mysterious exit', Mail and Guardian, 24 October 2014.
National Commissioner of the South African Police Service v. Southern African Human Rights Litigation Centre and Another (Constitutional Court of South Africa 2014), SAPS Written Submissions.
Open Society Foundations, 'Justice in the DRC Mobile Gender Courts Combat Rape and Impunity in Eastern Congo', 2013.
Southern Africa Litigation Centre, South Africa/Sudan: Seeking Implementation of ICC Arrest Warrant for President Bashir, Legal Papers and Judgments.
UNICEF, 'Darfur – overview'.

THE LEGACY OF THE INTERNATIONAL CRIMINAL TRIBUNAL FOR RWANDA

André KLIP

1. INTRODUCTION

To address the legacy of the International Criminal Tribune for Rwanda (ICTR) at this time seems to be a rather strange exercise as the ICTR is still working, albeit in the context of the Residual Mechanism. It is like writing an obituary for a person who is still alive.[1] The approach I have therefore partly chosen is to deal with the ICTR and its legacy from the perspective of how one would look back at the ICTR in some 25 years from now. How will the ICTR be assessed in 2040? This is a perspective that might enable us to look at the headlines and highlight what really had an impact on the development of international criminal law or the practice of international criminal tribunals and states. It is also an approach that focuses less on the technical legal details and may be more policy oriented.[2] On the other hand, it will be inevitable to deal with some current issues as well.

2. THE FIRST AFRICAN INTERNATIONAL CRIMINAL TRIBUNAL

To a certain extent the ICTR was the logical consequence of the establishment of the ICTY. Once the United Nations Security Council was willing to set up an

---

1 However, one author already wrote about the legacy of the ICTR in 2005, see Van den Herik 2005, p. 283.

2 I will therefore not meticulously analyse all detailed aspects of the case law of the ICTR, despite the fact that there might be many aspects on which that would be possible. See for such fine-tuning: Agbor, The Problematic Jurisprudence on Instigation under the Statute of the ICTR: The Consistencies, Inconsistencies and Misgivings of the Trial and Appeal Chambers of the ICTR, 13 International Criminal Law Review 2013, pp. 429–472, as well as of the same author Agbor, Instigation to Crimes Against Humanity, The Flawed Jurisprudence of the Trial and Appeal Chambers of the International Criminal Tribunal for Rwanda (ICTR), Martinus Nijhoff Publishers 2013.

international criminal tribunal for atrocities committed in Europe, it was more than logical to create a similar tribunal for a conflict in Africa pending at the same time. Together with its twin sister the ICTY, the ICTR also contributed strongly to the establishment of the ICC, as the existence of the two ad hoc tribunals made clear that it would be impossible for the future to create a separate tribunal for each conflict yet to come.[3] Both the ICTY and the ICTR thus influenced the way other initiatives were shaped, some of which got a hybrid nature (Special Panels for East Timor, the Special Court for Sierra Leone, the Extraordinary Criminal Chambers in Cambodia, as well as the Lebanon Tribunal). The hybrid courts were able to meet the criticism that the relevant national legislation played hardly any role and that the proceedings took place far away from the country involved.[4]

In 2040 we might also be able to identify that the ICTR had been the forerunner for the African Criminal Court, set up by the African community and not by the world community. The ICTR and the ICC did trigger initiatives to establish an African court of its own, the Malabo Protocol or Protocol herein.[5] An International Criminal Law section is established under the Malabo Protocol. Article 28A makes provision for the jurisdiction of the Court. It gives jurisdiction over crimes that fall within the statute of the ICC, as well as other crimes.[6] Another innovative aspect is the introduction of corporate criminal responsibility, as provided for in Article 46C. This might take away the pressure on stretching the legal concept of complicity and joint criminal responsibility as currently takes place in the case law of international criminal tribunals. Like the ICC Statute, the jurisdiction of the Court is based on the principle of complementarity (Article. 46H(1)). Analysing the Protocol from the perspective of whether it complies with the obligations for states deriving from the ICC Statute, there is no formal objection to the establishment of an African Criminal Court by the African Union.[7] On the contrary, it could perfectly fit into a system

3 Van den Herik 2005, p. 279 made the interesting observation that 'the establishment of the ICTR can be considered as one of the overriding reasons for establishing the ICC, precisely because it undermined the idea that the ICTY was a unique solution to a unique situation.'

4 However, we can see that all constructions have their pros and cons. Of the hybrids we can say that they were geographically closer to the people, because the hearings were conducted in the country. However, in East Timor hardly anyone attended, as the hearings were in Portuguese and English, languages the local population had no command of. The most important case of the Sierra Leone Special Court, the Taylor case, was held in The Hague for security reasons. Regarding the Cambodian courts, there were complaints that the national influence, both in applicable law and composition of the chambers might be too strong.

5 Protocol on Amendments to the Protocol on the Statute of the African Court of Justice and Human Rights, adopted at the 23rd Ordinary Session of the African Union, Malabo, Equatorial Guinea, 27 June 2014.

6 Some of which are really new, such as the crime of unconstitutional change of government (Art. 28E).

7 The presumption is that African states do not withdraw from the ICC Statute, but that they wish to provide a regional mechanism before the ICC gets involved. It may be further noted that also the draft protocol has only effect as with regard to new offences, committed after the

based on complementarity. On paper, the ICC crimes are covered and as the ICC should be understood as a court of last resort, for which there is only a task if the national courts cannot perform the job, it will perfectly be in compliance with the ICC Statute.[8]

The ICC has been criticised for focusing too much on the African continent and for that it would demonstrate a racial and colonial attitude towards the continent.[9] I am not convinced by the alleged bias, and regret that the responsibility of African states for African problems is implicitly denied.[10] A self-referral can only exclusively be made by one's own state. If African states are the only ones to refer cases to the ICC, the focus is automatically placed on those states and not on others. I would rather highlight the chances that exist for Africa and the fact that many ICC cases deal with African situations. Most cases that were brought to the ICC are the result of self-referrals.[11] Of most of the situations referred to, one cannot say that these deal with conflicts that are of a minor size. The ICC has only jurisdiction if the situation state is unable or unwilling to take on prosecution. In other words, states have it in their own hands whether the ICC will have a chance to become active. If African states do not take any initiative, there is a fair chance that the ICC might step in. So, in most cases, it is African states themselves that referred their situation to the ICC. Other cases were Security Council referrals (Darfur and Libya) and only the Kenyan case fell within the discretion of the Prosecutor. In two cases (Kenya and Libya), both in which it was not the initiative of the relevant situation state, the admissibility was challenged.[12] This could be seen as a sign that the assumption

entry into force of the Protocol and Statute. The Protocol therefore can have no effect for the pending cases.

8 However, as the grounds of admissibility in Art. 46H(2) of the Protocol are equal to Art. 17 of the ICC Statute, it would trigger the admissibility of two courts at the same time. This problem could be sorted out if the African Union itself were to become a party to the ICC Statute. The other alternative would be that AU states would withdraw from the ICC, which would have effect only for future cases.

9 See 'Much Ado About the Extraordinary AU Summit on the ICC', Africa Legal Aid, available at: www.africalegalaid.com/news/much-ado-about-the-extraordinary-au-summit-on-the-icc; and opening address by Evelyn A. Ankumah – Africa and the ICC: A Stakeholders Meeting on Unsettling and Emerging Issues, available at: www.africalegalaid.com/news/statement-by-evelyn-a-ankumah-africa-and-the-icc. See further Ssenyonjo 2013.

10 If I steal something and my neighbour does the same and I am prosecuted and my neighbour is not, the latter does not take away or reduce my own responsibility.

11 Uganda, Democratic Republic of Congo (DRC), the Central African Republic, Ivory Coast and Mali.

12 ICC's Pre-Trial Chamber I declared the Al-Senussi case inadmissible and the Gaddafi case admissible. See Decision on the admissibility of the case against Abdullah Al-Senussi, ICC-01/11–01/11–466, 11 October 2013 and Public redacted Decision on the admissibility of the case against Saif Al-Islam Gaddafi, ICC-01/11–01/11–344-Red, 31 May 2013. The Appeals Chamber upheld the decisions of the Pre-Trial Chamber, See ICC-01/11–01/11–565 and ICC-01/11–344. The Appeals Chamber rejected the inadmissibility claims in Judgment on the appeal of the Republic of Kenya against the decision of Pre-Trial Chamber II of 30 May 2011 entitled 'Decision on the Application by the Government of Kenya Challenging the

of jurisdiction without the initiative of the situation state is not taken for granted and that the states in question regard themselves capable of conducting the investigations and the trial.

Turning back to the motives behind the African Union's initiative for criminal jurisdiction for its own court instead of the ICC, it must be noted that the AU's reputation with regard to setting up effective international commissions and courts is rather dubious.[13] One might even say that a pattern exists to respond to unwelcome decisions, as can be seen with the SADC tribunal that has subsequently been lamed.[14] If the criticism towards the ICC is grounded in the fact that there are situations since 2001 that were more than qualified to come within the picture of the ICC, there is a point to make. However, they do not always relate to a state party (North Korea, Israel, Tibet, Chechnya, Syria). And some of them also have important links with a permanent member of the Security Council, which would make it almost impossible to get a decision to refer adopted.

There is another point of criticism in which I see some merit and this relates to the fact whether a case under investigation has a sufficient degree of gravity as required under Article 53 of the ICC Statute. Both the situations of Kenya and of Ivory Coast raise some doubts here. Are these really cases in which it is clear from the start that international crimes have been committed on a large scale? Both, despite the fact that quite some casualties occurred, deal with election-related violence over a limited period of time. Not with a government policy to erase a portion or portions of the population over several years. In the Ivory Coast case the referral was signed by the president who had just overthrown his predecessor who is now in jail in The Hague and out of sight in the country. To what extent has the case been referred because it is an easy manner to get rid of an unpleasant political opponent? In the context of today, the ICC has difficulties in managing its workload; it would do well to choose between various situations. In the list of priorities Ivory Coast and Kenya will certainly not rank on top. It

Admissibility of the Case Pursuant to Article 19(2) (b), ICC-01/09–01/11-OA, *Prosecutor v. William Samoei Ruto, Henry Kiprono Kosgey and Joshua Arap Sang*, 30 August 2011. See on the Libyan case further Bassiouni 2013.

13 See on the merger of the African Court of Justice and the African Court on Human and Peoples' Rights, Du Plessis, Implications of the AU decision to give the African Court jurisdiction over international crimes, Institute for Security Studies Paper No. 235, June 2012. At the AFLA Conference in Arusha (1 March 2013), I noted the sarcastic comment in one of the sessions that in Africa it is an unforgivable sin to set up something that functions. See in that respect the lamentable list of states not having submitted their regular reports to the African Commission on Human and Peoples' Rights: www.achpr.org/states/stats/.

14 The Southern African Development Community's Tribunal has effectively been suspended since 2012 as a result of some decisions that were unfavourable to Zimbabwe. See www.osisa.org/law/regional/last-week-save-sadc-tribunal. See further, 'Three illegal and arbitrary decisions taken in bad faith by the SADC Council of Ministers and Summit of Heads of State and Government', available at: www.politicsweb.co.za/documents/three-illegal-and-ultra-vires-decisions.

seems that the ad hoc tribunals were in a better position to make representative choices for the cases under their jurisdiction.

The ICTR contributed to spreading expertise on international criminal justice among Africans. Africans have been able to build up expertise in international criminal law as many have been working for the ICTR, its Office of the Prosecutor and the Defence. The prosecutor of the ICC is an African who worked at the ICTR. African states form the largest block of states that are states party to the ICC Statute. That is knowledge and influence, the latter expressed by the positions that Africans hold and by the votes in the Assembly of States Parties to the ICC.

3. THE GENOCIDE TRIBUNAL

Far and foremost the ICTR will be remembered as the genocide tribunal, as it reached the first conviction on genocide ever. The Akayesu case was the first and most prominent case in which many legal issues were decided.[15] But there were other aspects for which the ICTR was important. It also took the step to accept command responsibility for civil leaders. Practically it was able to try a large section of the de facto leaders in the genocide that was committed in Rwanda.[16] Cynical voices might say that this was not something the ICTR could be proud of, as some of the accused sought refuge and turned themselves in, in order to evade the death penalty in Rwanda.

Certainly not the least was the impact the ICTR had in placing gender based crimes on the agenda. In the judgement in the Akayesu case the ICTR for the first time established that a rape could amount to an act of genocide.[17] This was revolutionary at the time and welcomed by many. Of course later discussions came up whether the ICTR and its prosecutors had done enough to prosecute rape cases.[18] On this aspect – the number of prosecutions and the number of convictions reached in comparison to the sheer number of the crimes committed – it is unlikely that there will be any tribunal meeting a reasonable record. However, I do not think that this is the appropriate standard of measurement, as it is simply impossible to prosecute all crimes. By definition an (international) criminal court can never prosecute all crimes within its jurisdiction.

---

15 ICTR, *Prosecutor v. Akayesu*, ICTR-96-4-T, Judgment, Trial Chamber I, 2 September 1998, Klip/Sluiter, Annotated Leading Cases of International Criminal Tribunals II-399, with a commentary by William Schabas.

16 Van den Herik, 'The Contribution of the Rwanda Tribunal to the Development of International Law', Dissertation, Free University Amsterdam 2005, p. 263.

17 See further Kaites 2014.

18 See Trouille 2013.

Both ad hoc tribunals had a set of rules that offered little for the participation of victims and witnesses in the proceedings. Whilst some attempts were made to change this, these failed. Judge Pillay was quoted to have said: 'The Court is neither designed nor in a position to act as a public forum or claims commission for thousands of individual communications from victims of each situation'.[19] The fact that the rules applicable for ICTY and ICTR offered so little to victims certainly contributed to a new approach and to regard witnesses beyond a source of evidence.[20] However, the words of Pillay still echo, as the question is relevant whether the ICC is equipped to perform these duties. Numerous applications of victims and witnesses to participate and present their concerns at the hearings lame the work of chambers.[21] Other concerns relate to the changed nature of the proceedings, from a two party trial into a three or multiple party trial and its undesirable impact on the presumption of innocence: 'The presumption of victimhood and the presumption of the accused's innocence do not sit easily together.'[22] It seems as if, on the one hand, it has been inevitable to give in to claims 'to do something' about the position of victims.[23] On the other, the implementation has not been thought through thoroughly, both in terms of its practical and logistical demands: (ten) thousands of applications. As well as with regard to the changing nature of the proceedings: victims sharing their concerns without a finding that they are victims of the accused standing trial. The link between the concrete victim and the concrete accused may be lacking in proceedings at the ICC.[24]

4. INTENSE RELATIONSHIP WITH THE SITUATION STATE

Over the years the ICTR faced ups and downs with the situation state.[25] Rwanda has been a rather extraordinary situation state to the extent that it has been extremely active in the prosecution of offenders. Compared with other situations in the past, Rwanda stands out for its ambition in bringing perpetrators to justice. Even compared with another state that had been active in prosecuting its own nationals, Germany, the scale at which Rwanda has been conducting trials is much higher. Most other situation states have not done anything at all.

19 Quoted by Leyh 2011, p. 147.

20 Hankel 2013, p. 30.

21 Van den Wyngaert 2012.

22 Von Wistinghausen 2013, p. 170.

23 On the question why victim participation is necessary and why the goals pursued have not been fully answered yet, see Tonellato 2012.

24 Von Wistinghausen 2013, p. 170.

25 Situation state is terminology deriving from the ICC Statute, but it accurately describes what is relevant here.

Whereas some may have opted for other responses to the atrocities committed in the country, such as Truth and Reconciliation Commissions, Rwanda chose to prosecute in regular trials on a limited scale and around 1 million people were adjudicated in the gacaca proceedings.[26]

Over the years, relations with the ICTR, both with the bench and the Office of the Prosecutor (in particular Carla del Ponte), have been rather tense. Of all the small and big conflicts, it is worth mentioning the Barayagawiza affair of 1998–1999,[27] as well as the blockade to a re-nomination of Prosecutor Carla del Ponte in 2003. The latter was related with the accusations that the OTP concentrated its efforts too much on the Hutu population and that there was very little attention for the crimes that might have been committed by the ruling RPF party led by President Paul Kagame.

What is clear from this is that there was interdependence between the ICTR and the state of Rwanda. One could not do without the other. The ICTR needed the evidence that was located in Rwanda and could give the Rwandese authorities the necessary legitimacy for the procedures they were conducting. One of the last stages in which the ICTR was able to influence the course of events in Rwanda was with the applicable human rights standards for procedure to be referred from the ICTR to Rwanda, the so-called Rule 11*bis* proceedings. On quite a number of occasions the ICTR had refused to refer cases to Rwanda, as it considered the human right standards applicable in that state to be insufficient.

The ICTR applied as the standard of comparison for whether an accused may expect a fair trial in Rwanda the right ensured in Article 20 of the ICTR Statute.[28] The message it thereby gave was that an accused may not lose protection as a result of the referral. On the basis of this right to a fair trial, the Trial Chamber was initially convinced that Rwanda would violate this by not providing an independent tribunal. The practice of Rwanda in these cases at the time was that a single judge would try the case. Despite the fact that Rwanda did ratify relevant human rights obligations, the Trial Chamber noted in the Munyakazi case that it had a reputation of an interrupted cooperation with the ICTR and did not respond impartially to indictments of former members of the RPF by other national jurisdictions.[29] In other cases the same line of argumentation was used. It is stated that Rwandan legislation generally is in compliance with the requirements, but that the country's practice does raise serious concerns.[30]

---

26 See de Brouwer and Ruvebana 2013.

27 See on this episode Ryngaert 2013, pp. 129–132.

28 This section is partly taken from my commentary in Klip/Sluiter, Annotated Leading Cases of International Criminal Tribunals XXXI, pp. 91–94.

29 Decision on the Prosecutor's Request for Referral of Case to the Republic of Rwanda, *Prosecutor v. Munyakazi*, ICTR-97-36-R11bis, Trial Chamber III, 28 May 2008, Klip/Sluiter, Annotated Leading Cases of International Criminal Tribunals XXXI-20, para. 40.

30 Decision on Prosecutor's Request for Referral to the Republic of Rwanda, *Prosecutor v. Kanyarukiga*, ICTR-2002-78-R11bis, Trial Chamber II, 6 June 2008, Klip/Sluiter, Annotated Leading Cases of International Criminal Tribunals XXXI-29.

To a certain extent the decisions mark the final hour of revenge to the Rwandan response to the 1999 Barayagwiza decision, when Rwanda barred the Prosecutor from her Kigali office and took other measures that impeded cooperation with the Tribunal for quite a while. Despite the fact that this occurred years ago, for the Trial Chamber this is proof of the pressure the government may exert on judicial decisions. Additionally, it is referred to fierce responses to indictments by foreign judges of RPF members (the party of the Kagame government). The conclusion of the Trial Chamber was that the accused will be tried by a judge who will be susceptible to outside interference and pressure, especially from the executive. This is considered to be too much to expect of one individual to be able to resist the pressure of a state whose past practice has shown interference with judicial decisions.[31] However, only three weeks after the decision in the Munyakazi case, another Chamber held that 'although the concept of an independent judiciary is relatively new in Rwanda, this is insufficient to call into question the independence, impartiality and competence of the Rwandan judiciary to prevent transfer'.[32] The chambers did not concur on this issue, which is also reflected in a subsequent decision by the Appeals Chamber. The Appeals Chamber in the Munyakazi case followed the latter reasoning and held that the reactions to the 1999 Barayagwiza decision are insufficient to justify fear for interference with the independent judiciary.[33]

The Trial Chamber also feared that witnesses' rights would be violated. Quite a number of witnesses have been murdered over the years. Defence witnesses may fear their appearance will lead to an indictment for 'genocidal ideology.' In that context, the Trial Chamber was not convinced that the accused's fair trial right to obtain the attendance of, and to examine defence witnesses under the same conditions as witnesses called by the prosecution could be guaranteed in Rwanda.[34] Despite the fact that the Kanyarukiga Chamber noted that Rwanda has made notable progress in improving its judicial system, it was not satisfied that the possibility of monitoring the proceedings after referral would solve the

31 Decision on the Prosecutor's Request for Referral of Case to the Republic of Rwanda, *Prosecutor v. Munyakazi*, ICTR-97-36-R11bis, Trial Chamber III, 28 May 2008, Klip/Sluiter, Annotated Leading Cases of International Criminal Tribunals XXXI-21, para. 46.

32 Decision on Prosecutor's Request for the Referral of the Case of Ildephonse Hategekimana to Rwanda, *Prosecutor v. Hategekimana*, ICTR-00-55B-R11bis, Trial Chamber II bis, 19 June 2008, Klip/Sluiter, Annotated Leading Cases of International Criminal Tribunals XXXI-64, par. 46.

33 Decision on Prosecution's Appeal against Decision on Referral under Rule 11 bis, *Prosecutor v. Munyakazi*, ICTR-97-36-R11bis, Appeals Chamber, 8 October 2008; Klip/Sluiter, Annotated Leading Cases of International Criminal Tribunals XXXI-78, para. 28.

34 This was upheld by the Appeals Chamber, Decision on Prosecution's Appeal against Decision on Referral Under Rule 11 bis, *Prosecutor v. Munyakazi*, ICTR-97-36-R11bis, Appeals Chamber, 8 October 2008, Klip/Sluiter, Annotated Leading Cases of International Criminal Tribunals XXXI-71; Decision on the prosecution's appeal against decision on referral under Rule 11*bis*, *Prosecutor v. Kanyarukiga*, ICTR-2002-78-R11bis, Appeals Chamber, 30 October 2008.

problems relating to availability and protection of witnesses and not eliminate the risk of solitary confinement in case of life imprisonment.[35]

The Prosecutor put the matter to rest for some years. However, in view of the completion strategy new attempts were made to refer to Rwanda in 2010. The first case in which the Trial Chamber allowed the transfer to Rwanda was the Uwinkindi case:

> This Chamber notes that, in the intervening period, Rwanda has made material changes in its laws and has indicated its capacity and willingness to prosecute cases referred by this Tribunal. This gives the Referral Chamber confidence that the case of the Accused, if referred, will be prosecuted consistent with internationally recognised fair trial standards enshrined in the Statute of this Tribunal and other human rights instruments. The Referral Chamber is persuaded to refer this case after receiving assurances that a robust monitoring mechanism provided by the ACHPR will ensure that any material violation of the fair trial rights of this Accused will be brought to the attention of the President of the Tribunal forthwith so that remedial action, including revocation, can be considered by this Tribunal, or if applicable, by the Residual Mechanism.[36]

After this case that was decided in 2011, other cases were referred to Rwanda.[37] However, the actual implementation of the referrals had to wait until a monitoring system was set up.[38]

5. THE SUCCESSFUL TRIBUNAL

One way of looking at the achievements is whether the ICTR succeeded in reaching the goals for which it was set up. In Resolution 955 the Security Council laid down that the ICTR was to be established in order to bring an end to the commission of crimes, that it should prosecute those responsible, would further

---

35 *Prosecutor v. Kanyarukiga*, Decision on Prosecutor's Request for Referral to the Republic of Rwanda, ICTR-2002–78-R11bis, Trial Chamber, 6 June 2008, Klip/Sluiter, Annotated Leading Cases of International Criminal Tribunals XXXI-52, para. 103.

36 Decision on Prosecutor's Request for Referral to the Republic of Rwanda Rule 11 bis of the Rules of Procedure and Evidence, *Prosecutor v. Uwinkindi*, ICTR 2001–75–R11bis, 28 June 2011, para. 223.

37 Decision on Prosecutor's Request for Referral to the Republic of Rwanda, *Prosecutor v. Munyagishari*, ICTR-2005–89-R11bis, Referral Chamber, 6 June 2012. Other cases that were referred to Rwanda related to fugitives: *Prosecutor v. Kayishema*, ICTR-01–67-R11bis, transferred on 22 February 2012; *Prosecutor v. Sikubwabo*, ICTR-95–1D-R11bis, transferred on 26 March 2012; *Prosecutor v. Ntaganzwa*, ICTR-96–9-R11bis, transferred on 8 May 2012; *Prosecutor v. Ryandikayo*, ICTR-95-1E-R11bis, transferred on 20 June 2012; *Prosecutor v. Ndimbati*, ICTR-95–1F-R11bis, transferred on 25 June 2012; *Prosecutor v. Munyarugarama*, MICT-12–09-AR14, transferred on 5 October 2012.

38 See Order on the ICTR Monitoring Arrangements, *Prosecutor v. Uwinkindi*, ICTR 2001–75–R11bis, President, 29 June 2012.

national reconciliation and restore and maintain peace. This raises the question whether the standard of measurement is to measure its success or failure. It is for sure that the ICTR will be remembered as a very productive court.[39] However, it is difficult to state objective criteria to judge this. Is it the number of convictions? Is it the fact that no new atrocities were committed? These are all things that also depend on how one sees the effectiveness of criminal law and criminal justice. The general problem is that it is impossible to measure exactly the effects that the existence of any criminal court might have on the behaviour of individuals. With regard to its success, it seems to be reasonable to take the following factors into consideration: the resources of the tribunals in staff, money and time, access to the crime scene, the degree of cooperation the tribunal received from the key players, the distance from the court to crime scenes and the time that has lapsed since the commission of the crimes.

One of the prominent reasons to establish the ICTR was that it would contribute to reconciliation. It is questionable whether one can expect the work of a criminal court to immediately lead to reconciliation. There are some indicators of the opposite conclusion. Criminal trials have the tendency to bring the conflict back to life as all the details of the conflict and the specific atrocities committed will be discussed once again. In addition, the natural position of the accused is to defend himself – he may deny all charges, may state that what he did was no crime at all or may accuse the opposite side of having committed even worse offences. None of these positions will contribute to a mutual understanding of each other's position and interests. The ICTR demonstrated that it is possible to end impunity by means of an international criminal court.

As is the case with most tribunals, the most important decisions were the early decisions of the tribunal. The explanation for that is that in the early days for a tribunal questions of principle arise. After a couple of years of addressing most issues, a stable and consistent practice has emerged and most issues have been decided. Only rarely do entirely new issues pop up decades after the establishment of a new jurisdiction. In comparison with other international criminal tribunals of the time, the performance of the ICTR is reasonably good. It is most doubtful whether the ICC would have been similarly successful if it were in existence earlier. The Special Panels of the Dili District Court in East Timor are certainly an example of how international criminal justice should not be organised.[40] The SCSL can be characterised as the Charles Taylor court. The ECCC will be identified as the tribunal that came far too late. The Lebanon Tribunal started a case without an accused being present and will become the in absentia tribunal. The ICTY as the ethnic cleansing tribunal did perform on

---

39 If we look at how many of the first fifty volumes of the series Annotated Leading Cases of International Criminal Tribunals are dedicated to the ICTR, the ICTR scores a reasonable 13/50 (volumes 2, 6, 10, 12, 17, 18, 22, 24, 25, 31, 32, 36, 42) in the period 1999–2015.

40 See Freeland et al. in Klip 2011, pp. 15–27.

a similar level as the ICTR. The ICC still has not found the solution on which situations it should turn its attention to. It is simply overcommitted.

The ICTR (and ICTY) have demonstrated that the ad hoc model is still an attractive model, as it can prevent some of the problems that the ICC is currently facing. The ICC's Statute gives quite a dominant role to states in the selection of cases. This has led to a situation in which some states may refer a case to the competence of the ICC in order to get rid of a political opponent.

From a perspective of states that would wish to lame the ICC, it would be a perfect scenario to give it as many cases as possible, because it will spread the resources it can use with regard to one specific conflict.[41] It may sound contradictory, but complementarity may lame both the ICC as well as the activities of states and will be rather beneficial for perpetrators. The very existence of the ICC may give states an easy alibi to claim that they are unable to do the job and that the ICC should step in. In reality they might be unwilling, but either reason will function in practice as an excuse for not investigating. The ICC will only be able to combat this if it puts an emphasis on the admissibility threshold that the case is exemplary for international crimes.

One might also not question whether a state claiming to be willing and able should not receive the benefit of the doubt first, as complementarity is formulated as a cornerstone of the ICC system. In the years of its existence the ICTR gave guidance to national authorities in the way it conducted its investigations and trials. However, it seems to have little impact beyond Rwanda. It created a stable practice of investigations, prosecutions and sentencing. However, with regard to the latter, one must identify that the ICTR had predominantly the higher echelon of accused of the situation in Rwanda. In addition, they were also almost all charged with genocide. In that sense the fact that many life sentences were rendered by the ICTR was not a surprise. To phrase it in rhetorical terms: what penalty other than life imprisonment is appropriate for those convicted of genocide?

The ICTR might have been able to give more guidance both with regard to issues related to direct perpetration and the possible application of defences and excuses, as well as with sentencing if the Office of the Prosecutor would have indicted a wider range of perpetrators than the most responsible only. This, however, is a criticism applicable to all tribunals. Apart from the East Timorese Special Panels, all tribunals focused on the leadership only. This means that the legal issues decided related to leadership situations only. The ICTY case of Erdemović demonstrates how important it is that the ICTY could give guidance to national courts in those situations and how different the legal question at stake is. How many of the accused prosecuted before the international criminal tribunals over the last twenty years did actually kill or rape?

---

41 Similarly, there were times at the ICTY that it was profitable for the accused to turn themselves in all at once, as the ICTY could not cope with all cases at the same time.

Because of the many life sentences that it imposed, the ICTR will also give international criminal justice the lead in the way life imprisonment sentences are dealt with. This can be regarded as part of the leftovers: the execution issues, what to do with early release and pardon. It will be the Residual Mechanism that has to take care of this.[42]

6. CONCLUSION

In its more than twenty-year lifespan the ICTR has proven its reasons of existence. It has dealt with a high number of cases under difficult circumstances. An international criminal tribunal can only perform as well as the circumstances allow it to with regard to the quality and the expertise of its staff, the time and money it received to perform its tasks and the cooperation it received and obstruction it faced over the years. In that respect and in comparison to other international criminal tribunals that were implemented, the ICTR did reasonably well.

Whilst I took the perspective of looking at the ICTR in 2040, I must return to the facts of life today and that is that it is a little bit too early. The ICTR is still alive (compared to the life of a human being, it has retired now and is living in an elderly people's home), legacies begin after, but I am quite convinced that one day Africa and the world will miss the ICTR.

BIBLIOGRAPHY

BOOKS AND JOURNAL ARTICLES

Agbor 2013

Agbor, A.A., 'Instigation to Crimes Against Humanity, The Flawed Jurisprudence of the Trial and Appeal Chambers of the International Criminal Tribunal for Rwanda (ICTR)', Martinus Nijhoff Publishers, 2013.

Agbor 2013

Agbor, A.A., 'The Problematic Jurisprudence on Instigation under the Statute of the ICTR: The Consistencies, Inconsistencies and Misgivings of the Trial and Appeal Chambers of the ICTR', 13 International Criminal Law Review, 2013, pp. 429–472.

Bassiouni 2013

Bassiouni, C.M., 'Libya: From Repression to revolution: A record of armed conflict and International Law Violations, 2011–2013', Martinus Nijhoff Publishers, 2013.

De Brouwer and Ruvebana 2013

De Brouwer, A.M. and Ruvebana, E., 'The Legacy of the Gacaca Courts in Rwanda: Survivors' Views', 13 International Criminal Law Review, 2013, pp. 937–976.

42 Art. 26 of Security Council Resolution 1966 (2010).

Du Plessis 2012
Du Plessis, M., 'Implications of the AU decision to give the African Court jurisdiction over international crimes', 235 Institute for Security Studies Paper, June 2012.

Hankel 2013
Hankel, G., 'On Victims and Non-Victims: Observations from Rwanda', in Bonacker, T. and Safferling, C. (eds.), 'Victims of International Crimes: An Interdisciplinary Discourse', Springer, 2013.

Kaites 2014
Kaites, U., 'Genocidal Gender and Sexual Violence: The Legacy of the ICTR, Rwanda's ordinary courts and gacaca courts', Intersentia, 2014.

Klip 2011
Klip, K. and Sluiter, G. (eds.), 'Annotated Leading Cases of International Criminal Tribunals Vol. XXXI: The International Criminal Tribunal for Rwanda 28 November 2007–30 November 2008', Intersentia, 2011.

McGonigle Leyh 2011
McGonigle Leyh, B., 'Procedural Justice, Victim Participation in International Criminal Proceedings', Intersentia, 2011.

Ryngaert 2013
Ryngaert, C., 'State Cooperation with the International Criminal Tribunal for Rwanda', 13 International Criminal Law Review, 2013.

Ssenyonjo 2013
Ssenyonjo, M., 'The Rise of the African Union Opposition to the International Criminal Court's Investigations and Prosecutions of African Leaders', 13 International Criminal Law Review, 2013, pp. 385–428.

Tonellato 2012
Tonellato, M., 'The Victim's Participation at a Cross-roads: How the International Criminal Court Could Devise a Meaningful Victims' Participation while Respecting the Rights of the Defendant', 20 European Journal of Crime, Criminal Law and Criminal Justice, 2012, pp. 315–360.

Trouille 2013
Trouille, H., 'How Far Has the International Criminal Tribunal for Rwanda Really Come since *Akayesu* in the Prosecution and Investigation of Sexual Offences Committed Against Women? An Analysis of *Ndindiliyimana et al.*', 13 International Criminal Law Review, 2013, pp. 747–788.

Van den Wyngaert 2012
Van den Wyngaert, C., 'Victims Before International Criminal Courts: Some Views and Concerns of an ICC Trial Judge', 44 Case Western Reserve Journal of International Law, 2012, pp. 475–496.

Von Wistinghausen 2013
Von Wistinghausen, N., 'Victims as Witnesses: Views from the Defence', in Bonacker, T. and Safferling, C. (eds.), 'Victims of International Crimes: An Interdisciplinary Discourse', Springer, 2013.

JURISPRUDENCE

ICC 2014
ICC, Prosecutor v. Saif Al-Islam Gaddafi and Abdullah Al-Senussi, ICC-01/11-01/11-565, 24 July 2014.
ICC 2013
ICC, Prosecutor v. Saif Al-Islam Gaddafi and Abdullah Al-Senussi, ICC-01/11-01/11-466, 11 October 2013.
ICC 2013
ICC, Prosecutor v. Saif Al-Islam Gaddafi and Abdullah Al-Senussi, ICC-01/11-01/11-344-Red, 31 May 2013.
ICC 2011
ICC, Prosecutor v. William Samoei Ruto, Henry Kiprono Kosgey and Joshua Arap Sang, ICC-01/09-01/11-OA, 30 August 2011.
ICTR 2012
ICTR, Prosecutor v. Uwinkindi, ICTR 2001-75-R11bis, 29 June 2012.
ICTR 2012
ICTR, Prosecutor v. Ndimbati, ICTR-95-1F-R11bis, 25 June 2012.
ICTR 2012
ICTR, Prosecutor v. Ryandikayo, ICTR-95-lE-R11bi*s*, 20 June 2012.
ICTR 2012
ICTR, Prosecutor v. Munyagishari, ICTR-2005-89-R11bis, 6 June 2012.
ICTR 2012
ICTR, Prosecutor v. Ntaganzwa, ICTR-96-9-R11bis, 8 May 2012.
ICTR 2012
ICTR, Prosecutor v. Sikubwabo, ICTR-95-1D-R11bis, 26 March 2012.
ICTR 2012
ICTR, Prosecutor v. Kayishema, ICTR-01-67-R11bis, 22 February 2012.
ICTR 2011
ICTR, Prosecutor v. Uwinkindi, ICTR 2001-75-R11bis, 28 June 2011.
ICTR 2008
ICTR, Prosecutor v. Kanyarukiga, ICTR-2002-78-R11bis, 30 October 2008.
ICTR 2008
ICTR, Prosecutor v. Munyakazi, ICTR-97-36-R11bis, 8 October 2008.
ICTR 2008
ICTR, Prosecutor v. Hategekimana, ICTR-00-55B-R11bis, 19 June 2008.
ICTR 2008
ICTR, Prosecutor v. Kanyarukiga, ICTR-2002-78-R11bis, 6 June 2008.
ICTR 2008
ICTR, Prosecutor v. Munyakazi, ICTR-97-36-R11bis, 28 May 2008.
ICTR 1998
ICTR, Prosecutor v. Akayesu, ICTR-96-4-T, 2 September 1998.
MICT 2012
MICT, Prosecutor v. Munyarugarama, MICT-12-09-AR14, 5 October 2012.

TREATIES, LEGISLATION AND AGREEMENTS

Protocol on Amendments to the Protocol on the Statute of the African Court of Justice and Human Rights (Malabo Protocol), 27 June 2014.
Rome Statute of the International Criminal Court, 2187 UNTS 90/37, 17 July 1998.

OTHERS

ACHR, List of state reporting on implementation of the African Charter on Human and Peoples' rights.
Africa Legal Aid, 'Much Ado About the Extraordinary AU Summit on the ICC', 12 October 2013.
Africa Legal Aid, Statement by Evelyn A. Ankumah – 'Africa and the ICC: A Stakeholders Meeting on Unsettling And Emerging Issues', 30 July 2013.
Lee, R., 'Last week to save the SADC Tribunal', Open Society Justice Initiative for Southern Africa, 13 August 2012.
Pillay, Justice A.G., 'Three illegal and ultra vires decisions', Politics Web, 13 June 2011.
Van den Herik, L., 'The Contribution of the Rwanda Tribunal to the Development of International Law', Dissertation, Free University Amsterdam, 2005.

CAN THERE BE JUSTICE WITHOUT REPARATIONS?

Identifying Gaps in Gender Justice*

Renifa Madenga

1. INTRODUCTION

A key obstacle to gender justice identified by survivor witnesses at the International Criminal Tribunal for Rwanda (ICTR), is the disconcerting absence of reparations. Survivor witnesses of sexual violence interviewed for this study indicated that they had great expectations of receiving compensation for their pain, suffering, and great loss. This article focuses specifically on survivor witnesses who contracted HIV as a result of the rapes perpetrated during the Rwanda genocide. It discusses one of the findings of my PhD research.[1] Using the voices, experiences, and silences of survivor witnesses of the sexual violence in the 1994 Rwanda genocide, the study engaged survivor witnesses in a continuous dialogue since 2005 and used their voices and experiences to interrogate the International Criminal Justice System (ICJS) as partly represented by the ICTR. Voices of survivor witnesses on reparations, their experience, and their lived reality reveal an important point of reference to the missing link between reality and rhetoric within transitional justice interventions. Most importantly, the voices of the survivor witnesses refer to context specific notions of both individual and collective reparations which might take the gender agenda further for other tribunals already implementing the reparation regime;

* The research for this article was sponsored by the Southern and Eastern African Regional Centre for Women's Law (SEARCWL) as part of the author's field work in partial fulfilment of a final PHD thesis. It was made possible by the many treasured survivors, who generously shared their experiences as they interacted with the international criminal justice system as partly represented by the UN-ICTR. Although the authour worked as a case manager, trial attorney, legal advisor, appeals counsel, and gender focal person respectively at the ICTR from 1 July 2001 to 31 December 2014 the views expressed in this article do not necessarily reflect those of the UN or UN-ICTR.

1 Research topic: Using Women's Voices/Experiences/Silences to Interrogate the Efficacy of the International Criminal Justice System (ICJS) on Rape: *The Case of Rwanda 1994 Genocide.*

for example, the ICC and many other national courts. Victims[2] and witnesses called to testify at the ICC can now participate and receive compensation. This paper encourages an informed discussion in order to explore the notion of reparations which can assist public actors to look at timely reparations through the lens of survivors.

Over 21 years after the 1994 Rwanda genocide, survivor witnesses have remained without legal redress or reparations because, among other reasons, the provisions of the ICTR are limited. In this regard, the discussion focuses on the hopes, concerns, and fears of survivor witnesses who interacted with the international criminal justice system as partly represented by ICTR.

Concerns of victims have been echoed by public actors in international criminal justice. During my discussions with the prosecutor on 2 January 2014, he confirmed that one of the concerns which he feels was not addressed because of limitations in the provisions of the ICTR was reparations, and said that 'if the tribunal was to start again, that is one of the most important requests I would make to the Security Council … provisions to allow the prosecutor to apply for reparations for the victims. Both individual and collective reparations would in the case of ICTR have addressed both urgent, immediate needs and long term needs of our survivors.'

The concept of reparations in international criminal justice has been discussed by many scholars from different perspectives. My research focuses on how survivors of sexual violence fit into the framework of post-conflict and post-genocide reparations, and draws mainly on the voices of some of the survivors and studies that show the survivor witnesses' quest for gender sensitive reparations.

2. THE INTERNATIONAL CRIMINAL JUSTICE SYSTEM AND THE THEORY OF REPARATIONS

Over the last two decades, scholars and adjudicators in the international community have expressed an increased interest regarding the issue of reparations in post-conflict areas. Additionally, there has been an explosion of both scholarly writings and academic offerings following the genocides in Rwanda, the former Yugoslavia, and other places. Over the last half century, the plight of the Second World War (WWII) victims has generated and propelled the discussion on reparations – specifically the issue of German reparations

2 In the context of this research and this article, the words 'survivor', 'victims', and 'overcomer' are sometimes used interchangeably depending on how the interviewees referred to or regarded themselves. This aspect is discussed in detail in a research chapter entitled 'The Politics of Terminology Regarding Survivors of Sexual Violence during the 1994 Rwanda Genocide' and will not form part of this article. The term 'victims' is defined in Rule 85 of the International Criminal Court Rules of Procedure and Evidence (Rule 85 of the ICC RPE).

for atrocities committed during that war.[3] Following WWII, other mass atrocities, including the genocides in the former Yugoslavia and in Rwanda have prompted a closer look at how the literature and the international justice system conceptualise reparations and victim rights.

Article 75 of the Rome Statute enabled the International Criminal Court to order an individual perpetrator to make direct reparations to victims of international crimes.[4] The ICC reparation system was innovative in international law and marked a departure from the traditional inter-state approaches to the right granted to individuals to claim reparations for crimes under international law.[5]

In theory, the right to reparations for survivors of human rights violations has been well established in international humanitarian law.[6] The United Nations General Assembly has reaffirmed the rights of victims to reparations and it is now accepted that individuals have this right under international law. In 2005, the UN General Assembly introduced the 'Basic Principles and Guidelines on the Right to a Remedy and Reparation for Victims of Gross Violations of International Human Rights Law and Serious Violations of International Humanitarian Law.'[7] These principles are based on existing international obligations under international humanitarian law, calling for those involved in handling post-conflict and post genocide deliberations to provide adequate reparation 'proportional to the gravity of the violations and the harm suffered.'[8] Principle 14 recognises both the responsibility of the state and a 'person, legal person or other entity which is found liable for reparation' to provide reparations to the victim.[9] Principle 15 expressly incorporates the possibility that reparations may not only be made by states, but also by persons found liable for reparation to a victim.

---

3 Bauxbaum 2005.

4 The Rome Statute, adopted by 120 states on 17 July 1998 (International Criminal Court, 2006), established that the International Criminal Court would not be a replacement for national jurisdictions (but rather a means of intervention where a state lacks mechanisms to investigate and prosecute perpetrators of genocide and other crimes against humanity). Article 75 of the Statute highlights the issue of reparation for victims of genocide and crimes against humanity. See Noriega 2011.

5 Bottigliero 2004, p. 210.

6 Noriega 2011.

7 Van Boven, 'Basic Principles and Guidelines on the Right to a Remedy and Reparation for Victims of Gross Violations of International Human Rights Law and Serious Violations of International Humanitarian Law', United Nations Audiovisual Library of International Law, 16 December 2005, available at: http://legal.un.org/avl/ha/ga_60-147/ga_60-147.html (accessed 26 October 2015). In these guidelines different forms of reparation include restitution, compensation, rehabilitation, satisfaction, and guarantees of non-repetition.

8 'Justice for Victims: The ICC's Reparations Mandate', Redress, 20 May 2011, available at: www.redress.org/downloads/publications/REDRESS_ICC_Reparations_May 2011.pdf (accessed 26 October 2015).

9 For further discussion refer to Dwertmann 2010.

Previously, established human rights treaties, which set up state obligations, not only focused on investigating and prosecuting suspects, but also addressed the protection of citizens, remedies, and reparations to redress violations. States are obliged to provide victims with both procedural and substantive reparations, as well as the obligation to afford victims with adequate relief. Compensation and an effective route to obtain such relief are both parts of the general obligation to provide reparations.[10]

Lack of reparations in a system addressing conflict related sexual violence may be interpreted as reinstating or reinforcing the structural subordination and discrimination of women and men. It has been well noted that reparations may have the potential to trigger important changes even if reparations alone cannot transform the root causes of conflict-related sexual violence or the conditions that make such violence possible.[11]

3. WHAT DOES JUSTICE MEAN TO SOME OF THE ICTR SURVIVOR WITNESSES I INTERVIEWED?

Different survivor witnesses had differing views of what justice means and should be. However, the common theme was a quest for an empowering justice, one which dignifies their experience with compensation. When it comes to justice, women have a range of perceptions, closely linked to the injustices they see and experience around them. According to the women I interviewed, lack of provisions for reparations is in itself an injustice. A woman who survived the 1994 genocide in Rwanda described her experience when she left the ICTR after testifying in court by stating:

> When it comes to my experience at the ICTR court I find it difficult to understand justice the way it was dispensed. I was happy I had an opportunity to go and tell the truth about what happened to me in 1994. However, one thing left me very sad and disillusioned by the Arusha justice. After all the killings and rapes I saw, after what happened to me in Gisenyi, to walk out from court with nothing, no apology, no compensation, but just nothing, was heartbreaking to say the least. I told myself, this cannot be justice, I have not seen justice with nothing to show that your pain was acknowledged, there is no compensation, and there is no justice for us. The feeling

10 'Justice for Victims: The ICC's Reparations Mandate', Redress, 20 May 2011, available at: www.redress.org/downloads/publications/REDRESS_ICC_Reparations_May 2011.pdf (accessed 26 October 2015).

11 United Nations, 'Guidance Note of the Secretary –General: Reparations for Conflict-Related Sexual Violence', June 2014, p. 8; making further references to the Nairobi Declaration on Womens' and Girls' Right to Remedy and Reparation, Principle 3H; and comments by the International Criminal Court in *Prosecutor v. Thomas Lubanga Dyilo,* Decision establishing the principles and procedures to be applied to reparations, ICC-01/04–01/06–2904, Trial Chamber I, 7 August 2012, para. 222.

> is bad. You feel used wrongly. Your wounds are re-opened and you leave, bleeding again, and empty-handed. To me there is no justice without reparations.

Scholars like Juergen Shurr have stated that reparations are a form of justice, so that 'justice without reparation is not justice.' Shurr also criticised the failure of the Rwandan government and the ICTR to compensate the survivors and victims of genocide, even after the Rwandan government drafted the bill on compensation in 2001.

Even though international human rights and humanitarian law have established the right to reparations for survivors, the role of the ICTR in providing compensation is limited. Whilst the ICTR has been criticised for a lack of attention to sexual violence crimes,[12] the survivor witnesses have acknowledged the contributions of different NGOs. In the wake of the 1994 genocide, many NGOs took up the cause of women and girls' rights and some provided legal assistance, medical and counselling services to the best of their abilities. Given the limited provisions for reparations within the ICTR Statute, there have been different views from writers about the tribunal's role in those efforts. Shurr argues that even though it is impossible to fully compensate for crimes such as genocide, compensation is important for survivors as it serves as an acknowledgement of the crimes that were committed, and restores some sense of dignity for the survivors. Staub, Pearlman, Gubin, and Hagengimana argue that even before tackling the issue of reparations, 'peace' after a conflict is difficult to establish; people's attitudes towards each other need to change first; for each group, forgiveness does not come quickly or all at once, and it is only when the desire for revenge no longer exists, and when people move away from primarily identifying themselves as victims, that wounds begin to heal and a real move towards reparations can be made.[13]

One witness (GHT) from Butare feels the system has not been sensitive to survivors, particularly those who contracted AIDS as a result of the rapes perpetrated on them during the genocide:

> Many of us contracted AIDS when we were raped in 1994. Some of the Interahamwes who raped us already suffered from the disease. Very few of us went to Arusha and among the few who went to testify, not even one was compensated. We waited for justice for a long time and when I asked about it I was told there was no provision to compensate us. I thought it is like building a hospital and telling patients there are no painkillers. When the time came to have our day in court we hoped to have it, to start to talk about our real needs, ranging from medical needs for all the opportunistic

---

12 See NGO Coalition on Women's Human Rights in Conflict Situations, Rwandan and International NGO reports on ICTR, Amnesty International, *International Criminal Tribunal for Rwanda: Trials and Tribulations*, 1998; Women's Caucus for Gender Justice, *Summary of Panel Discussions on Victim and Witness Issues*, 27 July 1999, available at: http://www.iccwomen.org/archive/resources/vwicc/intro.htm.

13 Staub et al. 2005.

> diseases which come with AIDS, some money for food, clothes and toiletries. When it was explained that we cannot get even money for food when we came home, I thought why did I waste my time instead of focusing on my field?

While there is a growing emphasis on the importance of victims' rights in international human rights law and international humanitarian law towards restorative justice,[14] in practice, reparations have been hard to find in the international justice system, and theories and declarations supporting the need for reparations have sent mixed messages. In reports related to compensation to victims submitted to the Security Council, both judges of the ICTR and ICTY concluded that the statutes of the Tribunals do not give them the mandate to decide on such issues.[15]

Meanwhile, the eighth ICTY Annual Report confirmed the gradual formation of the right of victims to compensation under international law and recommended the International Commission for Compensation.[16] Attempts by the ICTR were made through the Office of the Registrar to provide assistance to witnesses and to contribute to projects in Taba Township, the locality where Akayesu was convicted by the ICTR of rape as genocide and crimes against humanity, and also the place where many survivors came from. Correspondences show this approach was not sustainable and the project's needs exceeded the Tribunal's capacity.[17] One of the public actors, who declined to be named, explained:

> Witnesses should be grateful that we are bending over backwards to assist them. We are not obliged to but we are going out of our way, people need to be thankful for that assistance and not expect too much. They must know that we work within the four corners of our mandate.

The ICTR has provided some 'assistance' to some of the victims of sexual violence who appeared as witnesses before the ICTR in the form of general medical services by a medical unit set up in Rwanda. Some authors have pointed

---

14 Restorative justice has been described as a concept that aims to involve the offender, the victim, and the community on a more or less equal basis in their search for repair, reconciliation, and justice. The concept includes measures of mediation, community service, restitution, and other forms of diversion aimed at providing redress to the victim and reconciliation between victim and offender. Dwertmann 2003, p. 275; Garkawe 2003, p. 345.

15 Recommendations made by the Tribunals included recommendations to the Security Council to consider a possible mechanism to deal with reparation to victims. Refer to ICTY's, *Victims' Compensation and Participation Report* prepared by the ICTY Rules Committee, Appendix to a Letter dated 12 October 2000 from the President of the ICTY addressed to the UN Secretary-General, annex to UN Doc. S/2001/1063 of 3 November 2000; ICTR, Letter of the President of the ICTR to the UN Secretary-General, Annex to a Letter from the UN Secretary-General to the Security Council, UN Doc. S/2000/1198 of 14 December 2000.

16 Eighth ICTY Annual Report UN Doc. A/56/352 of 17 September 2001, para. 49.

17 See Letter of the President of the ICTR to the UN Secretary-General. Annex to a letter from the UN Secretary-General to the Security Council, UN Doc. S/2000/1198 of 14 December 2000.

out that, in essence, the ICTR has accepted a duty on the basis of Rule 34 of its Rules;[18] however, these efforts are not enough under the standards set by international law on reparations for victims. Even when victims' rights are recognised in their national jurisdiction, the enforcement of such rights remains extremely difficult. As Witness ROR from Mugonero stated:

> Some of us have heard it all. We were told how after giving testimony in Arusha we could use the judgment to go to court here in Rwanda to get something. Many of us don't think justice is going to Arusha and coming back with nothing, then having to wait again. I waited since 1994 to give evidence in 2005 and now I am still waiting, how long should I wait and what am I still waiting for? Death? What I call justice is not waiting this long for nothing; we are tired of people talking about it and then pointing fingers blaming each other with no one taking responsibility to address the issue. What will transform my life is getting the material assistance I need to stop bleeding and start to rebuild my life.

Many of the survivors interviewed don't necessarily equate justice with prosecutions. In fact, in many instances, they reflected that recognition of what they have endured and finding means to build their lives often takes precedence over going to court. Given that prosecution alone will be inadequate to ensure justice, the justice system has to identify complementary interventions and build collaborations which manifest in gender sensitive forms of justice.

4. IDENTIFYING THE FORMS OF REPARATION

The Nairobi Declaration on Women's and Girls' Right to a Remedy and Reparation presents a compelling case for gender-sensitive reparations which take into account pre-existing gender relations and power imbalances in order to come up with a fair assessment of the harm inflicted upon different categories of survivors.

Reparations may take a number of forms, such as restitution, compensation, or rehabilitation, as well as guarantees of non-repetition of the offence.[19] Restitution can include restoration of liberty, return of property, and return to one's place of residence, but it is hard to access and assess as it is close to impossible to restore victim's original situation before the violation.[20]

---

18 The ICTR medical unit has been assisted by a voluntary trust fund. This is in contrast to the ICTY which only supports witnesses with basic support during their testimonies before the Tribunal. For an interesting discussion on this subject, see De Brouwer 2007, pp. 207, 217.

19 Schurr, 'Rwandan Genocide Survivors Still Waiting for Reparation', *Pambazuka News*, 14 September 2011, 547th ed., available at: www.pambazuka.net/en/category.php/features/76249 (accessed 25 October 2015).

20 'Justice for Victims: The ICC's Reparations Mandate', Redress, 20 May 2011, available at: www.redress.org/downloads/publications/REDRESS_ICC_Reparations_May 2011.pdf (accessed 26 October 2015).

Witness JKP from Kibuye explained:

> In my case things are very difficult. Though I was called to Arusha to tell my story and was given protective orders, the Interahamwe[21] who raped me and participated in the killing of my family lives in a village next to me and each time we meet and he says 'Amakuru' I ask myself where is the protection? In Arusha we didn't talk about him, we talked about his Commander. Can I have my children back? I cannot. So what does that help? All this justice sometimes makes my head spin. I just feel dizzy. One would think if you cannot have your children back you can have some little money to go and buy pain killers. If this justice cannot give me money, what about an apology?

Restitution for a victim depends on the content of the primary obligation that has been breached. As the first of the forms of reparation, it is of particular importance to determine whether the obligation breach is continuous; for example, an unlawful detention or disappearance will require the state to put an end to the situation as cessation or restitution.[22] What then would be appropriate for a survivor witness who lost her freedom to move around her village because the protective order she has is against the commander and not the neighbour, an Interahamwe, who has never been charged with rape?

Witness VOV from Bisesero explained:

> I have been ill since 1994 when I was raped. I still grieve over all the things I lost. All my 5 children. No one can do anything to bring my loved ones back. What about things which can have a solution? So I will never be compensated for my cow? Since I sometimes bleed I would sell milk and buy sanitary pads. I thought in Arusha the discussions would dwell on practicalities. How I would be compensated so that I replace my cow. I did not hear the word 'cow' at all and I could not ask for it since when they are there the accused persons talk through a lawyer and pretend they cannot talk. It is very strange how justice is dispensed in Arusha. Additionally, though there is a protective order, it is not against the Interahamwe who raped me, it is against his commander who will never come to Rwanda. Freedom is restoration. I want to walk freely in the village; some of the Interahamwe should be relocated. I want to rebuild my life and not be perpetually intimidated.

Compensation can include any 'economically assessable' damage resulting from the crimes. Compensation can be particularly important in cases where

---

21 In the context of Rwanda during the genocide, Interahamwe, literally translated, referred to people who 'work' or attack together. It was a general term used to refer to Hutu extremists from the ruling party who sensitised, trained, and mobilised to kill Tutsi and moderate Hutus during the 1994 Rwanda Genocide. It is widely documented that during the genocide, rapes were mostly perpetrated by the militia, Interahamwe, local authorities, soldiers, civilians, gendarmes, prisoners, and priests/pastors.

22 Redress, *Reparation: A Source Book for Victims of Torture and Other Violations of Human Rights and International Humanitarian Law*, 2003, available at: www.redress.org/downloads/reparation/SourceBook.pdf (accessed 26 October 2015).

restitution is no longer possible due to the nature of crime.[23] The function of compensation, as its title indicates, is purely compensatory. It is not concerned with the punishment of the responsible state; in this regard, the Inter-American Court of Human Rights held that compensation under international law did not recognise the concept of punitive or exemplary damages.[24]

However, in some cases, compensation is difficult to accomplish, as countries coming out of genocide have different priorities. In the case of Rwanda, the Executive Secretary of the National Unity and Reconciliation Commission has addressed the need for compensation, even though resources for compensation are very limited and access to it can be challenging.[25] Moreover, in the Rwandan context, an empirical study conducted by Brehm, Uggen and Gasanabo[26] indicates that gacaca embedded restorative justice, as perpetrators were asked to pay fines for offences against property.[27]

There have been different opinions among the people of Rwanda; one opinion emphasises that the government is more focused in establishing 'beautiful Kigali' than the welfare of genocide survivors.[28] Research published in June 2012 by the Legal Aid Forum in Rwanda (based on interviews with over 2,700 compensation claimants) confirms that awards by gacaca courts are the 'hardest to enforce', with 92 percent of all genocide-related judgments yet to actually be implemented.[29] Paul Jean Mugiraneza also argues that compensation for genocide survivors is very important, and criticises the failure of the Rwandan government in fulfilling these demands. He also emphasises that while the Rwandan government has established a legal framework supposedly aimed at providing compensation for genocide survivors, the commitment has been much more visibly enforced on a criminal justice level, but not on a more compensatory level that the survivors can see.[30]

One of the survivors who lives in Kigali Urban celebrated the reconstruction of Kigali and remarked that: 'some of the perpetrators will get lost if they come back home; for example, Kigali should make them ashamed, no one can destroy Rwanda, there is hope in Rwanda and from the ashes of the genocide we are raising the standard.'

---

23 Ferstman et al. 2009.

24 Redress, *Reparation: A Source Book for Victims of Torture and Other Violations of Human Rights and International Humanitarian Law*, 2003.

25 Ferstman et al. 2009.

26 Brehm, Uggen and Gasanabo 2014.

27 *Ibid.*

28 Ferstman et al. 2009.

29 'Right to Reparation for Survivors: Recommendations for Reparation for Survivors of the 1994 Genocide Against Tutsi', 2012, Redress, available at: www.redress.org/downloads/publications/121031right_to_rep.pdf (accessed 26 October 2015).

30 Mugiraneza, 'Rwanda Genocide: Why Compensation Would Help the Healing', *The Guardian*, 7 April 2014, available at: www.theguardian.com/global-development-professionals-network/2014/mar/04/rwanda-genocide-victims-compensation (accessed 26 October 2015).

Along with compensation, rehabilitation is also an important component of reparation, and the previously mentioned UN Basic Principles provides that 'rehabilitation should include medical and psychological care, as well as legal and social services.'[31] In *Barrios Altos v. Peru* (a case heard by the Inter-American Court of Human Rights in 1991 concerning the deaths of fifteen people and at least four injuries caused by a death squad composed of Peruvian Armed Force members in the Barrios Altos neighbourhood of Lima, Peru), the court approved the agreement signed by the state and the victims, wherein the state recognised its obligation to provide 'diagnostic procedures, medicines, specialized aid, hospitalisation, surgeries, labouring, traumatic rehabilitation and mental health' to victims of the Barrios Altos massacre. In other cases, the court provided assurance for the future medical treatment of victims, where there was a direct link between the condition and the violation.[32]

Rehabilitation is a form of restoration of a victim's physical and psychological health. Vandeginste[33] states that 'rehabilitation in a full reparation programme will normally require an initiative on the part of the State and its active involvement in the provision of medical and psychological care and of legal and social services.' Ruvebana and Brouwer[34] have also highlighted that gacaca was able to restore rehabilitation in the sense that during the gacaca proceedings, survivors and victims were allowed to relieve their frustration and were able to restore good relations among the community. Another form of reparation, reconciliation is a long-term process and does not happen overnight. Reconciliation at the societal level requires government to play an active role, but at the individual level it depends on different circumstances, like the magnitude of brutality suffered by the victims and survivors, their current living conditions, and the availability of additional support.[35]

It is not enough to have efforts towards reparations without guarantees that the offence will not be repeated to the satisfaction of the victims.[36] A central component of reparations is the public acknowledgment of the violation suffered by the victims and survivors. There are difficulties in conceptualising this form of reparation as a remedy awarded against an individual rather than a state.[37] One way to think about the concept is to analyse how scholars have highlighted the importance of the victims' right to know the truth and to hold

31 'Right to Reparation for Survivors: Recommendations for Reparation for Survivors of the 1994 Genocide Against Tutsi', 2012, Redress.

32 Redress, *Reparation: A Source Book for Victims of Torture and Other Violations of Human Rights and International Humanitarian Law*, 2003.

33 Vandeginste 2003.

34 De Brouwer and Ruvebana 2013.

35 *Ibid.*

36 'Right to Reparation for Survivors: Recommendations for Reparation for Survivors of the 1994 Genocide Against Tutsi', 2012, Redress.

37 *Ibid.*

the perpetrators accountable.[38] Vandeginste[39] claims that 'satisfaction' applies to those types of redresses that do not aim to set right specific individual losses or harm.

The main forms of 'satisfaction' are: the verification of the facts and the disclosure of the truth; an apology; sanctions against individual perpetrators, and commemorations of and tributes to the victims. From their empirical study, Ruvebana and Brouwer[40] illustrate that gacaca was still unable to fulfil the demands of survivors and victims in regards to reparation partially because of these forms of satisfaction. They also highlighted that reparation was essential for victims and survivors not only because of a need to be acknowledged, but also because many continue to live in poverty as a result of the genocide.[41] Rwanda holds an annual public memorial service in April for victims of genocide. Nevertheless, the empirical study by Jacqueline Lewis[42] indicated that during the memorial service, some Hutu students were uncomfortable – they believed that Hutus who were murdered because they refused to participate in genocide are not commemorated.[43] In these kinds of cases, the government should create a neutral atmosphere so that there is no increase in tension.

5. REPARATIONS AND RECONCILIATION

Reparations can be implemented at different stages of the reconciliation process. Vandeginste[44] has argued that the concept and terminology of 'reparations' is evolving and adopting a dynamic role. She argues that reparation measures can be implemented through reparation rights and reparation policies, individual and collective measures, financial and non-financial measures, and commemorative and reform measures.

Vandeginste[45] also argues that we might continue to find a strong legal basis for reparations in domestic law or in international human rights law. It is helpful to use different types of reporting mechanisms for civil society groups to design a reparation proposal or lobby for structural reparation measures. It is also important to stress the interaction between the enforcement of reparation rights and the adoption of reparation policies. In recent years, changes in the regulation regarding reparation have been implemented, but enforcing these

---

38 Redress, *Reparation: A Source Book for Victims of Torture and Other Violations of Human Rights and International Humanitarian Law*, 2003.
39 Vandeginste 2003.
40 De Brouwer and Ruvebana 2013.
41 *Ibid.*
42 Lewis, 'Mass Graves and a Thousand Hills: University Student Perspectives on the Gacaca Courts in Post-Genocide Rwanda', Inquiry Journal Paper 10 (2010).
43 *Ibid.*
44 Vandeginste 2003.
45 *Ibid.*

procedures has not yet developed far enough. Organisations like the Victims' Rights Working Group have questioned the effectiveness of the ICC in establishing effective procedures. They criticise the insufficient progress that has been made in clarifying the reparation process and establishing the principles on reparation required by Article 75(1) of the Rome Statute.[46]

The notion that the ICC should participate in awarding reparations was controversial due to concerns that the intermingling of civil matters with criminal proceedings would distract the court from its primary mission of fairly prosecuting individuals responsible for mass atrocities.[47] As the ICC has decided to approach reparation on a case-by-case basis, the Victims' Rights Group believes that this will result in inconsistent and weak reparation orders due to the different panels of judges.

Lack of sufficient information for victims has created frustration and confusion.[48] Currently, there has been a shift in focus towards the gender perspective of questions of reparations. The observations emphasised key reparations principles including a gender-inclusive approach; non-discrimination; the importance of effective consultation with victims/survivors including women and girls; a broad concept of harm; and the transformative function of reparations.[49] The importance of a gender-inclusive approach to reparation has also been emphasised by Zoglin,[50] when she highlights the importance of a gendered approach. She argues that women tend to lack courage to come forward, especially in relation to rape cases, raising the need to find a way to encourage them to participate during proceedings and reparations.

For individual and collective measures, Vandeginste[51] argues that, even though individual reparation is important, individual reparation measures are often insufficient and close to impossible. During the transitional justice schemes, collective reparation is more effective by providing access to communal facilities and initiatives like healthcare centres, funded education programmes, employment opportunities, etc. This argument has also been supported by Šoštarić[52] as he argues that reparations should be divided between individual

46 'Establishing Effective Reparation Procedures and Principles for the International Criminal Court', 2011, Victims' Rights Working Group (VRWG), available at: www.vrwg.org/VRWG_DOC/2011_Sept_VRWG_ReparationPaper.pdf (accessed 25 October 2015).

47 War Crimes Research Office, *The Case-Based Reparations Scheme at the International Criminal Court*, June 2010, available at: https://www.wcl.american.edu/warcrimes/icc/documents/report12.pdf (accessed 25 October 2015).

48 'Establishing Effective Reparation Procedures and Principles for the International Criminal Court', 2011, VRWG.

49 Women's Initiatives for Gender Justice (ICC Women), 'Statement of the Women's Initiatives for Gender Justice Change in Chambers' Approach to Reparations The Prosecutor vs. Germain Katanga', 1 September 2014.

50 Zoglin 2007, pp. 454–455.

51 Vandeginste 2003.

52 Šoštarić, 'War Victims and Gender-Sensitive Trust, Justice, Reparations and Non-Recurrence in Bosnia and Herzegovina', Perspective Series – Research Report, 2012.

and collective measures. Individual reparation recognises the importance of specific harm to the individual and an individual's worth as a citizen. Collective reparation aims to respond to collective harms and harms to collective cohesion.

Nevertheless, the combination of individual and collective approaches might have an impact on financial constraints, political and financial priority setting, and logical feasibility.[53] The problem also lies in identifying the correct enforcement of collective reparation or individual reparations. Even though individual reparation is beneficial in some cases, especially where atrocities have focused on a particular community or ethnicity, sex, or religion, collective measures seem more valuable. For example, in the recent ICC case of *The Prosecutor v. Germain Katanga*, where Katanga was convicted by a majority of Trial Chamber II as an accessory to the war crimes of directing an attack against a civilian population, pillaging, and destruction of property, as well as murder as a war crime and a crime against humanity, the chamber unanimously acquitted Katanga as an accessory to rape and sexual slavery as war crimes and crimes against humanity, as well as of the war crime of using child soldiers.[54] In terms of reparations, the ICC decided to implement individual reparations, which was unsettling to the Women's Initiative. The Women's Initiative argued that individual reparations may limit the potentially positive effect of reparations and introduce an unintended hierarchy of victims within situations under investigation by the ICC.[55] In relation to funds, there have been voluntary contributions and donations – not from the convicted person(s) – so utilising these resources collectively would be more efficient and meaningful.[56]

Vandeginst[57] indicates that during the implementation of reparation policies, non-financial packages can be implemented to meet victim needs and expectations, like providing people with death certificates for their disappeared loved ones, the facilitation of exhumations and reburials, and the expunging of criminal records. She also illustrates that there are two different types of commemorative reparation claims: firstly, a backward-looking claim showing the barbarity and humiliation associated with the past oppression; and secondly, a forward-looking claim seeking to alter the social and economic condition of disadvantaged groups. As indicated above, the forward looking approach has somewhat been addressed in Rwanda through the annual commemoration of the genocide in April where victims and survivors of the genocide are publicly

53 Vandeginste 2003.

54 Women's Initiatives for Gender Justice (ICC Women), 'Statement of the Women's Initiatives for Gender Justice Change in Chambers' Approach to Reparations The Prosecutor vs. Germain Katanga', 1 September 2014.

55 War Crimes Research Office, *The Case-Based Reparations Scheme at the International Criminal Court*, June 2010.

56 Women's Initiatives for Gender Justice (ICC Women), 'Statement of the Women's Initiatives for Gender Justice Change in Chambers' Approach to Reparations The Prosecutor vs. Germain Katanga', 1 September 2014.

57 Vandeginste 2003.

honoured, as well as the establishment of hundreds of memorial sites throughout Rwanda which to some extent provides survivors with a place to mourn and remember their loved ones who perished during the 1994 genocide.

The survivors have presented a compelling case for reparations. This has been buttressed by many scholars. For example, Vandeginste[58] has demonstrated the importance of reparations and why they are needed. The reparation component in transitional politics and law can be observed from different perspectives such as individual rights, reconciliation, acknowledging and repairing the suffering of victims, and political transition. The new government after a genocide or conflict should immediately take action for the past atrocities and guarantee individual rights and provide reparations to the victims.

5.1. THE LACK OF REPARATIONS NEGATES A GENDER-SENSITIVE APPROACH IN POST CONFLICT INTERVENTIONS

Acknowledging and attempting to alleviate the suffering of victims is an important aspect of reparation. It is important for a victim to be recognised as a human being with equal rights and dignity. According to Vandeginste,[59] political transition acts as a bridge between the past and the future through 'backward looking objectivity compensation for victims to forward looking objectivity of political reforms.' Relevant to the Rwandan context, the Nairobi Declaration on Women's and Girls' Right to a Remedy and Reparation provides a useful blueprint for devising comprehensive strategies to address sexual violence and related forms of gender based violence perpetrated against women and girls.[60] These kinds of reforms are important as they address the political and structural inequalities that negatively shape women's and girls' lives.[61]

It is encouraging that in the wake of the 1994 genocide, many NGOs took up the cause of women and girls rights and some provided legal assistance, medical and counselling services to survivors. To practically address the problems they faced after the genocide, the ICTR's role was much more elusive, and the government's role on the issue of reparations remains complicated. After the genocide, an estimated 70 to 80 percent of the surviving women in Rwanda were infected with HIV (AVEGA-AGAHOZO: 1999, de Brouwer 2005: 390),[62] and

58 *Ibid.*

59 Vandeginste 2003.

60 'Right to Reparation for Survivors: Recommendations for Reparation for Survivors of the 1994 Genocide Against Tutsi', 2012, Redress.

61 *Ibid.*

62 The AVEGA-AGAHOZO (Association of Genocide Widows, available at: www.avega.org.rw) carried out a survey of 1125 female genocide survivors in 1999. The finding was that some 80 percent are still severely traumatised. About 70 percent tested HIV positive. See Amnesty International, *Rwanda: Marked for Death*, AFR 47/007/2004, 5 April 2004, p. 3, in a survey

were in dire need of medical and rehabilitation services to deal with the trauma. Many factors strongly indicate that the majority of HIV/AIDS transmission took place through rapes perpetrated during the genocide.

In the midst of these challenges, witnesses and survivors of rape have struggled with finding ways to gain access to medical and psychological help, and to physically access promised medical care. One witness (Witness ROR Butare) explained some of the survival tactics developed among survivors:

> When I came back from Arusha, I decided to talk to others who were in my same situation. We agreed we are not going to sit and die, we were told we could go to Kigali and receive medication. That was better than before but we had to start to help ourselves ... We had to encourage each other to live and not give up living. Each time one of us needed medication we looked after her children. We were each other's keeper, caring for each other and trying to assist to meet the needs. What forced us to keep on living are our children. Most of the institutions supposed to assist can sometimes be rather illusive, however we encourage ourselves that we have to forge ahead and live to give our children a future and hope.

According to ROR, although ICTR has helped to bring international recognition to the existence of rapes and other sexual violence in Rwanda in 1994,[63] the ICTR does not have a comprehensive, easily accessible and effective rehabilitation, restitution, and compensation regime. Some survivors interviewed expressed concern that ICTR is closing down without guaranteeing any reparations for victims of the genocide and rape, and barely offers assistance to witnesses called to testify. One survivor witness (Witness KOK 2011) remembered her trip to Arusha with disappointment:

> I respected the dead by going to Arusha to narrate how they were killed, what I saw with my own eyes. I was not asked to talk about my own sickness whose symptoms were disturbing me on the trip to Arusha. That was my first trip on air and someone told me your thing (UN Beach craft) did not have a toilet ... When nobody talked about repairing my bladder, I knew we are forgotten, our issues are not the priority. You can only indicate your needs where you are part of a process.
>
> In those courts, people are doing their own thing which you do not quite understand. You can see that those who ask you questions have no serious problems themselves. There is really no space to talk about 'munda' (stomach aches), ruptured bottoms. 'Bagenzi bange nababuze' (I have lost my friends), who did not have a chance even to testify in Arusha due to continuous women's problems. Here, even if you injure a person slightly, we all expect you to say sorry, pay something to stop the

where 2000 women were tested, 80 percent were found to be HIV positive. See also, Mujawayo and Blewitt, 'Sexual Violence Against women: Experiences from AVEGA's work in Kigali', paper presented at the Silent Emergency Seminar in London, June 1999.

63 There is a lot of literature documenting many of such challenges thus supporting the voices of many survivors. Refer, among other publications, to Nowrojee 2005; Askin 2005.

> blood from flowing, yet in Arusha, you come back with nothing, no apology, not even 'matibiryo' (food).
>
> The only souvenir you bring is a heavy heart and the image of genocidaire who are well looked after, you have to carefully look to realize it's them; they look well looked after. We are the forgotten lot. What does your justice have for us who testify about how we were killed, and how we were denied the chance to die?

Even though Article 23(3) of the ICTR Statute says the tribunal is entitled, in addition to imprisonment, to order return of any property and proceeds acquired unlawfully, its implementation is rare, and the road towards its practical achievement is unclear. Rule 105, as read with Rule 88 of the Rules and Procedure of Evidence, sets out three requirements for restitution. Restitution could be ordered where an accused is convicted and where the unlawful taking of property has been established and the property can be associated with the crime. A request for restitution has to be made by the Prosecutor, or the Chamber orders it *proprio motu*.[64] This would then be followed by a cumbersome process involving a special hearing to determine the matter of restitution still pursuant to Rule 105.

At the ICTR, in both the Bagosora and Musema cases, the issue of restitution for victims was raised by the governments of Rwanda, Belgium (from Bagosora), and an NGO – African Concern – pursuant to Rule 74 procedure related to *amicus curiae*.[65] Compensation to victims could not be awarded by the tribunals because Rule 106 of the ICTR RPE specifically states that matters related to compensation fall within the jurisdiction of 'national courts' or other 'competent bodies.'[66] It has been suggested by some scholars that the rationale behind Rule 106 (common to both the ICTR and ICTY) for not providing a direct compensation mechanism within the tribunals is probably the fear that tribunals would be inundated with a potentially high number of claims while at the same time expected to deal with prosecution of serious crimes.

At one stage there was some judicial activism at the ICTR calling for the provision of compensation to victims. In 2000, the then Prosecutor of the ICTY and ICTR, Carla del Ponte, emphasised the deficits in the tribunals' legal system in relation to participation and payment of compensation, underlining that the system fell short of delivering justice to the people of Rwanda and the former

64 Rule 88(B) of the ICTR RPE as read with Rule 105 of the ICTR RPE.

65 Refer to The *Prosecutor v. Alfred Musema*, Decision on an application by African Concern for Leave to appear as Amicus Curiae, ICTR-96-13-T, 17 March 1999 (related to issues of restitution only); The *Prosecutor v. Theoneste Bagosora*, Decision on the Amicus Curiae application by the Government of the Kingdom of Belgium, ICTR67-96-7T, 6 June 1998 (restitution and compensation); *Prosecutor v. Theoneste Bagosora, Gratien Kabiligi, Alloys Ntabakuze and Anatole Nsengiyumva*, Decision on amicus Curiae Request by the Rwanda Government, ICTR-98-41T, 13 October 2004 (restitution only).

66 Rule 106 dealing with 'Compensation to Victims'.

Yugoslavia.[67] In 2002, Judge Navanethem Pillay, then President of the ICTR, called for compensation to victims, urging member states to compensate victims to facilitate recovery of Rwanda from the consequences of the genocide.

The UN General Assembly passed a resolution on 10 December 2004 calling for assistance to survivors of the 1994 genocide in Rwanda.[68] The resolution invited 'agencies, funds, and programmers' of the United Nations system to ensure assistance is provided in specific areas identified as priorities by the government of Rwanda, for instance: education for orphans, medical care, treatment for victims of sexual violence, including HIV positive victims, trauma and psychological counselling for genocide survivors and skills training and micro programmes aimed at promoting self-sufficiency and alleviating poverty. However, the plight of victims has barely changed.

Like many international criminal justice systems, the ICTR faces challenges on how to implement victim rights, particularly their right to reparations, because of a pervasive victim rights paradigm and its problematic history in the ICJS. As mentioned previously, the ICJS's history with the theory and practice of reparations has been problematic; reparations have been mentioned, at times implied, with no real action or power behind such statutes and declarations. In the Nuremberg and Tokyo Charters, reparations were not expressly mentioned.

Until the adoption of the ICC Statute, reparations for victims were not a formal part of international criminal justice. Before the ICC, some authors labelled the need or concern of victims in form of reparation as the 'missing link' of the international justice system.[69] Major developments and the codification of international legal standards for the rights of individuals, including the right to reparations, only gathered momentum in the second half of the 20th century.[70]

Many of the survivors expressed that victims are too often seen as passive, and rarely asked what kinds of restitution, reparations, or compensation they need in order to move on with their lives after traumatic experiences. There is no dialogue, and the victim is expected to understand and accept the modes of 'justice' that a particular tribunal prescribes.

Human rights treaties seemingly provide a remedy, both substantive and procedural, for individuals suffering injury from unlawful conduct by state authorities.[71] However, the limitations in the ICTR Statute denied the survivors

---

67 De Brouwer 2007, citing ICTY Press Address to the Security Council by Carla del Ponte, Prosecutor of the International Criminal Tribunals for the former Yugoslavia and Rwanda, to the UN Security Council, JL/P.I.S./542-e, The Hague, 24 November 2000.

68 UN General Assembly, Resolution 59/137 of 10 December 2004 on Assistance to survivors of the 1994 Genocide in Rwanda, Particularly Orphans, Widows and Victims of Sexual Violence, A/RES/59/137, 17 February 2004.

69 Ferencz 2000, p. 3.

70 Bassiouni 2006.

71 For example, both the European Convention on Human Rights and the American Convention on Human Rights allow, respectively, the European Court of Human Rights and the Inter-American Court of Human Rights to afford just satisfaction to victims.

the right to be granted compensation by this court. In her critique of the ICTR, del Ponte pointed out that:

> Voices of survivors and relatives of those killed are not sufficiently heard. Victims have almost no rights to participate in the trial process, despite the widespread acceptance nowadays that victims should be able to do so. And … it is regrettable that the Tribunal's Statute makes no provision for victim participation during trial, and makes only minimum provision for compensation and restitution to people whose lives have been destroyed.[72]

The issue of lack of reparations emerged in the findings amongst all respondents. In addition to referring to the social stigma and isolation, which accompanies survivor witnesses to and from the Tribunal, many participants coming from rural settings in Rwanda stressed the extreme economic hardships they still encounter many years after the genocide. In this regard, they underscored the issues of reparations to compensate for pain and suffering. Almost all the respondents I interviewed indicated that reparations in form of medical services, housing allowance, and education allowance would meet their needs or those of their children or adopted orphans. One witness (GOG-Cyangugu) expressed her sentiments:

> Many women survivors here do not want to talk about their status. The majority of female survivors I know here were sexually assaulted, some are infected with STDs including HIV, some miscarried, we meet at the market, and we talk even as we participate in 'Umuganda' (gatherings in Rwanda where people do community work). In the field, we have a common chorus. We complain of headaches and stomach aches. We know we are depressed and anxious. We know we are desperate since we are forgotten. I don't have an appetite; it is like living in a foreign body.
>
> I expected that part of the justice system is to ensure we get something to cater for our physical and mental needs. I got nothing, not even an apology, not even one 'amafaranga' (Rwandan francs) to build a decent hut, not even something to replace my cow slaughtered and eaten by those who killed my family. Your justice! Maybe it's because I have lost everything; sometimes I think I have lost my mind, I cannot understand how your justice works.

According to the Inter-American Court, 'this provision constitutes a rule of customary law that enshrines one of the fundamental principles of contemporary international law on state responsibility'. More than the European Court, the Inter-American Court has made broad use of its competence to award both monetary and non-monetary remedies. Human rights treaties also provide for specific provisions on compensation, for example to victims of unlawful arrest or detention. The Convention against Torture provides for an obligation to repair violations of the prohibition against torture.

72 ICTY Press Address to the Security Council by Carla del Ponte, Prosecutor of the International Criminal Tribunals for the former Yugoslavia and Rwanda, to the UN Security Council, JL/P.I.S./542-e, The Hague, 24 November 2000.

As mentioned previously, survivor witnesses have developed, from the varied experiences, both personal and collective strategies to help them cope, without further assistance from institutions and organisations. This is especially true for women who were forced by circumstances to live with their rapists, or the period of time when women were in a form of sexual slavery after having 'escaped' with the Interahamwe to refugee camps in DRC and Tanzania.

Almost all interviewed survivor witnesses feel there should be reparation hearings where the witnesses are called to give evidence before the imposition of sentences. According to the respondents, this can give them an opportunity to submit to the nature of reparation appropriate for them and their community. Most of the respondents explained that since the rapists were persons of authority or influence who raped or allowed their subordinates to rape, there is no reason why the accused persons cannot pay reparations.

5.2. REPARATIONS FOR SURVIVORS OF SEXUAL VIOLENCE IN RWANDA

The mechanisms improvised outside the ICTR Statute to provide medical assistance had their own limitations and recorded drawbacks. Rwanda, like other former colonial territories, is affected by a plurality of norms. Legal centralism and legal pluralism are analytical frameworks, which give way to different understandings of the position of women. The key to survivor witnesses feeling 'heard' is offering reparations. Another witness I interviewed (Witness XHX) told me:

> Understand me here; I am not talking only of not getting any reparation for pain and suffering. Your ICJS does not allow us to grieve for the loss of our loved ones.
>
> As you recall I lost all my five children, the youngest, as you recall was 3 days old when she was killed, my husband was killed atrociously and before my own eyes and subsequent to these events I was raped! I did not expect that my testimony would bring back my mother, husband or adorable children. However as someone who lost all that mattered, I expected that this would form the subject matter of the testimony and I would be told, 'we cannot do anything about your dead but since you are still living we have something for the living'. Your justice seems to have nothing for the dead and nothing for the living. When in court, I had all the opportunity to look at those who caused all this pain. They look well looked after. We also came to conclusions when we left Arusha. The system makes you feel like again you have lost something precious. It's difficult to explain this thing which you feel stolen, dignity. ('Agaciro') You feel like crying yet the system denies you the right to grieve publicly; yet it does not compensate you for all the loss.

'Agaciro' according to the Kinyarwanda interpreters means 'dignity', and from the context used by the witness, I was advised to equate the term to another concept – what many authors have explored within the context of the African philosophy of 'Ubuntu.'[73] Ubuntu (humaneness) refers to understanding diversity and the belief in a universal bond and sharing.[74] In the most fundamental sense it translates as personhood and 'morality'.[75]

Another witness (Witness VOV Kibuye/Gyshita) disclosed:

> I was 15 years old when the war started and was raped. I do not want to talk about the pain I suffered but the scars are deeper than the physical violations, they permeate your very inner dignity ('Agaciro'). Losing my virginity was like losing my identity for me particularly, I am not speaking on behalf of many other girls who suffered in the same manner during the genocide. I married a survivor and he has not come to terms with the loss and this has caused discord in our marriage.
>
> I felt the courts will remember all the loss we suffered and give us something to help wipe tears. Arusha is not like that, you can be shocked, me I laughed with shock, some of these things are unbelievable when you compare what you look like and what the person who wronged you looks like. If your law does not recognize the nature of the harm we suffered then to me it is not of any help. The judges thanked me for my testimony and that was all. I am still grieving.

The majority of the 76 survivor witnesses of sexual violence I interviewed define justice through reparations, rehabilitation, and reconciliation or other notions related to their lived experience and reality. One psychologist working in Rwanda noted a need for a process that allows rape victims to grieve for the lost aspects of their lives, by stating that 'rape is a loss; in most instances the loss is more painful than death since, it is best treated with a period of mourning and grief … social ceremonies for rape should be developed: rituals that, like funerals and wakes, would allow the mourners to recover the spirit that the rapist, like death, steals.'[76]

---

73 Tamale 2011, p. 7.

74 *Ibid.*

75 Metaphorically, it describes the significance of group solidarity, compassion, respect, human dignity, conformity to basic norms, and collective unity, and in its fundamental sense, it denotes humanity and morality. Its spirit emphasises a respect for human dignity, marking a shift from confrontation to conciliation. Tamale 2011, referring to Justice Yvonne Mokgoro of the South African Constitutional Court elaborating the concept of 'Ubuntu' by quoting from Sachs 2009, pp. 106–107. The same term was used during group discussions I had with UNILAC University students when we discussed issues to do with human dignity. I noted from the discussions that Rwanda as a nation has made significant progress in creating the space to discuss gender based violence, access to reproductive care, and issues of compensation.

76 Mukamana and Collins, 'Rape Survivors of the Rwandan Genocide', p. 8, buttresses by the discussions with Donatilla Mukamana and Dr Mudimutsa, at Ngurdoto, Tanzania during a workshop related to handling trauma.

6. CONCLUSION

Voices of survivor witnesses on reparations, their experiences, and lived reality reveal an important point of reference to the missing link between reality and rhetoric within international criminal justice systems as partly represented by the ICTR.

In this regard, survivor witnesses refer to context specific individual and collective reparations, which are relevant to their needs. Survivor witnesses called to testify at the ICTR were afraid that the high hopes they had placed on the ICJS as represented by the ICTR would not be fulfilled. Over 21 years after the Rwanda genocide and on the eve of the closure of the ICTR, survivor witnesses have not received compensation for pain, suffering, and irreparable loss. Justice, in their view, has remained a mirage, and the majority feel it is rather late in the day to continue pursuing it. Given the gravity of the crimes perpetrated on them during the genocide and the demands on their lives, many of them have this question: can there be justice without reparations? Will they one day be awarded something for their great loss and pain? Is it too late to do something about it? One of the survivors looked at me in deep reflection, shook her head and said softly: 'It is better late than never.'

There is a need to engage in dialogue to encourage international justice institutions like the ICC to continue to explore notions of gender sensitive reparations and reduce existing gender gaps. Meaningful participation in identifying context specific reparations should start with different categories of survivors taking ownership of the process; being granted space to define not only their notions of reparations, but also what is urgent and immediate, so that whilst waiting for long term reparations, survivors can actually survive.

BIBLIOGRAPHY

BOOKS AND JOURNAL ARTICLES

Askin 2005

Askin, K.D., 'The Treatment of Gender Crimes in the ICTR: Progress or Regression? The Akayesu Legacy at Risk', 3 Journal of international Criminal Justice, 2005.

Bassiouni 2006

Bassiouni, C.M., 'International Recognition of Victims' Rights', Human Rights Law Review, 2006.

Bauxbaum 2005

Bauxbaum, R.M., 'A Legal History of International Reparations', 23(2) Berkeley Journal of International Law, 2005.

Bottigliero 2004

Bottigliero, I., 'Redress for Victims of Crimes under International Law', Martinus Nijhoff, 2004.

Brehm, Uggen and Gasanabo 2014
Brehm, H.N., Uggen, C. and Gasanabo, J.D., 'Genocide, Justice, and Rwanda's Gacaca Courts', 30(3) Journal of Contemporary Criminal Justice, 2014.

De Brouwer 2007
De Brouwer, A.M., 'Reparation to Victims of Sexual Violence-Possibilities at the International Criminal Court and at the Trust Fund for Victims and Their Families', 20 Leiden Journal of International Law, 2007.

De Brouwer and Ruvebana 2013
De Brouwer, A.M. and Ruvebana, E., 'The Legacy of the Gacaca Courts in Rwanda: Survivors' Views', 13 International Criminal Law Review, 2013.

Dwertmann 2010
Dwertmann, E., 'The Reparation System of the International Criminal Court: its Implementation, Possibilities and Limitations', Martinus Nijhoff, 2010.

Ferencz 2000
Ferencz, B., 'The Experience of Nuremburg', in Shelton, D., 'International Crimes, Peace and Human Rights: the Role of the International Criminal Court', Transnational Publishers Inc., 2000.

Ferstman, Goetz and Stephens 2009
Ferstman, C., Goetz, M. and Stephens, A., 'Reparations for Victims of Genocide, War Crimes and Crimes Against Humanity', Martinus Nijhoff, 2009.

Garkawe 2003
Garkawe, S., 'Victims and the International Criminal Court: Three major issues', 3 International Criminal Law Review, 2003.

Lewis 2010
Lewis, J., 'Mass Graves and a Thousand Hills: University Student Perspectives on the Gacaca Courts in Post-Genocide Rwanda', Inquiry Journal, 2010.

Mukamana and Collins 2006
Mukamana, D. and Collins, A., 'Rape Survivors of the Rwandan Genocide', 17 International Journal of Critical Psychology, 2006.

Nowrojee 2005
Nowrojee, B., '"Your Justice Is Too Slow": How the ICTR Failed Rwanda's Rape Victims', in 'Women and Armed Conflict', Zubaan Books, 2005.

Staub et al. 2005
Staub, E., Pearlman, L.A., Gubin, A. and Hagengimana, A., 'Healing, Reconciliation, Forgiving And The Prevention Of Violence After Genocide Or Mass Killing: An Intervention And Its Experimental Evaluation In Rwanda', Journal of Social and Clinical Psychology, 2005.

Tamale 2011
Tamale, S. (ed.), 'African Sexualities: A Reader', Pambazuka Press, 2011.

Vandeginste 2003
Vandeginste, S., 'Victims of Genocide, Crimes Against Humanity, and War Crimes in Rwanda: The Legal and Institutional Framework of Their Right to Reparation', in Torpey, J. (ed.), 'Politics and the Past: On Repairing Historical Injustices', Rowman & Littlefield Publishers, 2003.

Zoglin 2007
Zoglin, K., Book review of 'What Happened to the Women? Gender and Reparations for Human Rights Violations', Ruth Rubio-Marin (ed.), International Journal of Transitional Justice, 2007.

JURISPRUDENCE

ICC 2012
ICC, Prosecutor v. Thomas Lubanga Dyilo, ICC-01/04-01/06-2904, 7 August 2012.
ICTR 2004
ICTR, Prosecutor v. Theoneste Bagosora, Gratien Kabiligi, Alloys Ntabakuze and Anatole Nsengiyumva, ICTR-98-41T, 13 October 2004.
ICTR 1999
ICTR, Prosecutor v. Alfred Musema, ICTR-96-13-T, 17 March 1999.
ICTR 1998
ICTR, Prosecutor v. Theoneste Bagosora, ICTR67-96-7T, 6 June 1998.

TREATIES, LEGISLATION AND AGREEMENTS

American Convention on Human Rights 'Pact of San Jose, Costa Rica' (B-32), 22 November 1969.
Convention against Torture and Other Cruel, Inhuman or Degrading Treatment or Punishment, UN Doc. A/RES/39/46, 10 December 1984.
European Convention on Human Rights, 4 November 1950.
International Criminal Court, Rules of Procedure and Evidence, ICC-ASP/1/3 (Part II-A), 9 September 2002.
International Criminal Tribunal for Rwanda, Rules of Procedure and Evidence, UN Doc. ITR/3/REV.1, 29 June 1995.
Rome Statute of the International Criminal Court, 2187 UNTS 90/37, 17 July 1998.

OTHERS

Amezcua Noriega, O., 'Reparation Principles under International Law and Their Possible Application by the International Criminal Court: Some Reflections', Transitional Justice Network Paper No. 1, August 2011.
Amnesty International, 'International Criminal Tribunal for Rwanda: Trials and Tribulations', 1998.
Amnesty International, 'Rwanda: Marked for Death', AFR 47/007/2004, 5 April 2004.
AVEGA-AGAHOZO, 'Survey on Violence Against Women in Rwanda', 1999.
ICTR, 'Letter dated 9 November 2000 from the President of the International Criminal Tribunal for Rwanda addressed to the Secretary-General', Annex, UN Doc. S/2000/1198, 14 December 2000.
ICTY, 'Address to the Security Council by Carla del Ponte, Prosecutor of the International Criminal Tribunals for the former Yugoslavia and Rwanda, to the UN Security Council', JL/P.I.S./542-e, 24 November 2000.
ICTY, 'Eighth Annual Report of the [ICTY]', UN Doc. A/56/352, 17 September 2001.
ICTY Rules Committee, 'Victims' compensation and participation', Appendix to a Letter dated 12 October 2000 from the President of the ICTY addressed to the UN

Secretary-General, Annex to Letter dated 2 November 2000 from the Secretary-General addressed to the President of the Security Council, UN Doc. S/2001/1063, 3 November 2000.

Mugiraneza, J.P., 'Rwanda Genocide: Why Compensation Would Help the Healing', The Guardian, 7 April 2014.

Mujawayo, E. and Blewitt, K.M., 'Sexual Violence Against women: Experiences from AVEGA's work in Kigali', Paper presented at the Silent Emergency Seminar in London, June 1999.

Nairobi Declaration on Women's and Girls' Right to Remedy and Reparation, International Meeting on Women's and Girls' Right to a Remedy and Reparation, March 2007.

REDRESS, 'Justice for Victims: The ICC's Reparations Mandate', 20 May 2011.

REDRESS, 'Reparation: A Source Book for Victims of Torture and Other Violations of Human Rights and International Humanitarian Law', 2003.

REDRESS, 'Right to Reparation for Survivors: Recommendations for Reparation for Survivors of the 1994 Genocide Against Tutsi', October 2012.

Schurr, J., 'Rwandan Genocide Survivors Still Waiting for Reparation', Pambazuka News, 14 September 2011.

Šoštarić, M., 'War Victims and Gender-Sensitive Trust, Justice, Reparations and Non-Recurrence in Bosnia and Herzegovina', Impunity Watch Perspective Series: Research Report, 2012.

UN General Assembly, Resolution on 'Assistance to survivors of the 1994 Genocide in Rwanda, Particularly Orphans, widows and Victims of Sexual Violence', A/RES/59/137, 17 February 2004.

UN, 'Guidance Note of the Secretary–General: Reparations for Conflict-Related Sexual Violence', June 2014.

Van Boven, T., 'Basic Principles and Guidelines on the Right to a Remedy and Reparation for Victims of Gross Violations of International Human Rights Law and Serious Violations of International Humanitarian Law', United Nations Audiovisual Library of International Law, 16 December 2005.

Victims' Rights Working Group, 'Establishing Effective Reparation Procedures and Principles for the International Criminal Court', September 2011.

War Crimes Research Office, 'The Case-Based Reparations Scheme at the International Criminal Court', International Criminal Court Legal Analysis and Education Project, June 2010.

Women's Caucus for Gender Justice, 'Summary of Panel Discussions on Victim and Witness Issues', 27 July 1999.

Women's Initiatives for Gender Justice (ICC Women), 'Statement of the Women's Initiatives for Gender Justice Change in Chambers' Approach to Reparations The Prosecutor v. Germain Katanga', 1 September 2014.

Women's Initiatives for Gender Justice (ICC Women), 'Statement on the First Reparations Decision by the ICC: The Prosecutor v. Thomas Lubanga Dyilo', 10 August 2012.

TRANSITIONAL JUSTICE AND THE ICC

Lessons from Rwanda

Leo C. Nwoye*

1. INTRODUCTION

This article explores the transitional justice mechanisms that were employed in Rwanda's post genocide era and extracts lessons that could be amenable to the International Criminal Court. A key question for the ICC to consider is how best to shape efforts internationally and domestically in order to ensure accountability for mass atrocities. Rwanda is one of the few African countries to have had its cases of international crimes prosecuted nationally as well as internationally. The solutions which arose in its milieu were the establishment of the International Criminal Tribunal for Rwanda (ICTR) by the UN Security Council (UNSC), whilst localised endeavours came in the form of, *inter alia*, the *gacaca* court system.

The salient lessons for the ICC are the following: (1) both international and grassroots transitional justice strategies can foster a sense of local ownership, though in different ways – with the international mechanisms focusing on the broad collective level by prosecuting those most responsible for orchestrating the Rwandan genocide, while the localised courts focused on the individual level; (2) there is a need for a customised approach to accountability; (3) whilst there are benefits in prosecution, this approach has some limitations; and (4) there is no 'one-size-fits-all' transitional justice system that can be used in any post-conflict situation. Yet, as a legal experiment that had no precedent, the legal pluralist system defined by a combination of the ICTR and the *gacaca* courts represents a possible model for delivering transitional justice that could be utilised and contextualised by the ICC in future post-conflict environments.

In 1994, Rwanda witnessed one of the worst mass atrocities ever perpetrated in history. Since then, there have been other ethnically infused political

* Assistant Appeals Counsel in the Office of the Prosecutor (OTP) at the Mechanism for International Criminal Tribunals (MICT), Arusha Branch. The views expressed in this article are the personal views of the author. The author would especially like to thank Dr Mathias Ruzindana for his comments.

upheavals on the African continent – in Kenya, Côte d'Ivoire, South Sudan, and more recently in the Central African Republic (CAR).

Transitional justice has acquired international recognition as it encompasses a multitude of short-term, distinct, though overlapping and often conflicting, judicial/non-judicial mechanisms/processes that address periods of conflict or repressive rule. A dominant subject in the area of post-conflict reconstruction and transitional justice has been legal pluralism. This is an arena where various legal systems cohabit within the same social space in order to advance just corollaries.[1] These legal systems can also co-occur nationally as well as externally, and whilst possessing largely dissimilar purposes, they become a unique type of legal pluralism. In truth, legal pluralism as a transitional justice approach may be more effective than a unitary legal system.

Internationally, the UNSC established the ICTR. It was directed to prosecute the persons responsible for genocide and other serious violations of international humanitarian law committed in Rwanda and by Rwandan citizens in neighbouring states, between 1 January 1994 and 31 December 1994.

Domestically, and in addition to the national criminal trials, the Rwandan government set up the *gacaca* court system in June 2002. This system was unconnected and detached from the ICTR. It emerged from the national justice system's inability to efficiently process the huge number of delayed genocide cases, especially as many of the legal workforce had been killed or had fled the country during the carnage.

Whereas the ICTR essentially uses a formal, adversarial, and retributive method of trial procedures, *gacaca* is an informal, customary Rwandan system of conflict resolution that was modified to meet the perceived needs of the post-genocide population. It was shaped to be culturally relevant to post-genocide Rwanda, unlike the ICTR, in its provision of transitional justice.

There have been notable censures as regards the efficacy, yield, and effectiveness of these distinct systems.[2] Nevertheless, Rwanda is amongst the few African states to have had its cases of genocide, war crimes, and crimes against humanity prosecuted nationally as well as internationally. Moreover, as is discussed below, Rwanda is one of few African countries that have experienced the trial of its citizens in foreign jurisdictions for international crimes.

There were two other legal courses established, and yet, whilst significant, they only operated peripherally. These are: Rwandan military trials, and international third-party prosecutions in foreign jurisdictions. The Rwandan domestic courts, the aforementioned supplementary mechanisms, and their contribution to transitional justice in Rwanda, however limited, are beyond the scope of this article.

1 Griffiths 1986, pp. 38–39; Merry 1988, p. 870.

2 For a comprehensive assessment on the ICTR and gacaca courts, see generally Nwoye 2014.

The ICC emerged largely in response to the creation and strategy of the ad hoc courts, filling the need for a permanent international judicial mechanism that would be able to address crimes against humanity and gross violations of human rights, supplementing local systems of governance the same way that the ICTR supplemented the *gacaca* system. Moreover, the ICC arose in response to cynicism regarding the ad hoc and temporary nature of the ICTR and International Criminal Tribunal for the former Yugoslavia (ICTY), with proponents wanting a permanent court at the international level.

In July 1998, the Rome Statute of the International Criminal Court was adopted by the international community and came into force on 1 July 2002. While the ICC now embodies the power to bring to justice those accused of genocide, war crimes, and crimes against humanity, its temporal jurisdiction does not precede the time at which it was ratified. Its judicial activity, unlike the ad hoc tribunals, is intended to complement domestic legal systems, but only when national courts are genuinely unwilling or unable to carry out the investigation or prosecution of a person accused of the crimes delineated in the Rome Statute.[3]

The ICC's creation has been endorsed by many countries on the African continent, as compared to other continents outside Europe. Indeed, nearly two-thirds of the African Union (AU) members are parties to the Rome Statute and were actively involved in its negotiation in the late 1990s. However, relations soured after a number of incidents. These were: Belgium's issuance of an arrest warrant for Abdoulaye Yerodia Ndombasi, the Democratic Republic of the Congo's (DRC) then-minister of foreign affairs; the indictment of the President of Sudan, Omar Al-Bashir, and the confirmation of charges against Uhuru Kenyatta (the winner of Kenya's 2013 presidential election) and three other prominent Kenyans for crimes against humanity, including murder and rape that were committed in the post-election violence: William Ruto, who would be elected Deputy President in 2013; Henry Kosgey, Former Minister of Industralization; and Francis Muthara, Former Head of Civil Service and Secretary to the Cabinet of President Mwai Kibaki.

Consequently, the AU has sought to withdraw from the Rome Statute, contending that the ICC is only targeting African states.[4] Conversely, it seems apparent that Africa itself is heavily divided on the issue – with East African leaders from Kenya, Sudan, and Uganda facing strong resistance from their West and Southern African counterparts like Ghana, Nigeria, and

3 Rome Statute, Art. 17(1)(a).

4 'Will Africa pull out of the ICC?', *BBC News*, 11 October 2013, available at: www.bbc.com/news/world-africa-24452288 (accessed 3 December 2014); 'African Union accuses ICC of "hunting" Africans', *BBC News*, 27 May 2013, available at: www.bbc.com/news/world-africa-22681894 (accessed 3 December 2014).

Botswana.[5] This is in spite of a recent AU resolution that, *inter alia*, all its incumbent heads of state shall not appear before any international court during their term of office and that any indictment served on them would weaken the sovereignty, peace, and stability of member states.[6] Rwanda has not signed the treaty ratifying the ICC and has become one of the ICC's severest detractors. This article will not consider its relationship with the ICC.

This article analyses the ICTR and the *gacaca* courts at a critical time. The ICTR has almost completed its cases and is closing down its operations – whilst the *gacaca* courts have completed their mandate. Therefore, there are major questions for the ICC as to how successful the systems were in promoting transitional justice and what lessons could be drawn from the Rwandan experience.

This article is organised into five sections. The second section briefly examines the ICTR and *gacaca* courts with respect to their creation and primary goals – analysing the processes as part of a legal pluralist system with respect to transitional justice, without framing the two entities in opposition to one another. It also appraises the ICTR and *gacaca* courts in holistically meeting transitional justice goals.

The third section provides a brief overview of the ICC, looking at the implications of seeking justice and preventing atrocities. It considers the ICC Prosecutor's discretion, exploring the gaps in the Rome Statute where the Prosecutor may decline intervention in situations where a country decides not to prosecute, in favour of other transitional justice processes. It also discusses the potential for the use of universal jurisdiction by domestic legal systems in Africa. The fourth section draws lessons and makes suggestions that could prove useful to the ICC. Finally, the fifth section makes concluding remarks.

2. TRANSITIONAL JUSTICE AND LEGAL PLURALISM IN RWANDA: THE COLLECTIVE LEVEL (ICTR) AND THE INDIVIDUAL LEVEL (GACACA)

Most of the literature focused on the role transitional justice plays in Rwanda puts the ICTR in contrast to the *gacaca* courts.[7] This is a fractured perspective

5 Greenberg, 'African Union Declaration Against the ICC Not What it Seems', *Foreign Policy on Focus*, 6 August 2009, available at: http://fpif.org/african_union_declaration_against_the_icc_not_what_it_seems/ (accessed 3 December 2014).

6 AU, Decision on Africa's Relationship with the International Criminal Court (ICC), Ext/Assembly/AU/Dec.1, October 2013.

7 See for example Westberg 2011, p. 331.

of this legal pluralist system that is more holistic in nature.[8] In several African states, as in Rwanda, the colonial authorities initiated their own court system whilst allowing native dispute resolution systems to continue functioning. This resulted in twin, parallel systems of laws and courts (i.e. legal pluralism).[9]

The legal pluralist system in Rwanda within which the ICTR and *gacaca* courts coexisted and operated had more impact and was more effective in accomplishing transitional justice goals than either the ICTR or *gacaca* courts in isolation.[10] The ICTR and *gacaca* courts also coexisted with Rwanda's national courts[11] and operated in semi-autonomous domains. There is no requirement for a partnership[12] or equity in power between the two systems, in order to fit the characterisation of an authentic legal pluralist system.

The UNSC has correctly stated that the success of transitional justice in any post-conflict society is dependent upon a number of factors, with the need to eschew the one-size-fits-all approach to transitional justice, and to instead rely on national assessments, in order to implement effective strategies.[13]

The National Unity and Reconciliation Commission (NURC) was created in March 1999 by the Rwandan government and given the broad mandate of promoting and nurturing reconciliation among Rwandans.[14] It postulates that six variables influence reconciliation in Rwanda: political culture, human security, citizenship and identity, transitional justice, historical understanding, and social cohesion.[15]

Transitional justice, according to the UN, can include both judicial and non-judicial institutions with arbitrary levels of truth-seeking, individual prosecutions, reparations, institutional reform, dismissals and vetting, and international involvement.[16] This is in contrast to the variables emphasised by the NURC as integral to transitional justice – notably individual healing, punishment, compensation, and forgiveness. Yet both sets of variables are vital for the attainment of transitional justice goals. Table 1 illustrates the differences between the UN and the Rwandan government's perception of transitional justice.

---

8 Clark 2007, p. 765.

9 Nwoye 2014, para. IV.

10 *Ibid*, p. 124.

11 Jones 2010, p. 84.

12 For example, the ICTR made use of *gacaca* records and judgements. The *gacaca* courts, conversely, did not make use of the ICTR judgments or decisions.

13 UNSC, 'The Rule of Law and Transitional Justice in Conflict and Post-Conflict Societies', 23 August 2004, UN Doc. S/2004/616.

14 NURC was created by Organic Law No. 03/1999 of 12 March 1999.

15 NURC, *Rwandan Reconciliation Barometer*, 2010, p. 86.

16 UNSC, 'The Rule of Law and Transitional Justice in Conflict and Post-Conflict Societies', 23 August 2004, UN Doc. S/2004/616, p. 1.

Table 1

	UN	Rwandan Government
Truth-Seeking	✓	
Reparations / Compensation	✓	✓
Institutional Reform	✓	
Dismissals / Vetting	✓	
International Involvement	✓	
Individual Healing		✓
Punishment	✓	✓
Forgiveness		✓

Table 1 reflects a domestic emphasis on the individual level, with the Rwandan government recognising the integral parts that individual healing and forgiveness play in transitional justice. In contrast, the international sphere emphasises the collective level – with the UN focusing on institutional reform and international involvement. The reparations and punishment variables can be found in both the domestic and international transitional justice frameworks. It is important to note however, that the early phase of the *gacaca* courts related to truth-seeking as it involved information gathering where allegations in the form of depositions were collected and validated.[17]

Transitional justice generally demands that the domestic systems take ownership of the process, with external, international, mechanisms supplementing these efforts. In the context of Rwanda, transitional justice can then be framed as a linked relationship between the ICTR and *gacaca* courts, rather than as either system operating in isolation. Equally, they can also be framed as a legal pluralist system seeking to support and achieve transitional justice goals – with their differences corresponding to their respective collective and individual levels.

2.1. THE ICTR'S CREATION, TRANSITIONAL JUSTICE AIMS, AND PREVAILING PERSPECTIVES

UNSC Resolution 955 sanctioned the establishment of the ICTR in 1994 and referred its principal aims, which are: '[to] contribute to ensuring that such violations are halted and effectively redressed'[18] through its prosecutions,[19]

17 Ingelaere 2008, pp. 41–42.

18 UNSC Res. 955 (8 November 1994).

19 ICTR Statute, Art 1. See also for example, *The Prosecutor v. Georges Ruggiu*, Sentencing Judgement, ICTR-97-32-I, Trial Chamber I, 1 June 2000, para. 32: 'The objective in creating

thereby 'contribut[ing] to the process of national reconciliation and to the restoration and maintenance of peace' in Rwanda.[20]

Since its commencement in 1997, the ICTR has hitherto completed 56 cases, acquitted 12 detainees, released two detainees, and has no trials currently in progress. It has released seven detainees after completion of their sentences. It also has six additional cases on appeal and has transferred ten cases to national jurisdictions. There are nine accused still at large.[21]

The ICTR has been censured for its high expense, slow pace, cultural incompetence, remoteness, its failure to genuinely endorse transitional justice for the Rwandan populace, and its perceived acquiescence of victor's justice.[22] Yet it cannot be controverted that the ICTR has provided a strong foundation for international criminal prosecution of genocide and war crimes, and has shaped the future of international post-conflict platforms. This is in spite of the apparent disparities between the ICTR and the goals enumerated by the UN. Nevertheless, the ICTR has largely attained a number of transitional justice aims as outlined by the UNSC, chiefly with respect to institutional reform, international involvement, and punishment.

As regards institutional reform, it is widely acknowledged that recent legal developments in Rwanda may be ascribed to the influence of the ICTR.[23] These include: the enhancement of due process and fair trial standards;[24] the adoption of genocide legislation congruent with the definitions of the 1948 International Convention on Genocide,[25] abolition of the death penalty,[26] the improvement of prison detention facilities, and the setting up of a dedicated Witness Protection Unit within the Judiciary.[27] In light of these reforms, the ICTR has been able to transfer cases to Rwandan national courts and other jurisdictions, on the proviso that, *inter alia*, the accused will receive a fair trial.[28]

With regard to the perception that the ICTR facilitates victor's justice, these standpoints are seemingly misinformed. The ICTR's genesis, mandate, and

---

the Tribunal is to prosecute and punish the perpetrators of the atrocities in Rwanda, to put an end to impunity and thereby to promote national reconciliation'.

20 UNSC Res. 955 (8 November 1994) (emphasis added).

21 ICTR, 'The Cases', available at: www.unictr.org/en/cases (accessed 19 December 2014).

22 Goldstein-Bolocan 2005, p. 370; Haskell and Waldorf 2011, p. 51.

23 See generally, Nwoye 2014, pp. 175–177.

24 Dieng 2011, p. 417.

25 See Organic Law on the Organization of Prosecutions for Offences constituting the Crimes of Genocide or Crimes against Humanity committed since 1 October 1990 (Organic Law No. 08/1996 of 30 August 1996).

26 Organic Law No. 31/2007 of 25 July 2007 – relating to the Abolition of the Death Penalty.

27 Dieng 2011, p. 420.

28 Pursuant to ICTR Rules of Procedure and Evidence (31 January 2010), Rule 11*bis*. See also UNSC Res. 1503 (28 August 2003). See also *The Prosecutor v. Jean-Bosco Uwinkindi*, Appeal Decision, ICTR-2001-75-AR11*bis*, Decision on Uwinkindi's Appeal against the Referral of his Case to Rwanda and Related Motions (16 December 2011); *The Prosecutor v. Jean-Bosco Uwinkindi*, ICTR-2001-75-R11*bis*, Decision on Prosecutor's Request for Referral to the Republic of Rwanda (28 June 2011); see also Dieng 2011, pp. 420–421.

make-up prevents it from being a 'victor's court' particularly as the Prosecutor can investigate and prosecute serious abuses of international humanitarian law on all sides of the conflict. Indeed, the ICTR OTP has conducted investigations on the allegations against the RPF with the Rwandan government's permission.[29] There were investigations conducted on 42 RPF soldiers – 19 were prosecuted for offences that were outside the ICTR's jurisdiction and 23 were tried for revenge crimes, after 1994, against non-combatants suspected of being genocide perpetrators.

The ICTR has no enforcement mechanism of its own and has to rely on state cooperation in the execution of its mandate[30] as regards the arrest and transfer of fugitives, the transfer and protection of witnesses, and the collection of evidence overseas.

It has also had a difficult working relationship with the Rwandan government, with the latter often accusing the ICTR of inefficiency and incompetence. The Rwandan government's assistance has been a mixture of antipathy and cooperation – with the ICTR's lack of enforcement powers giving the national government wide latitude to strategically decide on when and how to cooperate with the Tribunal.[31] In 2002, the Rwandan government demonstrated its ability to carry out its episodic threats, when witnesses were prevented from travelling to Arusha in order to testify, thereby delaying the ICTR trial process.[32] Relations have since improved.

While the ICTR enjoys primacy over all member state national courts by virtue of Article 8(2) of the ICTR Statute, as regards Rwanda – it has sought to forge a strong relationship through partnerships such as outreach programmes and capacity building; and the referral of cases to Rwanda for domestic prosecution. Primacy does not equate to, or guarantee, state cooperation, which cannot be forced. Moreover, how the ICTR is perceived in Rwanda will largely determine whether it is able to complete its transitional justice mandate. It was therefore crucial for the ICTR to make its work more visible and discernible, despite the complex political context it operated in.

The ICTR established its Outreach Program in 1999, which was designed to keep Rwandan citizens informed of the ICTR's objectives, importance, and accomplishments. Resolution 955 does not have capacity building in the mandate of the Tribunal. Instead, it encourages member states to improve cooperation in order to reinforce Rwanda's courts and judicial system.[33]

Whilst there have been efforts to assist capacity building in Rwanda,[34] the international community ultimately realised that the ICTR could proffer

29 Nwoye 2014, p. 174, nn. 405–406.

30 ICTR Statute, Art. 28.

31 Peskin 2005, p. 214.

32 Peskin 2008, pp. 212–215.

33 See UN Res. 955 (8 November 1994), para. 2.

34 The UNSC had called on the international community 'to assist national jurisdictions, as part of the completion strategy, in improving their capacity to prosecute cases transferred

considerable assistance in this regard. Indeed, since 2005, part of the ICTR's Outreach Program has provided training to Rwandan judges, lawyers, and human rights activists on a variety of legal topics and skills including investigation, prosecution, and administration.[35] The ICTR also has ties with NGOs and civil rights organisations in Rwanda.[36] It has also made valuable contributions to the improvement of the Rwandan judiciary over the past few years, through trainings and other outreach activities.

The ICTR opened an Information and Documentation Centre in Kigali in 2000, which is known as '*umusanzu mu bwiyunge*' or 'contribution to reconciliation'. The principal goal of the Centre is to 'bridge the information gap between the Tribunal and the Rwandan population.'[37] As Drumbl noted '[t]here is some indication that the more Rwandans learn of the ICTR's work, the more inclined they are to view the institution more favorably'[38] and this has been the case in Rwanda. The NURC has pointed out that 75.3% of Rwandans are aware of the purpose and nature of ICTR, of which about 59% consider the entity effective as a transitional justice mechanism.[39]

The results of the survey carried out by the NURC on this subject are reflected in Figure 1 below. These statistics represent a major shift of perspective by the Rwandan populace, particularly when compared to previous empirical studies.[40] However, recently, some in the Rwandan media, for example, Rwagatare, have suggested that 'the ICTR does not earn much praise in Rwanda ... The ICTR has done anything but what it was set up for'.[41] He offers no statistical or empirical substantiation for his assertions. Nonetheless, it seems clear that in spite of the challenges emanating from the Rwandan government, the establishment and operation of the ICTR has in large part been worthwhile.

from the ICTY and the ICTR and encourages the ICTY and ICTR Presidents, Prosecutors and Registrars to develop and improve their outreach programmes'. See UNSC Res. 1503 (28 August 2003).

35 Dieng 2011, p. 409.

36 *Ibid*, p. 410.

37 The ICTR also opened ten smaller information and documentation centres in other provinces of Rwanda. It is planned that following the completion of the ICTR's mandate, these centres will be handed over to the Rwandan government with the objective of preserving the ICTR's historical judicial output. See Dieng 2011, pp. 408–409.

38 Drumbl 2005, p. 47 (citations omitted).

39 NURC, *Rwandan Reconciliation Barometer*, 2010, p. 70.

40 For example, see Longman 2004, pp. 37–38. See also Des Forges and Longman, 'Legal responses to genocide in Rwanda', 25 October 2004, available at: http://faculty.vassar.edu/tilongma/justice.html (accessed 15 December 2014). A survey conducted in February 2002 revealed that 87.2% of participants in four communities claimed that they were not well informed or not informed at all about the ICTR.

41 Rwagatare, 'ICTR acquittals shocking but expected', *The New Times*, 12 February 2013, available at: http://allafrica.com/stories/201302120094.html (accessed 15 December 2014).

Figure 1. NURC Survey of the effectiveness of the ICTR as a transitional justice mechanism[42]

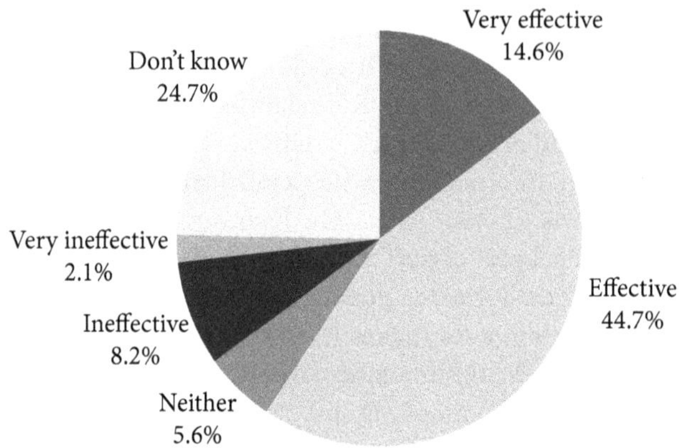

2.2. THE GACACA COURTS, TRANSITIONAL JUSTICE AIMS AND PREVAILING PERSPECTIVES

In its original form, *gacaca* is an informal, community-based system of dispute resolution with pre-colonial origins.[43] It exemplifies 'restorative justice principles because it does not seek to achieve justice by punishing the perpetrator, but to restore social order by finding communal, compromised solutions and by reintegrating the offender within the community.'[44] The 'new' *gacaca* process, just like its traditional form, focused on truth, justice, and reconciliation among Rwandans through community participation.[45] Yet the process differs from traditional *gacaca* in that it was formally recognised and organised by the government.[46] Its rules were not customary as they were codified in the Rwandan Transitional National Assembly Organic Law 40/2000 of 26 January 2001.

During its existence, the *gacaca* courts tried 1,951,388 cases[47] with a conviction rate of around 65%,[48] unlike the domestic justice processes, which

42 Adapted from NURC, *Rwandan Reconciliation Barometer*, 2010, p. 70.

43 Daly 2002, pp. 370–371 (citations omitted). See also Penal Reform International (PRI), 'Access to Justice in Sub-Saharan Africa: the Role of Traditional and Informal Justice Systems', January 2001, p. 51.

44 See generally Goldstein-Bolocan 2005.

45 Nagy 2009, p. 94.

46 Jones 2010, p. 8.

47 'Curtains fall on Gacaca', *The Independent*, 29 May 2012, available at: www.independent.co.ug/rwanda-ed/rwanda/5843-curtains-fall-on-gacaca (accessed 15 December 2014). This figure is likely to include all instances of trials and appeals. It also includes non-genocide cases such as looting committed during the attacks.

48 'Rwanda "Gacaca" Genocide Courts Finish Work', *BBC News*, 18 June 2012, available at: www.bbc.co.uk/news/world-africa-18490348 (accessed 15 December 2014).

dealt with only 10,026 cases between 1997 and 2004.[49] There is no institutional link between the *gacaca* courts and the national courts – yet cases classed as Category 1 genocide crimes may be transferred to the national courts, from the *gacaca* courts.

Like the ICTR, the *gacaca* courts have not been immune to criticism, which principally centred on fair trial violations and victor's justice. Concerns have been raised about the constitutionality of the *gacaca* law, as regards to legal precepts like fair trial,[50] legal representation,[51] the placing of the burden of proof,[52] the double jeopardy principle,[53] and competence of the lay *gacaca* judges.[54] Further, the *gacaca* system appears to have only dealt with crimes perpetrated by the Hutu population, and not the RPF.[55]

But these censures, which stem from a Western standpoint, are mostly unproven because the *gacaca* courts cannot be viewed purely as a legal institution, nor can it be considered without its reconciliation goals.[56] Clark states that '[t]he dominant discourse fails to account for the hybrid nature of *gacaca* and the hybrid methods and objectives it embodies. We therefore require a more nuanced interpretation of *gacaca* and its objectives if we are to offer more appropriate suggestions as to how it may be reformed to aid its effectiveness as a tool of post-genocide reconstruction.'[57]

In reality, there was no other alternative to the national courts (with their limited capacity at the time), other than *gacaca* – especially one that formed a foundation for justice and reconciliation whilst being culturally sensitive to the Rwandan people and the genocide context.[58] Public participation was a core aspect of the *gacaca* system, and was one of the most critical channels for promoting social cohesion.[59] Furthermore, the exclusion of legal representation in hearings was aimed at amplifying the community's sense of ownership over the process.

The *gacaca* courts have sentenced individuals to lengthy prison terms – hence, they must abide by certain legal principles including due process. The lack of legal representation is at variance with Article 18 of the Rwandan Constitution, which states: 'The right to be informed of the nature and cause of charges and

---

49 Ingelaere 2008.
50 Amnesty International, 'Rwanda: Gacaca: A Question of Justice', AI Index: AFR 47/007/2002, December 2002, p. 30.
51 *Ibid*, p. 14.
52 *Ibid*, p. 23.
53 *Ibid*, pp. 33 and 39.
54 *Ibid*, pp. 38–39; Westberg 2011, pp. 353–355.
55 Clark 2010, p. 211; Clark 2007, p. 806; Corey and Joireman 2004, p. 86.
56 Clark 2007, p. 807.
57 *Ibid.*
58 See also, Uvin and Mironko 2003, p. 219.
59 Clark 2007, pp. 808–809.

the right to defence are absolute at all levels and degrees of proceedings before administrative, judicial and all other decision making organs.'

Nevertheless, the concerns, whilst properly raised, did appear to have undermined the *gacaca* courts' potential to represent 'civic virtues of communal engagement, discourse and debate that are important for building trust and long-term peace.'[60] Gasibirege has argued that the discourse in *gacaca* proceedings is important for the wellbeing of the community as it helps them learn to determine difficult issues communally.[61]

The NURC has highlighted that the majority of Rwandans (93.7%) believe that the *gacaca* court processes revealed most of what occurred in the genocide – unlike the domestic justice system or the ICTR.[62] It posits that this percentage is reflective of the participant's belief in the impartiality of the *gacaca* judges, particularly as they may have attended a *gacaca* court session at least once.[63]

Some academics have asserted that the key objective of *gacaca* justice, unlike the ICTR, was restoration rather than retribution[64] – arguably this goes some way in countering the criticism that it was a form of victor's justice which focused on punishment over unity. Yet a literal reading of the title of the domestic law establishing the organisation, competency, and functioning of the *gacaca* courts show that they were 'charged with prosecuting and trying the perpetrators of the crime of genocide and other crimes against humanity, committed between October 1, 1990 and December 31, 1994.' It thus seems apparent that the key focus of the *gacaca* courts was essentially punitive.

With respect to transitional justice, the NURC cites that nearly 90% of citizens assert that punishments have been fair, with 70.8% believing that the genocide survivors have been fairly compensated (with few gender disparities reflected in the empirical data). Table 2 indicates the Rwandan government's synthesis of transitional justice outcomes delivered by *gacaca* from the perspective of the Rwandan people.[65] However, the NURC's study does not reveal whether persons of Hutu and Tutsi ethnicity regard transitional justice (and reconciliation) in the same way.

60 Clark 2010, p. 234.
61 Gasibirege 2002, pp. 93–127, 94, 101; see also Clark 2010, pp. 201, 232, 296.
62 NURC, *Rwandan Reconciliation Barometer*, 2010, p. 66.
63 *Ibid.*
64 Uvin and Mironko 2003, p. 227; Clark 2010, pp. 238–239, 249–250; NURC, *Rwandan Reconciliation Barometer*, 2010, pp. 61, 66.
65 NURC, *Rwandan Reconciliation Barometer*, 2010, p. 67.

Table 2

Transitional justice category	% of Respondents according to gender	
	Male	Female
Truth about the genocide was revealed	94.4%	93.2%
The gacaca judges were impartial during the process	83.5%	83.3%
Fair punishment for those convicted	89.2%	89.5%
Fair compensation for the genocide survivors	70.1%	71.6%
Government support and assistance during the process	68.7%	70.3%

Healing and forgiveness, as terms, can be challenging to define in a post-genocide environment. Clark identifies two main forms of healing through *gacaca* courts:[66] 'healing as liberation'[67] and 'healing as belonging.'[68] Both forms involve processes relating to the expression or reception of knowledge at *gacaca*, and often comprise notions of personal redemption or atonement through truth. Forgiveness, which involves the giving up of feelings of resentment and a desire for personal direct retribution, is necessary for a fresh start and to allow people to deal with memories of the past in a more constructive manner.[69]

The NURC highlights that most respondents have indicated that they have been healed from past events and that they are willing to forgive those who have hurt them, though this forgiveness has yet to occur.[70] The role of *gacaca* in promoting healing and forgiveness is a complex one. The NURC, however, links both individual healing and forgiveness to the remorsefulness of the perpetrators.[71]

Clark argues that the *gacaca* system cannot be effectively and comprehensively assessed from any socio-cultural context other than that within which the system exists.[72] The ways in which the Rwandan people perceive healing, forgiveness, and more broadly, justice, are then integral to any accurate assessment of *gacaca*'s effectiveness. The NURC contends that the large majority of Rwandans feel that healing and forgiveness are possible

66 Clark 2010, pp. 258–259.

67 *Ibid.* This involves individuals' discovery of a sense of inner liberty from sources of psychological and emotional turmoil, such as survivors' ignorance about what happened to their loved ones during the genocide.

68 *Ibid.* This relates to individuals' expressed desire to experience greater psychological and emotional completeness through reconnecting with their community.

69 Clark 2010, p. 43.

70 NURC, *Rwandan Reconciliation Barometer*, 2010, pp. 62–63.

71 *Ibid*, pp. 63–64.

72 Clark 2007, pp. 799–802.

following the genocide, though perpetrators' remorse is critical to their ability to forgive.[73]

It seems implicit from the NURC's report that the *gacaca* was not deemed as a sufficient vehicle for social cohesion. Some core weaknesses exist with respect to the promotion of social cohesion goals, for example, the participant's perception of victor's justice. Nonetheless, considering that reconciliation can stem from transitional justice, social cohesion becomes more akin to the former's outcome/process than the latter.

Transitional justice is a key component of reconciliation, and according to the NURC, it need not necessarily promote social cohesion outside the goals of healing, forgiveness, reparations, and punishment. Critics of *gacaca* have also queried the decision to allow a 'traumatised and still heavily ethnically-divided population' to wield justice over those who largely caused that trauma.[74] Before *gacaca*, post-conflict resolution mechanisms, such as war crimes tribunals and truth commissions, sought to limit the population's participation. It rationalised this by highlighting the perceived inability of victims to objectively facilitate justice.

The ICTR has operated in a similar fashion, seeking objectivity and promoting international participation over that of the population most directly impacted by the genocide. *Gacaca*, conversely, recognises that the community's participation is crucial to both reconciliation and justice – with social cohesion and national unity promoted by virtue of popular ownership and involvement in the *gacaca* system.[75]

The effectiveness of delivering transitional justice to the Rwandan population is thus linked to the connections between the collective and individual levels of transitional justice outcomes. Fundamentally, the potential for transitional justice to be achieved by either the ICTR or *gacaca* is dependent on the capacity and agency of the international community and the local community, respectively, in endorsing their transitional justice objectives.

2.3. ASSESSMENT OF THE ICTR AND GACACA

The divergent perspectives of transitional justice as articulated by the international community and the Rwandan government are particularly crucial in evaluating how the ICTR and *gacaca* courts have met transitional justice goals. There is evidence of a major shift in public opinion, with most Rwandans being aware of the nature and purpose of the ICTR and nearly 60% regarding

73 *Ibid*, p. 64.
74 Clark 2007, p. 808.
75 *Ibid*, pp. 807–819.

it as effective[76] – demonstrating that its outreach programmes are having an impact.

The scope of the ICTR's intervention may not appear vast, with only 64 cases[77] completed since its inception, as compared to the 1,951,388 cases tried in the *gacaca* courts. Yet, this is not an appropriate comparison given the crucial differences in the systems, especially as regards adherence to legal principles like burden of proof, fair hearing, and right to legal representation. The ICTR has received over 25,800 motions/submissions and has made over 7,700 decisions. It would not have been feasible for the ICTR to prosecute thousands of persons as this would entail more time, money, and personnel than the tribunal had at its disposal.

Moreover, the UNSC intended,[78] and requested the ICTR, to 'concentrate on the most senior leaders suspected of being the most responsible for [the] crimes' within its jurisdiction and refer the other perpetrators (who were considered to be middle and low ranking individuals) to 'competent national jurisdictions'[79] – primarily because of the enormous numbers involved and the temporary nature of the ICTR. Hence, the Prosecutor could not take on more cases because of the deadlines the UNSC predetermined[80] in order to allow the ICTR to meet its goals.[81]

Additionally, this comparison does not take into account, *inter alia*, the quality of justice dispensed, the pioneering status of the ICTR's work, and the complexities of trial at international level, involving international practitioners. As such, the approach taken by the ICTR is necessary and is reflected in the fact that both the ICTR and domestic courts have concurrent jurisdiction.[82]

The ICTR's work as a transitional justice mechanism has been hindered, to some extent, by its difficult working relationship with the Rwandan government. This highlights how the politics of post-genocide societies can shape or stymie the running of transitional justice mechanisms. The functioning of international justice depends, to a large degree, on the goodwill of domestic jurisdictions, and also on the diplomatic approach taken by the relevant international body. The ICTR's victor's justice label is seemingly a problem of state cooperation[83] – although as mentioned above, this is largely no longer an issue, with the ICTR building a relationship with the Rwandan government through its capacity

76 NURC, *Rwandan Reconciliation Barometer*, 2010, p. 70.

77 This figure denotes cases against individuals that have passed through the trial and appeal processes – resulting in either convictions or acquittals.

78 UNSC, Verbatim Record of the Security Council's 3453rd Meeting, UN Doc. S/PV.3453, 8 November 1994 (submissions of the French representative).

79 UNSC Res. 1534 (26 March 2004).

80 UNSC Res. 1503 (28 August 2003); UNSC Res. 1534 (26 March 2004).

81 UNSC Res. 1534 (26 March 2004).

82 ICTR Statute, Art. 8(1).

83 *Ibid*; Peskin 2005, p. 214.

building initiatives and outreach activities, as well as its referral of cases for domestic prosecution.

The *gacaca* system provided the Rwandan population with the ability to participate in the justice and reconciliation process, although the evidence implies that the degree to which transitional justice was sought included a heavy emphasis on punishment and reparations, rather than forgiveness and individual healing.[84]

The *gacaca* system afforded benefits to the Rwandan people in the political, social, and economic spheres. The direct impact on Rwanda by the *gacaca* courts has been considerable and relevant, including the economic benefits of reducing the financial drain on the overburdened legal system. Further, *gacaca* has, to a degree, promoted social cohesion by affording the accused with reduced sentences in return for remorsefulness – which also does not indicate a criminalisation and imposition of collective guilt on the Hutu majority.[85] And in turn, the promotion of social cohesion is derived from the just punishment and rapid reintegration of citizens. The cultural relevance of *gacaca* in requiring the perpetrators to confess and apologise publicly in front of their victims, their families, and local communities should serve as a significant deterrent for future crimes because of its public shaming element.[86]

Additionally, *gacaca* has promoted individual healing, apology, and the possibility of forgiveness. It created a forum for discourse and engagement with the ultimate aim of restoring fractured relationships.[87] Conversely, the intrinsic system of abstraction and remoteness of perpetrators from their communities as practised by the ICTR has had a negligible impact on individual healing and forgiveness. Yet it is also arguable that what the ICTR lacked in proximity, it gained in objectivity.

Nevertheless, the role of the ICTR in establishing and promoting a post-conflict agenda for the international community is irrefutable. While the number of cases tried by the ICTR was far more nominal, the global community's participation in delivering transitional justice was relevant and significant in complementing the localised justice delivered by the *gacaca* courts.

The ICTR largely met transitional justice goals as outlined by the UNSC. Furthermore, the ICTR has gone someway in addressing its broader goal of preventing similar events from occurring in the future – by sending a clear message that the continent will no longer tolerate the continuation of impunity. It has also set precedents relative to political accountability, and established that the international community has a moral obligation to single nation-states.

---

84 NURC, *Rwandan Reconciliation Barometer*, 2010, p. 66.
85 Clark 2010, pp. 238–239, 242–243, 249–252, 300.
86 Clark 2010, p. 205; Clark 2007, p. 798.
87 Clark 2010, pp. 194–195, 207–208.

However, it is difficult to gauge the ICTR's contribution to peace processes, particularly in the Great Lakes region of Africa.

The ICTR, as well as the ICTY, has given the prosecution of human rights violations a higher profile within the international community.[88] Grave crimes committed domestically are no longer considered to be solely of national concern – the international community can now get involved and have the jurisdiction to punish the perpetrators.[89] They have also updated the laws – with rape, *inter alia*, now being considered part of what is defined as genocide.

Additionally, recent developments in the Rwandan legal system, like the abolition of the death penalty and improvement of detention conditions, have been widely attributed to the influence of the ICTR. By facilitating the reconstruction of the domestic justice system, it can be argued that the ICTR has created a legacy that will continue after its closure.

The Rwandan government, unlike the UNSC, emphasises individual healing and forgiveness as key components of transitional justice, though the criteria for assessing these dimensions are complex. The NURC cites that individual healing has occurred in a significant percentage of the population as a direct result of *gacaca*, but the role of forgiveness is linked to the remorsefulness of the perpetrators.[90]

The perception by some sections, that the ICTR is a victor's court by proxy,[91] has, to a degree, hampered attempts at local ownership of the mechanism – yet there seems to have been a significant shift in the perception of the Rwandan population, with 59% considering the ICTR effective as a transitional justice mechanism (as reflected in Figure 1 above).[92] Conversely, the *gacaca* system has been regarded as a one-sided truth process in some quarters. It is arguable that these variances in opinion could open the door to revisionism on both sides – particularly in light of the fact that there is no nationally accepted version of Rwanda's history. Indeed, there have been contentious versions of the events in Rwanda,[93] differing depending on the group, whether or not they are in power at any particular stage.[94]

The ICTR's approach as regards the handover of files relating to RPF crimes for prosecution in Rwanda,[95] contrasts with the ICTY and the Special Court for Sierra Leone, which have prosecuted perpetrators from all sides of their

88 Glasius 2008, p. 49.
89 Rosenberg and Meredith 2010.
90 NURC, *Rwandan Reconciliation Barometer*, 2010, pp. 62–63.
91 See for example, Haskell and Waldorf 2011, pp. 51, 75–76; Peskin 2008, pp. 207–231.
92 NURC, *Rwandan Reconciliation Barometer*, 2010, p. 70.
93 See for example, Umutesi 2006, p. 157.
94 Prunier 1997, p. 80. As Temple-Raston observed, '[h]istory in Rwanda has always been malleable, growing out of story lines of one's own choosing. If one was Hutu, then the heroes were Hutu. If one was Tutsi, the opposite is true. In that story-telling, that exaggeration and embellishment came the seeds of conflict.' See Temple-Raston 2008, p. 17.
95 See *infra*, section 4.3.1.

respective conflicts and successfully targeted high-ranking government officials. Despite conjecture that this would subvert and destabilise these fragile post-conflict nations,[96] this did not transpire.

Some commentators have argued that the international community has not been as supportive or insistent on neutral prosecutions at the ICTR and the *gacaca* courts, and have advanced two reasons for this. First, many foreign governments still feel guilt at failing to stop the genocide and, in an effort to recompense for past wrongs, they provide financial aid to Rwanda with limited human rights conditionality.[97] Yet the Rwandan government can seemingly be moved by international pressure, as evidenced by the recent withholding of foreign aid[98] and the domestic judicial reforms made.

Second, some donor governments fear that seeking responsibility for RPF crimes might undermine the relative stability in Rwanda and the Great Lakes region – but this reasoning fails to take into account that the RPF's crimes may have contributed to violence in the DRC.[99]

Nevertheless, while the various inefficiencies of both the ICTR and *gacaca* have been well documented, this does not preclude their respective achievements of transitional justice outcomes, nor does one mechanism fortify the weaknesses of the other. Both systems have different goals with respect to transitional justice – with the ICTR symbolically delivering justice to key perpetrators and engaging the participation of the international community; and the *gacaca* system addressing the collective/individual level and engaging the participation of the local community. Both systems symbolise unprecedented legal experiments and the divergent criticisms exposing their limitations could be addressed in future incarnations of similar legal pluralist systems.

3. OVERVIEW OF THE ICC'S PROSECUTORIAL MANDATE

The ICC shares many goals with the ICTR (and ICTY), such as seeking justice by holding key perpetrators of international crimes accountable in accordance with internationally accepted standards of due process; deterring atrocities with the prospect of punishment for violations; and to a degree, building a truthful record of the crimes committed, as adjudicated. The ICC also has some major

96 For example, Haskell and Waldorf 2011, pp. 75–78; Moghalu 2005, p. 205.

97 Hayman, 'Milking The Cow: Negotiating Ownership of Aid and See Policy in Rwanda', June 2007, Global Economic Governance Working Paper 2007/26, 2, 9, 19; Zacklin 2004, p. 542.

98 'UK and the Netherlands withhold Rwanda budget aid', *BBC News*, 27 July 2012, available at: www.bbc.com/news/world-africa-19010495 (accessed 17 December 2014); 'UK stops £21m aid payment to Rwanda', *BBC News*, 30 November 2012, available at: www.bbc.com/news/uk-politics-20553872 (accessed 17 December 2014).

99 Haskell and Waldorf 2011, p. 75.

advantages over the ad hoc tribunals – its permanence, and broader temporal and geographic jurisdiction afford it a potentially bigger deterrent impact, and the ability to build on and develop jurisprudence that could serve as guiding principles for the future.

Yet, as specified earlier, the ICC has a stated objective that is fundamentally different from the ad hoc tribunals – in that it was created to prod and support responsible domestic investigations and prosecutions, with the prospect of international action only if states are unable or unwilling to authentically investigate or prosecute.

The ICC's success in encouraging responsible domestic investigations and prosecutions of international crimes will critically depend on its own credibility and legitimacy. If the ICC and its Prosecutor are viewed to act in highly politicised ways, 'their ability to catalyse domestic prosecutions and the legitimacy of its own prosecutions will be jeopardized.'[100] The ICC is far more likely to enjoy legitimacy and credibility if it proceeds in an impartial and non-political manner, against all countries, and not just certain targeted states in Africa.[101]

The ICC's success also depends on the sensitivity of the international community to national objectives and hindrances, as well as local factors like the capacity and will of states.[102] As such, the ICC has to steer delicately between sovereignty concerns and the pursuit of international accountability goals – and this is crucial to its effectiveness in providing constructive (not counterproductive) prompts to domestic accountability processes.[103]

3.1. THE ICC PROSECUTOR'S DISCRETION

The ICC Prosecutor is elected by the Assembly of States Parties[104] and his/her responsibilities entail, *inter alia*, determining cases for investigation and prosecution – choosing which situations and defendants to prosecute. The ICC Prosecutor can also exercise the discretion, granted by the Rome Statute, to permit countries to implement their own transitional justice mechanisms. The Office of the Prosecutor (OTP), which is to be an impartial and independent body,[105] can receive referrals and information about situations in which a crime under the jurisdiction of the ICC may have been committed.[106]

Matters can be brought to the attention of the OTP in one of three ways: (i) a state party can make a request to the Prosecutor to conduct an investigation into

100 Stromseth 2003, p. 27.
101 See *infra*, section 3.3.
102 Stromseth 2003, p. 28.
103 *Ibid.*
104 Rome Statute, Art. 42(4).
105 Rome Statute, Art. 42.
106 Rome Statute, Art. 42(4).

a matter – in its own or another country;[107] (ii) a situation may be referred to the Prosecutor by the UNSC, acting under its Chapter VII powers, if it resolves that a particular conflict is a threat to peace and security; and (iii) the Prosecutor can utilise her *propio motu* powers as conferred by Article 15 of the Rome Statute.[108]

According to Goldston, prosecutorial discretion, whether national or international, and at any level, involves making decisions on *inter alia*, the evidence, whether to prosecute, drop a case, which charges to bring, and whom to charge. Practical considerations like resources and time are, logically, a factor when these are made.[109]

Crucially, in the exercise of this discretion, prosecutors effectively decide where society's interest in justice lies. In the context of the ICC, this assignment is particularly challenging since the Prosecutor is essentially 'employed' by the Assembly of States Parties – 123 countries, all with variable notions of discretion and justice.[110]

The Rome Statute allows the OTP to decide on whether there is sufficient evidence to believe that any crimes under the Court's jurisdiction have been committed, and whether these crimes meet the 'seriousness' threshold and 'are of sufficient gravity to warrant the attention of the ICC'[111] – focusing on 'those bearing the greatest degree of responsibility.'[112]

According to Article 17 of the Rome Statute, cases are not permitted if they are already subject to an investigation or prosecution by the state in question.[113] This principle of complementarity, where nations can maintain their sovereignty whilst handling matters internally, offers countries the first chance to investigate and prosecute individuals suspected of committing crimes within the jurisdiction of the ICC before any intervention by the Prosecutor. Therefore, a state ought to be able to fashion its own transitional justice programme, thereby forestalling any ICC involvement – at least in theory.

Yet, in light of the ICC's prosecutorial mandate, the state would have to construct its transitional justice programme in a way that would convince the OTP that justice was being served. Such a programme would likely require investigative, retributive, and reparative components, at a bare minimum. The

107 Rome Statute, Art. 14(1).

108 Although this discretion is somewhat restricted. The OTP can commence a preliminary investigation of its own accord (Rome Statute, Art. 15(1)) – however it must obtain approval from the Pre-Trial Chamber in order to launch a full investigation (Rome Statute, Art. 15(3)). It must also inform the Chamber if after an investigation into a situation, it deems that the case is contrary to the 'interests of justice' (Rome Statute, Art. 53(1)).

109 Goldston 2010, p. 389. See also King 2012.

110 See generally Goldston 2010 and King 2012.

111 SáCouto and Cleary 2008.

112 International Criminal Court, *Policy Paper on the Interests of Justice*, September 2007, available at: www.icc-cpi.int/nr/rdonlyres/772c95c9-f54d-4321-bf09–73422bb23528/143640/iccotpinterestsofjustice.pdf (accessed 9 February 2014).

113 Rome Statute, Art. 17(1)(a).

notion that an investigation/prosecution may not serve the interests of justice, as well as the principle of complementarity, are two provisos the Prosecutor can choose to rely on if she refuses to prosecute a situation because the state is conducting its own domestic transitional justice processes.

3.2. POSSIBILITY FOR OTHER FORMS OF TRANSITIONAL JUSTICE

The subject of alternate forms of transitional justice was discussed at the Rome Conference of Plenipotentiaries in 1998.[114] However, what emerged was an accord that was mute on the use or proscription of alternative methods of accountability – with 'the drafters turn[ing] to the faithful and familiar friend of diplomats, ambiguity, leaving a few small avenues open to the Court and allowing the Court to develop an appropriate approach when faced with concrete situations.'[115]

The Rome Statute left openings in two provisions, namely Article 17 (whilst codifying the term 'complementarity', states that a case will only be admissible before the ICC in four scenarios[116]) and Article 53 (which defines the Prosecutor's duties and allows her to refuse to investigate or prosecute a case if doing otherwise would not serve the interests of justice[117]). The Rome Statute enunciates that the ICC is steered by the principle of complementarity – connoting that it will not get involved in a situation unless the nation in question is either unwilling or unable to do so itself.[118] Essentially, both of these

114 UN, Final Act of the United Nations Diplomatic Conference of Plenipotentiaries on the Establishment of an International Criminal Court, done at Rome on 17 July 1998, UN Doc. A/CONF.183/10, 17 July 1998; see also King 2012, pp. 16–17.

115 Robinson 2003, p. 483.

116 These are: (i) if a state with the relevant jurisdiction is already investigating or prosecuting a case; (ii) if a state with the relevant jurisdiction over the case investigated it but has decided not to prosecute the individual(s) the ICC seeks to prosecute; (iii) if the individual(s) in question have already been tried for the same crime(s); or (iv) if the OTP decides that the case is not sufficiently severe to warrant prosecution. Note, however, that with the situations noted at (i) and (ii), the ICC can still intervene if the nation shows an inability or unwillingness to conduct authentic investigations or prosecutions (Rome Statute, Art. 17(1)).

117 Rome Statute, Art. 53(1)(c) and (2)(c). The Statute does not define the phrase 'the interests of justice', which means that this term could be open for interpretation – with interpretation of the phrase being vital to the question as to whether the Prosecutor can accede to domestic transitional programmes that do not involve prosecution. A narrow interpretation of the idiom would mean, exclusively, criminal justice, hence prosecution would be the only preference. However, if it is broadly interpreted, there could be room for other retributive and restorative mechanisms to take centre-stage in the transitional process.

118 Rome Statute, Art. 17(1)(a). The Rome Statute elucidates that unwillingness includes considerations like: whether the domestic prosecution was a sham trial that was undertaken to protect the perpetrator(s) from responsibility; whether there has been an unreasonable and indefensible delay revealing, perhaps, a lack of will on the part of the state (e.g. Kenya); and whether the process is neutral and objective. Inability denotes the strength (or presence) of

provisions use language that enables the Prosecutor to stand back[119] and allow a country to embark on its transitional justice programmes.

3.3. UNIVERSAL JURISDICTION

The ICC does not exercise universal jurisdiction. In situations where the ICC cannot take certain cases, the principle of universal jurisdiction allows domestic proceedings to be instituted against perpetrators of international crimes, by any country, in its own courts, irrespective of where the crime was perpetrated. Legal arguments as regards the determination of universal jurisdiction and the required competence of individual jurisdictions to hear such cases are beyond the scope of this article.

As regards the Rwandan context, to date there have been prosecutions in connection with the 1994 Rwandan genocide in Belgium,[120] Canada,[121] Switzerland,[122] France,[123] and the Netherlands.[124] These prosecutions, whilst small in number, lessened the burden on the ICTR, Rwandan national courts,

---

the judiciary and whether the state has the necessary institutions to conduct prosecutions (Art. 17(2); see also Goldstone 2008.

119 In this scenario, the Prosecutor must notify the Pre-Trial Chamber of her decision (Rome Statute, Art. 53(1) and (2)(c)). Whilst the Pre-Trial Chamber is not required to give an opinion on the Prosecutor's decision, it may decide to so, in which case it must confirm the decision for it to be valid (Art. 53(3)(b)).

120 Higaniro, 'Higaniro Alphonse', Radio Netherlands Worldwide (International Justice Desk), 31 May 2001, available at: www.rnw.nl/international-justice/article/higaniro-alphonse (accessed 3 December 2014); Ntezimana, Mukangango and Mukabutera, Rwanda nuns in genocide trial', *BBC News*, 17 April 2001, available at: http://news.bbc.co.uk/2/hi/europe/1280947.stm (accessed 3 December 2014); Nzabonima, 'Etienne Nzabonima', TRIAL, available at: www.trial-ch.org/en/resources/trial-watch/trial-watch/profiles/profile/327/action/show/controller/Profile.html (accessed 3 December 2014); Ndashyikirwa, 'Samuel Ndashyikirwa', TRIAL, available at: www.trial-ch.org/en/resources/trial-watch/trial-watch/profiles/profile/328/action/show/controller/Profile.html (accessed 3 December 2014); Ntuyahaga, 'Rwanda major guilty of UN murders', *BBC News*, 4 July 2007, available at: http://news.bbc.co.uk/2/hi/africa/6270746.stm (accessed 3 December 2014); Nkezabera, 'Genocide banker jailed for 30 years', Radio Netherlands Worldwide (International Justice Desk), 1 December 2009, available at: www.rnw.nl/english/article/%E2%80%9Cgenocide-banker%E2%80%9D-jailed-30-years (accessed 3 December 2014).

121 Munyaneza, 'Desire Munyaneza', TRIAL, available at: www.trial-ch.org/en/resources/trial-watch/trial-watch/profiles/profile/423/action/show/controller/Profile.html (accessed 3 December 2014).

122 Niyonteze, 'Fulgence Niyonteze', TRIAL, available at: www.trial-ch.org/en/ressources/trial-watch/trial-watch/profils/profile/115/action/show/controller/Profile.html (accessed 3 December 2014).

123 Simbikangwa, 'Pascal Simbikangwa', TRIAL, available at: www.trial-ch.org/en/resources/trial-watch/trial-watch/profiles/profile/3552/action/show/controller/Profile.html (accessed 3 December 2014).

124 Mpambara, 'Joseph Mpambara', TRIAL, available at: www.trial-ch.org/en/resources/trial-watch/trial-watch/profiles/profile/757/action/show/controller/Profile.html (accessed 3 December 2014).

and *gacaca* courts – and thereby reduced the accountability gap. It also further symbolised international condemnation of the crimes perpetrated in Rwanda and was an example of international cooperation. Moreover, the ICTR's jurisprudence provided these domestic jurisdictions with a valuable tool for the exercise of universal jurisdiction.

Rwanda seemingly has mixed feelings towards the exercise of universal jurisdiction. On the one hand, it seeks to prosecute its nationals, who have been transferred to Rwanda by the ICTR or third-party states, for international crimes identical to the ICTR Statute.[125] Yet, conversely, it is also constrained by Rwanda's Constitution, which proscribes the extradition of Rwandan nationals.[126]

There has also been a general level of reluctance from African states to exercise this jurisdiction. To date, only a modest number of African countries have enacted domestic legislation implementing the Rome Statute's provisions.[127] Beyond reasons of legal capacity, it may be because of the concerns African states have about a perceived abuse of universal jurisdiction by European countries.[128]

Nevertheless, there are opportunities for national processes to be used by African countries to complement the ICC, or act as a substitute in adjudicating on crimes perpetrated by nationals of non-state parties in their territory. Additionally, this opportunity could be utilised in circumstances where there has not been any referral by the UNSC to the ICC, or even in circumstances where the ICC is unwilling or unable to investigate the crimes.

This extraterritorial judicial application has already begun in countries like South Africa,[129] Uganda,[130] and Senegal – and there is also mounting evidence

125 In accordance with Organic Law No. 11/2007 of 16 March 2007, commonly referred to as the 'Transfer Law.'

126 Constitution of Rwanda, Art. 25.

127 They are: Burkina Faso, CAR, Comoros, Kenya, Mauritius, Senegal, South Africa and Uganda. The DRC is a monist state, which means that international accords, in theory, have the same authority as constitutional law and can be directly applied as long as it is 'consistent with law and custom' (Arts. 153 and 215 of the DRC Constitution).

128 AU, Decision on Africa's Relationship with the International Criminal Court, Ext/Assembly/AU/Dec.1, October 2013, para. 3; AU, Decision on the Report of the Commission on the Abuse of the Principle of Universal Jurisdiction, Doc. Assembly/AU/14(XI), July 2008.

129 See generally, *National Commissioner of the South African Police Service v. Southern African Human Rights Litigation Centre and Another* [2014] CCT 02/14, available at: www.politicsweb.co.za/politicsweb/view/politicsweb/en/page71656?oid=771023&sn=Detail&pid=71616 (accessed 14 December 2014). The case is also known as the Zimbabwe Torture Docket case. Here the Constitutional Court of South Africa was asked to decide whether the South African Police Service (SAPS) is required to investigate allegations that high-ranking government and security officials in Zimbabwe committed acts of torture against other Zimbabweans (as per its Constitution, the Implementation of the Rome Statute of the International Criminal Court Act, and South Africa's international law obligations). The Court unanimously concluded that the SAPS had an obligation to investigate the complaints of crimes against humanity of torture allegedly committed in Zimbabwe, under the aforementioned laws.

130 Constitutional Court of Uganda, *Thomas Kwoyelo v. Uganda* [2011] UGCC 10, 21 September 2011.

that many non-party African states are practising international criminal justice at the domestic level.[131] Moreover, South Africa, Rwanda, and Uganda, have specialised international crimes divisions.

4. LESSONS FOR THE ICC

4.1. LESSONS FROM THE ICTR

The first, and probably crucial, lesson to be learned from the ICTR is that international transitional justice strategies can have options for encouraging local ownership and assisting reconciliation processes. In post-conflict environments, domestic processes are at the front line in addressing human rights violations, which are critical in preventing a recurrence of atrocities. Rwanda's initial experience with concurrent jurisdiction between the ICTR and national prosecutions demonstrate some of the tensions that can surface when a state is willing to prosecute but has limited capacity to do so. The Rwandan populace had felt physically and psychologically isolated from the ICTR, and had perceived the proceedings as competitive with Rwanda's own efforts, rather than complementary – thereby diminishing the educational and deterrent effects the ICTR hoped to have within Rwanda.[132]

Whilst the ICC does not have the same primacy over domestic proceedings that the ICTR has, there is still a possibility that similar tensions may arise. As such, international tribunals have a major role to play in the reconstruction of domestic institutions and legal systems; and it is imperative they forge a good relationship with national governments.

Outreach programmes potentially engender public awareness of the tribunal's work (from its proceedings, judgments, and parties). It stimulates discourse among the local populace about *inter alia*, truth, peace, justice, and reconciliation.

Capacity building is an important tool that makes a difference on the ground. Strengthening national legal institutions and capacities is essential to attaining any meaningful accountability for past atrocities and preventing future abuses. Its activities can enable a variety of important and valuable skills to be put into practice. It can be a one-off training workshop, or a long-term, iterative process – both of which are important routes to develop and strengthen key skills.

A more holistic approach to capacity building and outreach activities can be adopted at the outset and involve a range of agencies and professionals, including lawyers (prosecution and defence), judges, police, health professionals,

131 Du Plessis, Louw and Maunganidze, 'African efforts to close the impunity gap: Lessons for complementarity from national and regional actions', November 2012, ISS Paper 241, pp. 1–2.

132 Stromseth 2003, p. 29.

counsellors, academics, victim and witness advocates, and civil society groups – instead of having a compartmentalised approach. This way, beneficial synergies can be searched for and found in order to strengthen domestic capacity.

Capacity building and outreach activities can also target the population in general. It would serve to inform them on, *inter alia*, the ICC's work, the importance of the rule of law, due process at trial, the existence of international humanitarian law/ international criminal law, and the need for domestic capacity to deal with such crimes. A useful approach would be to involve both lawyers from the prosecution and defence – thereby explaining the differing perspectives in a case, the rights of an accused to a fair trial, and to be provided with detention facilities that meet internationally required standards. This can have the added effect of improving the domestic process whereby people are aware of the law and trial process (from both prosecution and defence standpoints).

It is also important for an international tribunal to engage candidly with the public, about the challenges and limitations in, *inter alia*, the trial process, convictions, sentences, and acquittals. This is particularly vital for witnesses who testified in cases and may not understand why their evidence was not believed – for example, it could be explained that an accused may be factually guilty but legally not guilty because of procedural irregularities.

Regrettably, at present, extensions to international tribunals' mandates to include outreach and capacity-building activities (which warrant an increase in budget) are usually not provided. This was also the case for the ICTR; as such, capacity-building initiatives rely solely on voluntary contributions by member states and creative thinking on the part of the ICTR to maximise such activities within the existing budget constraints.

Indeed, many of the ICTR's outreach initiatives would not have been possible without the assistance of the Rwandan government and the financial aid of sponsors, which include the European Union and the 'Friends of the ICTR.'[133] It is recommended that special budgets be set aside for such initiatives, as they form an important component of the tribunal's work. Furthermore, in a given context, the ICC should concurrently pursue capacity building alongside its prosecutorial mandate.

The second lesson is that transitional justice initiatives that aim to promote and nurture local ownership must have the appropriate backing, strategies, timing, and resources in order to attain any level of success.

The third lesson that can be taken from the ICTR experience is that local ownership becomes effectively unattainable if the tribunal does not have a good working relationship with the national government – especially as on a practical

133 Dieng 2011, p. 411. 'Friends of the ICTR' is an informal group of countries that provides support to the Tribunal and is represented by diplomats posted in Dar es Salaam, Kigali, and Nairobi. Membership has included: Belgium, Canada, France, Germany, Italy, the United States of America, and the Netherlands.

level, the tribunals rely heavily on countries to impart resources, witnesses, and criminals. The ICTR's outreach programme was, albeit intermittently, hindered to an extent by a problematic political relationship with the Rwandan government. It is therefore crucial to form partnerships with states – critical capacity building/outreach initiatives are a way of achieving this.

The fourth lesson is that international courts can play a crucial role in domestic prosecution of international crimes. The MICT, which is a residual mechanism that was established to conclude the ICTR's remaining tasks, has the function of monitoring the referred cases to Rwanda. It has provided regular reports of the proceedings. This process reinforces national courts by making them resistant to executive influence and setting their legal standards high.

It is also important for the international community to acknowledge and accept that even with the best intentions, international tribunals can never please everybody. If a tribunal is perceived as a victor's court it is arguable that attempts at locally possessing the transitional justice process may not succeed – although the Rwandan experience seems to demonstrate otherwise. Moreover, it is also arguable that there may always be a degree of victor's justice at play in international courts.

4.2. LESSONS FROM THE GACACA COURTS

The first lesson to be garnered from the *gacaca* courts is that they epitomise the very definition of local ownership of a transitional justice process. These courts were re-formulated by national leaders and it was implemented and administered by respected community leaders and authorities. Moreover, local participation was vital to the mechanism's ability to deliver transitional justice to the population. Local participation also helped reduce the risk of a repeat of the violence that had plagued the country for decades. In spite of some key concerns about the *gacaca* courts, the international community was generally supportive of the process, and provided funding, praise, and irregular legal and human rights succour.

The second lesson the ICC should take into account is cultural adaptation and its relevance. This was the *gacaca* system's key advantage over the ICTR. The ICTR's experience showed that it took the tribunal some time to understand and appreciate Rwanda's historical background; social, legal, and political contexts; cultural norms, practices, and hence the subtleties in its traditions. This process can take time for any external organisation and is a pertinent lesson for the ICC, as it prosecutes crimes from multiple states. Factoring this aspect in preparations can aid the prosecution of crimes as the investigators would be in a better position to elicit quality evidence. The ICC may consider opening additional branches in the countries in which it seeks to conduct its investigations – security permitting.[134]

The third and final lesson is that even if a state is willing to prosecute international crimes, the ICC will face difficult questions when appraising the sufficiency of the proceedings. Mechanisms operating like the *gacaca* courts can potentially endanger and destabilise a peace process – more so than an externally imposed system like the ICTR. Whilst the threats never materialised in the Rwandan example, the temporal insecurities emanating from the *gacaca* courts nonetheless unearth enduring fears of ethnic and economic enmity, as well as government dictatorial influence – which were instrumental to the genocide's origin.[135] Hence, whilst grassroots transitional justice mechanisms like *gacaca* may appeal – it is necessary to evaluate the legitimacy of these processes and their influencing factors.

This lesson raises what Stromseth terms as the 'prodding dilemma.'[136] The quandary is this: 'if the ICC sets the bar too low in assessing whether States are able or willing genuinely to investigate or prosecute, States with insufficient will to prosecute may come to the conclusion that minimal domestic efforts are sufficient, and the ICC's leverage in the next conflict may be reduced. On the other hand, if the ICC sets the bar too high, it may take cases away from domestic institutions that are trying, though imperfectly, to seek accountability, particularly if the problem is not the lack of will but lack of capacity.'[137] In such cases, the international community must consider supplementing domestic efforts.[138]

4.3. LESSONS FROM THE LEGAL PLURALIST STRUCTURE OF ICTR AND GACACA

4.3.1. *The Importance of Having a Customised Approach to Accountability*

After considering the widely-held perception that the ICTR is a conduit of 'victor's justice', it is critical to reflect upon the reasons behind the ICTR's standpoint, and whether the ICC, when faced with a similar situation, should take an analogous position. So, for example, if there was a similar post-genocide environment like Rwanda, and if the emergent government formulated a transitional justice programme similar to *gacaca* courts – could (and should)

134 The ICC currently has field offices in Kampala (Uganda), Kinshasa and Bunia (DRC), Abéché (Chad), and Bangui (CAR).
135 Magnarella 2005, pp. 817–821; Jean 2007, pp. 6–7.
136 Stromseth 2003, p. 30.
137 *Ibid.*
138 *Ibid.*

the ICC accede to this national recommendation, despite the fact that there are issues of victor's justice?

The answer, whilst complex, can be summarised in two points. First, while prosecution can serve a wide variety of purposes, especially following mass atrocities – it may not always be a sensible choice for a country. Second, demanding prosecution in every possible situation, whether by the ICTR, ICC, or domestically, whilst top-down, is also a very limited approach in that it overlooks the intricacies and difficulties of each conflict, thereby preventing the consideration of novel or underutilised alternative mechanisms of justice.[139]

An international tribunal is unfortunately in an unenviable position as it will often be criticised in its choices of whom to prosecute. A case in point is when the ICC-OTP announced the issuance of arrest warrants for five members of the LRA – whilst declining to indict any members of the government forces, in July 2005. It came under fierce criticism. Luis Moreno-Ocampo, the then Prosecutor responded to the censures, arguing that:

> Some people say that the only way to retain our impartiality is to prosecute both the LRA and the UPDF [the government forces]. However, I think that impartiality means that we apply the same criteria equally to all sides. A major criterion is gravity. There is no comparison of gravity between the crimes committed by the Ugandan army and by the LRA – the crimes committed by the LRA are much more grave than those committed by the Ugandan army.[140]

A similar response, by extension, applies to the Rwandan example. The number of deaths, and the viciousness in the way they were perpetrated by RPF soldiers, paled in comparison to the genocidal killings; and certain incidents may have been a military response to the recurring incursions from ex-FAR soldiers and ex-*Interahamwe*.[141] It is also arguable that the crimes committed by the RPF soldiers related more to war crimes, and were isolated incidents perpetrated by relatively junior and possibly 'roguish' elements of the RPF army – but then again there is the question of command responsibility. In truth, the full extent of the alleged crimes committed by the RPF may never been known – possibly for political reasons.[142]

---

139 Ludwin King, 'Does Justice Always Require Prosecution? The International Criminal Court and Transitional Justice Measures', August 2012.

140 Moreno-Ocampo 2006.

141 There were several incursions in the prefectures of Ruhengeri, Gisenyi, Gitarama, Kibuye, and Kigali – targeting the genocide survivors. These incursions stopped after the dismantling of refugee camps (see for example, Nsanzuwera 2005, p. 948.

142 But see 'Rwanda's Untold Story', *BBC News*, 3 October 2014, available at: www.bbc.co.uk/programmes/b04kk03t (accessed 3 October 2014). The ICTR's former Chief Prosecutor Carla del Ponte alleges that she was prevented from pursuing prosecution of members of the RPF. She said that the former UN Secretary General, Kofi Annan, had told her that the UNSC had made a political decision – with the US and the UK not endorsing her prosecutorial mandate.

This is not to understate the importance of prosecutions in post-conflict environments for all crimes and human rights abuses – it simply may not be suitable (or at times, possible) in all post-conflict settings. As referred to above, the ICTR Prosecutor investigated serious abuses of international humanitarian law on all sides of the conflict and deferred prosecution of crimes by the RPF soldiers to the military courts in Rwanda. As regards the latter, this approach is plausible given the fact that a military court is typically an appropriate forum in which to hear cases involving members of the armed forces, and it facilitated local ownership. Moreover, the perpetrators were relatively low-ranking soldiers, and proceeding with their cases would have been contrary to UN Resolution 1534 (2004).[143] Yet there is an inherent weakness in the use of military courts given that it would be the very epitome of victor's justice – in that the defeater is prosecuting the defeated.

It must also be borne in mind that post-conflict governments can influence or hinder the operations of transitional justice mechanisms. Nonetheless, the ICC should accede to the resolutions of states that permit authentic transitional schemas which include investigative, retributive, and reparative components. This would motivate states to take ownership of their own processes of accountability and transitional justice, customising these processes to the uniqueness of their environment: 'Deferral in appropriate situations will ... encourage countries to use autochthonous forms of justice and peace that could lead to greater confidence in the government and greater local buy-in of the other measures.'[144]

4.3.2. *Benefits and Limitations of Prosecution*

There are several benefits to prosecuting individuals suspected of human rights violations. It can help a nation that was divided by conflict by individualising guilt, thereby preventing accusations of collective guilt, i.e. that a whole ethnic group was responsible for the conflict.[145] It identifies the perpetrators as criminals, which demystifies any air of impunity and invincibility they may have had,[146] and confronts the 'mimetic structures of violence' that are entrenched in the minds of individuals who subsist in an environment of deep-seated chronic conflict.[147]

A major contribution of the ICTR to transitional justice (and reconciliation) in Rwanda is that of holding the principal perpetrators of the genocide

143 UNSC Res. 1534 (26 March 2004).

144 Ludwin King, 'Does Justice Always Require Prosecution? The International Criminal Court and Transitional Justice Measures', August 2012, p. 7.

145 Robinson 2003, p. 489.

146 Phillips and Albon 1999, p. 7.

147 Gallimore 2002, pp. 146–147.

accountable. By arresting and taking away these politically influential figures from public life and stigmatising them, the ICTR divested the perpetrators of their major leaders – thereby abating their military and political destabilisation of peace in Rwanda.[148] This also ruptured the mimetic cycle of violence and revenge that characterised the history of impunity in Rwanda.

Prosecutions are also vital for the families of victims. For many, the experience of seeing a perpetrator freed on the basis of receiving amnesty is incongruent with the notion of reconciliation.[149] Instead, they favour conventional trials and strict punishment for the violators of human rights, so they can see justice at work. In truth, people care little for 'symbolic', highly publicised justice – they simply want to see justice being meaningfully dispensed on a broad collective, intermediate, and individual level.

In a post-conflict environment, where a new administration gains power, it can drastically change the balance of power perceptions. Prosecutions can 'break the cycle' of the past and indicate a clean break with the previous regime – thereby heralding to the nation and the international community that this new government upholds the rule of law and respects human rights.[150] However, for the trials to be perceived as fair – perpetrators from all sides of the conflict must be brought to court.

Trials also aid a nation that was stricken with mass violence by acting as a deterrent, cautioning others that they will not profit from impunity if they engage in the same, or similar, conduct[151] – this is particularly critical for societies like Rwanda that have long tolerated impunity towards serious and systematic human rights abuses. Yet the deterrent effect of international trials is questionable. Since the establishment of a permanent international court, ad hoc tribunals, and even hybrid courts – there have been many conflicts around the world where mass human rights abuses have been committed and continue to be perpetrated.

However, there are seemingly some positive indications of the deterrent effect of international prosecution. Recently, Blaise Compaoré, the former President of Burkina Faso, stepped down from his presidency on 31 October 2014. This happened after attempting to extend his 27-year term sparked a series of mass demonstrations and riots in which government buildings, including the city hall, and his ruling Congress for Democracy and Progress party's headquarters were torched. He opted to resign and flee the country instead of aggressively cracking down on the protestors. It is likely that one of the reasons for his resignation was because he did not want the same fate that befell Laurent Gbagbo, the former President of Côte d'Ivoire. Hence, the upshot is that lives were saved.

---

148 Nsanzuwera 2005, p. 948.
149 Berinyuu 2004.
150 Ludwin King 2003, pp. 273, 275.
151 Scharf 1999, pp. 507, 512.

Nevertheless, more research needs to be carried out on the long term impacts of international courts on the ground level. However, in reality, the precise deterrent effects of international courts may take a long time to determine or may never be known. It is more difficult to empirically measure the absence of an action rather than its occurrence – how can one assess which is more aggressive: a dog that barks or one that does not?

Furthermore, even if a quantifiable decrease in human rights violations could be determined, it would be virtually impossible to determine the exact contribution of deterrence compared to other variables such as shifts in international norms, differing cultural settings, or changing domestic and international, political and economic, pressures.[152]

Contrary to the hopes of many, the deterrent effect of current international courts is likely to be minimal. As mentioned above, significantly strengthened domestic courts may be able to increase deterrence. Yet this does not indicate that international tribunals serve no purpose.

They are important in providing retributive justice or lessening abuses by incapacitating the most serious and key perpetrators – although, there should be harmonised sentencing guidelines for the ICC, or any other future international courts, which is based on reasonable and attainable goals.[153] Equally, for justice and practical reasons, international tribunals should drop explicit references to deterrence as a stated objective – even though it is an inherent goal of prosecutions. If an international tribunal is unable to meet certain goals, there is likely to be some criticism directed at the institution at a certain stage, thereby engulfing any evidence of what the institution has in fact attained in other areas.[154]

It is important to note that not all cost issues are insurmountable, particularly if a legal pluralist system is in operation. Effective cost management may simply be a case of re-allocating cases – with the most senior leaders suspected of being most responsible for crimes within the jurisdiction being prosecuted at the international level, and the lower ranking, intermediate individuals being prosecuted in the national courts or community courts (whichever is applicable). Furthermore, members of the armed forces can be prosecuted in the military courts. The key here is to categorise offenders (as was the case with Rwanda's Organic Law No. 08/1996[155]) so that depending on the level of offences and/or level of stature of the perpetrator there is a corresponding court.

Yet there are real issues about norms and standards – a delicate balance needs to be struck. It is important to acknowledge that requiring national justice to be

152 Bagaric and Morss 2006, p. 191.

153 Dietrich, 'Can International Courts Deter Human Rights Abusers?', 2 March 2007, as presented at the ISA Annual Convention, Chicago, Illinois.

154 *Ibid.*

155 Nwoye 2014, p. 174, nn. 405–406.

in accord with high international standards can cause problems. However, it is also equally vital for certain fundamental principles like justice and fairness to be upheld. Yet most countries do not have the resources to operate like the ICC or ICTR. This drawback must be addressed with additional funding for domestic capacity building.

Another strength of a legal pluralist system is the possibility of international assistance. By arresting these figures outside Rwanda, the ICTR extended the hand of justice beyond where the Rwandan justice system could reach – particularly as, at the time, Rwanda did not have extradition treaties with countries harbouring suspects. But then again, countries may simply refuse to hand suspects over because of, among other things, fair trial concerns, as was the case for Rwanda.[156]

Through its capacity building partnership with the ICTR (OTP and Registry Divisions), as well as making reforms in its domestic legal system, Rwanda was able to convince the ICTR Chamber and other states to extradite or transfer genocide suspects to Rwanda for trial. The ICC should consider a similar partnership with states that have persons who are subject to investigations and/or prosecutions.

Naturally, there are also limitations to prosecutions. Practical factors like resources and time frequently require consideration. This is especially so where

156 'Rwanda accused win UK court case', *BBC News*, 8 April 2009, available at: http://news.bbc.co.uk/2/hi/uk_news/7989534.stm (accessed 15 December 2014). Yet this decision has been challenged in light of the Uwinkindi ruling as noted above (n. 29), and the four suspects are now back in court undergoing a second legal battle against extradition from the UK. See Shirbon, 'Rwandan genocide suspects face UK extradition battle', Reuters, 5 June 2013, available at: www.reuters.com/article/2013/06/05/us-britain-rwanda-genocide-idUSBRE95417C20130605 (accessed 15 December 2014). Following the Uwinkindi ruling, the European Court of Human Rights decided that the right to a fair trial and humane treatment were adequately guaranteed as regards extradition to Rwanda. See *Ahorugeze v. Sweden*, App. no. 37075/09, ECtHR, 27 October 2011, available at: http://hudoc.echr.coe.int/sites/eng/pages/search.aspx?i=001–107183 (accessed 15 December 2014), paras. 39–40 and 127. Moreover, a number of other countries have since allowed extradition – the Netherlands. See 'Genocide suspect arrested in The Netherlands, to be extradited', *News of Rwanda*, 23 January 2014, available at: www.newsofrwanda.com/imitwe-ya-politiki/22023/genocide-suspect-arrested-in-the-netherlands-to-be-extradited/ (accessed 15 December 2014); 'Canada deports Rwanda genocide suspect Leon Mugesera', *BBC News (Canada)*, 24 January 2012, available at: www.bbc.com/news/world-us-canada-16694130 (accessed 30 March 2014); 'Rwanda: Danish Court Upholds Extradition of Rwandan Genocide Suspect', *Denmark (Hirondelle News Agency)*, 20 November 2012, available at: www.hirondellenews.com/ictr-rwanda/410-rwanda-other-countries/33903–201112-rwandadenmark-danish-court-upholds-extradition-of-rwandan-genocide-suspect (accessed 15 December 2014); 'Rwanda/Justice – Genocide Suspect Extradited from Norway to Stay in Custody', *Norway (Hirondelle News Agency*, 16 May 2013, available at: www.hirondellenews.com/ictr-rwanda/410-rwanda-other-countries/34196–160513-rwandajustice-genocide-suspect-extradited-from-norway-to-stay-in-custody, (accessed 15 December 2014). However, France has recently denied extradition, but not on fair trial concerns, 'French court rejects extradition of Rwanda', *SBS*, 27 February 2014, available at: www.sbs.com.au/news/article/2014/02/27/french-court-rejects-extradition-rwanda (accessed 15 December 2014).

the violence was committed by several hundred or even several thousand perpetrators (like in Rwanda). The prosecutions can exclude onlookers and countries outside the area that were also responsible for violence, thereby contributing to the above-mentioned 'illusion' of individualised guilt and collective innocence.[157] In such circumstances, prosecutions can be a 'slow, blunt instrument ... ill-suited for untangling the complex web of responsibility.'[158] Additionally, the character of prosecutions can produce a piecemeal historical record – in that each case relates to a particular set of events and deeds that cannot be said to comprehensively capture what happened during a conflict.[159] In this regard, it is arguable that they are less effective than truth commissions.

Moreover, in a situation where there is ongoing conflict, indictments can 'eliminate the full range of negotiated options for dealing with tyrants', thereby hindering, halting, and completely disrupting any previous peace process talks.[160] For example, as was the case for the ICC – the decision to issue the indictment for Muammar Gaddafi while the conflict in Libya was ongoing derailed peace-process talks.[161] The incentives for him to negotiate, step down, and seek exile disappeared once the indictment and a warrant for his arrest were issued,[162] because he knew that prosecution was likely to follow.

Because of their adversarial nature and cross-examination component, prosecutions tend to create conditions that deter people from coming forward and engaging in the process – particularly as this unfriendly environment may cause them to feel that they are being 'victimised' all over again.[163] Furthermore, they lack the negotiating power of amnesty that often proves crucial in bringing the perpetrators to the table.[164] Hence, many international prosecutions become very long, protracted processes as the prosecutors struggle to arrest those indicted and gather evidence.[165] This lethargic character of international prosecutions can negatively impact the process of transitional justice.

Yet, in the current global affairs climate, it would be difficult to fathom a situation where there are no prosecutions for mass human rights violations in many societies around the world, irrespective of the costs. Moreover, international justice, whilst an important undertaking, is by default, an expensive endeavour that necessitates more time and resources. Further,

---

157 Fletcher and Weinstein 2002, p. 580.

158 Mnookin 2012, p. 171.

159 Alvarez 1998, pp. 2031, 2100. Alvarez contends that truth commissions are apposite for the creation of comprehensive historical records.

160 Mnookin 2012, p. 170.

161 *Ibid.*

162 See ICC, *Situation in the Libyan Arab Jamahiriya*, Decision on the 'Prosecutor's Application Pursuant to Article 58 as to Muammar Mohammed Abu Minya Gaddafi, Saif Al-Islam Gaddafi and Abdulla Al-Senussi', ICC-01/11, 27 June 2011.

163 DeLaet 2006, pp. 55–76.

164 Sarkin 1999, p. 767.

165 Berinyuu 2004.

international pressure, including the possibility of international investigation or prosecution, has at times, prodded and underpinned what would have otherwise been half-hearted, inauthentic national efforts.

4.3.3. No 'One-Size-Fits-All' Transitional Justice System

The ICC's transitional justice approach is seemingly focused on prosecution with a 'one-size-fits-all' approach to accountability – notwithstanding that '[n]o mechanism will ever deliver perfect justice.'[166]

Admittedly, the Rome Statute does not envisage that international trials will work in isolation from, for example, grassroots justice and reconciliation efforts at the national level – however, the shortcomings of the prosecutorial approach (as mentioned above), may not make them an ideal alternative. Much depends on the country's transitional schema. If the truth of what transpired (including the origins of the conflict) is what the government and its populace seek – then perhaps a comprehensive and impartial investigation that includes the names of the perpetrators responsible for atrocities is required. It is crucial that a country is allowed to address what happened during the conflict in a manner that is best suited to its distinct post-conflict environment.[167]

Purely focusing on prosecution as the favoured mode of transitional justice ignores the nuances and complexities innate in any mid-conflict/post-conflict situation. This can be evident where, for example, there is a continuing conflict, yet national leaders resolve that the best way forward is to pursue peace.[168]

On the other hand, much would depend on the nature of the country, circumstances, and post-conflict environment. Kagame has stated: 'I don't understand what reconciliation would mean unless some of those responsible were brought to justice',[169] echoing the somewhat banal catchphrase of many commentators on post-conflict societies, that 'no reconciliation is possible ... without justice.'[170]

Nevertheless, the ICC must focus on prosecution over other alternative modes of accountability primarily because of its mandate. Yet it must not be

166 Blumenson 2006, p. 867.

167 Ludwin King 2003, p. 8.

168 An instance of this is in 2010 where Joseph Kabila, the President of the Democratic Republic of Congo defended his decision to engage with ICC indicted rebel leader Bosco 'The Terminator' Ntaganda, arguing, 'Why do we choose to work with Mr Bosco, a person sought by the ICC? Because we want peace now. In Congo, peace must come before justice'. See Smith, 'Congo Conflict: The 'Terminator' Lives in Luxury While Peacekeepers Look On', *The Guardian (UK)*, 5 February 2010, available at: www.theguardian.com/world/2010/feb/05/congo-child-soldiers-ntaganda-monuc (accessed 15 December 2014).

169 Taken from Harrell 2003, p. 37.

170 Institute for Contextual Theology, 'The Kairos Document: Challenge to the Church', 1985, available at: www.sahistory.org.za/article/kairos-document-1985–0 (accessed on 15 December 2014).

'close-minded toward alternative experiments in dealing with the past which are genuine democratic efforts advancing the goals of accountability.'[171]

5. CONCLUSION

Pursuing accountability through transitional justice objectives like justice, deterrence, and prevention in post-conflict environments is immensely arduous, particularly as they are sometimes at variance with each other. Fundamentally, any accountability process, whether national or international, judicial or non-judicial, is never going to be perfect in fully repairing the damage and healing the wounds – societal and personal – caused by the human rights abuses; or prevent future atrocities.

The lessons learned from Rwanda's transitional justice experience have, undoubtedly, been many and varied. Legal pluralist strategies symbolise a modern approach to transitional justice. Rwanda's example demonstrates the enormous challenge in developing effective approaches to accountability that meet various goals, address the unique needs arising in different post-conflict environments, and establish a constructive balance between national and international approaches. This necessitates careful consideration of the social, legal, and political contexts of the state or states involved, a clear enunciation of the objectives to be attained, an appraisal of other complementary processes to achieve accountability, and how to overcome the barriers faced. It would also necessitate a better understanding of how national and international mechanisms can (and do) interact optimally, and how different forms of international assistance can strengthen and support domestic efforts.[172]

The evolution of justice in the mass atrocities has demonstrated the importance of local ownership – through the engagement of local communities and agencies, and assuming more culturally and socially sensitive justice standards.

Just like the ICTR, the ICC represents 'foreign' involvement in a divided society, and can cause substantial scepticism about the international community's motives. Zacklin has argued that the international community's involvement in post-genocide Rwanda is an act of 'political contrition', emanating from the guilt of not intervening in the genocide sooner than they did.[173] Yet this guilt alone was not the basis for establishment of the ICTR. It also did not delineate the transitional justice schema the international community had for Rwanda. Additionally, it is improbable another ad hoc tribunal would be created given its great expense, temporal nature, and the existence of the ICC.

---

171 Robinson 2003, pp. 504–505.
172 Stromseth 2003, p. 4.
173 Zacklin 2004, p. 542.

A key theme emanating from this article is that transitional justice can be sourced on both collective and individual levels. Hence, when viewed from a legal pluralist standpoint, the majority of the censures, though not all, of the ICTR and *gacaca*, become minor – particularly as this twin system fosters worldwide understanding of the post-genocide environment, whilst promoting transitional justice on both the individual and collective levels.

The rebuilding of a society, especially one that was devastated by a genocide that was fuelled by enduring ethnic tensions, is a very difficult undertaking. It requires whole redefinitions and refocusing of relationships across societal lines, in terms of social, economic, and political aspects. It also necessitates the simultaneous encouragement of inner healing.

The post-conflict plan must thus have both internal and external elements so as to enable multilateral resource assistance whilst remaining socio-culturally relevant. The global society has traditionally intervened to stop violence and bloodshed. Peacebuilding and reconciliation are processes that must follow this typically military action.

The legal pluralist system in Rwanda, which encompassed the ICTR and the *gacaca* courts, did not characterise an envisioned or sound approach for attaining all transitional justice and reconciliation objectives. Yet its combination functioned to assist transitional justice and reconciliation on collective and individual levels. It also drew attention to areas in the system that can be addressed in future examples of transitional restoration.

Nevertheless, the ICC Prosecutor would be heedful that a homogeneous approach to transitional justice is not always the best policy, particularly as the prosecutorial mandate and obligation to take into consideration the interests of justice do not always match up.

The Rwandan example also underscores the importance of the ICC encouraging and endorsing domestic accountability efforts, and to develop novel forms of international assistance to those efforts. Indeed, willingness and capacity, as well as taking measures to prevent future abuses, will inevitably differ from state to state – but whilst difficult and challenging, international support is of crucial and continuing importance.[174] Yet it must also be borne in mind that the ICC is only one element of the system – a system that is a network of countries that have assumed responsibility to further international criminal justice in conjunction with, or to complement, the ICC's work. Hence, national courts can act as 'domestic international criminal [tribunals].'[175]

By developing innovative and complementary relationships between international and domestic players, and yet applying concerted international

174 Stromseth 2003, p. 36.

175 Du Plessis et al., 'African efforts to close the impunity gap: Lessons for complementarity from national and regional actions', ISS Paper, November 2012,p. 20.

pressure when needed,[176] the legal pluralistic structure formed can become a critical part of accountability in the coming years.

BIBLIOGRAPHY

BOOKS AND JOURNAL ARTICLES

Alvarez 1998
Alvarez, J.E., 'Rush to Closure: Lessons of the Tadic Judgment', 96 Michigan Law Review, 1998.
Bagaric and Morss 2006
Bagaric, M. and Morss, J. 'International Sentencing Law: In Search of a Justification and Coherent Framework', 6 International Criminal Law Review, 2006.
Berinyuu 2004
Berinyuu, A.A., 'Peace Building in Africa: Lessons from the Truth Commission', 20 International Journal of Humanities and Peace, 2004.
Blumenson 2006
Blumenson, E., 'The Challenge of a Global Standard of Justice: Peace, Pluralism and Punishment at the International Criminal Court', 44 Columbia Journal of Transnational Law, 2006.
Button 2010
Button, H., 'African Transitional Justice Universal Ideal or Political Reality?', 6 Atlantic International Studies Journal, 2010.
Clark 2010
Clark, P., 'The Gacaca Courts, Post-Genocide Justice and Reconciliation in Rwanda: Justice without Lawyers', Cambridge University Press, 2010.
Clark 2007
Clark, P., 'Hybridity, Holism and "Traditional" Justice: The Case of the Gacaca Courts in Post-Genocide Rwanda', 39(4) The George Washington International Law Review, 2007.
Corey and Joireman 2004
Corey, A. and Joireman, S.F., 'Retributive Justice: The Gacaca Courts in Rwanda', 103(410) African Affairs, 2004.
Daly 2002
Daly, E., 'Between Punitive and Reconstructive Justice: The Gacaca Courts in Rwanda', 34 New York University Journal of International Law and Politics, 2002.
DeLaet 2006
DeLaet, D., 'Gender Justice: A Gendered Assessment of Truth Telling Mechanisms', in Borer, J, T.A. (ed.), 'Telling the Truths: Truth Telling and Peace Building in Post-Conflict Societies', Notre Dame UP, 2006.

176 Stromseth 2003, p. 36.

Dieng 2011
Dieng, A., 'Capacity-Building Efforts of the ICTR: A Different Legacy', 9(3) Northwestern University Journal of International Human Rights, 2011.

Drumbl 2005
Drumbl, M.A., 'Lecture, Law and Atrocity: Settling Accounts in Rwanda', 31 Ohio Northern University Law Review, 2005.

Fletcher and Weinstein 2002
Fletcher, L.E. and Weinstein, H.M., 'Violence and Social Repair', 24 Human Rights Quarterly, 2002.

Gallimore 2002
Gallimore, T. 'Unresolved Trauma: Fuel for the Cycle of Violence and Terrorism', in Stout, C.E. (ed.), 'The Psychology of Terrorism: Clinical Aspects and Responses', Praeger Publishers, 2002.

Gasibirege 2002
Gasibirege, S., 'L'Élection des juges inyangamugayo: rupture ou continuité', in Eugène Ntaganda, E. (ed.), 'De la paix à la justice: les enjeux de la réconciliation nationale', Cahiers de Centre de Gestion des Conflits No. 6, 2002.

Glasius 2008
Glasius, M., 'We Ourselves, We are Part of the Functioning: The ICC, Victims, and Civil Society in the Central African Republic', 108 African Affairs, 2008.

Goldstein-Bolocan 2005
Goldstein-Bolocan, M., 'Rwandan Gacaca: An Experiment in Transitional Justice', Journal of Dispute Resolution, 2005.

Goldston 2010
Goldston, J.A., 'More Candour About Criteria: The Exercise of Discretion by the Prosecutor of the International Criminal Court', 8(2) Journal of International Criminal Justice, 2010.

Goldstone 2008
Goldstone, D.E., 'Embracing Impasse: Admissibility, Prosecutorial Discretion, and the Lessons of Uganda for the International Criminal Court', 22 Emory International Law Review, 2008.

Griffiths 1986
Griffiths, J., 'What is Legal Pluralism?', 24 Journal of Legal Pluralism, 1986.

Harrell 2003
Harrell, P.E., 'Rwanda's Gamble: Gacaca and a New Model of Transitional Justice', Writers Club Press, 2003.

Haskell and Waldorf 2011
Haskell, L. and Waldorf, L., 'The Impunity Gap of the International Criminal Tribunal for Rwanda: Causes and Consequences', Hastings International and Comparative Law Review, 2011.

Jean 2007
Jean, M., 'The Rwandan Genocide: The True Motivations for Mass Killings', 1 Emory Endeavors in World History, 2007.

Jones 2010
Jones, N.A., 'The Courts of Genocide: Politics and the Rule of Law in Rwanda and Arusha', Routledge, 2010.

Longman 2004
Longman, T., 'The Domestic Impact of the International Criminal Tribunal for Rwanda', in Ratner, S.R and Bischoff, J.L. (eds.), 'International War Crimes Trials: Making a Difference?', University of Texas School of Law, 2004.
Ludwin King 2003
Ludwin King, E.B., 'Trials and Truth Commissions in Argentina and El Salvador', in Stromseth, J. (ed.), 'Accountability for Atrocities: National and International Responses', Transnational Publishers, 2003.
Magnarella 2005
Magnarella, P.J., 'The Background and Causes of the Genocide in Rwanda', 3 Journal of International Criminal Justice, 2005.
Merry 1988
Merry, S.E., 'Legal Pluralism', 22(5) Law Society & Review, 1988.
Mnookin 2012
Mnookin, R.H., 'Rethinking the Tension Between Peace and Justice: The International Criminal Prosecutor as Diplomat', 18 Harvard Negotiation Law Review, 2012.
Moghalu 2005
Moghalu, K.C., 'Rwanda's Genocide: The Politics of Global Justice', Palgrave Macmillan, 2005.
Moreno-Ocampo 2006
Moreno-Ocampo, L., 'Keynote Address: Integrating the Work of the ICC into Local Justice Initiatives', 21(4) American University International Law Review, 2006.
Nagy 2009
Nagy, R., 'Traditional Justice and Legal Pluralism in Transitional Context: The Case of Rwanda's Gacaca Courts', in Quinn, J.R. (ed.), 'Reconciliation(s): Transitional Justice in Post-conflict Societies', McGill-Queen's UP, 2009.
Nsanzuwera 2005
Nsanzuwera, F., 'The ICTR Contribution to National Reconciliation', 3 Journal of International Criminal Justice, 2005.
Nwoye 2014
Nwoye, L.C., 'Partners or Rivals in Reconciliation? The ICTR and Rwanda's Gacaca Courts', 16 San Diego International Law Journal, 2014.
Peskin 2008
Peskin, V., 'International Justice in Rwanda and the Balkans: Virtual Trials and the Struggle for State Cooperation', Cambridge University Press, 2008.
Peskin 2005
Peskin, V., 'Beyond Victor's Justice: The Challenge of Prosecuting the Winners at the International Criminal Tribunals for the Former Yugoslavia and Rwanda', 4 Journal of Human Rights, 2005.
Phillips and Albon 1999
Phillips, T. and Albon, M., 'When Prosecution Is Not Possible: Alternative Means of Seeking Accountability for War Crimes', in Cooper, B., 'War Crimes: The Legacy of Nuremburg', TV Books, 1999.

Prunier 1997
Prunier, G., 'The Rwanda Crisis: History of a Genocide', 2nd ed., C Hurst & Co Publishers, 1997.
Robinson 2003
Robinson, D., 'Serving the Interests of Justice: Amnesties, Truth Commissions and the International Criminal Court', 14(3) European Journal of International Law, 2003.
Rosenberg and Meredith 2000
Rosenberg, T. and Meredith, M., 'Coming to Terms: South Africa's Search for Truth', Public Affairs, 2000.
SáCouto and Cleary 2008
SáCouto, S. and Cleary, K., 'The Gravity Threshold of the International Criminal Court', 23 Am. U. Intl. L. Rev., 2008.
Sarkin 1999
Sarkin, J., 'The Necessity of Establishing a Truth and Reconciliation Commission in Rwanda', 21(3) Human Rights Quarterly, 1999.
Scharf 1999
Scharf, M.P., 'The Amnesty Exception to the Jurisdiction of the International Criminal Court', 32 Cornell International Law Journal, 1999.
Stromseth 2003
Stromseth, J.E., 'Introduction: Goals and Challenges in the Pursuit of Accountability', in Stromseth, J.E. (ed.), 'Accountability for Atrocities: National and International Responses', International and Comparative Criminal Law Series, Transnational Publishers, 2003.
Temple-Raston 2008
Temple-Raston, D., 'Justice on the Grass: Three Rwandan Journalists, Their Trial for War Crimes and a Nation's Quest for Redemption', Free Press, 2008.
Umutesi 2006
Umutesi, M.B., 'Is Reconciliation Between Hutus And Tutsis Possible?', 60(1) Journal of International Affairs, 2006.
Uvin and Mironko 2003
Uvin, P. and Mironko, C., 'Western and Local Approaches to Justice in Rwanda', 9(2) Global Governance, 2003.
Westberg 2011
Westberg, M.M., 'Rwanda's Use of Transitional Justice after Genocide: the Gacaca Courts and the ICTR', 59 University of Kansas Law Review, 2011.
Zacklin 2004
Zacklin, R., 'The Failings of Ad Hoc International Tribunals', 2 Journal of International Criminal Justice, 2004.

JURISPRUDENCE

Constitutional Court of South Africa 2014
SACC, National Commissioner of the South African Police Service v. Southern African Human Rights Litigation Centre and Another, CCT 02/14, ZACC 30, 30 October 2014.

Constitutional Court of Uganda 2011
Constitutional Court of Uganda, Thomas Kwoyelo v. Uganda, Case no. 036/11, UGCC 10, 21 September 2011.
ECtHR 2011
ECtHR, Ahorugeze v. Sweden, Application no. 37075/09, ECtHR, 27 October 2011.
ICC 2011
ICC, Decision on the 'Prosecutor's Application Pursuant to Article 58 as to Muammar Mohammed Abu Minya GADDAFI, Saif Al-Islam GADDAFI and Abdulla AL-SENUSSI', ICC-01/11, 27 June 2011.
ICTR 2011
ICTR, Prosecutor v. Jean-Bosco Uwinkindi, ICTR-2001–75-AR11*bis*, 16 December 2011.
ICTR 2011
ICTR, Prosecutor v. Jean-Bosco Uwinkindi, ICTR-2001–75-AR11*bis*, 28 June 2011.
ICTR 2000
ICTR, Prosecutor v. Georges Ruggiu, ICTR-97–32-I, T Ch I, 1 June 2000.

TREATIES, LEGISLATION AND AGREEMENTS

AU, Decision on Africa's Relationship with the International Criminal Court (ICC), Ext/Assembly/AU/Dec.1, October 2013.
AU, Decision on the Report of the Commission on the Abuse of the Principle of Universal Jurisdiction, Doc. Assembly/AU/14(XI), July 2008.
DRC, Constitution of the Democratic Republic of Congo, 2005, 18 February 2006.
International Criminal Tribunal for Rwanda, Rules of Procedure and Evidence, UN Doc. ITR/3/REV.1, 29 June 1995.
Rome Statute of the International Criminal Court, 2187 UNTS 90/37, 17 July 1998.
Rwanda, Constitution of the Republic of Rwanda, 26 May 2003.
Rwanda, Law N° 03/99 of 12/03/1999 establishing the National Unity and Reconciliation Commission, 12 March 1999.
Rwanda, Organic Law N° 08/1996 of 30 August 1996 on the Organization of Prosecutions for Offences constituting the Crimes of Genocide or Crimes against Humanity committed since 1 October 1990, 30 August 1996.
Rwanda, Organic Law N° 31/2007 of 25 July 2007 relating to the Abolition of the Death Penalty, 25 July 2007.
Rwanda, Organic Law N° 11/2007 of 16 March 2007 Concerning Transfer of Cases to the Republic of Rwanda from the International Criminal Tribunal for Rwanda and from Other States, 16 March 2007.
Statute of the International Criminal Tribunal for Rwanda, SC Res. 955, UN Doc. S/RES/955, 8 November 1994.

OTHERS

Amnesty International, 'Rwanda: Gacaca: A Question of Justice', AFR 47/007/2002, December 2002.
BBC News, 'African Union accuses ICC of 'hunting' Africans', 27 May 2013.
BBC News, 'Canada deports Rwanda genocide suspect Leon Mugesera', 24 January 2012.
BBC News, 'Rwanda 'Gacaca' Genocide Courts Finish Work', 18 June 2012.
BBC News, 'Rwanda accused win UK court case', 8 April 2009.
BBC News, 'Rwanda major guilty of UN murders', 4 July 2007.
BBC News, 'Rwanda nuns in genocide trial', 17 April 2001.
BBC News, 'Rwanda's Untold Story', 3 October 2014.
BBC News, 'UK and the Netherlands withhold Rwanda budget aid', 27 July 2012.
BBC News, 'UK stops £21m aid payment to Rwanda', 30 November 2012.
BBC News, 'Will Africa pull out of the ICC?', 11 October 2013.
Dietrich, J.W., 'Can International Courts Deter Human Rights Abusers?', ISA Annual Convention, 2 March 2007.
Forges, A. and Longman, T., 'Legal responses to genocide In Rwanda', Vassar College, 25 October 2004.
Greenberg, D., 'African Union Declaration Against the ICC Not What it Seems', Foreign Policy on Focus, 6 August 2009.
Hayman, R., 'Milking The Cow: Negotiating Ownership of Aid and See Policy in Rwanda', Global Economic Governance Working Paper 2007/26, June 2007.
Hirondelle News Agency, 'Rwanda/Justice – Genocide Suspect Extradited from Norway to Stay in Custody', 16 May 2013.
Hirondelle News Agency, 'Rwanda: Danish Court Upholds Extradition of Rwandan Genocide Suspect', 20 November 2012.
ICC, Office of the Prosecutor, 'Policy Paper on the Interests of Justice', September 2007.
Ingelaere, B., 'The Gacaca Courts in Rwanda', in Huyse, L. and Salter, M. (eds.), 'Traditional Justice and Reconciliation After Violent Conflict: Learning from African Experiences', International Institute for Democracy and Electoral Assistance, 2008.
Institute for Contextual Theology, 'The Kairos Document: Challenge to the Church', 1985.
Ludwin King, E.B., 'Does Justice Always Require Prosecution? The International Criminal Court and Transitional Justice Measures', August 2012.
National Unity and Reconciliation Commission (NURC), Rwandan Reconciliation Barometer, October 2010.
News of Rwanda, 'Genocide suspect arrested in The Netherlands, to be extradited', 23 January 2014.
Penal Reform International (PRI), 'Access to Justice in Sub-Saharan Africa: the Role of Traditional and Informal Justice Systems', January 2001.
Plessis, M., Louw, A. and Maunganidze, O., 'African efforts to close the impunity gap: Lessons for complementarity from national and regional actions', ISS Paper, November 2012.
Radio Netherlands Worldwide (International Justice Desk), 'Genocide banker jailed for 30 years', 1 December 2009.

Radio Netherlands Worldwide (International Justice Desk), 'Higaniro Alphonse', 31 May 2001.
Rwagatare, J., 'ICTR acquittals shocking but expected', The New Times, 12 February 2013.
Shirbon, E., 'Rwandan genocide suspects face UK extradition battle', Reuters, 5 June 2013.
Smith, D., 'Congo Conflict: The "Terminator" Lives in Luxury While Peacekeepers Look On', The Guardian (UK), 5 February 2010.
Special Broadcasting Service (SBS), 'French court rejects extradition of Rwanda', 27 February 2014.
The Independent, 'Curtains fall on Gacaca', 29 May 2012.
TRIAL (Track Impunity Always), Desire Munyaneza Profile, The Trial Watch Project.
TRIAL (Track Impunity Always), Etienne Nzabonima Profile, The Trial Watch Project.
TRIAL (Track Impunity Always), Fulgence Niyonteze Profile, The Trial Watch Project.
TRIAL (Track Impunity Always), Joseph Mpambara Profile, The Trial Watch Project.
TRIAL (Track Impunity Always), Pascal Simbikangwa Profile, The Trial Watch Project.
TRIAL (Track Impunity Always), Samuel Ndashyikirwa Profile, The Trial Watch Project.
UN Security Council, 'The Rule of Law and Transitional Justice in Conflict and Post-Conflict Societies', Report of the Secretary-General, UN Doc S/2004/616, 23 August 2004.
UN Security Council, Resolution 1503 (2003), UN Doc. S/RES/1503, 28 August 2003.
UN Security Council, Resolution 1534 (2004), UN Doc. S/RES/1534, 26 March 2004.
UN Security Council, Verbatim Record of the Security Council's 3453rd Meeting, UN Doc. S/PV.3453, 8 November 1994.

LOOKING FORWARD, ANTICIPATING CHALLENGES

Making Sense of Disjunctures in Meanings of Culpability*

Kamari Maxine CLARKE

1. INTRODUCTION

The end of the first decade of the operation of the International Criminal Court has been met with celebration as well as extreme trepidation. While the celebration reflects the recognition of hard fought victories, the trepidation is related to the Court's critics, many of whom remain ambivalent about the way that the Court has parsed guilt and framed modes of responsibility. These modes of responsibility involve the ways that notions of culpability have been articulated through a language of individualisation – in which guilt is being attributed to those deemed the most criminally responsible, such as commanders and military leaders. However, the challenge is that notions of responsibility are also understood in collective terms, as well as through understandings that go well beyond the domain of the legal.

This essay is concerned with the emergence of new modes of responsibility as they are being unravelled in international criminal law domains. The goal is to explore the way that notions of 'culpability' are mediated through a range of formulations. While the Office of the Prosecutor (OTP) for the ICC may base culpability for contemporary violence in a narrow, a historical time frame that places responsibility in the hands of those who gave the orders or encouraged the violence, others assign modes of responsibility in relation to historical actors that they deem responsible for producing deep-seated structural inequality, such as colonial officers. These different assessments for assigning and comprehending guilt are often temporally driven and result in divergent ways of attributing culpability. These divergences result in what I have referred to elsewhere as an 'international criminal law (ICL) impunity

* An earlier version of this article was published in the *International Journal of Human Rights*.

gap'. This ICL impunity gap is the gap between the assignments of guilt that draw their meaning from the individualisation of criminal responsibility distinguished from modes of liability for parsing guilt that go beyond the individual.

Though the impunity gap has been invoked traditionally to refer to the gap in adjudication mechanisms between the international, regional, national and/or local mechanisms that shield some individual perpetrators from adjudication and enable the pursuit of adjudication for others, going beyond the individual analyses of guilt allows us to consider how and why collective and continuing crimes may trump new individualised conceptions of guilt in certain situations. Such examinations of the way that people parse guilt differently allow us to examine the differences that social time and legal time might offer; it likewise attends to the ways in which proximate actors are contradistinguished from commanders responsible for the actions of their subordinates and have implications for a substantial difference in how large portions of the Kenyan population are rethinking the popular international image of the perpetrator of crimes against humanity. For in the Kenyatta and Ruto cases under analysis, despite charges of culpability on the international stage, in 2013 a majority of the Kenyan people democratically elected them to be Kenya's President and Deputy President respectively. Both Kenyatta and Ruto remained in power, notwithstanding ICC indictments, and among various constituencies they took on a hero status, which calls into question the gap between the international court and Kenya's domestic imaginary.

In the remaining essay I consider the historical and juridical frames through which Kenyatta and Ruto were indicted: specifically, I analyse the historic circumstances surrounding the violence that erupted following the 2007 presidential election alongside legal arguments made by the ICC about culpability. To clarify, this democratic election followed the reign of President Mwai Kibaki (2002–2013), who prior to his leadership succeeded Daniel Moi (1978–2002) who ended a twenty-two year dictatorship. At stake in the ICC case against Kenyatta and Ruto was their alleged roles in the post-election violence following the election. In this sense, the essay shows that the logic of the African perpetrator figure is mediated through a distinct colonial-post colonial continuum in which effective relationships to historical injustices shape the way that people grapple with contemporary notions of individualised culpability.

2. MAKING SENSE OF THE PERPETRATOR

'Where all are guilty, no one is.'
– Hannah Arendt[1]

In his opening statement as one of the prosecutors of the Nuremberg Military Tribunal in November 1945, Justice Jackson stated: 'the idea that a state, any more than a corporation, commits crimes, is a fiction. Crimes always are committed only by persons. While it is quite proper to employ the fiction of responsibility of a state or corporation for the purpose of imposing a collective liability, it is quite intolerable to let such a legalism become the basis of personal immunity.' This statement forms the cornerstone of modern-day international criminal justice. Article 25 of the Rome Statute of the International Criminal Court – developed over half a century after the Nuremberg Tribunal started its first case – solidifies this position, determining that the Court shall have jurisdiction over natural persons. While historians of international criminal law often take Nuremberg as the starting point and trace the genealogy from there, the concept of individual criminal responsibility or culpability has long existed in national jurisdictions. Efforts to ascribe liability for collective crimes are a key feature of (international) criminal law. Liberal legalism (a key feature of Anglo-Saxon legal systems) dictates that individuals must be held accountable for their own crimes and not for those of others – it follows that the Western legal profession has a preference for direct, individual criminal responsibility. However, criminal trials (both domestically and internationally) have had to find ways to account for crimes that may have been collective in nature or have had collective elements.

On a national level, modes of liability such as aiding and abetting, conspiracy, etc. have long existed. However, due to the particular nature of international crimes, the tensions have been more pronounced. Prosecutors and judges have grappled with ways to establish the linkages between a particular accused actions (or failure to act) and a given set of acts. This tension in ICL – the matter of how to attribute individual guilt for collective crimes – remains among the most problematic issues of international criminal law. Yet the figure of the perpetrator of violence in the international imagination represents the imagery of an individual actor and/or high ranking leader who is mercilessly engaging in maiming and murder of thousands through their relentless commands. This figure is often described in human rights reports as an actor lacking feeling and brutally engaging in relentless prosecution. It often stands for a figure of violence representing African politics to the world embedded in irrational violence. In this light, this perpetrator imagery is often seen as a figure of African tragedy

1 Arendt 2003.

and uncivilised violence uncontrollable by reason and without respect for the sanctity of human life.

But the reality is that there is a gap related to the individualisation of criminal responsibility and collective conceptions of guilt. Epitomising this gap is the ongoing case of Kenya's William Ruto and the recently dropped case against Uhuru Kenyatta whose indictments by the ICC cohere and cohered for some with the international image of the African perpetrator. For others it contradicted such depictions. Such international characterisations operate in ostensible contrast to in-country politics in which it is clear that conceptions of culpability are lived not as permanent, synchronic or diachronic temporalities but in what Achille Mbembe has referred to as embodying multiplicities and synchronicities in their presences and absences.[2] Set against a backdrop in which Kenyatta and Ruto were cast as perpetrators notwithstanding an extensive history of colonial violence, this chapter makes visible a particular 'impunity gap' with regard to the Office of the Prosecutor's alleged perpetrators and popular sense of responsibility. This gap is evident via the longue durée of colonial violence which operates simultaneously and in opposition to the proximity of violence; such spaces lay bare the problem of legal time and the resulting implications for how culpability is imagined differently.

3. CULPABILITY AND THE CHALLENGE OF LEGAL TIME

The cornerstone of criminal law – national or international – is culpability. Culpability refers to the degree to which one can be held responsible for a particular act or set of results. Measuring culpability then, can be said to be the prime objective of criminal justice. Rooted in American and European legal traditions, individual culpability treats individuals as autonomous agents able to either obey or violate the law, and to bear the consequences of a violation of the law. In Anglo-Saxon legal tradition, known as the liberal justice model, culpability requires the existence of a criminal act (*actus reus*) coupled with the intentional commission of such an act (*mens rea*).[3] Elies van Sliedregt's work on individual criminal responsibility[4] approaches individualism as a concept rooted in western legal traditions, stemming from the understanding that a person is only culpable to the extent of his own free will or guilty mind (*mens rea*). Chrisje Brant, in her essay 'Guilty Landscapes' argues that individual guilt permeates western legal culture, and that criminal law takes individual guilt as its sole domain, rather than concepts such as

2 Mbembe 2001.
3 Hart 1958, pp. 401–441.
4 Van Sliedregt 2012.

collective guilt (a peoples' guilt) or even metaphysical guilt (the notion that man is guilty simply by being, which Brants argues have been banned to the terrains of art and philosophy).

The modern-day usage of individual criminal culpability can be considered an effort to pierce two traditional 'shields' from criminal culpability – the defence of superior orders and the principle of immunity for heads of state and senior state officials. While there is a tendency within international criminal legal scholarship to describe the development of international criminal law (ICL), and the modern-day international criminal justice system as merely another step in creating global law, a simple transplantation of domestic legal norms to the international level, the reality is more complex. Key proponents of ICL such as the late Cassese insist that 'international criminal law, to a great extent results from the gradual transposition on to the international level of rules and legal constructs proper to national criminal law or national proceedings.'[5] The choice to reject collective responsibility was seen by Cassesse as the central idea behind individualised liability decided in the *Tadić* decision, he argued that a 'defendant ought not to be punished for the acts of others'.[6]

The rejection of collective guilt in the international criminal legal system is both a matter of practicality in that it is not feasible to prosecute all who played a role, as well as a matter of principle and ideology with distinct historical roots.[7] While prior to the late twentieth century, the response to collective guilt was collective punishment (i.e. military retaliation and war) after the First World War. The victorious allies addressed the matter of settling accounts with the 'aggressors' (Germany and the Ottoman Empire) in the Treaty of Versailles. While there was talk of criminal trials, little came of them.[8] Rather, Brants argued that a 'key lesson learnt from Versailles was that collective guilt and collective sanctions do not result in peace, reconciliation, deterrence; rather the opposite.'[9] She argued that history has shown that collective guilt fuels frustration, extremism and eventually mass violence.' Many insisted that the Treaty of Versailles resulted in the collective punishment of the German people, created economic malaise, poverty and hunger, and led to the conditions for the rise of the Nazi Party and the Second World War.[10] Ultimately, through discussions amongst the victors of the Second World War on the way forward, a criminal procedure based in the Anglo-American tradition of fair trial, due process and by extension, individual culpability, was favoured as the solution

5 Cassese 2008, p. 7.
6 Casesse 2003.
7 Brants 2011, p. 60.
8 *Ibid.*
9 *Ibid*, p. 61.
10 Simpson 2007.

most likely to contribute to durable peace following the Nazi regime and the development of a legitimate regime in Germany.[11]

Justice Jackson, in his opening statement, employed similar reasoning. In his famous speech he proclaimed: 'That four great nations, flushed with victory and stung with injury stay the hand of vengeance and voluntarily submit their captive enemies to the judgment of the law is one of the most significant tributes that Power has ever paid to Reason.' Throughout this speech, Jackson made the case that individual responsibility was the most reasonable and necessary approach. 'This principle of personal liability is a necessary as well as logical one if international law is to render real help to the maintenance of peace.' He then insisted that 'an international law which operates only on states can be enforced only by war because the most practicable method of coercing a state is warfare… Only sanctions which reach individuals can peacefully and effectively be enforced.'[12] Thus, the Nuremberg solution is often taken to represent the 'triumph of liberal legalism and individual responsibility over vengeful politics and collective guilt'.[13] To date, the Nuremberg precedent heavily influences international criminal law.

International criminal law is strongly influenced by humanitarian law and international efforts to regulate armed conflict. Even where, as is the case with the development of the legal definition of crimes against humanity, the contextual requirement that the crime took place during an armed conflict has been removed, international crimes by their nature require that the conduct took place systematically, was organised, and occurred on a large scale. War crimes, for instance, as in Article 8 of the Rome Statute, fall within the jurisdiction of the ICC 'in particular when committed as part of a plan or policy or as part of a large scale commission of such crimes.'[14] Some like Mark Drumbl have argued that there is an element of collectivity in all international crimes. This collective element is the 'essence' of international crime.[15] In this sense, there is an inherent conundrum present in ICL – the jurisdiction is triggered by collectivity, but once a court is seized of jurisdiction, individual perpetrators – 'those most responsible' – are to be prosecuted. In short, the conundrum ICL presents is that the very acts which are criminalised (war crimes, crimes against humanity, genocide, aggression) are least suitable to individualised accounts of blame or guilt.[16]

---

11 Brants 2011, p. 61.

12 Justice Robert H. Jackson, Opening Statement Before the International Military Tribunal, 21 November 1945, available at: www.roberthjackson.org/the-man/speeches-articles/speeches/speeches-by-robert-h-jackson/opening-statement-before-the-international-military-tribunal/.

13 Simpson 2007.

14 Rome Statute of the International Criminal Court, Article 8.

15 Drumbl 2007; Brants 2011.

16 Simpson 2007.

Ascribing the guilt of many to a few results in evidentiary challenges when attempting to link an accused to the crimes (and prove this beyond a reasonable doubt).[17] Simpson has reflected that though putatively individualistic, international criminal law 'cannot escape into individualism entirely' and finds itself 'perpetually drawn back to group responsibility and communal guilt.' However, this challenge of communal guilt is also tied to the forces of history that drive communal action. Though not new to legal anthropology, the notion of legal time is scarcely interrogated in western jurisprudential circles, particularly with regard to how notions of culpability are conceptualised.

Scholars of international law like Simpson and Brant have explored questions of liability as a way to understand criminal responsibility but they, among many scholars of critical international law, have hardly examined how notions of legal time are not only conceptualised in particular ways but serve to restrict the analytic space in which criminal law can operate. To examine legal time through its strict understandings and demarcations in criminal law is to reflect on other temporal modes – such as continuing crimes – for addressing collective crimes. Continuing crimes (such as colonialism or apartheid) present us with less stable questions of *perpetratorhood* and create multivalent legal dilemmas. These dilemmas involve questions of jurisdiction, admissibility, and evidence, and further the parameters of an 'impunity gap' through which the notion of Kenyatta and Ruto as perpetrator is imagined as viable or unacceptable.

4. FOUNDATIONS FOR CONTINUING CRIMES IN THE KENYAN POSTCOLONIAL IMAGINATION

On 1 July 1895, the region that is now known as Kenya was declared to be a British-East African Protectorate.[18] British colonialism in Kenya produced a situation of uneven land distribution and a related problem of elite patronage. The colonial government forcefully evicted Africans from their ancestral lands and relocated them onto what became known as the 'Native Reserves.' The confiscated lands were referred to as the 'White Highlands', and represented some of the most fertile regions of Kenya. The British colonial administration imposed laws that also forced Kenyans to labour on European farms with poor social services. They imposed taxation laws, instituted racial segregation, restricted movement through the *kipande* identification system, and curtailed basic freedoms.

Despite their displacement, land and ritual oathing continued to be important for the unification of various Kenyan social groups. Land was not merely a means of economic production but was seen as a divinely inherited blessing

17 Van Sliedregt 2012.
18 Ogot 1974, p. 249.

that connected them to their ancestors. But as a result of the dispossession of Kenyans from their land, the *Mau Mau* struggle broke out in order to reclaim their land and promote equality in the region. The majority of the *Mau Mau* members were from the Kikuyu, Embu, and Meru communities, other Kenyans from various groups – such as the Akamba, Maasai, Abaluhya, Abagusii, and Luo, as well as various Kenyan Indian trade unionists – also participated in the struggle.[19] This struggle began as early as the late 1940s. It was most intense between 1952 and 1957 as its members intensified their mobilisation to establish the conditions for Kenyan independence in 1963. With Jomo Kenyatta, a former Mau Mau combatant,[20] as the new post-independence prime minister, there were great expectations that Kenyatta's government would sufficiently address the land question through a new land-redistribution policy. Hundreds of thousands of Africans – mainly Kikuyu – were either living as squatters on European farms in the Rift Valley or in relatively unproductive 'Native Reserves' away from their ancestral lands. Many hoped that Kenyatta's government would resettle them back to their ancestral lands. However, Kenyatta's government instituted a land-reconsolidation policy that vexed many of the poor squatters, peasants, and working classes.

Kenyatta eventually developed a series of strategies for the continual investment of European interests in Kenya while also brokering a deal for the transfer of land to Native Kenyans. In order to implement this plan he borrowed a loan from the British government in order to buy back land from the European settlers who chose to leave Kenya. Instead of overhauling the agrarian inequalities that were established during the colonial period and redistributing land among the majority of Africans who were either landless or land poor, Kenyatta's government introduced the infamous land policy known as 'willing buyer, willing seller', which required Africans to buy back their land. However, at independence, the majority of Africans were poor squatters, workers, and peasant farmers with very little capital. This post-independence policy was seen by many as a blatant injustice because only those who worked closely with the British and earned an income had the necessary resources to buy land or secure bank loans. Thus the early forms of stratification gave an unfair advantage to those who were on the colonial government's payroll during the Mau Mau struggle. But it also instilled feelings of injustice for many who felt that the terms for buying back land that was initially procured illegally were unjust.

---

19 Kinyatti 2009, pp. 144–50. The question of ethnicity in the *Mau Mau* struggle is one of the most controversial in the historiography. The debate revolves around whether the struggle was of a nationalist nature or just a Kikuyu affair. For details of this debate see Kinyatti 1977, pp. 287–311 and Atieno-Odhiambo 1991, pp. 300–307.

20 It is worth noting here that Kenyatta denied his involvement with the Mau Mau during the Kapenguria trial.

Over time, the formation of landless squatters unravelled and took on an ethnic dimension, especially during the 24-year reign of Daniel arap Moi. Both Kikuyu squatters and those members of the Kikuyu who acquired land in the Rift Valley legally were seen as 'foreigners' who needed to be forcefully evicted. The reality that various members of the Kikuyu elites – who eventually became known as the 'Mount Kenya Mafias' – had acquired immense wealth and power in Kenya's postcolonial period only made matters worse for those deemed to be 'foreigners' in the Rift Valley. To contextualise the violence that erupted following the 30 December 2007 elections one must consider the events leading to the elections, which seemingly reveal a nation fractured along ethnic-tribal lines, especially the way that a discourse of evicting the 'foreigners' became a rallying cry for Rift Valley politicians during election time.

Ethnic tensions ostensibly worsened when, amidst accusations of election rigging, competing parties – the Party of National Unity (PNU, led by sitting President Mwai Kibaki) and the Orange Democratic Movement (ODM, led by Raila Odinga) – both claimed electoral victory.[21] When Kenya's Electoral Commission announced that Mwai Kibaki was the winner of Kenya's 2007 elections, a two-month period of violence broke out throughout Kenya, particularly in pro-Odinga areas: the slums of Nairobi, the Rift Valley (Eldoret), and Nyanza (Kisumu).[22] In the end, rioting, excessive use of force (by police and security forces), burning, looting, sexual violence, and murder left 1,200 people dead and displaced thousands.[23] More than a year later, on 26 November 2009, the Prosecutor of the ICC requested authorisation from Pre-Trial Chamber II to investigate Kenya's 2007–2008 post-election violence. The Office of the Prosecutor argued that it had reasonable grounds to believe that 'crimes of murder, rape and other forms of sexual violence, deportation or forcible transfer of population and other inhumane acts' had been committed in Kenya from 2007 to 2008.[24]

On 15 December 2010, the Pre-Trial Chamber granted the relevant permission to indict Ruto and Kenyatta and others using the conception of superior responsibility. This legal frame involved the doctrine of hierarchical accountability wherein expectations of supervision pertain and a related liability for the failure to act – further established through the doctrine of 'command responsibility.' In the case against Kenyatta, charges were based on his supposed command of murders committed in Naivasha on 27 and 28 January 2008, and in Nakuru on 24 and 27 January.[25] For Ruto, the demarcated period was from

---

21 Cheeseman 2008, pp. 166–184.

22 Human Rights Watch, *High Stakes: Political Violence and the 2013 Elections in Kenya*, February 2013, available at: www.hrw.org/sites/default/files/reports/kenya0213webwcover.pdf (accessed 15 July 2013).

23 *Ibid*; See also Kagwanja & Southall 2009.

24 ICC, *Situation in the Republic of Kenya*, Request for authorization of an investigation pursuant to Article 15, Pre-Trial Chamber II, ICC-01/09-3, 26 November 2009.

25 *The Prosecutor v. Uhuru Muigai Kenyatta*, ICC-PIDS-KEN-02-010/14 (2014).

1 to 4 January 2008, and involved violence allegedly committed in the greater Eldoret area.[26]

Admittedly the ICC's temporal jurisdiction over the case was limited by Article 11 of the Rome Statute (*Jurisdiction ratione temporis*), which indicates that the 'Court has jurisdiction only with respect to crimes committed after the entry into force of this Statute.'[27] The ICC's judges examined its temporal jurisdiction over potential cases against Ruto and Kenyatta when it granted the prosecutor permission to commence an investigation over the situation. These considerations are also apparent in the temporal scope of the asserted crimes in relation to the evidence provided to cover the entire time period included in the prosecutor's initial charges. Expressly, Ruto was alleged to have held a series of meetings in which he distributed money and arms with the goal of commissioning the crimes of murder and displacement of supporters of the Party of National Unity (PNU) (led by sitting president at the time, Mwai Kibaki). Following this logic, these activities correspondingly fomented the violence following the 2007 election. With regard to Kenyatta, the Prosecutor alleged that he organised meetings with various government leaders, the police, and the leadership of the outlawed Mungiki sect; it was in those meetings that he supposedly provided funding, uniforms, and weapons to various pro-PNU youth to carry out their attacks. The Mungiki, whose name means 'a united people' in the Kenya Kikuyu language, is known as a mafia-oriented organisation in Kenya notorious for its participation in the 2007 post-election violence. Kenyatta is said to have mobilised their support for the purposes of 'defending' Kikuyu interests, leading the ICC to consider him criminally responsible for the violence the Mungiki perpetrated.[28]

Citing the gravity of the acts of violence and the absence of national proceedings, the Prosecutor argued that the cases originating from the investigation of violence during 2007 and 2008 should be admissible before the ICC.[29] The Kenyan government challenged this. Simultaneously, the African Union (AU) in partnership with the Kenya National Dialogue and Reconciliation (KNDR) team, under the leadership of former UN Secretary General Kofi Annan, recommended that the government establish the Commission of Inquiry

---

26 *The Prosecutor v. William Samoei Ruto and Joshua Arap Sang*, ICC-01/09-01/11-859 (2013). The Prosecutor did seek permission to amend the charges against Ruto/Sang to include events on 30 and 31 December 2007, but the Judges deemed this request inadmissible at the time it was made, as it was after the confirmation of charges hearing and no postponement was requested in order to amend the charges.

27 Rome Statute of the International Criminal Court, Article 11.

28 Interview 0037, Kamari Clarke, 18 July 2013.

29 ICC, *Situation in the Republic of Kenya*, Decision on the Prosecutor's appeal against the Decision on the Request to Amend the Updated Document Containing the Charges Pursuant to Article 61(9) of the Statue, Pre-Trail Chamber II, ICC-01/09-01/11-1123, 13 December 2013.

into Post-Election Violence (CIPEV).[30] Known as The Waki Commission, it recommended that a Special Tribunal for Kenya be set up within a given time frame to investigate and prosecute suspected perpetrators of crimes committed during the crisis period.[31] In October 2008, the report indicated that a meeting was held in the Statehouse to coordinate revenge on Luos and Kalenjins; it cited then-minister Uhuru Kenyatta as being criminally responsible for financing and mobilising electoral support through the Mungiki.[32] Similarly, the Luos and Kalenjins purportedly mobilised their support to attack the Kikuyus (the ethnic group to which Kenyatta belonged). The African Union-sponsored Waki Commission recommended that if the Kenyan government failed to set up a tribunal to investigate and adjudicate the cases, then the ICC should take over.

In early 2009, amidst increased ethnic party tensions, Kenyan parliamentarians tried to bring forward a bill to establish a Special Tribunal. In the end it received limited support and was defeated on two different occasions.[33] Parliamentarians from across the ODM (Raila Odinga) and PNU (Kenyatta and Kibaki's party) united to defeat it under the slogan: 'Don't be vague; let's go to The Hague.' The public statements made by various ODM and PNU politicians revealed their interest in seeking legal accountability for the other party. The prevailing argument was that no Special Tribunal in Kenya could be trusted to deal independently and impartially with issues that involve legal accountability for the post-election violence. On 8 March 2011, the ICC issued summons for the suspects to appear before the Court.[34] The Prosecutor named six persons (known as the Ocampo 6) suspected of bearing the greatest responsibility for crimes committed during Kenya's 2007 post-election period. The six were divided into two sets of cases representing two historically opposed factions divided along ethnic lines.

On one side were Major General Mohammed Hussein Ali, a Somali Kenyan who at the time of the post-election violence had been the Commissioner of the Kenyan Police; Uhuru Kenyatta (Kikuyu), then the Deputy Prime Minister and Minister for Finance as well as the chairman of President Kibaki's PNU; and Henry Kiprono Kosgey (Kalenjin in ethnicity), former Minister for Industrialization and a member of the National Assembly as well as the chairman of the ODM.[35] The opposing side included Francis Kirimi Muthaura, the Head of Public Service, Cabinet Secretary, and chairman of the National Security

30 Juma 2009.

31 Kagwanja & Southall 2009.

32 *The Waki Commission Report*, Commission of Inquiry into Post-Election Violence (CIPEV) 2008.

33 The first defeat was in 2009 when the government failed to obtain enough support in Parliament to pass the relevant laws to set up the Tribunal.

34 The Kenya National Dialogue and Reconciliation (KNDR) Monitoring Project, 'Progress in Implementation of the Constitution and other reforms', October 2011, Review Report (funded by Open Society Institute), 45.

35 Mueller 2014.

Advisory Committee; William Ruto, the Minister for Higher Education, Science and Technology, and ODM member of the National Assembly for Eldoret North; and Joshua Arap Sang, the head of operations at the Kalenjin-language radio station KASS FM, and a radio presenter at the time of the post-election violence (respectively of the Meru and Kalenjin ethnic groups).[36]

In January 2012, the Pre-Trial Chamber judges confirmed the charges of crimes against humanity against only four of the six indictees for Kenya's 2007–2008 post-election violence. The Chamber did not find that the evidence against Mr Kosgey met the necessary evidentiary threshold, so the charges against him were not confirmed. In Mr Ali's case the judges did not find that the evidence provided substantial grounds to believe that the National Police participated in the attacks in Naivasha and Nakuru, so the charges against him were also dropped, leaving Ruto and Sang on that case. By summer 2013, due to various setbacks in the Prosecution's evidence such as the loss of key witnesses for the Muthaura case, the charges against him were dropped, leaving only three indictees overall and only Kenyatta left in the second case. Though the mode of liability initially confirmed for Kenyatta/Muthaura was indirect co-perpetration, after the charges were dropped against Muthaura, the charge against Kenyatta was connected to him being 'individually responsible' for the violence in Naivasha on 27 and 28 January and in Nakuru on 24 and 27 January 2008.

The case against Ruto and Sang began in September 2013.[37] The case against Uhuru Kenyatta was continually adjourned and was finally dropped by the OTP on 5 December 2014.[38] The Ruto and Sang case is beset with controversies and complexities and was eventually dropped on 5 April 2016. In a poll conducted by Ipsos Synnovate in February 2014, more Kenyans opposed the ICC process than ever before: 46 percent of the Kenyan population was opposed to ICC

36 *Ibid.*

37 On 23 January 2012, the Pre-Trial Chamber II decided to move cases against Ruto, Sang, Muthaura, and Kenyatta to trial (see *The Prosecutor v. William Samoei Ruto and Joshua Arap Sang*, ICC-01/09-01/11-859 (2013); *The Prosecutor v. Uhuru Muigai Kenyatta*, ICC-PIDS-KEN-02-010/14 (2014)). Judges declined to confirm charges against Henry Kiprono Kosgey and Mohammed Hussein Ali. The charges against Francis Muthaura were dropped before being brought to trial. The recent decision to move the majority of the Kenyan cases to trial is bound to provide a window into another set of international juridical processes on the world stage and assessments on the extent to which the ICC has the potential to produce justice.

38 On 31 March 2014, Trial Chamber V(b) of the International Criminal Court adjourned the commencement date of the trial in the case against Uhuru Kenyatta to 7 October 2014 (see *The Prosecutor v. Uhuru Muigai Kenyatta*). The purpose of the adjournment is to provide the Government of Kenya with a further, time-limited opportunity to provide certain records, which the Prosecution had previously requested on the basis that the records are relevant to a central allegation to the case. ICC, Press Release: Trial adjourned until 7 October 2014, ICC-CPI-20140331-PR991, 31 March 2014, available at: www.icc-cpi.int/en_menus/icc/press%20and%20media/press%20releases/Pages/pr991.aspx (accessed 28 April 2014).

engagement, compared to 29 percent in 2013.[39] Interestingly, by fall of 2012 the once age-old competing parties/ethic groups came together to create the Jubilee Party, led by indictees Ruto (formerly of the ODM party) and Kenyatta (formerly of the PNU party). Despite the ICC indictment, in March 2013 the Kenyan people supported the Jubilee Party and voted for Uhuru Kenyatta as President of the Republic of Kenya and William Ruto as Deputy President, quickly leading to a drastic shift in public opinion on the ICC engagement, with more than half of the population becoming increasingly dismayed with the ICC indictments.[40]

While the question of who is responsible for violence committed against various victims has led to disagreements over the ICC indictments of perpetrators for crimes against humanity, especially those involving African sitting heads of states, longer histories of violence and questions of proximate violence have gained traction as the basis for the attribution of guilt. According to a report by the International Center for Transitional Justice, though victims understood that in ICC judicial contexts greater responsibility is borne by those who gave orders that led to violent outbreaks, more than half of those who responded to the question, 'Who should be prosecuted?', identified direct perpetrators or 'foot soldiers' of violence as being directly responsible.[41] Though supportive of the ICC concept, in principle, many victims also felt that instead of pursuing a lengthy ICC process in order to achieve compensation for violence and property loss, local and national mechanisms were preferable – even given the reality that in many ICC situation countries many did not feel fully satisfied with the domestic measures taken.[42]

In a 2013 survey that my research team and I conducted with victims of 2007–2008 post-election violence in Nairobi's low-income Kibera neighbourhood,[43] an overwhelming majority of Kibera residents insisted that criminal responsibility needs to be understood clearly through notions of collective guilt as clarified through the Mungiki phenomenon, the role of the police in post-election violence, and the way that the British colonial settlement of the Rift Valley led to the demise of both the Kikuyu and Kalejin-ethnic traditional networks. Despite this perception on the ground, international criminal law prioritises command/superior responsibility rather than holding proximate perpetrators accountable; the expectation is that direct perpetrators will be held accountable

39 Ipsos-Synovate, 'One Year into the Jubliee Government: A Reality-Check by Kenyans', 14 March 2014, available at: www.ipsos.co.ke/spr/downloads/downloads.php?dir=polls&file=KE_Ipsos%20SPEC%20Poll%20Report_One%20Year%20into%20the%20Jubilee%20Government%20Just%20What%20Are%20Kenyans%20Realities_14032014.MSWord.pdf (accessed 28 April 2014).

40 *Ibid.*

41 Robins, 'To Live as Other Kenyans Do: A Study of the Reparative Demands of Kenyan Victims of Human Rights Violations', International Center for Transitional Justice, July 2011, available at: http://ictj.org/sites/default/files/ICTJ-Kenya-Reparations-Demands-2011-English.pdf.

42 *Ibid.*

43 The survey was conducted during the author's fieldwork in Nairobi with a research team from September to December 2013.

under domestic criminal law. Accordingly, for some, the law falls short. This is not only because perpetrators of proximate violence are not being prosecuted in Kenya's national judiciaries; it is also attributable to the reality that international courts cannot situate crimes historically. Thus, as I will show, international legal processes have had the effect of producing images of African perpetrators that on one hand are being met with unease and on the other hand are seen for some as the only alternative for ending impunity in postcolonial Kenya. This duality exists both because international law is not seen by large numbers of Kenyans in our study as being capable of addressing the imbrication of continuing crimes and because they see Kenya's postcolonial elite as being structurally culpable. This structural culpability calls for a temporal analysis of modes of legal liability and is connected to a colonial-postcolonial continuum for parsing guilt.

5. COMMAND RESPONSIBILITY, LEGAL TIME, AND THE PROBLEM OF CONTINUING CRIMES

In the Rome Statute system, those most responsible for the commission of crimes over which the Court has jurisdiction can, in accordance with Article 25 of the Statute, be held individually responsible and liable for punishment. This criminal responsibility extends to individuals who commit such a crime jointly; those who order, solicit, or induce the commission of a crime; persons who aid, abet, or otherwise assist in the crime; and those who provide the means for the crime's commission.[44] Article 28 of the Rome Statute stipulates that a military commander or a person acting as a military commander with effective command and control over his forces shall be individually, criminally liable for the criminal conduct of his or her subordinates, provided he or she knew (or should have known) that the forces were committing or were about to commit such crimes. The article also concerns a commander who fails to take all necessary measures to prevent or suppress the commission of these crimes.[45]

Accordingly, the Rome Statute of the ICC sets out substantive laws and procedural rules through which to address violence. It ascribes guilt based on a particular period within the temporal jurisdiction of the Court and highlights questions of responsibility in individualist terms. Notwithstanding

---

44 Meloni 2007.

45 The requisite requires that the material elements of the crimes occur within the temporal jurisdiction of the Court (from 1 July 2002 onward); it also obliges that the crimes be committed with knowledge and intent. This doctrine of hierarchical criminal or command responsibility – established by The Hague Conventions (IV) and (X) of 1907 and first applied during the Leipzig War Crimes Trials after World War I – involves the reassignment of the guilt of thousands who committed violent acts to a single chief commander and a few top aides.

the stipulations for legal responsibility, many of the very victims on behalf of whom international judicial institutions seek to act protest the designations of criminal responsibility strictly in relation to individual responsibility, especially when there is an understanding that longer histories of imperial land disenfranchisement created (and were not products of) such forms of contemporary violence. Many of my respondents insisted that focusing on 2007–8 post-election violence failed to attend to deep-rooted historical and political issues. For example, Kiamu – a young Kenyan human rights advocate, maintains:

> One of the biggest weaknesses of Kenyan criminal law, we do not have a scheme for compensating victims of crime and the idea that these people of the 2007 violence are the only victims of crime, they're not the only victims of crime, I'm also a victim of crime I lost ten teeth, I nearly died; the state isn't compensating me. The best the state will do if they find the guys who beat me they might even hang them but they'll never pay me a coin for the injuries I've suffered. We've had victims in this country since the colonial times so if you're going to address the system of victims of political violence in Kenya we do it holistically. We begin with the day the British landed here, the evictions that the settlers did – today the biggest land-owners are settlers. All of these issues need to be addressed. We're not going to just come here and create a situation and it becomes an industry for everyone to make money and the reference point becomes 2007. My reference point is in the eighteenth century, and I think something needs to happen. If we're going to address the question of criminal politics of domination, exploitation and impoverishment and eviction then my reference point is not 2007 it goes much [further] back. And the ICC has no capacity to address that, so I'll not waste time on it.[46]

Kiamu has a strong conviction about the limits of culpability in domestic and international criminal law; we also see a critique concerning the inability of law to adequately encompass historical forms of violence. Despite these other conceptualisations of guilt, it is unlikely that the ICC will permit itself to consider activities that occurred prior to its temporal jurisdiction, thereby violating basic principles of legality.[47] Set against this vexed juridical backdrop, who should be held responsible for contemporary crimes of violence?

One of the most challenging examples of how courts wrestle with problems of strict temporality can be seen through attempts to address continuing and composite crimes as they force courts to address conduct that exists over a long time rather than in more familiar crimes such as murder. A continuing or composite crime is one that necessarily occurs over an extended period, such as the crime of apartheid. Apartheid, unlike murder, does not occur in a single instant. It involves legal policies, state action, social control and prolonged

46 Interview with author.
47 See Nissel 2004.

practices of exclusion and separation. Continuing and composite crimes also include specific, discrete acts that, by definition, must occur over a longer time frame. For example, the Rome Statute outlaws murder as a crime against humanity. By definition, to be a crime against humanity, the act of murder must occur as part of a widespread or systematic attack against a civilian population.[48] In contrast, when addressing regular crimes, such as murder, which occur in a discrete temporal instant, courts rarely, if ever, address the importance of temporal limits. However, with continuing and composite crimes, courts must regularly address the temporal scope of the conduct being prosecuted.[49]

5.1. CHALLENGES WITH CONTINUING CRIMES: THE RAINBOW WARRIOR CASE

The Rainbow Warrior is one of the most famous examples in the international case law concerning continuing violations. The case is important for the history of international tribunals recognising continuous crimes. In this case, two French agents were convicted by a New Zealand High Court for assisting in the sinking of the Rainbow Warrior, a Greenpeace ship docked off of the coast of New Zealand (which was going to protest French nuclear testing in the Pacific Ocean). France refrained from detaining the two agents and returned them to Hao, a French Pacific island, in violation of its agreement with New Zealand. In determining France's culpability for refusing to detain the agents, an international arbitration tribunal measured France's liability not just from the moment the agents were removed. Rather, the misconduct was deemed continuous and ongoing, and it included each day the agents remained outside of New Zealand's control.[50]

5.2. BRITISH SEIZURE OF US SLAVE SHIPS

A handful of cases involving the British seizure of US ships illustrates that courts will rule on the absolute moral wrongness of historical practices – here, slavery – but that courts remain largely unwilling to impose criminal liability except for specific acts and only after the conduct is clearly understood to be against the law. In this case the British authorities had seized over a few decades numerous

48 Nissel 2004, Art. 7(1)(a).

49 See also Nissel 2004.

50 See *Case Concerning the Difference Between New Zealand and France Concerning the Interpretation or Application of Two Agreements*, Concluded on 9 July 1986 Between the Two States and which Related to the Problems Arising from the Rainbow Warrior Affair (N.Z./Fr.), 20 R.I.A.A. 217 (1990).

American ships and freed the slaves that belonged to American nationals who were aboard.[51] The Governments referred to the Mixed Arbitration Commission that had the task of determining whether at the time each incident took place, slavery was 'contrary to the law of nations.' Umpire Bates held that the incidents during the 1830s to 1840s, when the slave trade was considered lawful under the law of nations, amounted to a breach on the part of the British authorities.[52] But the later incidents occurred when the slave trade had been 'prohibited by all civilized nations' and did not involve the responsibility of Great Britain.[53] Thus, the arbitration tribunal did not determine the timing of the wrongfulness of the acts – slavery was always wrong – but the (formal) illegality of the acts.'

In *Prosecutor v. Musema*, the International Criminal Tribunal for Rwanda allowed the Prosecutor to present pre-1994 evidence in order to establish the *mens rea* needed for genocide. Thus, the ICTR jurisprudence allowed pre-1994 evidence of intent but not of conduct.'[54] In this case as well as subsequent ICTR cases, such as *Prosecutor v. Nahimana* we see an example where the Court allowed the introduction of evidence from outside the jurisdictional temporal window.[55] But this compares with *Prosecutor v. Barayagwiza*, in which the court interpreted its jurisdiction restrictively, holding that no facts pre-dating or post-dating 1994 could be used to support a count in the indictment.[56]

Continuing and composite crimes force courts to address conduct that exists over longer time periods than other, more familiar crimes such as murder. They create legal dilemmas not just for questions of jurisdiction but also around questions of evidence and admissibility. The cases identified here address the limits of legal time and represent compelling examples of how courts have attempted to wrestle with problems of strict temporality. In the ICC cases relating to post-election violence in contemporary Kenya, it is clear that a close reading of the ICC's charges allow us to reflect on the tension between specific instances of criminality (violence), on the one hand, and histories of inequalities and perceived injustices that have occurred over extended periods, on the other hand.

Cross-cultural differences in concepts of time abound in the social science literature. In *The Elementary Forms of the Religious Life*, Émile Durkheim notes that 'time' is socially constructed and the form it takes in each society reflects the activities and rhythms of the society's culture, reinforcing the regularity of

---

51 Moore 1898; see Crawford 2001, p. 131.

52 *Ibid*, pp. 4349 and 4375.

53 *Ibid*, p. 2824.

54 Citing ICTR, *The Prosecutor v. Musema*, ICTR-96-13-A, Trial Chamber, Judgment and Sentence, P164, 27 January 2000.

55 Trial Chamber, 3 December 2003, ICTR-99-52-T, P103.

56 Appeals Chamber, 12 September 2000, ICTR-97-19-AR72.

those activities and rhythms.[57] E.E. Evans-Pritchard similarly asserts that, '[For the Nuer] time ha[ve] not the same value throughout the year … The Nuer have no expression equivalent to 'time' in our language, and they cannot, therefore, speak of time as though it were something actual, which passes, can be wasted, can be saved, and so forth.'[58] And Clifford Geertz, in 'Person, Time, and Conduct in Bali', sustains that a Balinese calendar 'is not used … to measure the rate at which time passes … [I]t is adapted to and used for distinguishing and classifying discrete, self-subsistent particles of time … The cycles and super cycles are endless, unanchored, uncountable, and, as their internal order has no significance, without climax. They do not accumulate, they do not build, and they are not consumed. They do not tell you what time it is; they tell you what kind of time it is.'[59]

Contemporary approaches such as David M. Engel's 'Law, Time, and Community', also examine competing, cyclical or 'iterative' versus linear conceptions of time shared by residents of a rural American town. These different conceptions of time influence the community's responses to litigation and the law. Carol J. Greenhouse examines representations of time within American legal culture and social life. For Greenhouse the relationship between cultural conceptions of time – 'social time' – and the organisation and management of legal institutions 'temporality and legality' are conceptually fused in the West. As such they produce the terms in which social life acquires meaning.[60] This scholarship on temporality has established the role of time as socially constituted. Let us turn to the example with John to demonstrate how temporality and legality played out in the conceptions of my informants. John – a known Kenyan journalist – points out that in 2007–2008 neither Kenyatta nor Ruto were heads of state, so it is not clear why they, over others, would be seen as bearing the most responsibility.

> Neither of them was running for president. I don't think there was [responsibility] if you look at the violence and protest in ODM strongholds. I think you would see 'no Raila no peace', not 'no Ruto no peace', and especially in Kalenjin stronghold. So how on earth do you then begin to design these cases against the two of them? I think that it is possible to finger Uhuru Kenyatta for post-election violence in Naivasha and Nakuru, I think that it is possible. It is much more difficult to [connect him] to the North Rift.[61]

By referring to the slogan, 'No Raila, No Peace', John was explaining that those who supported Raila were fighting for his presidency and not for Ruto's (who was

57 Durkheim 1915.
58 Evans-Pritchard 1940, pp. 102–103.
59 Geertz 1973, p. 393.
60 Greenhouse 1989.
61 Interview with author.

in the ODM leadership). After the election results and the announcement that Kibaki had won again, it became clear that Raila, through his ODM supporters mostly from the Luo ethnic group in the ODM strongholds (like Kibera), refused to accept a situation in which Raila was not going to be in power. Much of this was connected to the problem of the concentration of power among a few families and ethnic groups.

From the time Jomo Kenyatta took office from the colonial Home Guards in 1963 to the last election, power was seen as remaining within a very tightly sealed vacuum in which the Kikuyu and the Kalenjin constituted a small community that governed all others and shielded their political and economic elite from accountability to the people and to the law.[62] The violence of 2007–2008 was, in many ways, seen as a response to the unwillingness of others to concede to the monopolization of power by particular members of the elite once again. Yet the media contributed to the production of the concept of the perpetrator by depicting the situation as ultimately being about the ethnic Kalenjin mobilizing against the Kikuyu. As Bornu, a Kenyan political analyst, explained:

> Some say the Kalenjin rose up as a community – though it's not true at all! If you just go back to reports of the violence, the violence was up and down the railway line. There was looting and violence in Mombasa, there were Kikuyu and Kisii evictions in Maasai Land; there was no violence in Central Highlands but Nairobi and going all the way to the border! So the idea that the Kalenjin were some … atavistic, blood thirsty. Others just served to demonize them. … The ignorance about the Kalenjin was mind-blowing. I mean the Kalenjin were organised so effectively … But when you talk to people in Nakuru or Kikuyus who had family or whatever in Nakuru, there was a point at which the Kalenjin were invading and there was just utter fear. [Because of their fear, people didn't] know what kind of monster [was] coming to attack [them]. But the reality was that the violence was across the board and along party lines and also along a very anti-Kikuyu level. Then you'd have to provoke the question of why is everybody standing up, rising up against the Kikuyu? What is going on? But the Kalenjin were very insistent that the violence was spontaneous, and were very insistent that any form of planning or organization happened after the announcement of the election results, not before.[63]

Bornu's statement highlights that there was not only a sense that the violence was perpetrated across the board by many actors – police, local people, outside forces, militia, gangs – but also that it was inspired by deep-seated histories of disenfranchisement and the monopolization of power throughout Kenya. In Kiamu, John, and Bornu's statements, we can begin to see that at the heart of the impunity gap is the difficulty in ascribing guilt to particular individuals;

---

62 Home Guards were African village policemen who were working for the British colonial government in Kenya to quash the Mau Mau struggle. They had a reputation of being extremely vicious in their anti-Mau Mau campaigns.

63 Interview with author.

some feel that the ICC's focus on command responsibility not only overlooks the guilt of those who actually engaged in criminal conduct, but that, in the Kenyan cases, it also produces a framework in which the cases are argued in a way that overlooks the temporality of collective responsibility for age-old political problems.

Understanding the inter-ethnic consolidation of Ruto's United Republican Party (URP) with Kenyatta's National Alliance Party (TNA), which came together to produce the Jubilee Party and its victory, is central to grasping the emergence of an impunity gap in the Kenyan national imaginary. It is worth asking how would-be 'perpetrators' of Kenya's 2007 post-election violence, according to the ICC, could facilitate the consolidation of historically opposed ethnic groups, whose candidates then won Kenya's 2013 presidential elections. On one hand, the histories of land dispossession during and following British colonialism produced the conditions through which Kenyatta and Ruto's Jubilee coalition could be perceived as settling a more than fifty-year-old history of injustice. On the other hand, since Kenya gained independence, political and economic power in government has circulated among the Kikuyu and Kalenjin elite to the exclusion of other groups. The recognition of these two realities suggests that the violence actually attests to the way that histories of dispossession became sedimented along various patronage lines. Thus, the attacks against the Kikuyus represented the mobilization of particular ethnic patronage networks to try to change the Kikuyu and/or Luo and Kalenjin monopolization of power in postcolonial Kenya. It is the realization of the deep-seated complexities of culpability playing out through a sense of communal responsibility to protect that has contributed to the recognition of the centrality of proximity and patronage. This sensibility of collective responsibility – instantiated through oathing, but later sedimented through patronage – informs the production of a popular national imaginary in which Ruto and Kenyatta are not widely seen as 'perpetrators' awaiting indictment of the ICC but as national heroes to be protected and celebrated.

My informant's answer to the related question of who should be held accountable instead highlights the extent to which collective responsibility is relevant. According to Ngogi, a local Kenyan activist:

> The financing of that violence involved the entire Kikuyu diaspora as well as [the] domestic population. People from southeast London to Texas were holding meetings and sending cash to support the cause. They were planning meetings all over this city. There w[as] supposed to be at one point a huge incident in Umoja and Eastlands where especially Luos were going to be flushed out of the houses that they allegedly occupied. Kikuyu shopkeepers in Umoja raised a lot of cash and it just so happened that the peace deal came before they were able to carry out the plan.[64]

---

64 *Ibid.*

Some of the Kenyans that we spoke with during fieldwork in Nairobi[65] alleged that Kenyatta and Ruto actually defended the powerless. From these interviews it became clear that the complexity of financing violence as a part of the co-perpetration of violence was not only central to parsing responsibility. Rather, the act of financing and arming fellow Kenyans was seen as a response to the call to protect the collective whole – the Kikuyu against Raila's supporters, the Luo, for example. Accordingly, what the Office of the Prosecutor (OTP) saw as Kenyatta's legal culpability was actually seen by members of the Kikuyu elders as a necessary act of communal responsibility in which he – as well as others in Kenya and throughout the diaspora – were perceived to be taking critical steps to protect his community from ethnic-inspired violence and to ensure Kikuyu prominence/dominance in Kenyan politics.

Uhuru Kenyatta's rapid rise to power is seen as an indicator of the importance of the notion of collective responsibility, in which it is understood that Kenyatta was obligated to contribute to the financing of the violence in order to protect his community against other ethnic forces set on displacing them from their land. With this rationale, Kenyatta's community saw him as protecting the collective, and thus they do not see him as culpable. The overt problem is that admitting to the existence of Kenyatta's participation and the role of others in actually financing the violence would be seen as a legal admission of guilt during the designated post-election period of violence. Instead, Kikuyus often make vague admissions by describing Kenyatta's actions as collectively appropriate. Statements such as, 'Uhuru stepped in because Mwai Kibaki was asleep.' Or, 'Kibaki was too weak, Mwai Kibaki was useless', and 'Uhuru is our hero because he took responsibility when it really mattered'.[66] These claims – with their legal implications – speak to the affective sentiments of solidarity and alliance through which contemporary Kenyans are asserting a new narrative about political violence in their country. According to interview participants, because of reprisal violence on the part of Luos against any ethnic group they felt had supported the Kibaki victory, the Kikuyu's in coordination with Kikuyu elders, mobilized forces to protect themselves in various places; hence the mobilization of the Mungiki forces. Actions taken in the Ruto camp, and by extension the Kalenjins (and Kenyatta through his Kikuyu networks), in terms of mobilization – i.e. financing and executing violent acts – were ultimately seen by participants as being in support of two principle players: Kibaki and Raila. The compromise related to this standoff eventually resulted in the creation of a new position, Prime Minister, as part of the power-sharing agreement in which historically

65 Concentrated ethnographic fieldwork and survey data collection for this project was funded by the National Science Foundation and conducted by the author and three researchers from May to December 2013 and then again in summer 2014. Surveys were disseminated in Kibera and Nashava, Kenya and focus groups were conducted in various sites throughout Western and Southern Kenya.

66 Interview data collected in Nairobi from May to December 2013.

opposed parties came together.[67] Thus, among a particular contingent, Kibaki and Raila were seen by many as the most invested parties in the post-election violence, and, therefore, though not seen as those engaged in proximate violence, when respondents were pressed to parse responsibility according to principles of international law, many argued that Kibaki and Raila should have been the ones seen as bearing the greatest responsibility and not Kenyatta and Ruto.

6. PROXIMITY, INTIMACY, AND REDIRECTING THE CULPABILITY OF THE PERPETRATOR

When we asked Marcus, a villager from Kibera, whether he thought Kenyatta was the most responsible, he, like many, responded by insisting that many Kenyans believed that Prosecutor Moreno Ocampo was interested in prosecuting those listed on the Waki Commission's list because the OTP was outsourcing a significant amount of its investigations to NGOs and others, who many discredited as being incompetent and far from thorough. As Marcus elaborates:

> So, how do these guys end up at the ICC? If not through a process of kind of political roulette, how does he end up there? That is completely arbitrary; you have twenty people or twenty plus people fingered for the violence by Waki, he narrowed it down too. I think a lot of people will be asking questions about why isn't so and so and why isn't so and so on the list, but I don't know by what logic somebody like John Michuki could have escaped? He was Internal Security Minister, the one who directly banned any type of street demonstrations. He was very much involved at the National Security, NSAC, and on top of that Michuki had said on multiple occasions he was directly ordering the police to shoot to kill Mungiki. But if you are not going to touch Michuiki, I don't see how then you are going to deal with reprisal violence in the North. The other person who should be at the ICC, I mean one would think, would be Maina Njenga [the head of the Mungiki] himself.[68]

By referring to the perception that the OTP accepted the names outlined in the Waki Commission report, Marcus suggests that the logic was political and, in some cases, arbitrary. He continued:

> If you are talking about the criteria for these kinds of charges to warrant a case at the ICC, I think one of the things that Luis Moreno Ocampo has been at pains to show is that there was a structured violence, that there was an organization with a hierarchy and so on. It is called Mungiki and its head is Miana Njenga. In many ways one can then begin to understand that there is something legitimate about the angle of Uhuru Kenyatta and William Ruto.[69]

---

67 Nicoll and Delaney 2013, pp. vii–ix.
68 Interview with author.
69 *Ibid.*

Yet, despite this concession about the plausibility of guilt, a range of actors, such as the police chief, members of the police force, and Mungiki gangs, were also seen as contributors to violence but were actually dropped from the list. Also part of the story, and as my informant explained, was that the police were part of this process. The existence of the police also raises questions about why the ICC's prosecution did not pursue the head of the Kenyan police force. Here the presumption was that the violence should not be attributed to one or two commanders. The planning for the violence was said to precede the elections and was mobilized as part of the defence of the Kikuyu. The reality is that there is not only a sense that the violence was perpetrated across the board by many actors – police, local people, outside forces, militia, gangs – but also that the violence was inspired by deep-seated histories of disenfranchisement in which various persons saw themselves as carrying out their obligations to protect their community. But despite the recognition of the responsibility to protect, the point, ultimately, is that they, and not Kenyatta and Ruto, were the ones who were seen as being engaged in inflicting proximate violence. Marcus maps out the forms of proximate violence relevant to the Mungiki phenomenon:

> There are a number of men that were targeted because of their ethnic leanings, and the link between those ethnic groups to certain political leanings. And because of that they were attacked in certain sex-selective ways. You know having their penises amputated, or having them sodomized, and because then when you think about them from the political reasons why it happened then they qualify as gender crimes … Sexual and gender-based crimes post-election have been downplayed. They're taken as serious crimes related to the election violence. The police have been implicated and other security agents that some victims have described in detail, that it is for sure the people that raped them were security agents that had been deployed to that area or to those places during the period of the chaos.
>
> So, for instance, in Kibera a number of victims have described the attire that the men that raped them were in and for some of them they described it in detail; they talk about the way the teargas canisters were dangling and making noises, those are some of the noises they remember. So we were concerned that our own security agents have been implicated and that the government has not done anything.[70]

As we see, the realities of intimate violence – rape, castration, sodomy – remain part of the ways that victims of violence are also conceptualizing guilt. Those responsible for violence against their bodies are those who actually committed the crimes: the man who raped, the boy next door who killed his neighbour, and the foot soldiers of the security forces who maimed. Yet the problem for many is that because of the ICC indictment it is the Kenyan government through the figure of Kenyatta and Ruto that is being held responsible for those alleged perpetrators of violence in the police and security forces.

---

70 *Ibid.*

In response to our question about whether Kenyatta and Ruto should assume responsibility for the 2007–2008 post-election violence, journalist, Ngugi turns around the question and asks us:

> Responsibility for what? Some of the worst violence happened in Western Kenya and, yes, it is often mentioned that Kisumu [is] burning, but it's actually not considered a media epicenter of the violence. And in both cases [they] let the state security forces off the hook. In Kakamega, Bungoma, in Kitale, the vast majority of people that were killed were killed by police bullets, usually found in [their] back; they were running away. If you omit that, then all the violence becomes is a long-held ethnic dispute. You know all the rhetoric that influenced – is it called Agenda Four items[71] – it is absolute *bullshit*.[72]

Here by referring to 'Agenda Four' items Ngugi is referring to part of the national dialogue and reconciliation efforts that took place after the 2007–2008 violence. Four agendas were proposed to address the way forward for Kenya. The fourth and final agenda item was to address 'long-term issues and solutions' and include items such as land reform, national unity, etc. The Agenda Four items were the last items agreed to in the Annan-brokered peace agreement. They had to do with further long-term peacebuilding concerns. But Ngugi's point is that the issue is a lot more complex than simply ethnicity and land. The issues are also about the perceptions of narrative erasures – the production of false narratives that are seen as being part of the maintenance of state power. He suggests that the violence was not simply 'routine' ethnic violence, as it was often framed. He insists that the security forces – those in proximate relations to daily citizens – were actively involved, and people from Western region were being targeted.

> I spent a lot of time, January and part of February, in the North Rift, in places like Kiptere, just around Eldoret town in the outskirts of Eldoret. I was scooping spent cartridges, G3 cartridges. I mean the cops had gone completely amuck ... because even the security forces ... were divided along party and ethnic lines.

He emphasizes how ethnically segmented the divisions became:

> If you went to the police station in Eldoret town, I remember the first time I went there on a Sunday and a policeman comes striding out. I am coming into the compound and she is coming out and she is loudly announcing, 'This is an ODM zone, so understand where you're coming.' I needed security to go into a place called

71 Following the violence over Kenya's disputed 2007 General Elections, the Kenyan Dialogue and Reconciliation forum was created to facilitate mediation among the various parties. As part of this process four agendas were identified as areas of focus for national dialogue and reconciliation. Agenda 4 focused on long-term issues and solutions such as land reform, legal and institutional reform, unemployment and several more. (See the National Accord and Reconciliation Act 2008 signed in Nairobi, Kenya on 1 February 2008).

72 Interview with author.

> Munyaka, which was a Kikuyu settlement, and she told me, 'Eh listen my friend this not the place, and now you have to make special arrangements, you are not going to find people here that are going to go in there.' The cops, General Service Unit, Administrative Police, and so on who were shooting up the place in Kiptere and so on were imported and it was very specific because they were Kenyan police and, again according to locals, again another narrative that's never discussed, Ugandans. But if you went to Moi referral hospitals and you found anyone who was working at Moi referral hospital in January/February 2008, [they say] there was an invasion by Administration Police-looking types of the hospital at one point, and they said these people could not speak Kiswahili. That is one of the stories you will also here in Kisumu.[73]

In this passage Ngugi counters what he sees as false narratives – or massive omissions of facts – in which the proximate role of the police, the security forces, and the use of foreign forces like the Ugandans were underplayed. He insists, rather, that the state security machine played a major role in the violence and were in fact the largest perpetrators. He argues that when you remove these major players from the story, the violence begins to look like a long-standing ethnic dispute. It involved a range of actors engaged in intimate killing whose affiliations were conveniently segmented along ethnicity and party alliances; but some of the worst forms of violence involved the police and security forces from nearby states that were imported to perpetrate violence. The implications debunk Kenyatta and Ruto's criminal responsibility for the perpetration of violence by suggesting that Kibaki had requested assistance from Museveni, who responded by sending security forces from Uganda to parts of the Rift and Western Kenya. The report that the 'police-looking types' did not speak Kiswahili was taken as further evidence that they were not Kenyan and had been 'imported.' He also seems to suggest that even Kenyan security forces were stationed in different areas, or at least 'imported' into certain hot spots like Eldoret, based on ethnicity/political affiliation. Given the way the security forces are 'divided along party and ethnic lines', the Kibaki government was calculating in its deployment of the forces. Thus Ngugi suggests that there was more at play than different ethnic communities fighting each other. The key point is that the violence was based on much more than ethnic patronage. It was about the fight to overtake government – at all costs – or for the Kibaki government to maintain power within it.

Of the most pronounced redirections of culpability – from Ruto and Kenyatta to the police, security services, or neighbours accused of stealing – were those accused of perpetrating the most intimate forms of violence: sexual violence ranging from rape to castration and sodomy. Proximity mattered in those contexts and notions of culpability were directly tied not to individual

---

73 *Ibid.*

commanders who directed and enabled violence but to those who themselves engaged in proximate violence.

7. CONCLUSION

Articulating guilt through narrow terms like superior responsibility limit the representational life of those deemed most responsible for violence. International criminal legal concepts of culpability rely not only on rational reasoning for clarifying the line of command, but they also depend on a particular production of the guilty perpetrator without whom violence would not be possible. Thus far we have seen that the different levels of perpetration: senior level and the execution level of proximate violence are not separate but are interconnected. How one may attribute guilt, and by extension how the perpetrator of violence is conceived becomes difficult when questions of historical collective responsibility are introduced.[74] This is especially a challenge because international crimes normally involve a plurality of individuals acting within the framework of a common plan. In this context, the direct perpetrators or proximate actors who physically commit the criminal acts – typically occupy low-ranking positions are set alongside those who orchestrate systematic commission and execution of violence. These notions of culpability and the related liability understood in legal circles are often argued in relation to strict temporal designations. And this is where the problem lies.

New international law assertions of culpability are not enough to make sense of the deep roots of violence. There is an affective dimension – an emotional connection to colonial injustices and proximate action that remains part of the postcolonial condition. But large numbers of the Kenyan public see the postcolonial complexities that have taken shape as being misdirected by the International Criminal Court indictments. Ultimately this has had implications for the construction of the African perpetrator as the Kenyan President or the Deputy President and the limits of the law in attributing histories of violence according to contemporary approaches to command responsibility.

The construction of international criminal law has involved the production of strict understandings and demarcations in time through which to attribute guilt. Rather than reflecting on historical developments or broader root causes, ICC jurisprudence has adopted a relatively strict view of temporality with the recognition that non-retroactivity or the principle of *nullum crimen sine lege* – no crime except what is proscribed by law – is one of the central principles of law. The criminalization of acts occurring over long periods of time is seen as potentially threatening this principle because it is hard to define what precisely

74 *Ibid.*

is being punished and when exactly the conduct becomes criminal. But this is where the problem lies.

The impunity gap represents an abyss between legal presumptions of temporally relevant responsibility, and the growing grassroots conception of who is actually criminally responsible for acts of violence – including historically relevant institutions such as colonial agents and discriminatory segregation politics. I have shown how – in relation to these historical realities – the impunity gap highlights a hierarchical/vertical disjuncture due to the limitations of attributing conduct from one person to the other – distinguishing between foot soldiers and 'those most responsible' – and the problem of legal time as it relates to strict applications of the temporality of violence. What the ICL impunity gap reveals is the difference between social and legal justice and the varying understandings of guilt and responsibility. It highlights the afterlife of a failure to balance power historically in postcolonial Kenya, set alongside the use of the law to rectify histories of dispossession manifest in acts of violence. We also see how fraught with meaning the assignment of culpability to one perpetrator really is – especially in contexts in which the state has failed to adequately address the needs of those victimised by violence.

Whether the disjuncture occurs because of a difference with attribution based on proximate violence, or because of the inability to reconcile contemporary violence in relation to guilt attributed within a strictly narrow temporal period in 2007–2008, the reality is that this impunity gap exists in the Kenyan political landscape because people recognize that legal time and the individualization of criminal responsibility do not account for the deep histories that produced the conditions under which police violence, ethnic rivalries, and land dispossession were made possible.[75] Rather, there is a realization that inscriptions of power in colonial Kenya were central to the play of power in post-independence Kenya. And since independence, power has never been balanced or distributed beyond those ethnic groups – the Kikuyu and Kalenjins – that inherited power. Yet, the other reality is that in postcolonial Africa, the afterlife of imperialism, colonialism, and the violence of dispossession persist deeply in the psychic life of social justice. And alongside ethnic divisions, there is also an awareness of the ways that imperial injustices remain part of the postcolonial reality – a continuity of structures of economic, legal and political power. And while the image of the African perpetrator as warlord and killer has been constructed through the law to produce a narrative of the merciless mercenary, the African head of state as perpetrator has been subject to another moral imaginary that represents a new shift.

75 The TJRC report tried to address these very questions, but the process was significantly delayed and marked with internal wrangling, which served to discredit the process significantly.

The Kenyan cases being pursued by the ICC demonstrate an alternate conceptualization of culpability. What they show us is that the impunity gap can actually be explained through affective sentiments of historical solidarity that suggest that not only do Africans want to end violence, impunity, and the abuses of the postcolonial elite, but they also want to reassert a new narrative imaginary about the political nature of contemporary violence in Kenya.

The new imaginary of collective crimes understood through a colonial-postcolonial continuum competes with the ICC perpetrator figure. It represents a new socio-cultural realization tied to particular historical attachments that reflect the reality that we live in a world where meanings of justice extend beyond the law. What we see is that the colonial–postcolonial continuum is complexly interconnected. Senses of the continuity with the past and present are tied to an emotional afterlife that shapes the subordination of liberal legalism to the realities of post-coloniality. These notions of continuity show how people understand collective responsibility in relation to affective and historically influenced domains. These affective forms structure engagements with justice and reproduce forms of desire, freedom, and ways of rejecting hegemony in daily life. In that process they produce an affective continuity in which agents struggle for the power to articulate meaning and produce relevance. Seen as thus, exploring the work of the temporal imagination in the legal practice can be enriched through bringing it into dialogue with transnational fields of power – such as international law – historically situated subjects who imagine transformative possibilities in contemporary democracy. The Jubilee Party victory of 2013 demonstrates how social justice can exceed the juridical. On one hand, the political elite were able to implement an UhuRuto promotional strategy and politicize ethnicity, leading to a merger and consolidation of the Jubilee Party and its deployment of a strategic narrative of colonial victimhood. On the other hand, we are seeing the emergence of a renewed sense of ethnic solidarity based on a different 'moral imaginary' within their respective to the culpability for violence in postcolonial Africa. The contemporary period is characterized by a rupture with the past in which the imagination and the imaginary is 'no longer mere fantasy'[76] but is constructed within a landscape of social practices and relations of power. Thus, when set alongside a broader temporal continuum, how one imagines the culpability of a perpetrator involves the new negotiations between individual agency in the reading of colonial and postcolonial history in relation to globally defined fields of possibility in which social knowledge contributes to the production of new meanings of justice.

To understand the play of the imagination and the conditions of possibility through which legal logic is reconceptualised, the interrogation of the figure of the perpetrator calls for new theoretical models for explaining how through conceptions of continuing crimes new global imaginaries of conflict and violence

[76] Appadurai 1996.

are being deployed to address histories of protest against liberal legal forms and their institutions. They are being deployed to rethink continuing challenges of violence and their impact on proximate social worlds and are providing the vocabulary for managing the globalization of the rule of law and the discourses of justice in terms that are meaningful.

Ultimately, the competing discourses that are embedded in conceptions of culpability are actually reflective of a turn in the modernity of international justice and its reassertion as an ontological problem – that of the existence of temporal continuities that have traditionally been written out of modern legality. The insistence of temporal linkages through colonial-postcolonial continuums call on us to rethink how articulations of temporal jurisdiction presumed to be 'natural' and rational are just as shaped by ideologies of constructing rationality as they are by actual connections. With this insight, the attribution of the perpetrator figure is a question of how temporal continuity as an ontological question is negotiated in complex sites of international meaning making.

BIBLIOGRAPHY

BOOKS AND JOURNAL ARTICLES

Appadurai 1996

Appadurai, A. 'Modernity at Large: Cultural Dimensions of Globalization', University of Minnesota Press, 1996.

Arendt 2003

Arendt, H., 'Responsibility and Judgment', Schocken, 2003.

Atieno-Odhiambo 1991

Atieno-Odhiambo, E.S., 'The Production of History in Kenya: The Mau Mau Debate', 25(2) Canadian Journal of African Studies, 1991, pp. 300–307.

Brants 2011

Brants, C., 'Guilty Landscapes', in Bailliet, C. and Franko Aas, K. (eds.), 'Cosmopolitan Justice and its Discontents', Routledge, 2011.

Cassese 2008

Cassese, 'International Criminal Law', Oxford University Press, 2008.

Cheeseman 2008

Cheeseman, N., 'The Kenyan Elections of 2007: An Introduction', 2(2) Journal of Eastern African Studies, 2008, pp. 166–184.

Crawford 2001

Crawford, J., 'The International Law Commission's Articles on State Responsibility: Introduction, Text and Commentaries', Cambridge University Press, 2001.

Drumbl 2007

Drumbl, M., 'Atrocity, Punishment and International Law', Cambridge University Press, 2007.

Durkheim 1915
Durkheim, E., 'Elementary Forms of Religious Life', Hollen Street Press, 1915.

Evans-Pritchard 1940
Evans-Pritchard, E.E., 'The Nuer: A Description of the Modes of Livelihood and Political Institutions of a Nilotic People', Oxford University Press, 1940.

Geertz 1973
Geertz, C., 'The Interpretation of Cultures', Basic Books, 1973.

Greenhouse 1989
Greenhouse, C.J. 'Just in Time: Temporality & the Cultural Legitimation of Law', 98 Yale L.J., 1989.

Hart 1958
Hart, H.M., 'The Aims of the Criminal Law', 23(3) Law and Contemporary Problems, 1958, pp. 401–441.

Juma 2009
Juma, M.K., 'African mediation of the Kenyan post-2007 election crisis', 27(3) Journal of Contemporary African Studies, 2009, pp. 407–430.

Kagwanja and Southall 2009
Kagwanja, P. and Southall, R., 'Introduction: Kenya – A democracy in retreat?', 27(3) Journal of Contemporary African Studies, 2009, pp. 259–277.

Mbembe 2001
Mbembe, A., 'On the Postcolony', University of California Press, 2001.

Meloni 2007
Meloni, C., 'Command Responsibility. Mode of Liability for the Crimes of Subordinates or Separate Offence of the Superior?', 5(3) Journal of International Criminal Justice, 2007, pp. 619–637.

Moore 1898
Moore, J.B., 'History and Digest of the International Arbitrations to which the United States has been a Party', US Government Printing Office, 1898.

Mueller 2014
Mueller, S.D., 'Kenya and the International Criminal Court (ICC): politics, election and the law', 8(1) Journal of Eastern African Studies, 2014, pp. 25–42.

Nicoll and Delaney 2013
Nicoll, A. and Delaney, J. (eds.), 'Kenya's election: risk of renewed violence', 19(1) International Institute for Strategic Studies, 2013.

Nissel 2004
Nissel, A., 'Continuing Crimes in the Rome Statute', 25 Michigan Journal of International Law, 2004.

Ogot 1974
Ogot, B (ed.), 'Zamani: A survey of East African history', East African Publishing House and Longman Group, 1974.

Simpson 2007
Simpson, G.J., 'Law, War & Crime: War Crimes, Trials and the Reinvention of International Law', Polity Press, 2007.

Van Sliedregt 2012
Van Sliedregt, E., 'Individual Criminal Responsibility in International Law', Oxford Monographs in International Law, 2012.

Wa Kinyatti 2009
Wa Kinyatti, M., 'History of Resistance in Kenya: 1884–2002', Mau Mau Research Centre, 2009.
Wa Kinyatti 1977
Wa Kinyatti, M., 'Mau Mau: The Peak of African Political Organization in Colonial Kenya', 5(2) Kenya Historical Review, 1977, pp. 287–311.

JURISPRUDENCE

Arbitral Tribunal 1990
Arbitral Tribunal, Rainbow Warrior (New Zealand v. France), 20 R.I.A.A. 217, 30 April 1990.
ICC 2013
ICC, Prosecutor v. William Samoei Ruto and Joshua Arap Sang, ICC-01/09–01/11-1123, 13 December 2013.
ICC 2013
ICC, Prosecutor v. William Samoei Ruto and Joshua Arap Sang, ICC-01/09–01/11-859, 16 August 2013.
ICC 2009
ICC, Situation in the Republic of Kenya, Request for authorization of an investigation pursuant to Article 15, ICC-01/09–3, 26 November 2009.
ICTR 2003
ICTR, Prosecutor v. Ferdinand Nahimana, Jean-Bosco Barayagwiza and Hassan Ngeze, ICTR-99–52-T, 3 December 2003.
ICTR 2000
ICTR, Prosecutor v. Jean-Bosco Barayagwiza, ICTR-97–19-AR72, 12 September 2000.
ICTR 2000
ICTR, Prosecutor v. Musema, ICTR-96–13-A, 27 January 2000.

TREATIES, LEGISLATION AND AGREEMENTS

(Hague) Convention (IV) respecting the Laws and Customs of War on Land and its annex: Regulations concerning the Laws and Customs of War on Land, 18 October 1907.
(Hague) Convention (X) for the Adaptation to Maritime Warfare of the Principles of the Geneva Convention, 18 October 1907.
Kenya, National Accord and Reconciliation Act 2008 1 February 2008.
Rome Statute of the International Criminal Court, 2187 UNTS 90/37, 17 July 1998.

OTHERS

Commission of Inquiry into Post-Election Violence, 'The Waki Commission Report', 2008.

Human Rights Watch, 'High Stakes: Political Violence and the 2013 Elections in Kenya', February 2013.

ICC, 'Kenyatta case: Trial adjourned until 7 October 2014', ICC-CPI-20140331-PR991, 31 March 2014.

ICC, 'The Prosecutor v. Uhuru Muigai Kenyatta Case Information Sheet', ICC-PIDS-KEN-02–010/14 /15_Eng.

Ipsos-Synovate, 'One Year into the Jubilee Government: A Reality-Check by Kenyans', 14 March 2014.

Jackson, Justice Robert H., 'Opening Statement Before the International Military Tribunal', 21 November 1945.

Robins, S., 'To Live as Other Kenyans Do: A Study of the Reparative Demands of Kenyan Victims of Human Rights Violations', International Center for Transitional Justice, July 2011.

The Kenya National Dialogue and Reconciliation (KNDR) Monitoring Project, 'Progress in Implementation of the Constitution and other reforms', October 2011.

BUILDING THE BASE

Local Accountability for Conflict-Period Sexual Violence

Kim Thuy Seelinger and Julie Freccero

1. INTRODUCTION

Sexual violence during periods of armed conflict occurs in many forms. On one hand, it may be committed strategically as a war crime, crime against humanity, or act of genocide – as when tens of thousands of men and women were raped or sexually tortured during the war in Bosnia twenty years ago,[1] or during Rwanda's 100-day genocide in 1994, when thousands of women were raped or had their genitals mutilated.[2]

On the other hand, sexual violence during wartime may also happen for non-strategic, non-military reasons – as in 'opportunistic' violations committed by fellow civilians, intimate partners, or errant armed actors.[3] In this sense, it may be rooted in localised gender norms that preceded the conflict and which will, in all likelihood, persist after it.

The pursuit of legal accountability for different kinds of conflict-period sexual violence has traditionally implicated different actors. For the past twenty years, the investigation and prosecution of sexual violence as a war crime, crime against humanity, or act of genocide, have typically been taken up by actors linked to international tribunals. On the other hand, local actors responsible for addressing day-to-day crimes of sexual violence during peacetime – healthcare providers, police officers, prosecutors, community leaders and civil society organisations – become the frontline responders when these basic crimes occur during conflict periods as well.

What bears new and deeper consideration is the extent to which these local actors may hold the key to accountability for *international* crimes of sexual

1 Stigmayer 1994. For a discussion of the psychological and political aspects of survivors experiences, see Skjelsbaek 2012.

2 Bijleveld et al. 2009.

3 See Hossain et al. 2014; Palermo, Bleck and Peterman 2014, pp. 602–12; and Wirtz et al. 2013, available at: www.conflictandhealth.com/content/7/1/13.

violence, as well. The truth is, local nurses in a rural health clinic and police officers on routine duty in the streets of the capital have a fundamental role in the documentation, investigation, and prosecution of sexual violence committed as a war crime, crime against humanity, and act of genocide.

This may provoke scepticism in some. It is true that basic response to sexual and gender-based crimes is limited in many areas of the world, where medical care providers and police officers are not always sensitive to, or skilled in addressing sexual offences or gender-based violence generally. It is also true that acute insecurity, collapse of infrastructure, lack of mobility, and heightened resource constraints during conflict periods can cripple even the most functional healthcare and law enforcement systems.

However, we are not where we were twenty years ago. Significant gains have been made in terms of domestic legislation of gender-related offences, local response to crimes of sexual violence, and funding for survivor support programmes. So what do we know about the state of basic documentation of sexual violence in local health clinics and police stations? What are the primary challenges to reporting, investigation, and prosecution of sexual offences generally? What lessons can be drawn from recent conflict periods in order to adapt basic response and documentation of sexual violence in future conflict periods?

This article explores ground-level efforts to secure legal accountability for sexual violence in four countries: Kenya, Liberia, Sierra Leone, and Uganda. It draws on a recent study conducted by the Human Rights Centre at the University of California, Berkeley (HRCe), as well as an historic report-back workshop held in Kampala, Uganda, in August 2015. The article introduces the 'local actors' who play a key role in response to day-to-day sexual violence during peacetime and how they also play a key role in the documentation, investigation, and prosecution of conflict-period sexual violence. Then, after drawing on relevant findings from the HRCe's four-country study, the chapter presents signs of legislative and institutional progress in the case study countries. It closes with four considerations for the improvement of local capacity to address sexual violence as a war crime, crime against humanity, and act of genocide.

2. LOCAL ACTORS: WHO THEY ARE AND WHY THEY ARE IMPORTANT

For the past twenty years, pursuit of conflict-period crimes of sexual violence that may constitute war crimes, crimes against humanity, and acts of genocide has fallen primarily to investigation and prosecution teams from international and hybrid tribunals such as the International Criminal Court for the Former Yugoslavia (ICTY), the International Criminal Tribunal for Rwanda (ICTR), the

Special Court for Sierra Leone (SCSL) and the Extraordinary Chambers of the Courts of Cambodia (ECCC).

Most recently at the International Criminal Court, the Office of the Prosecutor (OTP) has charged sexual violence as a war crime and crime against humanity in several cases ranging from the Central African Republic to Kenya.[4] However, the OTP's success has been limited by the tremendous difficulties of collecting and preserving evidence of sexual violence many years after its occurrence, identifying and protecting witnesses, and establishing a clear link between physical perpetrators of sexual violence and the higher level commander on trial.[5]

In ICC 'situation countries', local actors who are tasked with response, support, and justice in cases of day-to-day sexual violence – the healthcare providers, police officers, prosecutors, community groups and civil society organisations – are also the frontline responders when it occurs during periods of armed conflict.

As such, these local actors play a critical role in the pursuit of accountability for conflict-period atrocities that violate the Rome Statute, as well. This is not only because of the principle of complementarity, which posits that the ICC and national governments should work hand in hand to address the full spread of international crimes committed in a given situation, but also for pragmatic reasons.

First, domestic actors – healthcare workers, police officers, prosecutors, local civil society groups – are closer to the evidence, the witnesses, and physical perpetrators. They are present during the conflict period; they are better able to record violations contemporaneously; they have a better chance of assisting victims and witnesses during the crisis period or of finding them after the fighting is over. In some cases, the acts they document and the evidence they collect can help illuminate broader patterns of violence across a jurisdiction, or capture local knowledge about troop movement or relationships among armed actors.[6] These threads of information may later indicate that individual crimes were also part of a larger war crime, crime against humanity, or genocidal effort. They can thus lay a foundation for later prosecution of international crimes – either by a local or international tribunal. Assuming there is no political

4 For example, Jean-Pierre Bemba from the Central African Republic was charged with two counts of crimes against humanity (murder and rape), as well as with three counts of war crimes (murder; rape and pillaging). *The Prosecutor v. Jean-Pierre Bemba Gombo.* Now-President Uhuru Kenyatta of Kenya was charged with five counts of crimes against humanity (murder; deportation or forcible transfer of population; rape; other inhumane acts; persecution, including by means of rape and other inhumane acts.) The case, *The Prosecutor v. Uhuru Muigai Kenyatta,* was withdrawn in December 2014.

5 For an excellent review of sexual violence investigation and prosecution at the ICC, see Hayes 2015.

6 For a discussion of the use of 'pattern evidence' in cases of sexual violence, see Aranburu 2010.

interference in the process, local investigators and prosecutors should have more immediate and long-term access to victims and witnesses than international entities would have.

Second, domestic actors may have more flexibility to pursue crimes of sexual violence committed during periods of armed conflict. Where an act is simply a violation of domestic penal laws – as in a case of intimate partner violence or a non-strategic rape of one civilian by another, local investigators and prosecutors can pursue the case accordingly. Where an act is later understood to constitute a war crime, crime against humanity, or act of genocide, prosecutors in countries that have ratified and domesticated the Rome Statute could prosecute an act of sexual violence as such. Or, if it is not feasible to gather evidence of the additional contextual and linkage elements that the Rome Statute requires, local prosecutors can still pursue the direct, individual act of sexual violence using the most appropriate domestic laws criminalising sexual offences.

The ability of local actors to detect, respond to, and document crimes of sexual violence committed during periods of armed conflict can thus determine not only the likelihood of later prosecution under domestic penal laws but also as war crimes, crimes against humanity, and acts of genocide. It is therefore essential to understand their day-to-day challenges during peacetime in order to improve access to justice for survivors of conflict-period sexual violence as well. In developing this understanding, we also deepen our understanding of the true potential and limitations of 'complementarity' as a practice.

3. THE STUDY

To improve understanding of domestic-level accountability for sexual violence, the Human Rights Center conducted a four-country study from 2011 to 2014, in Kenya, Liberia, Sierra Leone, and Uganda. The goal of the study was to identify and describe major barriers and approaches to legal accountability for sexual violence in these four countries. The specific objectives were to identify key challenges and strategies related to reporting, investigating, and prosecuting cases of sexual violence. In addition, the study aimed to gather relevant lessons learned during recent periods of armed conflict or political violence.

Kenya, Liberia, Sierra Leone and Uganda were selected as case studies because of their diverse political contexts, their histories of sexual violence reported and documented during conflict periods, and significant policy and programmatic responses to sexual violence. Fieldwork sites included capital cities as well as relatively rural cities or towns that had been directly affected by conflict-related violence.[7]

Research teams at the Human Rights Center first conducted desk research on the nature of sexual violence during and after periods of conflict, and on accountability and support mechanisms available in each country. Researchers then conducted a total of 279 semi-structured interviews with representatives of governments, UN agencies, and civil society organisations in Kenya (N=59), Liberia (N=115), Sierra Leone (N=27), and Uganda (N=78). Study participants included both policymakers and practitioners working in healthcare, law enforcement, the judiciary, prosecution units, civil society organisations and traditional justice systems. Participants were selected based on their roles or expertise within the organisations and institutions involved in sexual violence response during and/or after the conflict periods.

Using a semi-structured interview guide, researchers asked study participants about the major challenges and strategies relevant to their own work on sexual violence cases, as well as their broader views on barriers to accountability for sexual violence. With participants who had worked on sexual violence issues during conflict periods, researchers also explored conflict-specific challenges and practices employed during those time periods. The interview data was coded and analysed to identify common themes related to the reporting, investigation, and prosecution of cases of sexual violence across the four case study countries.

The final report, 'The Long Road: Accountability for Sexual Violence in Conflict and Post-conflict Settings'[8] was launched in August of 2015 at the Missing Peace Practitioners' Workshop on Accountability for Sexual Violence in Kampala, Uganda. The three-day workshop, hosted by the Human Rights Center and the Uganda Fund as part of the Missing Peace Initiative,[9] brought together over seventy practitioners from Kenya, Liberia, Sierra Leone, Uganda, South Sudan and eastern DRC to discuss the findings of the four-country study, exchange practices and resources across countries, and brainstorm priority measures for improving the documentation and prosecution of sexual violence as an international crime.[10]

---

7 Interview sites included Kisumu, Nakuru, and Nairobi in Kenya; Monrovia, Paynesville, Owensgrove District, Kakata, Totota, Gbarnga, Ganta, and Saclepea in Liberia; Freetown, Port Loko, and Kenema in Sierra Leone; and Gulu and Kampala in Uganda.

8 Seelinger and Freccero, 'The Long Road: Accountability for Sexual Violence in Conflict and Post-Conflict Settings', August 2015, available at: https://www.law.berkeley.edu/centers/human-rights-center/programs/sexual-violence-program/.

9 The Missing Peace Initiative, co-chaired by the Sexual Violence Program of the Human Rights Center, the United States Institute of Peace (USIP), the Peace Research Institute Oslo (PRIO), and Women in International Security (WIIS) convenes academics, policymakers, and practitioners to examine the issue of sexual violence in conflict, identify gaps in knowledge, and improve response.

10 For more information about the Missing Peace Practitioners' Workshop, see: https://www.law.berkeley.edu/centers/human-rights-center/programs/sexual-violence-program/.

This article provides an overview of key findings from the study as well as priority actions for improving accountability for sexual violence in conflict and post-conflict settings. In addition, based on research findings and later discussions at the Missing Peace Practitioners' Workshop in Kampala, it offers key considerations for improving the reporting, investigation, and prosecution of sexual violence as an international crime.

4. ACCOUNTABILITY CHALLENGES DURING RECENT CONFLICT

During periods of conflict in Kenya, Liberia, Sierra Leone, and Uganda, efforts to bring about legal accountability for sexual violence were minimal. Local reporting, investigation, and prosecution of sexual violence during conflict were hindered by ongoing security challenges, limited staffing and resources, and a general breakdown of systems and services. The following provides an overview of the key barriers to accountability during periods of active conflict or political violence.

4.1. REPORTING

According to key informants across the four case study countries, conflict periods both exacerbated existing barriers to reporting and created new challenges. For example, key informants reported that survivors may face additional layers of stigma in situations where rape had been committed by a member of a particular rebel, military, or ethnic group. For example, in Northern Uganda, women and girls who were forcibly married to or raped by LRA members were especially stigmatised and, in some cases, were rejected from their communities. Due to the potential social consequences of reporting, few survivors were willing to come forward to speak about their experiences both during and after the conflict.

In addition, community leadership structures for receiving reports of violence and addressing disputes were dismantled. For example, in Sierra Leone and Uganda, informants noted that in some displacement camps, there were no community leaders, while in others, several community leaders were crowded into the same areas, creating confusion in leadership roles.

Many survivors, particularly those raped by soldiers or rebel group members, did not know their rights or how to report incidents. Furthermore, in all case study countries, the state was implicated in the violence, which meant there were few safe channels for reporting to the police and few ways to ensure the safety of survivors afterward.

> If a soldier raped a woman, the woman had to report to the military, you know, to the same soldiers. And so women kept silent.
> – Practitioner, NGO, Uganda

> You must understand that Kibera is mostly [opposition-party] territory. So it was the police themselves who were standing on the main road there, shooting into our homes. Who were we to report to?
> – Staff, safe shelter, Kenya

Conflict situations also posed major structural barriers to reporting and seeking services. Many police and health facilities were closed or operated at limited capacity due to severely damaged physical infrastructure and staffing shortages. Even when government facilities were functioning, staff and survivors both faced significant access challenges, including, for example, transportation disruptions, roads blocked by fires, or the fear of being stopped by armed actors.

Finally, in the midst of conflict and emergency, sexual violence response was not prioritised. Governments and NGOs were more concerned with maintaining security and order and providing food, water, shelter, and basic medical care, particularly in the early stages of the conflicts. Informants reported that the police often did not view sexual violence as a serious issue requiring immediate response when compared to murder and forced displacement.

> In a time of chaos and upheaval, rape was the least concern in the eyes of law enforcement. To them, they were there to maintain order, maintain peace, and protect lives and property. But rape isn't visible...
> – Practitioner, NGO, Kenya

Strategies to improve reporting in conflict settings focused on creating accessible reporting channels and facilitating access to services. These included operating 24-hour hotlines offering immediate counselling and transportation to the hospitals offering post-rape care, and training teams of community-based first responders to assist and refer survivors.

4.2. INVESTIGATION

Research identified a number of evidence-collection challenges during periods of armed conflict or emergency. Due to security and mobility challenges mentioned previously, survivors often reported health facilities long after incidents occurred or not at all. In addition, the health sectors' capacity to provide care for sexual violence survivors was curtailed by the limited number of skilled providers in conflict-affected areas. Many providers fled the areas where violence broke out, were unable or afraid to travel to work, or were sent to areas with even greater needs. As one provider in Kenya explained:

> During the postelection violence, we had so many patients who were admitted ... but our staff were also suffering. Our staff could not even come to work because it was dangerous at that time.
>
> – Nurse, hospital, Kenya

In conflict settings, police and healthcare providers are often overwhelmed with emergency response and depleted resources, making it difficult to manage the lengthy examination and investigation processes required in sexual violence cases. Police may have limited access to survivors and witnesses during the investigation process in a conflict setting, as people are displaced from their homes and it may be difficult to contact. Specific considerations for the documentation and management of sexual violence cases in emergency settings is rarely included in police and health sector guidelines. One exemplary exception is Kenya's 2009 National Guidelines on the Management of Sexual Violence for healthcare providers produced by the Ministry of Health. Based on lessons learned from the post-election violence period and advocacy efforts by civil society, the guidelines were revised to include a short section on response in humanitarian settings which emphasised the importance of collecting forensic evidence.

Another significant barrier to accountability for conflict-periods sexual violence is the fact that evidentiary requirements for proving sexual violence as a war crime, crime against humanity, or act of genocide are simply not well understood by healthcare providers or police on the ground. It is therefore unlikely that they will recognise, collect or document relevant evidence properly. Further, domestic investigation of sexual violence committed by state actors is also unlikely in areas where the current government is implicated in the violence perpetrated during conflict.

4.3. PROSECUTION

At the time of research, there had been no meaningful efforts by state prosecutors to try conflict-period sexual violence in the domestic court system, either as domestic or international crimes. The only efforts to address sexual violence through the domestic courts have been initiated by civil society organisations. For example, in Kenya, a coalition of civil society organisations led by the Coalition on Violence against Women (COVAW) and the Kenya Section of the International Commission of Jurists (ICJ-Kenya) filed a constitutional complaint, claiming that the government failed to uphold its obligation to protect Kenyan citizens from sexual violence during the period of post-election violence. The public interest litigation, which is still pending, aims to establish the government of Kenya's active responsibility in the commission of sexual violence and seeks an expanded understanding of justice for survivors that includes psychosocial support, physical security, and apology from the state.

Also, creative use of universal jurisdiction allows local documentation of atrocities to still be useful where local prosecution of international crimes is not feasible. One striking example was found with the Global Justice and Research Project, a Liberian group that collects survivor testimony as documentation of atrocities committed during the country's back-to-back civil wars. The group works in collaboration with Swiss Group Civitas Maxima to transmit the evidence to European authorities that can prosecute the crimes in *their* domestic courts. In 2014, these combined efforts led to the arrest of a former NPFL commander in Belgium and a former leader of the United Liberation Movement rebel group in Switzerland.

5. SIGNS OF PROGRESS

Despite significant challenges, there are several reasons for optimism about the developing potential of domestic actors to address sexual violence committed during armed conflict, including that which may constitute a violation of the Rome Statute. One key development comes in the form of legal and institutional frameworks: Kenya, Liberia, Sierra Leone and Uganda have benefited from strong new legislation, institutional development with respect to sexual offences and international crimes. These provide a stronger foundation in which local actors from government and civil society can work.

5.1. NEW LAWS

Domestic legislation governing sexual and gender-based violence has evolved significantly in the four case study countries since their most recent periods of conflict or political unrest. Many with recent amendments expand lists of offences or the specific definition of rape. Further, the four countries demonstrated varying degrees of progress towards domesticating the Rome Statute.

In terms of sexual and gender-based violence laws, the Kenyan Parliament enacted the Sexual Offences Act (SOA) in 2006, prior to the post-election violence of 2007–2008. It is a remarkably comprehensive law: not only does it assert an expansive list of criminalised offences (from rape to child pornography), but it also prescribes the manner in which cases are to be investigated, victims are to be supported in court, and convicted persons' identities are to be tracked through various databases. Unfortunately, a task force reviewing sexual violence cases in 2012 found that no files contained sufficient evidence for prosecution under the SOA.[11]

In Liberia, the penal code in effect during the conflict periods defined sexual offences in limited terms that did not encompass many incidents that occurred during the civil wars, such as gang rape and the rape of men and boys. This was rectified years later through the Rape Amendment Act of 2006, still referred to as the 'New Rape Law'. Though passed less than a decade ago, the amendment had been conceived of years earlier due to brutal acts of sexual violence that Liberian female law reform advocates had observed during the civil wars. Those acts included rape with objects, rape committed by male and female perpetrators, gang rape, and sexual offences committed under threats of violence and/or after intoxicating the survivor. All of these are now criminal offences. The law also designates eighteen as the age of consent and is written broadly enough to encompass sexual acts against men and boys.[12]

During the conflict in Sierra Leone, criminalisation of sexual offences was based on an antiquated British law – the Offences against the Persons Act of 1861, which penalises but does not clearly define rape. The law also criminalises other forms of sexual contact such as abduction, sexual contact with minors, and indecent assault. The offences accounted only for female victims.[13] In 2012, Sierra Leone had passed the Sexual Offences Act (SOA). The SOA criminalises offences ranging from rape to caretaker sexual abuse of a person with a mental disability. Notably, it criminalises all non-consensual sexual activity, including sexual activity involving a husband and a wife. Furthermore, it contains specific systems-oriented prescriptions, such as expectations for police response and prohibiting fees for medical treatment and reporting.

Uganda's Penal Code of 1950, which was in effect during the conflict with the Lord's Resistance Army, lacked meaningful address of sexual violence. However, it did list rape, defilement, prostitution, and other sexual offences in its 'Offences against Morality' section. The Code was amended in 1990 and again in 2007 to reflect changes in penalties for offences and to broaden the coverage of laws on defilement and similar acts.[14] The Code is still in effect, criminalising the rape of female victims, defilement (defined as the rape of a

11 Amran, 'Post-Election Violence Suspects May Face International Law', *Standard Digital News*, 18 August 2012, available at: www.standardmedia.co.ke/?articleID=2000064300; Maliti, 'Kenyan Prosecutor: Insufficient Evidence Has Made Prosecuting Post-Election Violence Cases Difficult', *International Justice Monitor*, 26 October 2012, available at: www.ijmonitor.org/2012/10/kenyan-prosecutor-insufficient-evidence-has-made-prosecuting-post-election-violence-cases-hard/.

12 Cummings 2011, pp. 223, 236.

13 United Kingdom and Ireland Offences Against the Person Act (1861), Cap 100, s. 48–55.

14 Uganda Penal Code Act of 1950, Uganda Legal Information Institute, Cap 120, ss. 123–151. See also Uganda's Penal Code (Amendment) Act (2007).

minor), indecent assault, and 'unnatural offences' (defined as 'carnal knowledge of a person against the order of nature').[15] In 2009 and 2010, the Ugandan Parliament passed a slate of thematic laws criminalising domestic violence (DV), trafficking in persons, and female genital mutilation/cutting (FGM/C). The Ugandan Parliament is also now considering a Sexual Offences Bill and the Witness Protection Bill.

Legal frameworks for prosecuting sexual violence as an *international* crime, as outlined in the Rome Statute, were progressing slowly but steadily. All four countries are signatory to the Rome Statute.[16] At time of fieldwork, though, only Kenya and Uganda had domesticated it.

Kenya's International Crimes Act (2008) adopts the Rome Statute's definitions of war crimes, crimes against humanity, and acts of genocide[17] and lays out the terms of cooperation between Kenyan state entities and the ICC. The act applies only to international crimes committed after 1 January 2009, the date it came into force. Similarly, in Uganda, the International Criminal Court Act (2010) adopts the Rome Statute's definitions of international crimes,[18] including the statute's references to forms of sexual violence. Both were adopted after the countries' recent periods of conflict and neither law is understood to have retrospective application.

5.2. NEW INSTITUTIONS

Another reason for optimism is the investment of time and resources into the development of relevant expertise in both the police and prosecution bodies in the countries studied. This often came in the form of new sub-institutions: specialised police and prosecution units to respond to crimes of sexual and gender-based violence.

In terms of police, researchers observed the establishment of specialised units focused on sexual and gender-based violence. They ranged from police teams focused mainly on supporting victims of sexual violence to dedicated corps with exclusive mandate over investigations of sexual and gender-based violence cases.

For example, within the Uganda Police Force (UPF), cases of sexual and gender-based violence have typically been handled by two law enforcement

---

15 Uganda Penal Code 1950, para. 145.

16 Kenya signed 11 August 1999 and ratified 15 March 2005. Liberia signed 17 July 1998 and ratified 22 September 2004. Sierra Leone signed 17 October 1998 and ratified 15 September 2000. Uganda signed 17 March 1999 and ratified 14 June 2002. See www.icc-cpi.int/en_menus/asp/states%20parties/Pages/the%20states%20parties%20to%20the%20rome%20statute.aspx.

17 Kenya International Crimes Act (2008), Article 4.

18 Uganda International Criminal Court Act (2010), Articles 7, 8 and 9.

entities: the Child and Family Protection Unit (CFPU) and the Directorate of Criminal Investigations (CID), respectively.[19] CFPU officers support victims of sexual and gender-based violence in arbitration, networking, guidance and counselling. In those cases, general officers from the CID typically conduct the investigations, calling upon colleagues from the CFPU for support with interviewing or survivor care as needed. In 2013, a special Gender-based Violence Department was established within the CID to strengthen its internal competence in investigating these crimes.[20]

In Sierra Leone, 'Family Support Units' (FSUs) were established within the Sierra Leone Police Force as early as 2001. Once thought of as just an access point for women and girls to report domestic violence, FSUs now respond to a broader range of cases related to sexual and gender-based violence. FSU officers register claims and conduct investigations when a survivor of sexual and gender-based violence reports to a police station. Moreover, they also conduct countrywide outreach about these crimes through media and other educational programmes.[21]

The most permanent and specialised police unit researchers observed was in Liberia, where a dedicated police unit called the Women and Children's Protection Service (WACPS) was established in 2005.[22] Housed under the Criminal Investigations Division of the Liberia National Police, WACPS is mandated to 'investigate all forms of violence disproportionately affecting women, such as domestic violence, sexual abuse, prostitution, illegal adoption and child abandonment, and human trafficking.'[23] In practice, whenever a complaint involves a woman or a child, WACPS is expected to respond.[24] It is seen as more approachable and better sensitised to do so – in comparison to 19% of the overall national police force, 33% of WACPS officers are female.[25]

---

19 In 1995, the UPF first created 'gender desks', or reception desks in police stations for women filing complaints of gender-based violence. However, in 1998, the UPF broadened the mandate to include children and the family and changed the name to the Child and Family Protection Unit (CFPU).

20 The Gender-based Violence Department of the Directorate of Criminal Investigations was not functional at the time of fieldwork (September and October 2013). See also a statement by CIID Director Grace Akello in a Ugandan news report during the August 2015 Missing Peace Kampala Workshop, available at: www.newvision.co.ug/news/672690-police-to-institute-sexual-violence-unit.html.

21 For example, in cooperation with social workers of the Ministry of Social Welfare, Gender and Children's Affairs, FSU officers in Sierra Leone also run a phone hotline to assist survivors calling in for support.

22 UNICEF, 'News Note: New Women and Children Protection Section for Liberia's Police', 1 September 2005, available at: www.unicef.org/media/media_28159.html.

23 Griffiths 2011.

24 Anonymous interview with police official, Liberia, August 2013.

25 Bacon, 'Building an Inclusive, Responsive National Police Service: Gender-Sensitive Reform in Liberia, 2005–2011', Innovations for Successful Societies, Princeton University, available at: www.princeton.edu/successfulsocieties; anonymous interview with police representative, Liberia, August 2012. Note that interviewees mentioned that even within this specialised

In terms of prosecution models for sexual offences, researchers observed a few different models that ranged from the ad hoc delegation of sexual and gender-based violence cases to specific prosecutors with experience handling these offences, to the establishment of one intensive, fully-dedicated prosecution unit.

For example, Uganda's Directorate of Public Prosecution has created a 'Sexual Offences Section' in Kampala, consisting of four full-time prosecutors who also handle other kinds of cases.[26] In Kenya, the Office of the Director of Public Prosecutions has a similar gender-based violence unit whose prosecutors work on a variety of other cases until called upon for expertise on sexual and gender-based offences.[27]

Liberia, on the other hand, has adopted a more intensive approach to specialised prosecution. Liberia's 'Sexual and Gender-based Violence Crimes Unit' (known locally as the 'Crimes Unit' or 'SGBV CU') was established in 2009. The unit's mandate is to improve prosecutorial response to complaints of sexual offences, based on a victim-centred approach.[28] The staff includes not only prosecutors, but case support staff as well as staff focused on the welfare of the survivor engaging the formal legal system. The team conducts outreach about legal rights related to gender violence; it also runs a hotline through which it runs a referral and advice service.

6. CONSIDERATIONS FOR IMPROVING DOMESTIC ACCOUNTABILITY FOR CONFLICT-PERIOD SEXUAL VIOLENCE

In light of research findings and the report-back discussion held in Kampala in August 2015, we offer the following considerations for improving the potential of local accountability for sexual violence that occurs during periods of armed conflict.

unit, it can be hard to recruit and retain female officers. In Liberia, police rotations require years of service out in the rural counties – there is not always separate living space for female officers. Also, informants explained that it is very difficult to move with one's children for each assignment, so many women do not apply to the police force.

26 Anonymous interview with prosecutor, Uganda, September 2013.

27 Anonymous interview with prosecutors, Kenya, March 2014.

28 Abdulai, *Evaluation: Strengthening of Prosecution of SGBV Offenses through support to the Sexual and Gender Based Violence Crimes Unit (SGBV CU)*, UNFPA, Monrovia, November 2010, p. 14.

6.1. IMPROVING REPORTING DURING CONFLICT

Reducing such barriers to reporting during conflict is, first and foremost, critical in order to ensure that survivors can access medical care and psychosocial support. However, facilitating reporting during conflict is important for another reason: it can serve as an opportunity to collect evidence that may prove essential to later prosecution. Contemporaneous documentation of survivors' individual experiences of sexual violence can contribute to the prosecution of international crimes of sexual violence after an acute emergency period has ended and it becomes clear that a survivor's individual experience may have been part of a larger, strategic attack.

It is also important to facilitate the reporting of sexual violence during conflict because many of the local civil society organisations receiving reports and providing counselling, shelter, and other emergency assistance to sexual violence survivors during conflict also have a major role to play in accountability after emergency periods are over. They can keep survivors updated on relevant political and legal developments as opportunities to contribute testimony in cases of international crimes may arise years later. Civil society organisations that have had a long-term presence in the community and have established trust among community members are uniquely situated to reach survivors and facilitate their participation in these processes.

Addressing day-to-day barriers to reporting sexual violence during peacetime is essential to improving reporting during future periods of conflict or emergency for two reasons. First, research findings indicate that conflict settings often exacerbate pre-existing barriers to reporting sexual violence within communities, such as stigma, transport challenges, and constrained police and health-related resources. Second, making reporting more accessible and raising community awareness of how to report sexual violence during peacetime may increase chances of reporting during conflict, as survivors will already be familiar with reporting channels and processes.

So what are the primary barriers to reporting sexual violence today? Our research in Kenya, Liberia, Sierra Leone, and Uganda identified barriers that fall within three main categories: social factors, structural factors, and community perceptions of the police.

Stigma was consistently noted as a major social barrier to reporting sexual violence. Across the case study countries, adult survivors reportedly face greater stigma and blame for sexual violence than child survivors do, which can inhibit adults from reporting or seeking services.

> The stigma surrounding a survivor reduces as her age gets lower. You can't blame a one-year-old or a five-year-old, but when you start to get to puberty, the blame starts to shift: 'She was acting that way, showing her body off.'
> – Practitioner, NGO, Liberia

Informants also reported that social and economic pressure from community and family members to settle cases informally, fear of perpetrators, and preferences for community-based resolution also prevent many survivors from reporting sexual violence to the police and the formal legal system. In addition, limited community awareness of legal rights and of how to report incidents can further inhibit survivors from filing cases. For example, community members and survivors themselves may not know what steps to take to file claims or preserve evidence, and they may not think that the sexual violence they have suffered is a crime.

> For some of them, as long as you are not a virgin, you were not raped. [You] need to explain to them that even if a woman has twenty children, when she is forced to have sexual intercourse against her will, it is rape...
> – Representative, UN agency, Liberia

Structural barriers to reporting include transportation challenges and long distances to adequate healthcare and police services, particularly in rural areas. In addition, actual and perceived costs of services, such as medical treatment or police paperwork, hinder survivors from accessing health and legal systems.

Finally, informants told researchers that the community's perceptions of the police impact survivors' willingness to report their experiences. They noted that there is often a lack of confidence in the police to handle sexual violence cases sensitively and effectively. This was particularly true in areas where the police force was directly implicated in the violence perpetrated during conflict, as these experiences reportedly had a long-term negative impact on community members' trust in the police force.

Research findings emphasise the need to create a more enabling environment for survivors to seek accountability through the legal system. Strategies to this end include long-term community mobilisation and sensitisation efforts, use of radio, theatre, and billboards to educate communities about sexual violence.

Finally, our research highlighted the need to create accessible reporting channels that aim to reach survivors where they are. The establishment of 24-hour hotlines and teams of community-based volunteer who serve as first responders or advocates can help to facilitate reporting in peacetime, and may prove even more critical in emergency settings given exacerbated access challenges. Workshop participants also discussed the importance of healthcare facilities operating temporary mobile clinics in conflict or disaster-affected areas, and offering regular, free ambulance services to reach survivors who are unable to travel to health facilities.

Such interventions to reduce day-to-day barriers to reporting are necessary to improve the chances of reporting during emergency periods, thereby enhancing the potential for accountability for sexual violence as an international crime later.

6.2. RETHINKING WITNESS PROTECTION

The provision of safe shelter and witness protection is the linchpin of accountability. Without a sense of security, survivors and other witnesses often do not feel comfortable reporting their experiences or participating in investigation and prosecution. Survivors may need a range of protection options over time. A person may seek temporary harbour when fleeing imminent or fresh harm. She may need higher security shelter if she fears escalation or retaliation after reporting violence. She may need longer-term protection if she pursues a case against her aggressor in court – trial can last months, and then what?

The need to offer meaningful protection at these various stages challenges both state and civil society actors in the case study countries. Most temporary safe houses researchers learned about were run by small private organisations with donor funding.

More formal witness protection is a consistently complex and resource-intensive endeavour, and witness protection programmes in these countries are rare. The sole example of a formal, state-run programme in these case studies was found in Kenya, where the National Witness Protection Agency became operational in 2011. It offers shelter, support, and even relocation to victims and witnesses who are under threat for their engagement in criminal cases. This includes victims and witnesses involved in sexual violence cases.

Research highlights a few unique challenges may arise in the protection of survivors affected by conflict-period violence.

First, shelters and safe houses face the same infrastructural and security risks during periods of armed conflict as any other institutions, so their ability to remain operational and house survivors fleeing harm can be limited. A shelter risks physical destruction; its staff may be unable to come to work due to insecurity or immobility during acute emergency periods; it may have trouble accessing basic food and supplies required for operation.

In addition, numbers may swell. The threat or impact of mass crimes can cause large numbers of men, women, and children to seek safety. Most of the safe houses researchers observed were already under-resourced and over capacity. Some were able to make adjustments during emergency periods, such as the Filadelfia Women's Crisis Centre in Nakuru, Kenya, which made bed space for hundreds of people on the church floor and enlisted community volunteers to assist with cooking and cleaning. However, the reach and capacity of these shelters is still severely limited.

Furthermore, relative risks can change. Sheltering a woman from an abusive spouse already poses myriad challenges in times of peace (where to house her confidentially, which security measures to use, how long to house her, whether her children may accompany her). Sheltering someone from a rebel group, armed actor, or even the state apparatus may pose dangers of a greater order. A simple fence or alarm system may offer no protection in times of armed conflict, should armed actors seek those who flee from them. Perpetrators may be more heavily armed than local police, or they may outnumber them. Finally, threats to victim or witness security may persist long after the conflict period has ended, particularly if there is a later possibility of prosecution before an international tribunal.

Overall, the provision of safe shelter and meaningful witness protection for conflict-period violence requires new thinking and creative approaches. This may require creative collaboration between state and civil society actors.

6.3. SUPPORTING THE HEALTH SECTOR

The health sector plays a critical role in accountability for sexual violence through evidence collection. Healthcare facilities are often the first place where survivors seek assistance. In addition to providing therapeutic, clinical care, healthcare providers are also responsible for conducting the forensic medical examination, documenting their findings in an official medical report, and collecting physical material from a survivor's body. They are also required to liaise with the police to transfer the evidence and testify in court when requested.

Survivors who wish to bring their cases into the formal legal system rely on critical information from doctors, nurses, and other healthcare providers. Informants across the four case studies consistently noted that the medical report documenting the results of the examination is the most important, and often the only, evidence available in sexual violence cases apart from a survivor's own testimony.

During conflict and other humanitarian crises, healthcare providers can also play a critical role in documenting the nature and extent of sexual violence that occurs. Recent increased interest in accountability for sexual violence as an international crime has placed greater expectations on healthcare providers to carry out an evidence-collecting role in conflict and emergency settings in order to support later prosecution. For example, aggregated hospital records indicating multiple sexual assaults in a locality might provide evidence of patterns of violence affecting an entire community. This might help to detect a widespread or systematic attack against a civilian population.[29] Further, healthcare facilities could take steps to make medical records, de-identified and aggregated by specific time periods, available to police investigators and prosecutors of international crimes after a conflict period has ended for use in post-conflict prosecutions of international crimes.

In addition to making use of the data already collected at healthcare facilities, there may be additional measures that healthcare providers could take to document information that would be useful as evidence of war crimes or crimes against humanity. For example, it may be useful to integrate certain questions into the interview when taking the patient's history, such as whether or not the perpetrator was wearing a uniform or whether he or she made specific threats related to the patient's ethnicity or political affiliations.

Documentation of these additional layers of information can be an added burden and challenge for medical care providers working in crisis situations. Fortunately, new tools such as the International Protocol for the Documentation and Investigation of Sexual Violence in Conflict are emerging to guide healthcare providers in the capture of sexual violence as an international crime.

Still, the role of healthcare providers as evidence-collectors in conflict and emergency settings raises several practical and ethical concerns. On a practical level, it is important to understand the health sectors' potential to contribute evidence to cases of international crimes of sexual violence within the context of current capacity limitations and barriers to evidence collection by healthcare providers in day-to-day cases of sexual violence.

One of the most common challenges to evidence collection by healthcare providers identified through our research the fact that survivors often seek care from health facilities days or weeks after an incident, once injuries have largely healed or physical evidence has been washed away. Informants also spoke of various resource constraints and capacity limitations that inhibit effective evidence collection. Health facilities often lack the basic supplies for collecting and storing evidence, and few health care providers in case study countries have the training to conduct the forensic medical examination, complete the required documentation, and collect evidence, particularly outside of the larger referrals hospitals.

> Doctors simply do not know what to collect and how to handle evidence. The survivor may require treatment, but also [needs] justice... There are medical guidelines on evidence collection since 2009, but they have not trickled down.
> – Forensic expert, Nairobi, Kenya

---

29 Anastario et al. 2014; Aranburu 2010.

Across study locations, we learned about several challenges related to the medical certificate, which is completed by a healthcare provider to document the findings of the medical examination. For example, there was often confusion among stakeholders and healthcare providers themselves regarding who can complete the forms. In some locations, such as Kenya and Uganda, policies had been changed to enable providers other than doctors, such as nurses and clinical officers, to conduct the exam; however, these new requirements were not yet fully understood on the ground. Informants also noted challenges related to poor quality of documentation, as healthcare providers do not always fill out the medical report forms completely or accurately. Further, survivors sometimes encounter challenges in accessing the medical certification forms because they are not readily available at police or health facilities, or because survivors are asked to pay for copies despite regulations stating that the provision of forms is free.

According to informants, some healthcare providers are reluctant to document and collect evidence because they do not view it as part of their mandate or feel that they simply do not have time to complete the extended examination and lengthy documentation given the demand for care and limited staffing available. Others do not want to be required to testify in court because they do not feel adequately prepared or supported to do so and find the court process intimidating.

Finally, insufficient coordination between healthcare providers and law enforcement, in addition to limited training among police and health staff in the proper storage and transfer of evidence, creates challenges in maintaining the chain of custody across actors.

> Sometimes an officer will take evidence to the county attorney, but then it goes missing and no one can find it.
>
> – Representative, specialized police force, Liberia

Strategies for improving evidence collection through the health sector included the distribution of pre-assembled 'rape kits' to health facilities, national guidelines on the clinical management of sexual violence for health care providers, and payments by NGOs to providers as incentives to complete the forms and testify in court. In addition, sector-specific and cross-sectoral training bringing together healthcare providers, police, prosecutors, and judges have been implemented to improve the management of medico-legal evidence and establish local protocols.

In light of current practical challenges and capacity constraints with regards to evidence collection, the dual role of healthcare providers in humanitarian settings, in particular, raises ethical questions as well. In conflict settings, as healthcare providers are often overwhelmed with demands for emergency medical care, while grappling with damaged infrastructure, limited supplies and staffing shortages, they have even less time to complete lengthy documentation and carefully collect evidence. In such circumstances, what forms of evidence can healthcare providers reasonably be expected to collect and document, that does not detract from their primary mandate to provide emergency medical care to the community?

Moreover, by increasing the expectation that healthcare providers support later prosecution of international crimes, what implications would this have for their safety in conflict situations? How might this also impact the safety of the survivors seeking their care?

Further dialogue among healthcare providers and policymakers, the police, and prosecutors of international crimes is needed to identify priority evidence that could be collected by healthcare providers in conflict settings to support post-conflict prosecutions. Protocols for evidence collection should be context-specific, practical in application, and ensure that the safety of healthcare providers and survivors is not compromised.

6.4. DEVELOP AND COORDINATE EXPERTISE ON SEXUAL VIOLENCE AND INTERNATIONAL CRIMES

A final take-away from HRCe's research on domestic accountability mechanisms is the need to increase local capacity and competence in investigating and prosecuting both sexual and gender-based violence and international crimes, and to coordinate these sources of expertise so they can work in concert. This means supporting and evaluating the effectiveness of strategies like the establishment of specialised health and police units focused on sexual and gender-based violence and also developing ways to coordinate and combine their expertise with entities focused on international crimes investigation and prosecution. It also means helping to build the capacity of civil society groups in the proper documentation of international crimes and sexual violence.

In the health sector, one-stop centres at both public and private hospitals provide comprehensive medical care and psychosocial support to survivors of sexual violence. They often fill a gap in general medical service provision. More importantly, they are known within their communities for providing specialised services so they are accessed relatively often by survivors. During periods of conflict and emergency, these facilities may receive a high volume of cases from surrounding areas. For this reason, they may serve as a repository of critical information and data that can be used later as evidence in cases of international crimes of sexual violence.

In terms of investigation and prosecution, researchers observed that special health, police, prosecution, and even judicial units focused on sexual and gender-based violence have begun to emerge in the four countries studied, as well. These include the Children and Family Protection Units of the Uganda Police Force, the

Sexual and Gender-Based Violence Division of Kenya's Office of the Director of Public Prosecutions, and 'Criminal Court E' for sexual offences in Liberia's capital.

Similarly, two out of the four case study countries have developed specialised institutions that focus on international crimes. In Kenya and Uganda, the Directorates of Public Prosecution have established specialised prosecution teams focused on international crimes. In Uganda, the International Crimes Division of the High Court is also technically operational. As with specialised police units, this concentration of expertise in international criminal law within a specific team of lawyers or judges is intended to ensure that *someone* can be tasked with these cases should they arise.

A word of caution: creating purely parallel specialisation of investigation and prosecution may risk creating two separate institutional paths – one for the pursuit of sexual violence crimes under domestic penal provisions, and one for the investigation, prosecution, and adjudication of international crimes. In an increasingly bifurcated system that generates separate investigating and prosecuting entities with separate training and mandates, *international* crimes of sexual violence may fall between the tracks unless there is meaningful and sustained cross-training and mutual support among specialised units. In those locales that have only specialists in sexual and gender-based violence, it is unclear whether necessary training or capacity to handle international crimes of sexual violence yet exists.[30] For this reason, enhanced coordination and collaboration between expert units within and across sectors is critical.

7. CONCLUSION

Findings from HRCe's recent research and its subsequent workshop discussion in Kampala highlight the challenges many local nurses, doctors, police officers, community groups, and prosecutors face in addressing sexual violence in their day-to-day work. The hurdles are numerous. Some are as fundamental as severe resource constraints and the scarcity of victim support and protection. Others are more complex, such as the need for better cross-sectoral coordination and training on the preservation of the chain of custody for evidence. Emerging strategies such as the formation of specialised health, police, and prosecution units are promising, but require evaluation and support.

Most of these mundane, quotidian challenges and strategies do not figure into higher level discussions about complementarity between the International Criminal Court and national jurisdictions. However, a realistic appraisal of the potential for complementary efforts in domestic courts requires a clear, practical sense of how local systems and actors function and what their needs are. This is particularly true when considering crimes of sexual violence, which are already

[30] For further discussion about specialised police, prosecution, and court units, Seelinger 2015.

complex cases during peacetime. Even if overall evidentiary requirements may differ under basic criminal code provisions and the Rome Statute, the local clinic nurse or rural police officer may still be the first to document an individual sexual violation committed during conflict. Local documentation and response in these individual cases, when taken in the aggregate, may later hold the key to pattern detection or ground-level memorialisation of actors' specific actions or stated motives. As such, with full domestication of the Rome Statute, these records also become key to later prosecution of sexual violence committed as an international crime in *national* courts.

BIBLIOGRAPHY

BOOKS AND JOURNAL ARTICLES

Agirre Aranburu 2010

Agirre Aranburu, X., 'Sexual Violence beyond Reasonable Doubt: Using Pattern Evidence and Analysis for International Cases', 4 Law and Social Enquiry, 2010.

Anastario et al. 2014

Anastario, M.P. et al., 'Time Series Analysis of Sexual Assault Case Characteristics and the 2007–2008 Period of Post-Election Violence in Kenya', 9(8) PLOS ONE, 2014.

Bijleveld, Morssinkhof and Smeulers 2009

Bijleveld, C., Morssinkhof, A. and Smeulers, A., 'Counting the Countless: Rape Victimization during the Rwanda Genocide', 19(2) International Justice Review, 2009.

Cummings 2011

Cummings, S.K., 'Liberia's 'New War': Post-Conflict Strategies for Confronting Rape and Sexual Violence', 43(1) Arizona State Law Journal, 2011.

Griffiths 2011

Griffiths, C., 'Mapping Study on Gender and Security Sector Reform Actors and Activities in Liberia', Geneva Centre for the Democratic Control of Armed Forces (DCAF), 2011.

Hayes 2015

Hayes, N., 'La Lutte Continue: Investigating and Prosecuting Sexual Violence at the ICC', in Stahn, C. (ed.), 'The Law and Practice of the International Criminal Court', Oxford University Press, 2015.

Hossain et al. 2014

Hossain M. et al., 'Men's and Women's Experiences of Violence and Traumatic Events in Rural Côte d'Ivoire Before, During and After a Period of Armed Conflict', 4(2) BMJ Open, 2014.

Palermo, Bleck, and Peterman 2014

Palermo, T., Bleck, J. and Peterman, A., 'Tip of the Iceberg: Reporting and Gender-Based Violence in Developing Countries', 179(5) American Journal of Epidemiology, 2014.

Seelinger 2015

Seelinger, K.T, 'Domestic Accountability for Sexual Violence: The Potential of Specialized Units in Kenya, Liberia, Sierra Leone, and Uganda', International Review of the Red Cross, 2015.

Skjelsbaek 2012

Skjelsbaek, I., 'The Political Psychology of War Rape: Studies from Bosnia and Herzegovina', War Politics, and Experience Series, Routledge, 2012.

Stigmayer 1994

Stigmayer, A., 'The Rapes in Bosnia-Herzegovina', in 'Mass Rape: the War against Women in Bosnia-Herzegovina', University of Nebraska Press, 1994.

Wirtz et al. 2013

Wirtz, A.L. et al., 'Development of a Screening Tool to Identify Female Survivors of Gender-Based Violence in a Humanitarian Setting: Qualitative Evidence from Research among Refugees in Ethiopia', 7 Conflict and Health, 2013.

JURISPRUDENCE

ICC 2014

ICC, Prosecutor v. Uhuru Muigai Kenyatta, ICC-01/09–02/11, 5 December 2014.

ICC 2014

ICC, Prosecutor v. Jean-Pierre Bemba Gombo, ICC-01/05–01/08, 13 November 2014

TREATIES, LEGISLATION AND AGREEMENTS

Kenya, International Crimes Act, 24 December 2008.

Uganda, International Criminal Court Act, 25 May 2010.

Uganda, Penal Code (Amendment) Act, 17 August 2007.

Uganda, Penal Code Act, 15 June 1950.

United Kingdom and Ireland, Offences against the Person Act, 6 August 1861.

OTHERS

Abdulai, E.S., 'Evaluation: Strengthening of Prosecution of SGBV Offenses through support to the Sexual and Gender Based Violence Crimes Unit (SGBV CU)', UNFPA, November 2010.

Amran, A., 'Post-Election Violence Suspects May Face International Law', Standard Digital News, 18 August 2012.

Bacon, L., 'Building an Inclusive, Responsive National Police Service: Gender-Sensitive Reform in Liberia, 2005–2011', Innovations for Successful Societies, 2012.

ICC, List of 'The States Parties to the Rome Statute'.

Maliti, T., 'Kenyan Prosecutor: Insufficient Evidence Has Made Prosecuting Post-Election Violence Cases Difficult', International Justice Monitor, 26 October 2012.

Seelinger, K.T. and Freccero, J., 'The Long Road: Accountability for Sexual Violence in Conflict and Post-Conflict Settings', UC Berkeley School of Law Human Rights Centre, August 2015.

Ssenyonga, A., 'Police to institute sexual violence unit', New Vision, 26 August 2015.

UNICEF, 'New Women and Children Protection Section for Liberia's Police', News Note, 1 September 2005.

SAFETY AND SECURITY OF PROTECTED WITNESSES AND ACQUITTED AND RELEASED PERSONS

Lessons from the International Criminal Tribunal for Rwanda

Roland Kouassi AMOUSSOUGA GÉRO

1. INTRODUCTION

The Netherlands' recent deportation of Mr Mathieu Ngudjolo Chui, the first person to be acquitted by the International Criminal Court, has brought to light the acute and multi-faceted challenge of providing safety, security, and justice to persons who have served as witnesses before, and/or have been acquitted or released by, an international criminal court.

Mr Ngudjolo Chui, a national of the Democratic Republic of Congo (DRC) and alleged former leader of the Front des Nationalistes et Intégrationnistes (FNI), was indicted by the ICC for crimes against humanity and war crimes. He was arrested and transferred to the ICC in February 2008, where he was detained in the ICC Quarters in Scheveningen Prison. In December 2012, Mr Ngudjolo Chui was acquitted of all charges by Trial Chamber II.[1] Mr Ngudjolo Chui expressed concerns about his safety should he return to his native DRC. Yet he was provided a one-way ticket, escorted to Schiphol Airport, and handed over to Dutch authorities there. Mr Ngudjolo Chui applied for asylum and was placed in a retention centre for almost five months. His Dutch lawyers successfully protested in court. Mr Ngudjolo Chui was released and stayed in a hotel in The Hague at the expense of the ICC for the duration of the ICC Prosecutor's appeal against his acquittal. In February 2015, the ICC Appeals Chamber confirmed Mr Ngudjolo Chui's acquittal.[2]

---

1 *The Prosecutor v. Mathieu Ngudjolo*, ICC-01/04-02/12, Trial Chamber II, Judgment, 18 December 2012.

2 *The Prosecutor v. Mathieu Ngudjolo*, ICC-01/04-02/12, Appeals Chamber II, Judgment, 7 April 2015.

Immediately after Presiding Appeals Judge Sanji Monageng finished reading the judgment, and upon exiting the courtroom, Mr Ngudjolo Chui was apprehended by Dutch authorities in civilian clothes and taken to Schiphol Airport because he, allegedly, no longer had the right to remain on Dutch soil. The authorities planned to deport him to his native DRC on a flight that was due to depart at 1800 hours. Mr Ngudjolo Chui was allowed a few minutes with his ICC counsels only after the repeated insistence of his defence team, reportedly with Dutch authorities and ICC Registry officials present. It is further reported that Mr Ngudjolo Chui was subsequently denied access to his counsels in his Dutch asylum case, and was interrogated in the absence of his counsels. Minutes after he boarded the flight (to the DRC), expulsion was barred after Mr Ngudjolo Chui's Dutch counsels submitted another application against his expulsion.[3]

Some months later, Mr Ngudjolo Chui's application for asylum was rejected, and no state was willing to host him. Once again, he was given a one-way-ticket to the DRC, where he feared persecution. On this occasion, he was successfully deported; while handcuffed and accompanied by six police officers.[4] Mr Ngudjolo Chui was treated like a convict, not an acquitted person.[5]

Whether or not Mr Ngudjolo Chui is safe in the DRC, his story deserves to be told. It is an example of a more general problem, an omission within the ICC and more generally, the international criminal justice regime.[6] Who should take responsibility for persons who have been acquitted by the ICC or who have testified before the Court, made statements against some powerful people in their home countries, and for whom it is therefore not safe to return? A court like the ICC does not have much to offer in this regard. It is not a state, and has no territory to host the persons concerned.

The ICC only has a detention centre, which is not an appropriate place to host acquitted persons who cannot return to their native countries, or witnesses who have testified. Perhaps the host state could assume responsibility or, in the alternative, other ICC states parties could. But what to do when no state is willing to offer witnesses or acquitted persons a safe haven? This article explores how the Arusha-based International Criminal Tribunal for Rwanda (ICTR) sought to render justice for such persons, and what lessons the ICC, and other international criminal tribunals, could learn from the ICTR's experience.

---

3 Africa Legal Aid E-Reporter, 'ICC Appeals Chamber Confirms Ngudjolo Chui Acquittal: a Challenge to the ICC Host State', March 2015, available at: www.africalegalaid.com/newsletter.

4 Statement by Ankumah at Africa Legal Aid Conference on Universalizing the Rome Statute of the International Criminal Court, 18–19 May 2015, Johannesburg, South Africa.

5 *Ibid.*

6 Van der Mei, 'Ngudjolo Chui: Acquitted by the ICC but not Free', 13 March 2015, available at: http://law.maastrichtuniversity.nl/newsandviews/ngudjolo-chui-acquitted-by-the-icc-but-not-free/.

2. THE EXPERIENCE OF THE ICTR

On 10 December 2014, President Meron of the Mechanism for International Criminal Tribunals (MICT),[7] while updating the United Nations Security Council on the work and progress of MICT, highlighted the challenges posed by persons acquitted by the ICTR and those released after having served their sentences. He considered the question of resettlement to be a crucial matter of humanitarian concern for the international community. According to him, these individuals, having been exonerated or served the sentences imposed by the ICTR, deserved the opportunity to be resettled and to rebuild their lives.[8]

The ICTR's experience over the past 21 years shows that dispensation of international criminal justice can only be successful in meeting those challenges if and when there is political will and a clear demonstration of cooperation from member states. Since its inception, the ICTR has encountered obstacles in the relocation of protected witnesses, acquitted persons, and released prisoners. Indeed, those challenges are made critical by the absence of specific provisions in the ICTR Statute that could have directly placed an express obligation on the shoulders of member states to assist in the relocation of protected witnesses, acquitted persons, and released prisoners.

The ICTR Statute is silent on the issue. Article 28 contains a provision on the cooperation and judicial assistance that member states must offer to the Tribunal in the investigation and prosecution of persons accused of committing serious violations of international humanitarian law. This provision, however, is limited in scope. It obliges member states to comply, without undue delay, with any request for assistance, or an order issued by the Trial Chamber dealing with investigation and prosecution,[9] but it does not apply to requests for relocation following an acquittal or a completion of a sentence. As a result, the Registry, the organ responsible for the administration of the Tribunal, has been required to play a central role in tackling those challenges.

---

7 The MICT was established by UN Security Council Resolution 1966 (22 December 2010) S/RES/1966, available at: www.refworld.org/docid/4d270e432.html. To complete the remaining work of the International Criminal Tribunal for Rwanda and the International Criminal Tribunal for the former Yugoslavia after the completion of their respective mandates. The MICT has two branches, one in Arusha, Tanzania, and one in The Hague, Netherlands.

8 See Address of Judge Theodor Meron, President of the International Criminal Tribunal for the former Yugoslavia And President of the International Residual Mechanism for Criminal Tribunals to the United Nations Security Council, 10 December 2014, available at: www.unmict.org.

9 This includes: (a) the identification and location of persons, (b) the taking of testimony and the production of evidence, (c) the service of documents, (d) the arrest or detention of persons, and (e) the surrender or transfer of the accused to the ICTR.

3. RELOCATING ICTR PROTECTED WITNESSES

The issue of relocation of protected witnesses has posed considerable challenges since the Tribunal's inception. One major problem is that the ICTR has not been as successful as its sister tribunal, the International Criminal Tribunal for the Former Yugoslavia (ICTY), in concluding cooperation agreements with member states for the relocation of protected witnesses. So far, the Tribunal has not been able to rally effective support from member states to extend protection to its vulnerable witnesses by way of accepting them on their territories.

A small number of member states showed support of the ICTR's intervention in favour of some critical prosecution witnesses or potential witnesses. The ICTR, through the offices of the Prosecutor and the Registrar, undertook to exploring and negotiating specific arrangements for their relocation in foreign countries. States like Australia and Canada exchanged letters with the ICTR in which they confirmed their willingness to receive a few vulnerable and protected witnesses. The United Kingdom also accepted, in principle, to sign an agreement with the ICTR.

As a matter of general principle, the Rwandan government does not support the 'external' relocation to foreign countries of protected prosecution witnesses who reside in Rwanda. The government is of the view that Rwandan citizens should not be encouraged to flee the country. Moreover, since the government has stated it is committed to ensuring the security and safety of its citizens, it sees no reason for the ICTR to remove and relocate its citizens who were called to travel from Rwanda to Arusha for testimony purposes. As a result, the Rwandan government made it mandatory for the ICTR to return all witnesses who were authorised to leave Rwanda for court duties.

However, internal relocation of such witnesses has been effectively implemented with the full cooperation of the Rwandan government. The relocation of witnesses or potential witnesses who resided abroad, to foreign countries falls within the category of exceptional resettlement measures involving independent referral programmes for individuals in compelling humanitarian situations established and managed by some member states. Other measures include the UNHCR's resettlement programmes for eligible refugees and stateless persons who fear persecutions in their countries of origin.

4. RELOCATING ACQUITTED AND RELEASED PERSONS

So far, the ICTR has relocated 6 out of 14 acquitted persons. After a protracted process involving extensive bilateral negotiations, Ignace Bagilishema (former bourgmestre of Mabanza) and Jean Mpambara (former bourgmestre of

Rukara) were relocated to France. Others were relocated to different European countries: Emmanuel Bagambiki (former préfet of Cyangugu) and Augustin Ndindiliyimana (former General) were relocated to Belgium. André Rwamakuba (former Minister of Education) was relocated to Switzerland. These relocations reunited the individuals with their families who were living abroad. Hormisdas Nsengimana (priest) was accepted by and relocated to Italy. In spite of protracted negotiations with other member states, as well as with the United Nations High Commission for Refugees (UNHCR), the ICTR was not able to find countries that were willing to accept any of the remaining 8 acquitted persons.[10] These acquitted persons are still in Tanzania under the care of the ICTR, along with three persons who were convicted and have served their sentences.[11] Although technically free, the freedom of these 11 individuals remains restricted due to various factors beyond their or the ICTR's control. They are consigned to reside in 'safe houses' provided by the ICTR in Arusha, Tanzania, but remain unable to settle in Tanzania. As such, they live in legal and social limbo with no place to go or any means of rebuilding their lives. For example, Mr André Ntagerura, who was acquitted in February 2004. He and others have spent well over a decade in Arusha, partly in custody and partly as free men. The fact that the 11 individuals remain virtually stateless in Tanzania, without visas, residence permits, identity documents, or employment rights, and with bleak prospects of being reunited with their families, represents a serious violation of their basic human rights, including their right to liberty.

One of the implications of their living in Tanzania without means of their own is that they do not have adequate access to health care. Most of them are advanced in age and their conditions require regular access to health care. Overall, their situation also represents a critical challenge to the implementation of international criminal justice, as well as to the ICTR's duty to adhere to the requirements of international human rights law and humanitarian considerations. Mindful of this difficult humanitarian situation, the Tribunal has continued to seek the assistance of member states in order to relocate the remaining eleven individuals.

In an effort to ensure enjoyment of the basic human rights of the acquitted and released persons, the ICTR has sought to reunite them with their families in the countries in which their families have settled. In this regard, the Tribunal has approached countries in which family members of acquitted and released persons have acquired rights of residence or citizenship, and requested those

10 André Ntagerura (former Minister of Transport); Gratien Kabiligi (former General); Protais Zigiranyirazo (businessman); Casimir Bizimungu (former Minister of Health); Jerome Bicamumpaka (former Minister of Foreign Affairs); Justin Mugenzi (former Minister of Commerce); Prosper Mugiraneza (former Minister of Civil Service); and Francois Xavier Nzuwonemeye (former commander of the reconnaissance battalion).

11 Anatole Nsengiyumva (former Colonel); Tharcisse Muvunyi (former Commander); and Innocent Sagahutu (former Captain).

countries accept their relocation, either in Europe or North America. The assumption underlying the reunification strategy adopted by the ICTR is that these persons will resettle quicker if placed within their family support structures, and are not likely to be of substantial financial burden to the countries concerned.

Unfortunately, efforts to relocate the persons concerned have failed. The ICTR has also explored possibilities of relocation to Scandinavian states. However, those efforts have not yet yielded positive results. The ICTR also approached some African governments who expressed their willingness to consider applications from the ICTR for relocation of a small number of acquitted and released persons on their territories. As part of the application, the ICTR provided notes verbales and individual profile forms for each of the individuals, which contained details on their educational and professional backgrounds, and information relating to their cases.

The ideal solution would have been for these persons to return to their country of origin and citizenship: Rwanda. On numerous occasions, the ICTR urged them to consider that option. For its part, the Rwandan government has said that they are welcome to return. So far, these individuals have not exercised that option, and it does not appear that they will any time soon. They repeatedly expressed their reluctance to return to Rwanda, citing their fear of reprisal by the Rwandan government. They argue that in addition to the fear of persecution, their resettlement in Rwanda would be difficult considering the manner in which they have been vilified by the government, victims' organisations, and the Rwandan media since their acquittal. For those who were convicted and have served their sentences, the Rwandan community considered the sentences to be too light. They also pointed out that they no longer have immediate family in Rwanda, and that they lost all their properties when they left the country. While they have lived orderly and exemplary lives in Tanzania, they cannot stay in Tanzania indefinitely since they do not possess valid visas to remain and reside in the country under the terms of exceptional and temporary arrangements concluded between the ICTR and the Tanzanian government.

At the request of the ICTR, the Security Council has addressed issues concerning the status of acquitted and released persons on a number of occasions. On 21 December 2011 it adopted Resolution 2029, in which it 'noted with concern that the International Tribunal continues to face problems in the relocation of acquitted persons and convicted persons who have completed serving their sentences.'[12] In the preamble of Resolution 2054 of 29 June 2012, the Security Council again 'noted with concern that the International Tribunal continues to face problems in the relocation of acquitted persons and convicted

12 S/RES/2029/2011, available at: www.un.org/en/sc/documents/resolutions/2011.shtml.

persons who have completed serving their sentences, and emphasized the importance of successful relocation of such persons.'[13] In both resolutions, the Security Council commended member states that have accepted the relocation to their territories of acquitted persons or convicts who have completed serving their sentences. The Security Council also reiterated its call upon other member states in a position to do so, to cooperate with the Tribunal and render all necessary assistance to it in the relocation process. Unfortunately, the Tribunal has yet to see any positive outcomes of these resolutions.

Having fled Rwanda in 1994, the persons concerned have endured very long detention periods while awaiting completion of their trials and appeals, including equally lengthy periods of confinement in safe houses in Arusha after release. They live in a state of indigence. The fact that most of them are quite advanced in age diminishes their attractiveness within the labour market. It was the ICTR's expectation that should African governments accept one or more of these individuals, they would assist with the maintenance and upkeep based on a modest living standard. The ICTR continued to advocate for the need of the international community to establish a special fund to assist in the settlement of a relocated person, where necessary, by providing some start-up resources. At this stage, it is unknown whether member states will ever accede to such a request. The commitment is yet to be registered.

The ICTR also hoped that a relocation arrangement would offer secure residence rights and privileges to the accepted individual(s). It appealed, in vain, to prospective states to grant them a form of permanent residence rights for the purposes of obtaining identity, travel, and work documents. In cases where there is an acceptance of the relocation of a person to the territory of the willing state, the ICTR expects the state's assistance in the process of introducing and integrating him or her into the social and economic fabric of the country, as some of these individuals are professionals with various backgrounds in social, military, business, and public services.

In the view of the ICTR, these individuals should be considered immigrants due to their sui generis status. They are neither refugees nor asylum seekers, although the spirit of the protection afforded to refugees and asylum seekers should be extended to them as well. A number of states including the Netherlands, Canada, and France have refused to accept acquitted or convicted persons on national public safety and political grounds. According to these states, they do not qualify as refugees under the refugee convention.

The ICTR has repeatedly appealed to willing states to ensure that their treatment, in case of acceptance for relocation, would conform with that of other similarly situated individuals and that they should enjoy the same privileges and protections.

13 S/RES/2054/2012, available at: www.un.org/en/sc/documents/resolutions/2012.shtml.

It is also worth noting that at this point in time, the ICTR acquitted persons are not immune from being subjected to the application of the 'exclusion clauses' by the UN High Commission for Refugees (UNHCR), which require careful and assiduous examination. This situation gives rise to legitimate questions as to the actual consideration and legal weight that are given to ICTR acquittal decisions by all external stakeholders, including member states and UN agencies. The absence of political will and provisions for such obligations assigned to member states in the ICTR's statutory provisions renders this challenge quite daunting.

Countries that have refused to allow these persons to relocate to their territory often cite similar reasons as a justification for their denial. In its experience, the ICTR has found that a number of reasons are typically used by member states when declining requests to host an acquitted or released person. A reason often given by countries for their refusals is that the applicant(s) (the acquitted or released person) do not meet one of the requirements for obtaining a visa – the inability of the acquitted or released persons to provide an explanation regarding their anticipated source of income or means of subsistence. The other requirement that is often not met is sufficient proof of a strong link or connection to the country.

Further, some of the requested countries do not consider that a judgment of acquittal by the ICTR completely exonerates persons of criminal wrongdoing during the genocide. The position often taken by such states is that the acquitted or released persons' mere involvement in the interim government or military during the 1994 genocide implicates them in wrongdoing, making them responsible for crimes committed during that period.[14]

Another of the reasons given most often concerns the potential disruption of public order. In most European countries, a government can deny a visa to someone on the basis that his or her mere presence in the country would threaten public order. In the present cases, some European governments claim that public order would be threatened by way of the strong reaction manifested in demonstrations and protests organised by the Rwandan survivors/refugees and victims groups in their countries.

There is a clear indication that consideration for maintenance of excellent diplomatic relationship between Rwanda and prospective host countries continues to play a large role in the potential host states' unwillingness or refusal to accept acquitted persons and released convicts.

---

14 Following an application for permanent residency in Canada filed on 21 May 2009 by one acquitted person, Andre Ntagerura, the Canadian Minister of Citizenship and Immigration in his response, decided to exclude all former members of the previous Rwandan government under President Habyarimana between October 1990 and April 1994 from asylum or residency in Canada on the ground that they had engaged in systematic or gross human rights violations, or genocide, war crimes, or crimes against humanity.

5. LESSONS LEARNED FROM THE ICTR

As noted, there are many lessons to be learnt from the ICTR's experience in its efforts to protect the rights of acquitted and released persons. If one asks whether the ICTR has ensured that justice was rendered for such individuals, the answer may well be that it was partially the case, given the limited scope and nature of the ICTR Rules and Statute. However, one of the critical tests for assessing the success of the ICTR is the daunting challenge that it faces in its attempts to ensure that acquitted and released persons are justly treated after their release. There are three major lessons to be learned from the ICTR's experience.

The first lesson worth noting is that over the past twenty years, the ICTR has acknowledged that its mandate and responsibility as a court does not end at the point of acquittal or release of the convicts. Taking into consideration the complexity of the political dynamics surrounding the discharge of its mandate, there are many non-judicial steps to climb before the ICTR's legacy can be deemed successful or not. In essence, relocating released convicts and acquitted persons to their home state or foreign countries of their choice has proven to be an extreme challenge.

While notable progress was registered with respect to the conclusion of agreements with member states for the enforcement of the sentences handed down by the ICTR, so far only a few states have agreed to receive a handful of acquitted and released persons. ICTR statutes, rules and procedure, as well as policies, do not impose an obligation on member states to accept released convicts or acquitted persons. At best, there remains a heavy burden on the Registry, as it bears the responsibility for the safety and security of accused persons, acquitted and released persons while under the custody and protective care of the Tribunal. The unwritten, but implied, obligation to negotiate and find states willing to receive them and to provide them with financial and administrative assistance in getting travel documents and securing funds for their transportation to the relocation state, if and when necessary, also remains with the Registry.

The second lesson is that although Rwanda, which is their country of origin, is willing to welcome them back, the acquitted and released persons did not wish to return to Rwanda or to the countries of their arrest, the latter of which have not been willing to accept them back either. It is gainsaying that, although UNHCR has further recognised the fact that although acquitted of criminal responsibility by the Tribunal, these persons may hold well-founded fears of persecution, and that their return to Rwanda therefore may not be possible. As a result, UNHCR underscored that the ICTR acquitted persons were not immune from being subjected to the application of its 'exclusion clauses', which requires careful and assiduous examination.

The third lesson is found in the willingness of the hosting state of Tanzania to go beyond the framework of its own domestic laws on asylum and the provisions of Article XX (relating to the suspect or accused) of the hosting agreement signed with the United Nations[15] to facilitate the operation of the Tribunal from its inception until its closure. Such a commitment was remarkable and underlined the highest consideration that the host country places on seeing that the ICTR does not completely fail to deliver justice to acquitted and released persons.

Mindful of its own domestic laws and the strict provisions of the Host Country Agreement, which requires that acquitted and released persons leave Tanzania within two weeks following their release, the Tanzanian Government has gone beyond what is permissible under the law by allowing the acquitted and released persons to stay in the country beyond the mandatory time set out in the Host Country Agreement. Tanzania has provided the ICTR with concrete support and cooperation by accepting to grant temporary asylum in the country to one of the acquitted persons, namely Mr Ntagerura, who was acquitted in 2004 pending his relocation to a third country. The Government requested to be kept informed of any subsequent developments with regard to any re-settlement formalities as soon as they are completed, while allowing the remaining acquitted and released persons to remain in Arusha under the care of the ICTR pending their relocation elsewhere.

6. POSSIBLE SOLUTIONS AND WAY FORWARD

The current situation, and the similar foreseeable situation of future acquitted persons and released prisoners who have or will have completed their sentences while still in Arusha, are indeed important challenges that must be urgently addressed. For political reasons, acquitted and released persons are often considered by many member states as potential threats to law and order.

It goes without saying that the ICTR's inability to find suitable states for these individuals will no doubt constitute a continued burden and a spoiler on its incredible legacy, as well as a critical challenge for the hosting state Tanzania. This shared burden should not solely be upon the ICTR. It remains, fundamentally, a collective challenge facing the international community, including Tanzania, at the completion of the ICTR's mandate. Furthermore, such a failure might seriously hamper the foundation of the joint effort of the ICTR and the Tanzanian government to ensure a lasting contribution to national reconciliation, restoration, and maintenance of peace and security in Rwanda and the Great Lakes Region, and to the development of an effective international

15 Agreement between the United Nations and the United Republic of Tanzania concerning the Headquarters of the International Tribunal for Rwanda, signed in New York on 31 August 1995, in United Nations/A/51/399-S/1996/778–24 September 1996.

criminal justice system. Thus, the issue of finding relocation states for acquitted and released persons remains a critical challenge for the international community in its attempts to accord justice to them.

Moreover, the ICTR considers that allowing persons acquitted by an international criminal tribunal to resume their lives is a fundamental expression of the rule of law. There is a legitimate expectation that individual member states of the United Nations or the ICC states parties will enforce orders and judgments of the ICTR and of the ICC. Although the Host Country Agreement that the United Nations concluded with the Tanzanian government expressly provides that on conviction or on release, the person shall be sent out of Tanzania as soon as practicable, the Tanzanian government has tacitly recognised the daunting challenge facing the ICTR. Notwithstanding the infringement of its national law, the Tanzanian government shows its deepest commitment to contributing to a temporary solution and relief on humanitarian grounds, by allowing the continued stay of these individuals in Arusha, under the care of the ICTR, until such a time as the ICTR completes negotiation for their relocation and resettlements outside Tanzania.

Regrettably, this is not an option chosen by the ICC and its hosting state, the Netherlands. Rather, ICC and Dutch authorities apparently dismissed the fears expressed by Mr Ngudjolo Chui that his security will be in danger if he goes back to the DRC. It is of paramount importance that viable and sustainable solutions are found for acquitted and released persons whenever they express legitimate fears of persecution should they return to their country of citizenship or residence.

While contrasting the lessons learned from the ICTR's experience with that of the ICC in Mr Ngudjolo Chui's acquittal, one may argue that the Netherlands as a host state could learn from Tanzania's example. Others may argue that the Netherlands is a state that cannot violate its own national laws to accommodate an ICC acquitted person's needs, as priority must be given to Dutch asylum law, which ultimately prevailed in the case of Mr Ngudjolo Chui.

These two situations give rise to some fundamental questions, which need to be addressed, such as how to reconcile the seemingly conflicting interests of the national laws of hosting states with those of international criminal institutions and the need to render justice to acquitted and released persons under a credible framework of the existing international criminal justice system.

Whatever solutions might be envisaged will certainly entail a bold commitment from the international community, specifically from the United Nations Security Council for the ICTR, the Assembly of States Parties for the ICC, and from willing individual member states, as a renewed pledge to assist the International Criminal Court/Tribunal in discharging its full mandate of justice to the victims and the suspects. Such a commitment must also be supplemented by a readily available and actionable mechanism for the resettlement of acquitted and released persons.

We may not have all the answers but we can at least attempt to explore possible solutions. The first proposed solution entails the development of a global international policy on the resettlement of acquitted and released persons by international criminal tribunals/courts in which there is a clear recognition of the international criminal institution's responsibility to ensure that acquitted and released persons are treated with respect and duly accorded the right to be primarily resettled/relocated in their country of origin. However, in the event that the acquitted or released persons may have a well-founded fear of persecution within the meaning of the Refugee Convention of 1951, he/she should be resettled to either the host state of the international criminal tribunal/court or the country of arrest.

The second proposal calls for a credible international initiative by the Security Council or the Assembly of States Parties (ASP) to the ICC, aimed at facilitating the conclusion of practical arrangements with UNHCR concerning the resettlement within its own eligible programmes of acquitted and released persons by international criminal courts/tribunals.

Finally, a third solution would involve the absorption of internationally acquitted persons into independent referral programmes for individuals in compelling humanitarian situations managed by some individual member states, as well as the expansion of the scope of existing agreements on the enforcement of sentences to include the resettlement of acquitted and released persons.

7. CONCLUSION

As the ICTR draws ever closer to the completion of its work and closure, the issue of relocating acquitted persons and released convicts is now becoming a daunting challenge, particularly with respect to acquitted persons and convicts who have been released on Tanzanian soil. Leaving these individuals behind in Tanzania after the closure of the ICTR is not a viable option since the Host Country Agreement between the United Nations and Tanzania does not provide any means by which ICTR detainees released in Arusha may be allowed permanent settlement. The Agreement also makes it clear that immunities cease for accused persons who are acquitted or otherwise released by the Tribunal. The cooperation of member states as required by Article 28 of the Statute does not extend to the relocation of acquitted persons.

Acquitted persons and released convicts fled Rwanda in 1994, their close family live outside Rwanda, and they fear for their security if returned to Rwanda. UNHCR has indicated that despite their acquittals or the fact that they have served their punishments for the wrongs they committed during the genocide in 1994, they may have well-founded fears of persecution should they return to Rwanda, and their return may therefore not be possible. UNHCR has so far been willing to consider their applications for refugee status, but their applications have, like all other applications, been subject to the exclusion clauses of the Refugee Convention.

The effectiveness of any international criminal tribunal or court, such as the ICTR or the ICC, will remain seriously challenged until their member states show a firm commitment to support the institutions when faced with such a daunting challenge. Hosting states like the Netherlands and Tanzania have additional strategic and historical burdens, imposed upon them by the nature of the alleged crimes and the complexity of the personality of the suspects brought onto their territories, and who are subjects of international criminal proceedings. As a result, these states must contribute to finding long-term solutions to such challenges. Forceful deportation of acquitted or released persons back to their country of origin or the place of arrest, where they have legitimate fear for their safety and security sends a wrong and negative signal that will, in the long term, erode the foundation of international justice on the African continent, where all ICC cases have so far originated.

Host countries must therefore be encouraged to devise strategies within their national immigration regulatory framework(s) to accommodate special provisions for such humanitarian contingencies. These special circumstances in which the acquitted or released persons find themselves as a result of the international criminal proceedings instituted against them in hosting states is a good enough reason to call for such provisions. Above all, hosting states of international criminal tribunals should have the moral duty to ensure that such a challenge to the international criminal justice system does not obscure the progress achieved in the field of criminal accountability and in the global fight against impunity.

Acquitted and released persons should not be forcibly deported to a country where they fear persecution. This affects the integrity of international criminal justice. The Assembly of States Parties to the International Criminal Court should follow in the footsteps of the UN Security Council, and consider the question of resettlement of acquitted and released persons. This is indeed a crucial matter of humanitarian concern for the international community and the future of international criminal justice.

A supportive response from UN and ICC member states with respect to third country admission of acquitted and released persons would go a long way towards making a remarkable and positive contribution to supporting the burden-sharing premise underpinning the international criminal justice system. It will also reinforce its legitimacy and ensure that justice is even-handedly and properly administered to the victims, the accused persons, the innocent, and the convicted persons who have paid their debt to the international community by serving their sentence. This will further constitute a clear affirmation of member states' commitment to contribute to the global efforts towards combating impunity and supporting the international criminal justice system in its pioneering initiatives aimed at delivering effectively and efficiently on its global mandate.

BIBLIOGRAPHY

JURISPRUDENCE

ICC 2012
ICC, Prosecutor v. Mathieu Ngudjolo, ICC-01/04–02/12, 18 December 2012.
ICC 2012
ICC, Prosecutor v. Mathieu Ngudjolo, ICC-01/04–02/12 A, 7 April 2012.

TREATIES, LEGISLATION AND AGREEMENTS

Agreement between the United Nations and the United Republic of Tanzania concerning the Headquarters of the International Tribunal for Rwanda, UN Doc. A/51/399 – S/1996/778, 24 September 1996.
Statute of the International Criminal Tribunal for Rwanda, SC Res. 955, UN Doc. S/RES/955, 8 November 1994.
Statute of the International Residual Mechanism for Criminal Tribunals, SC Res. 1966, UN Doc. S/RES/1966, 22 December 2010.
United Nations Security Council, Resolution (concerning the ICTR), UN Doc. S/RES/2029 (2011), 21 December 2011.
United Nations Security Council, Resolution (concerning the ICTR), UN Doc. S/RES/2054 (2012), 29 June 2012.

OTHERS

Africa Legal Aid, 'ICC Appeals Chamber Confirms Ngudjolo Chui Acquittal: a Challenge to the ICC Host State', March 2015.
Africa Legal Aid, Statement by Evelyn Ankumah – 'Universalizing the Rome Statute of the International Criminal Court', 7 May 2015.
United Nations Mechanism for International Criminal Tribunals, Address of Judge Theodor Meron, President of the International Criminal Tribunal for the former Yugoslavia And President of the International Residual Mechanism for Criminal Tribunals to the United Nations Security Council, 10 December 2014.
Van der Mei, A.P., 'Ngudjolo Chui: Acquitted by the ICC but not Free', Maastricht Law News & Views, 13 March 2015.

BRIDGING THE LEGAL GAP

The International Initiative for Opening Negotiations on a Multilateral Treaty for Mutual Legal Assistance and Extradition in the Domestic Prosecution of Atrocity Crimes

Anne-Sophie MASSA

1. INTRODUCTION

Hardly a week goes by without pictures and reports of atrocities committed around the globe. Frequently, those atrocities amount to crimes the international community views as the most serious and heinous ones and for which it has voiced its unanimous condemnation at multiple occasions, namely the crimes of genocide, crimes against humanity and war crimes.[1]

Those atrocity crimes fall within the jurisdiction of the International Criminal Court, which, after a decade of judicial activities, has delivered a significant contribution to the fight against impunity. Nevertheless, the core of the criminal system as enshrined in the Rome Statute is based on the principle of complementarity, under which the International Criminal Court is only called to play a subsidiary role and supplement the domestic investigation and prosecution of atrocity crimes.[2] The primary responsibility to bring the perpetrators of these atrocity crimes to trial therefore rests with states. The General Assembly recently recalled the complementary nature of the International Criminal Court and the corollary responsibility of states to domestically investigate and

1 The Rome Statute of the International Criminal Court speaks of 'the most serious crimes of concern to the international community as a whole' (recitals 4 and 9 of the Preamble), or 'most serious crimes of international concern' (Article 1). See Rome Statute of the International Criminal Court, adopted on 17 July 1998 and entered into force on 1 July 2002. As of 8 September 2015, the Rome Statute counts 123 contracting parties.

2 Benzing 2003, p. 596.

prosecute atrocity crimes,[3] and emphasised, in this context, 'the importance of international cooperation and judicial assistance in conducting effective investigations and prosecutions'.[4]

Due to the very nature of atrocity crimes however, suspects, witnesses and evidence do not find themselves on the territory of a single state. Suspects may have found safe haven in a foreign country, witnesses may have fled and been granted refugee status far away from home, evidence may be scattered all over the world. Mutual legal assistance and extradition are therefore crucial tools in the investigation and prosecution of atrocity crimes at the domestic level. Without an effective level of cooperation between states, the fight against impunity for atrocity crimes stands the risk of remaining an abstract reality, which is simply not acceptable.

In contrast with some recent treaties that have been adopted, for instance under the auspices of the United Nations in the fields of corruption or transnational organised crime, and which contain a set of procedural provisions dealing explicitly and in a detailed manner with mutual legal assistance and extradition, the international legal framework for cooperation in relation with atrocity crimes remains inadequate. The Genocide[5] and Geneva Conventions,[6] adopted in the aftermath of the Second World War, do not foresee modern forms – if any – of mutual legal assistance and therefore appear outdated in this regard. In practice, the lack of appropriate legal framework for cooperation between states has hindered the prosecution of atrocity crimes at multiple occasions, leaving the judicial authorities of the concerned states powerless in the face of the international duty resting on them to end impunity for the crimes of genocide, crimes against humanity and war crimes.[7]

In order to fill this existing legal gap, the Netherlands, together with Argentina, Belgium and Slovenia, has been advocating for the adoption of a new multilateral treaty on mutual legal assistance and extradition for atrocity crimes that would bring the necessary legal improvements in order to ensure an

---

3 A/RES/68/305 (2014) on the Report of the International Criminal Court, adopted on 9 September 2014, para. 5.

4 Ibid, para. 7.

5 Convention on the Prevention and Punishment of the Crime of Genocide, adopted on 9 December 1948 and entered into force on 12 January 1951. As of 8 September 2015, 146 states were parties to the Convention.

6 Geneva Convention for the Amelioration of the Condition of the Wounded and Sick in Armed Forces in the Field (First Geneva Convention), Geneva Convention for the Amelioration of the Condition of the Wounded, Sick and Shipwrecked Members of the Armed Forces at Sea (Second Geneva Convention), Geneva Convention Relative to the Treatment of Prisoners of War (Third Geneva Convention), Geneva Convention on the Protection of Civilian Persons in Time of War (Fourth Geneva Convention), adopted on 12 August 1949 and entered into force on 21 October 1950. As of 8 September 2015, 196 states were parties to the Conventions.

7 For a few examples of situations in which cooperation requests were denied due to the absence of an appropriate legal basis, see Ferdinandusse 2014, available at: www.asil.org/insights/volume/18/issue/15/improving-inter-state-cooperation-national-prosecution-international.

effective interstate cooperation in the domestic prosecution of atrocity crimes, with the ultimate goal that safe havens would cease to exist for those responsible of these crimes.

In this context, the present contribution seeks to shed light on this international initiative for opening negotiations on a new multilateral treaty on mutual legal assistance, by presenting its origins, its main objectives, its proposed content, its latest developments and its way forward.

2. THE EARLY DAYS

Taking stock of its experience in the domestic investigation and prosecution of atrocity crimes since the 1990s, the Netherlands observed that the legal framework for interstate cooperation was 'formed by a patchwork of partly outdated treaties'.[8] Together with Belgium and Slovenia, which shared its views, the Netherlands therefore decided to convene an expert meeting in The Hague in November 2011 with the aim of gathering international legal experts and practitioners of all regions of the world and exploring the extent to which a legal gap existed in the international legal framework concerning mutual legal assistance between states for the national adjudication of atrocity crimes and, if needed, the way it could best be addressed. The experts, representing the ministries of justice, prosecution services or ministries of foreign affairs of 19 states across five continents,[9] unanimously concluded that a gap indeed existed, which caused legal as well as practical obstacles for a fully functioning interstate cooperation. The option of adopting a new multilateral treaty on mutual legal assistance and extradition was brought to the table in the course of the discussions among the experts on how to bridge this gap in the most appropriate manner.

On the basis of these conclusions, Belgium, the Netherlands and Slovenia launched the Initiative for Opening Negotiations on a Multilateral Treaty for Mutual Legal Assistance and Extradition in the Domestic Prosecution of Atrocity Crimes. They were soon joined by Argentina, which co-sponsored the initiative.

---

8 See 'A Legal Gap in the International Legal Framework Concerning the National Adjudication of International Crimes?', Background Paper by The Netherlands, p. 3, in *A Legal Gap? Getting the evidence where it can be found: Investigating and prosecuting international crimes*, Report, expert meeting, The Hague, 22 November 2011, published by the Hague Institute for the Internationalisation of Law and the Government of the Netherlands and available upon request.

9 Argentina, Australia, Belgium, Canada, Colombia, Czech Republic, Denmark, Finland, France, Germany, Japan, Norway, Slovenia, South Africa, Sweden, The Netherlands, The Philippines, United Kingdom and the United States.

In order to raise awareness among states on the initiative and the objectives it pursues, the co-sponsoring states decided to carry out several rounds of demarches. The initiative was also presented in a variety of fora, and multiple side-events were organised. At the occasion of the 11th session of the Assembly of States Parties to the Rome Statute of the International Criminal Court in 2012, Belgium, the Netherlands and Slovenia presented a joint statement in the specific context of the segment on complementarity. They were heard by other states, and the importance of strengthening international cooperation and judicial assistance found an echo in the preamble of the resolution adopted by the Assembly.[10]

A few months later, a draft resolution was submitted by Argentina during the 22nd session of the Commission on Crime Prevention and Criminal Justice of the United Nations in Vienna. This document, which was co-sponsored by 23 countries,[11] acknowledged the insufficient nature of the legal basis for mutual legal assistance and extradition in cases of crimes of genocide, crimes against humanity and war crimes, and called for the strengthening of the legal framework for international cooperation with a view of facilitating and promoting the investigation and prosecution of atrocity crimes.[12] Although the resolution was ultimately not adopted, it nevertheless triggered an intensive and constructive debate among the states' representatives present. This session of the commission also provided an excellent opportunity to present the initiative. To this aim, a side-event, at the occasion of which both the late Ugandan Senior State Attorney, Madam Joan Kagezi, and the then Dutch Secretary of State for Security and Justice, H.E. Fred Teeven, delivered a keynote speech on their professional experience in the domestic prosecution of atrocity crimes, was organised by the permanent missions of Belgium, the Netherlands and Slovenia. While Madam Joan Kagezi stressed that regional tools were not satisfactory enough due to the fact that evidence, witnesses and suspects do not all remain in one region, H.E. Fred Teeven highlighted that 'justice begins at home' and that 'tolerating individuals suspected of committing these crimes on our territory undermines the rule of law, both in our countries and in the wider world'.[13]

In October 2013, a Strategic Meeting took place in The Hague, in the presence of representatives of all regional groups, as well as with the special attendance

---

10 Resolution ICC-ASP/11/Res.6, recital 3 of the Preamble: '*Recalling* the primary responsibility of States to investigate and prosecute the most serious crimes of international concern and that, to this end, appropriate measures need to be adopted at the national level, and international cooperation and judicial assistance need to be strengthened, in order to ensure that national legal systems are capable of genuinely prosecuting such crimes.'

11 Argentina, Austria, Belgium, Chile, Cyprus, Estonia, Hungary, Latvia, Liechtenstein, Lithuania, Luxembourg, Poland, Norway, Peru, Georgia, The Netherlands, Romania, Slovakia, Slovenia, Macedonia, Mongolia, Andorra and Sweden.

12 E/CN.15/2013/L.5, recital 10 of the Preamble and para. 1.

13 Speech delivered in Vienna on 22 April 2013.

of H.E. Adama Dieng, the UN Under Secretary-General and Special Adviser to the UN Secretary-General on the Prevention of Genocide, and former Registrar of the International Criminal Tribunal for Rwanda. The latter, in his allocution, brought a valuable support to the initiative by speaking out for the adoption of a new multilateral treaty:

> I would like to reiterate my belief that I personally consider the negotiation of a multilateral treaty regime of fundamental importance and therefore be dealt with as a matter of priority by the international community. As I have consistently reminded [s]tates whenever I have had such an opportunity, atrocity crimes, are the most serious crimes of international concern and all [s]tates have the obligation to investigate and prosecute them effectively. It therefore goes without saying that the adoption of a new treaty regime will enhance state cooperation and capability to effectively prevent and punish these crimes.

Two months later, the states co-sponsoring the initiative organised a side-event *en marge* of the Assembly of States Parties to the Rome Statute of the International Criminal Court, at the occasion of which Madam Joan Kagezi, as keynote speaker, reaffirmed her wholehearted support for the initiative. They also presented a Joint Statement calling for the opening of negotiations on a new MLA treaty for the domestic prosecution of atrocity crimes and opened it for signature. 39 states formally expressed their support for the initiative by signing the statement.[14] In March 2014, a new Strategic Meeting gathering the supporting states was organised in The Hague. It was decided that the statement would be transformed into a permanent declaration disconnected from any particular forum, which would be opened to signature and could be joined by any state at any time until the conclusion of the whole process.

As in the previous year, Argentina, Belgium, the Netherlands and Slovenia advocated for the adoption of a new instrument aimed at providing states with better tools to domestically prosecute atrocity crimes within the framework of the Commission on Crime Prevention and Criminal Justice of the United Nations in Vienna. To this end, a side-event was organised at the occasion of the 23rd session of the commission, which took place in May 2014. At the same time, the importance of improving interstate cooperation in the prosecution of atrocity crimes and the relevance of the initiative in this regard were stressed by Madam Lieve Pellens, member of the Belgian Federal Prosecutor's Office, who, in the context of the thematic discussion on international cooperation in criminal matters, shared her experience as national magistrate and highlighted

---

14 Albania, Andorra, Argentina, Austria, Belgium, Bosnia and Herzegovina, Bulgaria, Chile, Costa Rica, Cyprus, Czech Republic, Finland, Georgia, Greece, Hungary, Ireland, Liechtenstein, Lithuania, Luxembourg, Macedonia, Malawi, Moldova, Mongolia, the Netherlands, Norway, Panama, Paraguay, Peru, Samoa, Senegal, Serbia, Seychelles, Slovakia, Slovenia, South Africa, Suriname, Sweden, Trinidad and Tobago, and Uruguay.

the practical obstacles arising from the inadequate nature of the current legal basis for cooperation regarding atrocity crimes.

The Permanent Declaration, together with an annex listing possible topics to be covered by the new treaty and an explanatory note informing states in further detail on the practical need for a new instrument dealing with mutual legal assistance and extradition for the domestic prosecution of atrocity crimes and addressing specific issues raised by states, was handed over to national authorities worldwide in the context of a new round of demarches that was carried out during autumn 2014. These documents were also presented en marge of the 13th session of the Assembly of States Parties to the Rome Statute of the International Criminal Court in the course of a side-event aimed at providing states with the most recent state of play regarding the initiative. At this occasion, H.E. Adama Dieng, as keynote speaker, reiterated his full support for the initiative.

Looking specifically at the outreach within the French-speaking world, two events in particular may be highlighted. First, a meeting gathering representatives of countries of the International Organization of *la Francophonie* was organised in April 2014 in The Hague by the co-sponsors of the initiative. Secondly, the *Sommet de la Francophonie*, which took place in November 2014 in Dakar, expressly recognised the necessity of facilitating the development of an appropriate legal framework for cooperation between states and in that sense acknowledged the importance of the initiative. The Declaration adopted at the end of the Summit indeed affirms:

> *Restons mobilisés dans la lutte contre l'impunité afin que les personnes soupçonnées de crimes soient jugées et que les victimes accèdent librement à la justice et obtiennent réparation. Soulignons, à ce propos, l'importance de coopérer avec la justice pénale internationale et de faciliter le développement des procédures de coopération judiciaire entre les États, indispensable à la poursuite des auteurs des crimes les plus graves.15*

In April 2015, the General Assembly of the United Nations, in its Resolution 69/270 on the cooperation of the United Nations with the International Organization of *la Francophonie*, endorsed the declaration made in Dakar and

> welcome[d] the importance given by the States members of the International Organization of la Francophonie to cooperating in the area of international criminal

15 'Noting the need to remain mobilized in the fight against impunity so that those suspected of having committed crimes be tried and victims benefit from a free access to justice and obtain reparations. Underlying, in this regard, the importance of cooperating with international criminal justice and of facilitating the development of procedures for judicial cooperation between states, indispensable to the prosecution of those responsible for the most serious crimes' (translation by the author).

justice and facilitating the development of judicial cooperation procedures between States, which is essential in prosecuting perpetrators of the most serious crimes.[16]

3. THE MAIN OBJECTIVES

Having sketched the origins of the initiative and its early developments, it is essential to understand the main goals pursued by the co-sponsors of this ambitious project. What would be the advantages of a new multilateral treaty on mutual legal assistance and extradition? How would it improve the international cooperation in the fight against impunity for atrocity crimes? Would such treaty really make a difference in comparison with the current legal framework?

The importance of international cooperation for the purpose of investigating and prosecuting atrocity crimes is anything but new. Already in 1973, the General Assembly proclaimed a set of principles of international cooperation in the detection, arrest, extradition and punishment of persons guilty of war crimes and crimes against humanity and, in this context, requested from states that they 'co-operate with each other on a bilateral and multilateral basis with a view of halting and preventing war crimes and crimes against humanity, and [that they] take the domestic and international measures necessary for that purpose', in particular in relation to extradition and the exchange of information.[17]

However, and as previously mentioned, the existing legal framework pertaining to international cooperation with regard to atrocity crimes is inadequate. The initiative backed by Argentina, Belgium, the Netherlands and Slovenia, and which aims at opening negotiations for the adoption of a new multilateral treaty for mutual legal assistance and extradition in the domestic prosecution of atrocity crimes stems from this observation.

Whereas not all states require the same level of formality for international legal cooperation, experience has shown that the absence of a proper legal basis has either prevented various states from executing a request for assistance, how willing they might have been to cooperate, because their constitution demands a treaty basis for mutual legal assistance and extradition, or caused serious delays and complications in the execution of the said request.[18] In this sense, the existence of a formal agreement, whether bilateral or multilateral, has proved to significantly expedite the process of obtaining a reply to a request for assistance.

As a multilateral instrument nevertheless, the proposed treaty would certainly provide a more coherent approach for all states dealing with cooperation in the context of atrocity crimes and it would, in this regard, draw

16 A/RES/69/270 (2015), para. 15.
17 A/RES/3074 (1973), paras. 3, 5 and 6.
18 Ferdinandusse 2014.

on the UNGA Resolution 3074 (1973). The system put into place would be more efficient than the current ad hoc system of bilateral treaties, developed in the absence of an appropriate multilateral legal framework.

Further, enhancing mutual legal assistance is not only essential for the investigation and prosecution of atrocity crimes; it is also an extremely useful and effective tool to designate direct channels of communication to expedite the judicial cooperation and to exchange best practices, know-how and expertise.

Finally, it must be noted that the coming into existence of a new treaty would send a strong and remarkable message toward the outside world, reaffirming the importance attached by the international community as a whole to the efficient prosecution of – and by the same token, the end of impunity for – atrocity crimes.

4. THE PROPOSED CONTENT

The main purpose of this initiative, as already mentioned, is to provide an appropriate legal framework in order to enhance the cooperation between states regarding the domestic prosecution of atrocity crimes. In this regard, it is essential to keep in mind that evidence lies at the heart of criminal cases, and that without evidence, there can be no trial. In particular, due account must therefore be given to the specificities attached to criminal cases involving this category of crimes. On the one hand, witnesses do not often find themselves on the territory of the state where the atrocities were perpetrated, but have rather fled to other countries. This means that the way to receive testimonies is strewn with severe hurdles. On the other, criminal cases are not only built on testimonies. Evidence of a different nature, such as material, is equally indispensable. To this end, documents, assets and bank records, letters or telephone taps may reveal of essential importance. Still, such key pieces of evidence are often to be found on the territory of more than one state. Mutual legal assistance and extradition are therefore crucial tools in order to greatly increase the chances of successful investigation and prosecution of atrocity crimes at the domestic level.

However, the existing gap in the legal framework for international cooperation creates serious legal and practical obstacles for both mutual legal assistance and extradition, whereas there should be no safe havens for atrocity crimes. The provisions on mutual legal assistance and extradition regarding atrocity crimes are indeed extremely limited, if not inexistent.[19] The Genocide Convention contains a provision requiring states to 'grant extradition in

19 On this issue, see for instance Ferdinandusse 2014.

accordance with their laws and treaties in force', but does not provide more detailed provisions on mutual legal assistance.[20] The four Geneva Conventions contain an *aut dedere aut judicare* obligation,[21] but only war crimes committed in the context of an international armed conflict fall within the scope of this obligation. Finally, no international instrument of conventional nature regulates mutual legal assistance as far as crimes against humanity are concerned, with the exception of specific crimes, such as torture, which benefit from a distinct treaty regime.

In contrast with these older conventions where a serious lacuna may be noticed, more recent treaties contain modern and detailed provisions on mutual legal assistance and extradition. This shift in focus has been observed since the 1980s, with the adoption of the Convention on the Prevention of Torture.[22] This trend found its consecration in the early 2000's, as reflected by the consecutive adoption of the United Nations Convention against Transnational Organized Crime (UNTOC),[23] the United Nations Convention against Corruption (UNCAC)[24] and the Convention on Enforced Disappearances.[25]

In light of these observations, the objective of the initiative is to set a new treaty that would embark all modern mutual legal assistance and extradition provisions from more recent conventions, and would for instance include provisions explicitly and specifically dealing with the issues of extradition, freezing of assets, seizure and confiscation, protection of witnesses, transfer of criminal proceedings, disposal of confiscated proceeds of crime or property, taking of evidence or statements from persons, service of judicial documents, searches and seizures, identification or tracing proceeds of crime, property, instrumentalities or other things for evidentiary purposes, facilitation of the voluntary appearance of persons in the requesting state party, designation of central authority and channel of communication, videoconference, assistance to and protection of victims, training and technical assistance.

As the main purpose of the initiative is to set up a *practical* tool enabling all states to enhance their capacity for the investigation and prosecution of

---

20 Convention on the Prevention and Punishment of the Crime of Genocide, Art. 7.

21 First Geneva Convention, Art. 49; Second Geneva Convention, Art. 50; Third Geneva Convention, Art. 129 and Fourth Geneva Convention, Art. 146. On this point, see the *Final Report of the International Law Commission on the obligation to extradite or prosecute (aut dedere aut judicare)*, 2014, Yearbook of the International Law Commission, para. 9.

22 Convention against Torture and Other Cruel, Inhuman or Degrading Treatment or Punishment, adopted in New York on 10 December 1984 and entered into force on 26 June 1987. As of 8 September 2015, 158 states were parties to the Convention.

23 Adopted in New York on 15 November 2000 and entered into force on 29 September 2003. As of 8 September 2015, 185 states were parties to the UNTOC.

24 Adopted in New York on 31 October 2003 and entered into force on 14 December 2005. As of 8 September 2015, 176 states were parties to the UNCAC.

25 International Convention for the Protection of All Persons from Enforced Disappearance, adopted in New York on 20 December 2006 and entered info force on 23 December 2010. As of 8 September 2015, 50 states were parties to the Convention.

atrocity crimes at the domestic level, it would not entail extensive negotiations on new concepts or provisions. The aim is certainly not to redefine the crimes covered by the treaty but rather to refer to the definitions already agreed upon in conventional and customary law. Similarly, provisions regulating mutual legal assistance and extradition would be extensively grounded on existing ones, present in the recent above-mentioned treaties, and adapted to the specificities of the cooperation in the investigation and prosecution of atrocity crimes.

5. LATEST DEVELOPMENTS AND WAY FORWARD

Alongside an ongoing round of demarches worldwide, important events in connection with the initiative for a new multilateral treaty took place over the last months. On 22 April 2015, for instance, a conference on the 'Rights for Peace: Challenges and Opportunities' was held in Brdo, Slovenia. In the context of one of the panels organised at this occasion on how to step up action against atrocity crimes, H.E. Fatou Bensouda, Prosecutor of the International Criminal Court, in the course of her keynote address,

> note[d] with praise the initiative of Slovenia, jointly with other [s]tates, to consider the possibility of adopting a new international instrument on mutual legal assistance and extradition aimed at effective domestic investigation and prosecution of international crimes.

Two months later, on 23 June 2015, a Strategic Meeting convened in The Hague by Argentina, Belgium, the Netherland and Slovenia, gathered representatives of the supporting states. Alongside a presentation by the Dutch Ministry of Justice that highlighted the obstacles with which it is confronted in its daily work in the execution of cooperation requests pertaining to atrocity crimes, H.E. Hassan B. Jallow, Chief Prosecutor of the International Criminal Tribunal for Rwanda and the Mechanism for International Criminal Tribunals and Under Secretary-General of the United Nations, pronounced a keynote speech at the occasion of which he pledged his unfailing support for the initiative:

> There is an urgent need for an international convention on mutual legal assistance for the most serious international crimes. Such a treaty will ensure that [s]tates not only complement one another, but will also encourage national authorities to cooperate more smoothly. As we move forward with this idea, and because of the very serious

nature of these crimes, we should all begin to think about bold new and innovative ways to make such a treaty effective, efficient, and universal.[26]

The goal of the meeting was also to provide supporting states with an update pertaining to the initiative and its evolution, as well as to hold a constructive discussion on how to bring this project one step further. The delegations present were extremely active in the discussion and fuelled it with valuable suggestions on the way forward.

The autumn/winter 2015 was an excellent occasion for the Netherlands, together with Argentina, Belgium and Slovenia, to continue its advocacy activities. Various important side-events were planned and organised *en marge* of the 14th Session of the Assembly of States Parties of the International Criminal Court in November 2015, as well as at the occasion of the 32nd International Conference of the Red Cross and Red Crescent that will be held in Geneva in December 2015. In addition, presentations of the initiative in the context of experts meetings took place, for instance during the 20th Annual Conference of the International Association of Prosecutors that was held in Zürich in September 2015. At this occasion, H.E. Serge Brammertz, Chief Prosecutor of the International Criminal Tribunal for the former Yugoslavia, convinced of the need for a new treaty on mutual legal assistance and extradition for atrocity crimes, highlighted its added value to his fellow prosecutors in the course of a special meeting on war crimes and international criminal justice. The International Association of Prosecutors, which gathers practitioners who deal with cooperation requests on a daily basis and are confronted with obstacles that delay or even prevent the execution of such requests, appears to be the perfect place to raise awareness among those who best experience the need for, and who best would benefit from a new instrument on mutual legal assistance and extradition for atrocity crimes that would bring practical tools to easily overcome these hurdles.

At the same time, the co-sponsoring states are currently in the process of identifying regional venues where politicians and diplomats, but even more importantly practitioners and experts in the field, may be properly informed about, and sensitised on the initiative and the positive practical implications that it would have regarding the international cooperation for the domestic prosecution of atrocity crimes.

---

26 See the Statement published on the website of the United Nations Mechanism for International Criminal Tribunals in this regard, available at: www.unmict.org/en/news/prosecutor-jallow-delivers-keynote-speech-multilateral-treaty-mutual-legal-assistance.

6. CONCLUSION

As was shown throughout this contribution, the initiative has, over the years, benefitted from a growing diplomatic and political support. As of today (October 2015), 48 states, representing all regions of the world,[27] have formally expressed their support toward the setting up of an instrument aimed at improving interstate cooperation in the investigation and prosecution, at the domestic level, of the crimes of genocide, crimes against humanity and war crimes.

The community of states that now support the initiative is not only composed of contracting parties to the Rome Statute. Whereas it fits perfectly into the international criminal justice system enshrined in the Rome Statute, i.e. the principle of complementarity under which it remains the primary responsibility of states to prosecute the perpetrators of atrocity crimes, the proposed project is aimed more widely at all states, irrespective of their membership of the International Criminal Court, and intends to provide them with the tools necessary to comply with their international obligations pertaining to the end of impunity for atrocity crimes, as well as to empower their national judiciaries.

In this sense, one of the ultimate goals of the initiative is to increase in a significant manner the chances of successful investigation and prosecution when performed by national authorities, by rendering the cooperation between states, not only possible, but also fully efficient. Another goal is to place at the disposal of states that have suffered violent conflicts, an instrument to help them deal with their past, instead of leaving this task to other states or international criminal jurisdictions.

Modern and detailed provisions setting up a legal framework for extradition and other forms of mutual legal assistance do exist. They may be found in recent conventions dealing with, for instance, corruption and transnational organised crimes. With regard to the most serious crimes of international concern – which are the crimes of genocide, crimes against humanity and war crimes – this is not the case. Setting up a new multilateral treaty, which would bridge the current gap, is viewed by Argentina, Belgium, the Netherlands and Slovenia, as well as by a growing number of like-minded states, as the most suitable course of action to enable a full practical implementation of the commitment made by the international community: *no safe havens for perpetrators of mass atrocities*. Future will tell whether states will make the choice of bringing this commitment into reality.

---

27 Albania, Andorra, Argentina, Austria, Belgium, Bolivia, Bosnia and Herzegovina, Bulgaria, Chile, Costa Rica, Côte d'Ivoire, Cyprus, Czech Republic, Finland, Georgia, Greece, Guinea, Hungary, Ireland, Kazakhstan, Liechtenstein, Lithuania, Luxembourg, Macedonia, Malawi, Moldova, Mongolia, the Netherlands, Norway, Panama, Paraguay, Peru, Poland, Saint Kitts and Nevis, Samoa, São Tomé and Príncipe, Senegal, Serbia, Seychelles, Slovakia, Slovenia, South Africa, Suriname, Sweden, Trinidad and Tobago, Uruguay and Vietnam. Those states have expressed their support by signing either the ASP12 Joint Statement, or the Permanent Declaration, or both.

BIBLIOGRAPHY

BOOKS AND JOURNAL ARTICLES

Benzing 2003

Benzing, M., 'The Complementarity Regime of the International Criminal Court: International Criminal Justice between State Sovereignty and the Fight against Impunity', 7 Max Planck Yearbook of United Nations Law, 2003.

Ferdinandusse 2014

Ferdinandusse, W., 'Improving Inter-State Cooperation for the National Prosecution of International Crimes: Towards a New Treaty?', 18(5) ASIL, 2014.

TREATIES, LEGISLATION AND AGREEMENTS

Convention (I) for the Amelioration of the Condition of the Wounded and Sick in Armed Forces in the Field (First Geneva Convention), 75 UNTS 31, 12 August 1949.

Convention (II) for the Amelioration of the Condition of Wounded, Sick and Shipwrecked Members of Armed Forces at Sea (Second Geneva Convention), 75 UNTS 85, 12 August 1949.

Convention (III) Relative to the Treatment of Prisoners of War (Third Geneva Convention), 75 UNTS 135, 12 August 1949.

Convention (IV) on the Protection of Civilian Persons in Time of War (Fourth Geneva Convention), 75 UNTS 287, 12 August 1949.

Convention against Torture and Other Cruel, Inhuman or Degrading Treatment or Punishment, UN Doc. A/RES/39/46, 10 December 1984.

Convention on the Prevention and Punishment of the Crime of Genocide, GA Res. 260 (III), 78 UNTS 278, 9 December 1948.

International Convention for the Protection of All Persons from Enforced Disappearance, GA Res. A/RES/61/177, UN Doc. A/61/177, 20 December 2006.

Rome Statute of the International Criminal Court, 2187 UNTS 90/37, 17 July 1998.

United Nations Convention against Corruption, GA Res. 58/4, UN Doc. A/58/422, 31 October 2003.

United Nations Convention against Transnational Organized Crime, GA Res. 55/25, UN Doc. A/55/383, 15 November 2000.

OTHERS

Assembly of States Parties to the Rome Statute of the ICC, 12th Session, Joint Statement on an 'International Initiative for Opening Negotiations on a Multilateral Treaty for Mutual Legal Assistance and Extradition in Domestic Prosecution of Atrocity Crimes (crimes of genocide, crimes against humanity and war crimes)', November 2013.

Assembly of States Parties to the Rome Statute of the ICC, Resolution ICC-ASP/11/Res.6, 'Complementarity', 21 November 2012.

Commission on Crime Prevention and Criminal Justice (Economic and Social Council), 'International cooperation in the fight against the crime of genocide, crimes against humanity and war crimes', E/CN.15/2013/L.5, 28 March 2013.

Dakar Declaration, 15th Francophonie Summit, November 2014.

International Law Commission, 'Final Report on the obligation to extradite or prosecute (aut dedere aut judicare)', Yearbook of the International Law Commission vol. II, 2014.

Permanent Declaration on an 'International Initiative for Opening Negotiations on a Multilateral Treaty for Mutual Legal Assistance and Extradition in Domestic Prosecution of Atrocity Crimes (crimes of genocide, crimes against humanity and war crimes)'.

The Netherlands, 'A Legal Gap in the International Legal Framework Concerning the National Adjudication of International Crimes?', in 'A Legal Gap? Getting the evidence where it can be found: Investigating and prosecuting international crimes', Report, expert meeting, The Hague Institute for the Internationalisation of Law and the Government of the Netherlands, 22 November 2011.

UN General Assembly, Resolution on 'Cooperation between the United Nations and the International Organization of la Francophonie', A/RES/69/270, 2 April 2015.

UN General Assembly, Resolution on 'Principles of International Cooperation in the Detention, Arrest, Extradition and Punishment of Persons Guilty of War Crimes and Crimes against Humanity', A/RES/3074, 30 November 1973.

UN General Assembly, Resolution on 'Report of the International Criminal Court', A/RES/68/305, 9 September 2014.

UN Mechanism for International Criminal Tribunals, 'Prosecutor Jallow Delivers Keynote Speech on Multilateral Treaty for Mutual Legal Assistance for International Crimes at the Netherlands Ministry of Foreign Affairs', 23 June 2015.

www.ingramcontent.com/pod-product-compliance
Ingram Content Group UK Ltd.
Pitfield, Milton Keynes, MK11 3LW, UK
UKHW051917100926
8556IPUK00021B/1229

9 781780 684178